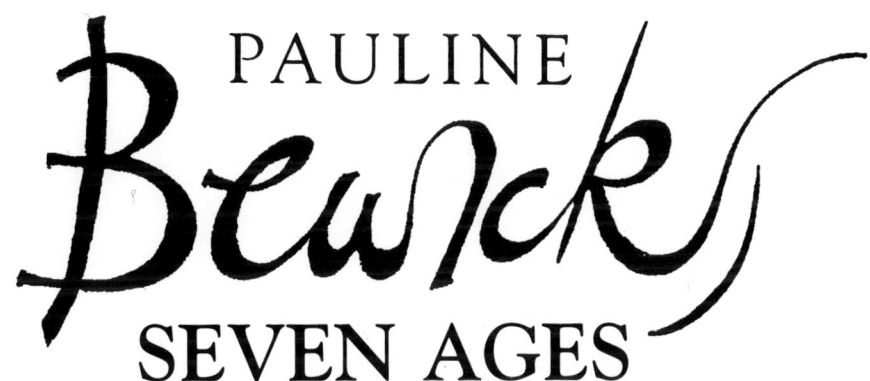

PAULINE Bewick
SEVEN AGES

A Comprehensive Catalogue of the Waterford, Kerry and Travelling
Permanent Collections (*first working proof*)

Alan Hayes, EDITOR

ISBN 10: 1-903631-87-4
ISBN 13: 978-1-903631-87-4

First published in November 2006 by Arlen House

Arlen House
PO Box 222
Galway
Phone/Fax: 00 353 86 8207617
Email: arlenhouse@gmail.com

Distributed in North America by Syracuse University Press

Syracuse University Press
621 Skytop Road, Suite 110
Syracuse, NY 13244–5290
Phone: 315–443–5534/Fax: 315–443–5545
Email: supress@syr.edu

Designed in Dublin by DP Imaging

Printed in Dublin by Betaprint

Cathal Ó Searcaigh

Pauline Bewick: Showing her Colours

"When I paint green it doesn't mean grass.
When I paint blue it doesn't mean sky.
It is through colour that I am".

This is Henry Matisse expressing the poetic impulses that
freed his art from a conventional representational realism.

The paintings in this book, like the artist herself, have a lovely self-assurance about them, an elegance. They have a lovely sensuality of shape, the swell and curve of femininity, the poise of style, the restraint of craft. In these paintings passion and precision, craft and ardour, come together in a glorious chant of exultation.

Colours have emotional values and energies. They give us sensations. We all have preferred colours. Colours that please us, pleasure us, promote our confidences. We also have colours that dismay and disillusion us. We, each of us, have public colours and private colours. Colours for the church and colours for the closet. As for myself, blue is the colour of my public world, pink the colour of my private world.

Pauline Bewick is a tremendous colourist. Her pictures are symphonic arrangements. Arias of blue, allegros of green, rondos of red. Her colours pulse and vibrate. If we look clearly we can see their auras. If we listen intently we hear their harmonies. In that respect they are profoundly spiritual presences beckoning us into their contemplative spaces. They make us aware while looking at them, listening to them, of being alive in a profoundly refreshing way. They restore us, enriched to the real world of our everyday existence, equipped with a new awareness and a new vision of that world.

Creativity for Pauline Bewick, seems to me, to be an expression of gratitude, a hymn of colour to her home-place, Kerry. In that sense her work is devotional; a psalm in praise of place. I look at her pictures and I get the feeling that they are surges of the spirit – sudden recognitions of the world of light, but equally an awareness and indeed an apprehension of the dark. A homage to the yin and yang of Kerry.

Someone told me that in Russian you can refer to a loved one as "my native place", a phrase reserved in other languages for the place where you were born. But we can understand that. Love is the very place where we are born. We become childlike in the sense that our eyes become more keen, our ears more alert, our hearts more compassionate. We become more attuned and attentive. By the evidence of her pictures, Pauline Bewick has been born, again and again, over the past 70 years in the arms of her beloved Kerry.

It is clear that Pauline made contact with her vital creative energies in Kerry. She first arrived there as a 2 year old with her mother 'Harry' who had run away from her English husband and family. Something pushed her in the right direction. A lucky meeting of fate and talent. "It takes little talent to see clearly what lies under one's nose", W. H. Auden said, "A good deal of it is to know in which direction to point that organ". Auden was wrong. It takes genius to see clearly what lies under one's nose. Pauline Bewick is attentive to the immediate. She is a visionary of the real, a mystic of the domestic. She, like Christina Rossetti, knows full well, "that could we but look with seeing eyes, this very spot might be paradise". Anyway, paradise is not a place, but a condition. A simple being alive, a clear-sighted mindfulness. Pauline is blessed with that gift.

Pauline remembers things by their colours. In that sense she resembles Marcel Proust. She evokes her life memories by colour much in the same way that Proust evoked his by smell. Colour activates and arouses her memories of things past. In Greek mythology Mnemosyne was the spirit of remembering. The Greeks held her to be the foremost muse. Memory is genius, having the capacity to explore one's buried self, the shreds and the fragments, the bits and pieces of this and that, joy, sorrow, grief, happiness, loneliness. It's akin to archaeology … this excavation of the psyche. We have many lost worlds buried deep in the earth of our psyche, a whole Atlantis of feelings. Nothing is ever forgotten by the body. Pauline uses colour to dig, to unearth, to discover the ages of her Being, the artifacts of her feelings. The full range of her excavations is to be admired in this book.

This is a beautiful product from Arlen House, a lucky bag of the devine, a rattlebag of mysteries, Alan Hayes, publisher of Arlen House, is committed to publishing beautifully designed essential books, books which are visually and verbally stimulating. I wish Pauline and Arlen House unlimited luck as this book takes flight.

Gort a' Choirce
Donegal

September 2006

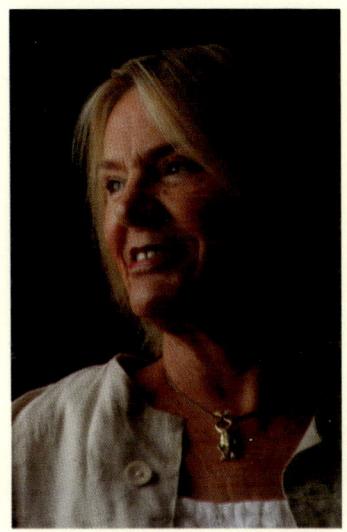

the second time neither I nor the river was the same

- Hereclites

Timeline of Important Dates

4 September 1935	Born in Northumbria, England to Alice Graham Bewick and John Corbett Bewick
late 1937/early 1938	Alice runs away from the Bewick family, takes pseudonym 'Harry', ends up in Kenmare, County Kerry. Pauline does her first sketches in Kerry
1938	Death of John Corbett Bewick. Harry returns briefly to the UK for the funeral
1941	First oil paintings done in Kerry
1943	Move to Belfast, Portrush, Londonderry
1944-49	Return to Britain, to progressive schools, Wales and England, then conventional school in Wargrave
1949	Return to Ireland travelling around in a van, brought boat from England to Cork and Passage West, then settled briefly in Killarney at the Lodge of the Cahernane Hotel
1950	Move to Dublin to enroll in the Art School, purchase of 51 Frankfort Avenue
1952	Depart Dublin Art School
1952	Met Pat Melia at the D'Arcy sisters party
1953	Performs as a nightclub singer at Clover Club, O'Connell Street, is offered work with the Pike Theatre as stage designer and actor
1956	First trip to Paris with Pat
1957	First solo exhibition
1958-62	Split with Pat and move to London
1963	Pat and Pauline marry
1964	Rent flat in Upper Mount Street, Dublin
1965	Purchase house in Heytesbury Lane, Dublin
1966	Daughter Poppy born
1970	Daughter Holly born
1972	First visit to Tuscany
1973	Pat appointed to Killarney hospital and family move back to Kerry
1976	Move to permanent home outside Glenbeigh
1979	Death of Harry Bewick
1985	50th birthday inspires collection of major exhibition, From Two to Fifty, book *Pauline Bewick: Painting a Life* by James White and film by David Shaw-Smith
1989-1991	Move to the South Pacific Islands for two years
4 September 2005	Celebrates 70th birthday
11 November 2005	Exclusive announcement on Pat Kenny's *Late Late Show* of major donation of her master works of art to the State
14 November 2006	Official opening by President Mary McAleese of Pauline Bewick's Seven Ages collection at the Waterford Institute of Technology

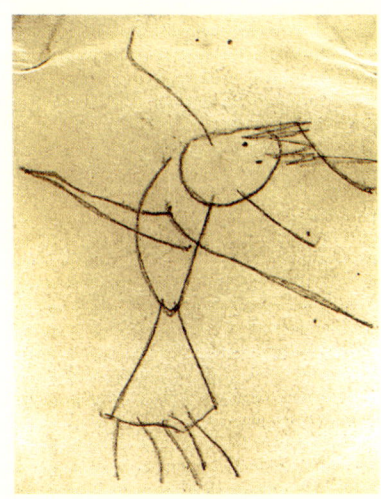

DANCING GIRL KENMARE
1938 • pencil
Kerry Collection

LITTLE GIRL WITH LONG HAIR
1938 • pencil
Kerry Collection

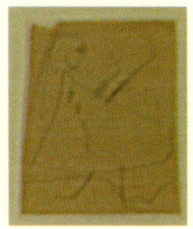

GIRL WITH BUTTONS ON HER DRESS
1938 • pencil
Kerry Collection

The last memory of England was breathing through a gas-mask. There was a threat of war. Harry, my mother, had left Corbett Bewick and ran away with myself and Hazel. She met a Kerry woman, Pat Newling, who was opening a new hotel in Letchworth. Pat offered her a farmhouse in Ireland outside Kenmare after she offered to foster Lucy and Michael, Pat's niece and nephew who'd just been orphaned. We went to Gleninchaquin, County Kerry to pick them up from the cottage of their postman uncle, Buttons. Our first game together, Lucy, Michael, Hazel and I, was 'Cot'. Later it changed to 'Tig'. That broke the ice and we had a wonderful childhood together, though I was always trailing behind, being five or six years younger than the others. Our kitchen was lit by candle and lamplight and Harry laid out all her art materials from her art school days on the table. 'Dancing Girl Kenmare' is the first sketch I ever did.

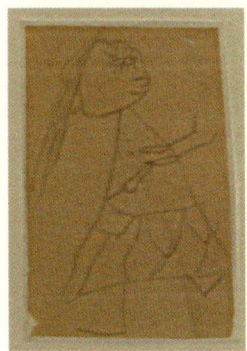

GIRL WITH LONG EYELASHES AND ROUND NOSE
1938 • pencil
Kerry Collection

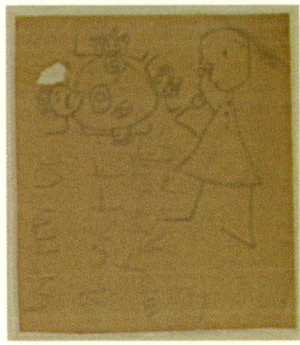

WAITRESS AT THE LANSDOWNE
ARMS HOTEL, KENMARE
1938 • pencil
Kerry Collection

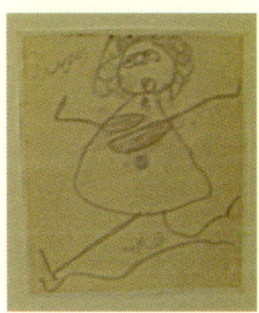

WOMAN RUNNING
1938 • pencil
Kerry Collection

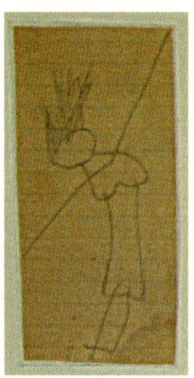

GIRL DANCING WITH BREASTS
1938 • pencil
Travelling Collection

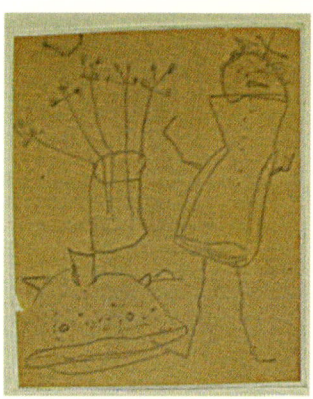

WAITRESS WITH FLOWERS
1938 • pencil
Travelling Collection

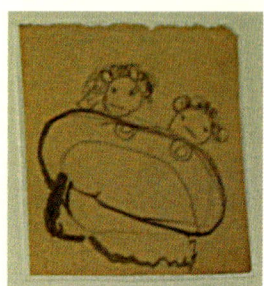

TWO GIRLS WITH CURLY HAIR AT A TABLE
1938 • pencil
Travelling Collection

The earliest pencil drawings from 2½ years of age.

Up to this day whatever happens in life has to go down on paper to prove it's happened,
or to hope that it won't happen!

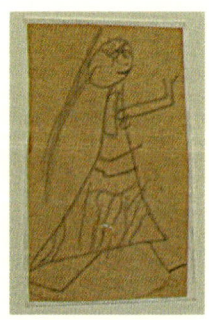

THIN GIRL WITH LONG EYELASHES
1938 • pencil
Travelling Collection

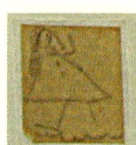

LITTLE GIRL WITH TWO BUTTONS
1938 • pencil
Travelling Collection

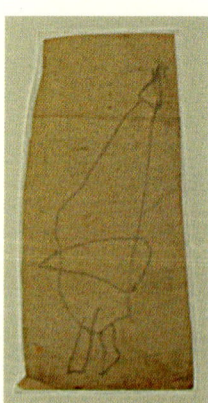

GIRL IN A PIXIE HAT
1938 • pencil
Travelling Collection

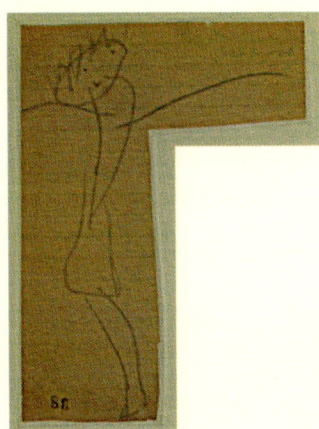

GIRL DANCING, ARMS UP
1938 • pencil
Waterford Collection

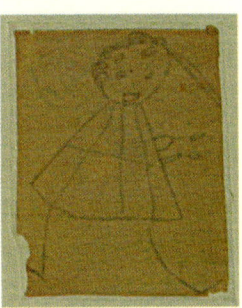

GIRL IN A DRESS, WITH ROSY CHEEKS
1938 • pencil
Waterford Collection

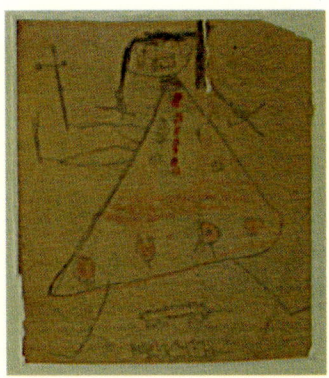

GIRL WITH FLOWERY DRESS
1938 • pencil
Waterford Collection

The waitress who served our meal in the Lansdowne Arms Hotel, Kenmare
was amazed at Harry's order. 'Anything raw?'
She laughed. They'd never seen vegetarians before.

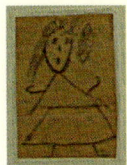

GIRL WITH BLOUSE AND SKIRT
1938 • pencil
Waterford Collection

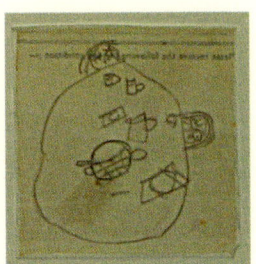

TWO GIRLS EATING AT THE TABLE
1938 • pencil
Waterford Collection

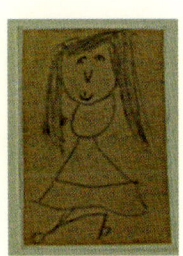

GIRL WHISTLING
1938 • pencil
Waterford Collection

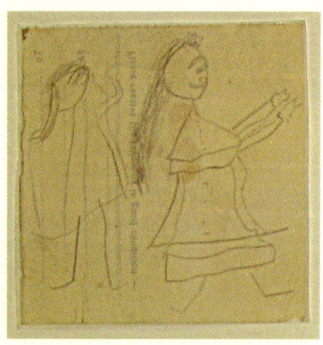

TWO GIRLS AT A WEDDING
1939 • pencil
Kerry Collection

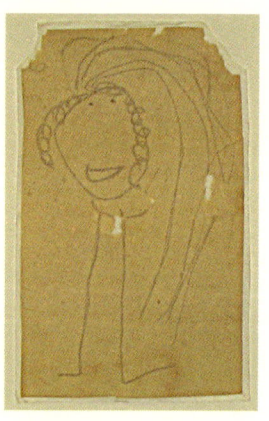

BRIDE LAUGHING, WITH VEIL
1939 • pencil
Kerry Collection

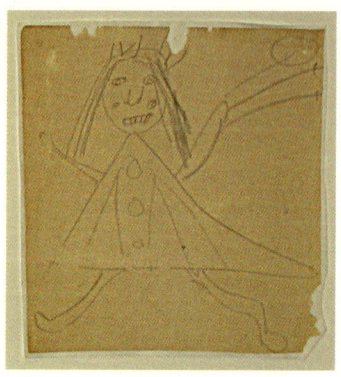

BRIDE WITH THREE BUTTONS
1939 • pencil
Kerry Collection

The first wedding at the church was like a fairytale.

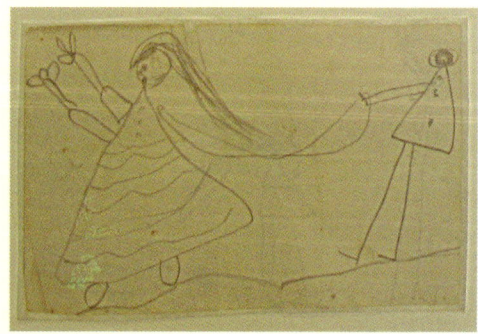

BRIDE WITH TRAIN HOLDER ON A HILL
1939 • pencil
Kerry Collection

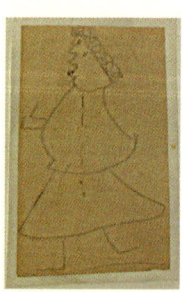

ONE GIRL, SIDE VIEW
1939 • pencil
Kerry Collection

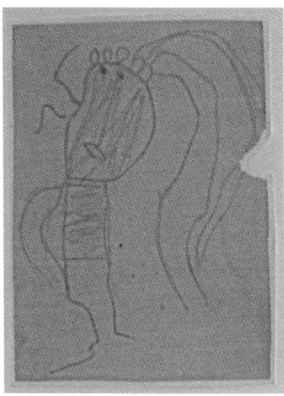

BRIDE WITH VEIL, I
1939 • pencil
Travelling Collection

TWO GIRLS, SIDEVIEW
1939 • pencil
Travelling Collection

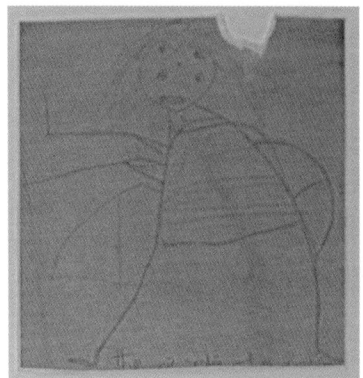

TWO SETS OF ARMS
1939 • pencil
Travelling Collection

Harry's praise was huge when I started doing profiles.

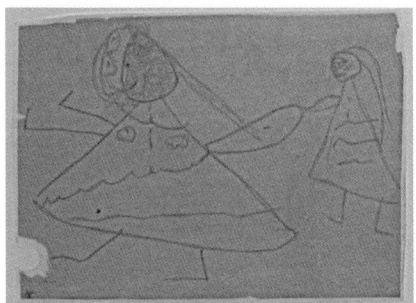

BRIDE AND TRAIN HOLDER
1939 • pencil
Travelling Collection

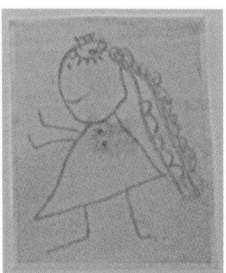

BRIDE WITH VEIL, II
1939 • pencil
Travelling Collection

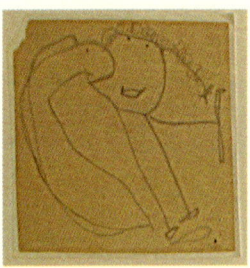

BRIDE WITH VEIL III
1939 • pencil
Waterford Collection

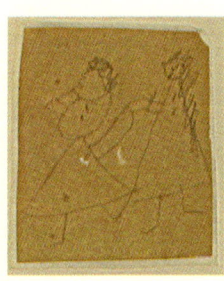

GIRL HOLDING BRIDE'S VEIL
1939 • pencil
Waterford Collection

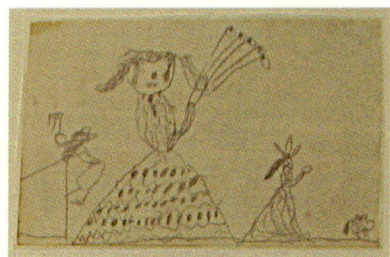

BRIDE WITH PATTERNED DRESS
1939 • pencil
Waterford Collection

Our painting sessions would stop for us to have a bath in a Guinness barrel in water heated over the open fire. It would become a steam bath once the lid was put on. Other activities were washing our clothes in the stream where inevitably we'd lose something, and would find a sock or vest later covered in crustations down at the sea. Harry wrote a book about our life in Kenmare, *A Wild Taste*.

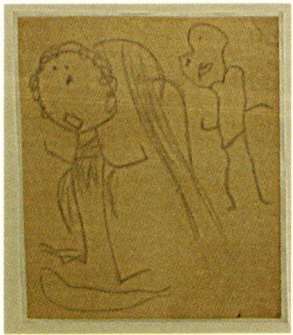

BRIDE AND GROOM
1939 • pencil
Waterford Collection

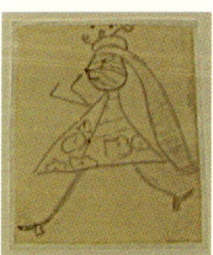

BRIDE WITH HAT AND VEIL
1939 • pencil
Waterford Collection

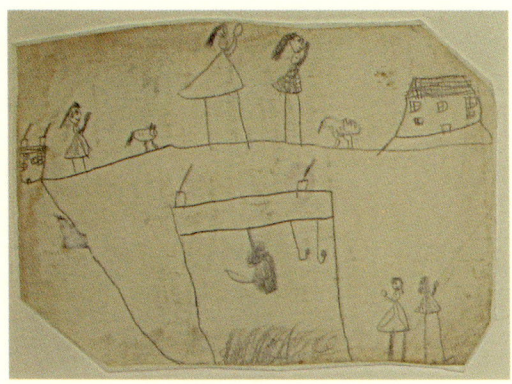

COOKING POTS AT OUR FARM
1940 • pencil
Kerry Collection

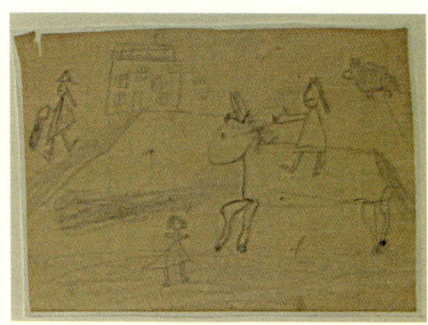

ME, HAZEL AND HORSE
1940 • pencil
Kerry Collection

Cooking bread over the fire, and this is Hazel on Shamrock, our horse.

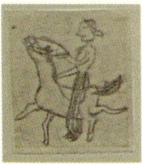

MAN ON A HORSE
1940 • pencil
Kerry Collection

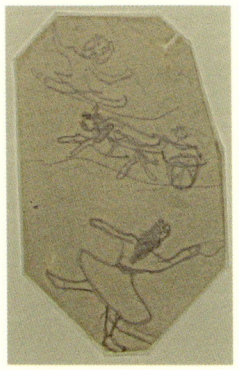

CIRCUS IN KENMARE
1940 • pencil
Kerry Collection

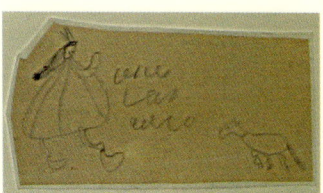

GIRL WITH DOG AND WRITING
1940 • pencil
Kerry Collection

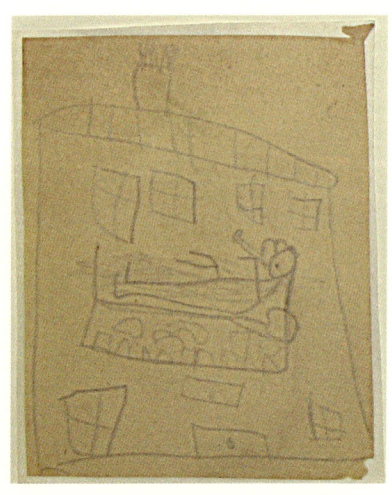

GIRL IN BED
1940 • pencil
Travelling Collection

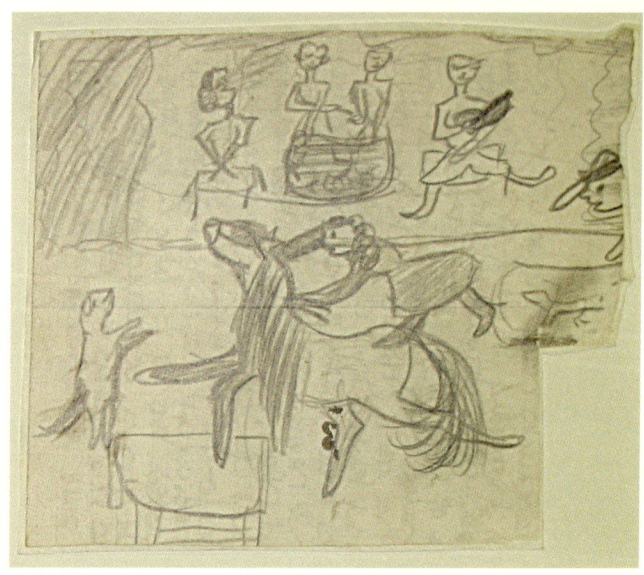

CIRCUS IN KENMARE, BARE BACKED RIDER
1940 • pencil
Travelling Collection

My bed in Cillagh East.
Duffy's circus often came to town. A woman whispered, 'there's only an inch between herself and decency'.
Pat Newling smoking with her rosy cheeks.

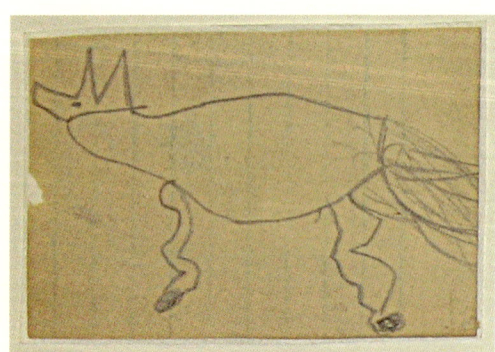

HORSE
1940 • pencil
Travelling Collection

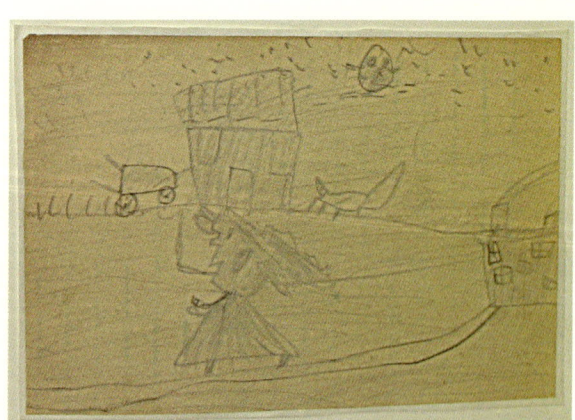

PAT NEWLING SMOKING
1940 • pencil
Travelling Collection

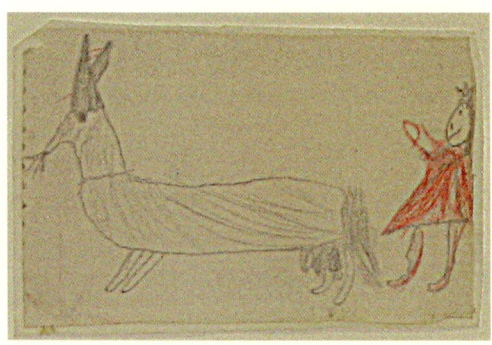

COW AND GIRL
1940 • pencil
Waterford Collection

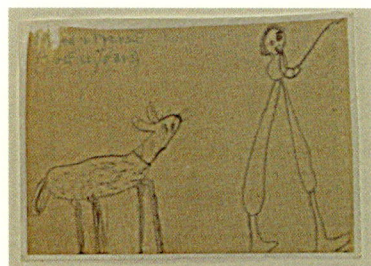

MAN AND HORSE
1940 • pencil
Waterford Collection

Harry's voice still rings in my ears. 'That's marvellous!' 'You're a genius!'

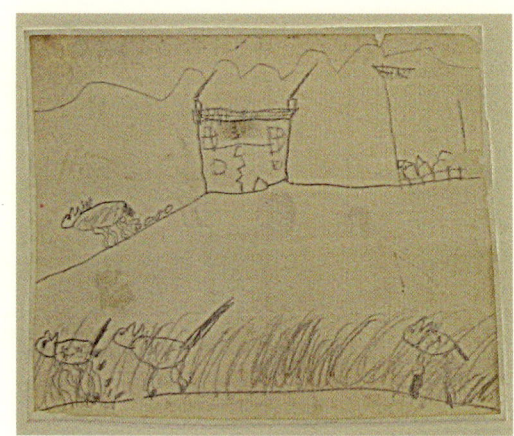

OUR FARM AND ANIMALS
1940 • pencil
Waterford Collection

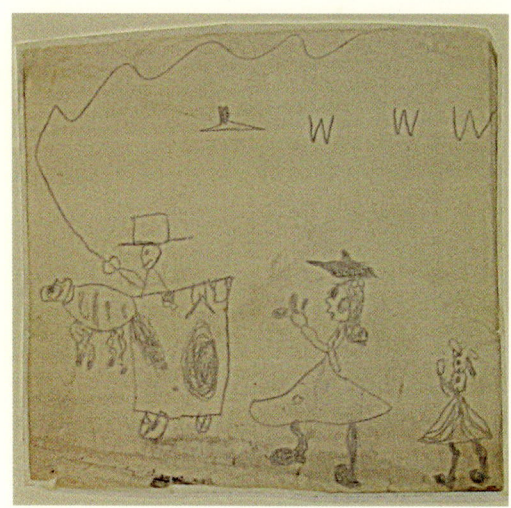

MAN, HORSE AND CART
1940 • pencil
Waterford Collection

Harry got wood offcuts from Arthur's sawmills in Kenmare and we were free and thrilled to use them. She had fallen in love with Ireland and added the names in Gaelic under each picture when finished.

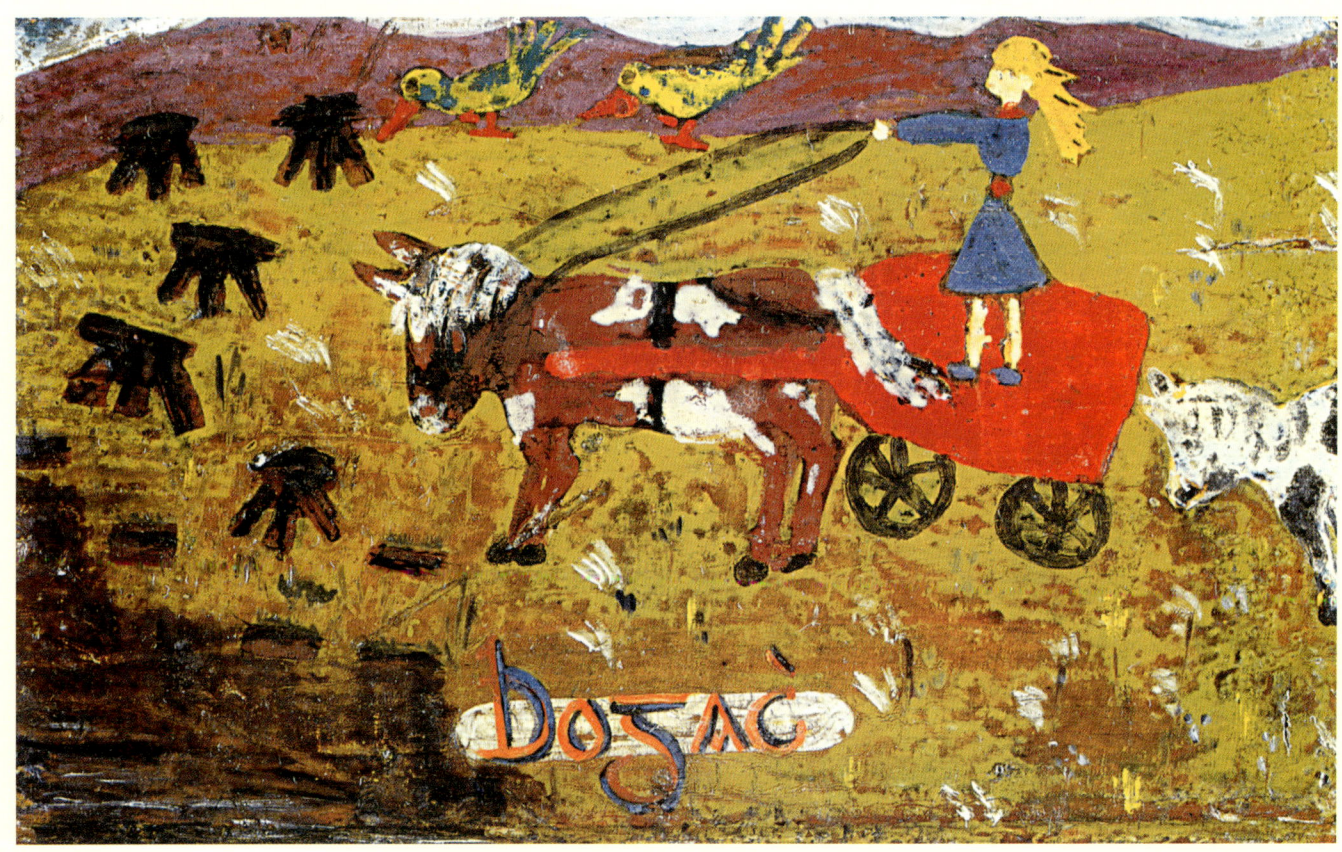

Bogac, Our Bog
1941 • oil on board • 4" x 6"
Travelling Collection

I did this in secret for Harry's birthday. We had our own bog. Each year we would go up to it with our horse Shamrock to cut the turf. I was too small so the soft turf provided great *marla* to make figures. Using heather for the mouth, bog cotton for the hair and blue milkwort flowers for the eyes. They dried into little sculptures and lasted for ages on the windowsills.

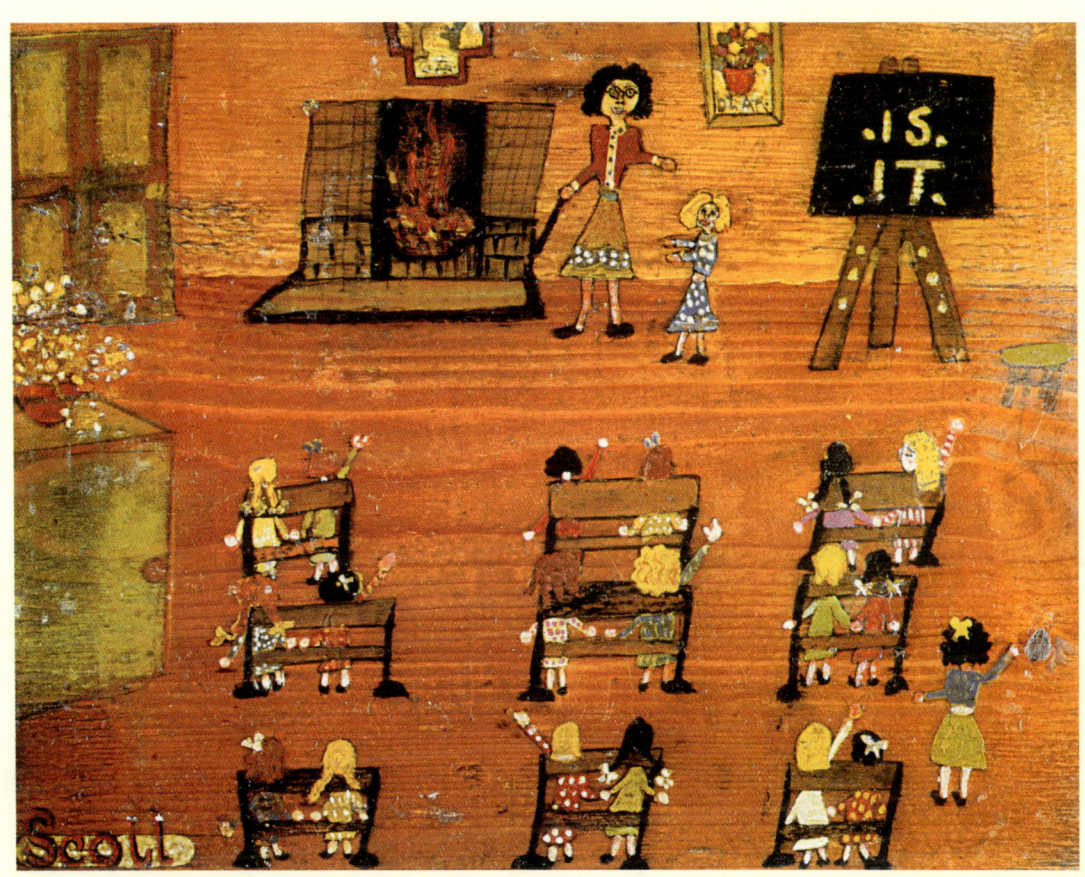

SCOIL, DOURUS SCHOOL
1942 • oil on board • 8" x 10"
Travelling Collection

Going to school I would call for Maisie Downey who lived a mile along the high road and barefooted off we'd go. Each child brought a piece of turf which kept the classroom warm. Miss Murphy never made a fuss because I couldn't spell. Instead she praised me for drawing a bird and for making 'a shop' outside on the wall during religious classes. Pine cones and dried horse-dung were buns. The class would rush out at break.
'How much are the buns?'
'A Pingin'.

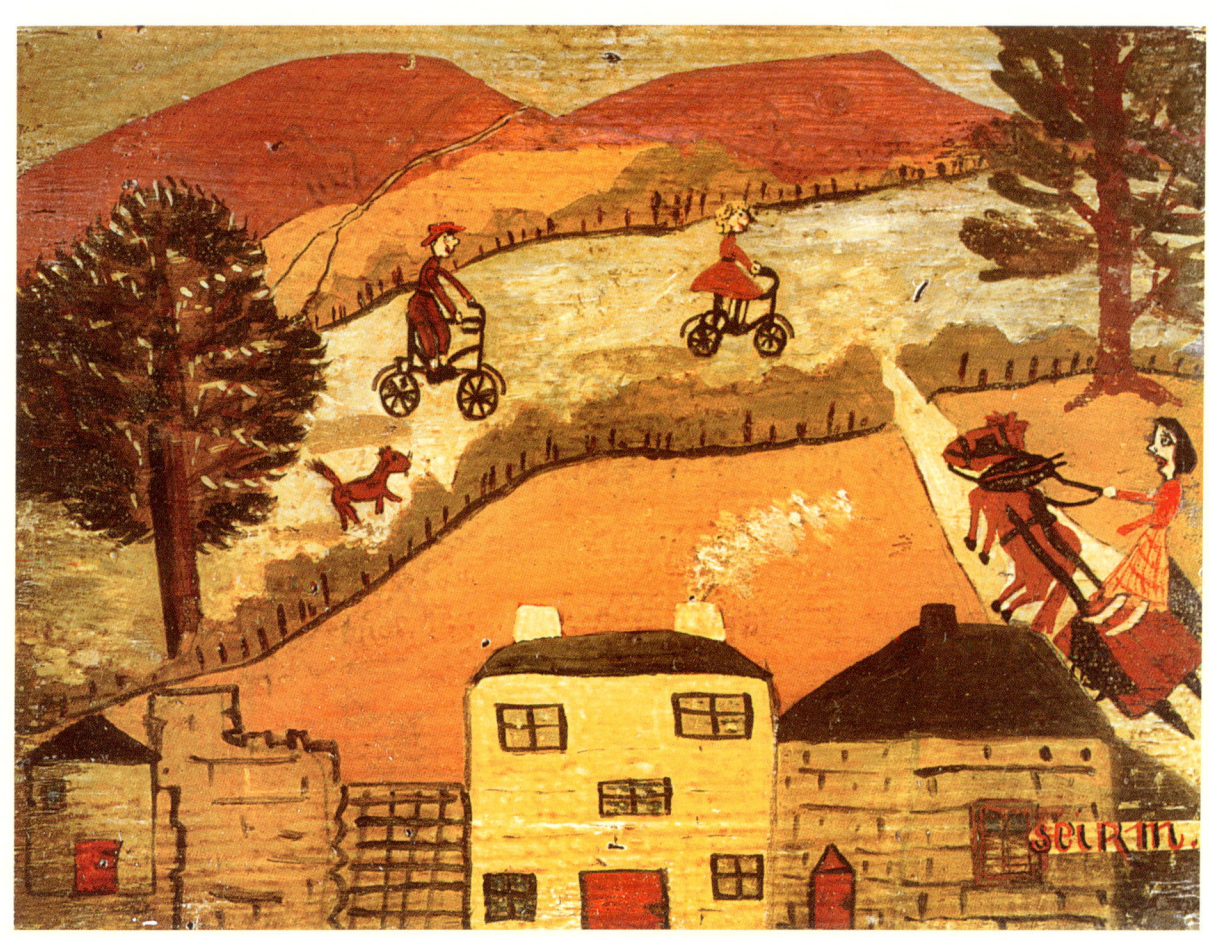

Downey's House, Feirm
1942 • oil on board • 8" x 10"
Waterford Collection

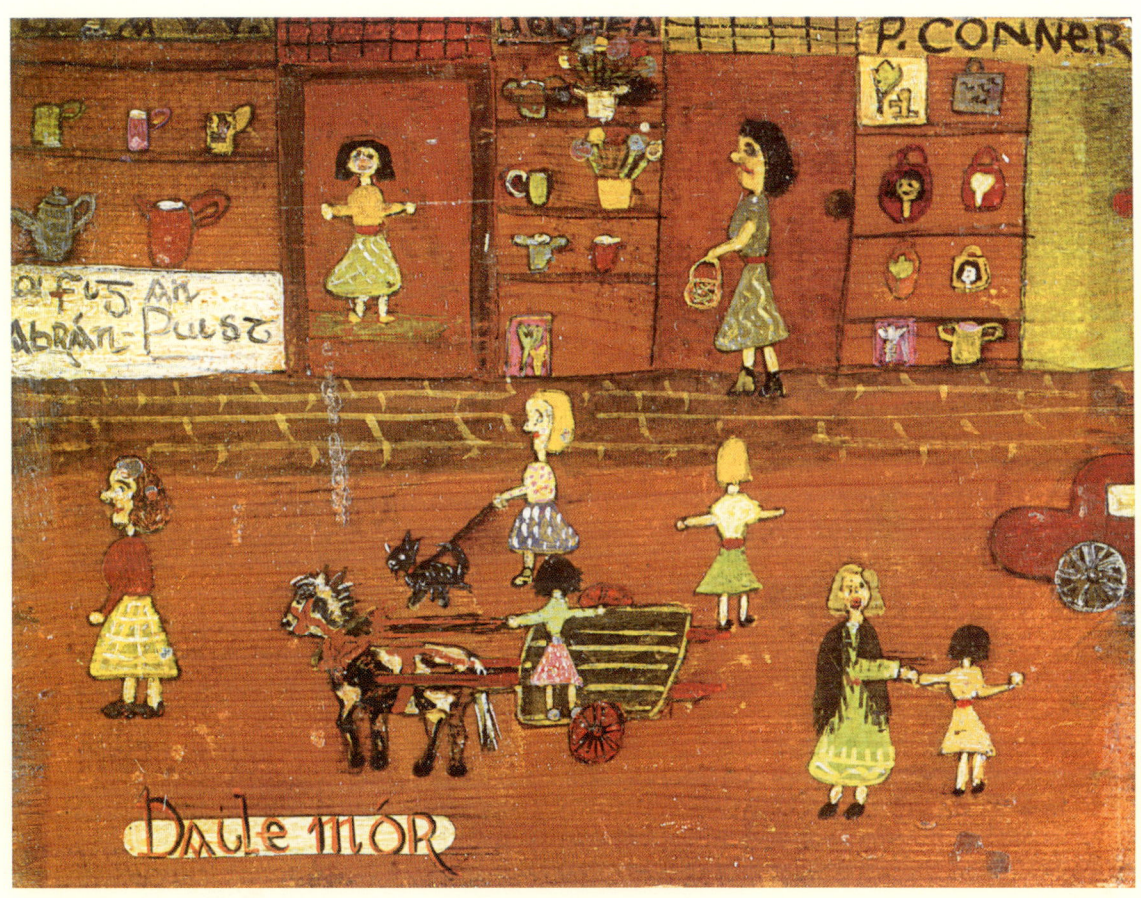

KENMARE, BAILE MÓR
1942 • oil on board • 8" x 10"
Waterford Collection

Our visits to the town, to the shops and Arthur's sawmills and going home with Shamrock and the cart full of flour, yellow meal and paraffin, and to renew our glass radio batteries with acid. We had the only radio for miles. Harry often sternly said 'don't lick the batteries'. Because of that they became fascinating and one day on my own in the room with the radio the temptation was too much. I went behind the radio and ran my tongue from the bottom of the battery to the top. At first nothing! Then a dreadful tingling! I shouted to Hazel, 'I licked the batteries'. 'You licked the batteries!' She grabbed my arm and we flew down the hill to Harry. 'Pauline's licked the batteries!'. 'What? You licked the batteries!' Up the hill again to have my mouth washed out.

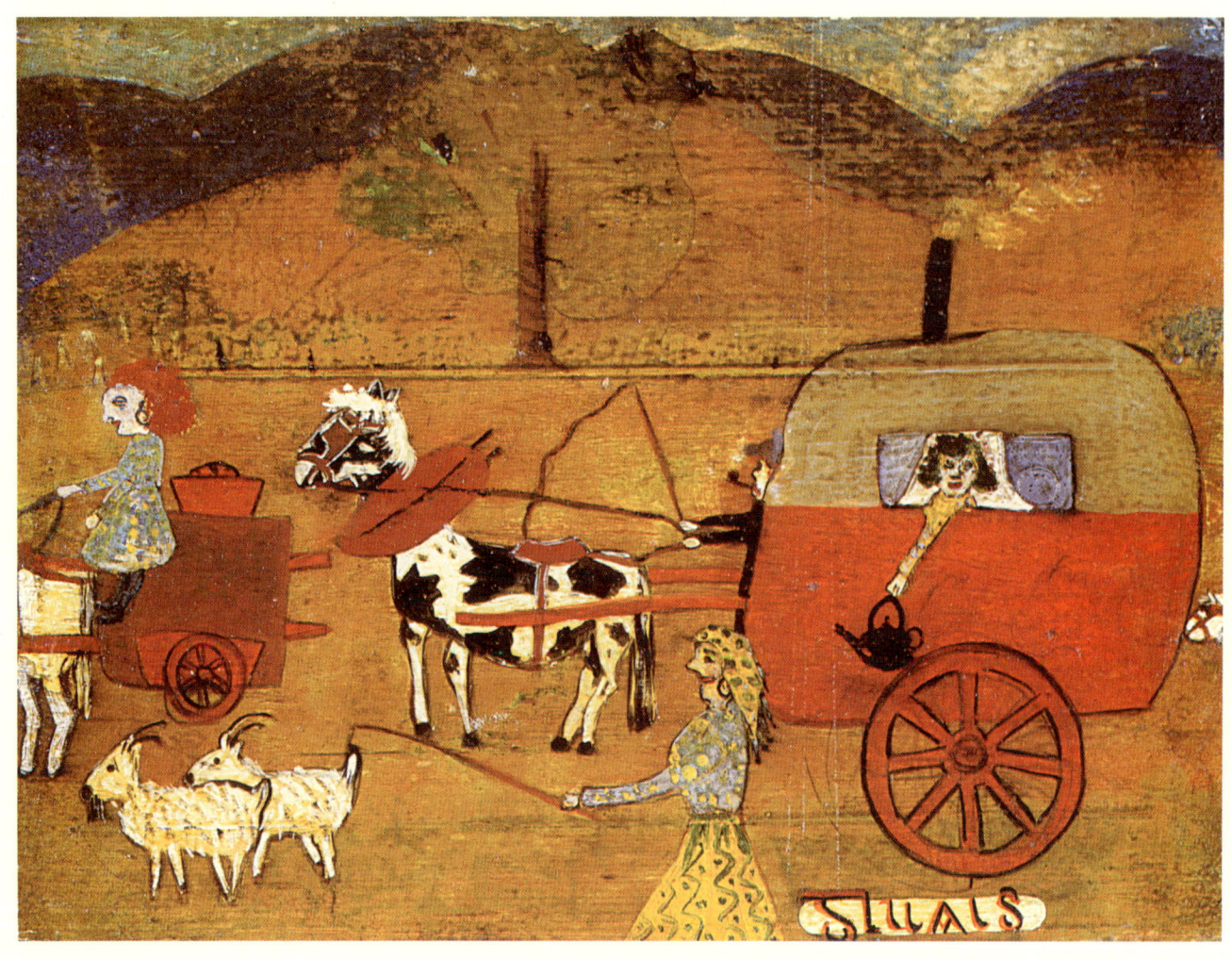

GLUAIS, TRAVELLERS
1942 • oil on board • 8" x 10"
Travelling Collection

The travellers' wooden-wheeled caravans could be heard rattling along the low road.
Sometimes they would call to beg.

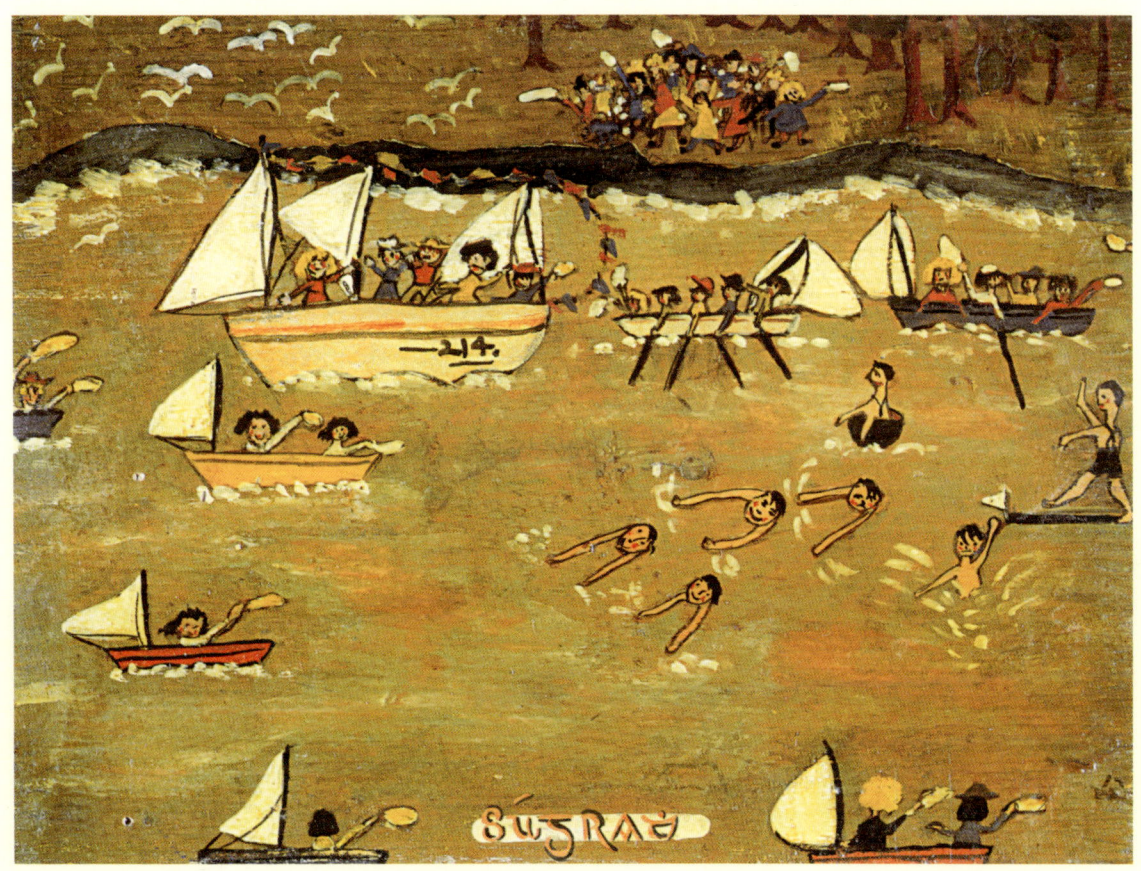

SÚGRADH, REGATTA
1942 • oil on board • 8" x 10"
Kerry Collection

The regatta had barrel races, boat races and the slippery pole, thick grease was smeared on the pole, they always fell off into the sea. Crowds gathered on the pier and the big rock opposite.

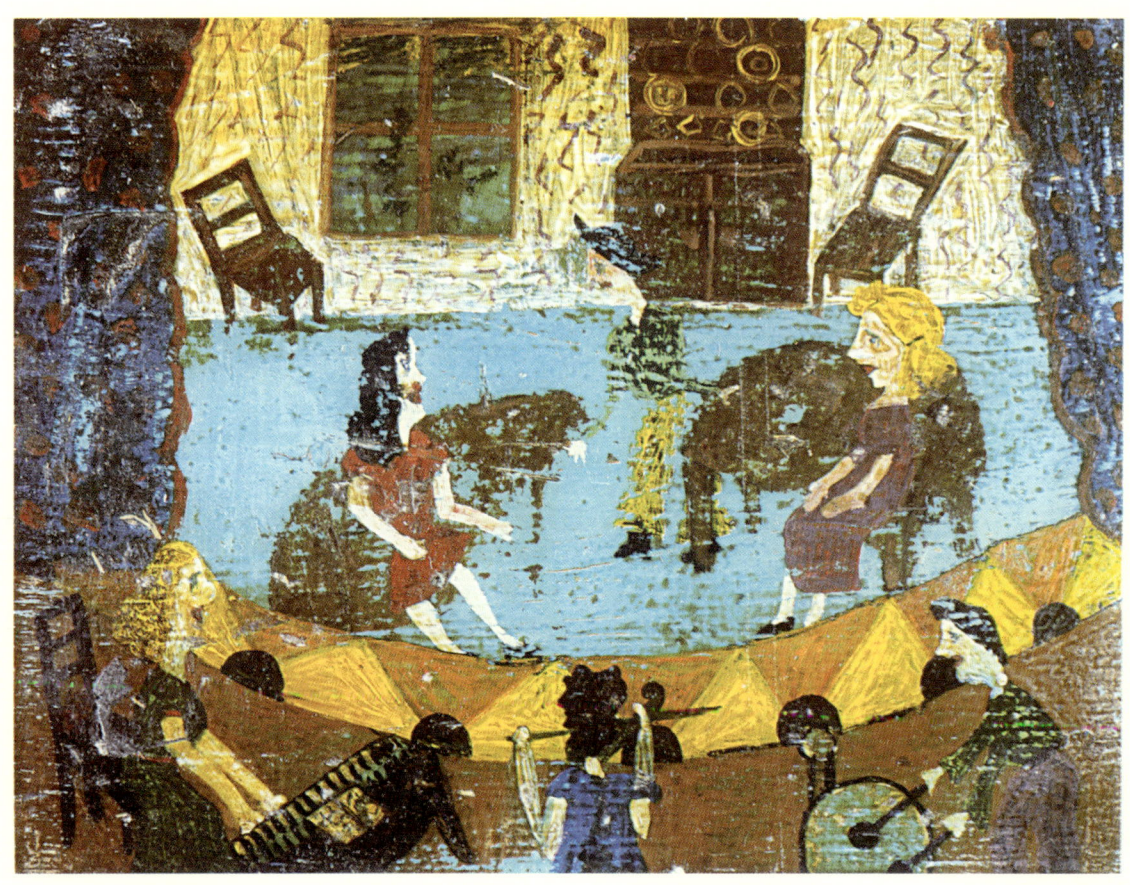

PLAY AT THE CARNEGIE LIBRARY, KENMARE
1943 • oil on board • 8" x 10"
Kerry Collection

Even if there was a storm we would go to the cinema to see films like *Tarzan* where we sat under a drip and comments would be made when somebody farted. 'There's a *fierce* smell of early York'. The Carnegie Library put on plays where we saw Anew McMaster playing Oedipus Rex who gouged out his eyes. The actors stayed at the Lansdowne Arms.

THE ABBEYGALE FAMILY

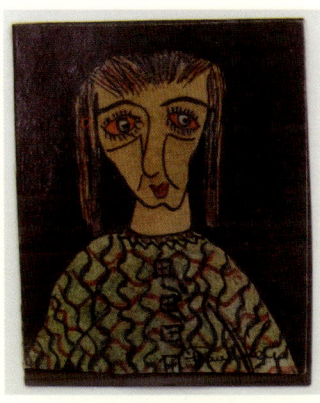

DAUGHTER
1944 • ink on card varnished • 3" x 3"
Travelling Collection

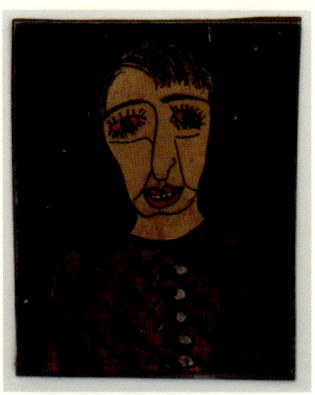

MOTHER
1944 • ink on card varnished • 3" x 3"
Travelling Collection

All of a sudden life changed. Lucy died from galloping meningitis, like her parents. Michael was rushed to Switzerland for the air, and to learn the hotel business. Harry no longer felt comfortable living on in Cillagh East. We sold our animals, and went to Belfast where we lived behind an advertisement board in a caravan. I caught the tram to school, played on the rubbish dump with a little girl who also lived in a barrel-topped caravan. Her father was a legless street artist. Briefly we lived in Londonderry in a workman's caravan on the side of a road, and a caravan on the cliffs of Portrush. Then Harry decided to fulfil her dream and get a job to educate me in the AS Neill method of progressive schooling. Hazel had gone to Newcastle to live with her Bewick grandparents where she studied to be a dietician. Harry became the vegetarian cook in the two progressive schools we went to, Blackbrook in Wales and St Catherine's in Bristol.

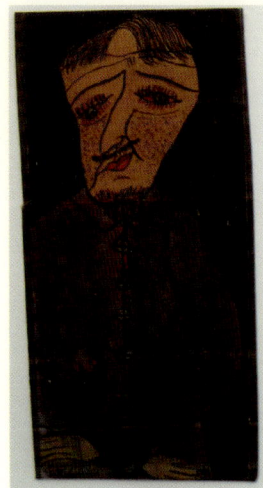

FATHER
1944 • ink on card varnished • 5" x 4"
Travelling Collection

We invented together story after story of the Abbeygale family. They lived in a cave, and had yellow skin and red whites to their eyes.

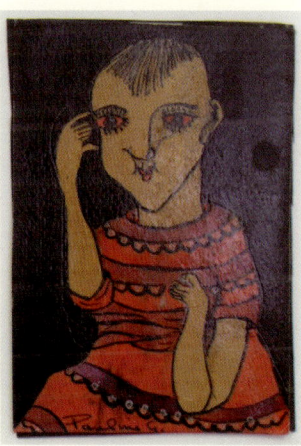

SON
1944 • ink on card varnished • 4" x 3"
Travelling Collection

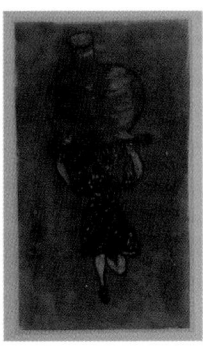

WATER CARRIER
1945 • pastels and inks • 9" x 5"
Kerry Collection

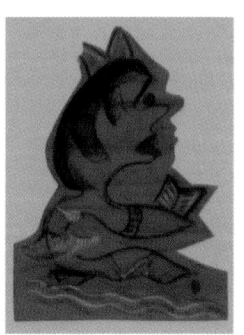

BY THE SEA
1945 • pastels and inks • 9" x 7"
Kerry Collection

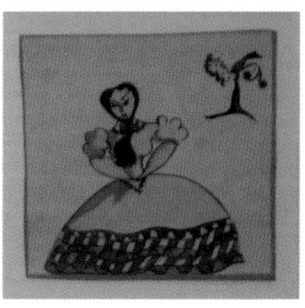

YELLOW DRESS
1945 • pastels and inks • 6" x 7"
Kerry Collection

'Don't call yourself Bewick! Why not use your middle name Gale'.
So I was to sign my pictures 'Pauline G' for quite some time.
Later she had me believe I was not Corbett Bewick's daughter, having conceived me, she said,
from a young man she met in a wheatfield.

There were always pencils, paints and paper, no matter how little money Harry had.
The drawings and paintings when finished, were popped into an old battered case.

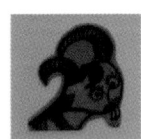

GOAT
1945 • pastels and inks • 9" x 7"
Kerry Collection

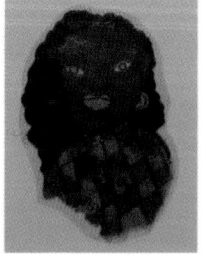

INDIAN WOMAN
1945 • pastels and inks • 9" x 7"
Kerry Collection

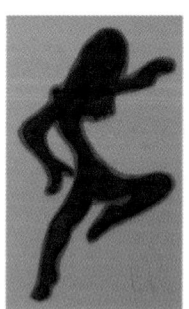

DANCER
1945 • pastels and inks • 9" x 5"
Kerry Collection

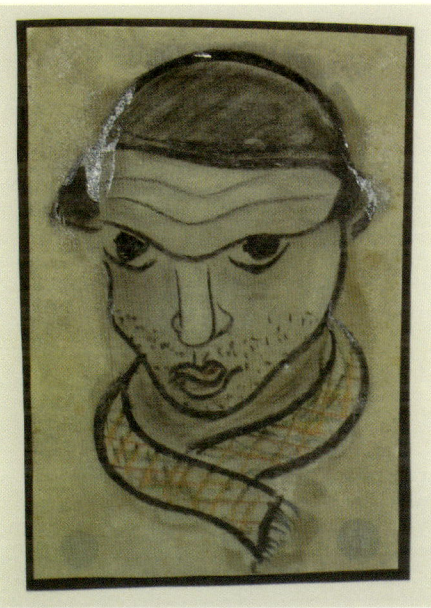

JAMES MASON
1945 • pastel • 8" x 5"
Kerry Collection

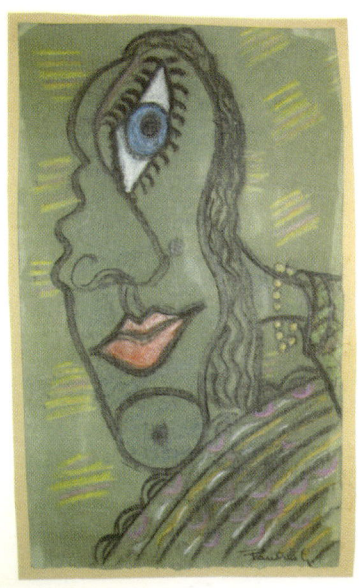

PEEPING TOM
1945 • pastel • 7" x 4"
Travelling Collection

The film stars of the day were drawn, fear of a peeping tom, and happy dancing girls, all flew out.
On the front lawn of St. Catherine's progressive school, like Isadora Duncan who Harry raved about, I danced
naked to Tchaikovsky's Sugar Plum Fairy waving a blue veil thinking how graceful I was!

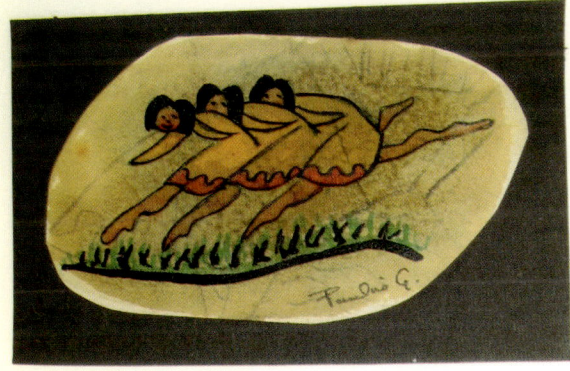

PATTERN FOR DANCING GIRLS I
1945 • ink on card varnished • 2" x 4"
Waterford Collection

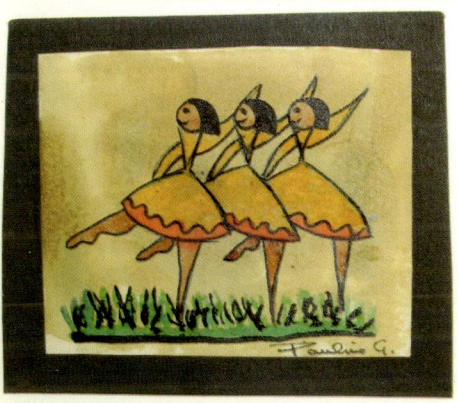

PATTERN FOR DANCING GIRLS II
1945 • ink on card varnished • 3" x 3"
Waterford Collection

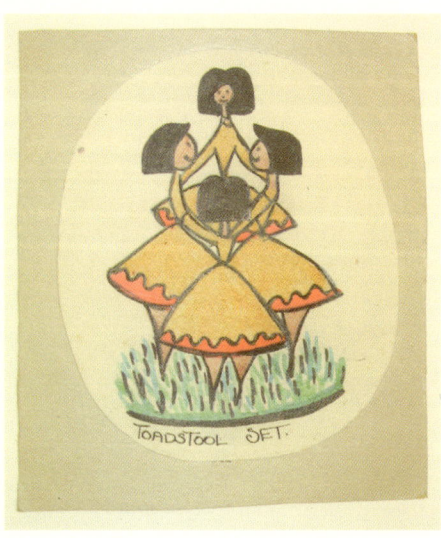

PATTERN FOR DANCING GIRLS III
1945 • ink on card varnished • 4" x 4"
Travelling Collection

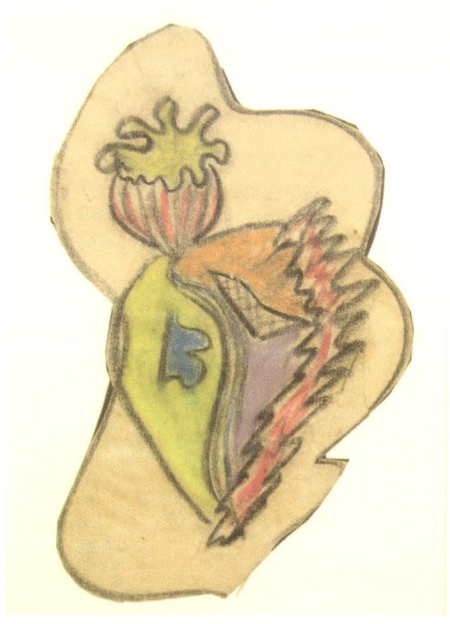

THISTLE
1945 • pastel • 7" x 5"
Waterford Collection

'That's wonderful', Harry said, 'do another and make it neater!'

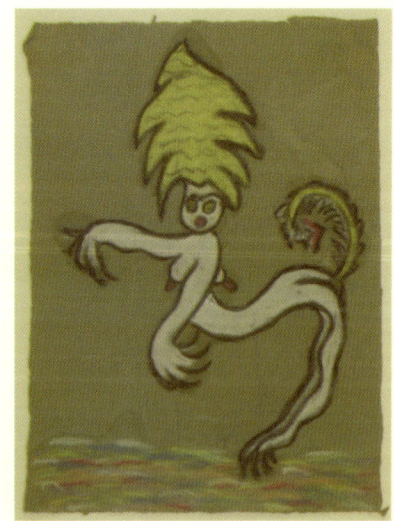

WHITE FILLY I
1945 • pastel • 7" x 5"
Waterford Collection

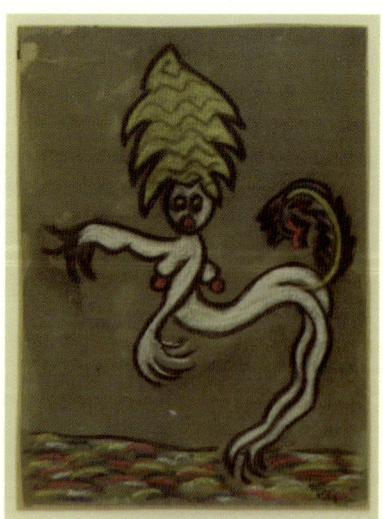

WHITE FILLY II
1945 • pastel • 7" x 5"
Waterford Collection

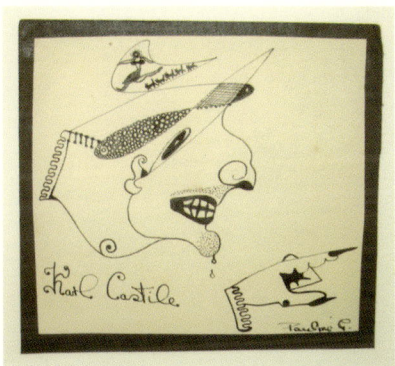

HEADMASTER POINTING
1946 • ink • 4" x 5"
Travelling Collection

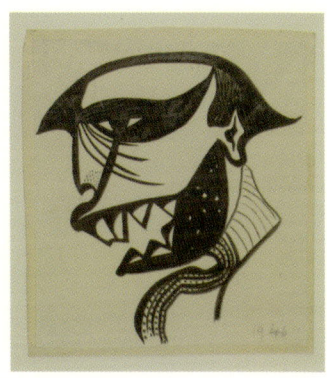

JAMES MASON WITH TEETH
1946 • ink • 6" x 6"
Kerry Collection

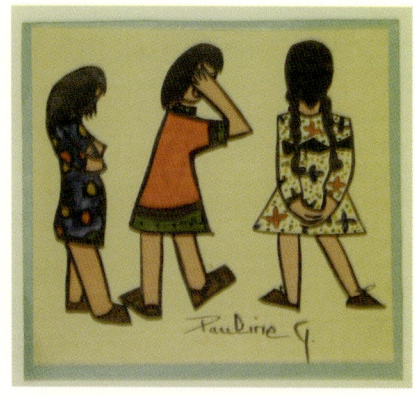

SCHOOL GIRLS
1946 • poster colours • 5" x 6"
Travelling Collection

Karl Castille, headmaster of Blackbrook Progressive School.

Conversations about quakers that I would overhear between Harry and the teachers.

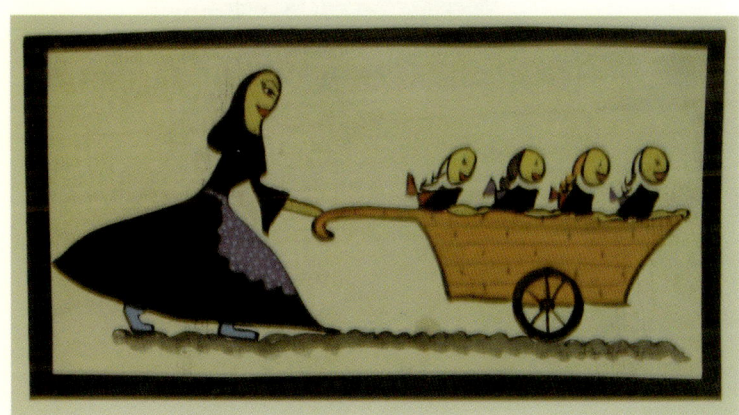

QUAKER AND BABIES
1946 • poster colours • 4" x 8"
Travelling Collection

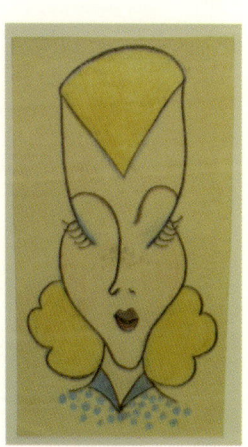

PRETTY BLONDE
1946 • crayon • 6" x 3"
Kerry Collection

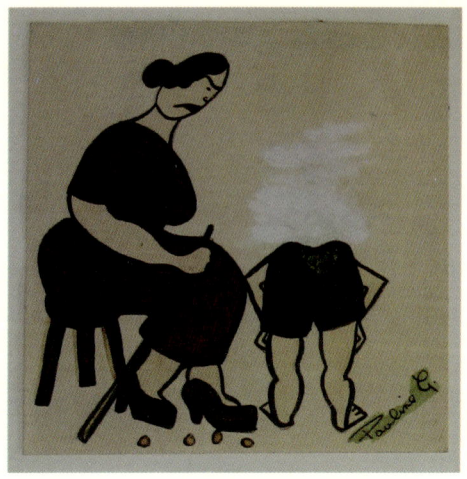

NAUGHTY BOY
1946 • poster colours • 6" x 6"
Waterford Collection

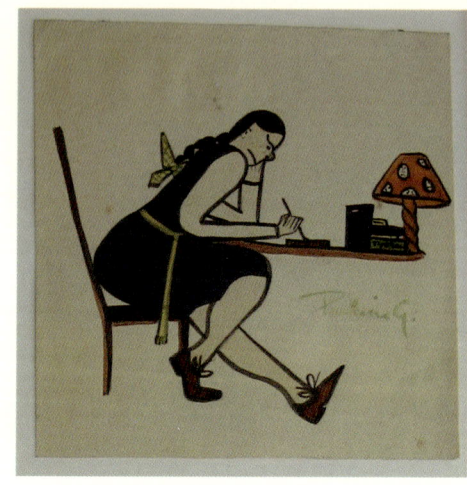

HOMEWORK
1946 • poster colours • 6" x 6"
Waterford Collection

Imaging conventional living, schooling with homework, beatings, and Father reading the newspaper.

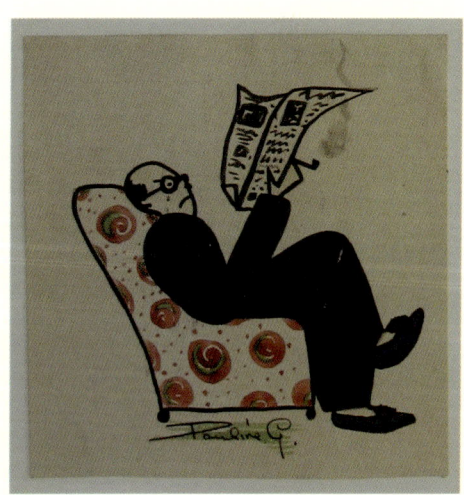

MAN IN TEARS
1946 • poster colours • 6" x 6"
Waterford Collection

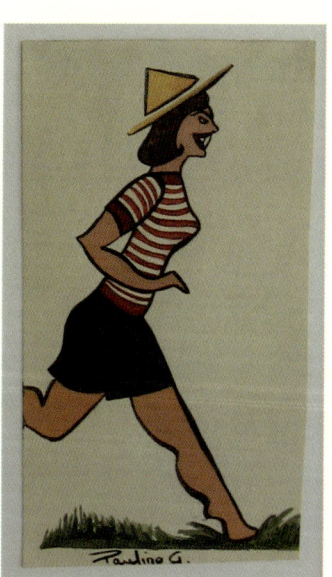

RUNNING
1946 • poster colours • 8" x 4 "
Waterford Collection

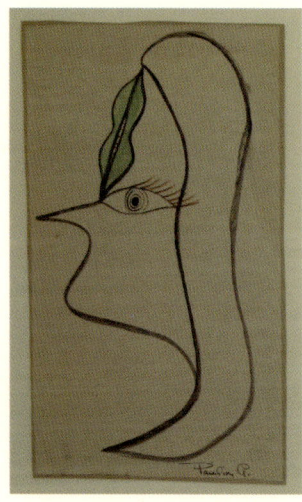

WOMAN
1946 • poster colours • 11" x 6"
Kerry Collection

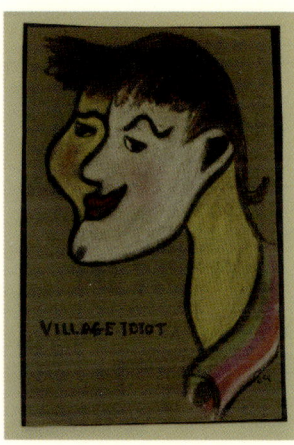

VILLAGE IDIOT
1946 • pastel • 6" x 4"
Waterford Collection

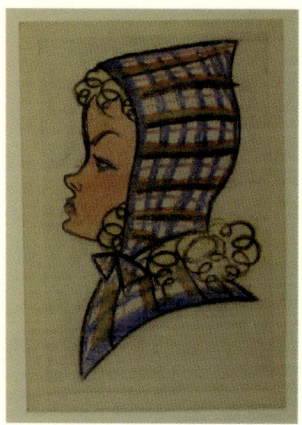

GIRL IN A PIXIE HAT
1946 • pastel • 6" x 4"
Waterford Collection

The fears and characteristics of the teachers were worked out on paper.

During school holidays we lived in another caravan in Saltford where we picked up a stray kitten, Salty.

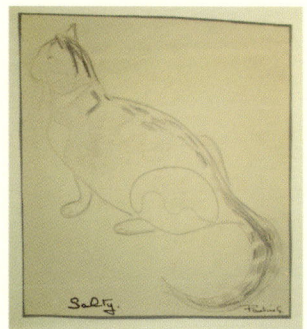

SALTY
1946 • pencil • 7" x 7"
Travelling Collection

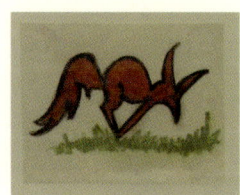

FOX
1946 • poster colours • 3" x 4"
Kerry Collection

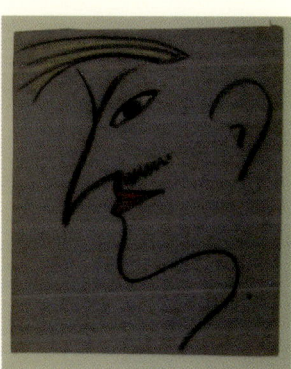

MAN
1946 • poster colours • 9" x 7"
Kerry Collection

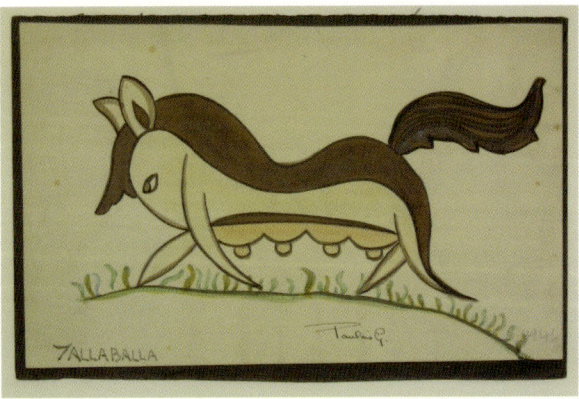

YALLABALLA
1946 • ink • 6" x 10"
Kerry Collection

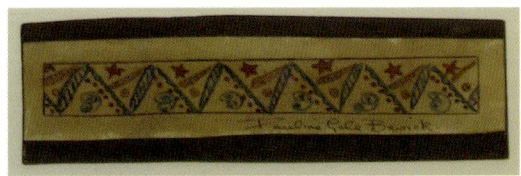

PATTERN
1946 • ink • 1" x 7"
Kerry Collection

Karl didn't hide the fact he loved women. Looking back at this picture he must have had a cruel side.

'Now you can burn your own spinach', laughed Harry and John Watling as they both resigned from the progressive school.

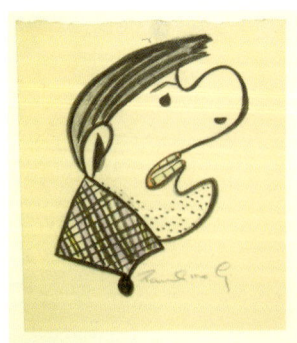

CHECKERED COLLAR
1946 • ink and pencil • 6" x 6"
Waterford Collection

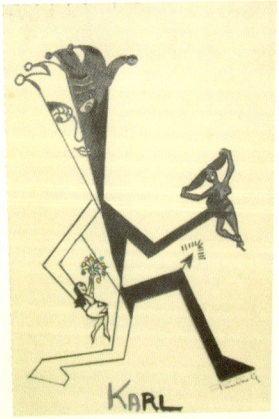

HEADMASTER WITH TWO WOMEN
1946 • Indian ink • 7" x 5"
Waterford Collection

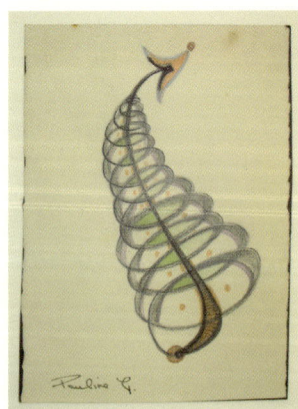

SPIRAL
1946 • poster colours • 6" x 4"
Travelling Collection

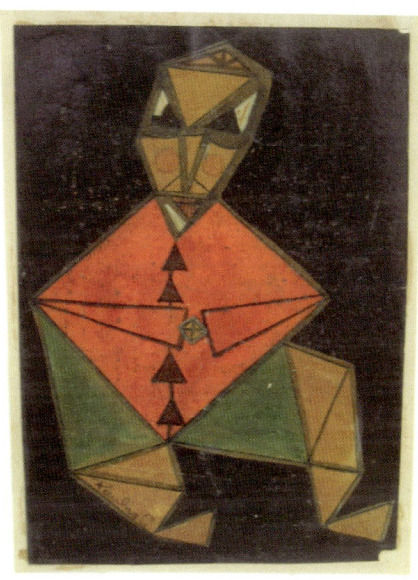

CHINAMAN
1947 • ink • 7" x 5"
Waterford Collection

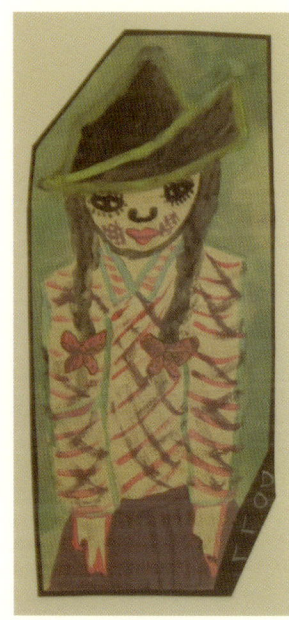

DOLL
1946 • poster colours and ink • 9" x 4"
Kerry Collection

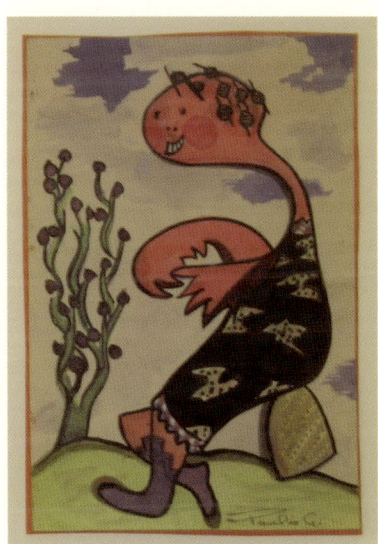

CURLERS IN HER HAIR
1946 • poster colours and ink • 7" x 5"
Kerry Collection

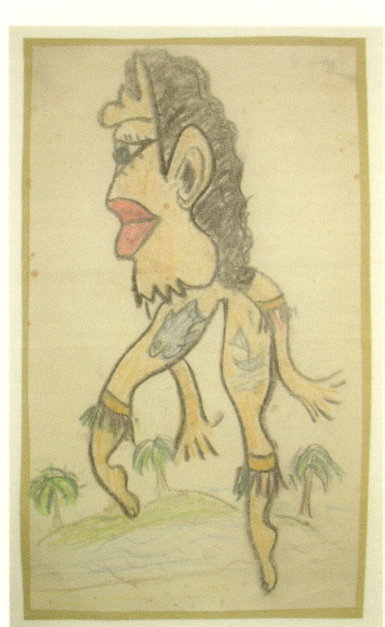

DANCER
1947 • pastel • 8" x 6"
Travelling Collection

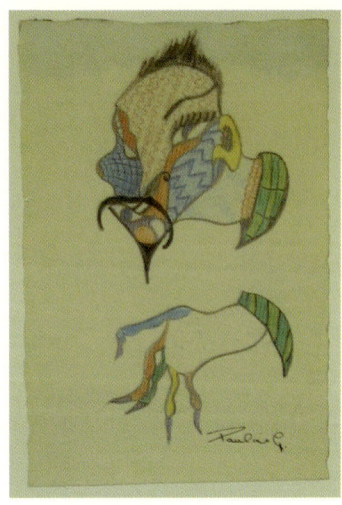

DESIGN MAN
1947 • pencils • 6" x 4"
Travelling Collection

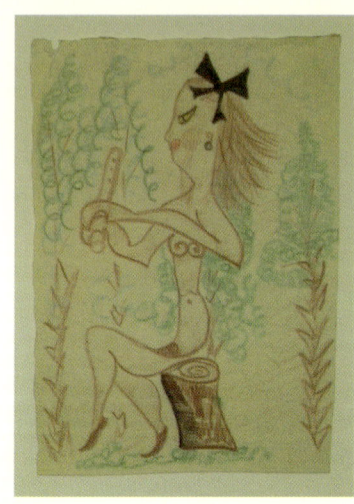

PLAYING THE FLUTE
1947 • pencils • 6" x 4"
Travelling Collection

We sold the caravan, bought a houseboat and went up Kennet and Avon Canal.

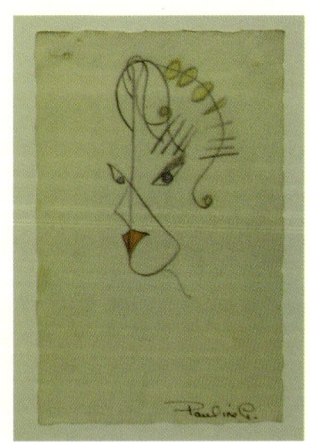

MUSIC GIRL
1947 • pencils • 7" x 4"
Travelling Collection

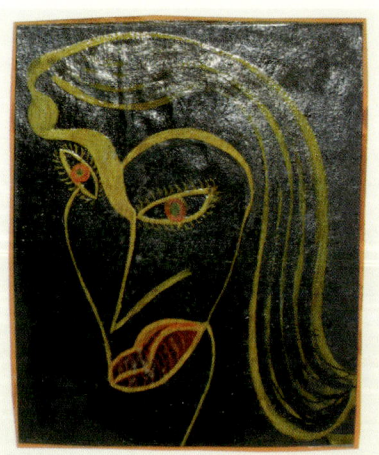

FED UP
1947 • ink varnished • 6" x 5"
Kerry Collection

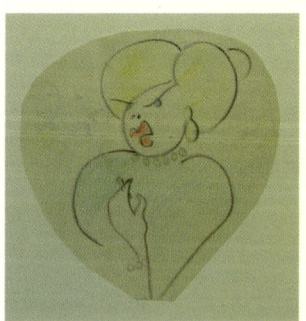

DOLLY
1947 • pencils • 6" x 6"
Travelling Collection

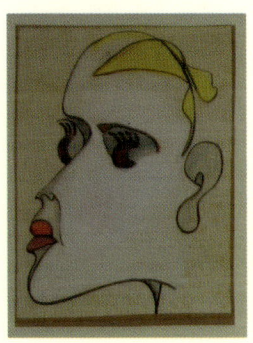

PALE WOMAN
1947 • inks and pastel • 8" x 6"
Kerry Collection

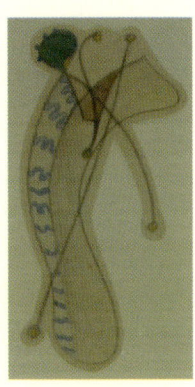

DESIGN
1947 • inks and pastel • 6" x 12"
Kerry Collection

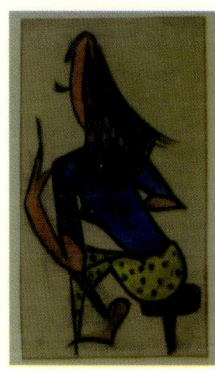

ON A STOOL
1947 • inks and pastel • 11" x 6"
Kerry Collection

The Kennet and Avon canal had not been used for sixty years. Duck-weed clogged our propeller and lay like a carpet on the surface of the water. Harry opened the window of our boat which shot Salty into the water. The hole closed over, we were hysterical with worry. She swam all the way around the boat under the duck-weed and emerged on the bank. Each day we had to move on from our mooring. Salty was missing. We called and called. She didn't appear. Five miles up the river near Divises, Salty lay curled up asleep. She stretched and jumped up on the boat as if nothing had happened. The Divises newspaper wrote all about our trip, mostly about Salty.

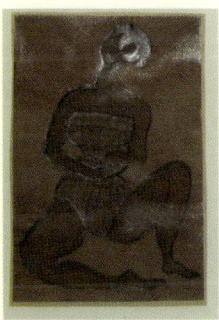

BATHER
1947 • inks and pastel • 8" x 5"
Kerry Collection

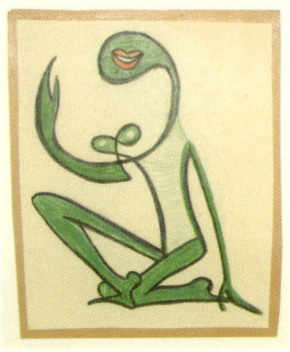

GREEN WOMAN
1947 • pencil • 5" x 5"
Waterford Collection

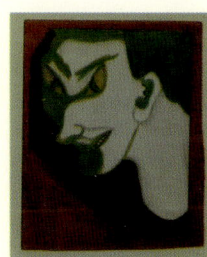

GREEN MAN
1947 • ink and pastels • 5" x 4"
Kerry Collection

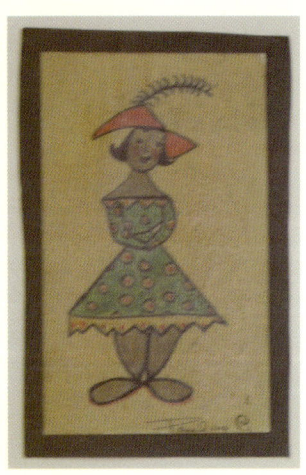

GREEN DRESS
1947 • ink varnished • 5" x 3"
Travelling Collection

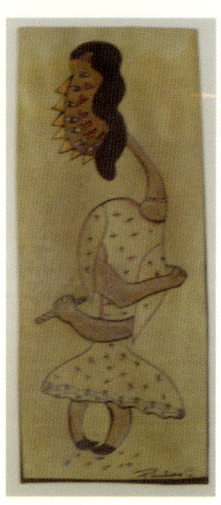

ROCK SWEET
1947 • ink varnished • 8" x 4"
Travelling Collection

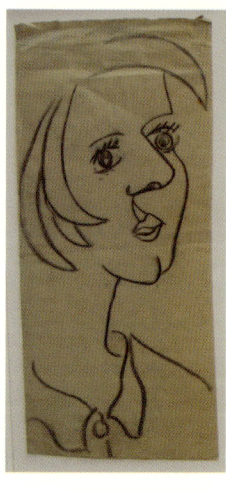

ONE BUTTON
1947 • ink, pencil and charcoal • 11" x 5"
Waterford Collection

In these days I didn't made life-long friends as we were always on the move, always meeting new faces.

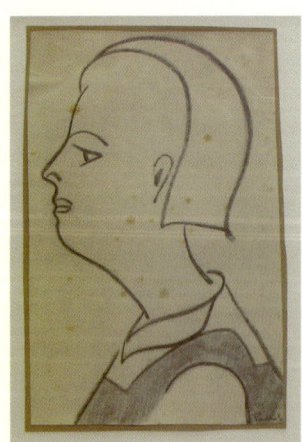

SCHOOL GIRL
1947 • ink, pencil and charcoal • 7" x 5"
Waterford Collection

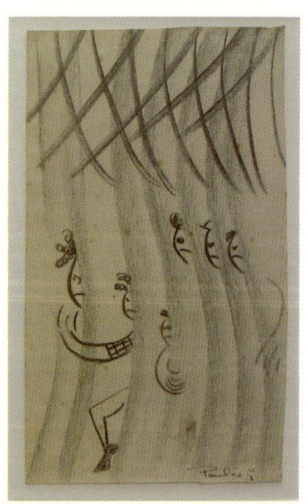

HIDE & SEEK
1947 • ink, pencil and charcoal • 10" x 6"
Waterford Collection

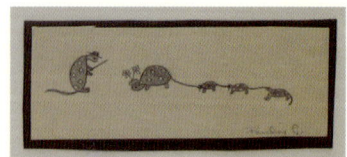

TURTLES
1947 • ink, pencil and charcoal • 1" x 4"
Waterford Collection

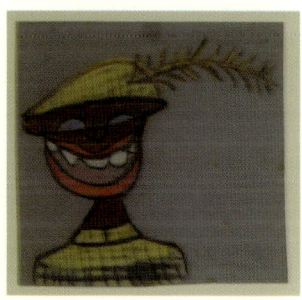

SAMBO
1947 • pastel, crayon and ink • 7" x 7"
Travelling Collection

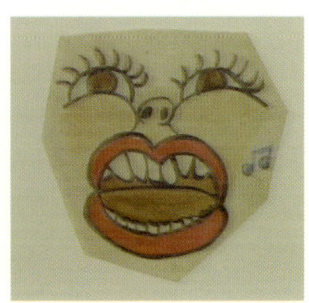

SINGER
1947 • pastel, crayon and ink • 3" x 3"
Travelling Collection

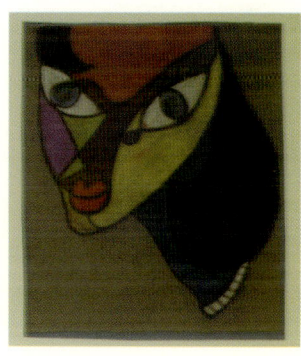

LOVELY LADY
1947 • pastel, crayon and ink • 7" x 6"
Travelling Collection

The little table in the boat was spread with paper and colours as we travelled mile upon mile up the canal.

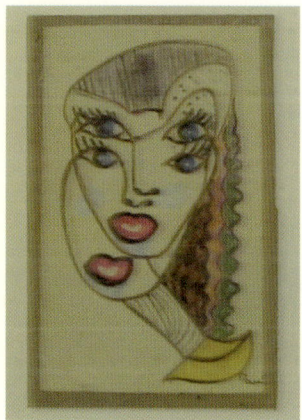

DOUBLE VISION
1947 • pastel, crayon and ink • 4" x 3"
Travelling Collection

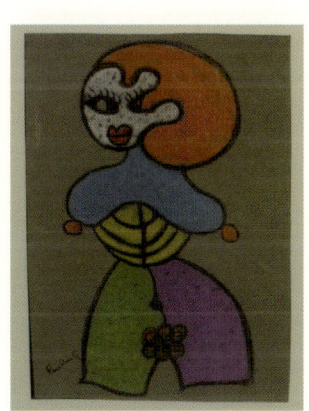

MODEL
1947 • pastel • 6" x 5"
Kerry Collection

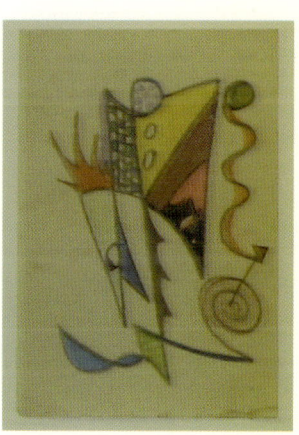

PATTERN
1947 • pastel, crayon and ink • 5" x 3"
Travelling Collection

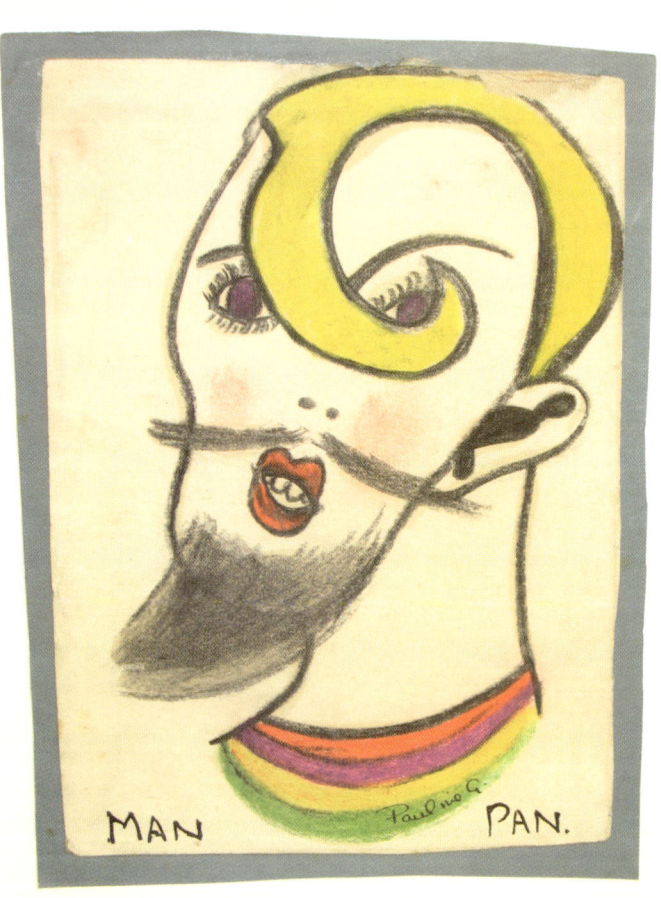

PAN
1947 • pastel • 6" x 5"
Waterford Collection

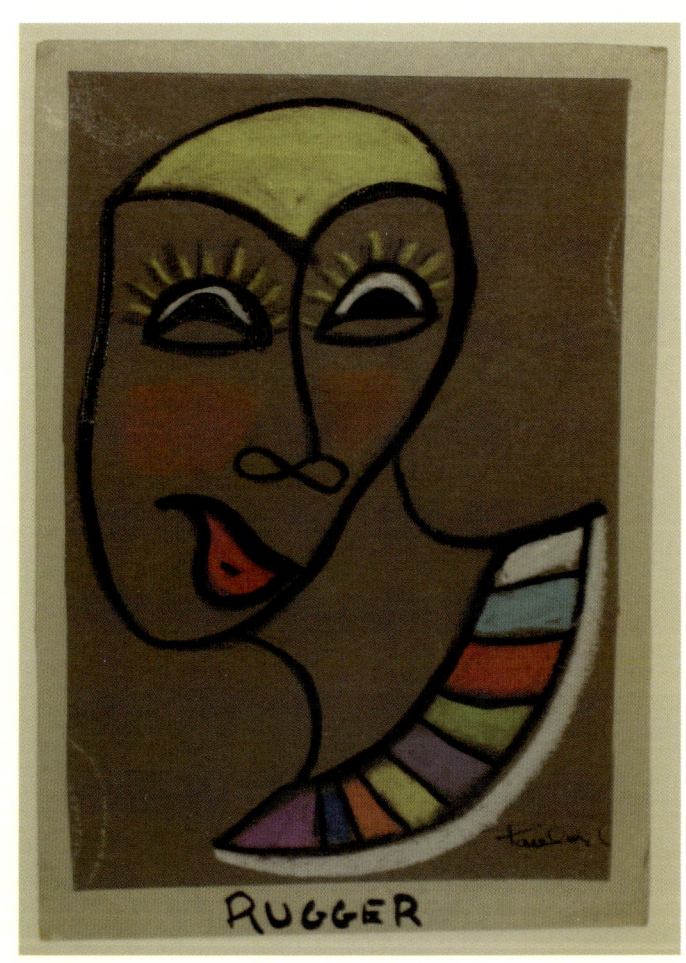

RUGGER
1947 • pastel and ink • 6" x 4"
Kerry Collection

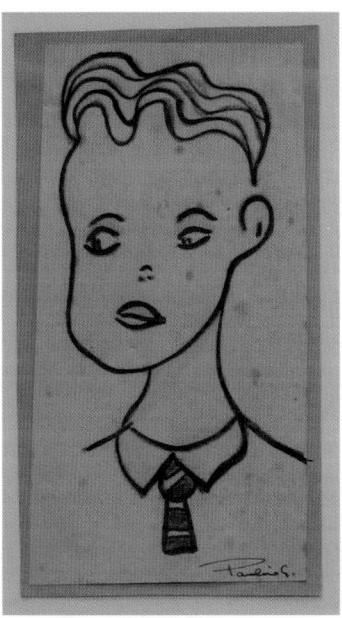

SCHOOLBOY
1947 • ink, pencil and charcoal • 6" x 3"
Waterford Collection

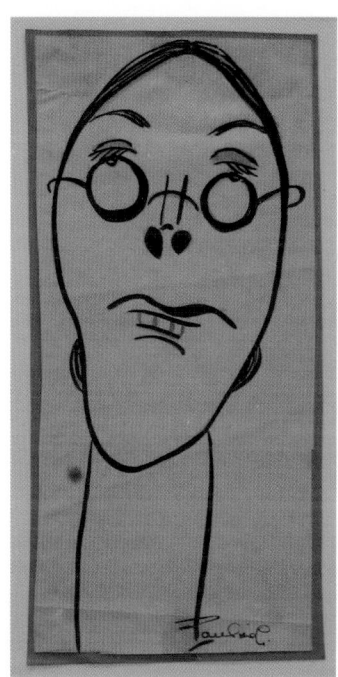

ROUND SPECS
1947 • ink, pencil and charcoal • 8" x 4"
Waterford Collection

Harry said: 'don't wash up, you draw'.

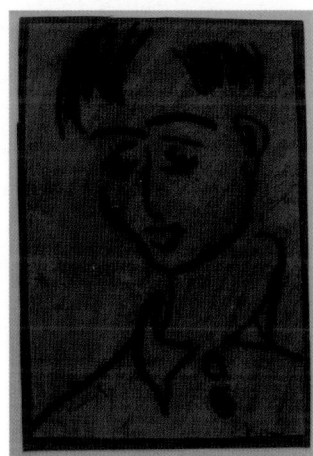

TWO BUTTONS
1947 • ink, pencil and charcoal • 6" x 4"
Waterford Collection

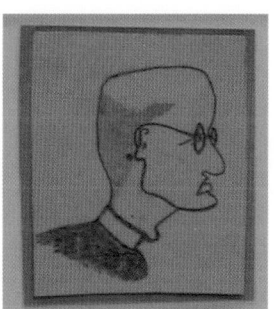

ADAM'S APPLE
1947 • ink, pencil and charcoal • 2" x 2"
Waterford Collection

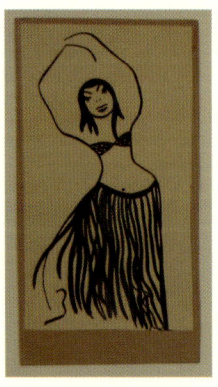

HULA
1947 • ink • 7" x 4"
Kerry Collection

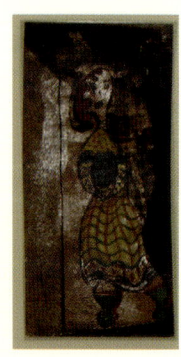

THROUGH A DOOR
1947 • ink • 6" x 3"
Kerry Collection

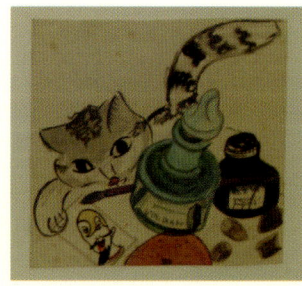

SALTY AND PEN
1947 • ink • 6" x 6"
Kerry Collection

We got to Henley on Thames and we settled at Bushmill's Boathouse and I went to school - this time a conventional one. They got me to design their sunken garden, but many's the corner I stood in for lack of concentration. The boat was heaven, ideas, conversations, wishes and fears poured out.

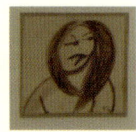

CROSS
1947 • ink • 2" x 2"
Kerry Collection

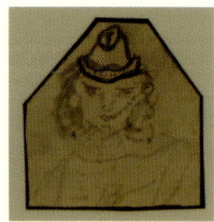

CRYSTAL WOMAN
1947 • ink • 3" x 3"
Kerry Collection

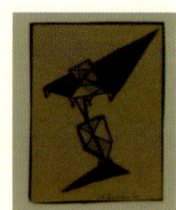

SMOKING
1947 • ink • 4" x 4"
Kerry Collection

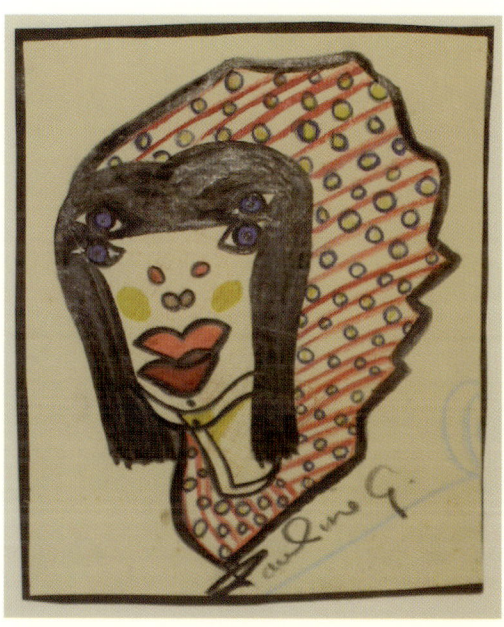

SEEING DOUBLE
1947 • pencil and ink • 5" x 5"
Kerry Collection

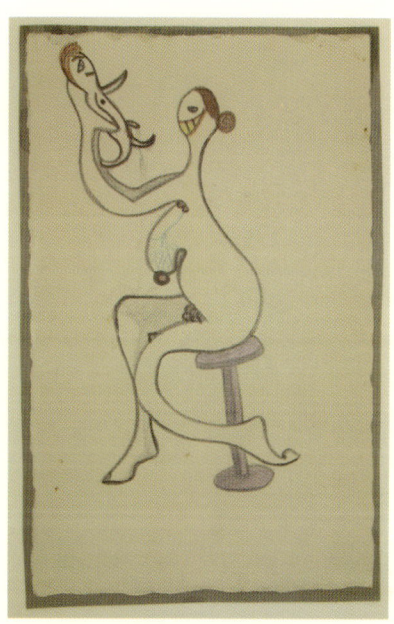

MOTHER AND SON
1947 • pencil • 7" x 4"
Travelling Collection

Prophetic as she is like a hula dancer.

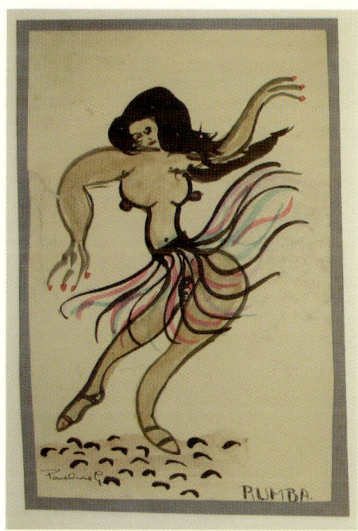

RUMBA
1947 • ink varnished • 8" x 5"
Waterford Collection

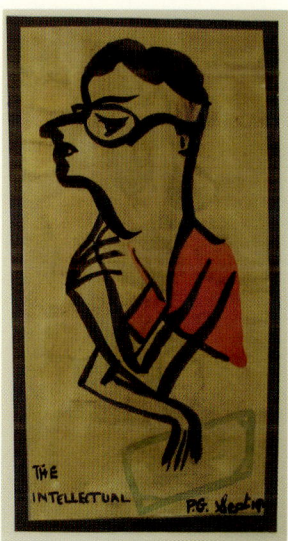

INTELLECTUAL
1947 • ink varnished • 8" x 4"
Waterford Collection

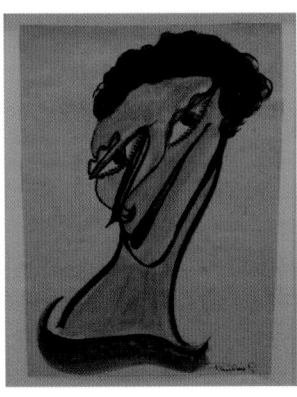

SMILE
1947 • ink and poster colours • 9" x 6"
Waterford Collection

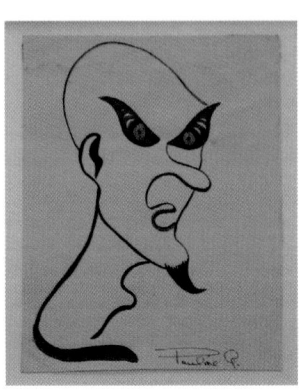

MR
1947 • ink and poster colours • 9" x 14"
Waterford Collection

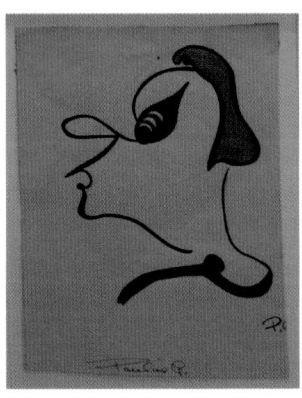

MRS
1947 • ink and poster colours • 9" x 14"
Waterford Collection

Tahiti and the South Pacific, Margaret Mead and Western Samoa were conversations I would paint to, that she and John Watling would discuss.

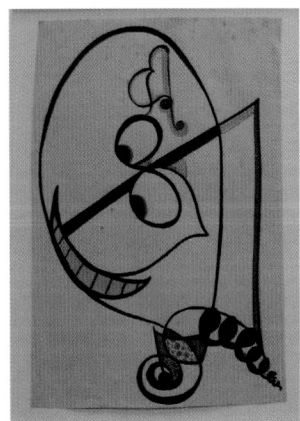

PENCIL NOSE
1947 • ink and poster colours • 9" x 6"
Waterford Collection

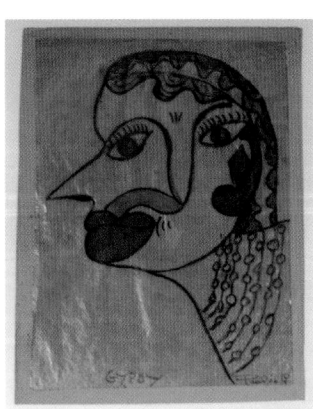

GYPSY
1947 • ink varnished • 10" x 8"
Travelling Collection

VARIOUS CHARACTERS
1948 • indian ink and charcoal • 11" x 6" and similar dimensions
Travelling Collection

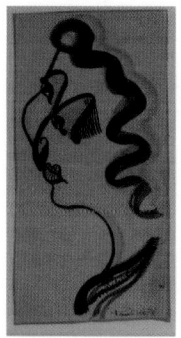
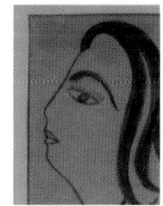
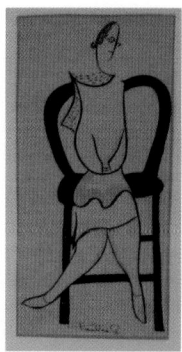
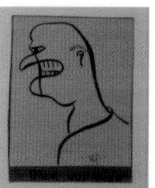

John Watling fell in love one day when he was walking through Henley with Harry.
Her name was Nicandra McCarthy, model for Augustus John.
Nicandra became a constant presence in our lives,
her high heels, long red hair, the one brown dress with blue and white horses all over it,
impressed me as much as the bride in Kenmare.

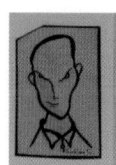
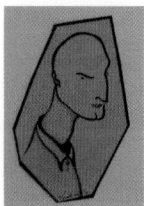
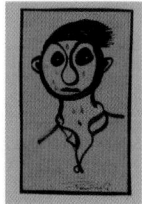
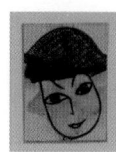
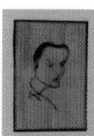

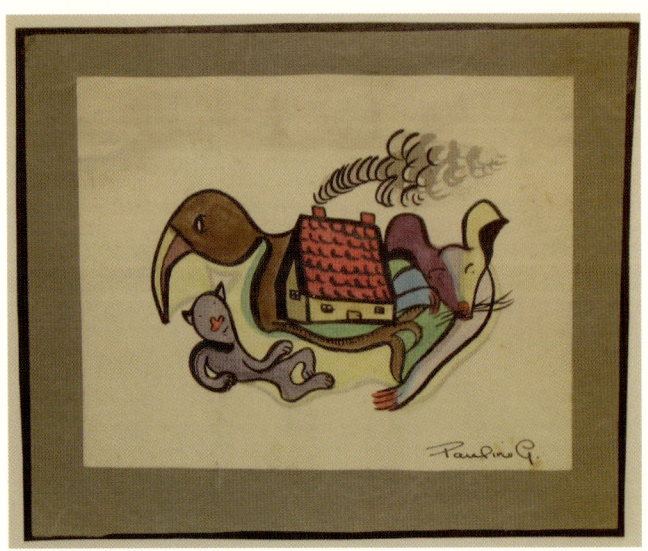

ANIMAL HOUSE
1948 • ink • 4" x 5"
Kerry Collection

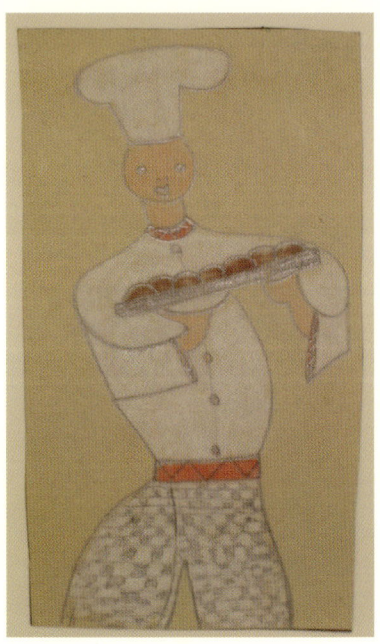

BAKER
1948 • pencil and pastel • 7" x 4"
Kerry Collection

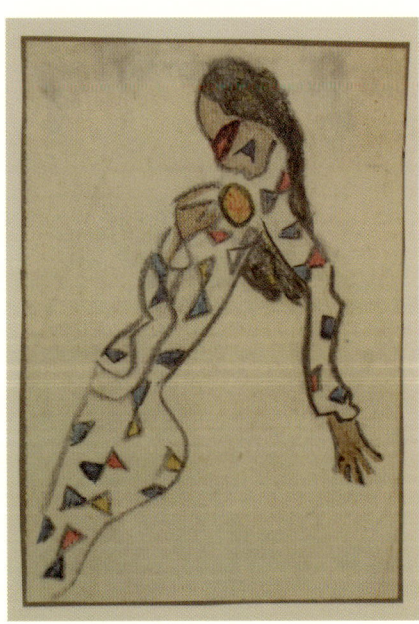

BLACK HAIRED NICANDRA
1948 • pastel • 6" x 4"
Kerry Collection

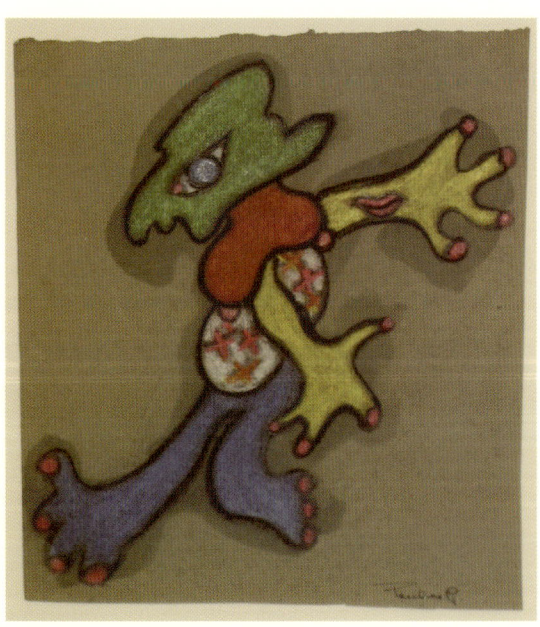

DANCING PHANTOM
1948 • pastel • 7" x 6"
Kerry Collection

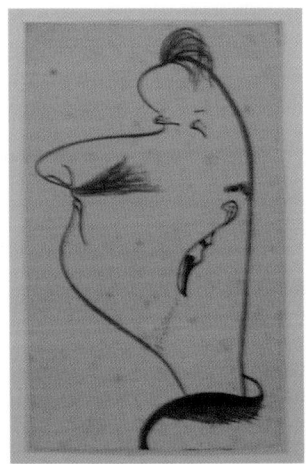
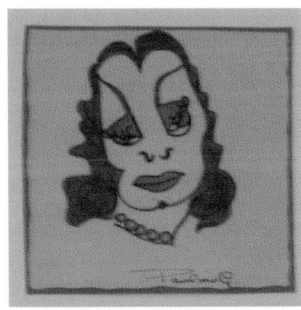
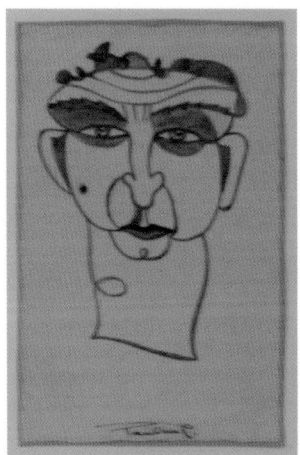

Mr and Mrs Rudd lived on the boat next to us. His wife asked, 'what shall I give him for his tea? I could give him a salad, potatoes, lasagne, spaghetti …' Eventually Harry said, 'boil the bugger an egg'.

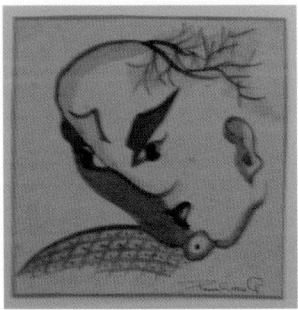
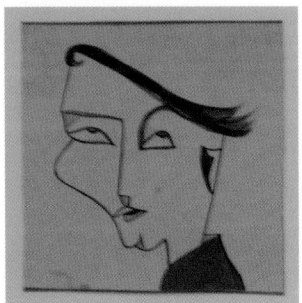
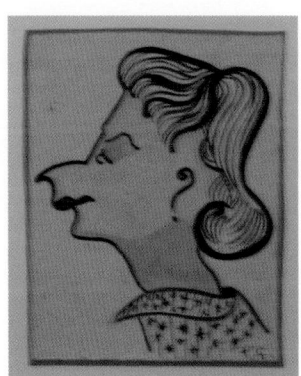

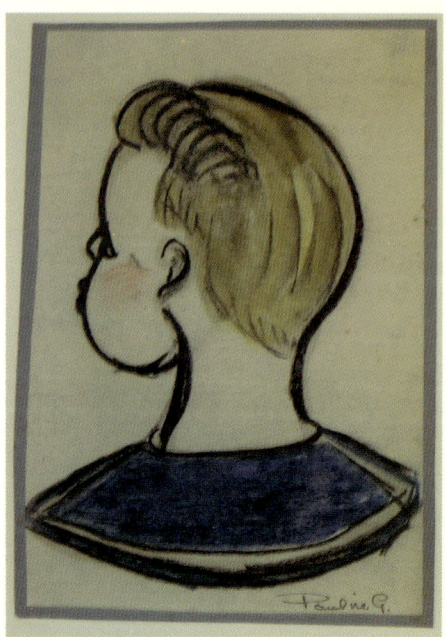

THE CHRISTMAS PARTY I
1948 • pastels • 9" x 6"
Travelling Collection

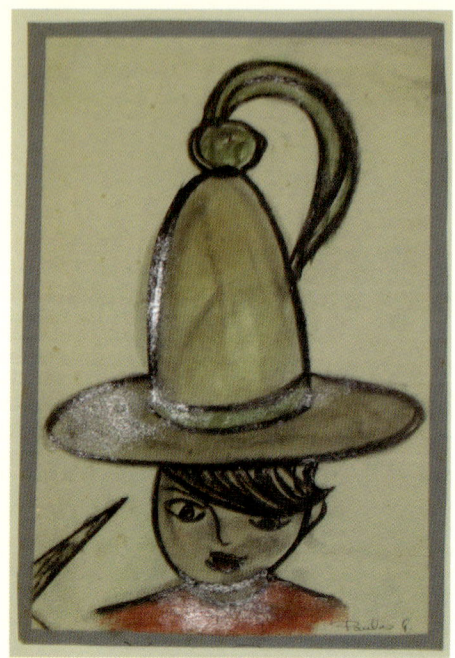

THE CHRISTMAS PARTY II
1948 • pastels • 9" x 6"
Travelling Collection

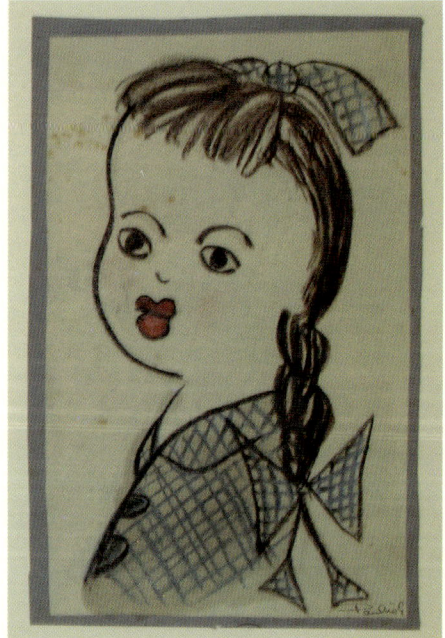

THE CHRISTMAS PARTY III
1948 • pastels • 9" x 6"
Travelling Collection

Characters from a Christmas party, including
Colm William Wallace. Harry laughed when I
said 'Collie Willie Wally is a naughty boy'.

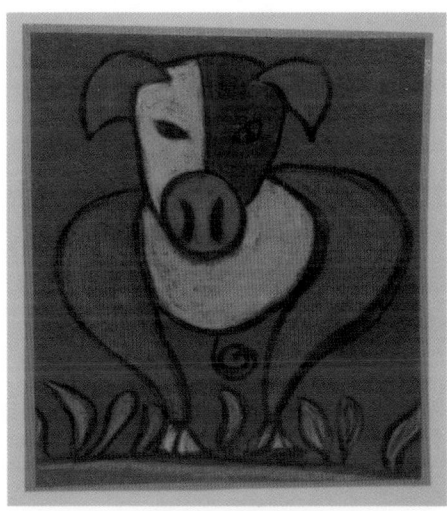

COLOURED PIG
1948 • pastel • 4" x 4"
Kerry Collection

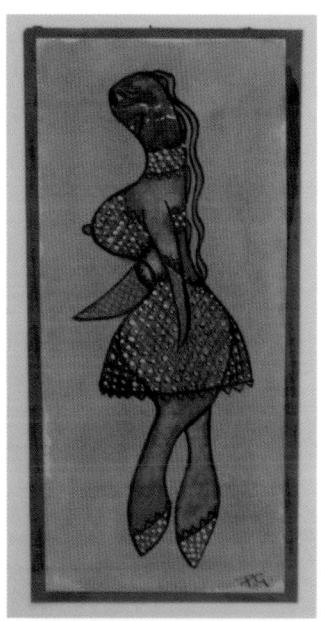

EARTH MOTHER DRESSED UP
1948 • ink varnished • 7" x 3"
Kerry Collection

From our boat we would see swimmers with hairy chests and bikinis.

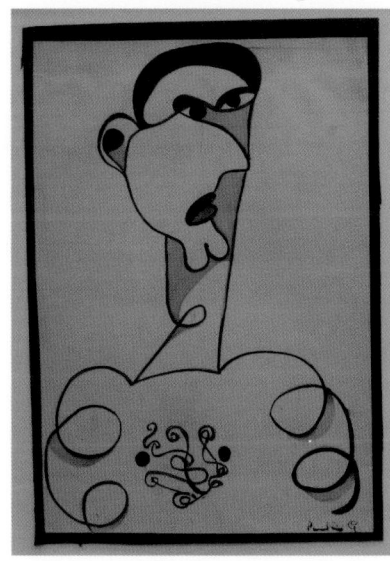

HAIRY CHEST
1948 • ink and poster colour • 10" x 7"
Waterford Collection

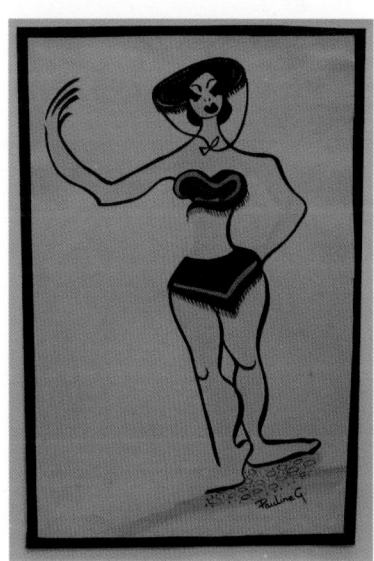

BIKINI
1948 • ink and poster colour • 9" x 6"
Waterford Collection

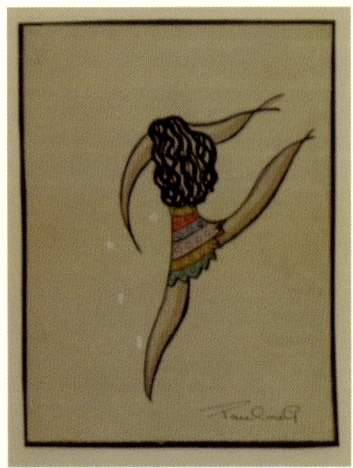

DANCER
1948 • ink • 6" x 5"
Kerry Collection

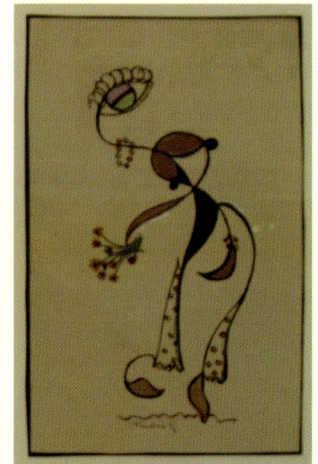

DILLETANTE
1948 • ink • 8" x 5"
Kerry Collection

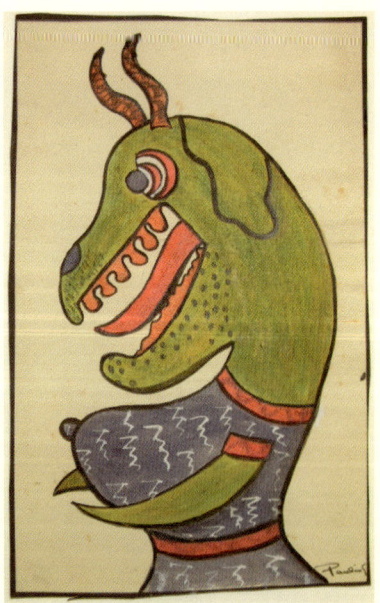

GREEN GRANDE DAME
1948 • ink • 7" x 4"
Travelling Collection

The green grande dame was a friend of my mother's.

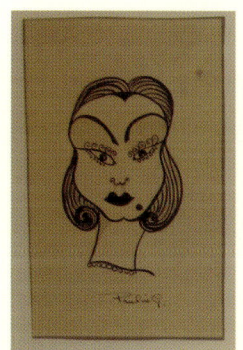
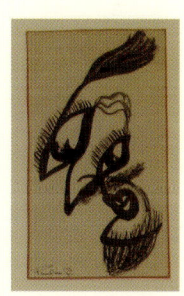
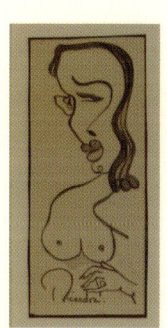
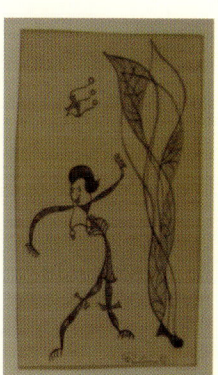

At times I envied my friends living in beautiful houses.
'Why can't I eat like the others, instead of sandwiches of railway bank herbs?'

Pictures came from conversations overheard.
Harry laughed and praised as she mounted and titled the pictures, popping them into the suitcase.
The flow was, as it is today, continuous.

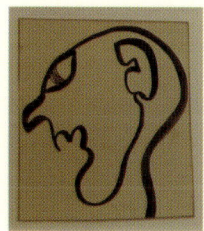
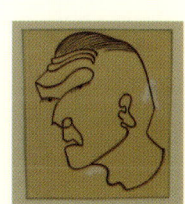
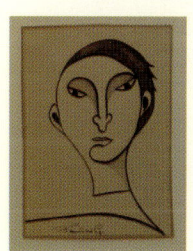
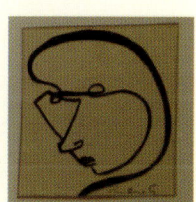

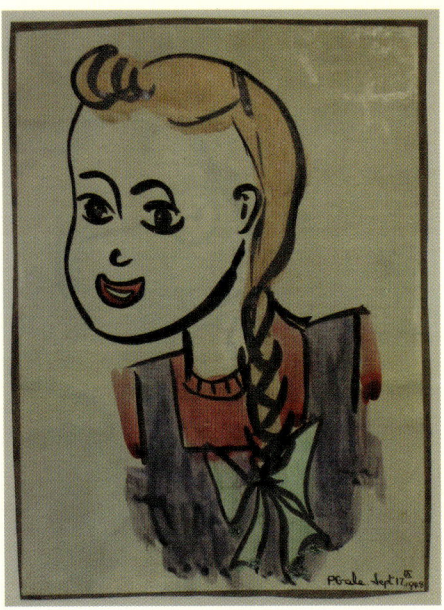

INNOCENT
1948 • ink • 6" x 4"
Kerry Collection

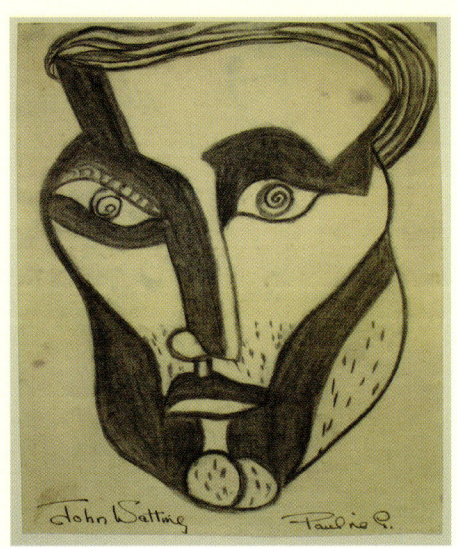

JOHN WATLING
1948 • charcoal • 8" x 6"
Waterford Collection

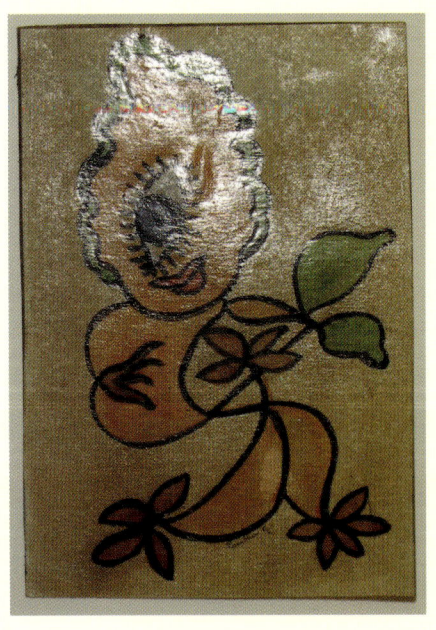

LEMON LADY
1948 • ink varnished • 6" x 4"
Kerry Collection

There was nothing to fear from John, he filled the place with jokes, laughter, dirty songs and his beautiful Nicandra. I don't know why I painted him looking scary.

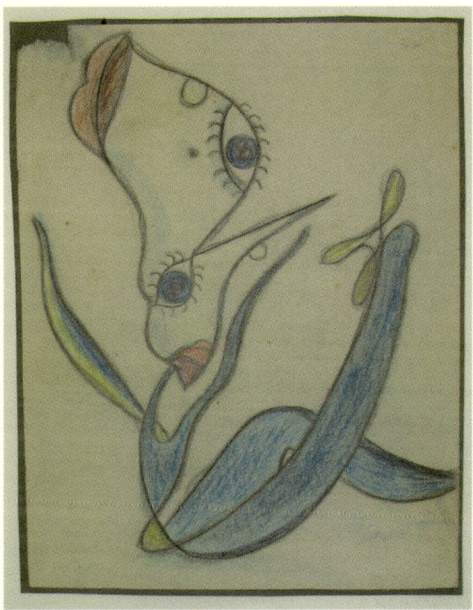

LIPPY LADY
1948 • pastel • 8" x 6"
Waterford Collection

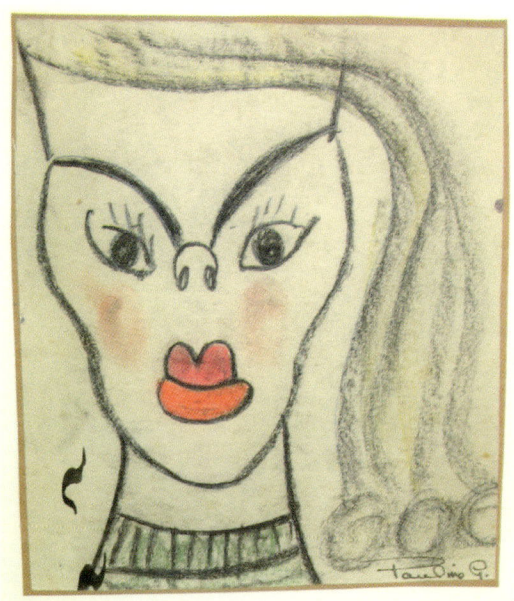

ME
1948 • pastel • 7" x 6"
Waterford Collection

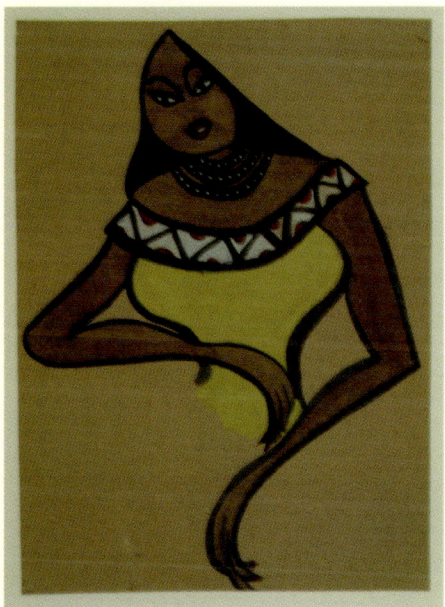

MEXICAN
1948 • poster colour and ink varnished • 10" x 7"
Travelling Collection

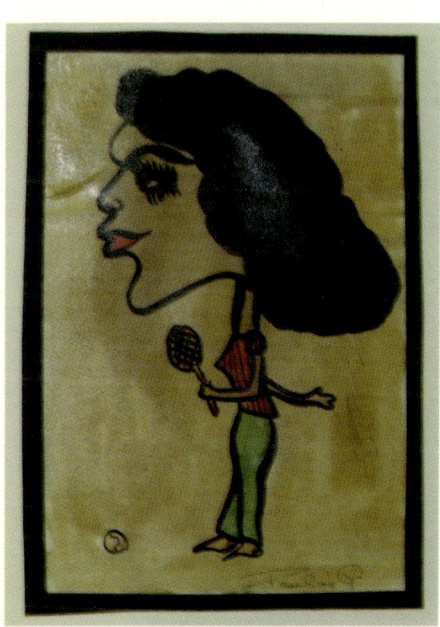

TENNIS PLAYER
1948 • poster colour and ink varnished • 8" x 5"
Travelling Collection

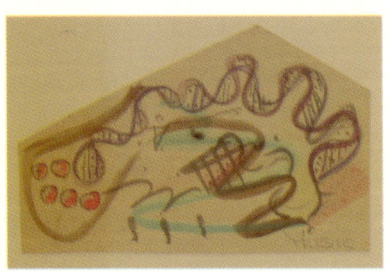

MUSIC I
1948 • ink • 4" x 7"
Kerry Collection

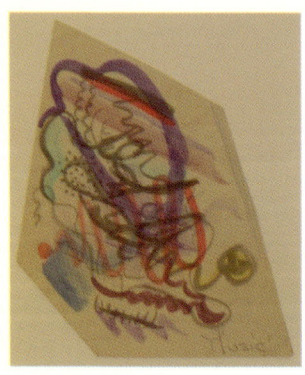

MUSIC II
1948 • ink • 6" x 6"
Kerry Collection

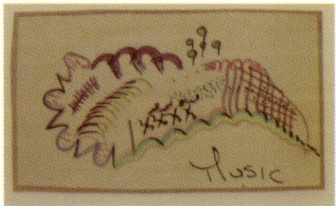

MUSIC III
1948 • ink • 3" x 6"
Kerry Collection

Detecting the hidden side of not only Nicandra, but of people all around, seemed to be a therapeutic thing to do.

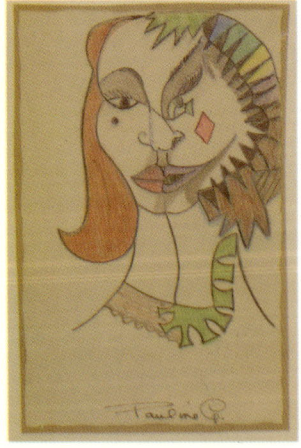

NICANDRA TWO FACED
1948 • coloured pencil and ink • 7" x 4"
Kerry Collection

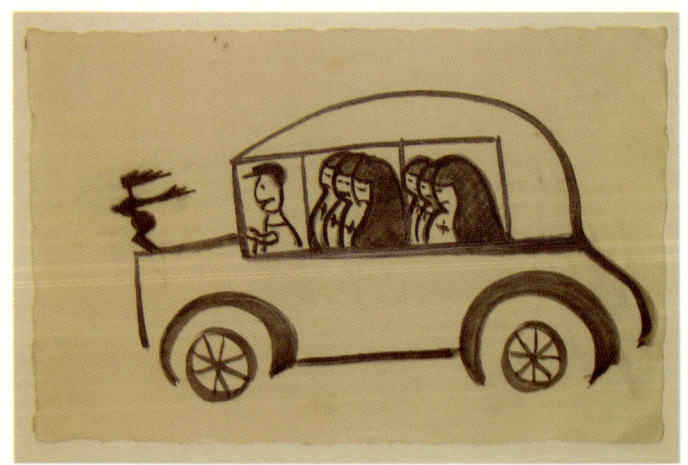

NUNS IN A TAXI
1948 • ink • 4" x 7"
Waterford Collection

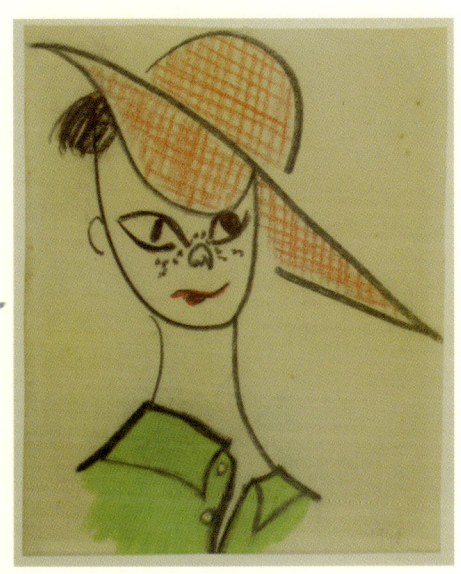

PARTY BOY
1948 • pastel • 8" x 7"
Kerry Collection

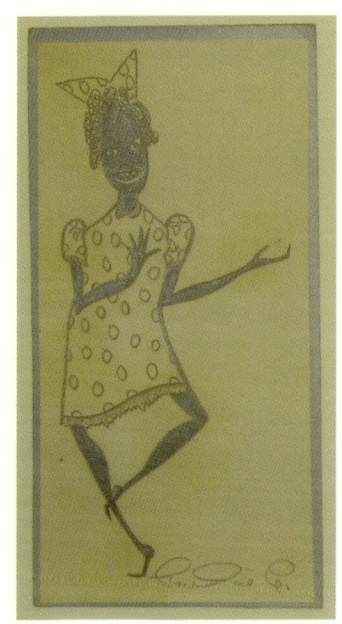

PICKANINNY
1948 • pencil and ink • 9" x 4"
Kerry Collection

Imaging what went on in this policeman's head under his helmet.

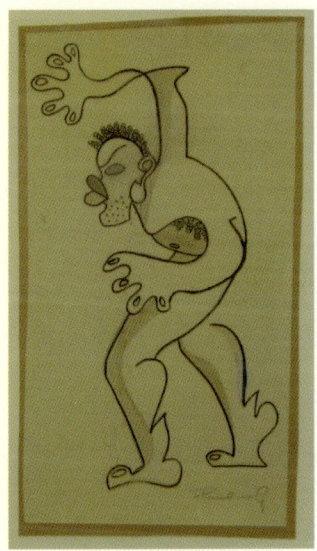

BOXER
1948 • pencil and ink • 8" x 4"
Kerry Collection

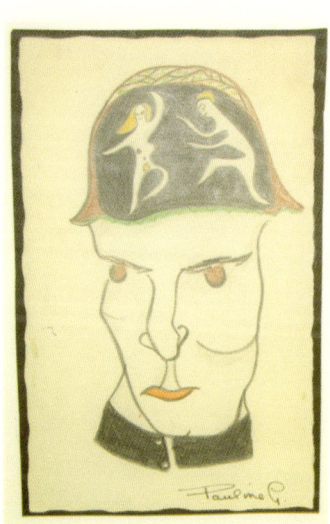

POLICEMAN
1948 • pencil • 7" x 4"
Waterford Collection

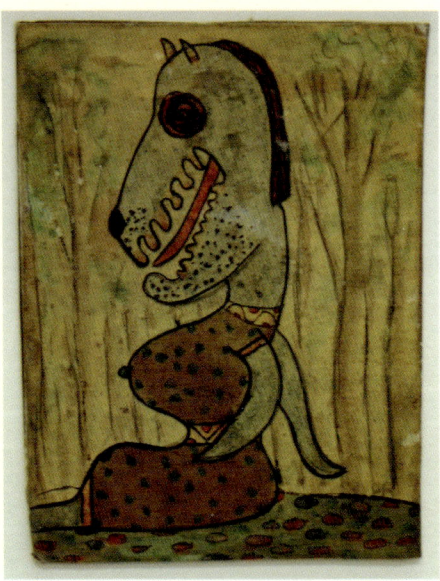

PREHISTORIC LADY
1948 • ink varnished • 5" x 4"
Waterford Collection

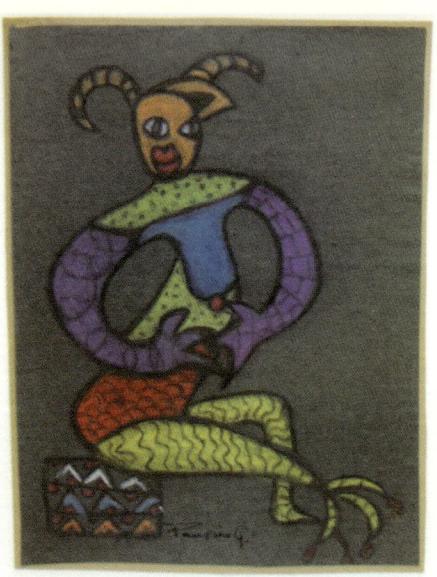

YUBA
1948 • ink • 6" x 5"
Waterford Collection

Karl Castille, the headmaster had a multi-faceted nature. Even after leaving school, he
continued to appear in drawings.

If a picture was good but messy, Harry said 'it's marvellous, but do it again'.
Then she would varnish or spray the pictures.

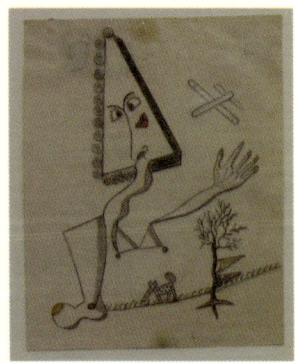

HEADMASTER I
1948 • pencil • 6" x 5"
Travelling Collection

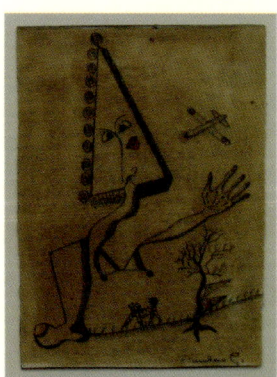

HEADMASTER II
1948 • pencil varnished • 6" x 4"
Travelling Collection

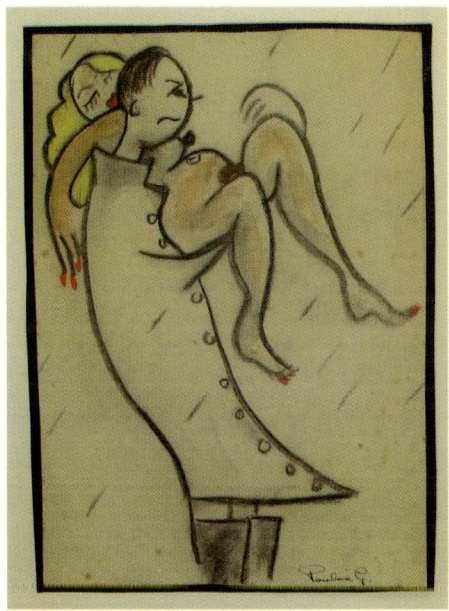

FROM THE RAIN
1948 • pastel and ink • 10" x 7"
Travelling Collection

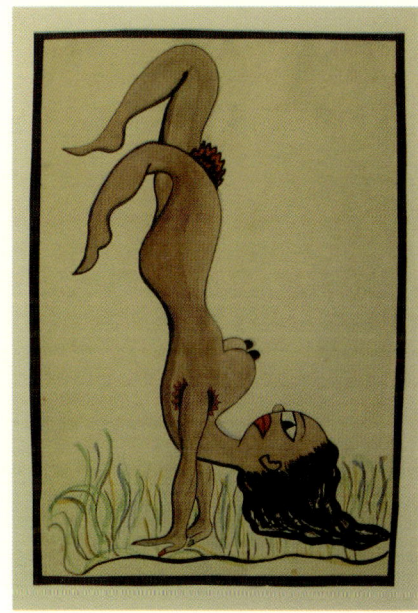

HANDSTAND
1948 • pastel and ink • 9" x 6"
Travelling Collection

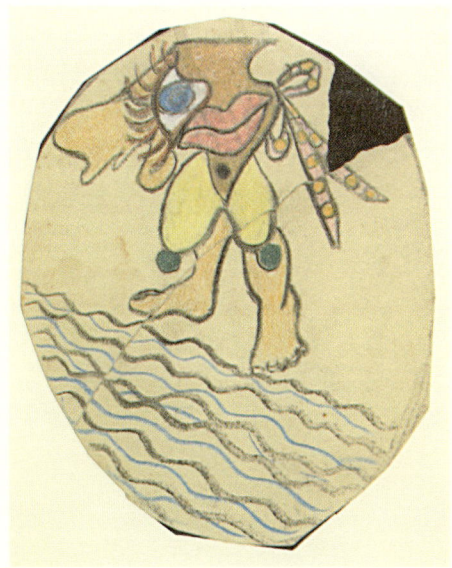

WALKING ON WAVES
1948 • pastel • 5" x 4"
Waterford Collection

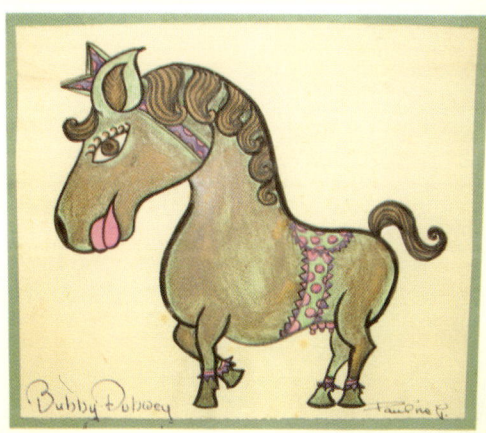

BUBBY DUBWEY
1948 • ink • 6" x 7"
Waterford Collection

VARIOUS CHARACTERS
1948 • pastel and ink • 6" x 4" and similar dimensions
Waterford Collection

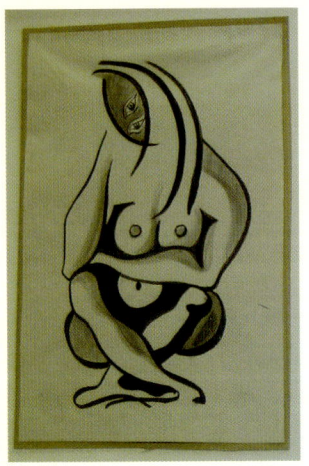 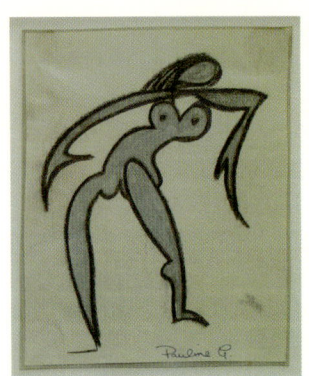 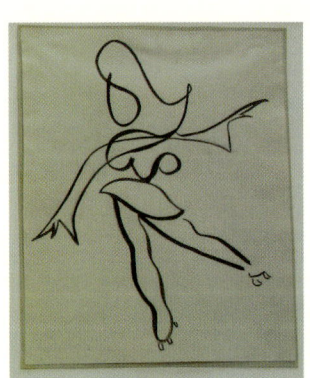 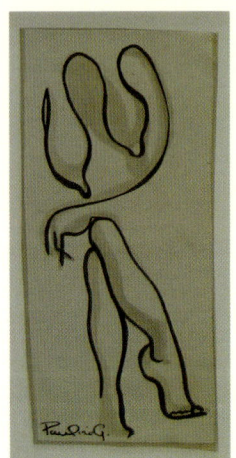

The Thames flooded and Harry fell off our boat when cleaning the desk. But for the fact that she clung on to a branch she may not have survived. I came back from school to hear her story. In the boat, space being so cosy, I would hear such conversations as conscientious objectors, Bertrand Russell and the pros and cons of abortion.

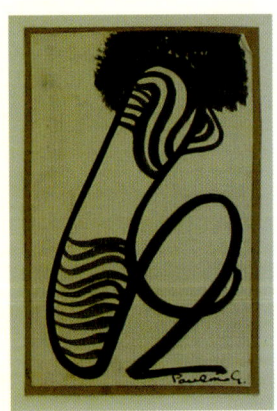 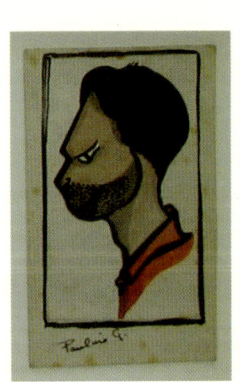 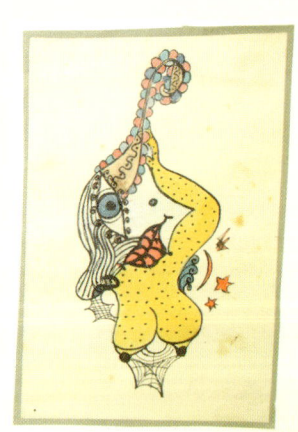

VARIOUS CHARACTERS
1948 • pastel and ink • 6" x 4"
Waterford Collection

WOMAN, MOON AND STARS I
1948 • ink varnished • 5" x 3"
Waterford Collection

WOMAN, MOON AND STARS I
1948 • ink varnished • 4" x 2
Waterford Collection

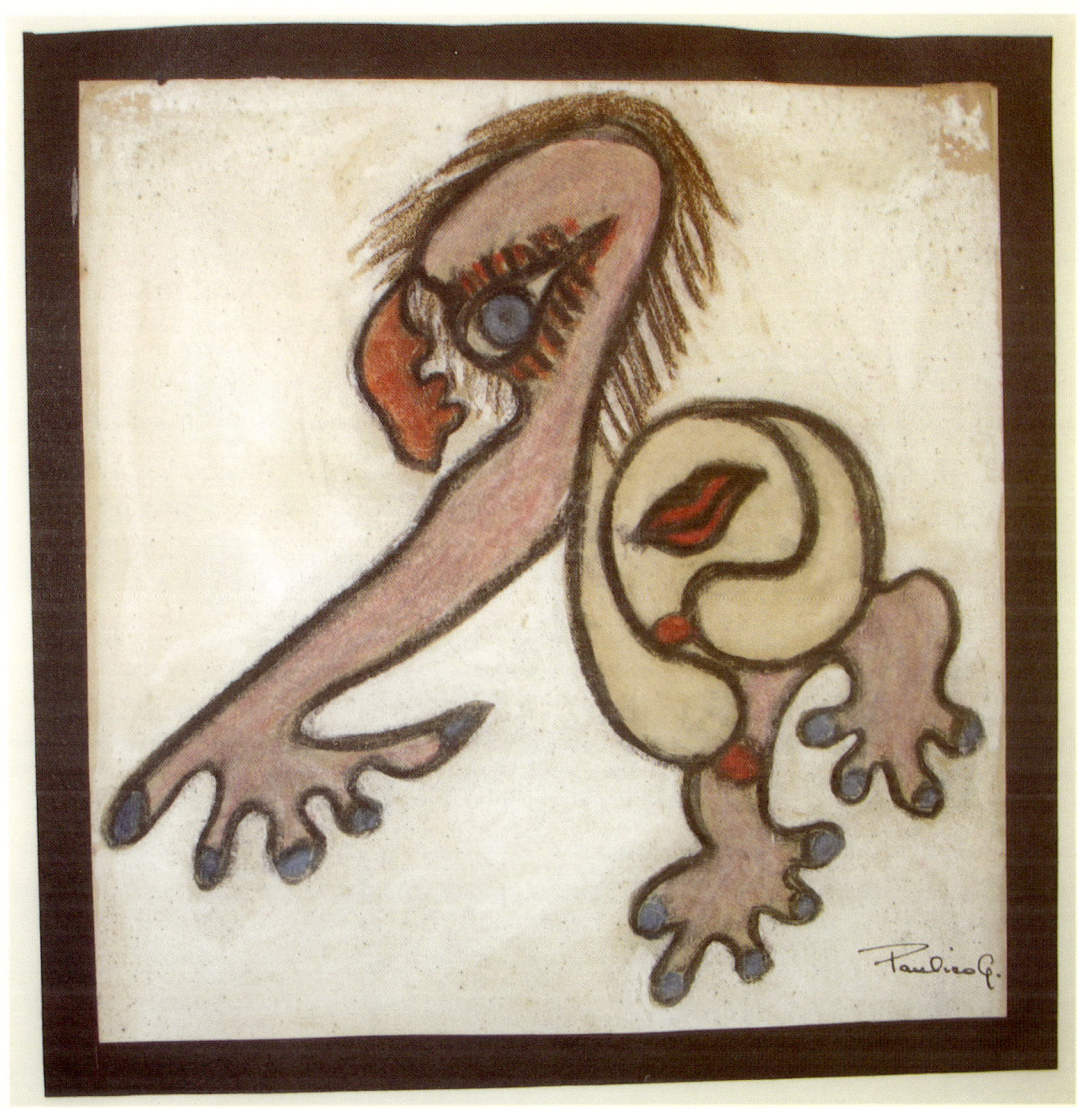

ABORTION
1948 • pastel • 6" x 6"
Travelling Collection

This pastel was what I imagined abortion to be.

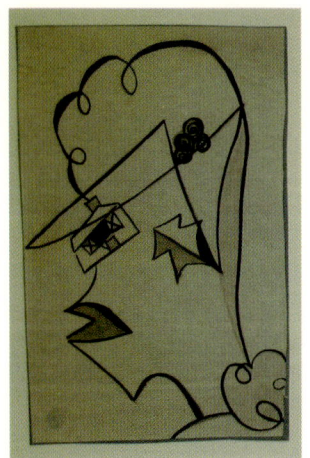
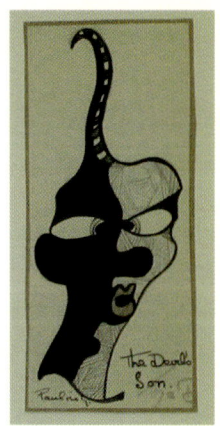
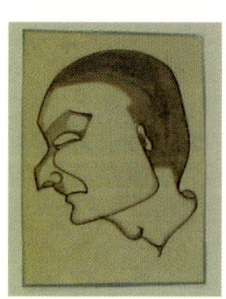
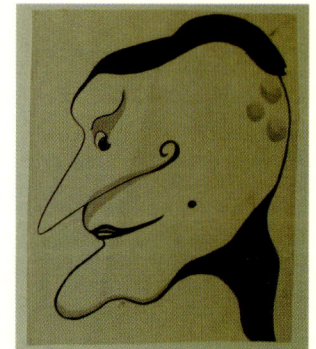

Drawing was more important than homework to Harry.

I would turn out one picture after another while the water of the Thames plop, plop, plopped against the boat.

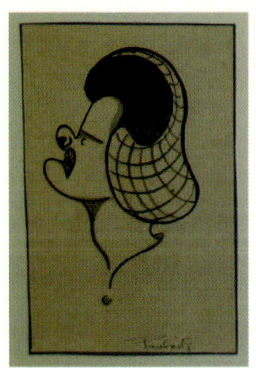
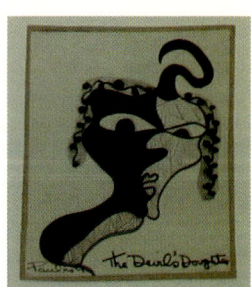
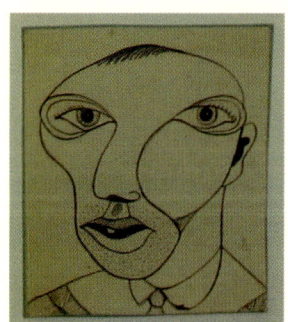
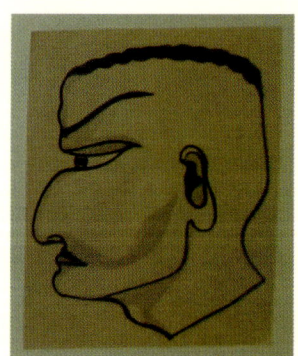

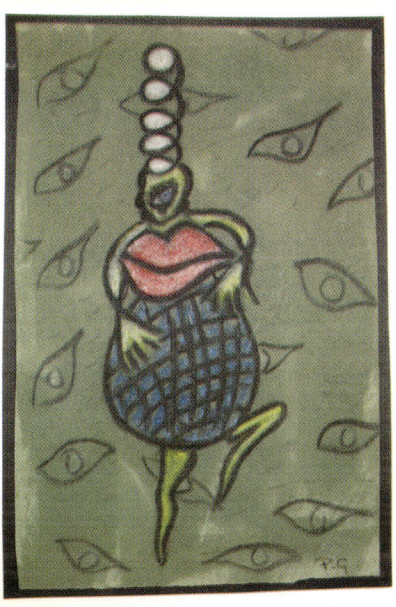

DANCING WORLD
1948 • pastel • 7" x 5"
Travelling Collection

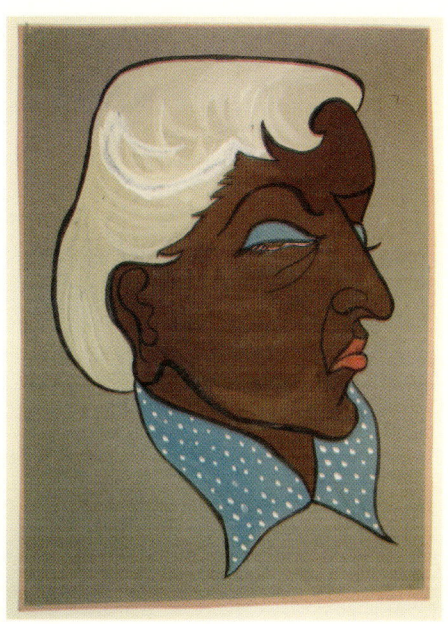

HARRY
1948 • poster colours • 8" x 6"
Travelling Collection

Harry painted as a coloured woman.
Another helmet full of thoughts.

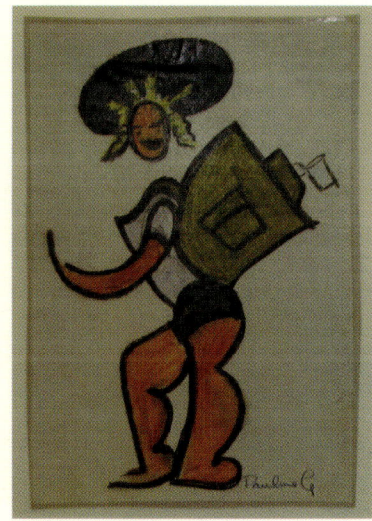

HITCHHIKER
1948 • oil, pastel and ink • 7" x 5"
Kerry Collection

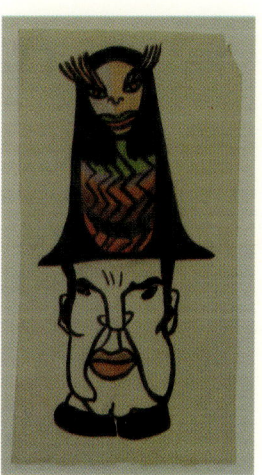

POLICEMAN
1948 • oil, pastel and ink • 6" x 3"
Kerry Collection

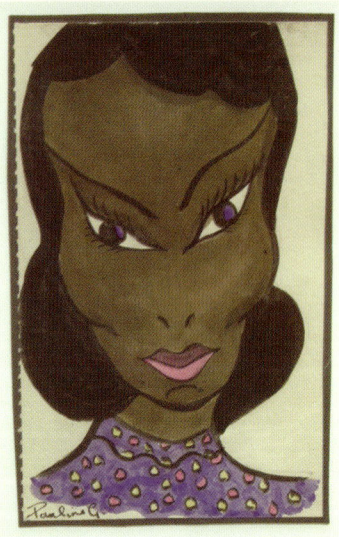

LADY IN PURPLE PINK
1948 • ink • 5" x 3"
Waterford Collection

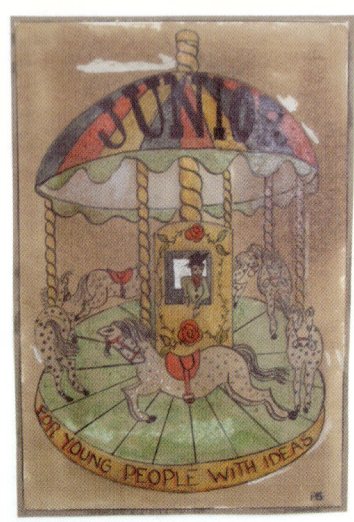

MERRY GO ROUND
1948 • inks varnished • 7" x 5"
Travelling Collection

A competition for *Junior* magazine. I won £12 pounds for 'Merry Go Round'.

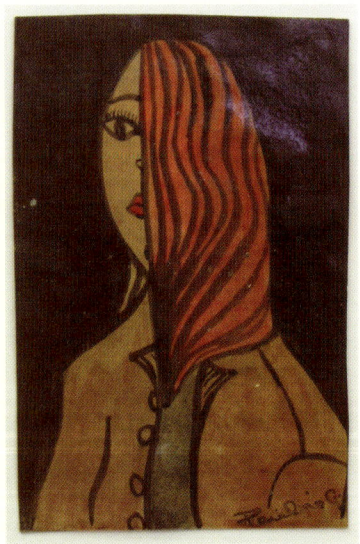

NICANDRA, HAIR OVER FACE
1948 • ink varnished • 4" x 3"
Travelling Collection

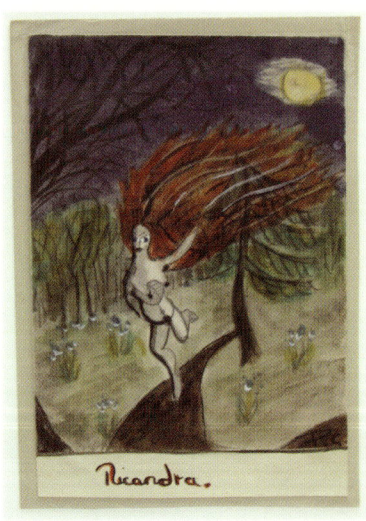

NICANDRA RUNNING
1948 • ink • 5" x 3"
Waterford Collection

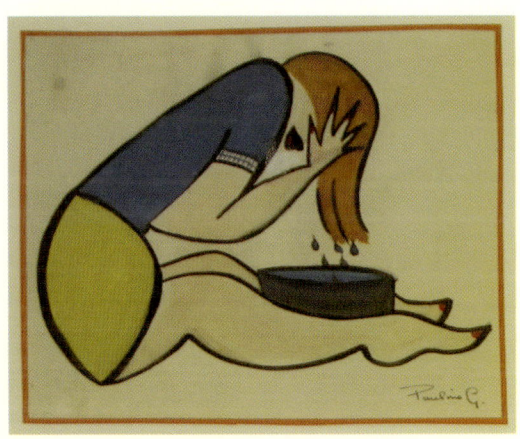

LILLY WASHING HER HAIR
1948 • poster colour • 5" x 6"
Travelling Collection

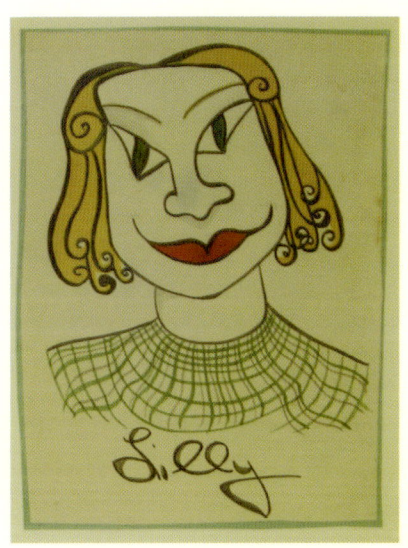

LILLY
1948 • ink • 8" x 6"
Travelling Collection

John Watling loved another girl called Lilly.
Remembering Mr Butterfield who was the only progressive school teacher we called formally.
He taught us boat-building and was the only one who had no mistress.

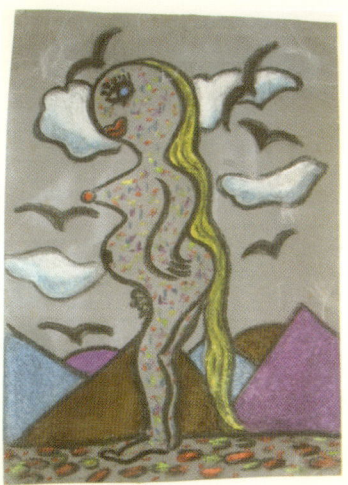

MOTHER EARTH
1948 • pastel • 8" x 6"
Travelling Collection

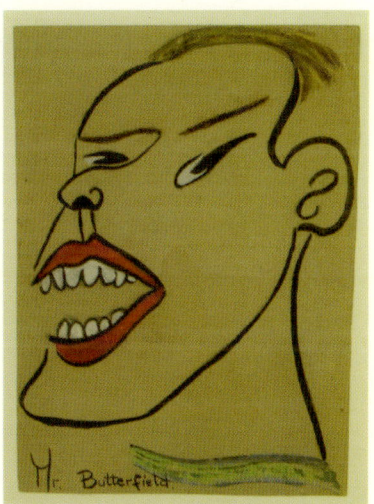

MR BUTTERFIELD
1948 • ink and pastel • 11" x 8"
Travelling Collection

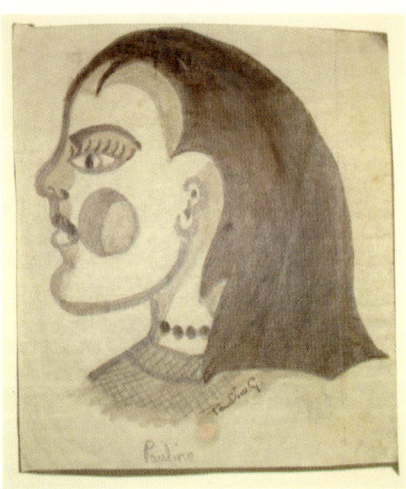

PAULINE
1948 • ink and pencil • 6" x 5"
Travelling Collection

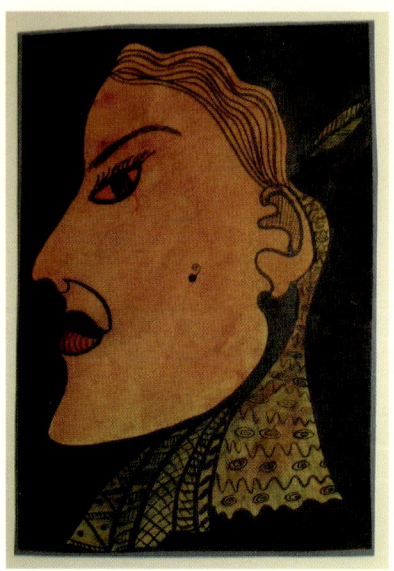

PROFILE I
1948 • ink varnished • 6" x 4"
Waterford Collection

Lilly had another admirer, a sailor who terrified me and I didn't know why.

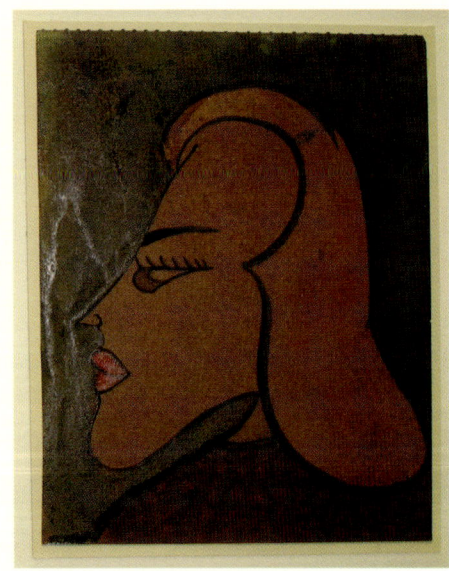

PROFILE II
1948 • ink varnished • 6" x 5"
Waterford Collection

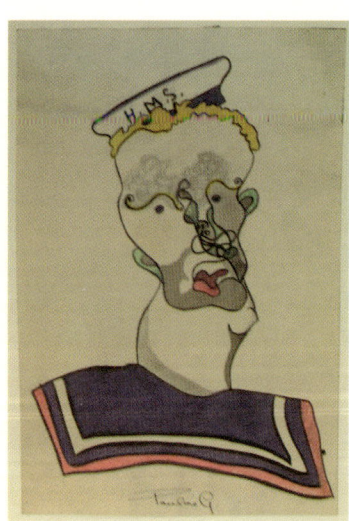

SAILOR I
1948 • ink • 9" x 6"
Travelling Collection

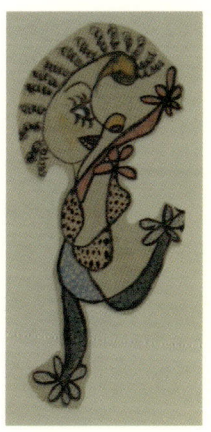

RAG DOLL
1948 • ink • 9" x 5"
Kerry Collection

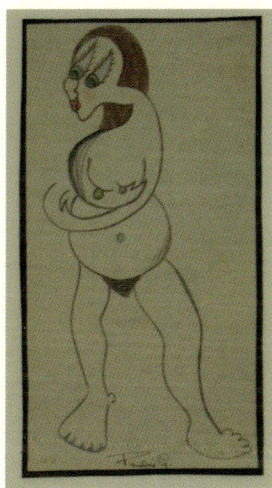

SURPRISED
1948 • ink • 10" x 5"
Kerry Collection

Harry didn't flaunt her free thinking – she just was.
Authority figures were not to be feared, everybody had equal status.

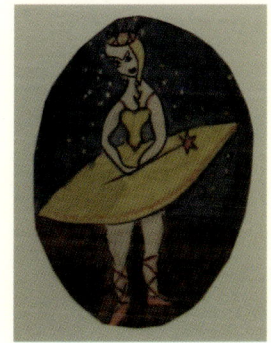

GOOD FAIRY
1948 • ink • 5" x 4"
Kerry Collection

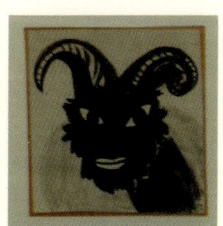

GOAT MAN
1948 • ink • 3" x 3"
Kerry Collection

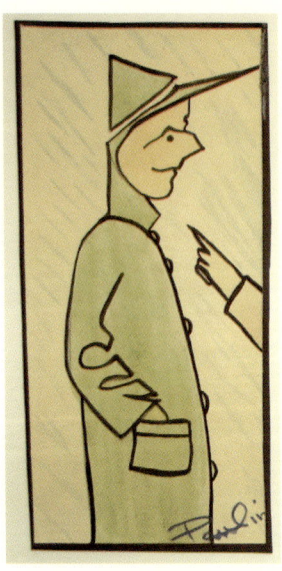

RAIN
1948 • ink • 8" x 4"
Waterford Collection

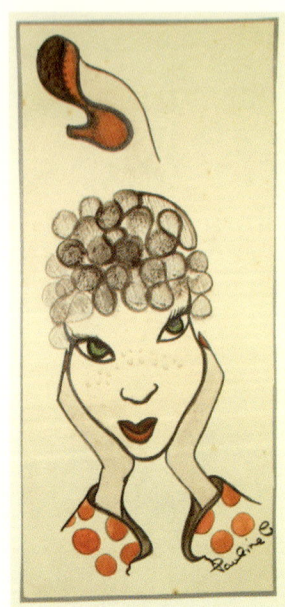

MODEL
1948 • ink • 9" x 4"
Waterford Collection

Why did I do so many women being saved in the woods?

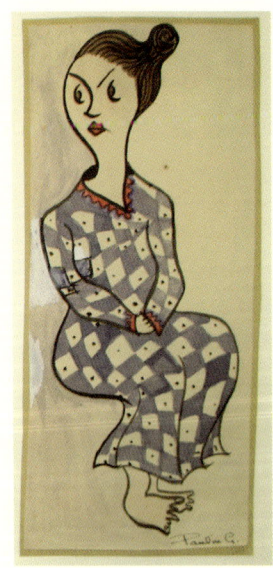

DISAPPROVAL
1948 • ink • 8" x 4"
Waterford Collection

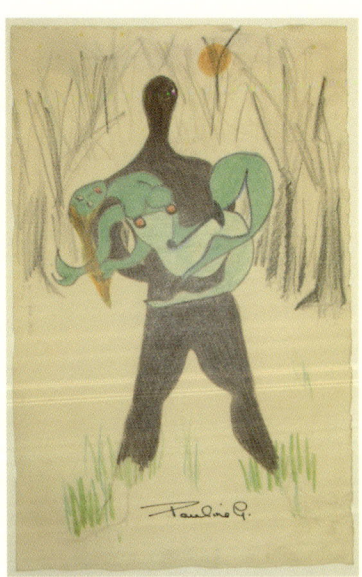

SAVED IN THE WOOD
1951 • pencil • 7" x 4"
Travelling Collection

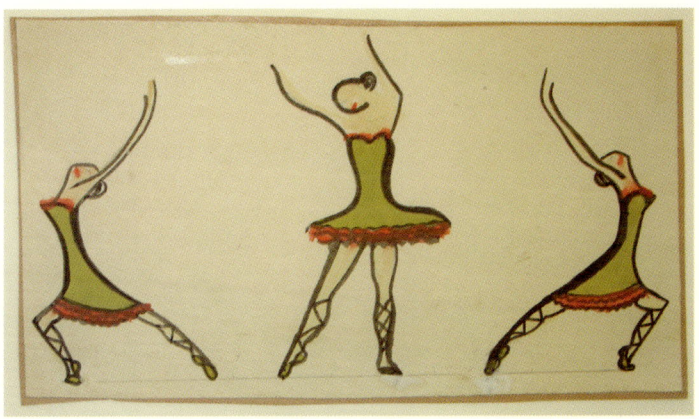

BALLET DANCERS
1949 • pencil and ink • 6" x 3"
Travelling Collection

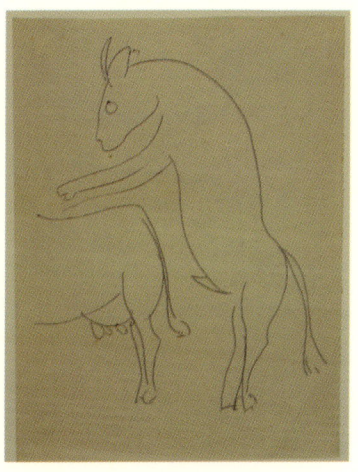

BULL AND COW
1949 • biro • 8" x 6"
Kerry Collection

Memories of our dexter bull having to stand on the wall of the dung-heap
as he was too short to mount the cow.

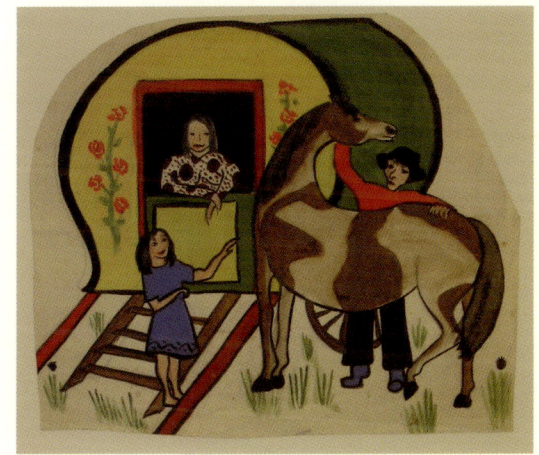

TRAVELLERS' CARAVAN I
1949 • poster colour • 9" x 11"
Kerry Collection

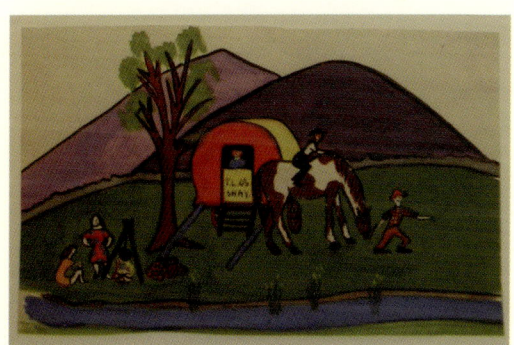

TRAVELLERS' CARAVAN II
1949 • poster colour • 6" x 9"
Kerry Collection

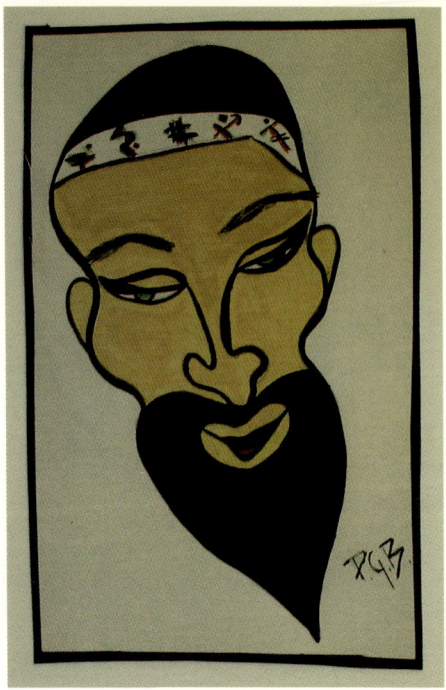

CHINAMAN
1949 • ink • 7" x 5"
Waterford Collection

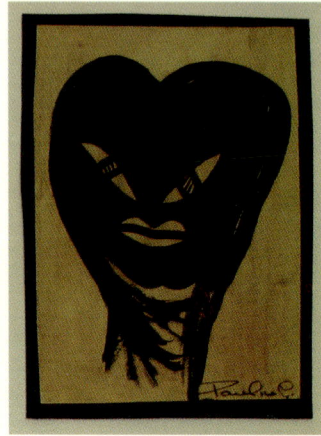

MASK
1949 • ink • 4" x 3"
Waterford Collection

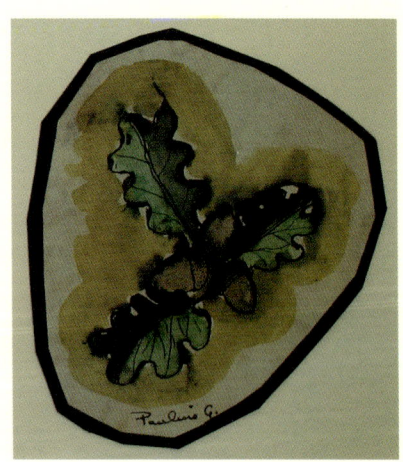

OAK
1949 • ink • 4" x 4"
Waterford Collection

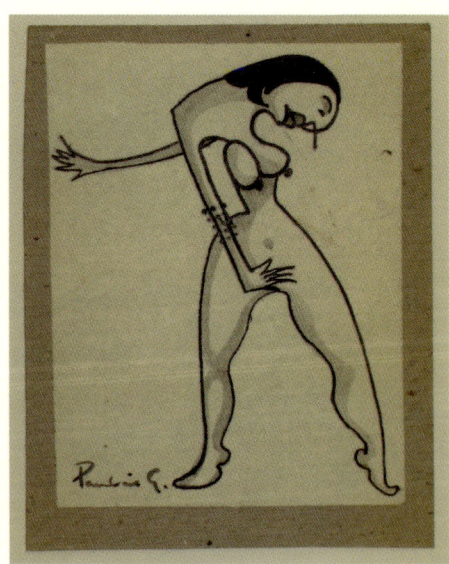

DANCE STEP
1949 • ink • 5" x 4"
Kerry Collection

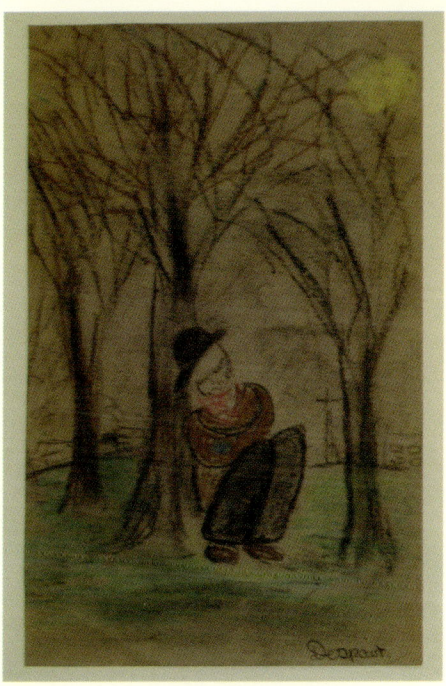

DESPAIR
1949 • pastel • 10" x 6"
Travelling Collection

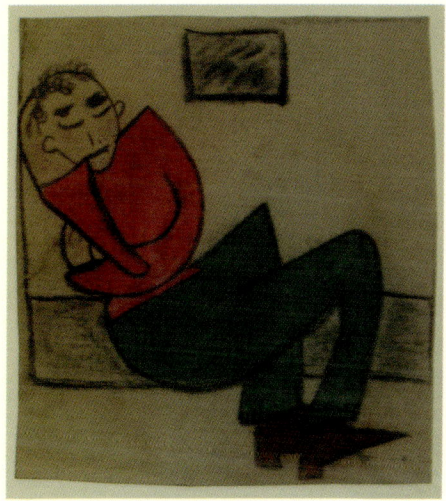

SLEEP
1949 • pastel • 8" x 7"
Travelling Collection

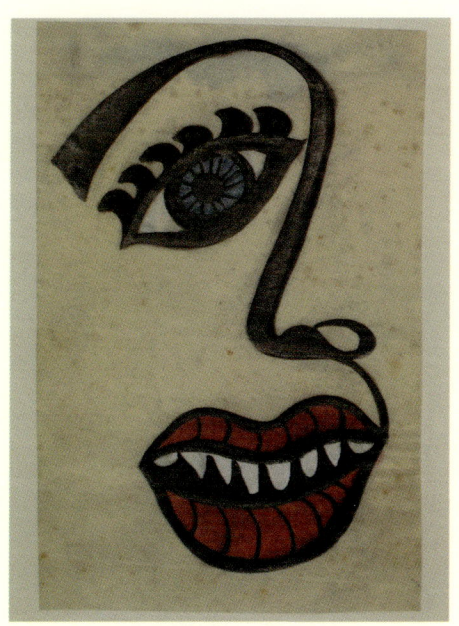

EYES, NOSE AND MOUTH
1949 • ink • 7" x 5"
Kerry Collection

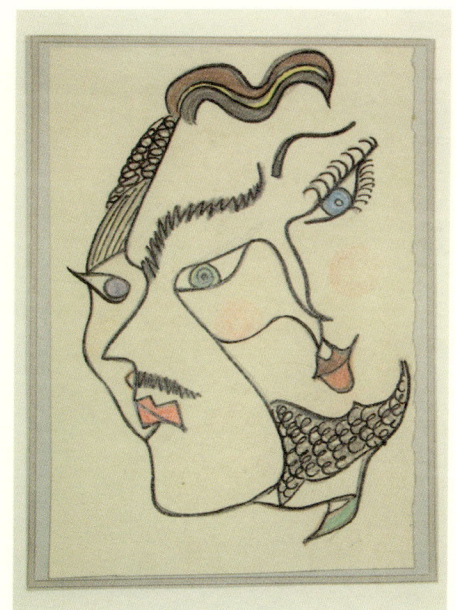

FAMILY TIES
1949 • pencils and ink • 5" x 4"
Travelling Collection

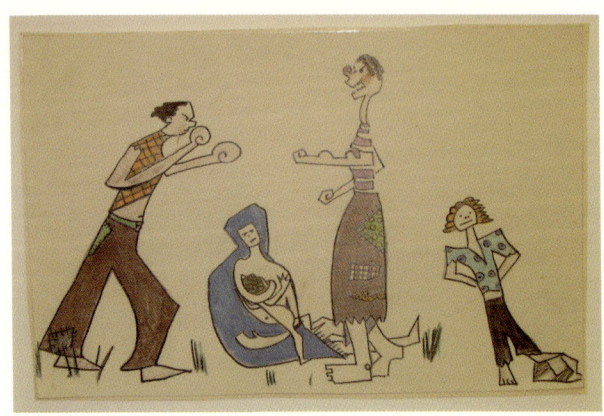

FIGHTING TRAVELLERS
1949 • pencil and ink • 6" x 9"
Waterford Collection

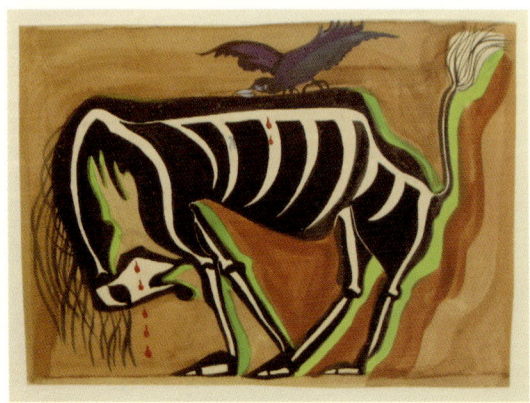

HORSE AND CROW
1949 • poster colours • 6" x 8"
Kerry Collection

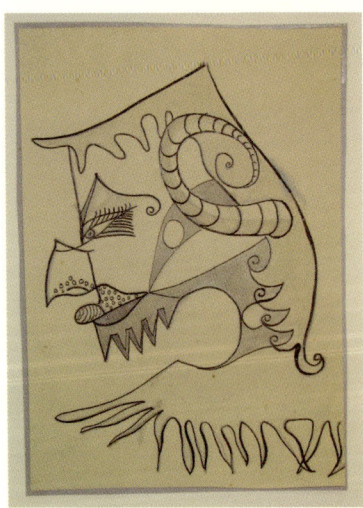

MAN WITH A HORN
1949 • ink and pencil • 7" x 5"
Waterford Collection

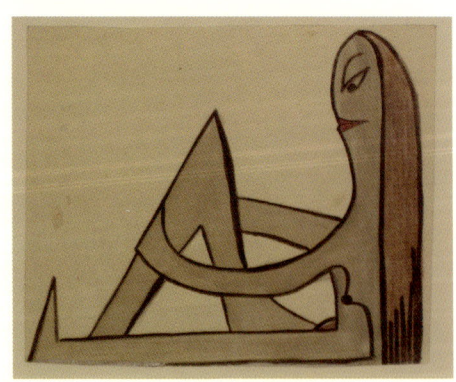

LADY BOOKEND
1949 • ink • 4" x 5"
Kerry Collection

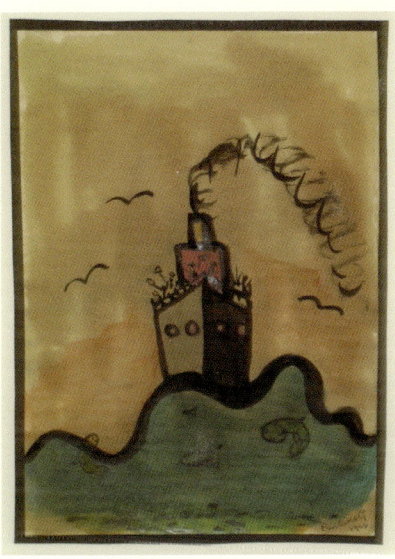

CROSSING THE IRISH SEA
1949 • ink varnished • 8" x 6"
Kerry Collection

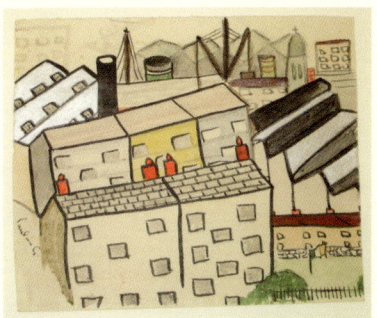

MONTENOTTI
1949 • ink • 5" x 6"
Travelling Collection

Back to Ireland. We stayed in a guesthouse in Montenotti.
Over breakfast one of the farmers at our table threw his crusts and tea-dregs under the table,
as you would for your dog on the farm.

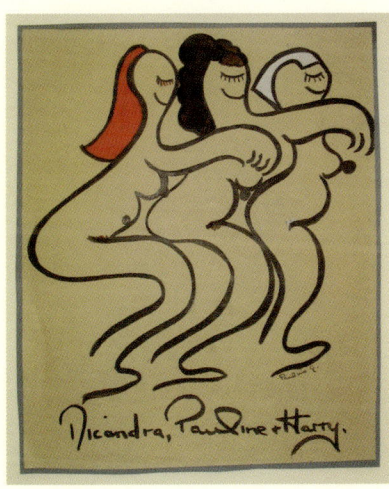

NICANDRA, PAULINE AND HARRY
1949 • ink • 8" x 7"
Waterford Collection

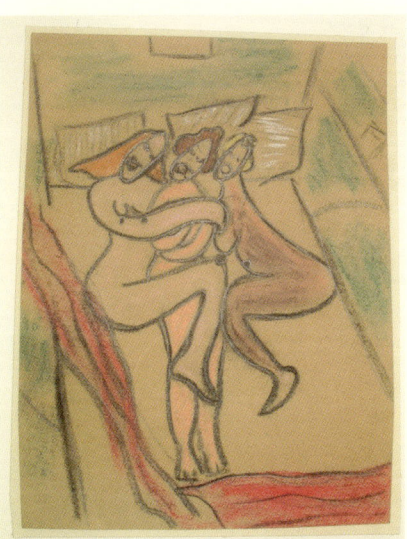

NICANDRA, HARRY AND ME IN A VAN
1949 • ink • 8" x 7"
Travelling Collection

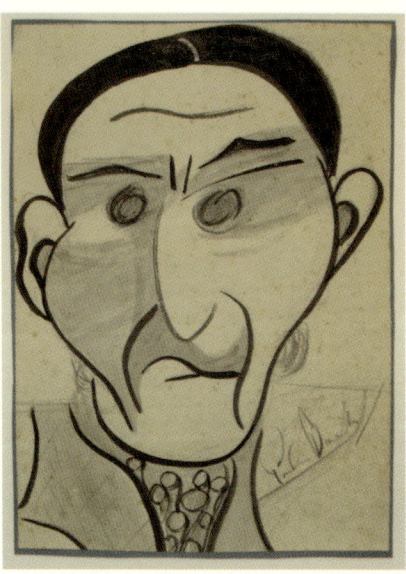

MRS HEALY
1949 • ink and charcoal • 9" x 7"
Kerry Collection

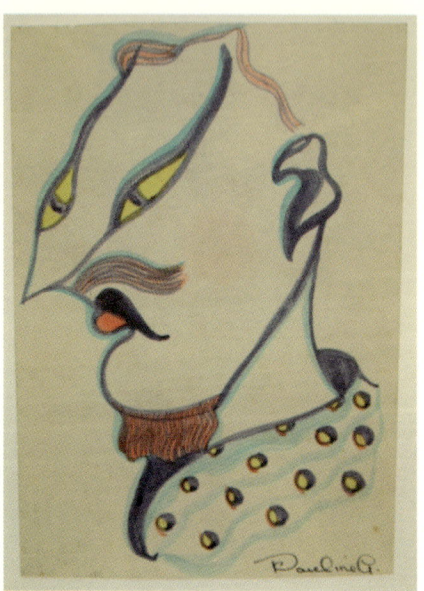

ORIENTAL
1949 • ink • 6" x 4"
Waterford Collection

Mrs Healy of Cillagh East, Kenmare, 'the higher up the mountain, the more the monkey shows his arse'.

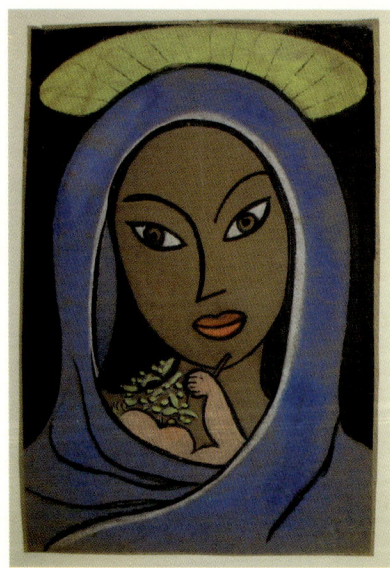

OUR LADY
1949 • pastel • 11" x 7"
Waterford Collection

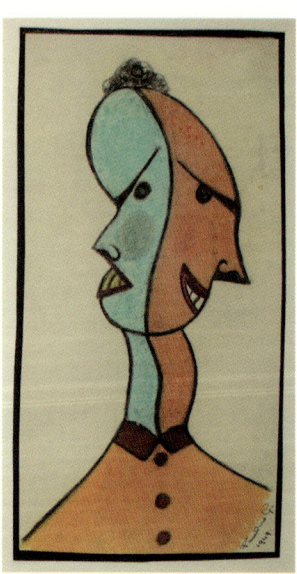

JANUS
1949 • pastel • 10" x 5"
Waterford Collection

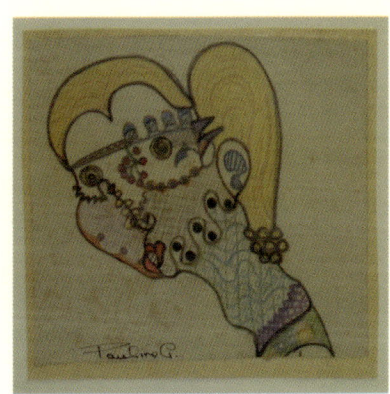

MUDDLED WOMAN
1949 • pencil • 5" x 5"
Kerry Collection

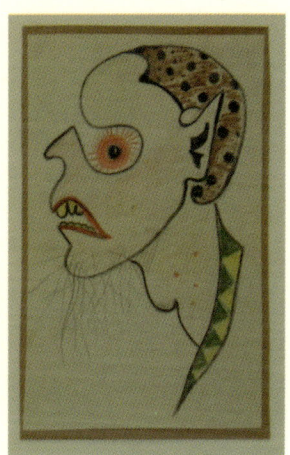

SPOOKY MAN
1949 • pencil • 6" x 4"
Kerry Collection

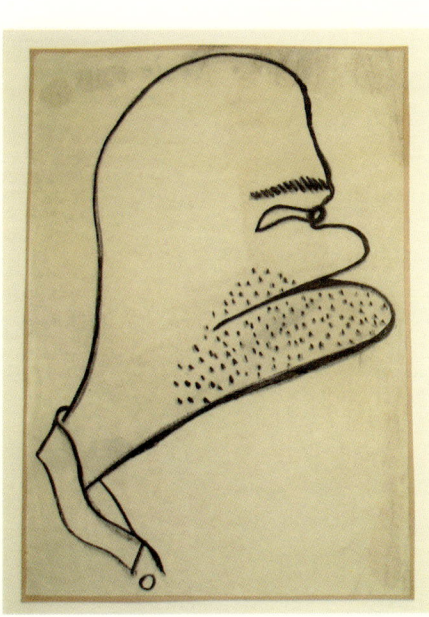

NO TEETH
1949 • ink • 8" x 6"
Waterford Collection

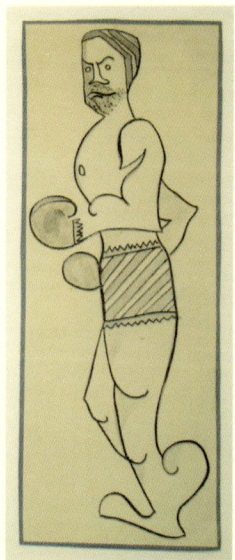

BOXER
1949 • ink • 10" x 4"
Waterford Collection

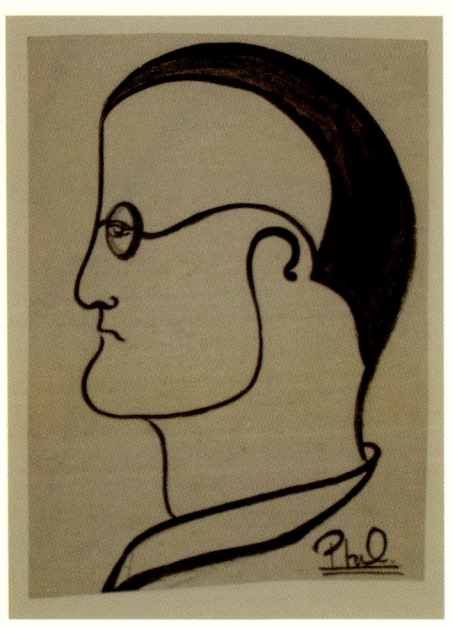

PHIL
1949 • ink • 6" x 4"
Kerry Collection

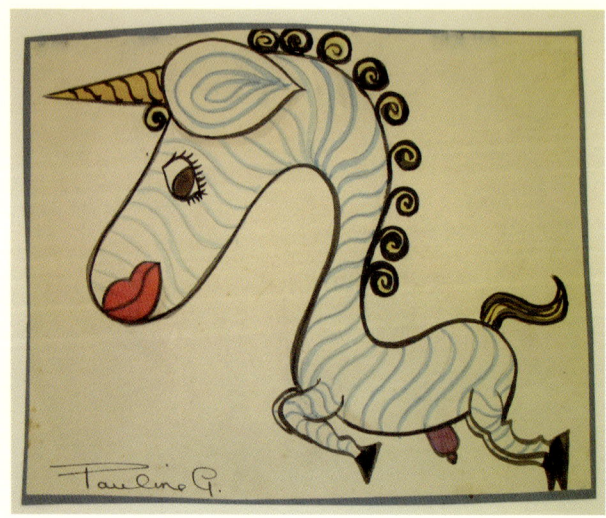

STRIPED UNICORN
1949 • ink • 6" x 7"
Travelling Collection

Phil Arthur who owned the sawmills in Kenmare

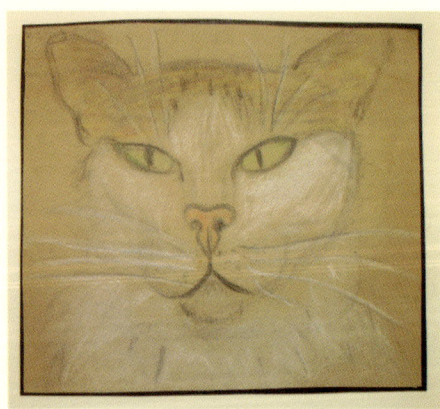

SALTY
1949 • pastel • 6" x 6"
Travelling Collection

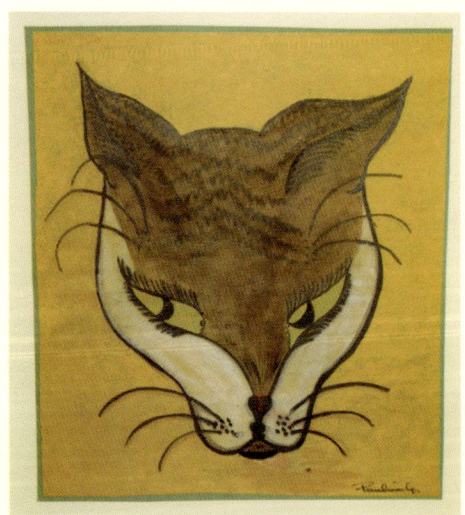

SALTY, FRONT FACE
1949 • ink • 6" x 5"
Waterford Collection

EIGHT STUDIES OF SALTY
1949 • ink and charcoal • 8" x 5" and similar dimensions
Waterford Collection

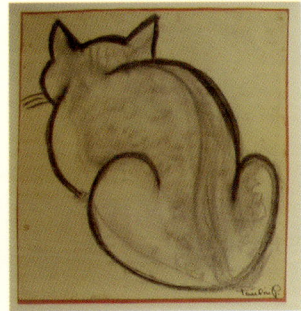
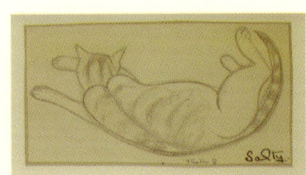
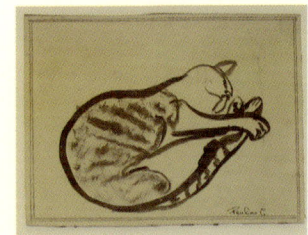
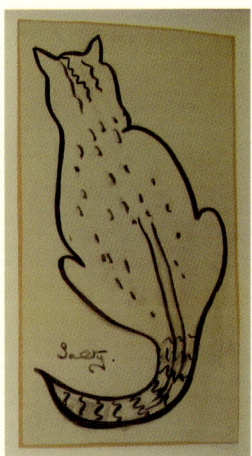

Cats, cats, we were never without cats.
One of our cats had given birth on the B&I steamboat crossing the Irish Sea.
The ship's nurse made more fuss of her than any of us who were vomiting all
over the place.

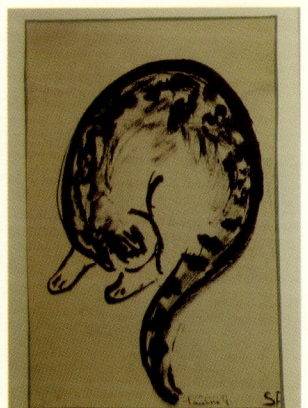
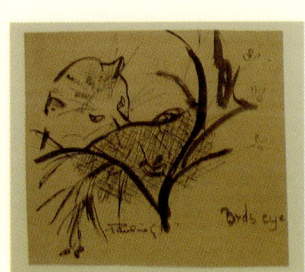
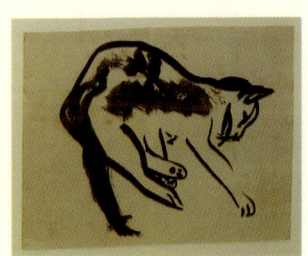
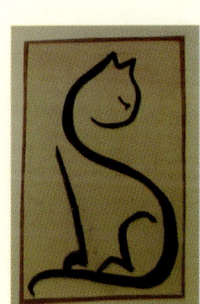

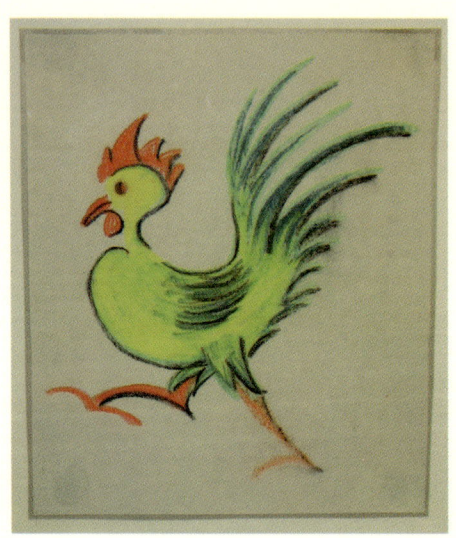

STRUTTING COCK
1949 • pastel • 6" x 5"
Waterford Collection

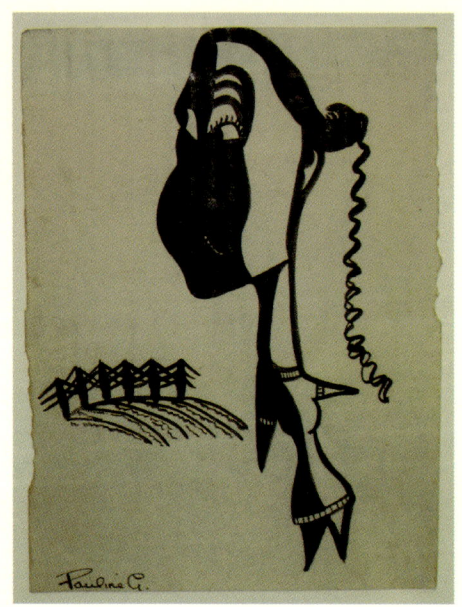

SUSPICION
1949 • ink • 7" x 5"
Waterford Collection

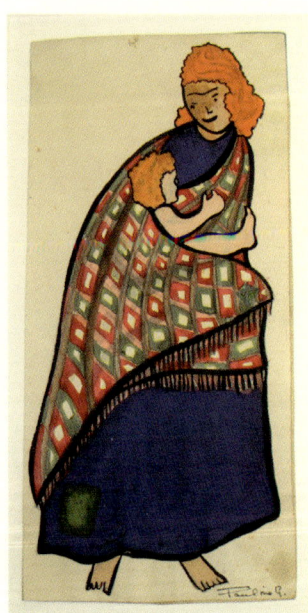

TRAVELLING LADY
1949 • poster colour • 9" x 5"
Waterford Collection

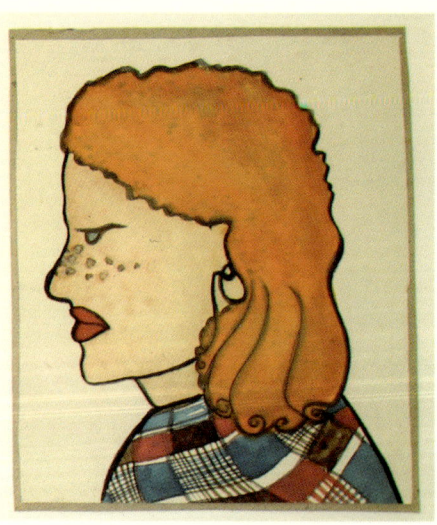

CHILD
1949 • poster colour • 5" x 4"
Waterford Collection

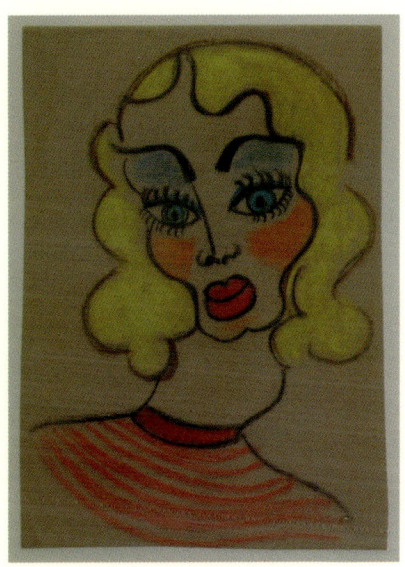

BLONDE
1949 • pastels • 11" x 8"
Kerry Collection

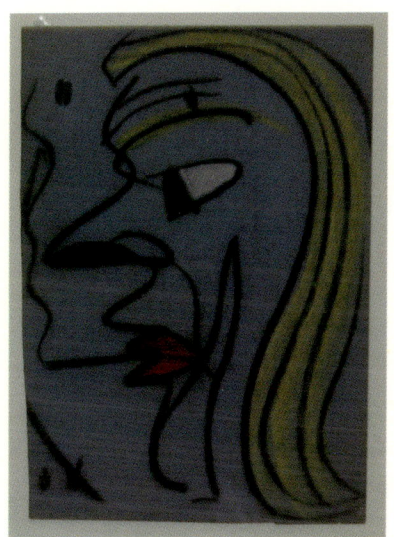

BLONDE SMOKING
1949 • pastels • 10" x 7"
Kerry Collection

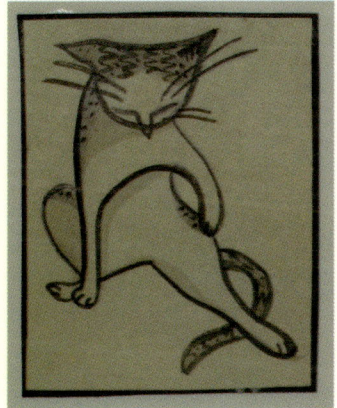

CAT I
1949 • ink • 3" x 3"
Waterford Collection

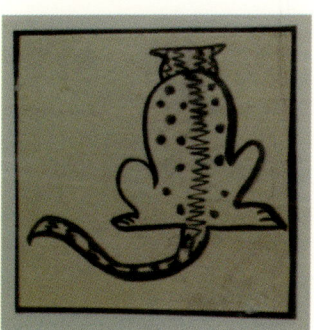

CAT II
1949 • ink • 3" x 3"
Waterford Collection

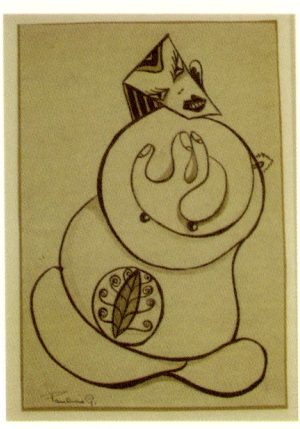

SHEELA NA GIG
1949 • ink • 10" x 7"
Waterford Collection

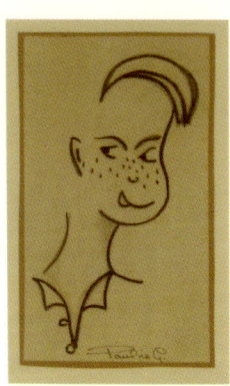

FRECKLES
1949 • charcoal and ink • 6" x 4"
Kerry Collection

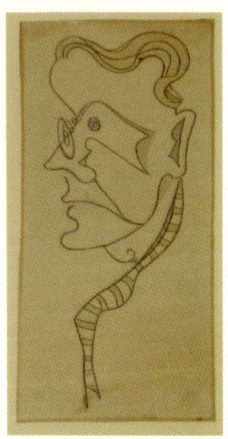

MONOCLE
1949 • charcoal and ink • 10 " x 5"
Kerry Collection

Harry and I settled at the Lodge Gate of the Cahernane Hotel now owned by Pat Newling.
The Hotel had a huge piano where I pretended to be a composer, banging out loud music.
One night a man fell down the stairs, having been given poitin.
He was so relaxed, no harm came to him. Maybe he was 'worm man'?

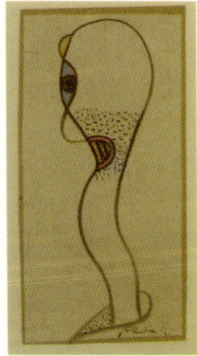

WORM MAN
1949 • charcoal and ink • 6" x 4"
Kerry Collection

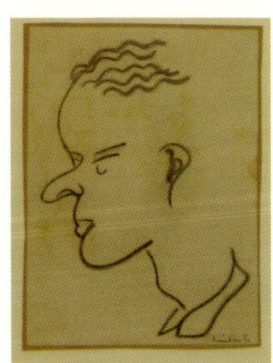

BIG NOSE
1949 • charcoal and ink • 6" x 5"
Kerry Collection

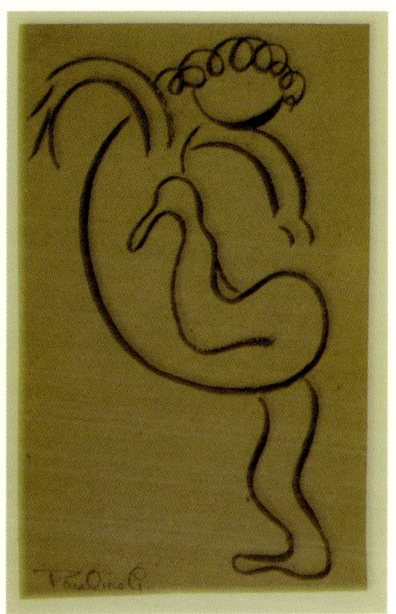

1, 2, 3, KICK!
1949 • ink • 8" x 5"
Travelling Collection

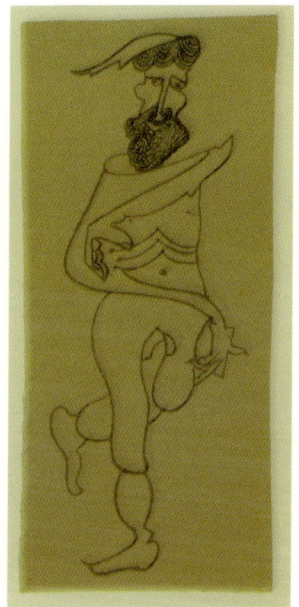

BEARDED DANCER
1949 • ink • 8" x 3"
Travelling Collection

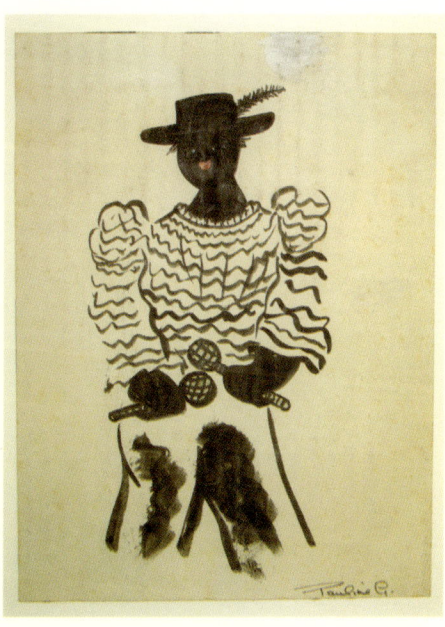

CALYPSO
1949 • ink • 7" x 5"
Travelling Collection

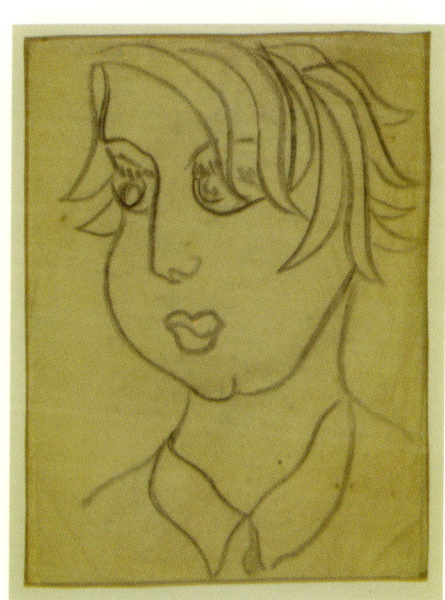

CHUBBY CHEEKS
1949 • charcoal • 10" x 8"
Travelling Collection

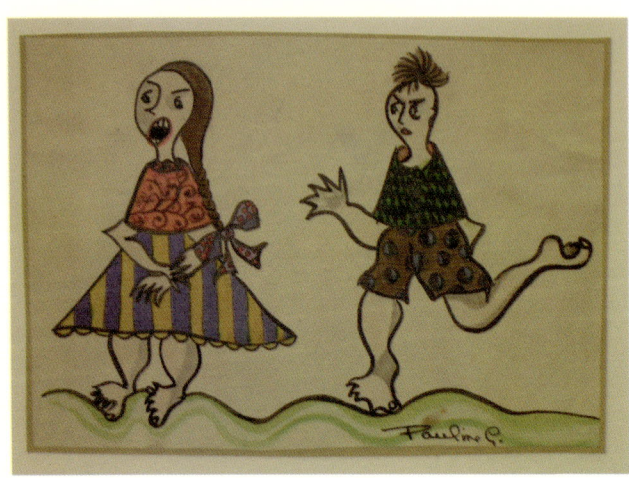

COMING
1949 • ink • 5" x 7"
Kerry Collection

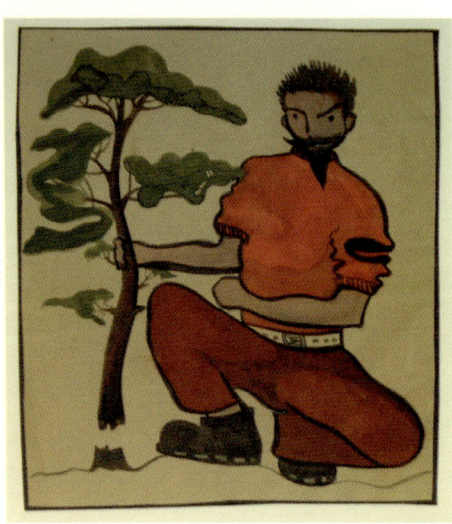

GIANT
1949 • poster colour • 8" x 7"
Travelling Collection

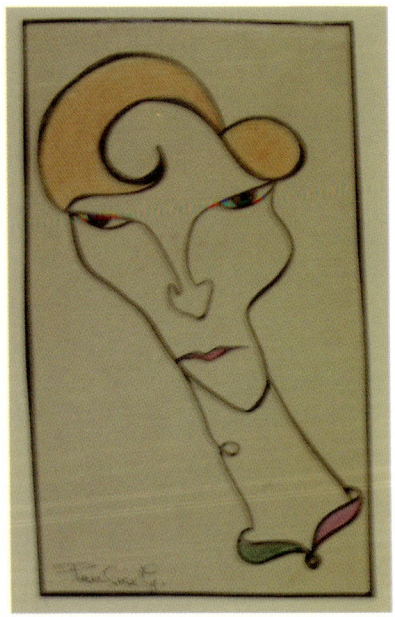

JERRY
1949 • ink • 7" x 4"
Travelling Collection

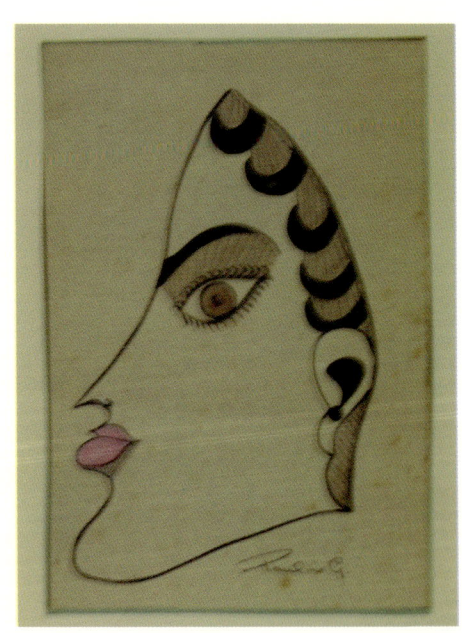

ANN
1949 • ink • 6" x 4"
Travelling Collection

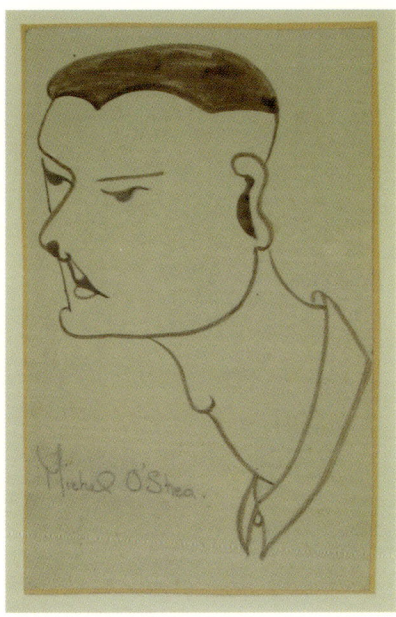

MICHAEL O'SHEA
1949 • ink • 8" x 5"
Travelling Collection

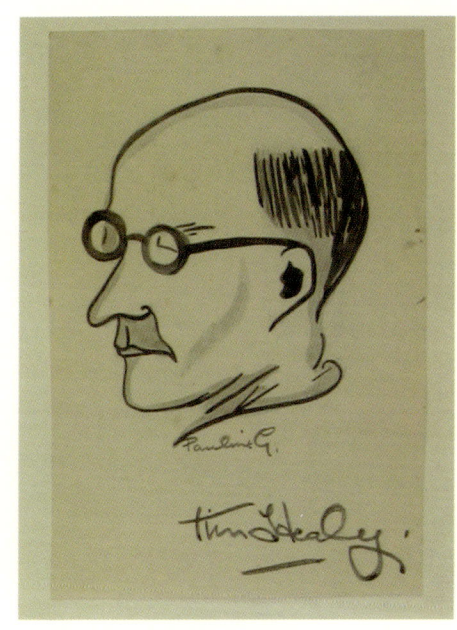

TIM HEALY
1949 • ink • 6" x 4"
Travelling Collection

Michael O'Shea from Kenmare who Harry fostered.

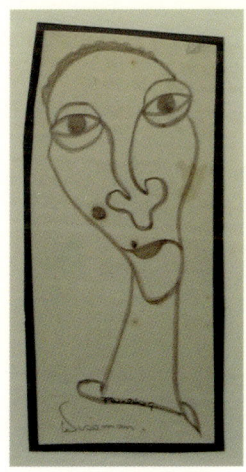

WISEMAN I
1949 • ink • 5" x 2"
Travelling Collection

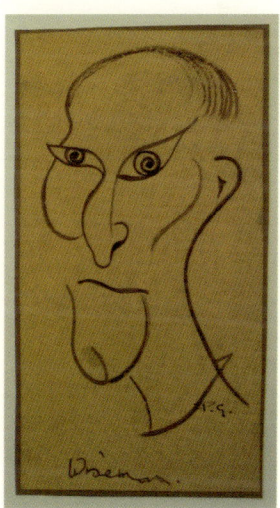

WISEMAN II
1949 • ink • 8" x 4"
Travelling Collection

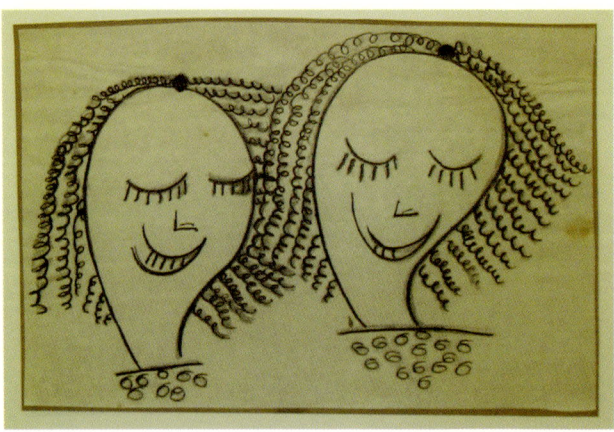

WE ARE THE PHONEY TWINS
1949 • poster colours • 6" x 9"
Travelling Collection

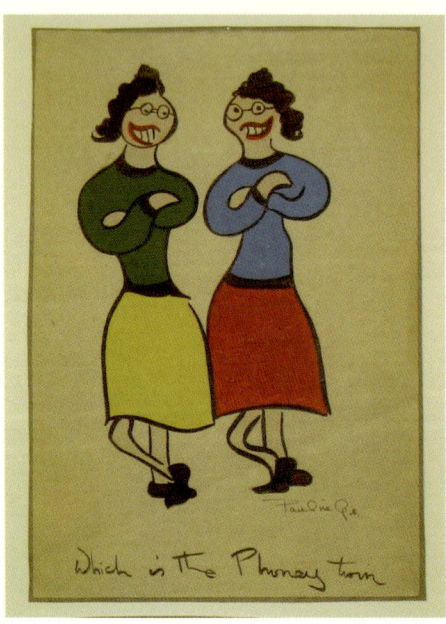

THE PHONEY TWINS
1949 • poster colours • 10" x 7"
Travelling Collection

An advertisement for hair perming appeared in many magazines, the caption being:
'Which is the Tony Twin?'
We called them 'the phoney twins'.

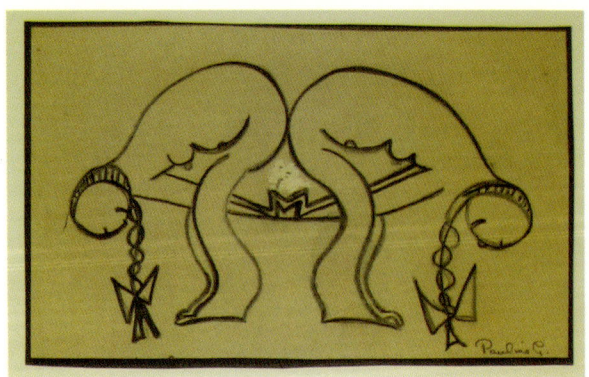

LET'S CHARCOAL EACH OTHER'S ARSEHOLES
1949 • poster colours • 5" x 9"
Travelling Collection

Let's charocoal each other's arsehole – a song John Watling would sing to peals of laughter from Harry and I.

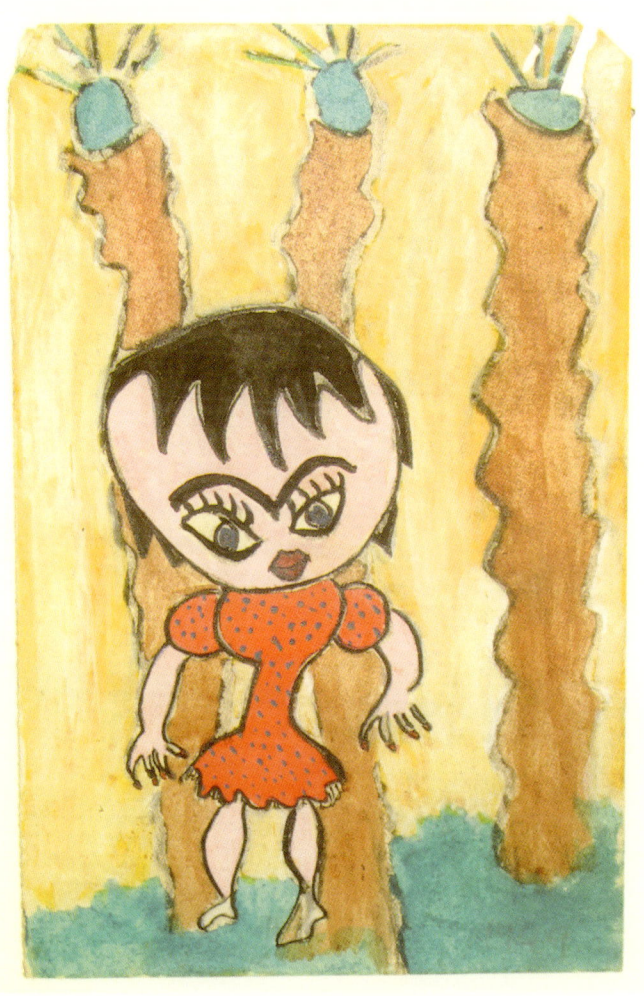

POLLARDED TREES AND GIRL
1949 • ink • 7" x 4"
Waterford Collection

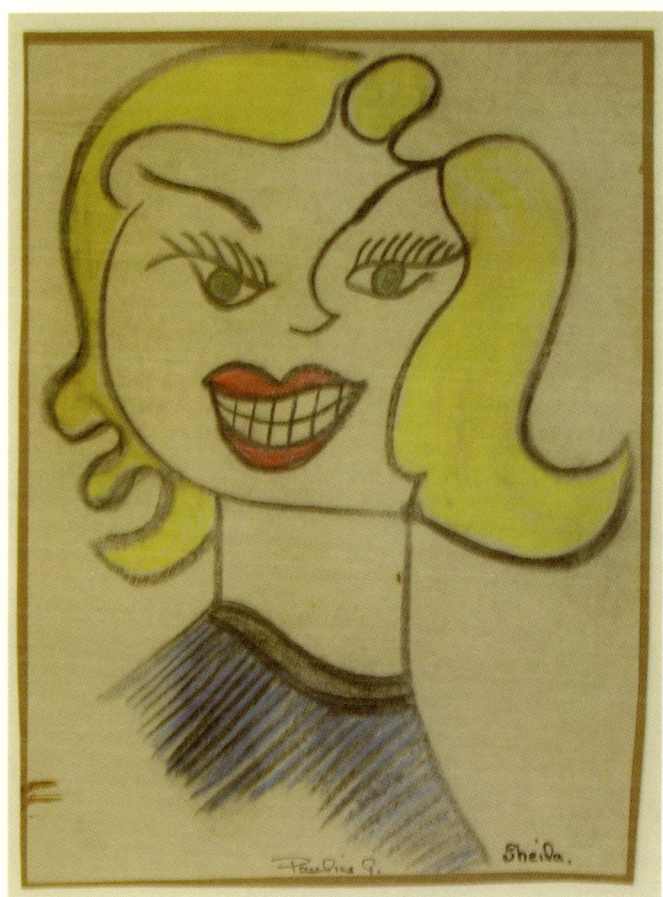

SHEILA
1949 • pastel • 10" x 7"
Travelling Collection

Sheila, daughter of Phil Arthur, became my best friend.

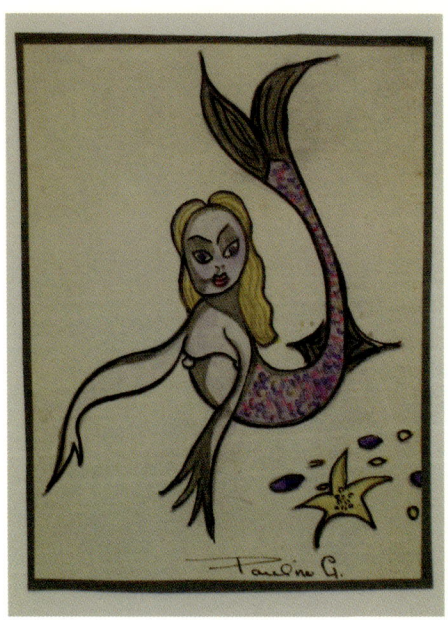

MERMAID
1949 • ink • 5" x 4"
Kerry Collection

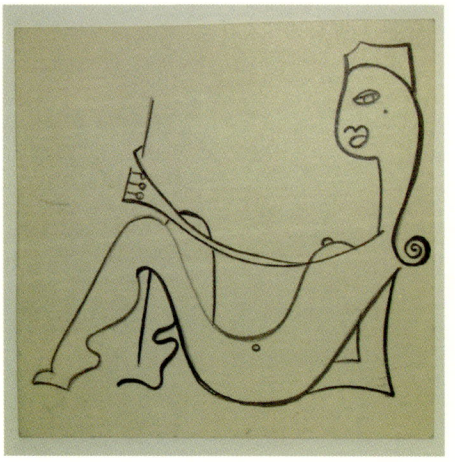

MIRROR, MIRROR
1949 • ink • 5" x 5"
Waterford Collection

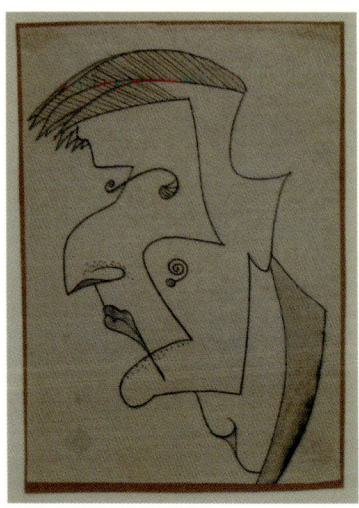

MR
1949 • ink and pencil • 7" x 5"
Kerry Collection

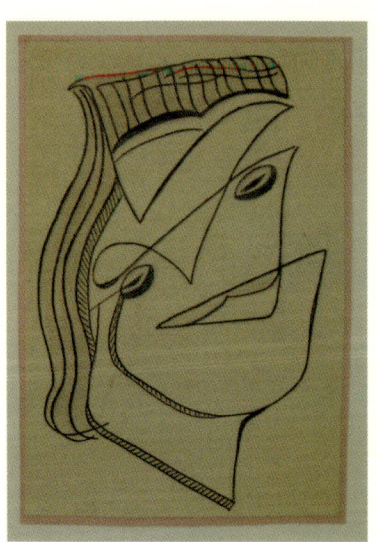

MRS
1949 • ink and pencil • 8" x 5"
Kerry Collection

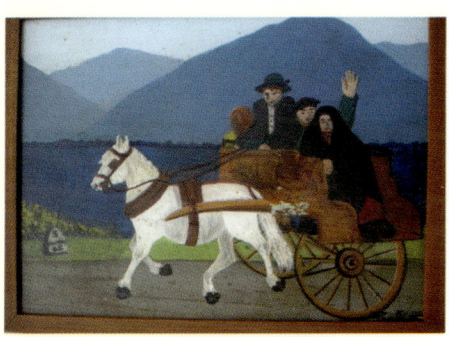

MUCKROSS
1949 • oil on board • 12" x 16"
Kerry Collection

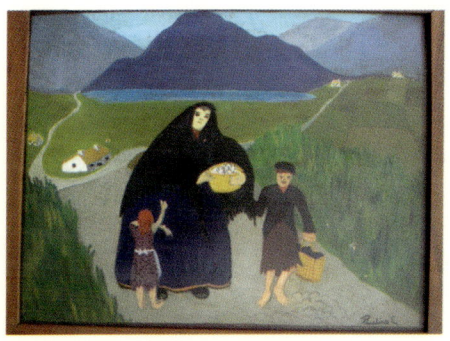

OLD IRISH LADY
1949 • oil on board • 12" x 16"
Travelling Collection

Harry decided to move on again and enroll me in the Dublin Art School. She borrowed from the Building
Society to buy No 51 Frankfort Avenue. The first person we met was puppeteer Desmond McNamara.
His friends all had beards and were very arty. 'She *must* have seen Picasso'.
Bursting into tears, 'If they're going to be all *so* intellectual, it'll be frightening in the art school'.
The first person I met was Maura Laverty's daughter, Barry. She became a life-long friend.

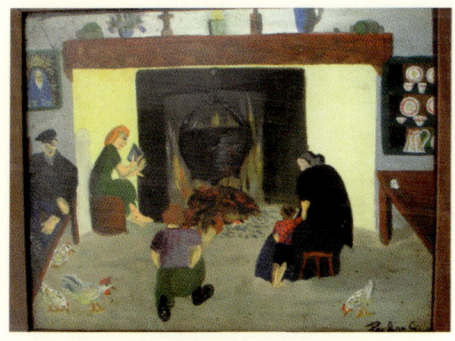

AN IRISH KITCHEN
1949 • oil on board • 12" x 16"
Waterford Collection

We painted boards and sold them to
tourists for a pound each from the
Cahernane Hotel.

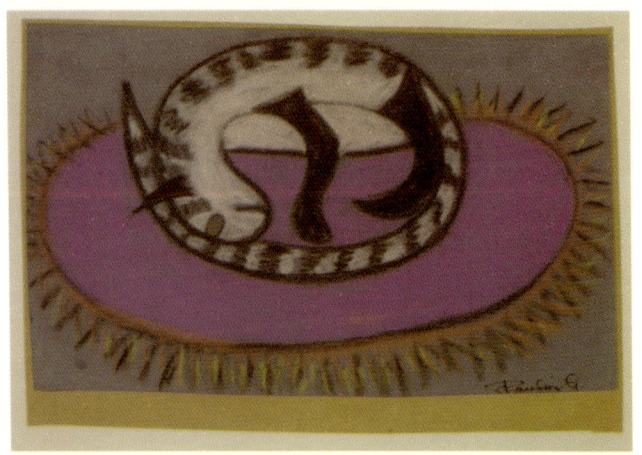

CAT ON PURPLE RUG
1950 • pastel • 6" x 11"
Kerry Collection

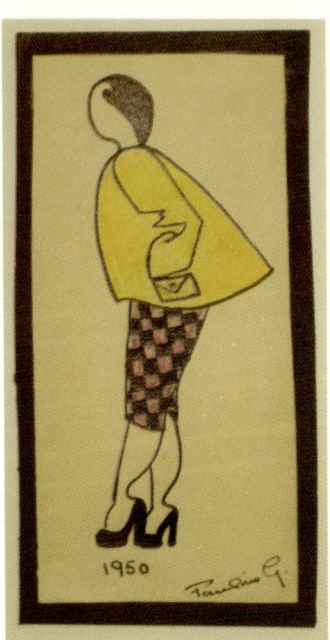

1950 FASHION
1950 • ink and pastel • 6" x 3"
Kerry Collection

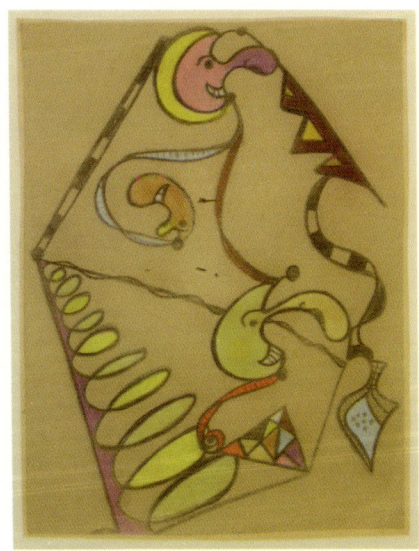

HALLOWEEN
1950 • pastel • 11" x 8"
Kerry Collection

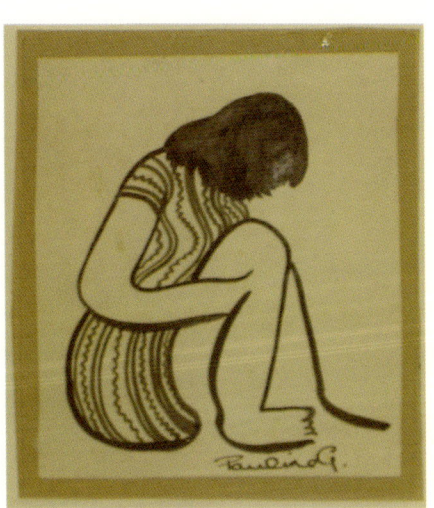

GIRL THINKING
1950 • ink • 4" x 3"
Kerry Collection

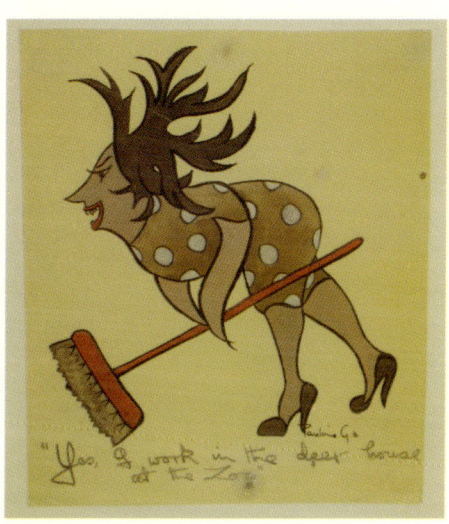

WORKER AT THE ZOO
1950 • poster colour • 7" x 6"
Kerry Collection

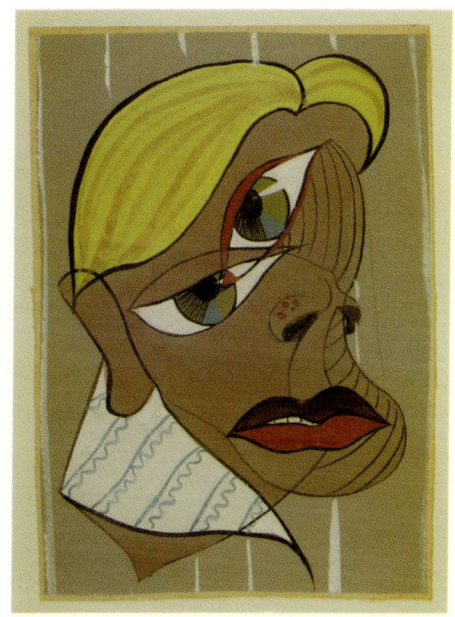

ABBEY ACTOR
1950 • poster colour
Waterford Collection

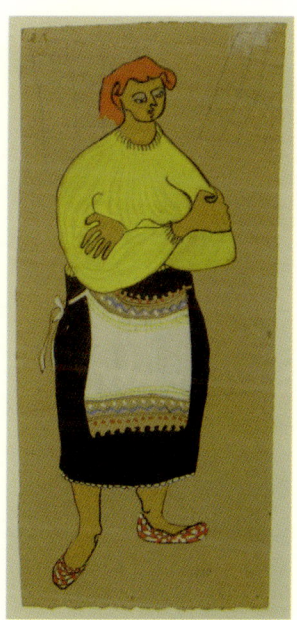

ABBEY ACTRESS
1950 • poster colour
Waterford Collection

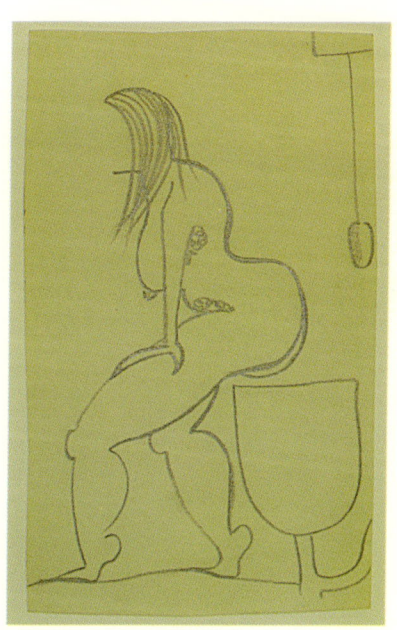

AT THE LAV
1950 • pencil • 7" x 4"
Travelling Collection

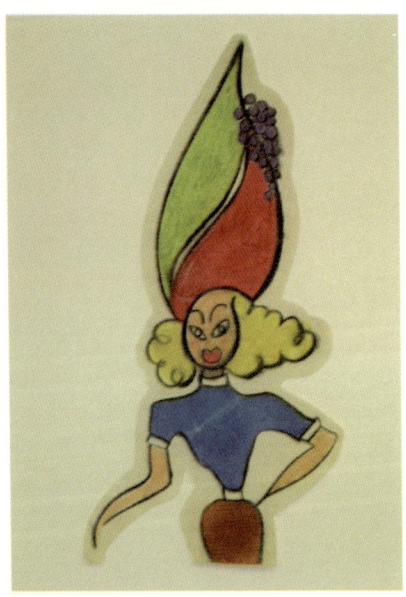

CARMEN MIRANDA
1950 • pastel • 14" x 7"
Travelling Collection

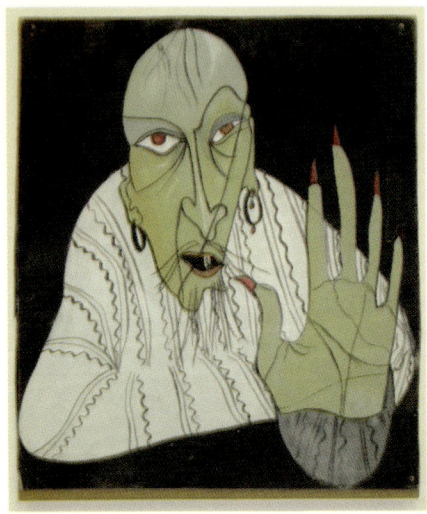

FORTUNE TELLER MAN
1950 • ink • 9" x 8"
Travelling Collection

City life had theatrical excitement all the time. Harry took down the railings outside.
'Conduct your house', a neighbour told her.

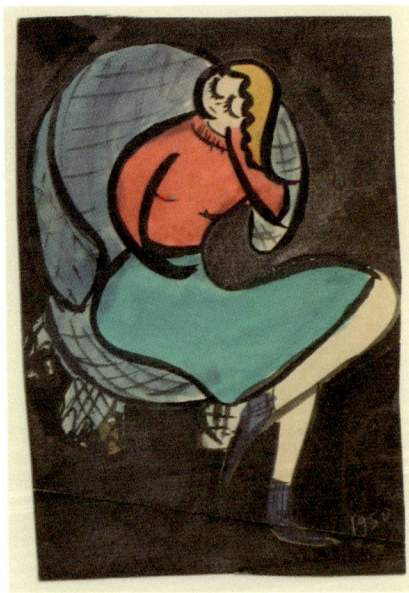

GIRL IN ARMCHAIR
1950 • ink • 6" x 4"
Travelling Collection

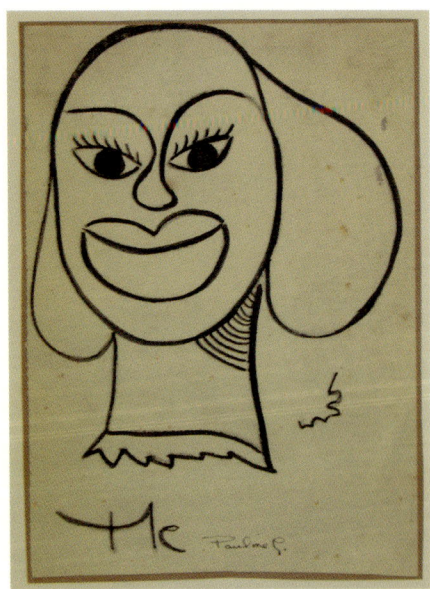

ME
1950 • ink • 9" x 7"
Waterford Collection

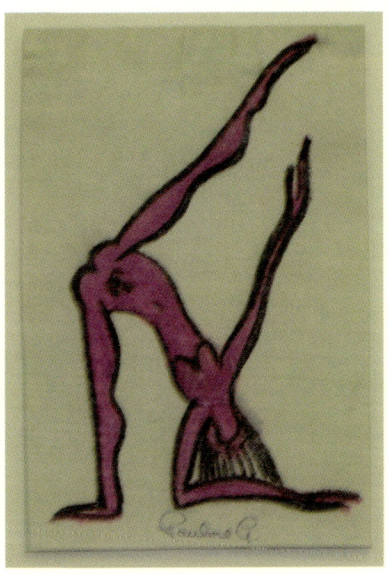

PURPLE DANCER I
1950 • pastel • 7" x 5"
Travelling Collection

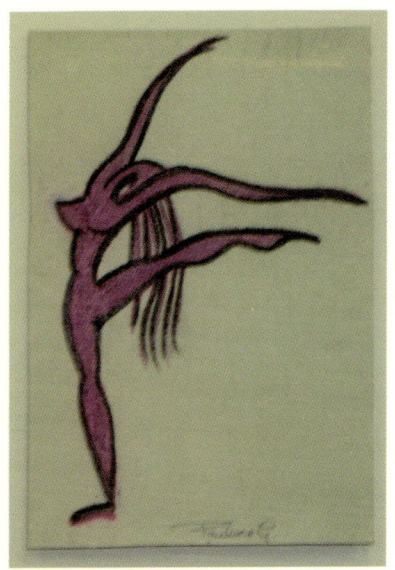

PURPLE DANCER II
1950 • pastel • 8" x 6"
Travelling Collection

We saw Siobhan McKenna in the old Abbey Theatre. Harry just loved her.

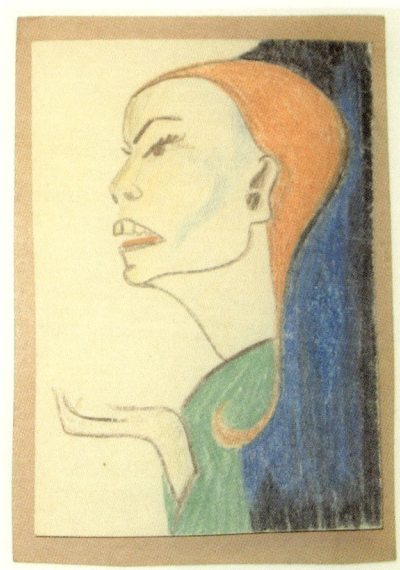

SIOBHAN
1950 • pencil and ink • 4" x 3"
Travelling Collection

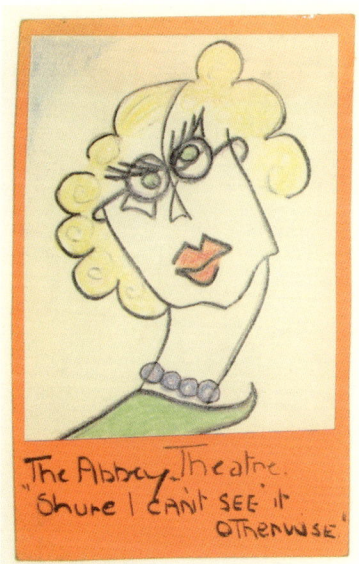

AUDIENCE WOMAN
1950 • pencil and ink • 5" x 3"
Travelling Collection

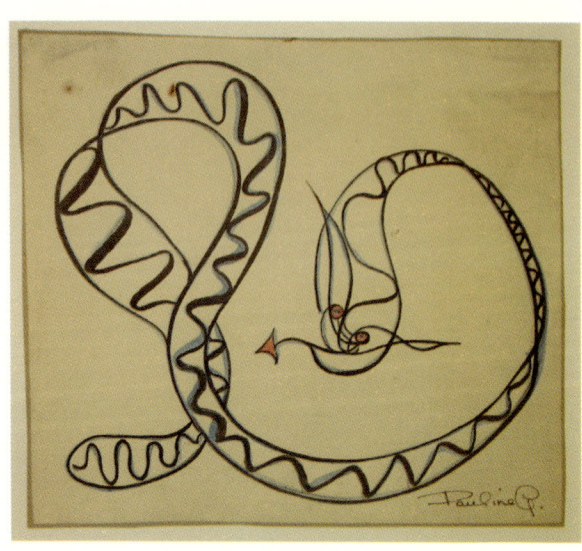

SNAKE
1950 • pastel • 8" x 9"
Waterford Collection

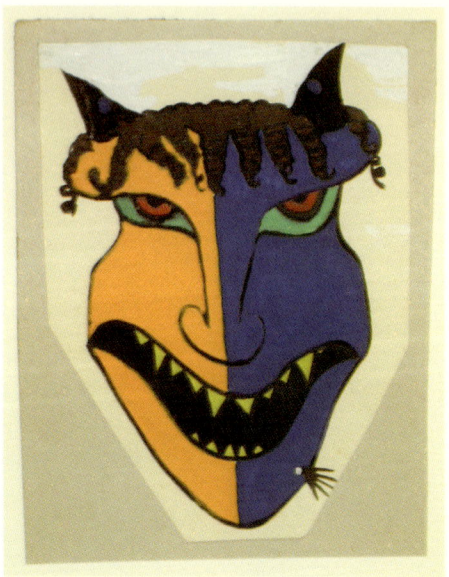

THEATRE MASK
1950 • poster colour • 4" x 3"
Waterford Collection

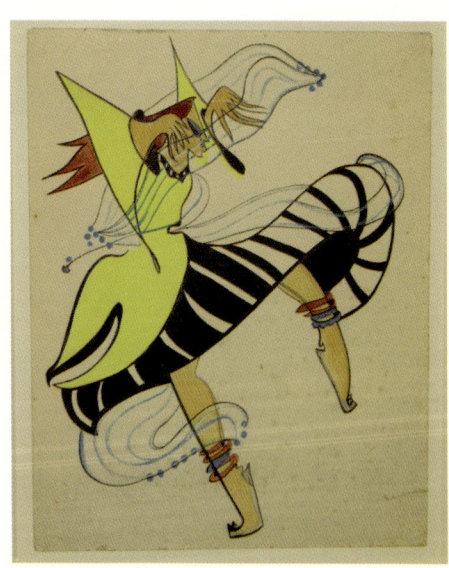

WHIRLY DANCER
1950 • poster colour • 12" x 10"
Waterford Collection

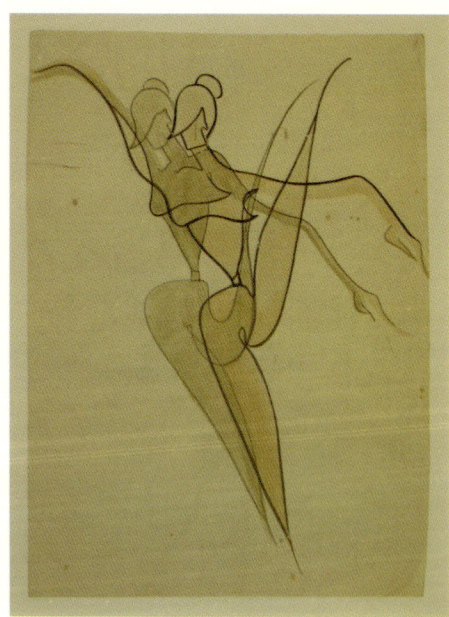

SHADOW DANCE
1950 • ink • 13" x 10"
Kerry Collection

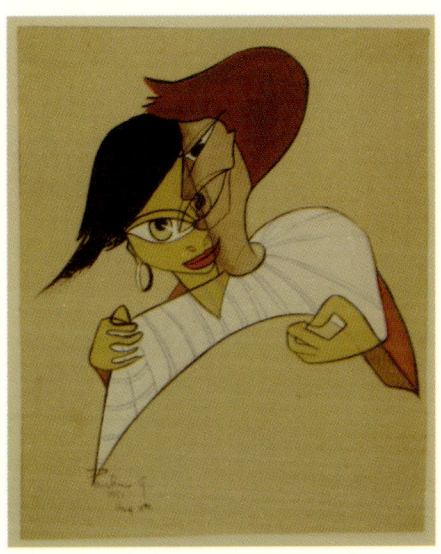

SWISS CHALET HOP
1951 • poster colour • 10" x 8"
Kerry Collection

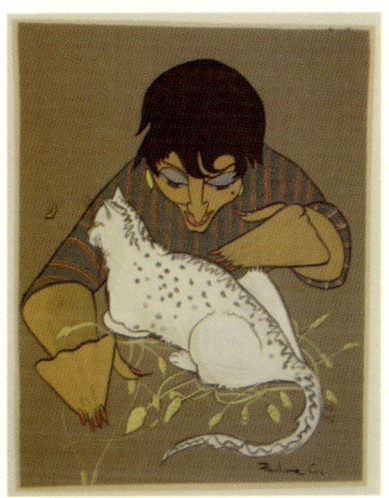

WOMAN AND CAT
1951 • ink • 14" x 11"
Kerry Collection

Pat Cahill was one of the lodgers in 51 Frankfort Avenue. We begged her to tell our fortunes; 'what tops you, what hangs over your head, your life, your love, your wish and whats *booound* to be true'.
Dancing cheek to cheek with the architects, Des, Benny and Brian thrilled us.

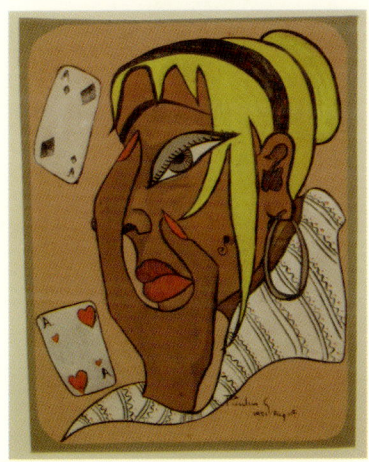

FORTUNE TELLER WOMAN
1951 • ink • 12" x 9"
Waterford Collection

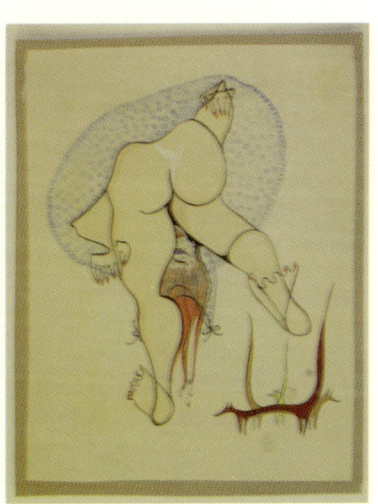

OOPS!
1951 • ink • 13" x 10"
Travelling Collection

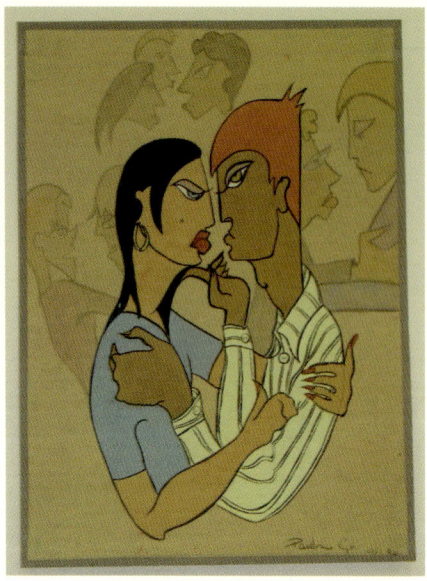

DANCING AT THE HOP, DUBLIN
1951 • gouache • 11" x 9"
Travelling Collection

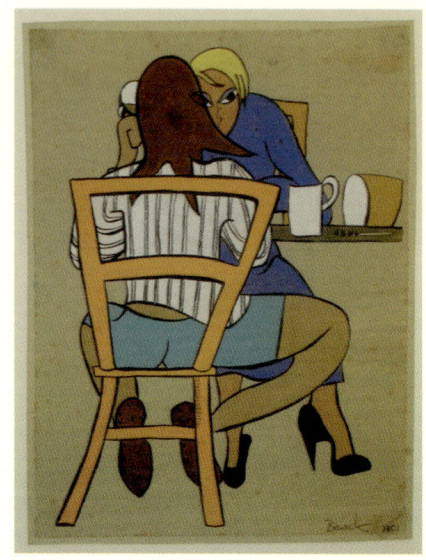

CUPS OF TEA IN FRANKFORT AVENUE
1951 • ink • 11" x 8"
Waterford Collection

We started to get serious crushes at the Hops.
Barry's mother, Maura Laverty came looking for us once in Stephen's Green. 'Is this what Pearse died for?'

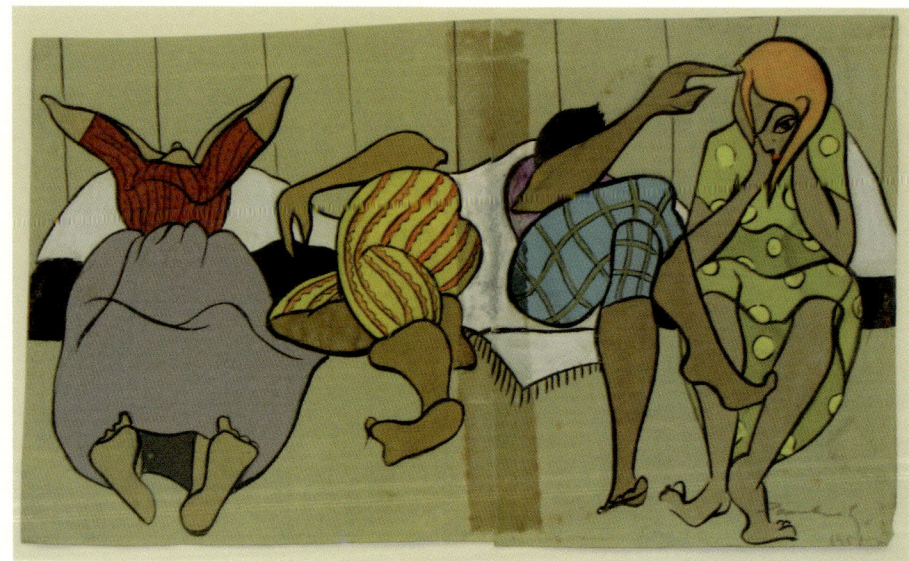

AFTER LATE NIGHT PARTIES
1951 • ink • 7" x 12"
Travelling Collection

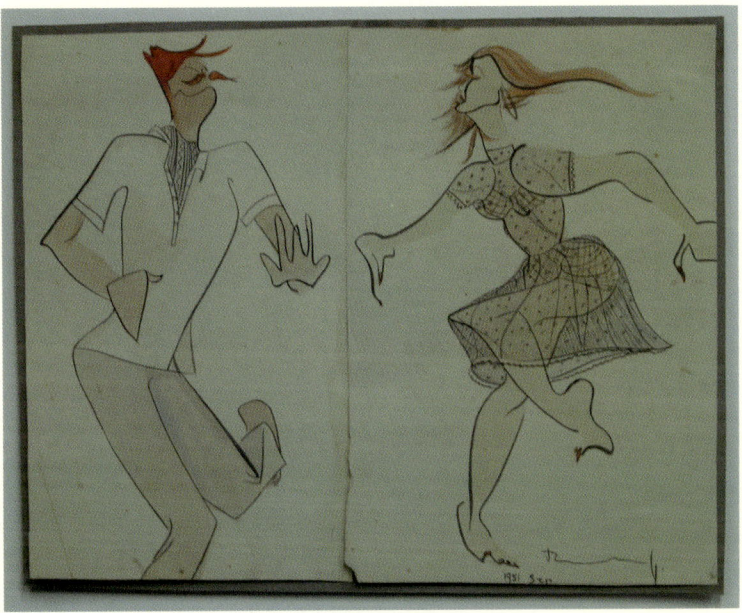

JAZZ DANCERS
1951 • ink • 10" x 13"
Travelling Collection

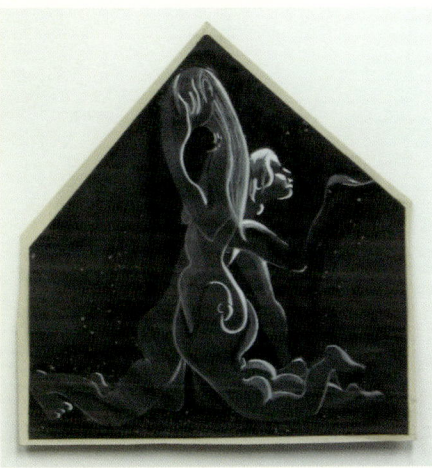

FAMILY IN A TRIANGLE
1952 • poster paint • 12" x 12"
Travelling Collection

Scraper board produced fine white lines onto a black background. Different techniques have different inspirations.

At Art School we learned more about each other while we sat on the hot pipes and gossiped.

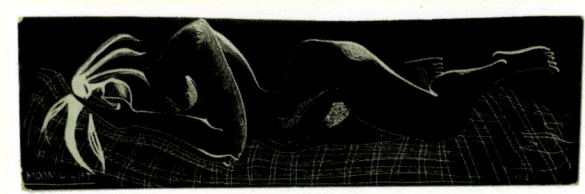

SLEEPING NUDE 1
1952 • 3" x 12"
Waterford Collection

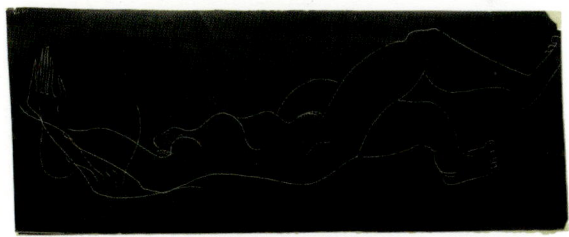

SLEEPING NUDE II
1952 • 4" x 10"
Waterford Collection

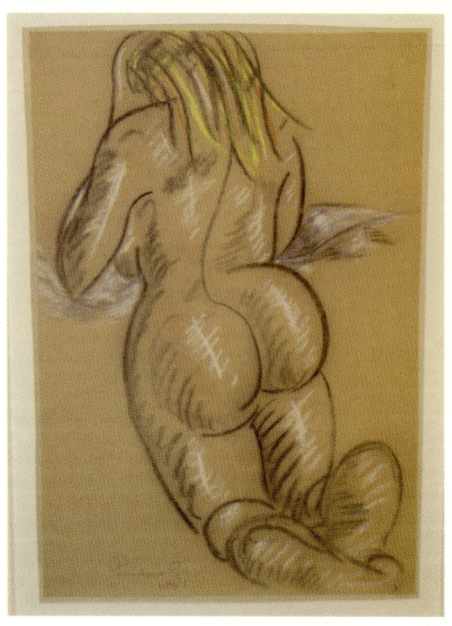

PAT C. KNEELING
1951 • pastel • 12" x 8"
Waterford Collection

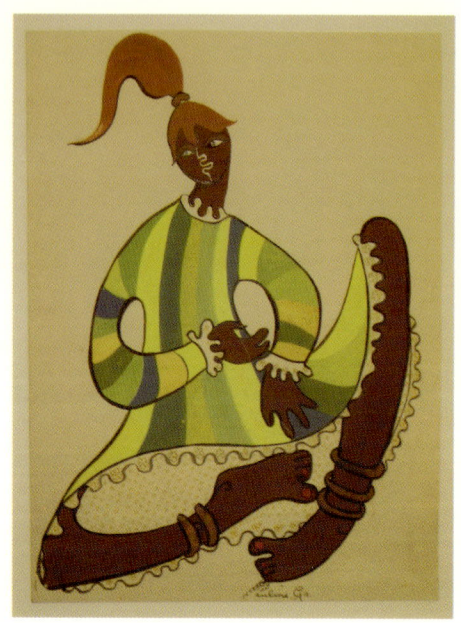

BLACK DOLL
1952 • poster colour • 11" x 8"
Kerry Collection

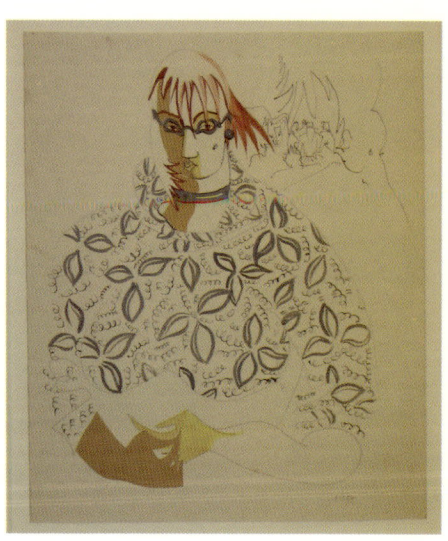

FAT INTELLECTUAL
1952 • poster paint • 12" x 10"
Kerry Collection

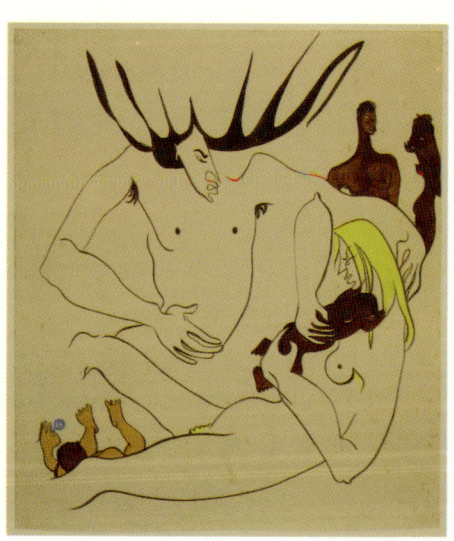

MIXED RACES
1952 • poster colour • 11" x 10"
Kerry Collection

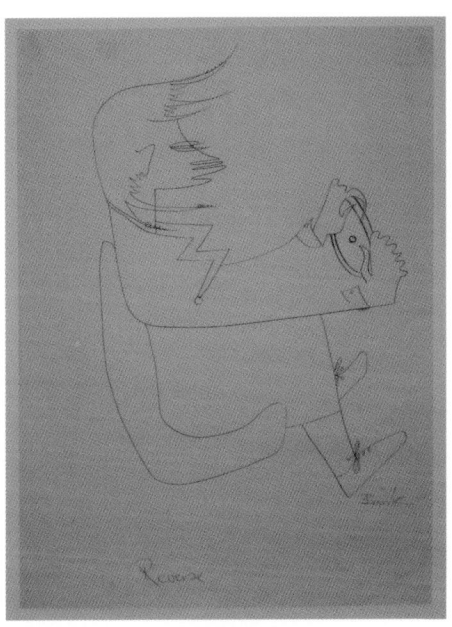

REVERSE
1952 • ink • 13" x 10"
Kerry Collection

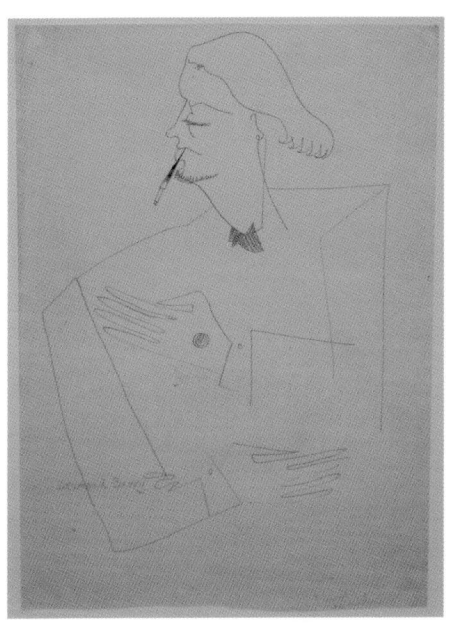

DESMOND BARRY
1952 • ink • 14" x 10"
Waterford Collection

Falling in love got more serious, first with Desmond Barry and then Pat.

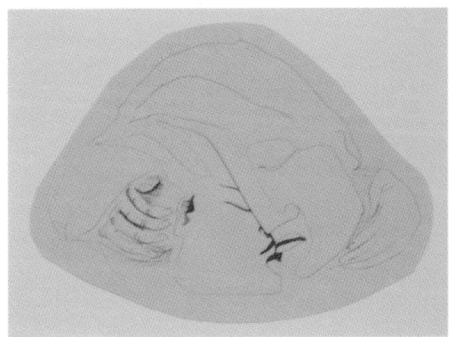

KISS
1952 • fountain pen and egg • 4" x 5"
Travelling Collection

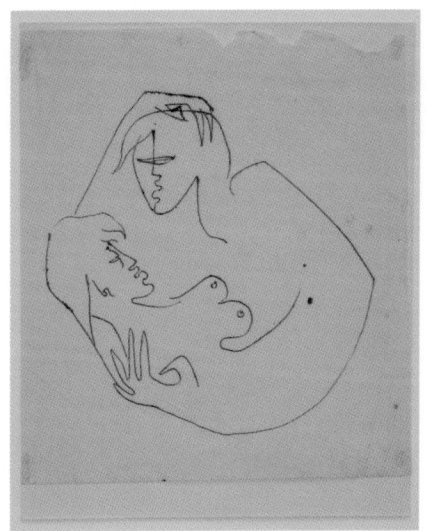

LOVERS
1952 • biro • 8" x 7"
Travelling Collection

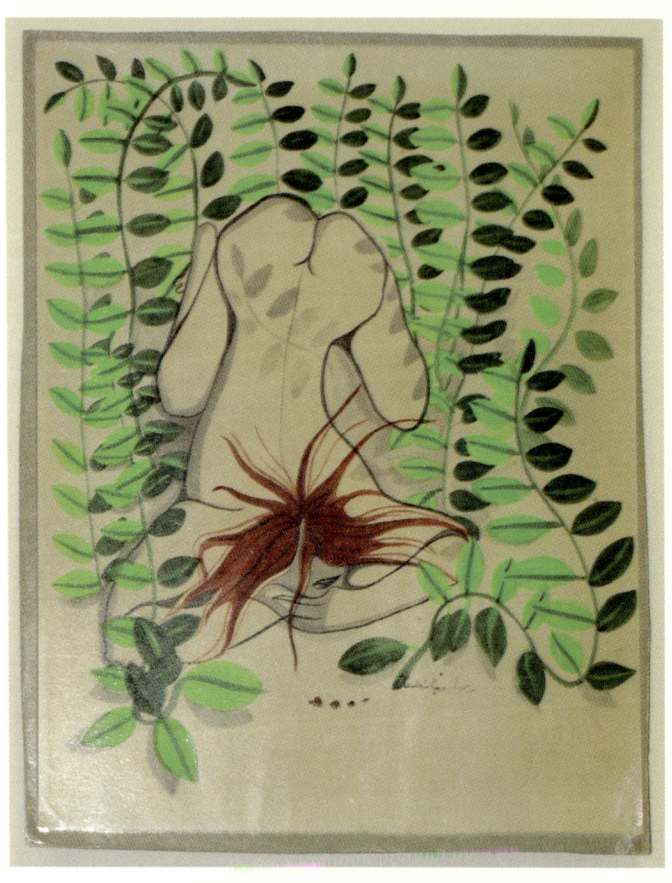

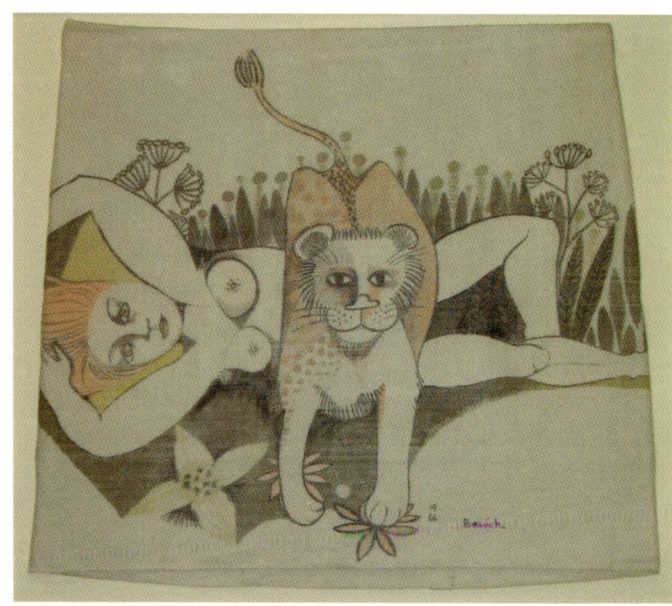

LOOKING AT LADYBIRDS
1952 • poster colour • 9" x 7"
Travelling Collection

LIVING ART SKIRT
1952 • ink on linen • 13" x 16"
Travelling Collection

The Exhibition of Living Art was looked after by Colonel Knox.
'She doesn't even wear a bra, and enters disgusting pictures like this. It's a disgrace', I was told during a game of compliments and insults.

Being rejected I made a linen skirt and painted a picture on it, and wore it to the opening.

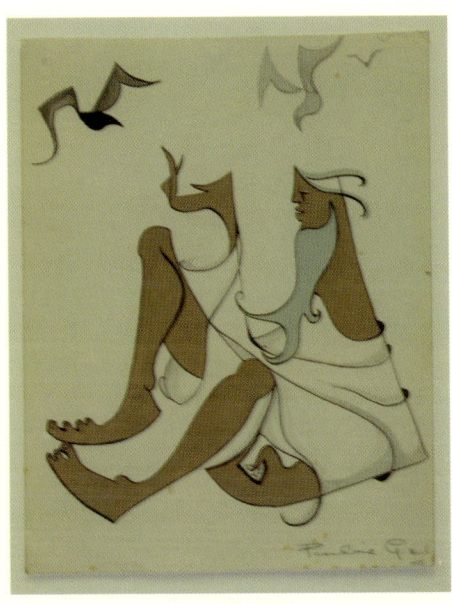

ICARUS
1952 • poster paint • 11" x 9"
Travelling Collection

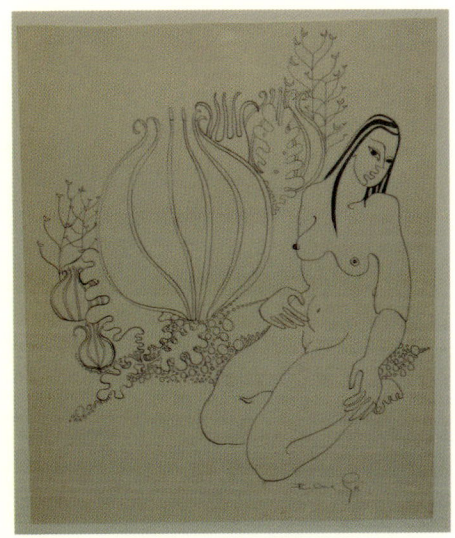

NUDE WITH GOURD
1952 • ink • 10" x 9"
Waterford Collection

Cover of *Icarus* magazine from Trinity College.

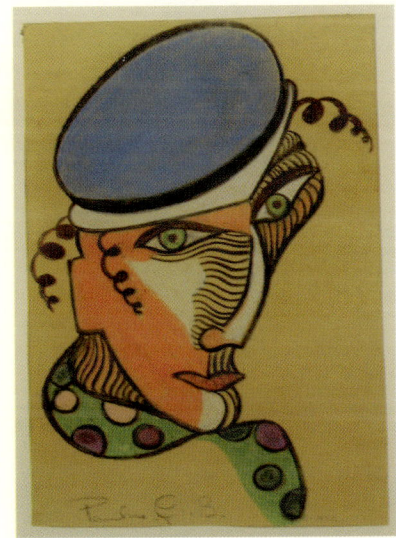

SAILOR II
1952 • pastel • 12" x 8"
Waterford Collection

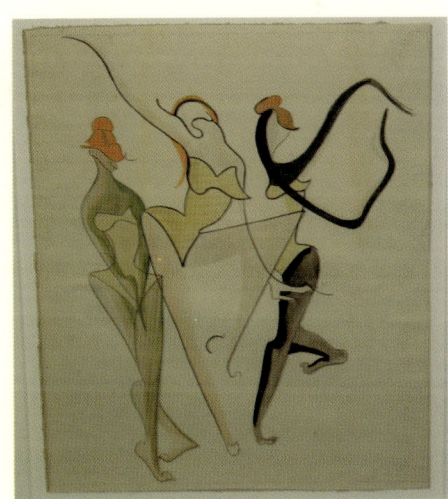

THREE DANCERS
1952 • poster paint • 12" x 10"
Waterford Collection

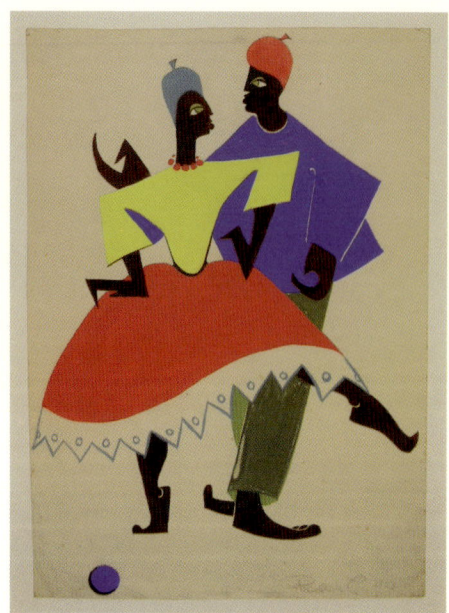

BLACK DANCERS
1953 • poster colour • 13" x 10"
Kerry Collection

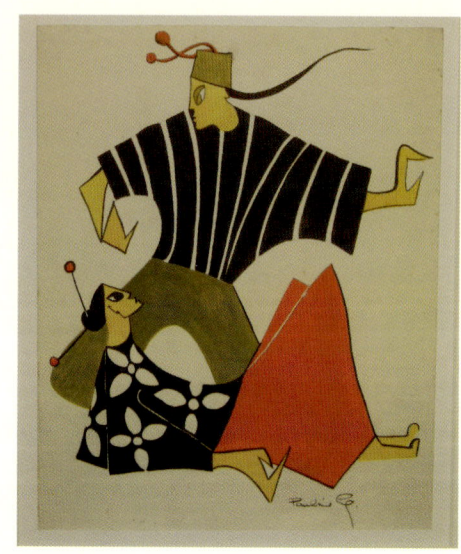

CHINESE DANCERS
1953 • poster colour • 12" x 10"
Kerry Collection

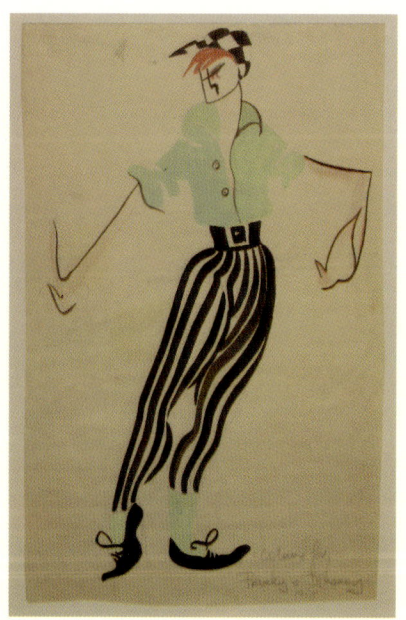

COSTUME FOR FRANKIE AND JOHNNY
1953 • ink • 13" x 8"
Kerry Collection

Designs for Alan Simpson and Carolyn Swift
of the tiny Pike Theatre in Herbert Lane

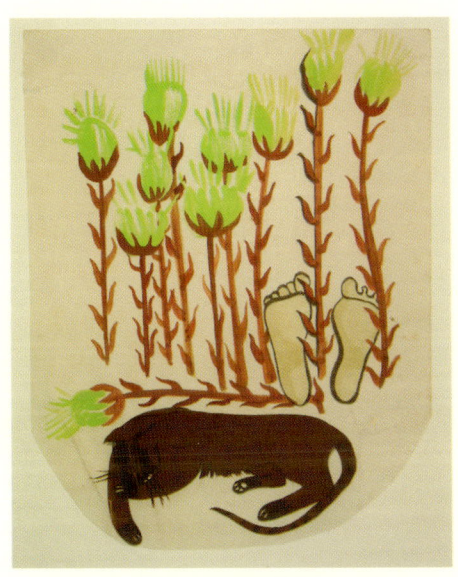

CAT AT HER FEET
1953 • ink • 7" x 5"
Kerry Collection

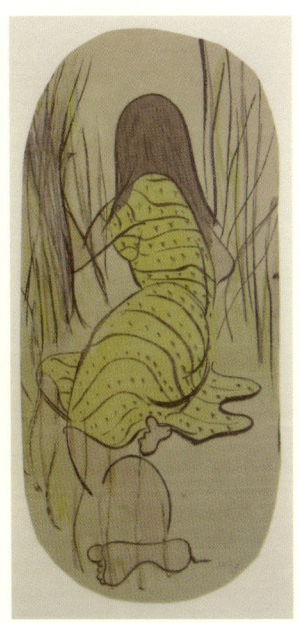

LOOKING THROUGH RUSHES
1953 • poster colour • 10" x 5"
Kerry Collection

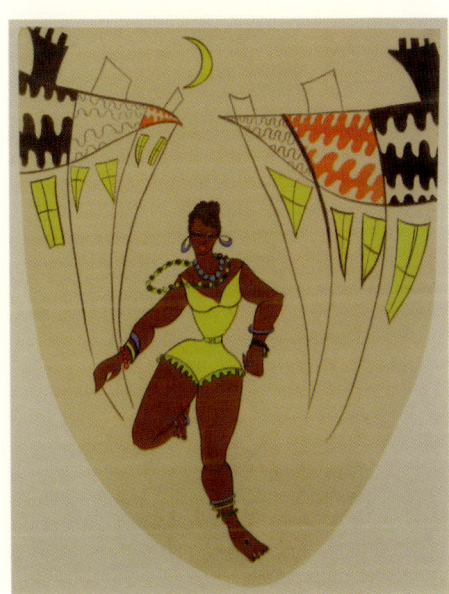

NEGRESS ON STAGE
1953 • poster colour • 14" x 10"
Kerry Collection

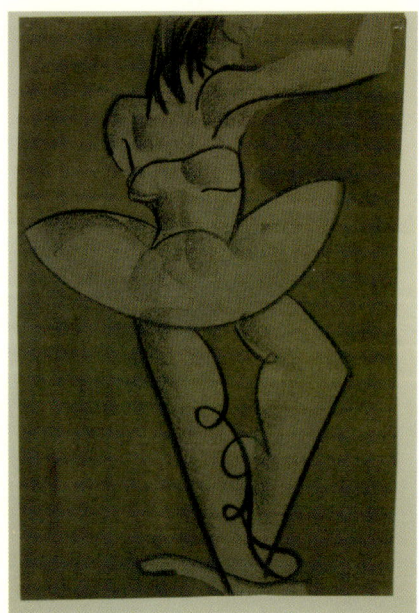

BALLET DANCER
1953 • charcoal • 12" x 8"
Waterford Collection

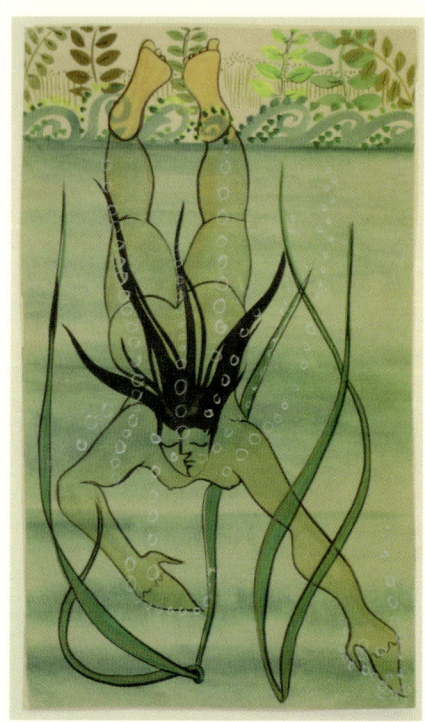

DIVING
1953 • poster colour • 9" x 5"
Travelling Collection

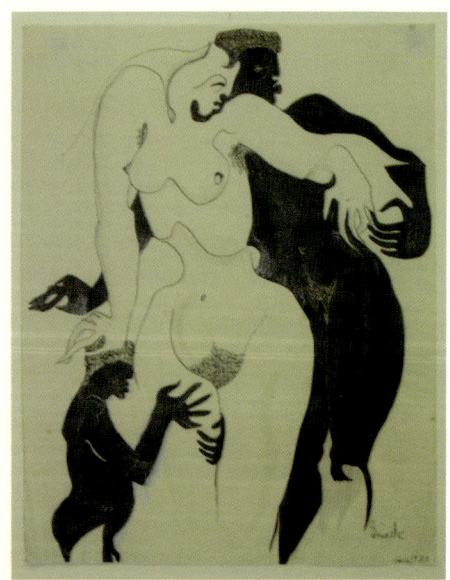

COLOUR BAR I
1953 • ink • 10" x 8"
Travelling Collection

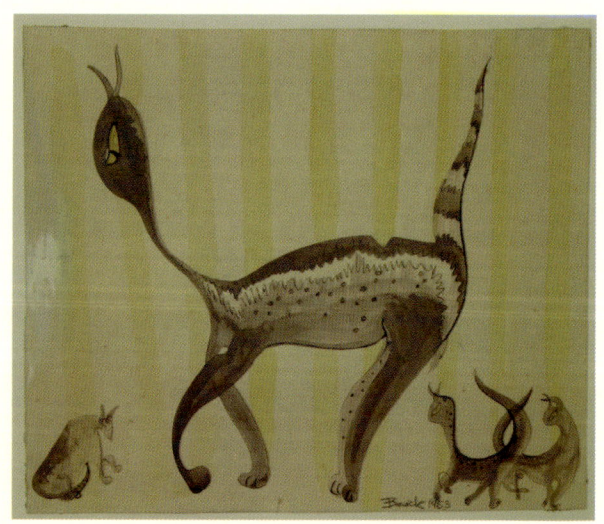

CAT AND THREE KITTENS
1953 • ink • 9" x 11"
Waterford Collection

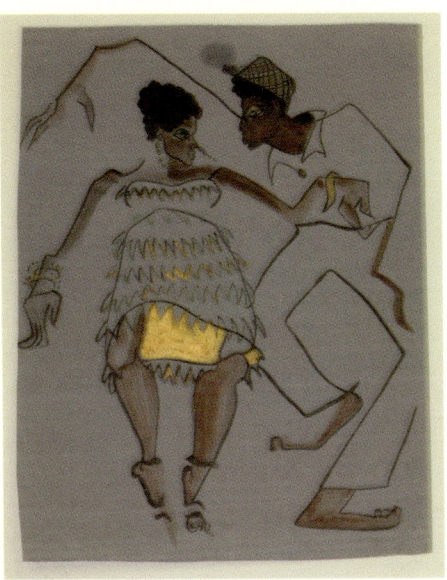

DOROTHY DANDRIDGE
1953 • ink • 10" x 8"
Travelling Collection

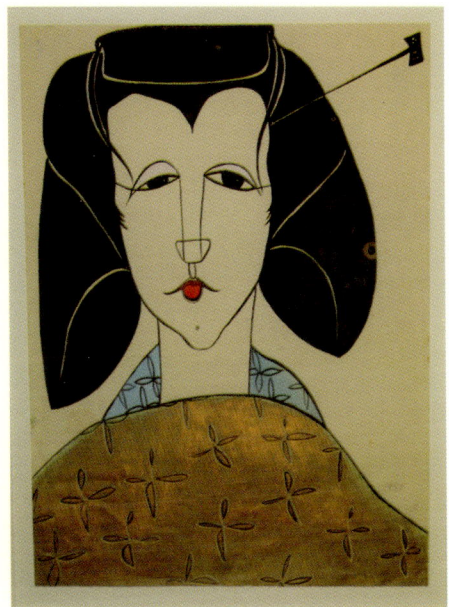

JAPANESE DANCER
1953 • ink • 14" x 10"
Waterford Collection

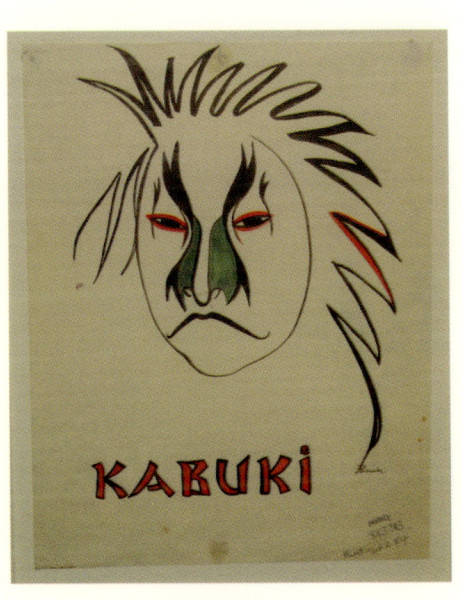

KABUKI
1953 • poster colour • 10" x 8"
Waterford Collection

We saw Dorothy Dandridge and the Kabuki
dancers on stage in Dublin. They were
magical.

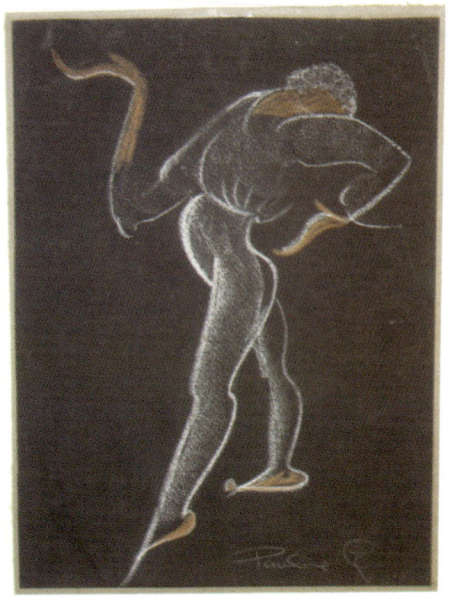

MARCEL MARCEAU
1953 • pastel • 12" x 9"
Waterford Collection

Mime artist Marcel Marceau came over from Paris.

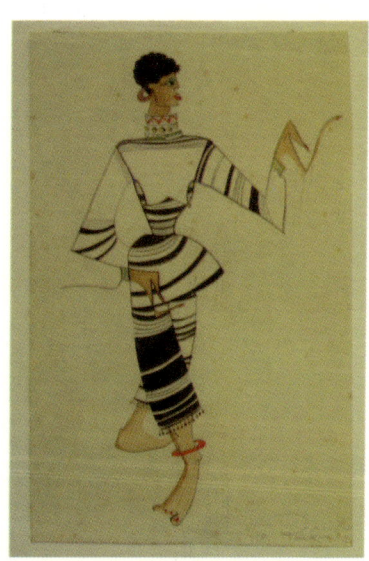

ON STAGE IN STRIPES I
1953 • ink • 12" x 8"
Travelling Collection

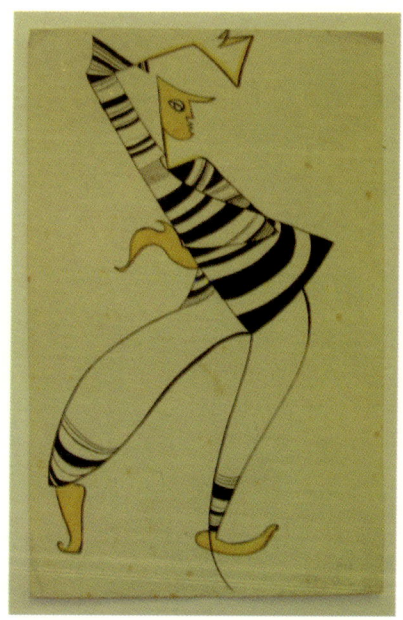

ON STAGE IN STRIPES II
1953 • ink • 14" x 9"
Travelling Collection

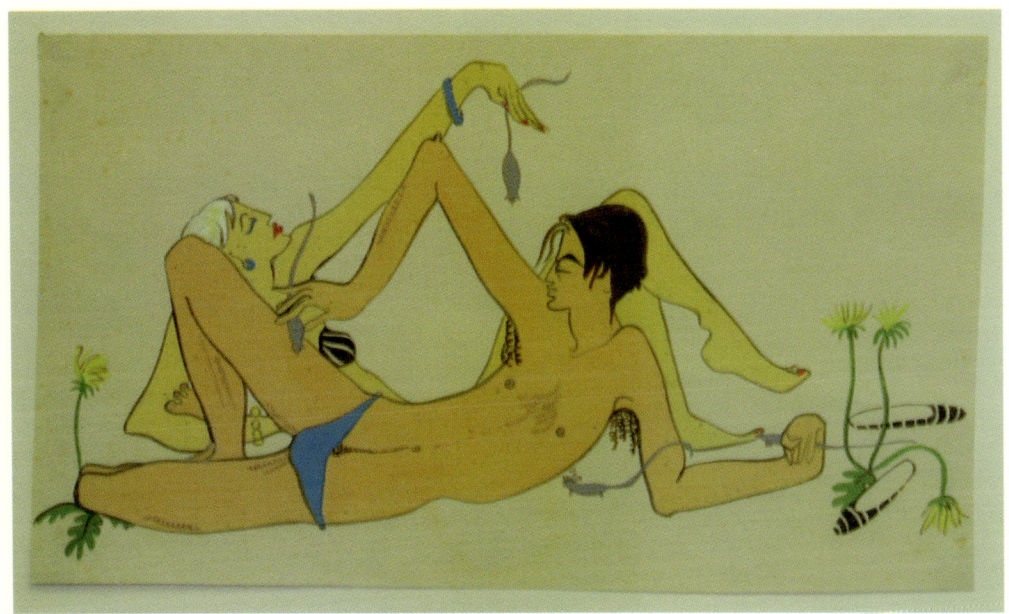

PAT AND I WITH MICE
1953 • poster colour • 7" x 13"
Travelling Collection

Pat has a caring nature.

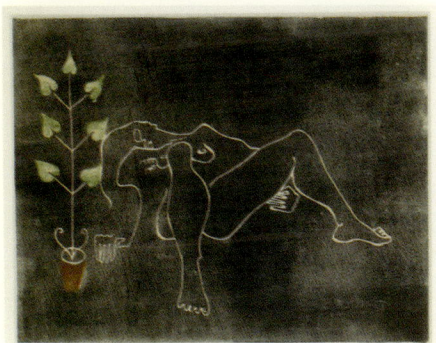

ASLEEP IN THE GLASSHOUSE I
1954 • lino cut • 9" x 12"
Kerry Collection

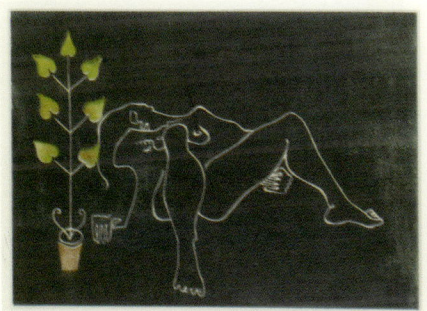

ASLEEP IN THE GLASSHOUSE II
1954 • lino cut • 9" x 12"
Kerry Collection

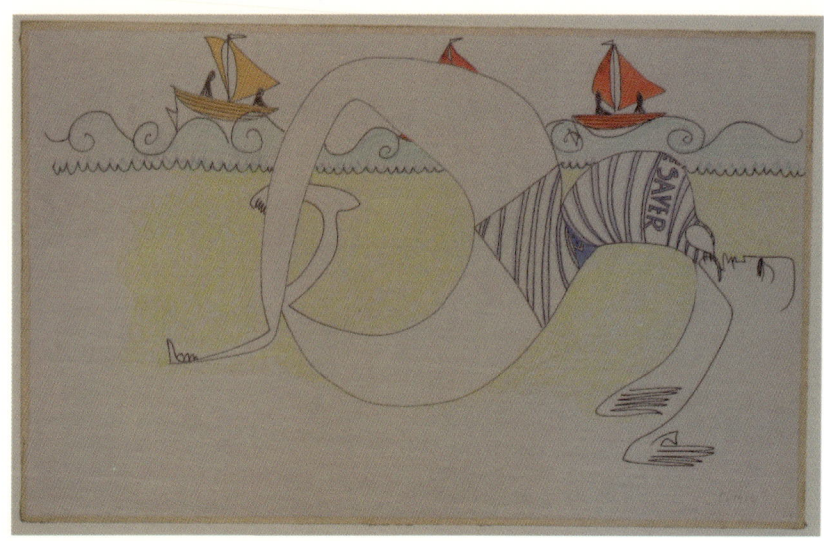

LIFE SAVER
1954 • ink and pencil • 10" x 16"
Kerry Collection

Having bought a second-hand book for two shillings on the quays called *Philosophical Transactions*, a word on a page would inspire a picture. The editor of *Ambit* magazine, London, commissioned work to publish. However he was shocked to see so many pages of this rare book defaced!

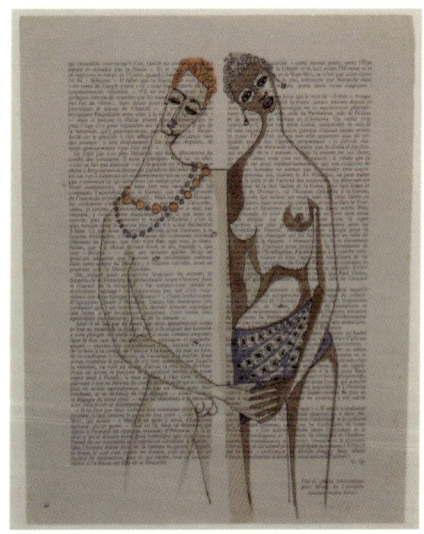

COUPLE ON FRENCH BOOK
1954 • ink • 12" x 9"
Kerry Collection

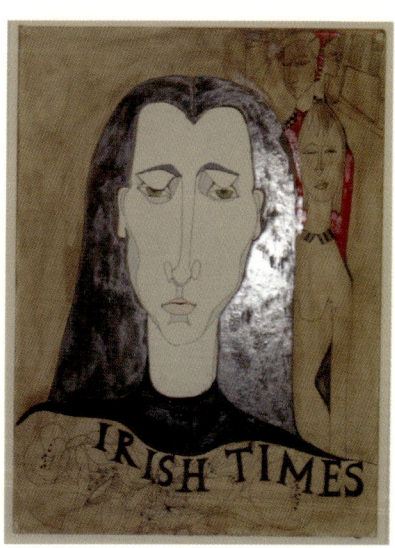

READING THE IRISH TIMES
1954 • ink varnished • 20" x 15"
Kerry Collection

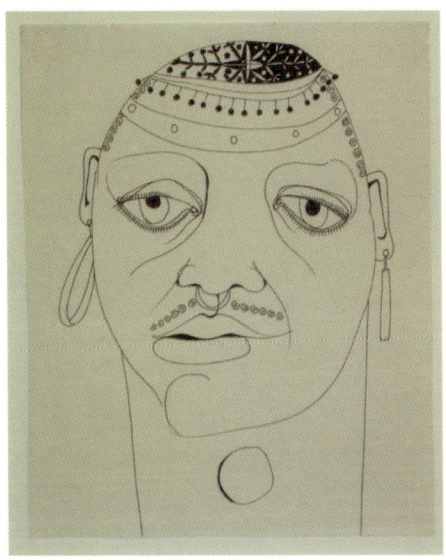

AFRICAN
1954 • ink • 8" x 7"
Travelling Collection

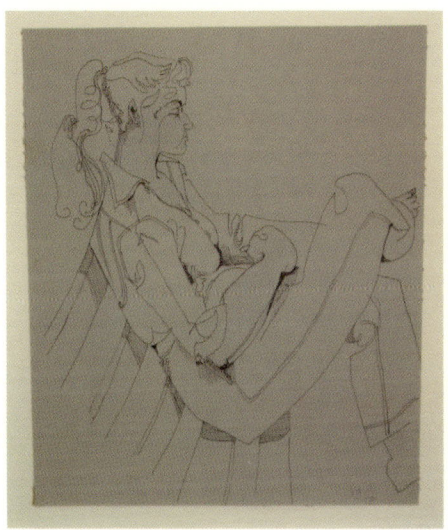

BARRY LAVERTY ON BENCH
1954 • ink • 10" x 8"
Waterford Collection

Barry Laverty wore a shiny, bouncy ponytail and wore trousers. I admired her for it.
Sean Keating remarked, 'strutting around the art school with their bums encased in trousers'.

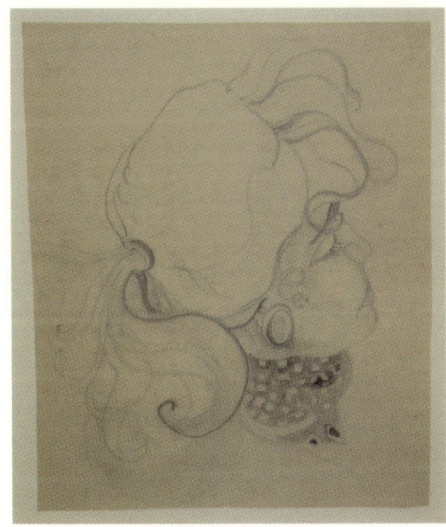

BARRY LAVERTY
1954 • pencil • 9" x 8"
Waterford Collection

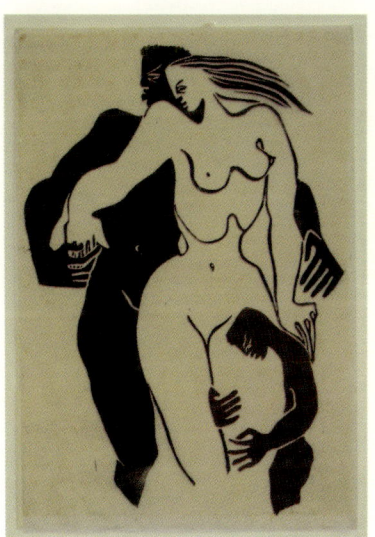

COLOUR BAR II
1954 • lino cut • 14" x 10"
Travelling Collection

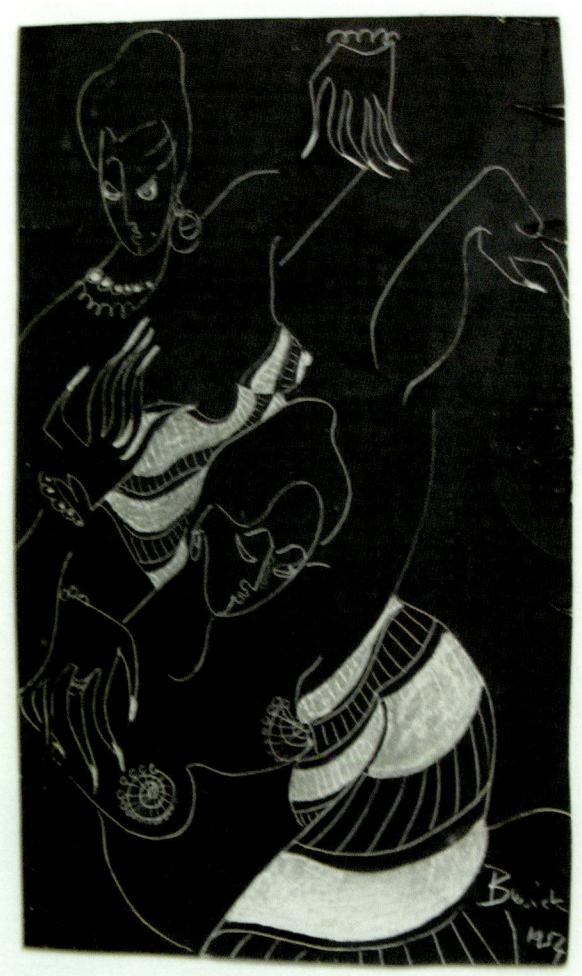

DECORATIVE DANCING
1954 • scraperboard • 6" x 3"
Waterford Collection

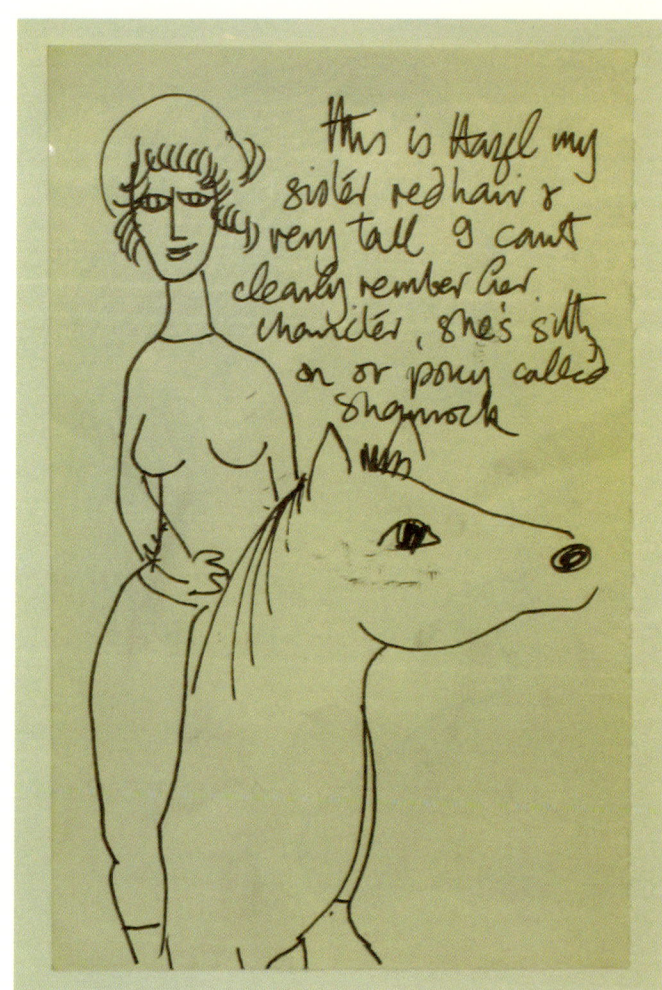

HAZEL ON A HORSE
1954 • ink • 5" x 3"
Travelling Collection

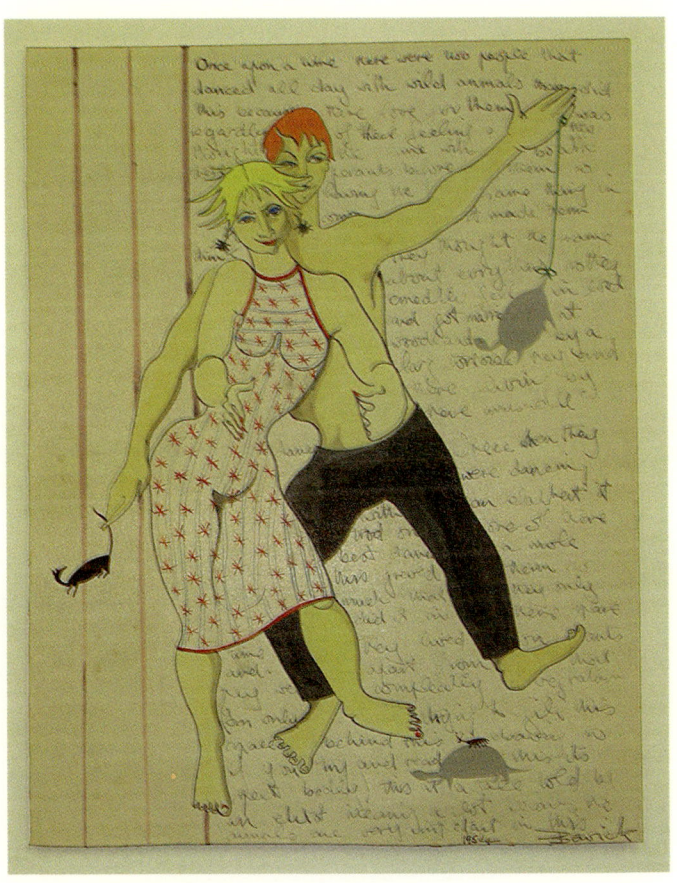

MARRIAGE AT WOODLANDS
1954 • poster colour • 12" x 9"
Travelling Collection

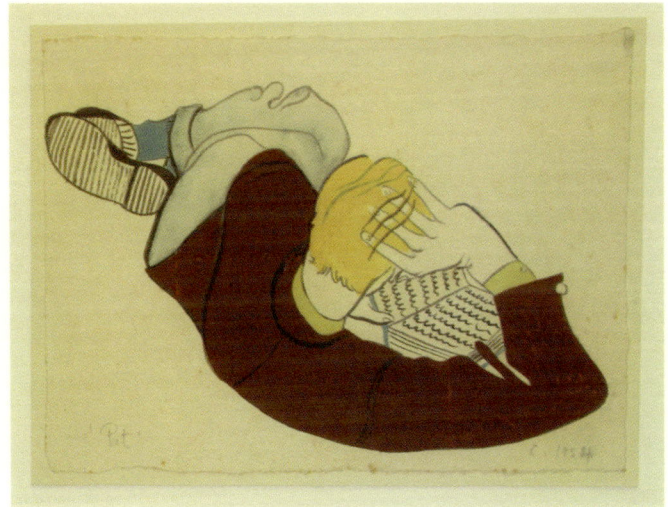

PAT READING
1954 • poster colour • 6" x 8"
Travelling Collection

Pat read aloud to me then, as he still does to this day.

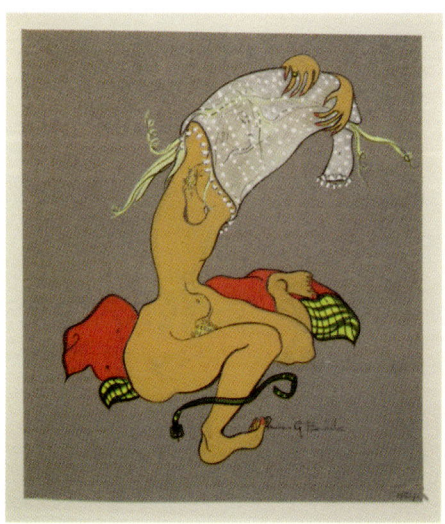

SEE THROUGH NIGHTDRESS
1954 • poster paint • 10" x 9"
Waterford Collection

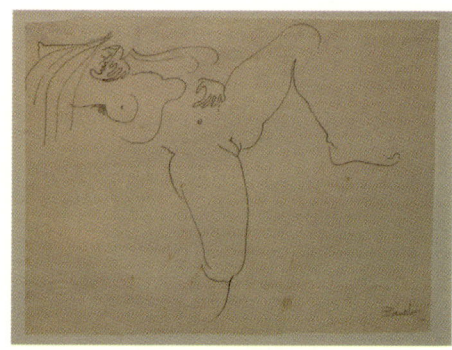

RECLINING NUDE
1955 • ink • 7" x 10"
Kerry Collection

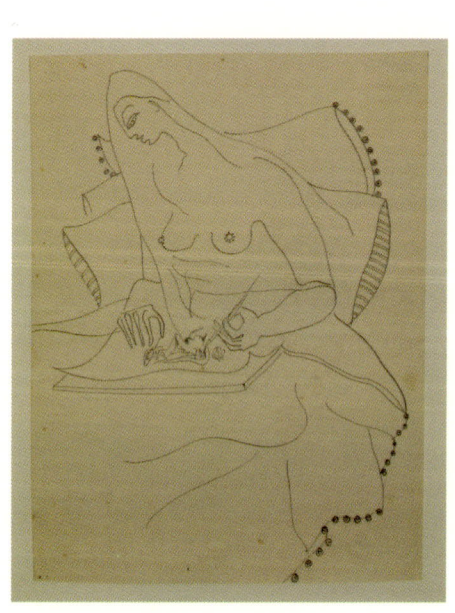

DRAWING IN BED
1955 • ink • 10" x 7"
Kerry Collection

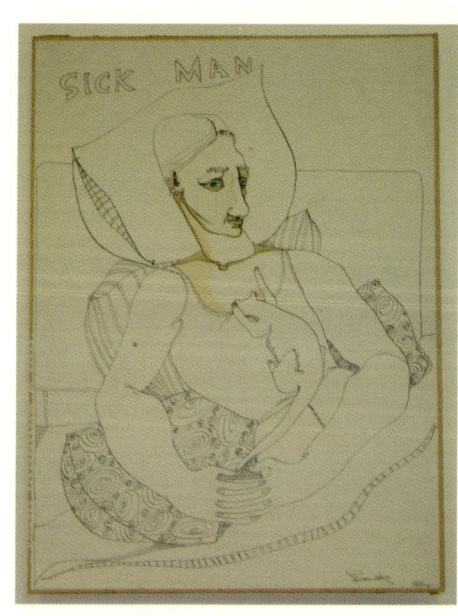

SICK MAN
1954 • ink • 15" x 12"
Travelling Collection

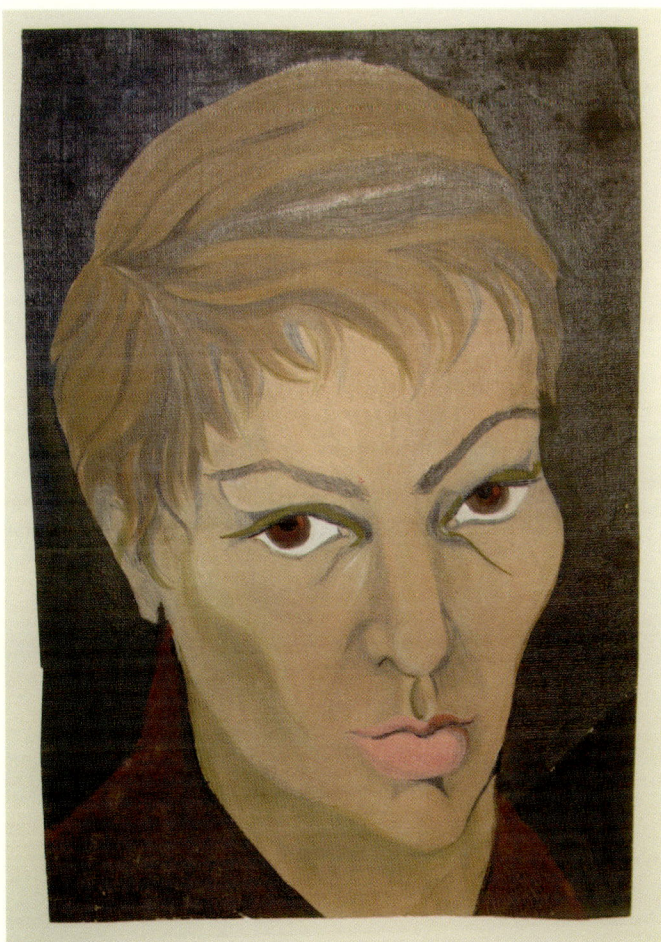

SELF PORTRAIT
1954 • oil • 13" x 9"
Waterford Collection

Oils were not easy to use, because I couldn't lean my hand on the wet surface of the canvas. The overpowering smell wouldn't allow one to become immersed.

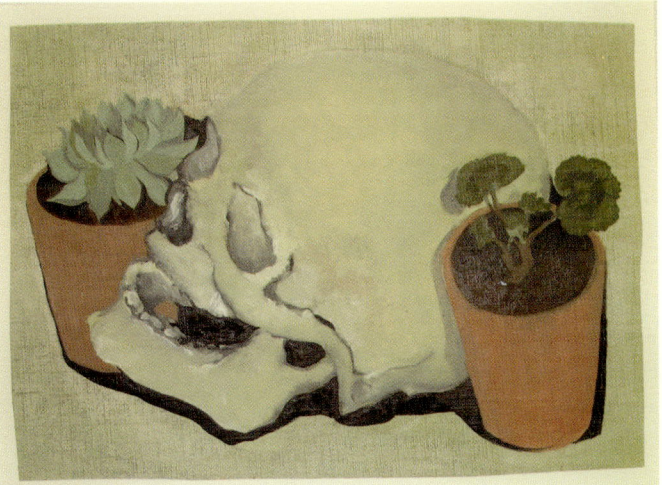

STILL LIFE WITH SKULL
1954 • oil • 9" x 13"
Waterford Collection

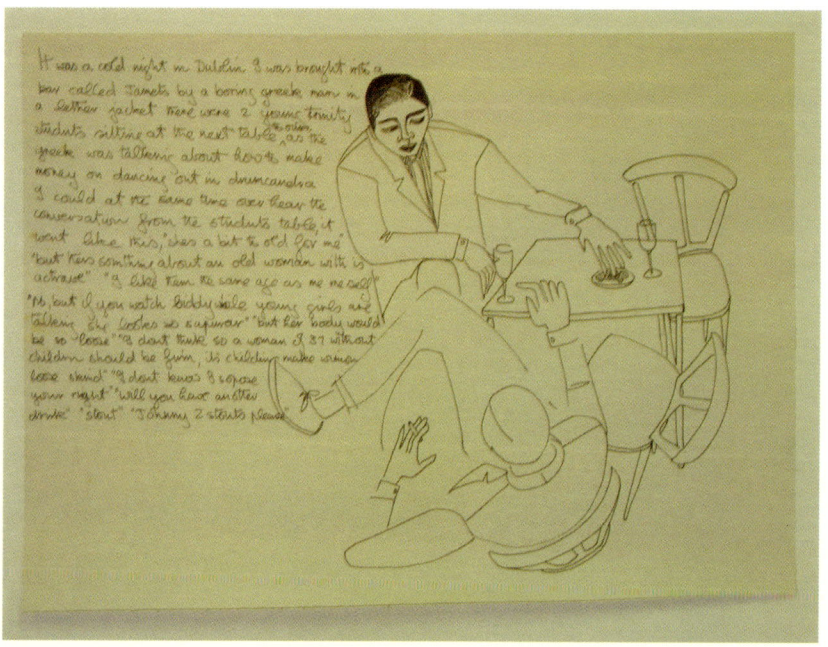

TWO MEN IN JAMMETS
1954 • ink • 10" x 15"
Travelling Collection

It was a cold night in Dublin. I was brought into a bar called Jammets
by a boring Greek man in a leather jacket. There were two young
Trinity students sitting at the next table to ours. As the Greek was
talking about how to make money on dancing out in Drumcondra I
could at the same time overhear the conversation from the students'
table. It went like this 'she's a bit too old for me', 'but there's something
about an old woman with is actrave', 'I like them the same age as me,
myself', 'no, but if you watch Biddy while young girls are talking, she
look's so superior', 'but her body would be so loose', 'I don't think so. A
woman of 37 without children should be firm', 'it's children that make
wimon loose skind', 'I don't know, I supose', 'you're right', 'will you have
another drink', 'stout', 'Johnny, two stouts please'.

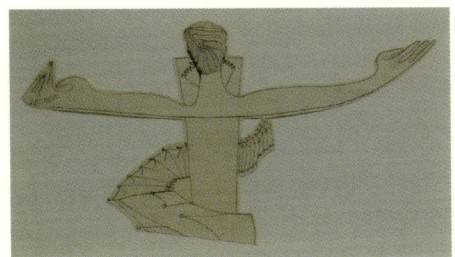

DIVE
1955 • ink • 6" x 11"
Waterford Collection

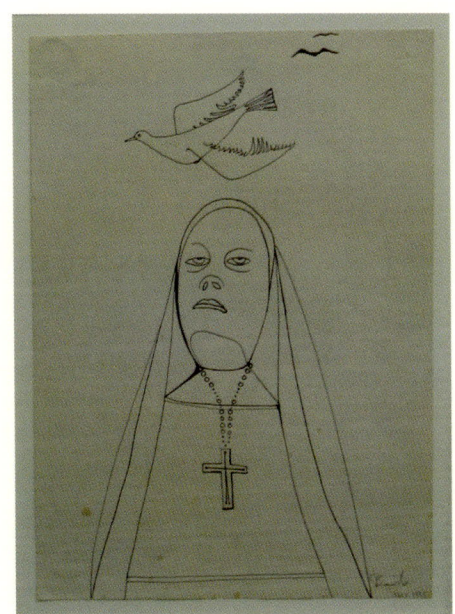

NUN
1955 • ink • 10" x 7"
Waterford Collection

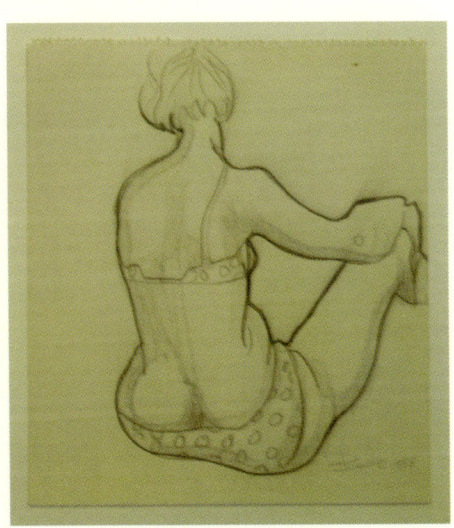

HARRY, BACK
1955 • conte • 12" x 11"
Travelling Collection

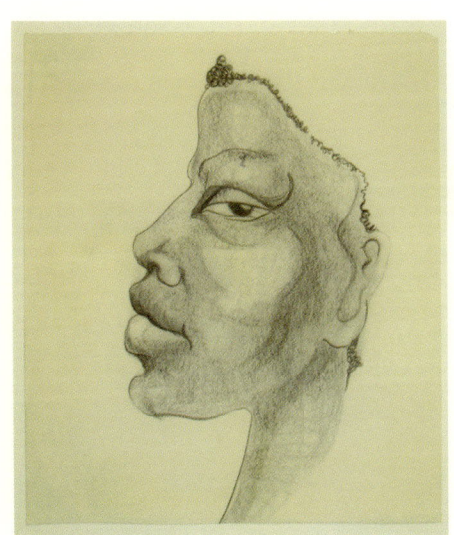

NEGRO PROFILE
1955 • conte • 12" x 11"
Waterford Collection

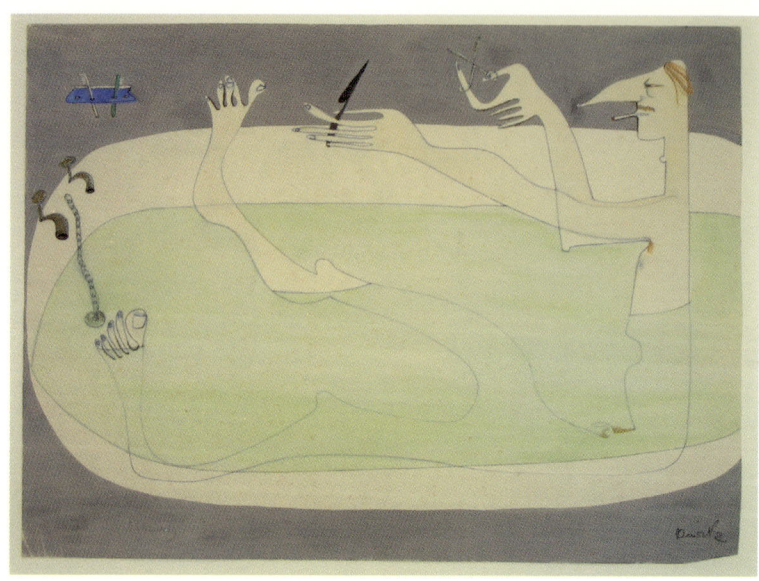

HODDY IN THE BATH, IMAGINED
1955 • poster colour and ink • 10" x 13"
Travelling Collection

Hoddy played the piano for the Pike Theatre. One day I fell over him asleep, rolled up into one of the canvas sets. He was the jazz critic on the *Irish Times*. 'Today I bought a box of tinned food that had lost their labels. So I never know what I'm going to eat before I open the tin'. He would strike up the piano, T.P. McKenna, Milo O'Shea, Deirdre McSharry and I would burst into song 'boulevadiers in Paris today, all go for le Jazz'.

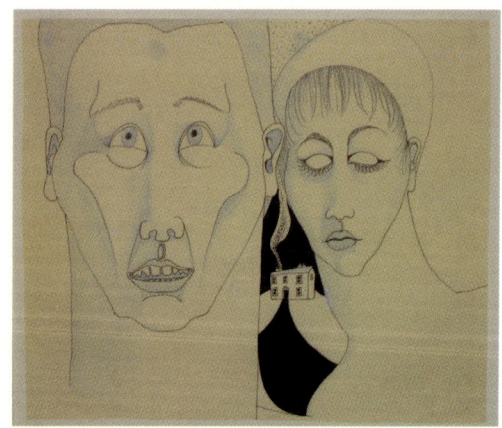

BLUE PARTNERS
1956 • ink and pencil • 11" x 13"
Kerry Collection

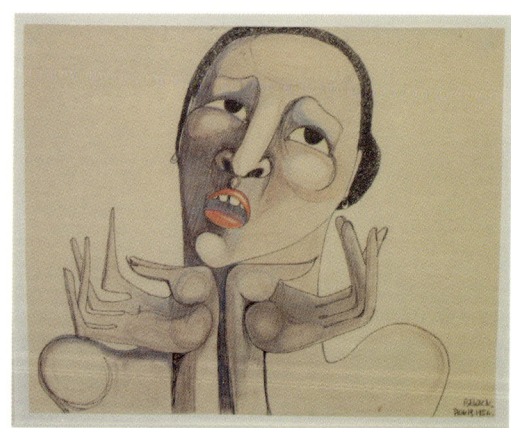

BLUES SINGER
1956 • ink and pencil • 12" x 15"
Kerry Collection

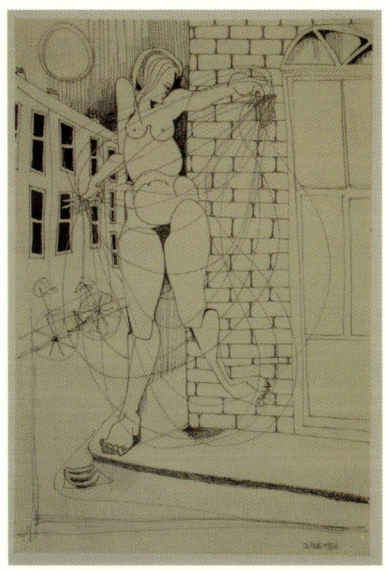

COMPLICATED SKIPPING
1956 • ink • 17" x 12"
Kerry Collection

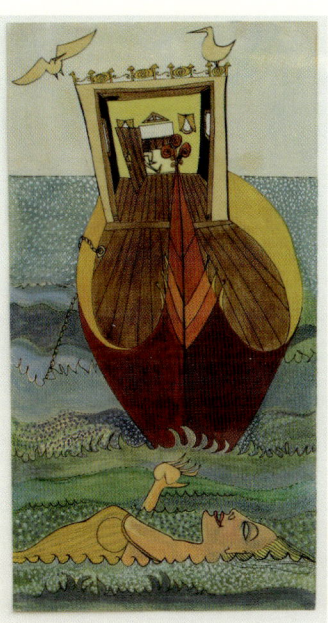

DREAM HOUSE
1956 • ink varnished • 15" x 8"
Kerry Collection

I often pictured an idyllic abode and idyllic life alone.
Pat and I stayed in the Hotel du Dragon on our first trip to Paris
together, baguette and camembert picnic by the Seine.

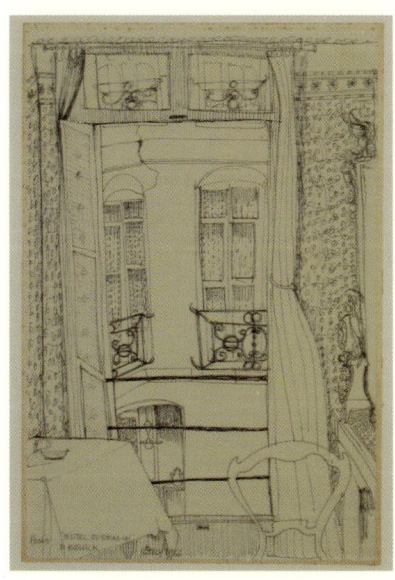

HOTEL DU DRAGON, PARIS
1956 • ink • 18" x 12"
Kerry Collection

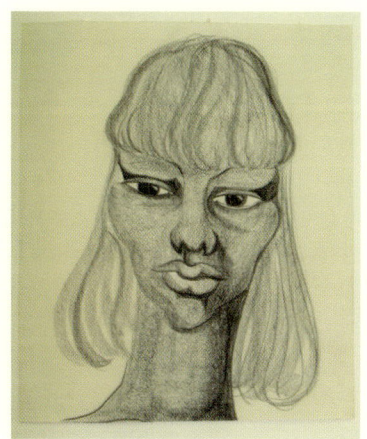

ME
1955 • conte • 12" x 11"
Travelling Collection

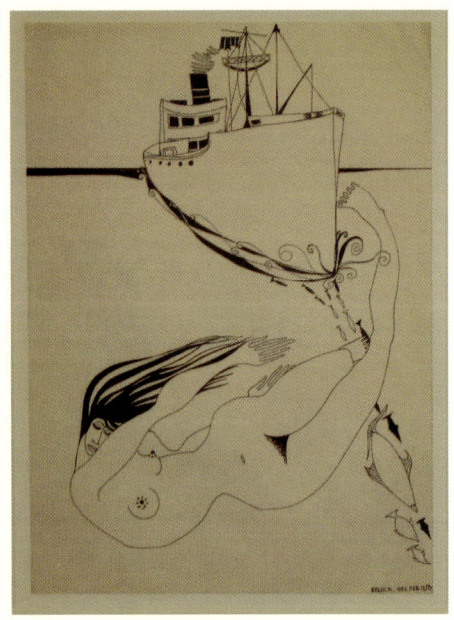

SWIMMER
1956 • ink • 15" x 11"
Kerry Collection

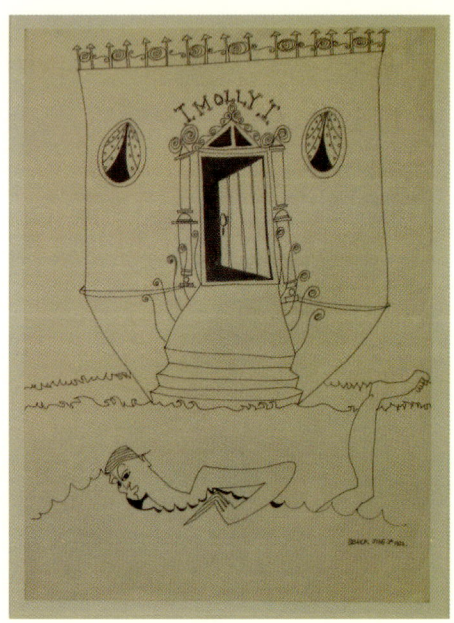

BOATS
1956 • ink • 15" x 11"
Kerry Collection

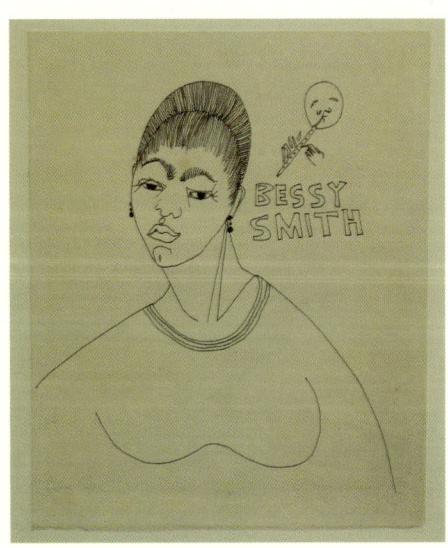

BESSY SMITH
1956 • ink • 8" x 7"
Travelling Collection

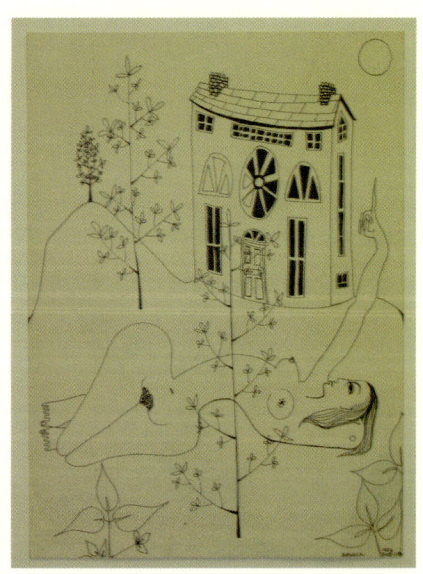

DREAM HOUSE
1956 • ink • 15" x 11"
Travelling Collection

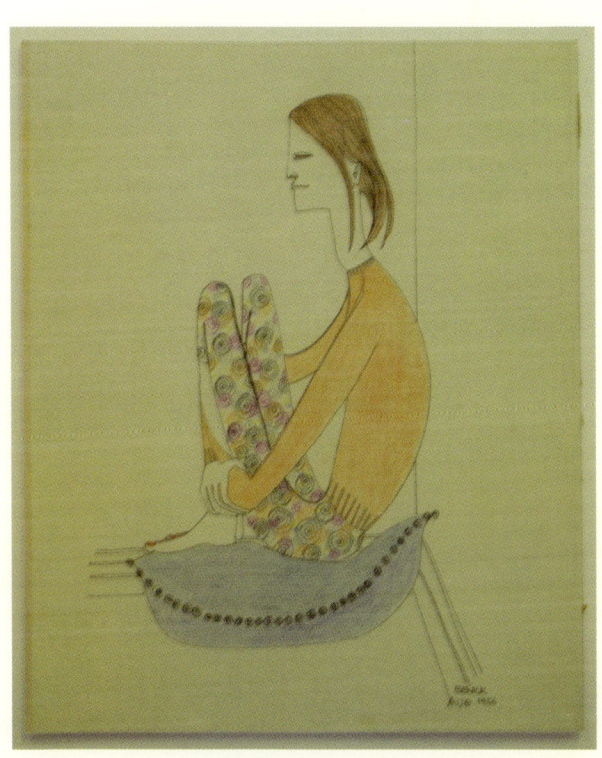

BARRY AT NO 51
1956 • ink and pencil • 12" x 10"
Travelling Collection

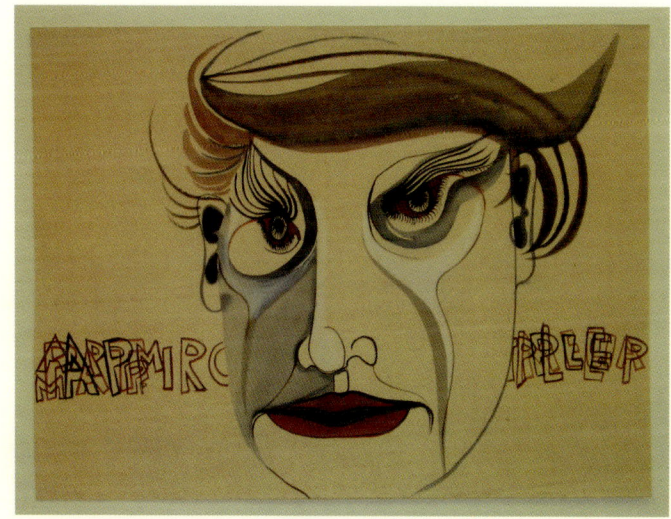

CROSS MAN
1956 • ink • 12" x 16"
Travelling Collection

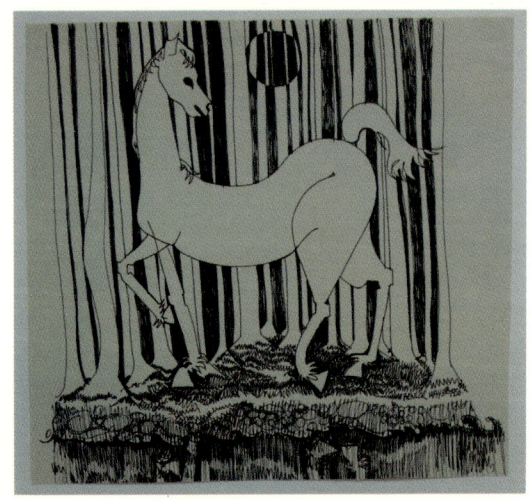

HORSE IN THE WOOD
1956 • ink • 11" x 11"
Waterford Collection

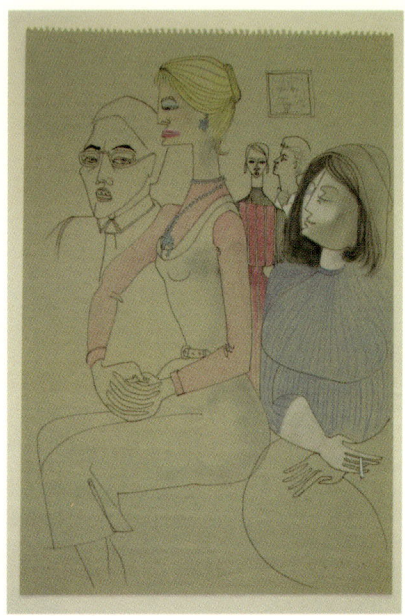

IN O'DONOGHUE'S PUB
1956 • pencil and ink • 18" x 12"
Travelling Collection

In O'Donoghue's pub listening to the Dubliners getting famous.

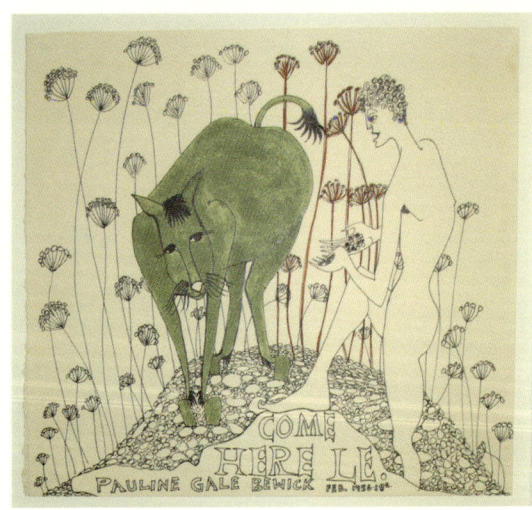

LE
1956 • ink • 10" x 12"
Waterford Collection

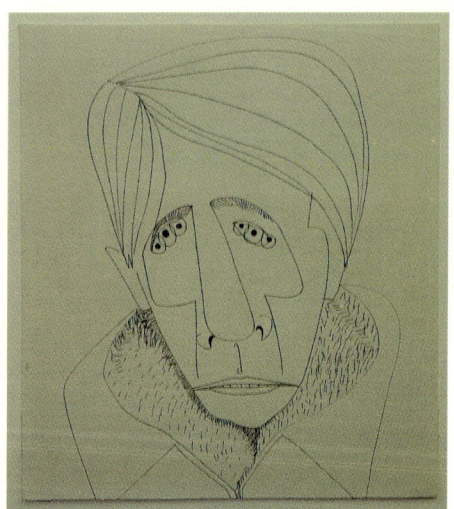

PAT CROSS-EYED
1956 • ink • 12" x 11"
Travelling Collection

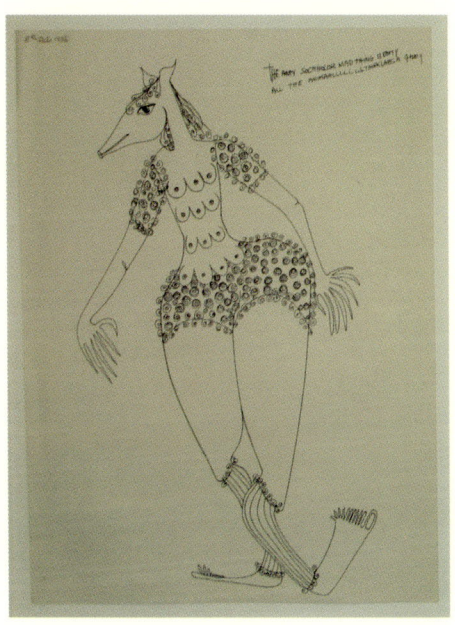

MAD THING
1956 • ink • 15" x 11"
Waterford Collection

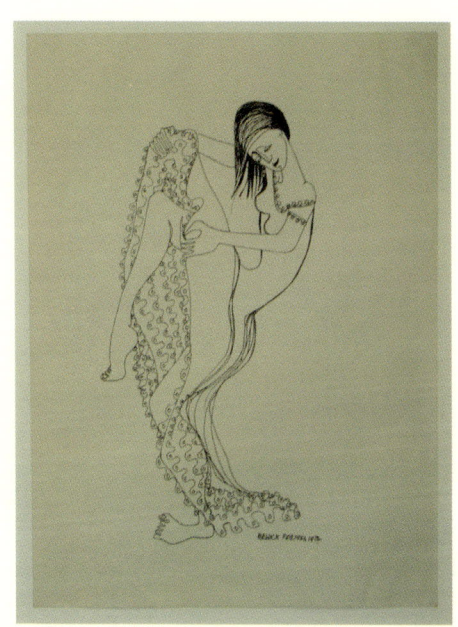

DANCER
1956 • ink • 15" x 11"
Waterford Collection

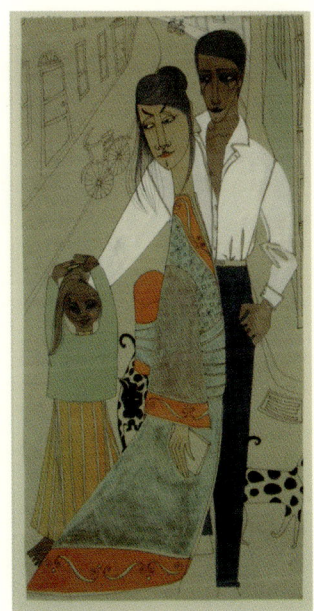

MIXED FAMILY
1956 • ink • 18" x 9"
Waterford Collection

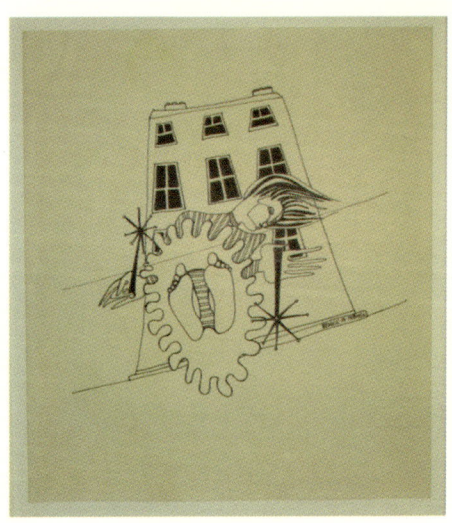

SEE-THROUGH PAVEMENT
1956 • ink • 12" x 11"
Waterford Collection

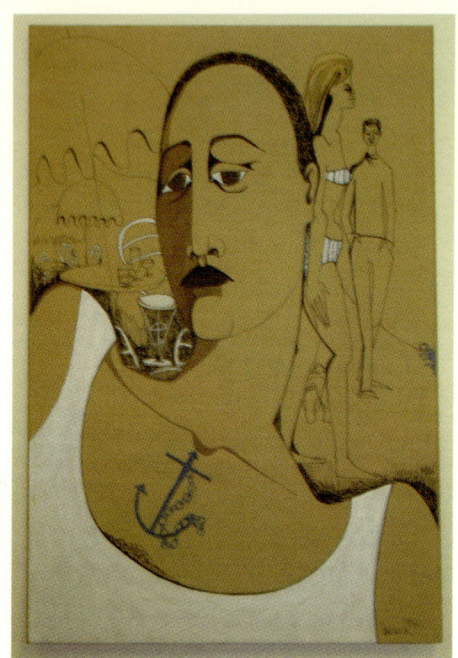

TATTOOED LIFE-SAVER
1956 • ink • 17" x 12"
Travelling Collection

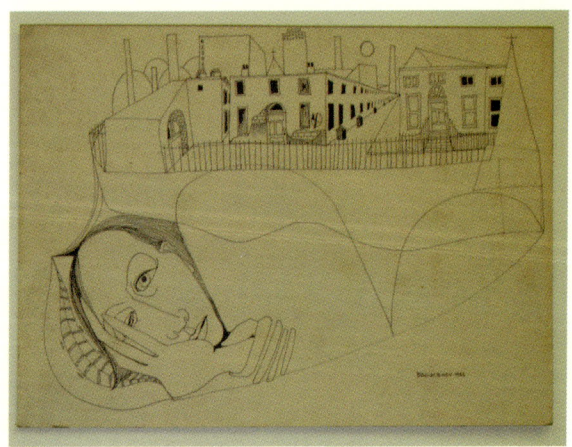

WORRIED ABOUT SLUMS
1956 • ink • 11" x 15"
Travelling Collection

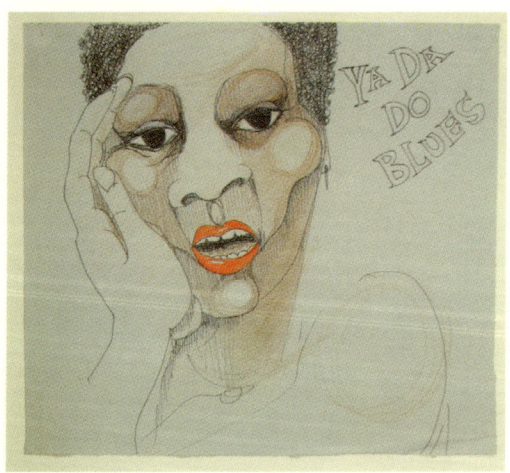

YA DA DO BLUES
1956 • ink and pencil • 9" x 10"
Waterford Collection

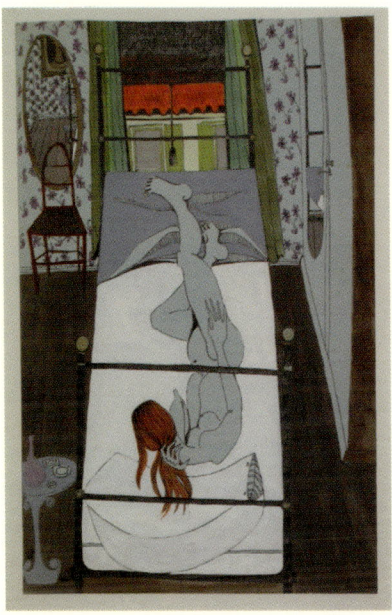

FRENCH FLAT
1957 • poster colour • 17" x 12"
Kerry Collection

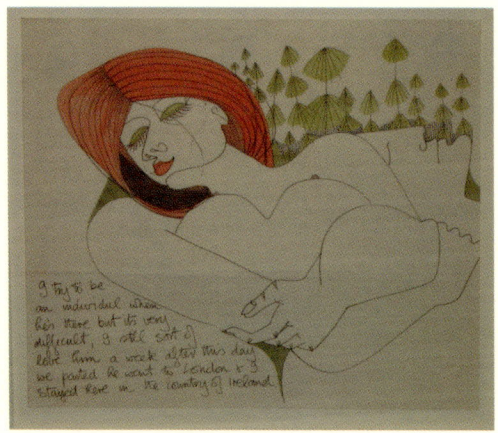

THOUGHTS OF HIM
1957 • ink • 9" x 11"
Kerry Collection

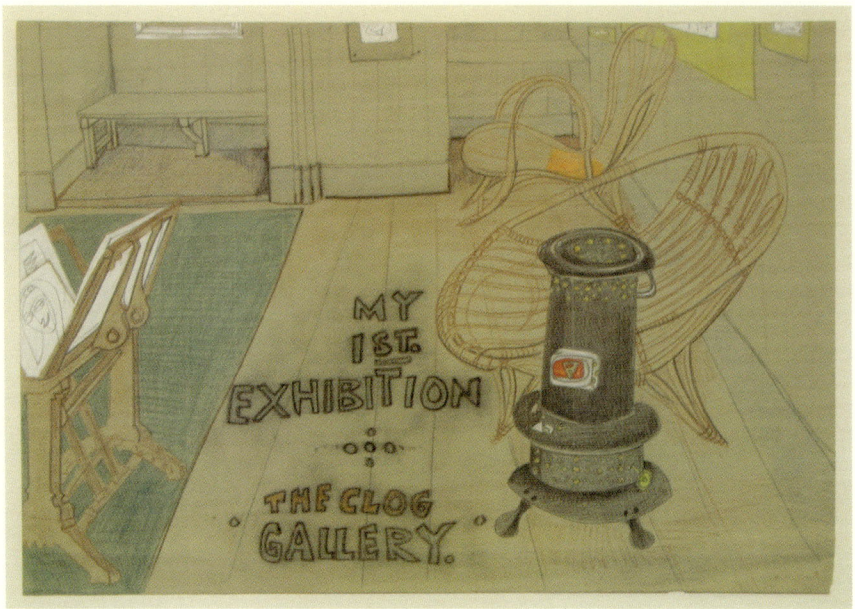

MY FIRST EXHIBITION
1957 • pencil • 12" x 17"
Travelling Collection

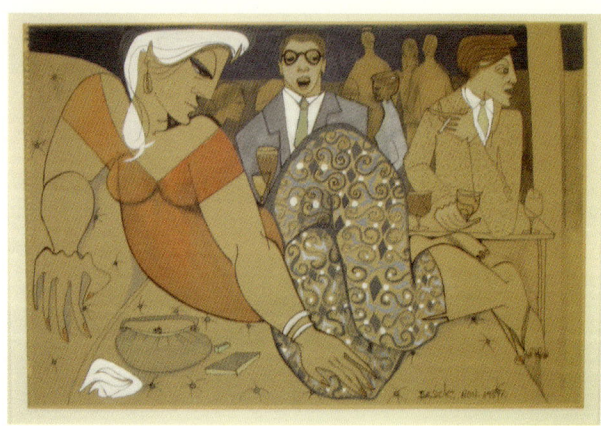

ME, SEBASTIAN AND PAT IN JAMMETS
1957 • ink • 12" x 18"
Travelling Collection

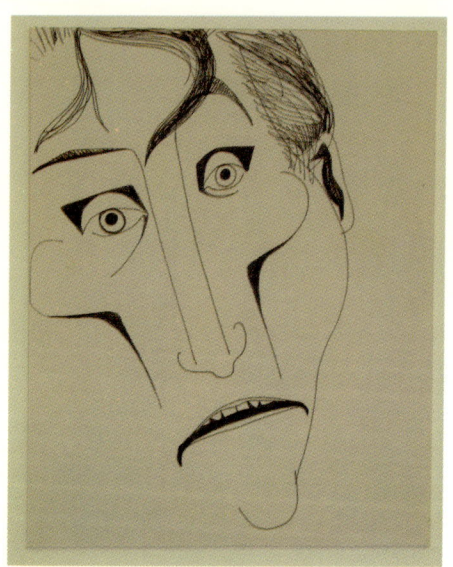

JOHN MOLLOY
1957 • ink • 10" x 8"
Travelling Collection

Comedian John Molloy never stopped codding around.

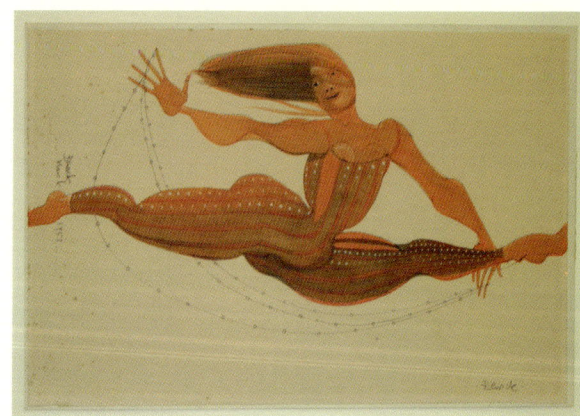

ORANGE DANCER
1957 • ink • 19 " x 12"
Waterford Collection

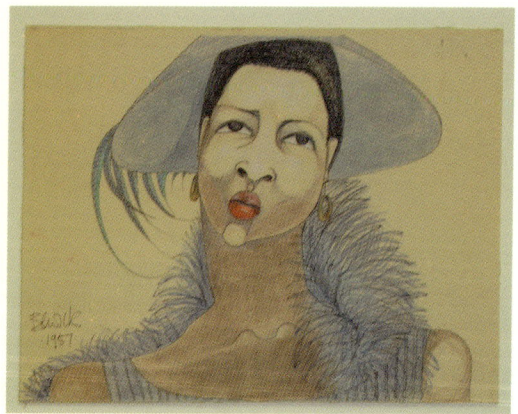

SINGING THE BLUES
1957 • ink and pencil • 12" x 16"
Travelling Collection

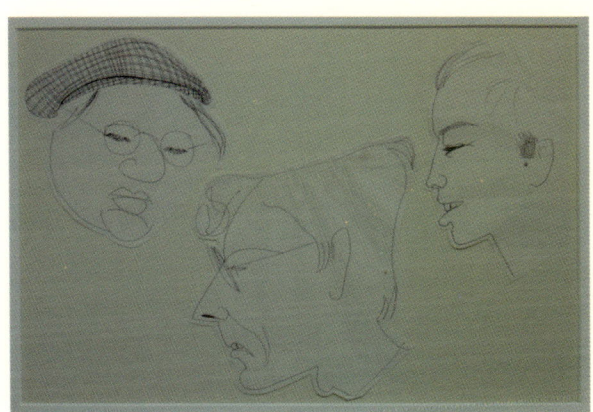

PHILIP, JOHN, SEBASTIAN
1957 • ink • 15" x 23"
Waterford Collection

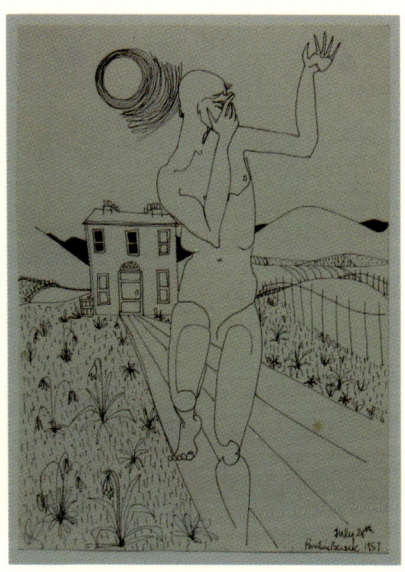

RUNNER
1957 • ink • 12" x 9"
Waterford Collection

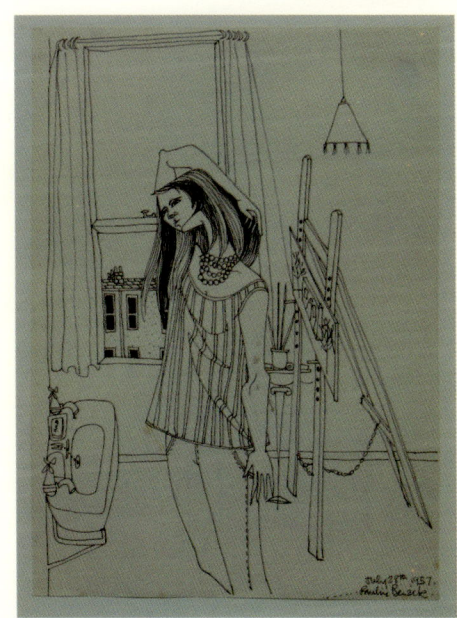

ARTIST
1957 • ink • 12" x 9"
Waterford Collection

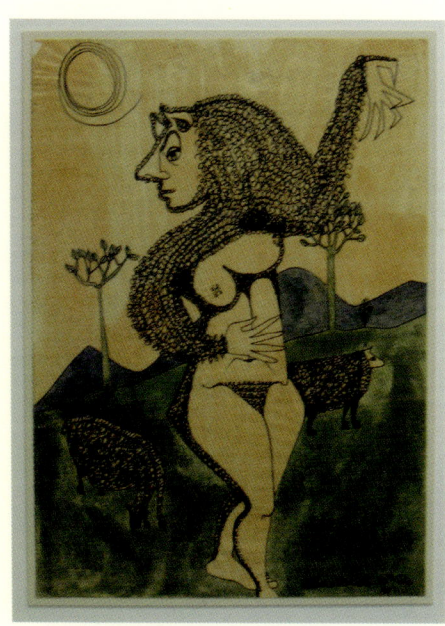

SHEEP WOMAN
1957 • ink varnished • 11" x 8"
Waterford Collection

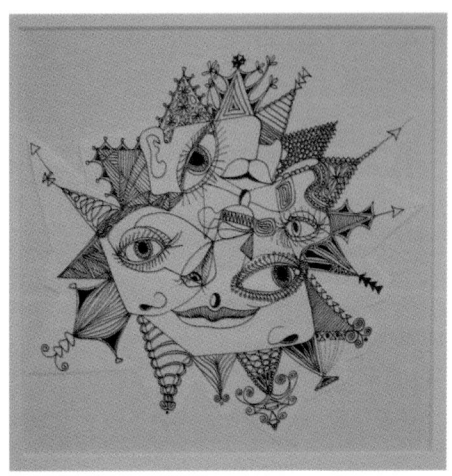

STAR HEAD
1957 • ink • 13" x 13"
Waterford Collection

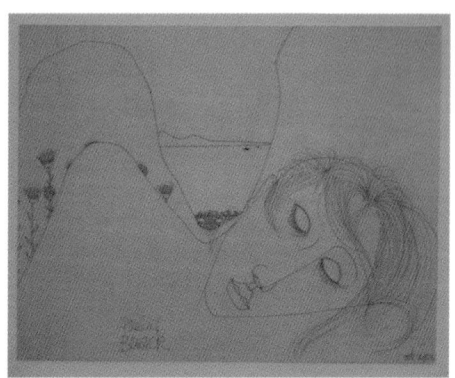

ASLEEP IN GLEESK
1958 • ink • 14" x 18"
Kerry Collection

John Watling lent us the holiday house he built in Gleesk, Co Kerry.

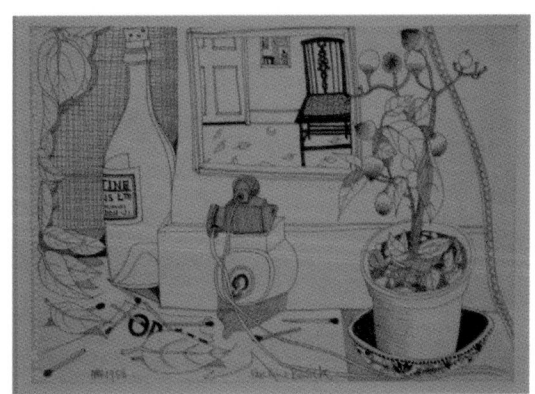

ELECTRIC PLUG ETC
1958 • ink • 10" x 14"
Kerry Collection

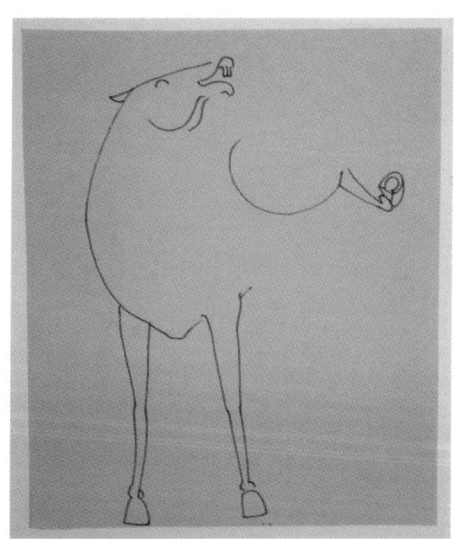

KICKING HORSE
1958 • ink • 8" x 7"
Kerry Collection

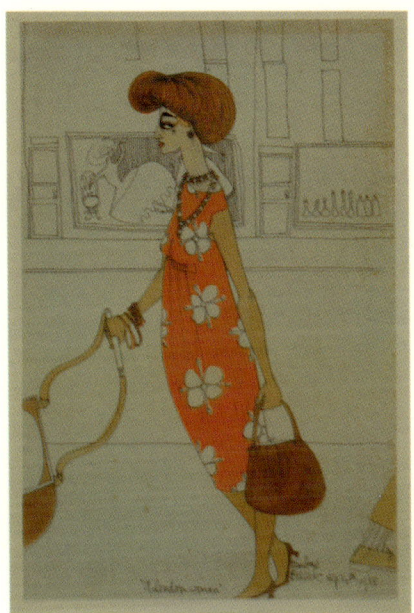

A LONDON WOMAN
1958 • ink • 18" x 12"
Kerry Collection

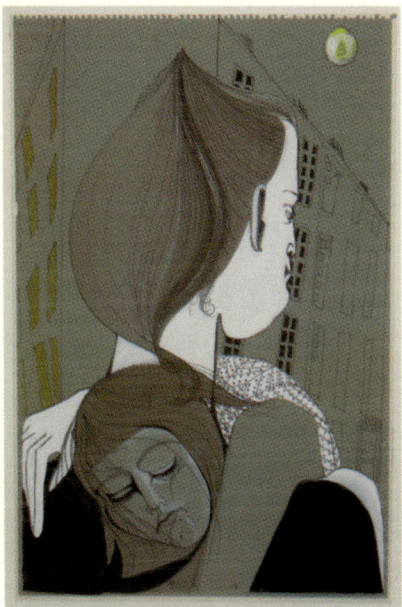

MOTHER AND DAUGHTER
1958 • ink • 18" x 12"
Kerry Collection

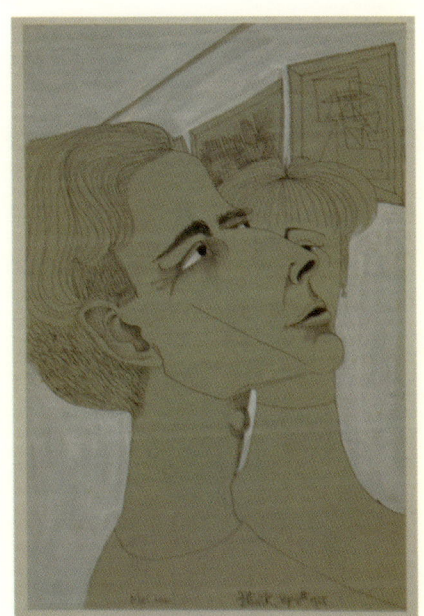

MR CHASE
1958 • ink • 17" x 12"
Kerry Collection

Mr Chase of the Zwemmer Gallery, London
showed my work.

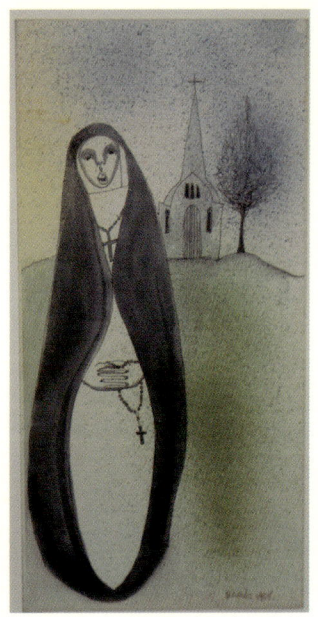

NUN
1958 • ink • 17" x 8"
Kerry Collection

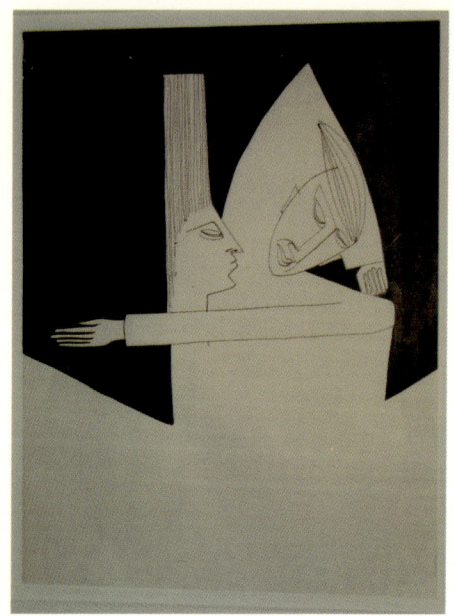

PAT AND I
1958 • ink • 11" x 14"
Kerry Collection

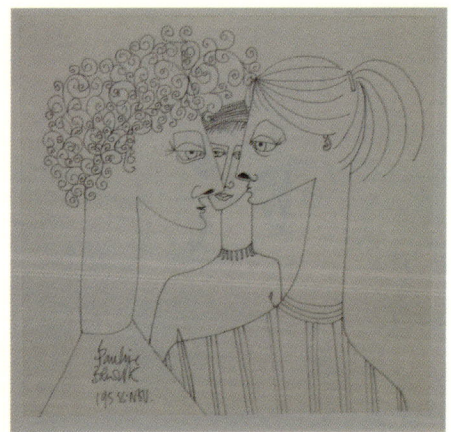

THREE GIRLS
1958 • ink • 9" x 10"
Kerry Collection

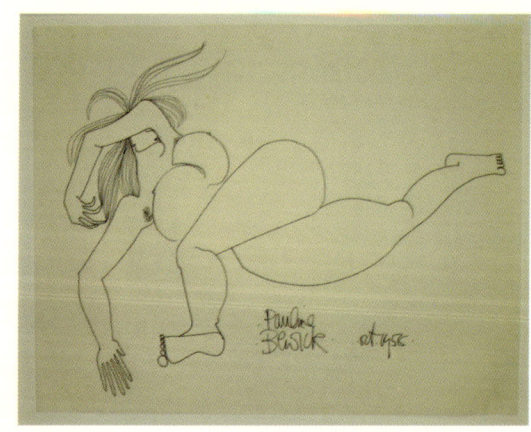

ASLEEP
1958 • ink • 11" x 14"
Waterford Collection

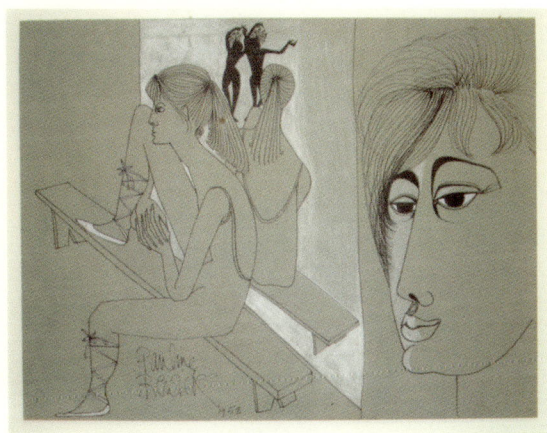

BALLET CLASS
1958 • ink and pencils • 12" x 16"
Waterford Collection

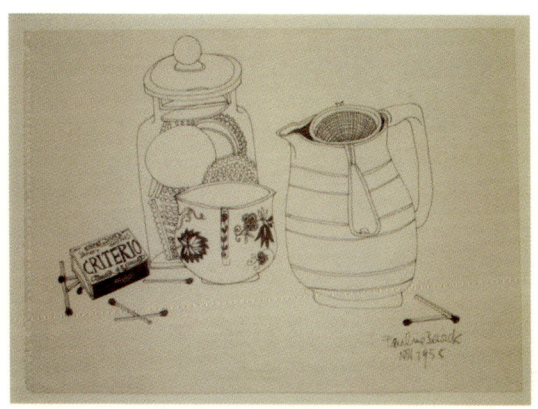

COFFEE TIME
1958 • ink • 10" x 14"
Waterford Collection

The still life works were usually drawn while waiting and waiting …

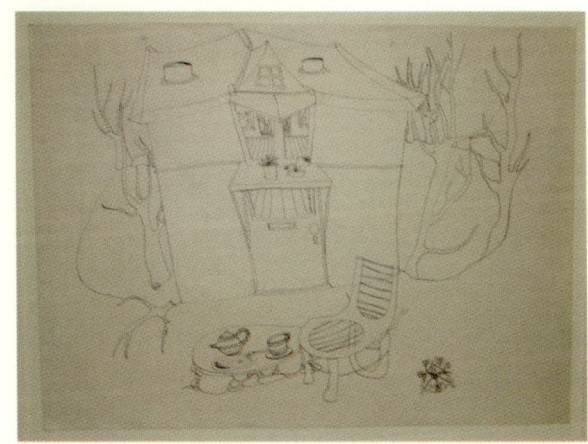

IMAGINARY HOUSE
1958 • ink • 11" x 15"
Waterford Collection

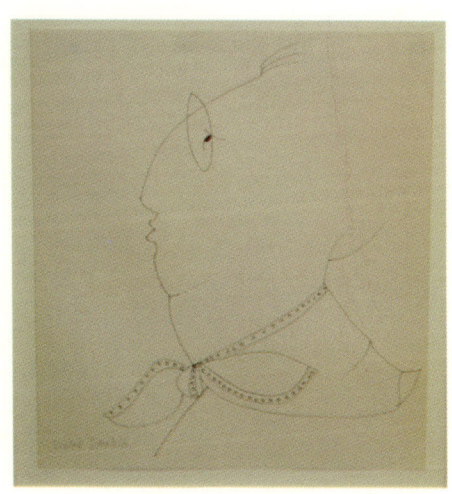

LESLIE DAIKEN
1958 • ink • 11" x 10"
Travelling Collection

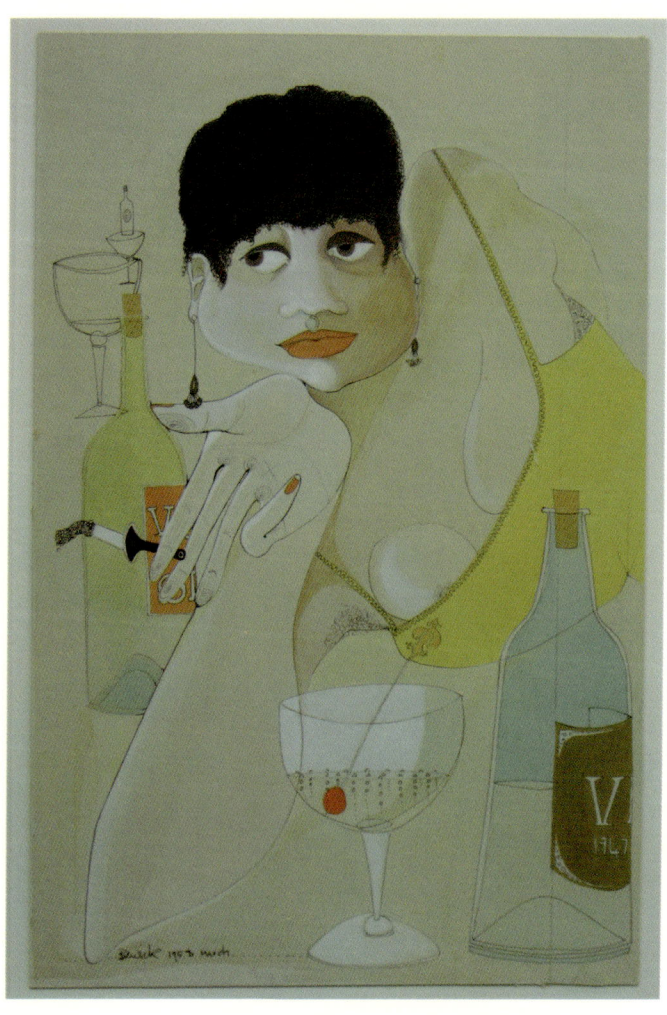

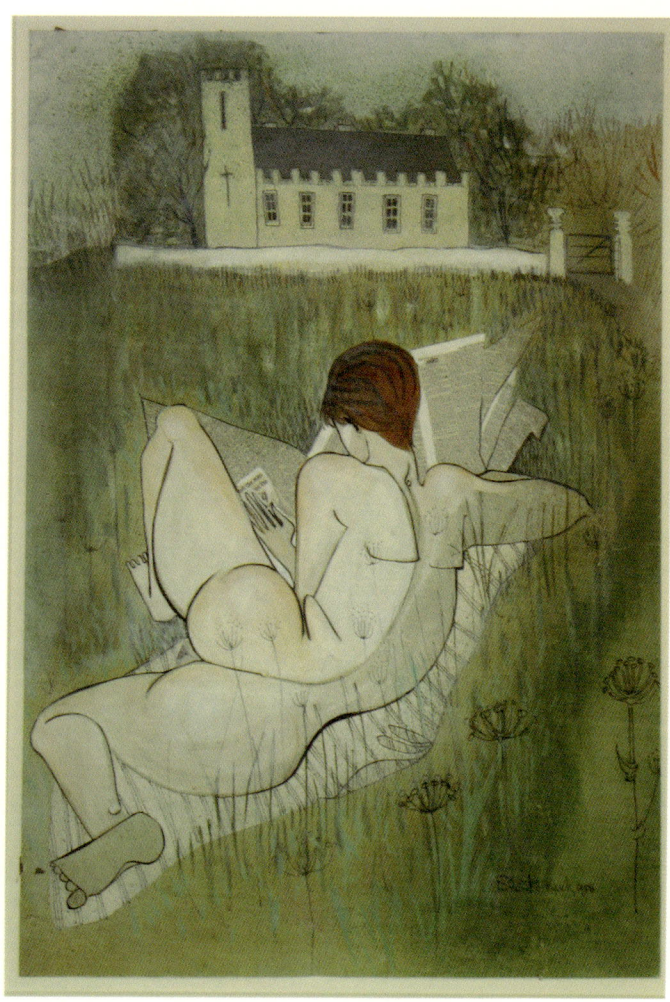

BECHET BUBBLES
1958 • ink • 18" x 12"
Travelling Collection

HOLIDAY IN LARAGH
1958 • ink • 24" x 17"
Travelling Collection

Another trip to Paris where Pat and I danced to Sidney Bechet.
'À poil' everyone shouted, while his mistress stirred the bubbles out of his champagne.

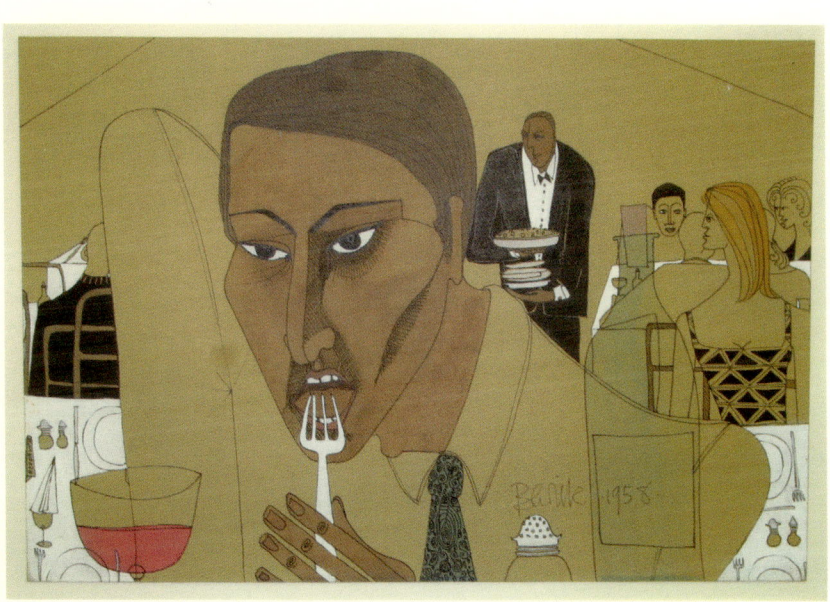

INDIAN RESTAURANT
1958 • ink • 12" x 17"
Waterford Collection

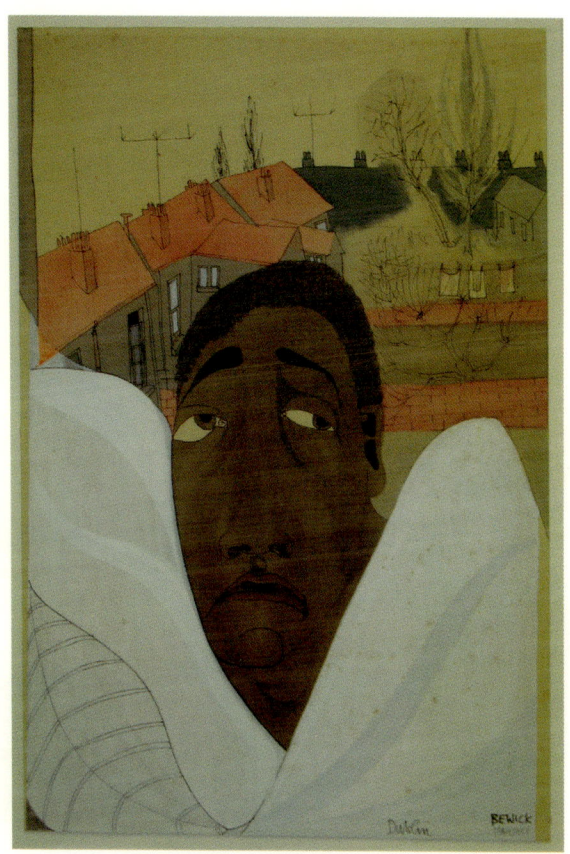

NEGRO IN DUBLIN
1958 • ink • 18" x 12"
Travelling Collection

Negro in Dublin – we took in lodgers. I worried about their loneliness.

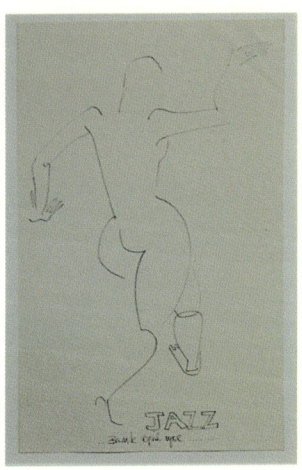

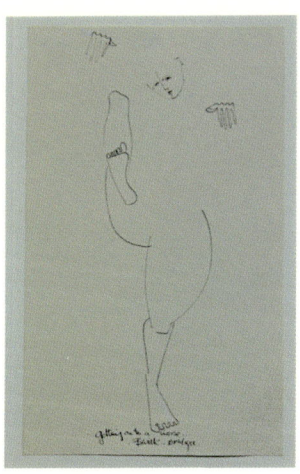

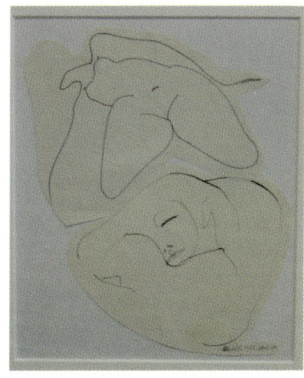

JAZZ DANCER
1958 • ink • 13" x 8"
Travelling Collection

GETTING ON A HORSE
1958 • ink • 13" x 8"
Travelling Collection

NUDE / MOTHER AND CHILD
1958 • ink
Travelling Collection

Line doodles.

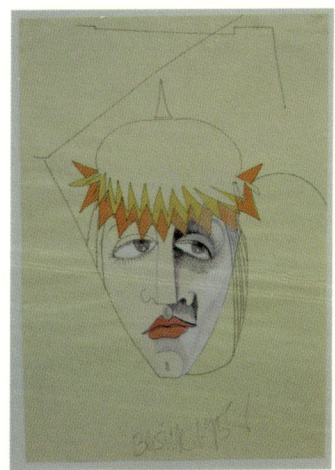

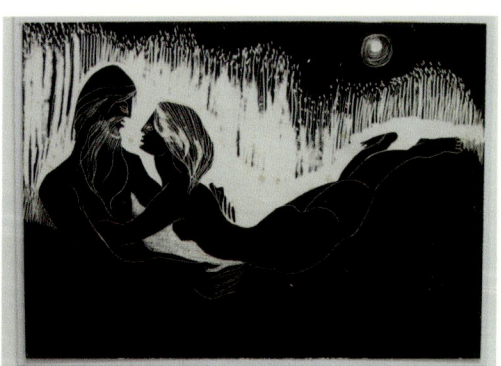

STAGE SICK
1958 • ink • 17" x 12"
Waterford Collection

LOVERS IN A WHEATFIELD
1958 • scraperboard • 7" x 10"
Waterford Collection

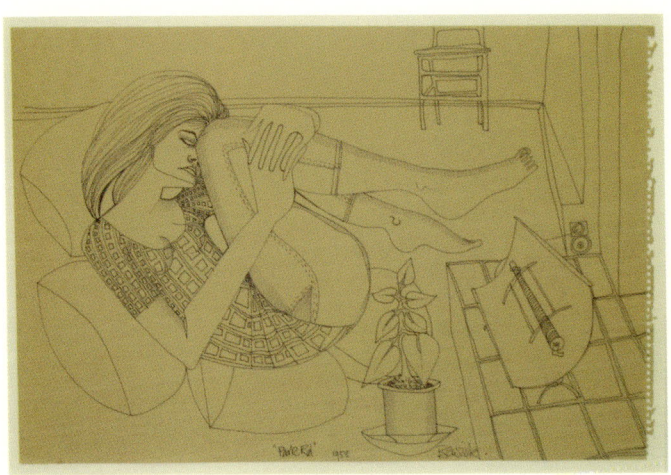

PARK ROAD
1958 • ink • 12" x 18"
Travelling Collection

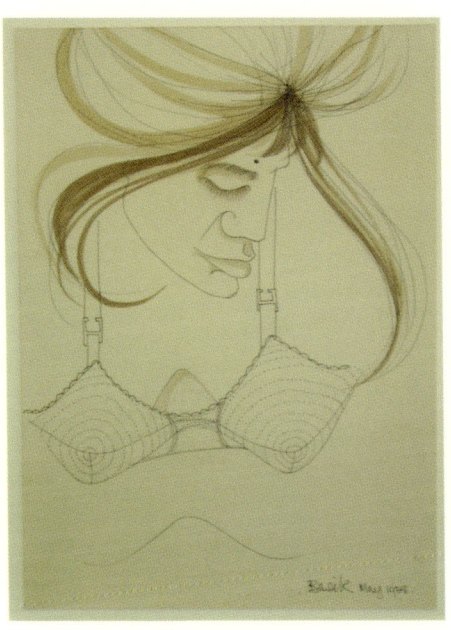

P. G. IN A BRA
1958 • ink • 14" x 10"
Travelling Collection

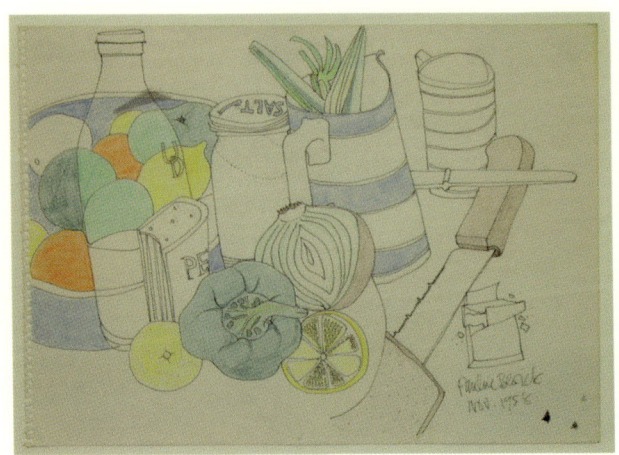

STILL LIFE WITH GREEN PEPPERS
1958 • ink and pencil • 10" x 14"
Travelling Collection

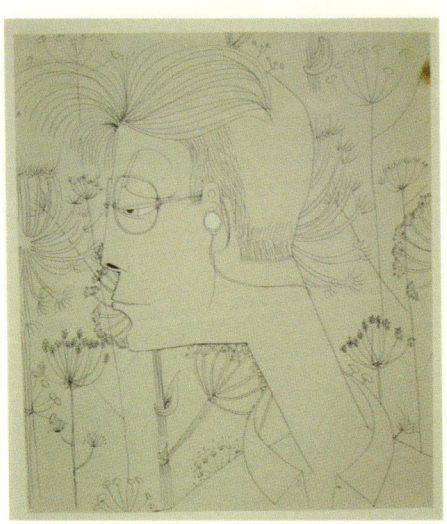

UNIVERSITY MAN
1958 • ink • 12" x 11"
Waterford Collection

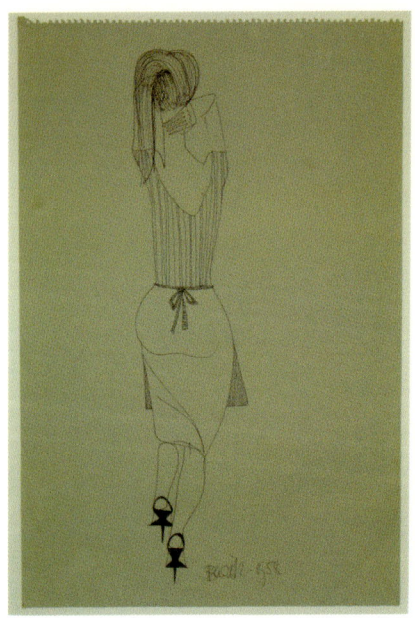

WAITRESS
1958 • ink • 18" x 12"
Waterford Collection

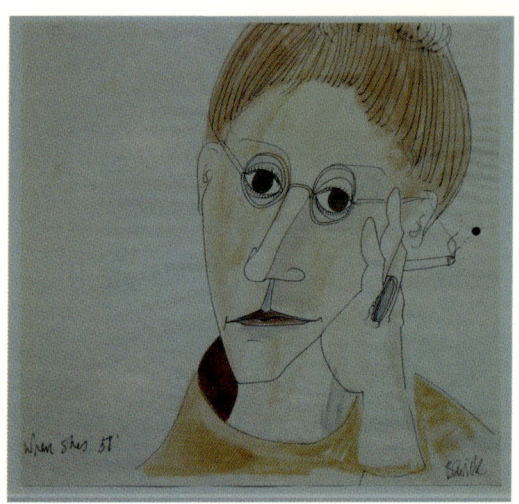

WHEN SHE IS 58
1958 • ink • 14" x 15"
Travelling Collection

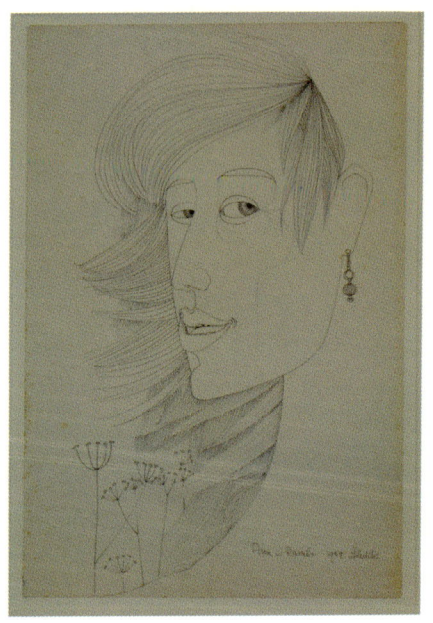

ANN IS RUSSELL'S
1959 • ink • 22" x 15"
Kerry Collection

How I imagined Leslie McWeeney when she is 58.

In 1958 there was no work in Dublin and Pat and I had gone our different ways. I went to look for work in London. Edward Fitzgerald let me stay in a tiny room in Chalcot Crescent with no windows but a hatch that led into a kitchen. Eventually I got a job with the BBC drawing and writing the 'Little Jimmy' series.

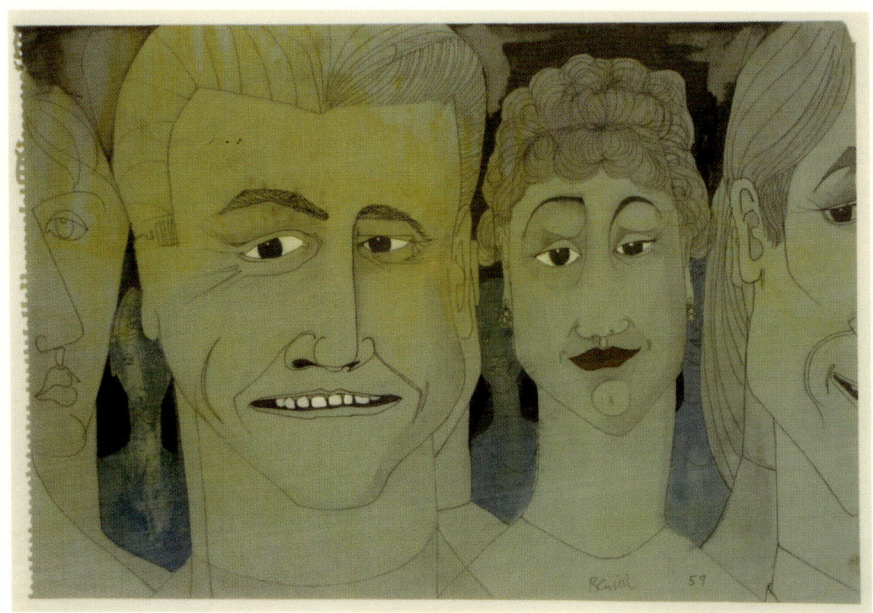

AT THE CINEMA
1959 • ink • 12" x 18"
Kerry Collection

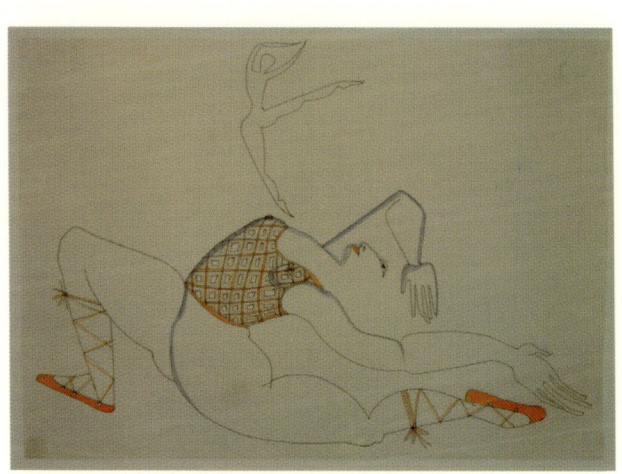

BALLET DANCERS
1959 • ink • 11" x 16"
Kerry Collection

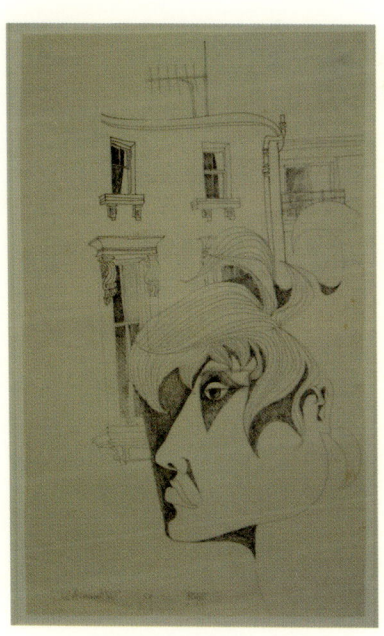

CHALCOT CRESCENT, NW1
1959 • ink and roller • 22" x 15"
Kerry Collection

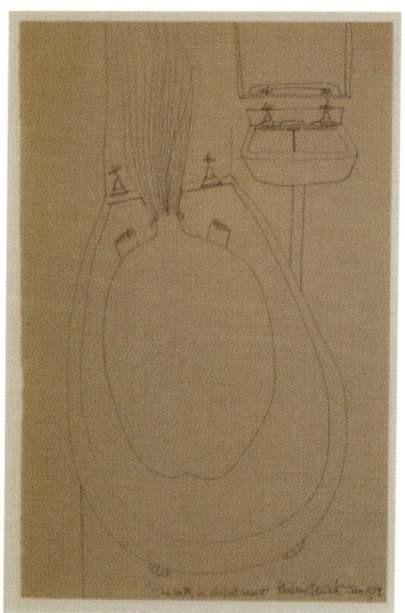

BATH
1959 • ink • 15" x 9"
Kerry Collection

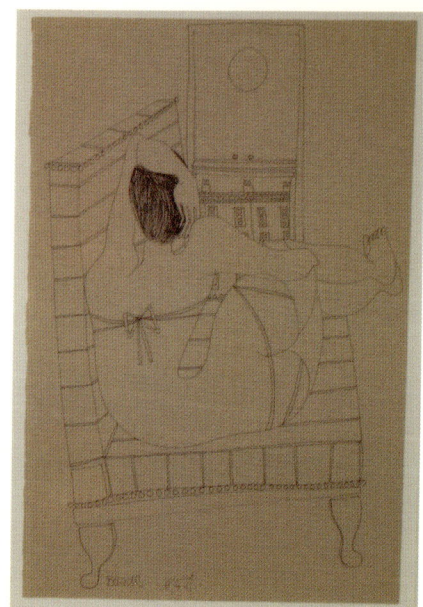

CHALCOT CRESCENT
1959 • ink • 15" x 9"
Kerry Collection

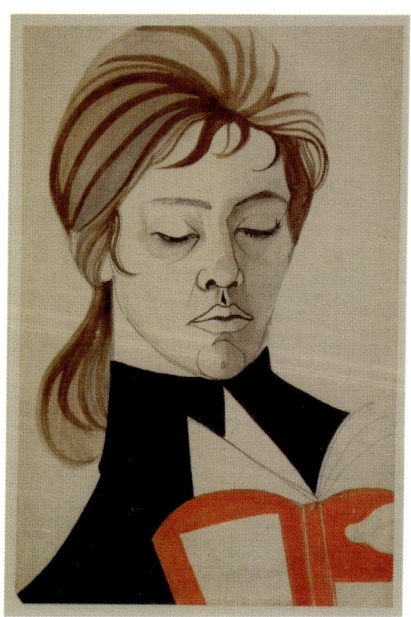

PAULINE GOODWIN
1959 • ink • 22" x 15"
Kerry Collection

Pauline Goodwin studied Catholicism in order to argue with knowledge. Before London, she had lived with us in 51 Frankfurt Avenue.

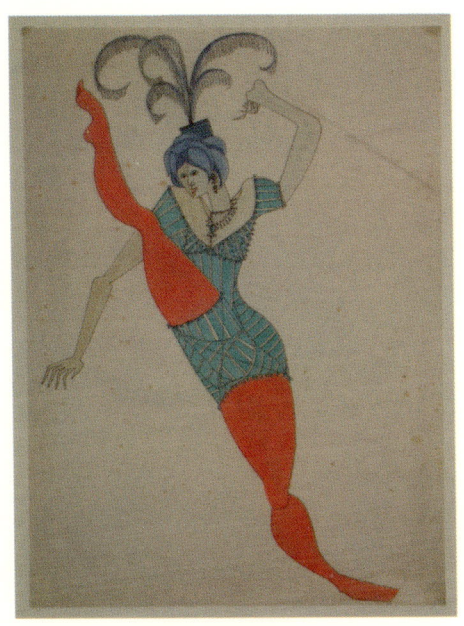

CHORUS GIRL
1959 • ink • 19" x 14"
Kerry Collection

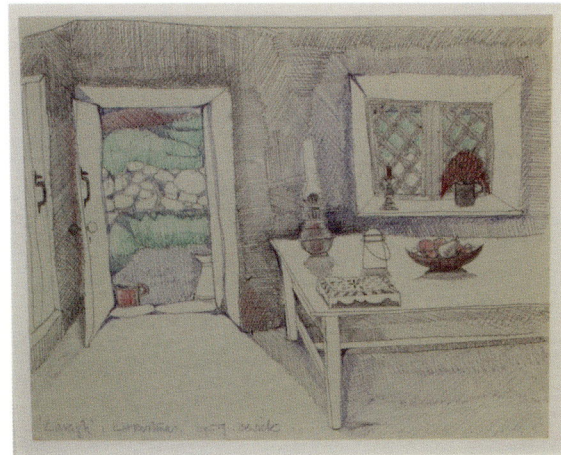

HARRY'S HOUSE, LARAGH
1959 • biro • 9" x 12"
Kerry Collection

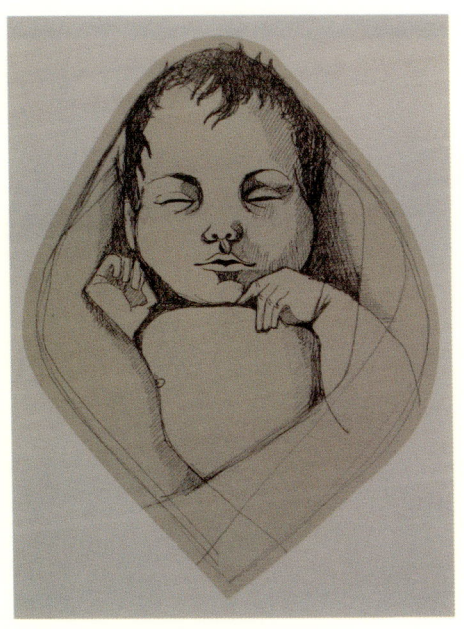

KUNU, TED'S BABY
1959 • ink • 11" x 8"
Kerry Collection

Regular trips back to Laragh, Glendalough, Co Wicklow where Harry now lived, to sleep off London.

Ted, a friend of Sally Travers, brought his naked baby, Kunu, to visit us. He showed us how to stand for ages on our heads. Ted was an eccentric man who had dreadlocks, stuck bird feathers in his hair and his child was naked, never had a nappy and did its business on newspapers.

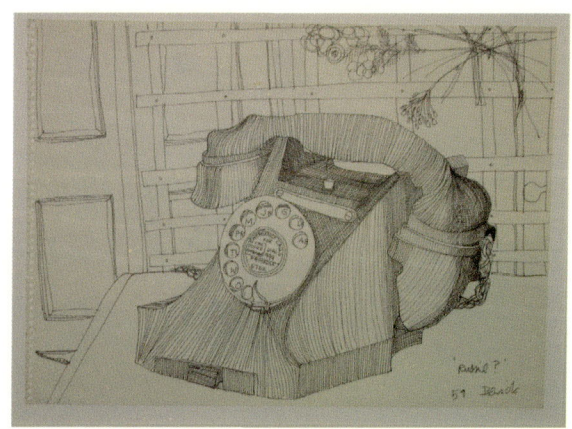

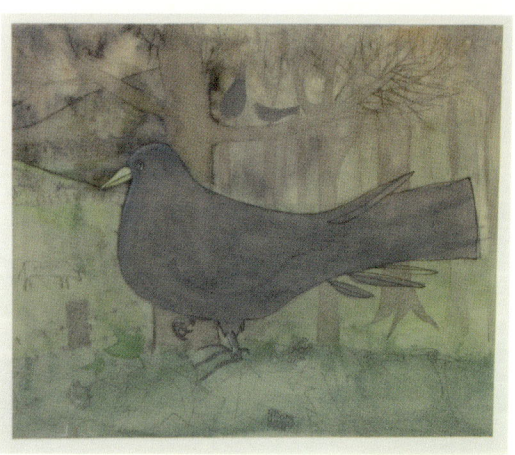

TELEPHONE
1959 • ink • 10" x 14"
Kerry Collection

URBAN BIRDS
1959 • ink • 9" x 10"
Kerry Collection

Another 'waiting' for something to happen still life.

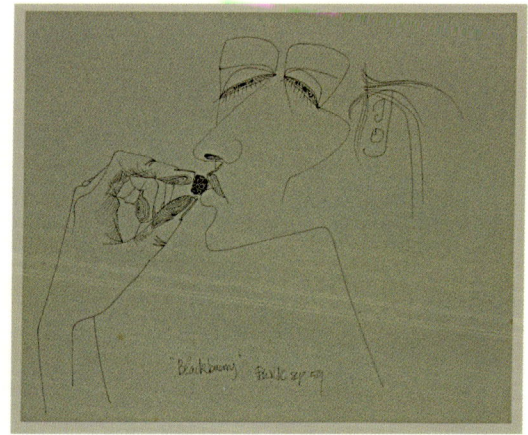

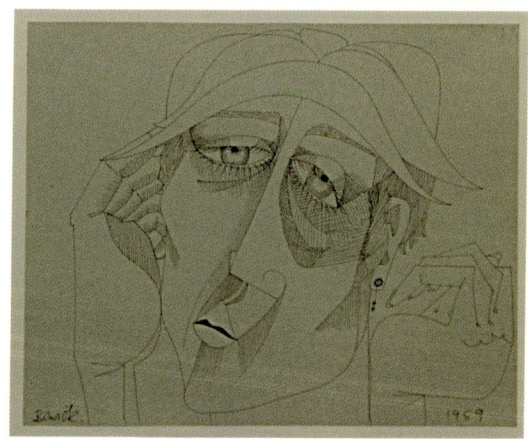

BLACKBERRY EATER
1959 • ink • 9" x 12"
Kerry Collection

WOMAN
1959 • ink • 9" x 12"
Kerry Collection

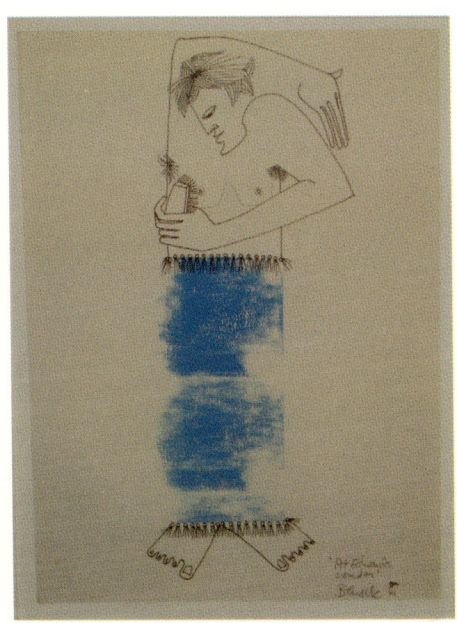

UNDER ARM SCRUB
1959 • lino ink • 14" x 11"
Kerry Collection

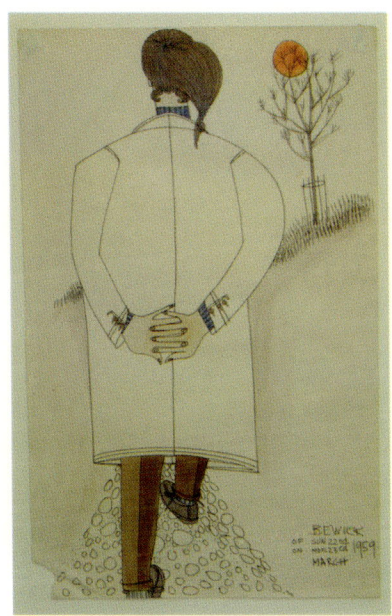

BARRY ON PRIMROSE HILL
1959 • ink • 14" x 9"
Travelling Collection

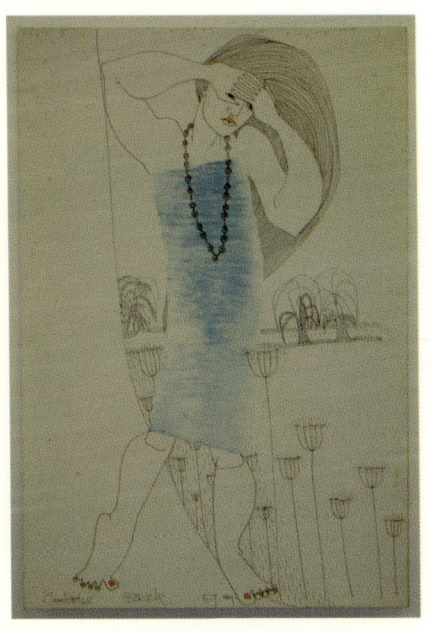

AT CAMBRIDGE
1959 • lino inks • 22" x 16"
Travelling Collection

Primrose Hill, beside Chalcot Crescent was the place to get air from my little dark room when Barry and friends would visit.

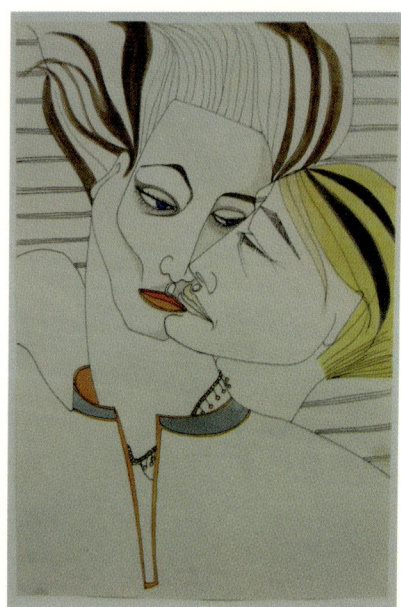

CITY LOVERS
1959 • inks • 17" x 11"
Travelling Collection

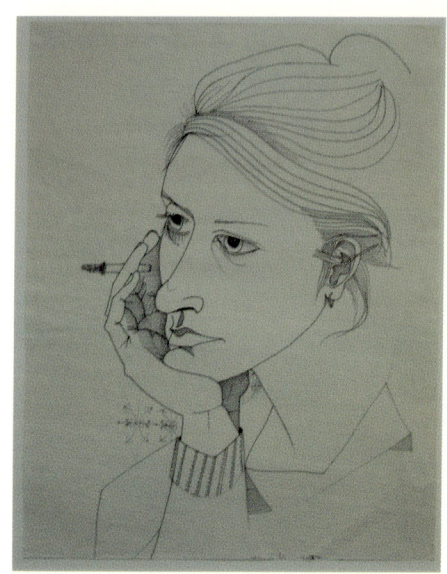

LESLIE McWEENEY
1959 • ink • 18" x 14"
Travelling Collection

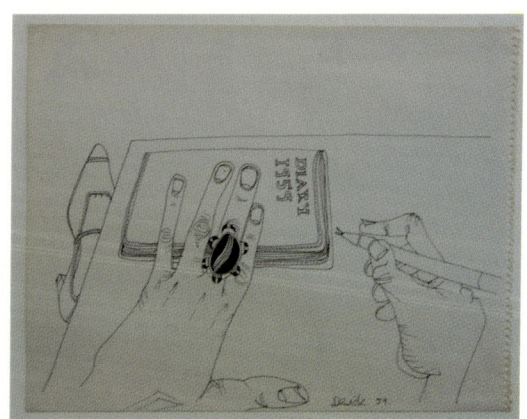

DIARY, 1959
1959 • ink • 10" x 14"
Travelling Collection

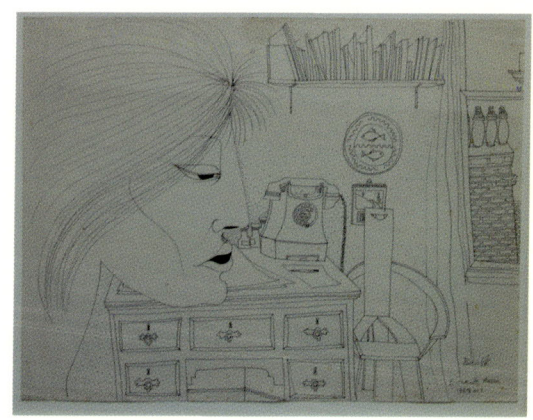

EDWARD'S ROOM
1959 • ink • 15" x 20"
Travelling Collection

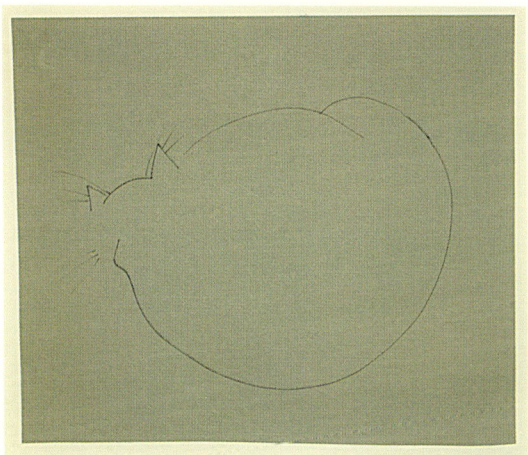

FAT CAT
1959 • ink • 9" x 10"
Waterford Collection

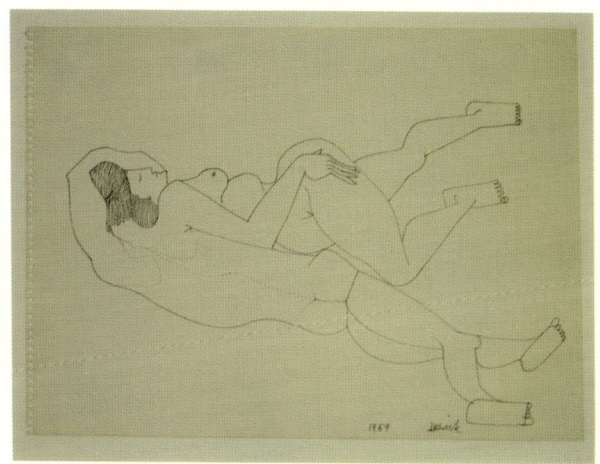

COUPLE LYING
1959 • ink • 10" x 14"
Waterford Collection

Taking air in Primrose Hill, an old man once said, 'you're lying in my spot. I've been coming here to this spot for twenty years'.

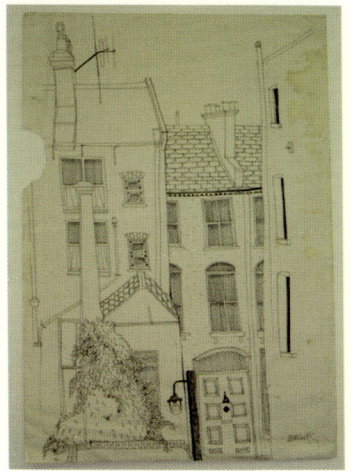

CHALCOT CRESCENT
1959 • ink • 22" x 15"
Travelling Collection

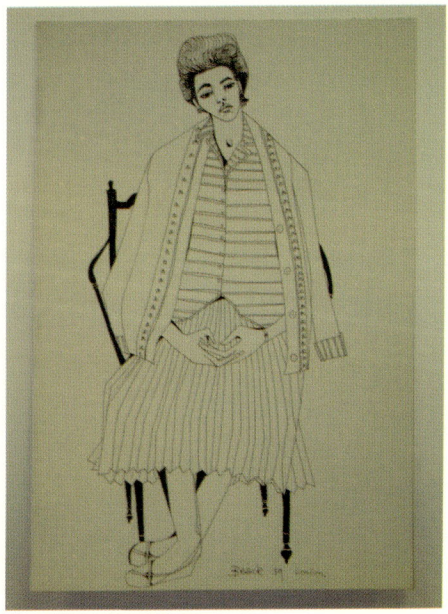

GILLIAN
1959 • ink • 20" x 14"
Travelling Collection

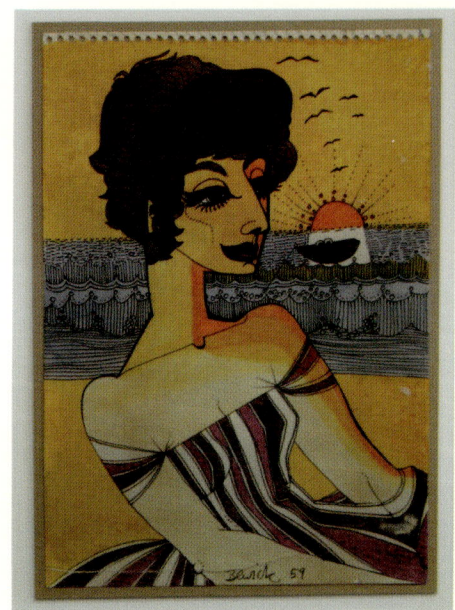

GIRL BY THE SEA
1959 • ink • 10" x 17"
Travelling Collection

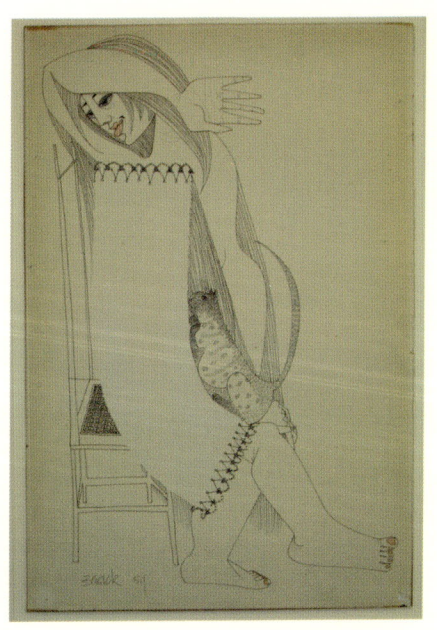

GIRL AND A CAT ON A CHAIR
1959 • ink and roller • 22" x 15"
Waterford Collection

Gilliam Solomons got cross when I asked someone
at her dinner party 'What religion are you?'
'You don't ask people that in London'.

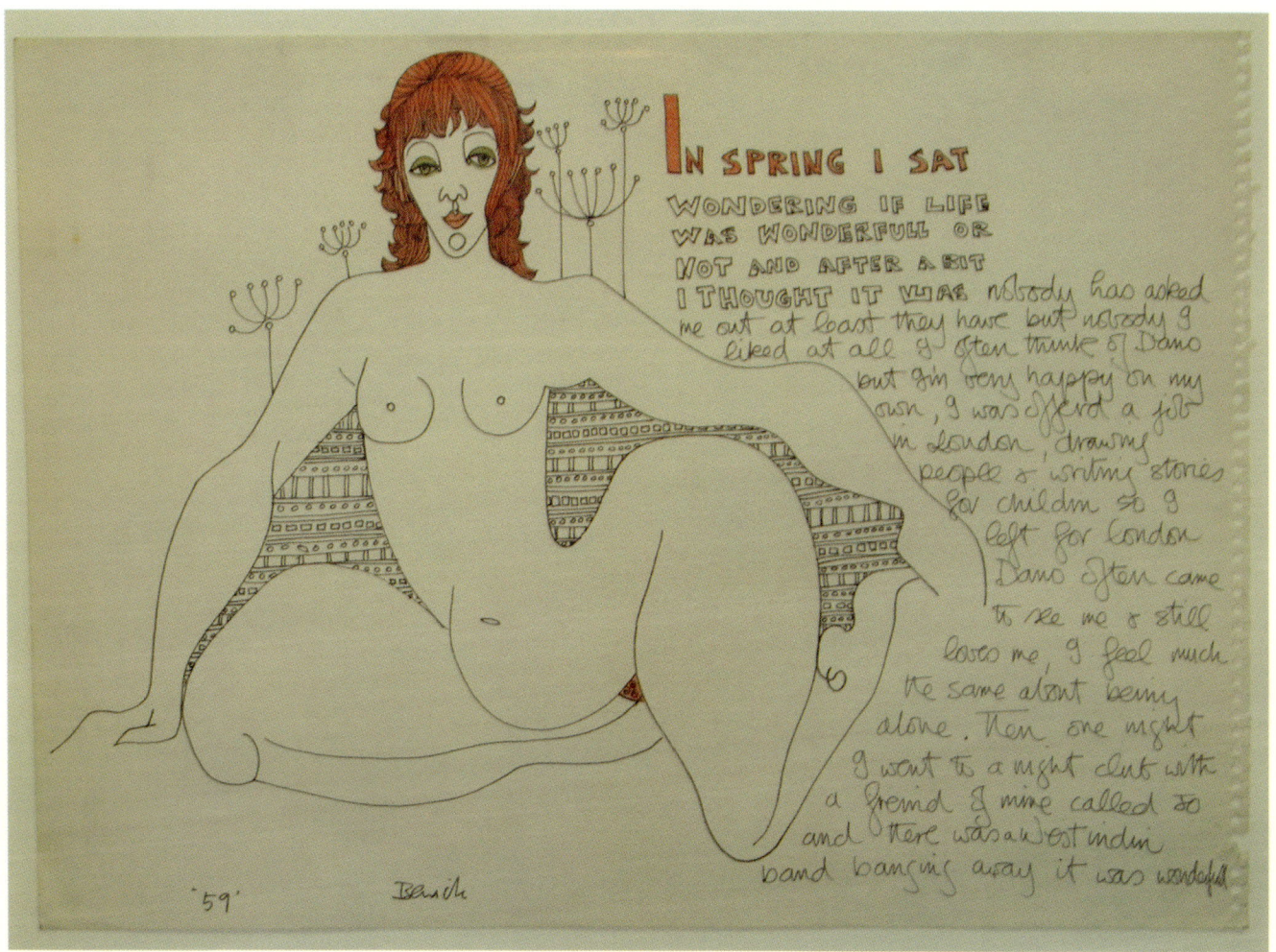

IN SPRING
1959 • ink • 10" x 14"
Travelling Collection

In Spring I sat wondering if life was wonderful or not, and after a bit I thought it was. Nobody has asked me out, at least they have but nobody I liked at all, I often think of Dano [Pat] but I'm very happy on my own. I was offered a job in London drawing people and writing stories for children, so I left for London. Dano often came to see me and still loves me. I feel much the same about being alone. Then one night I went to a nightclub with a friend of mine called Joe [Edward] and there was a West Indian band banging away. It was wonderful.

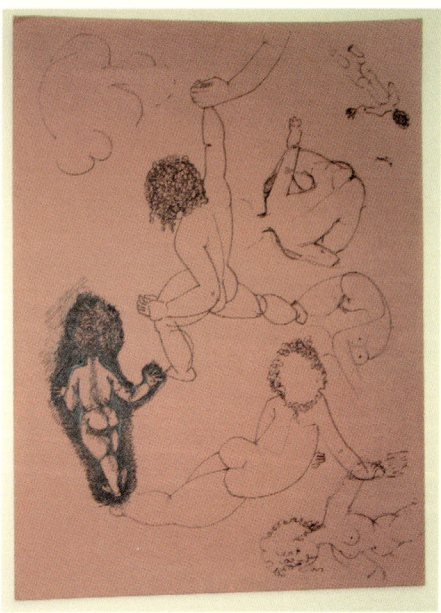

KUNU WALKING
1959 • ink • 20" x 15"
Travelling Collection

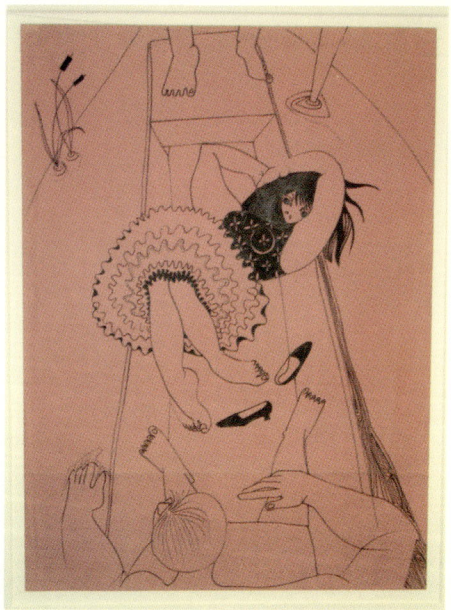

PUNTING IN CAMBRIDGE
1959 • ink • 20" x 15"
Waterford Collection

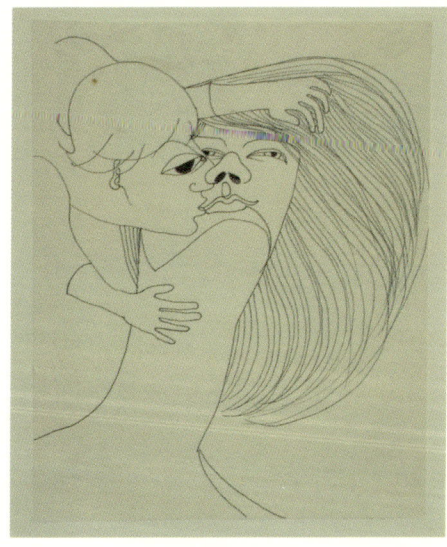

MOTHER AND CHILD
1959 • ink • 8" x 7"
Waterford Collection

It was lovely to have a friend like Edward.
We went to balls in Oxford and Cambridge
with no strings attached, as he was gay.

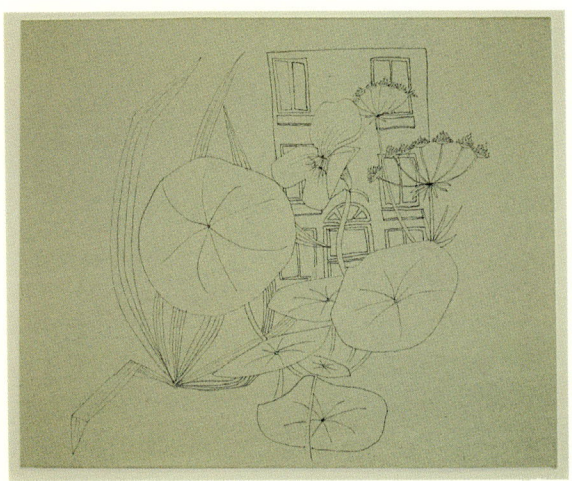

NASTURTIUMS
1959 • ink • 9" x 11"
Waterford Collection

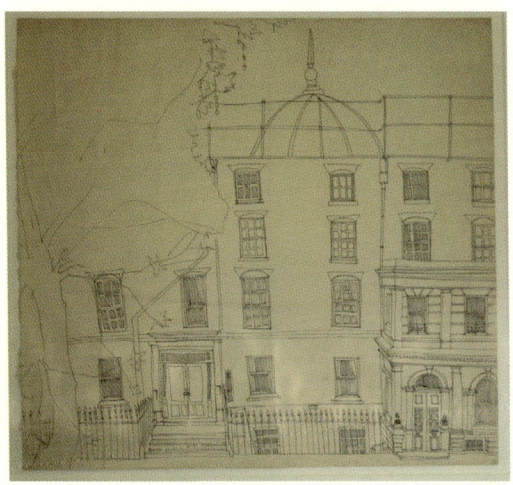

7 PARK ROAD
1959 • ink • 21" x 15"
Waterford Collection

Edward's boyfriend lived in Park Road.

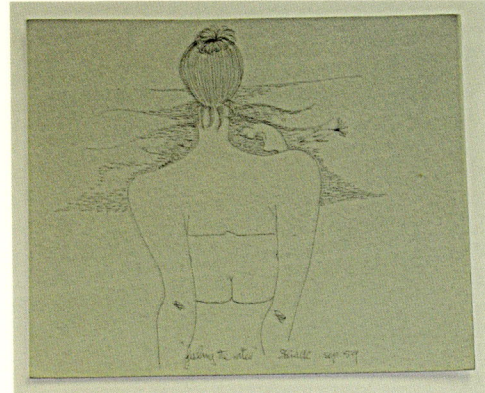

FEELING THE WATER
1959 • ink • 9" x 12"
Travelling Collection

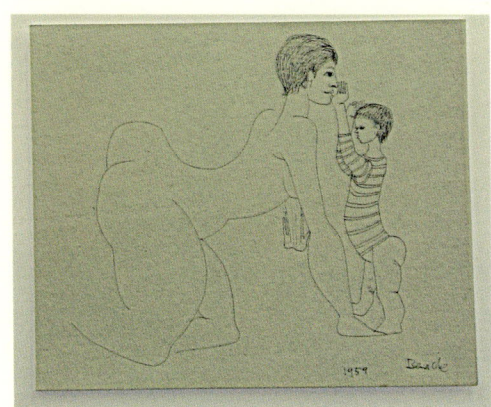

MOTHER AND CHILD
1959 • ink • 9" x 12"
Travelling Collection

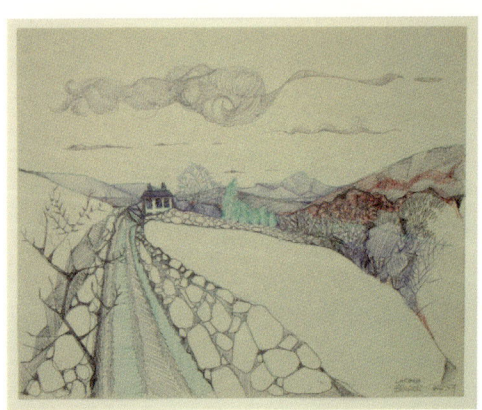

PETER'S HOUSE, LARAGH
1959 • biro • 9" x 12"
Waterford Collection

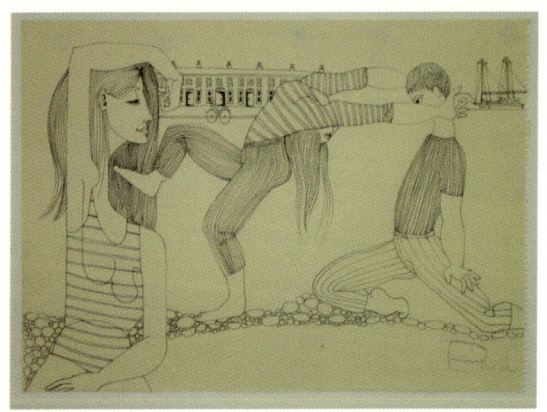

PLAYING ON THE BEACH
1959 • ink • 12" x 18"
Waterford Collection

Peter Murray lived near Harry in Laragh.

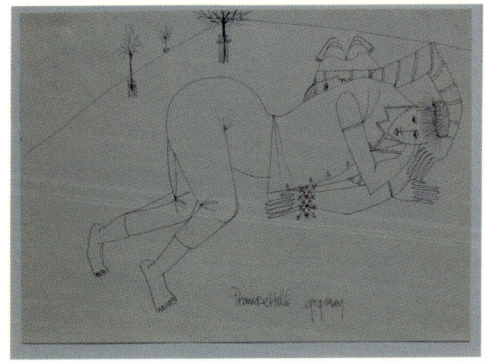

PRIMROSE HILL
1959 • ink • 10" x 14"
Waterford Collection

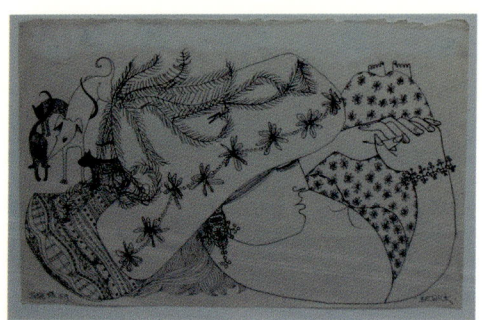

DAME AU CHAPEAU
1959 • ink • 10" x 14"
Waterford Collection

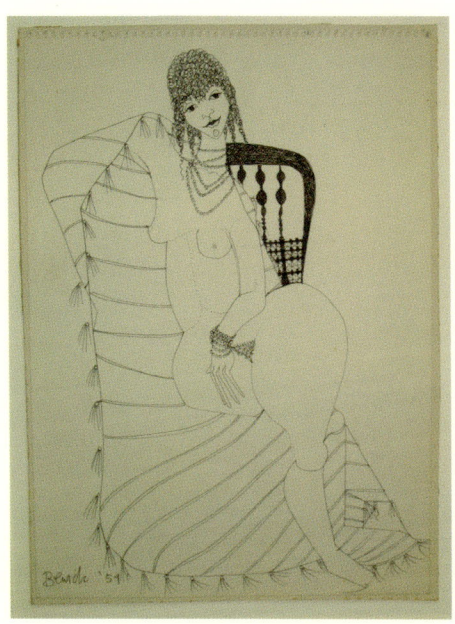

ON A STRIPED RUG
1959 • ink • 14" x 10"
Waterford Collection

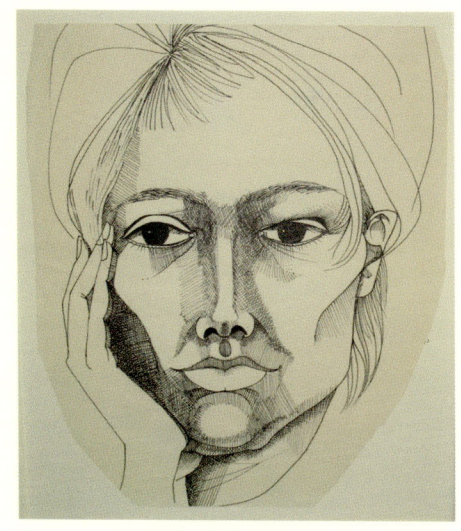

SELF-PORTRAIT
1959 • ink • 12" x 11"
Waterford Collection

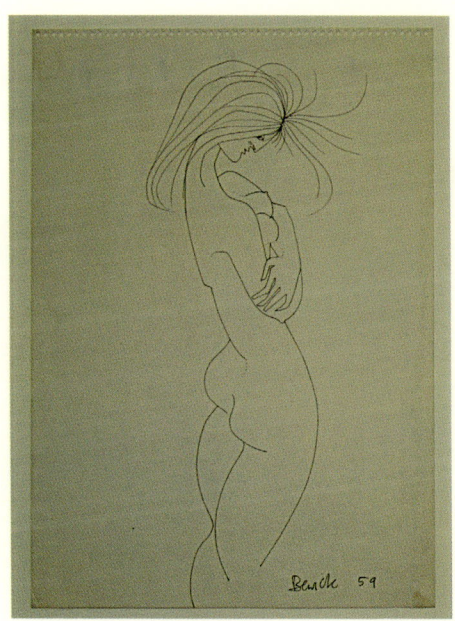

PROFILE
1959 • ink • 14" x 10"
Waterford Collection

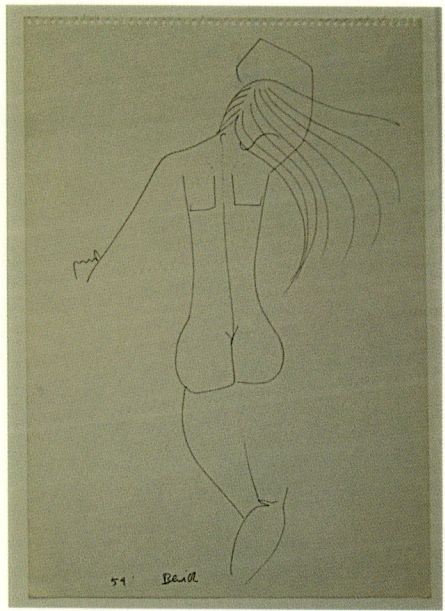

BACK
1959 • ink • 14" x 10"
Waterford Collection

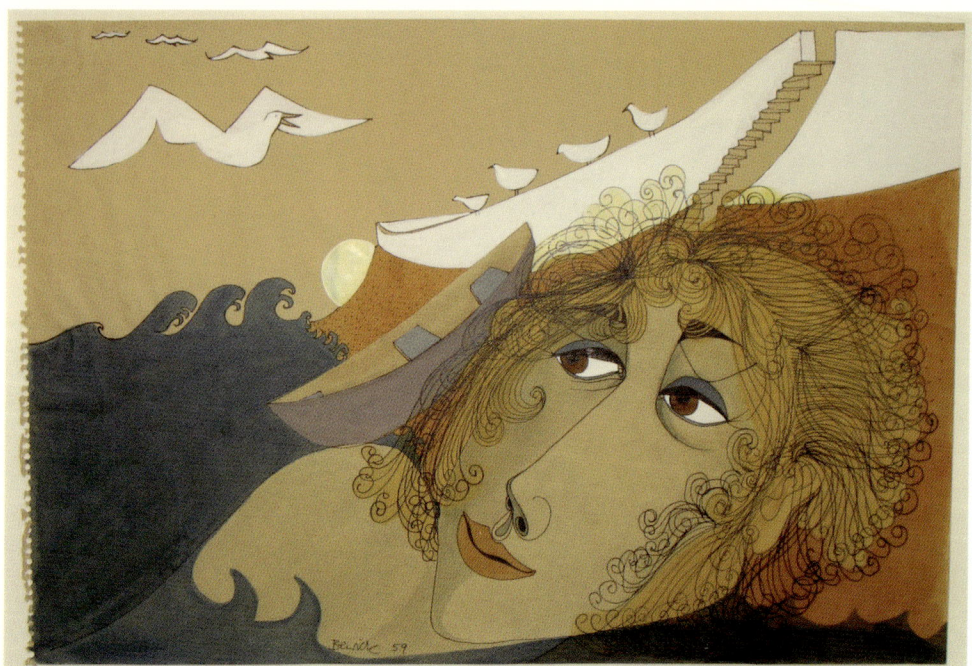

A SWIM AT BRIGHTON
1959 • ink • 12" x 18"
Waterford Collection

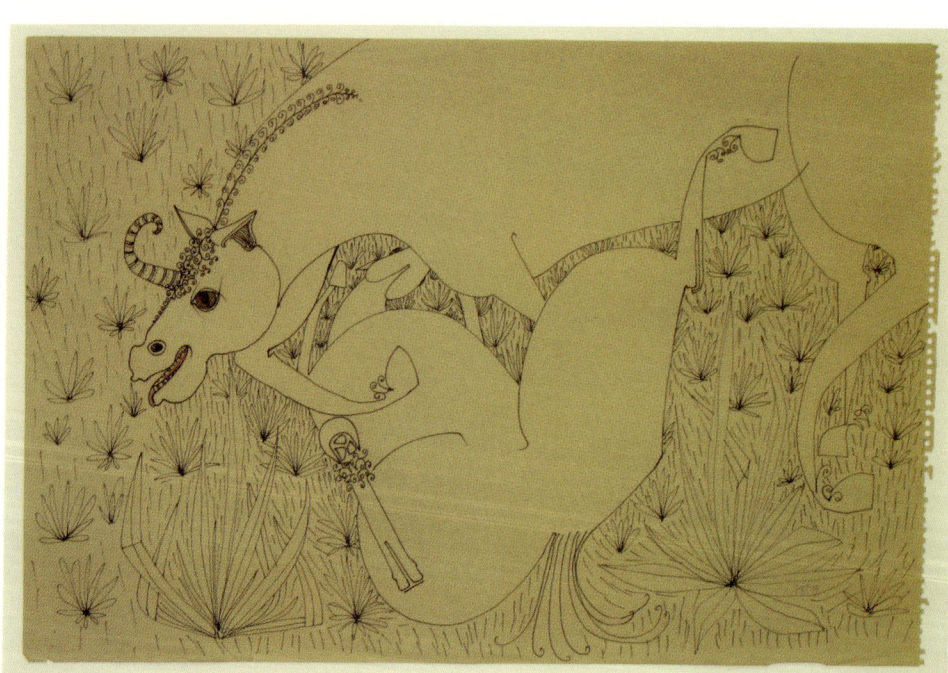

UNICORN AND HORSE
1959 • ink • 12" x 18"
Travelling Collection

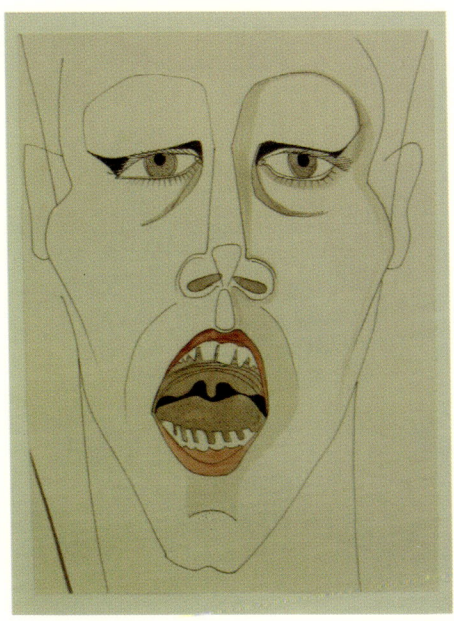

UVULA
1959 • ink • 10" x 8"
Travelling Collection

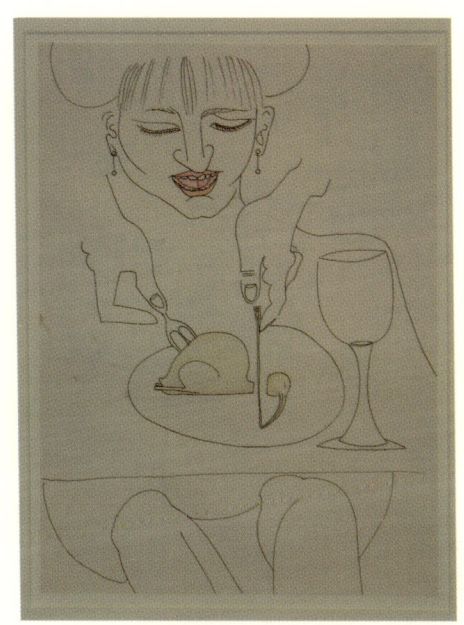

CARVING A SNIPE
1960 • ink • 20" x 15"
Kerry Collection

'Poor snipe', Barry said, but she still ate it.

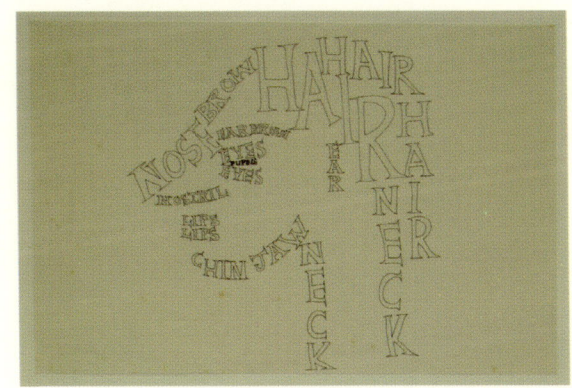

WORD FACES 1
1959 • ink • 10" x 15"
Waterford Collection

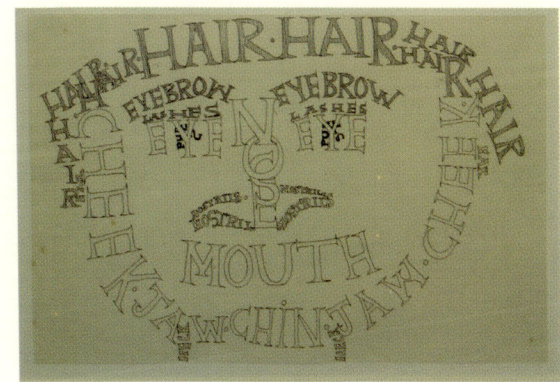

WORD FACES II
1959 • ink • 10" x 15"
Waterford Collection

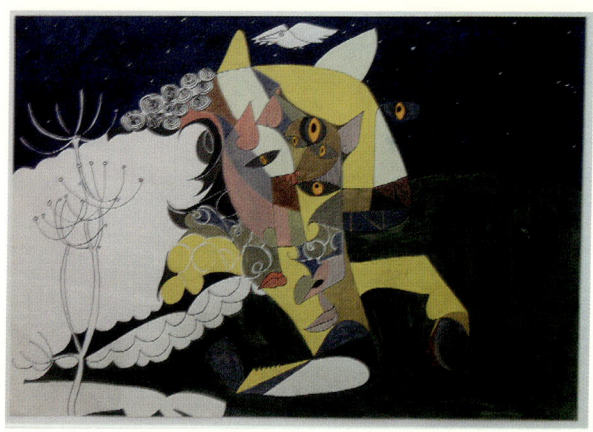

SHEEP MAN
1960 • poster colour varnished • 15" x 22"
Kerry Collection

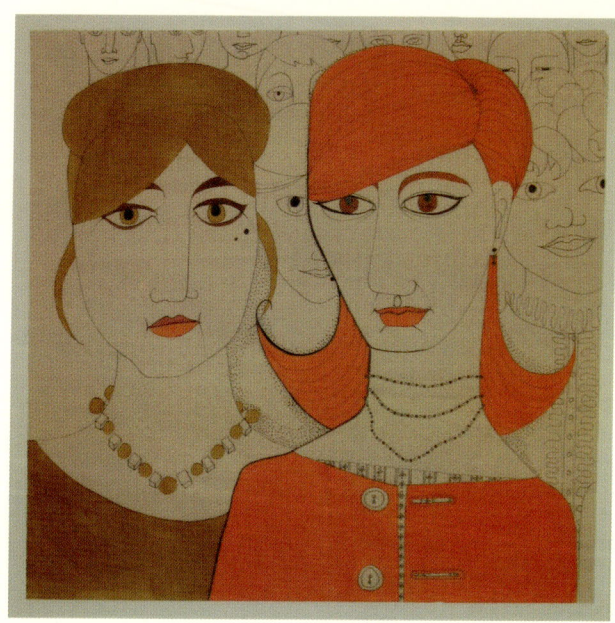

TWO OF AN AUDIENCE
1960 • ink • 14" x 14"
Kerry Collection

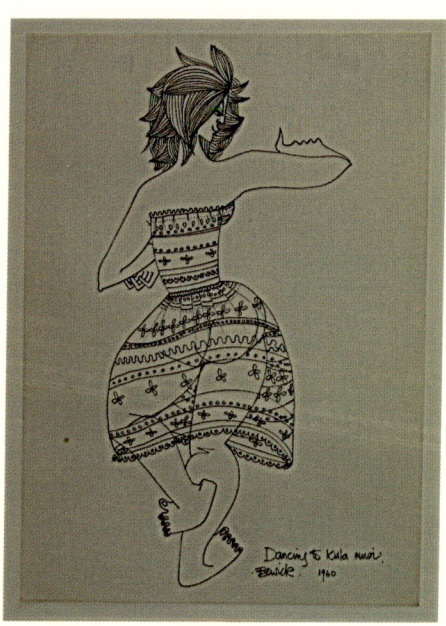

DANCING
1960 • ink • 14" x 10"
Kerry Collection

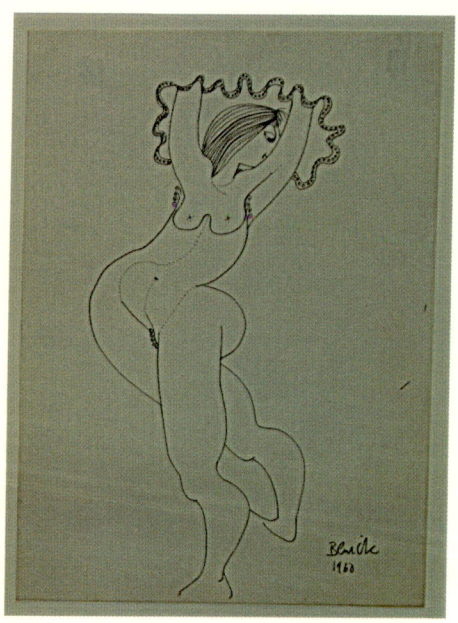

UNDRESSING
1960 • ink • 14" x 10"
Kerry Collection

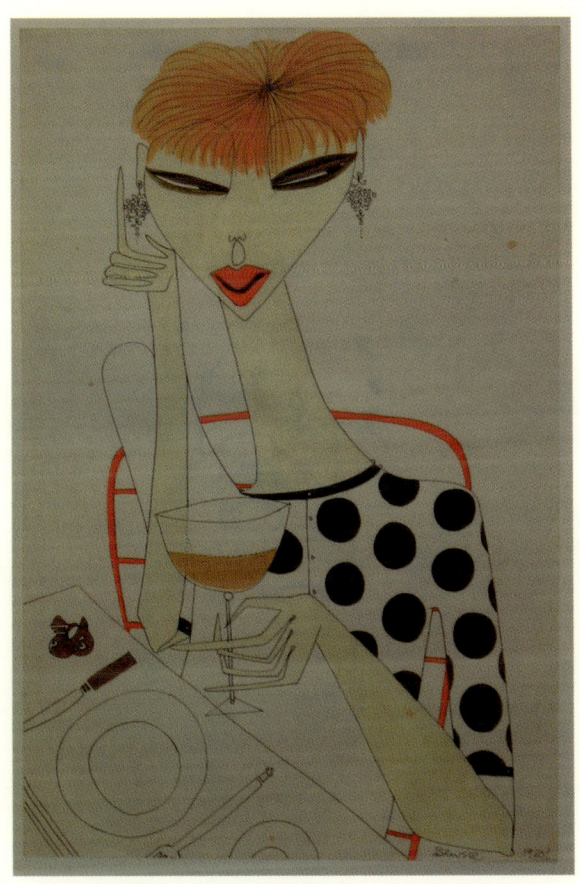

LUNCH LADY
1960 • poster colour • 17" x 11"
Kerry Collection

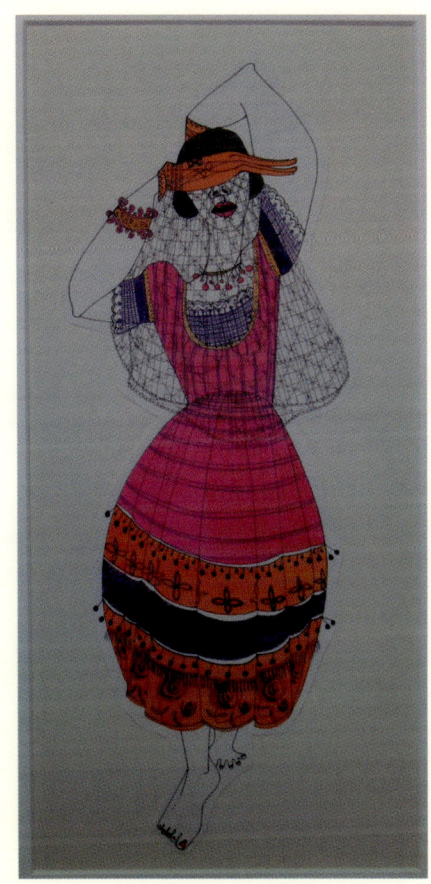

ETHNIC LADY
1960 • ink • 21" x 9"
Waterford Collection

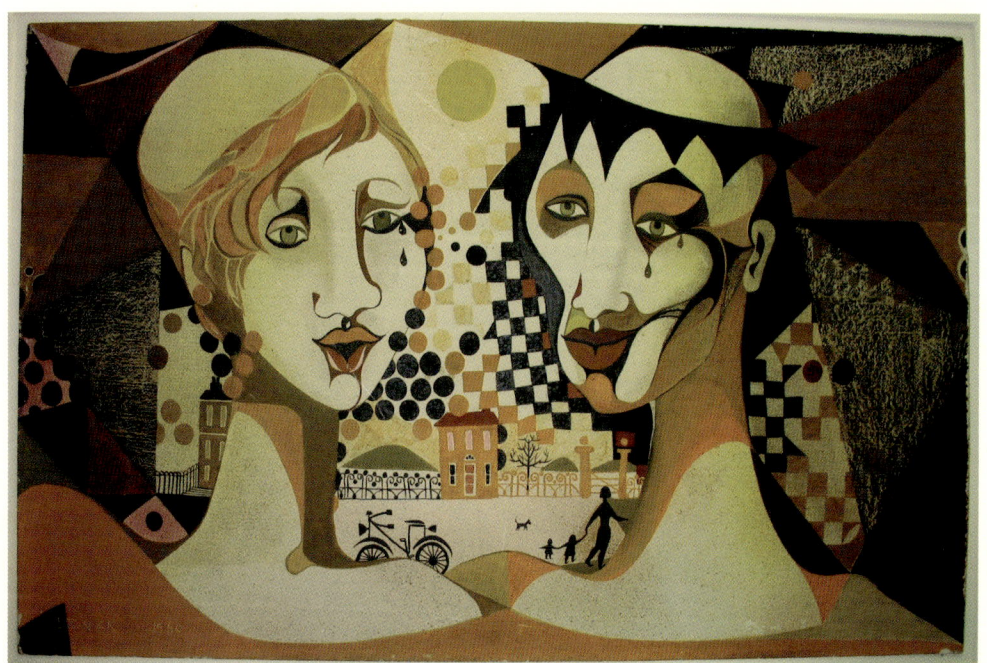

CLOWN SWEETHEARTS
1960 • oil and ink • 22"x 35"
Travelling Collection

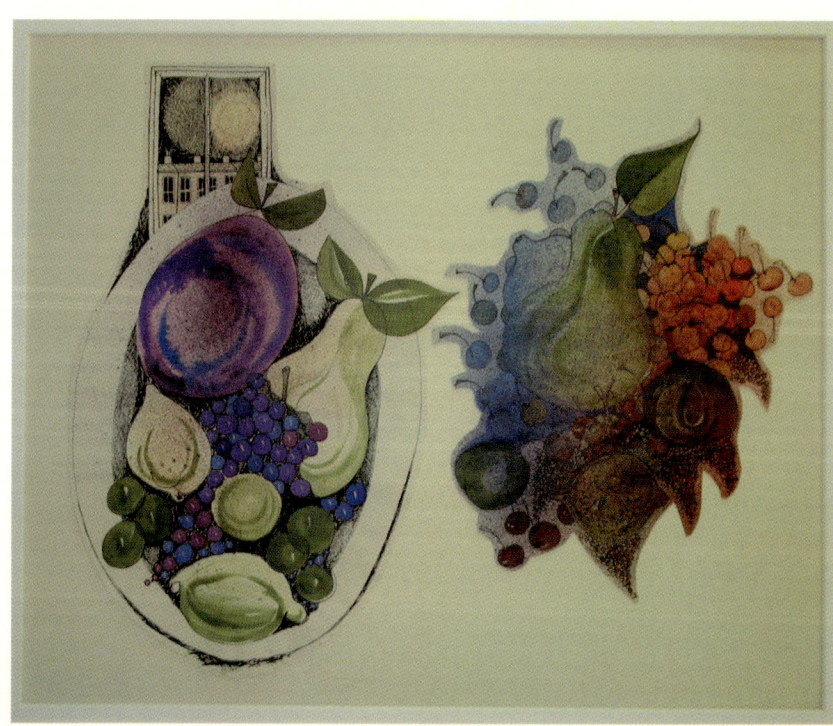

FRUIT BOWL AND FRUIT
1960 • pencils • 19" x 24"
Waterford Collection

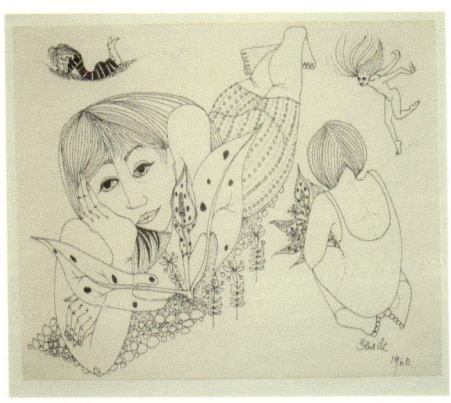

GIRL AND JACK-IN-THE-PULPIT
1960 • ink • 9" x 11"
Travelling Collection

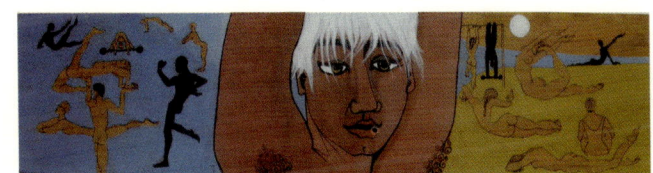

GYMNASTICS BY THE SEA
1960 • ink and poster colour • 5" x 21"
Waterford Collection

Nico was in Russell's steel band, a witty Trinidadian. 'You need a lot of stairs to understand that'.
'A Rolls Royce don't walk that way'. 'My mother said "son, when you grow up, find a friend with the AA"'.

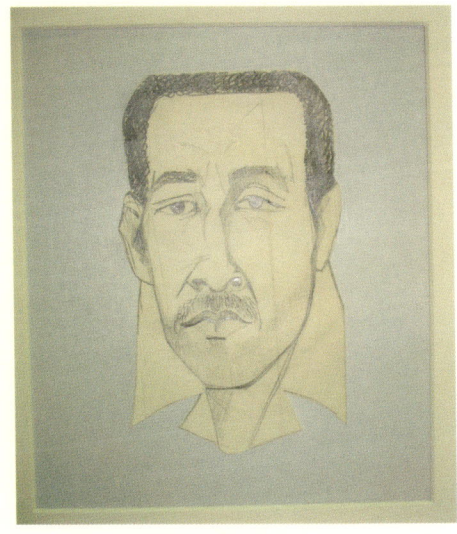

NICO
1960 • ink • 10" x 6"
Travelling Collection

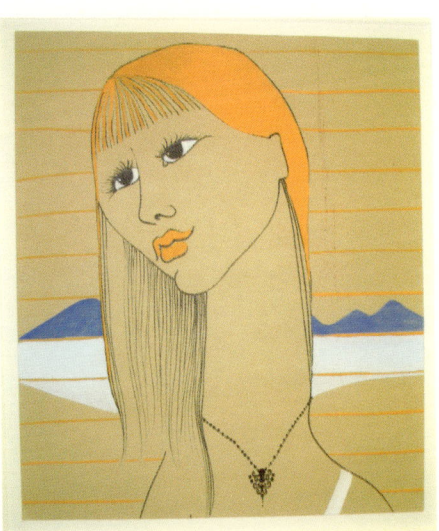

ORANGE HAIR AND LIPS
1960 • poster colour • 12" x 11"
Waterford Collection

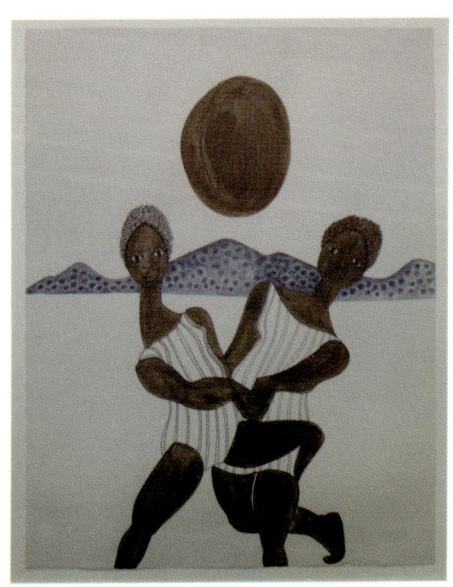

PLAYING IN THE DESERT
1960 • ink • 18" x 14"
Travelling Collection

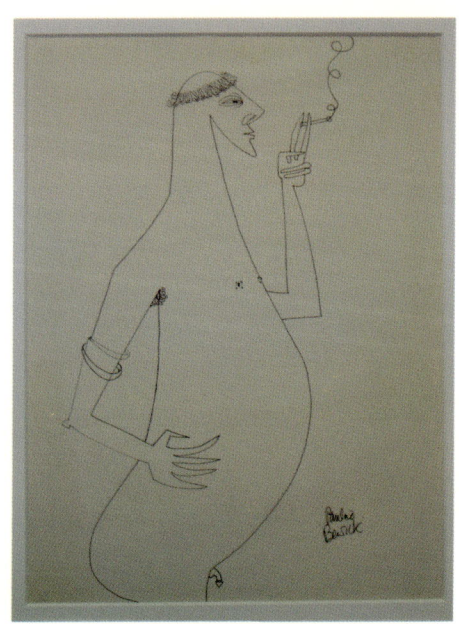

SMOKING MONK
1960 • ink • 19" x 14"
Travelling Collection

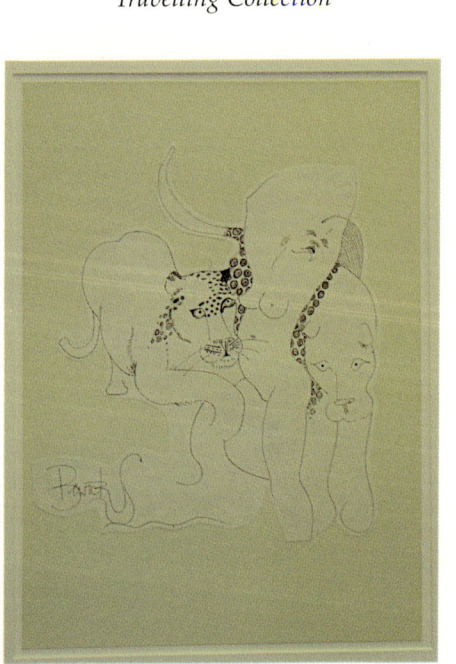

TWO TIGERS AND A WOMAN
1960 • ink • 21" x 19"
Waterford Collection

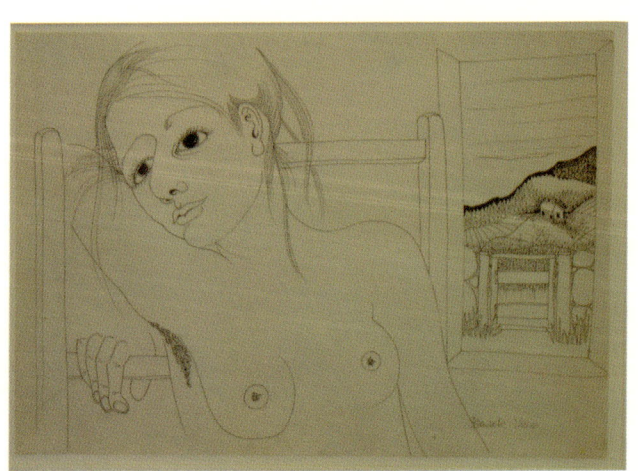

GIRL IN LARAGH
1961 • ink • 15" x 21"
Kerry Collection

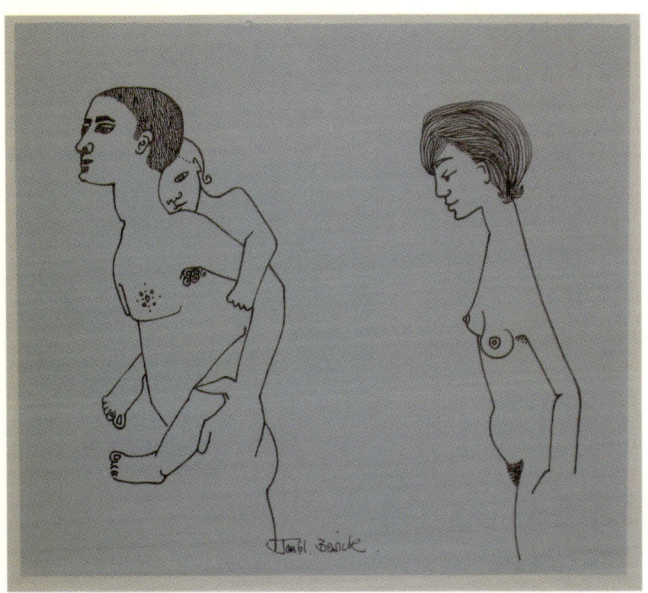

PIGGYBACK I
1961 • ink • 11" x 12"
Kerry Collection

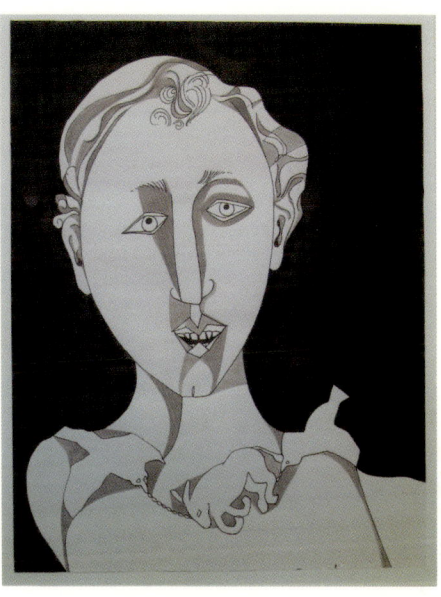

ALAN
1961 • watercolour • 18" x 14"
Travelling Collection

Alan and Leslie were brother and sister. He is a photographer, and Leslie and I were in art school together.

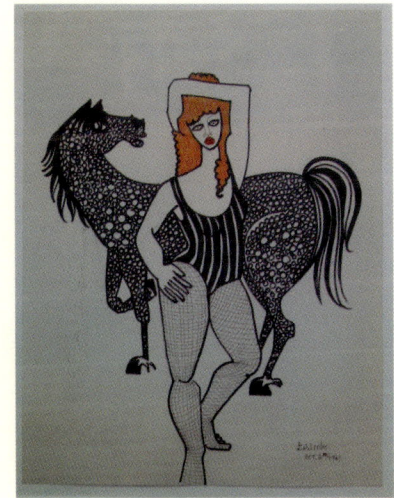

CIRCUS RIDER
1961 • marker • 18" x 14"
Waterford Collection

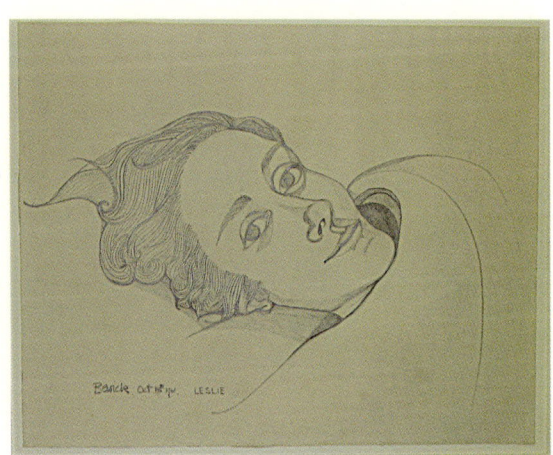

LESLIE
1961 • pencil • 14" x 18"
Travelling Collection

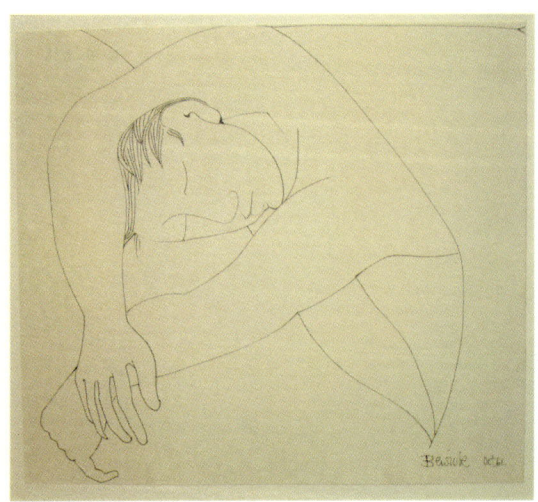

MAN ASLEEP
1961 • ink • 11" x 12"
Waterford Collection

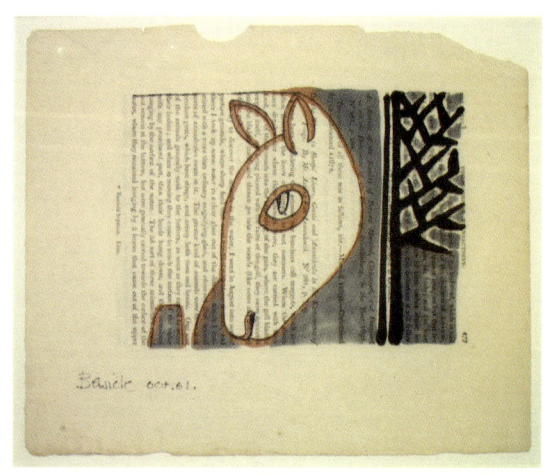

SHEEP
1961 • ink and newsclipping • 11" x 9"
Travelling Collection

Another page from *Philosophical Transactions.*

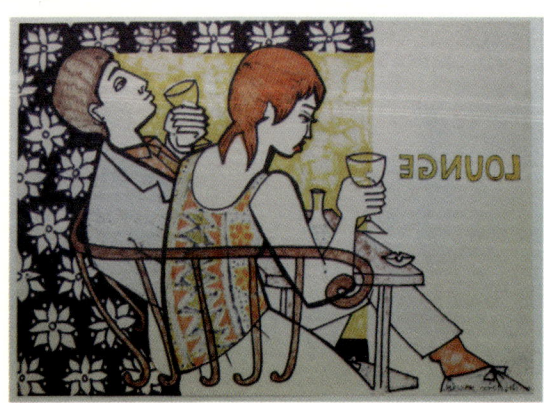

THROUGH THE WINDOW
1961 • ink • 14" x 20"
Waterford Collection

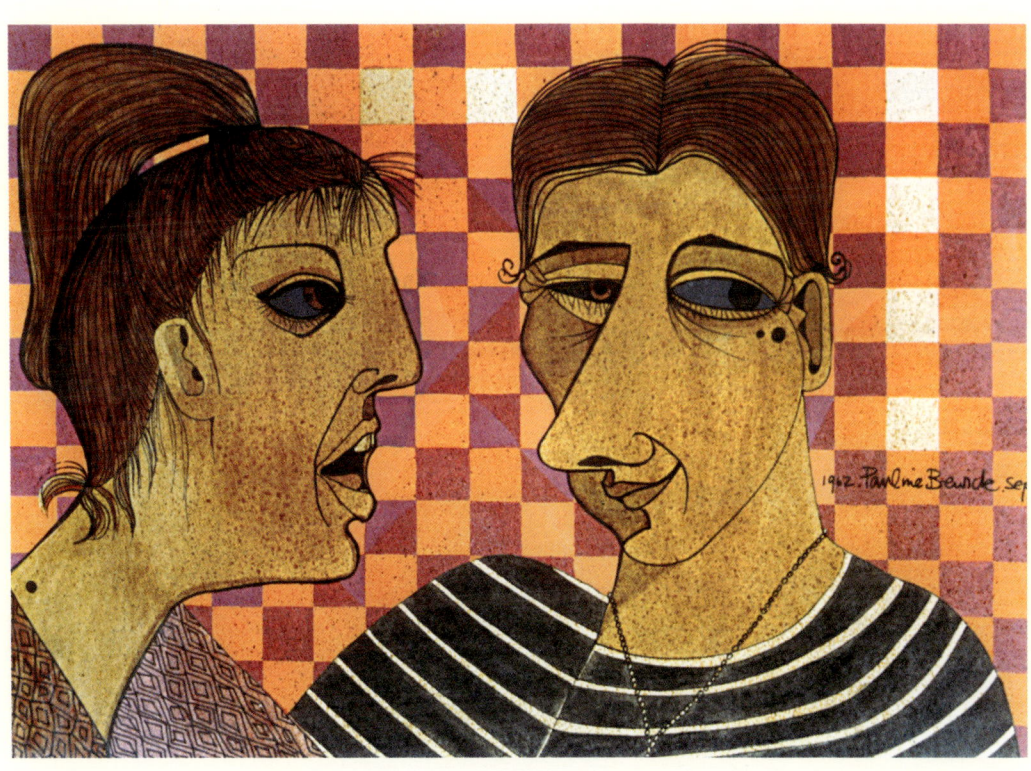

Brow Beating
1962 • ink varnished • 14" x 20"
Kerry Collection

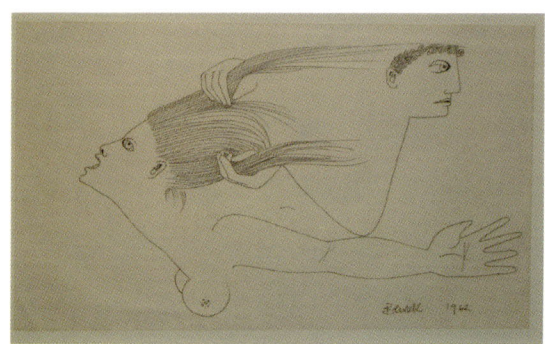

HUSBAND AND WIFE
1962 • ink • 10" x 17"
Kerry Collection

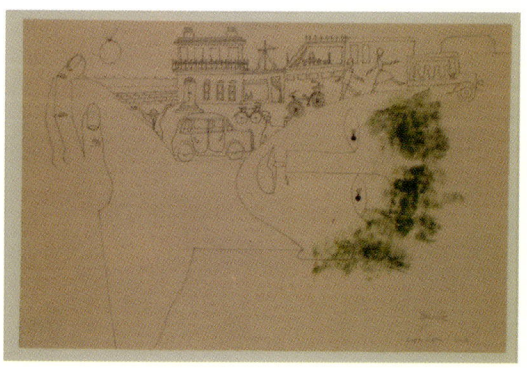

TOWN I HATE, COUNTRY I LOVE
1961 • ink • 12" x 19"
Kerry Collection

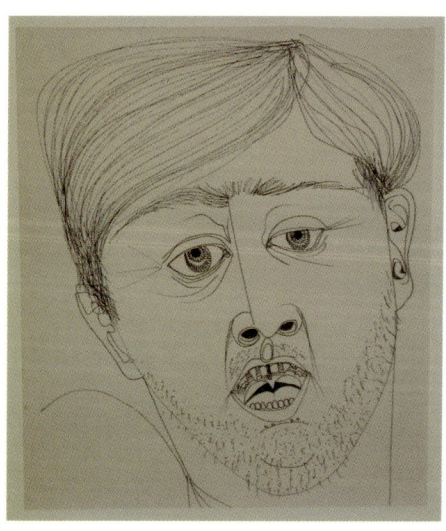

PHILIP
1962 • ink • 12" x 11"
Kerry Collection

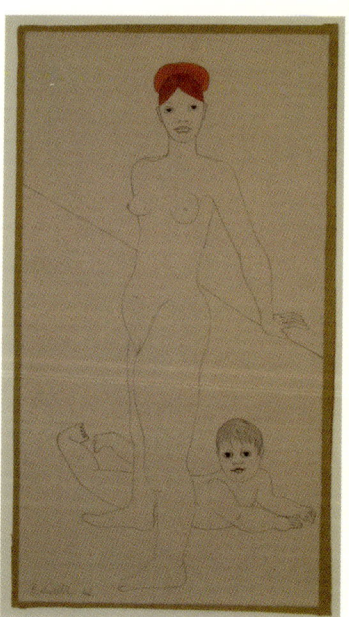

RED-HAIRED MOTHER AND SON
1962 • ink • 19" x 11"
Kerry Collection

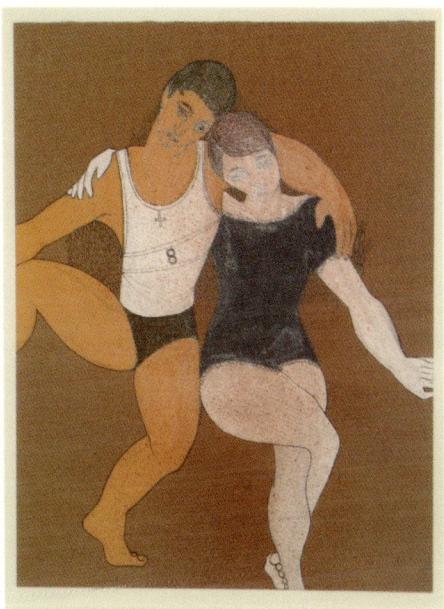

SEASIDE COUPLE
1962 • ink • 15" x 12"
Kerry Collection

Back with Pat, we lived in Beaufort St with Barry and Philip. We planned a trip on their boat, the Carningly, to travel the Mediterranean. Pat left the boat in France to go back to work. Continuing on we met Costas in Hydra where a new love developed. He bought me sandals and made me kiss the sandal-maker.

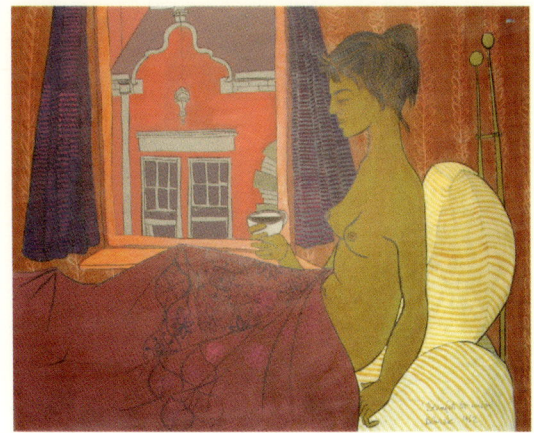

BEAUFORT STREET, LONDON
1962 • ink • 16" x 19"
Travelling Collection

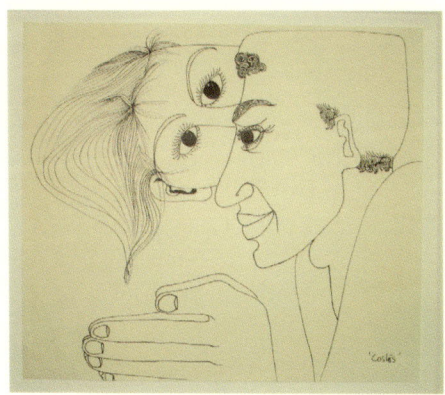

COSTAS I
1962 • ink • 10" x 11"
Waterford Collection

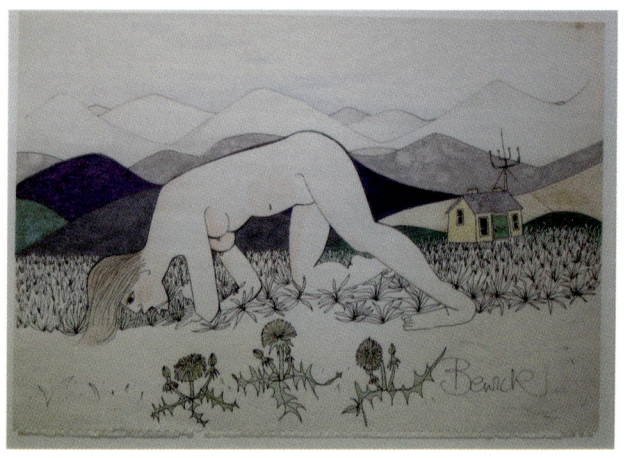

EATING GRASS
1962 • marker, pencil and ink • 14" x 21"
Travelling Collection

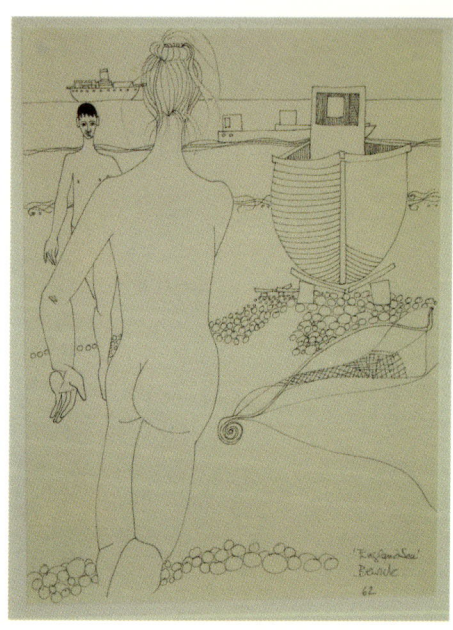

ENGLISH SEASIDE
1962 • ink • 16" x 12"
Travelling Collection

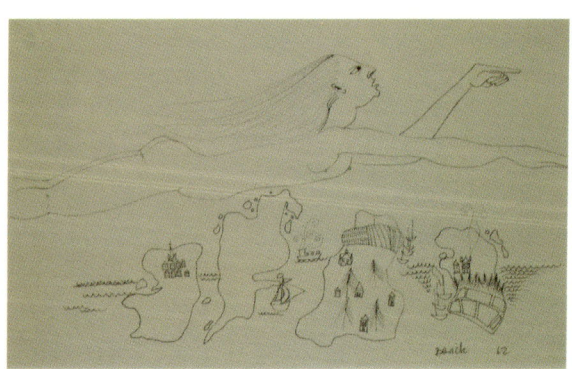

FLYING OVER ISLANDS
1962 • ink • 10" x 17"
Travelling Collection

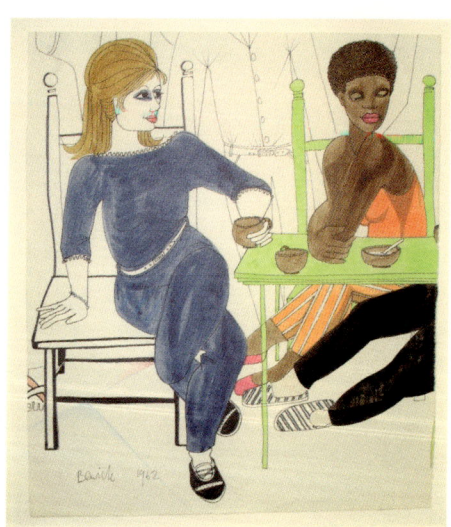

GIRLS AT GREEN TABLE
1962 • ink • 12" x 11"
Waterford Collection

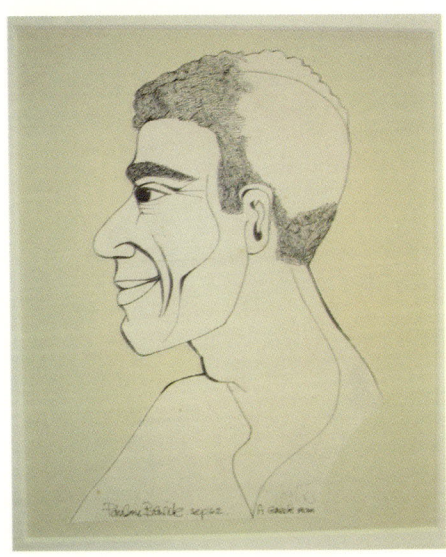

GREEK MAN COSTAS II
1962 • ink • 12" x 8"
Travelling Collection

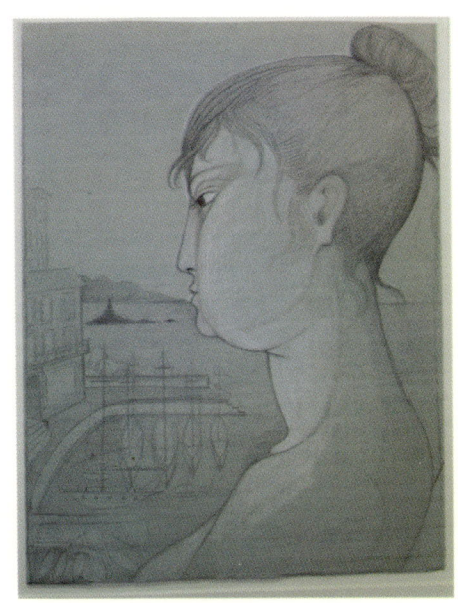

HYDRA
1962 • pencils • 18" x 14"
Waterford Collection

Costas got cross at a drawing I did of Eros because he had an erect penis.
I began to think Costas was too macho.

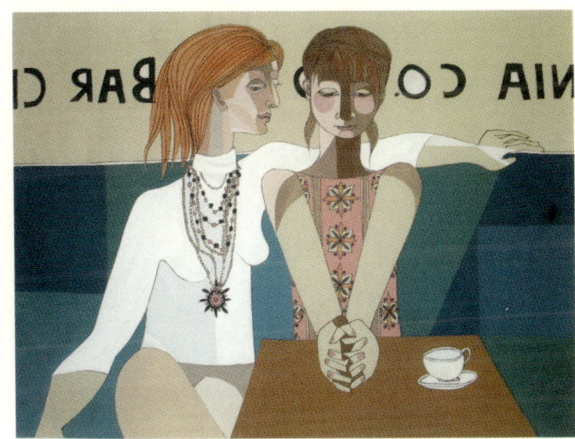

JILL AND FRIEND
1962 • poster colour and ink • 12" x 16"
Waterford Collection

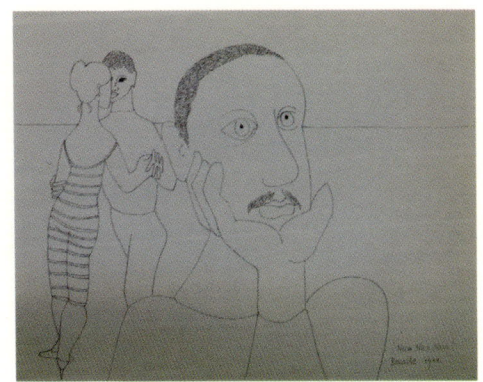

NICO, NICO, NICO
1962 • ink • 14" x 18"
Waterford Collection

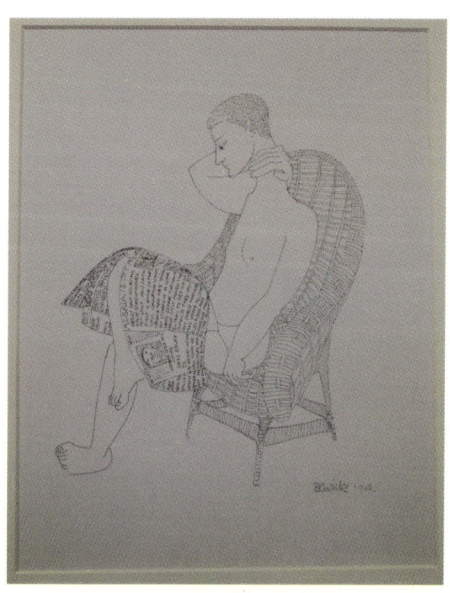

READING THE PAPER
1962 • ink • 18" x 14"
Travelling Collection

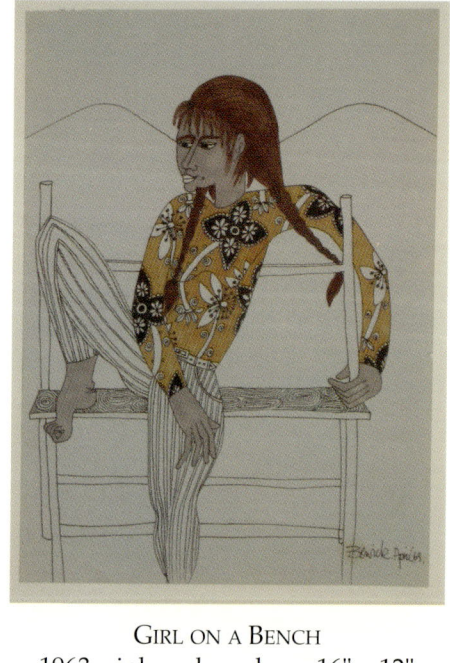

GIRL ON A BENCH
1963 • ink and marker • 16" x 12"
Kerry Collection

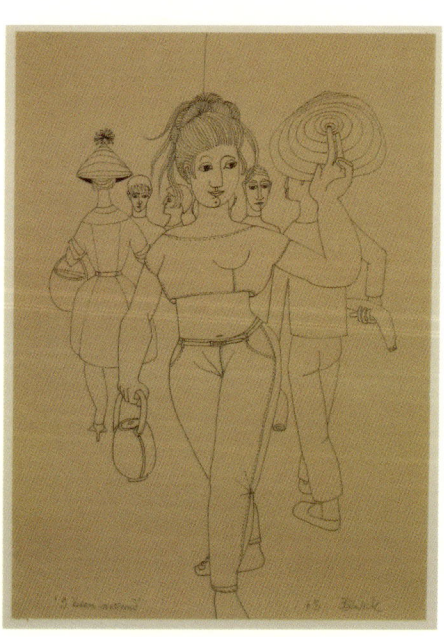

I BEEN AROUND
1963 • ink • 16" x 12"
Kerry Collection

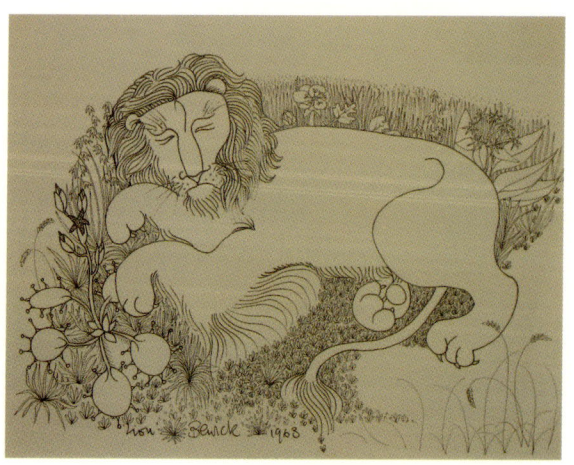

LION ASLEEP
1963 • ink • 14" x 18"
Kerry Collection

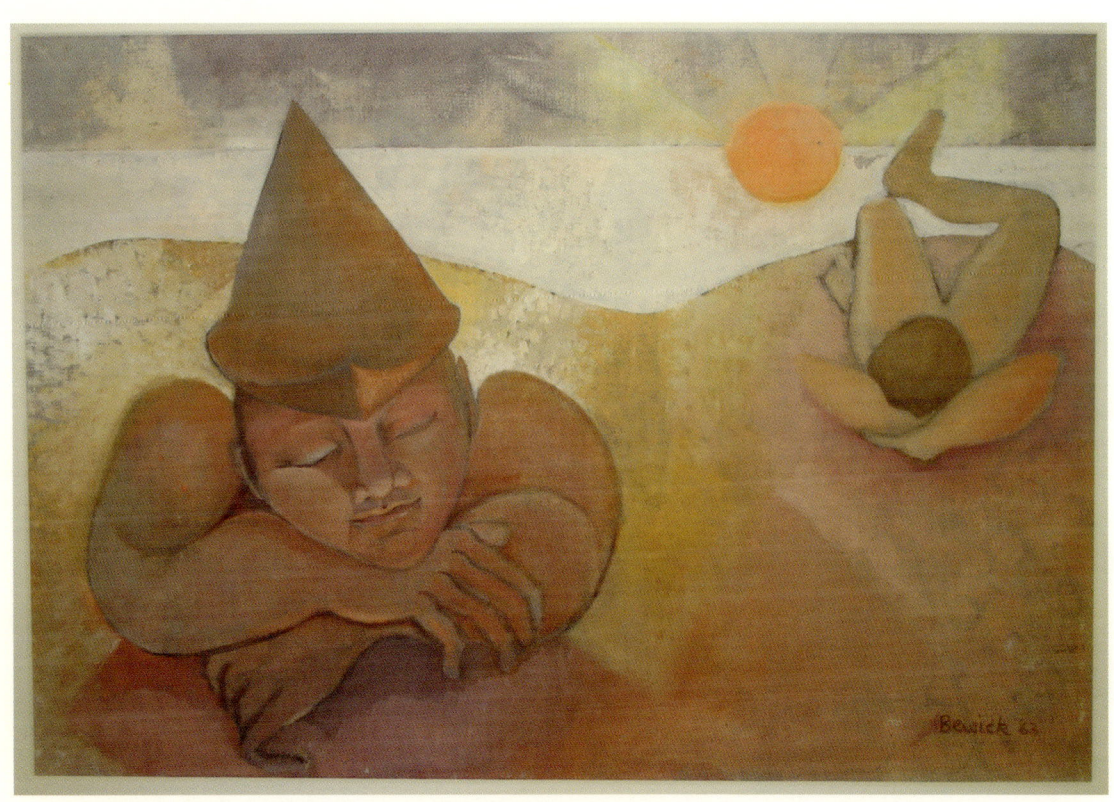

TWO PEOPLE ON THE BEACH
1963 • oil • 20" x 30"
Kerry Collection

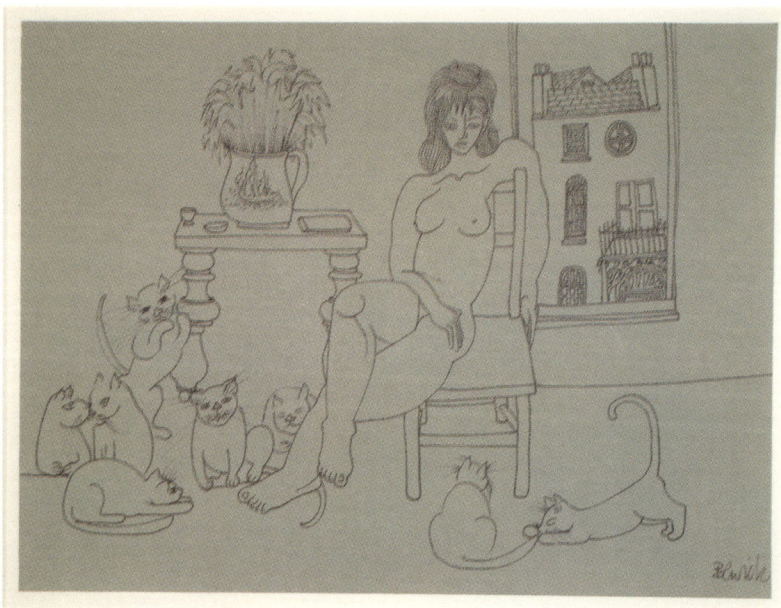

WITH HER CATS
1963 • ink • 12" x 16"
Kerry Collection

Pat and I made up and came back to Dublin.

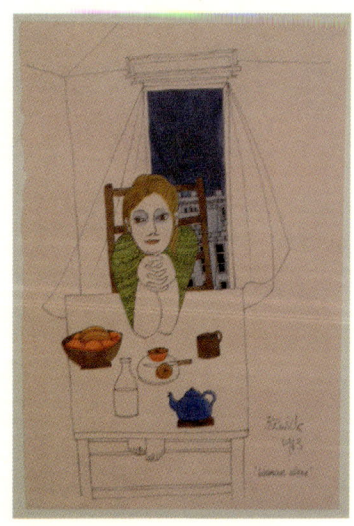

WOMAN ALONE
1963 • ink • 14" x 12"
Kerry Collection

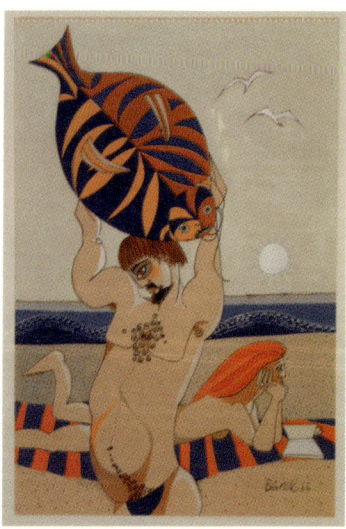

FAT MAN, FLAT FISH
1963 • poster colour and ink • 18" x 12"
Kerry Collection

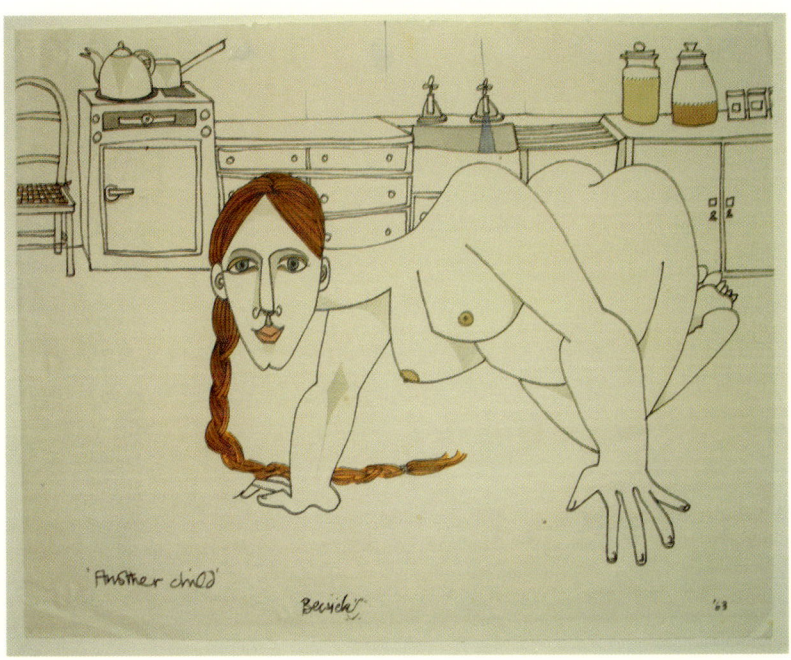

ANOTHER CHILD
1963 • ink • 11" x 14" ink
Travelling Collection

Imagined pregnancy.
Pat wanted children but the world
was too awful a place for them.
It haunted me that one day I would
regret not having any.

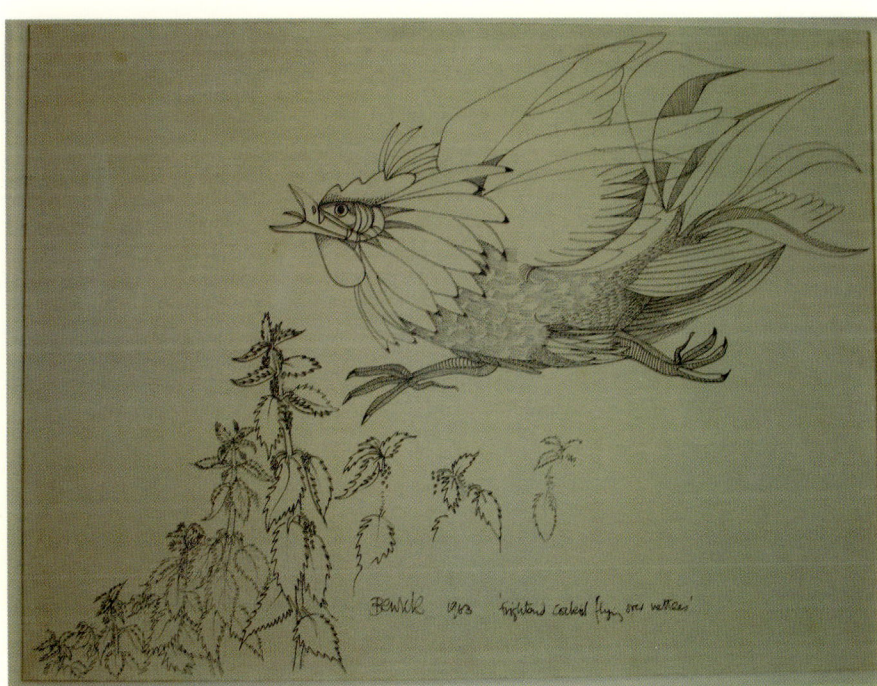

FRIGHTENED COCKEREL FLYING OVER NETTLES
1963 • ink • 22" x 30"
Travelling Collection

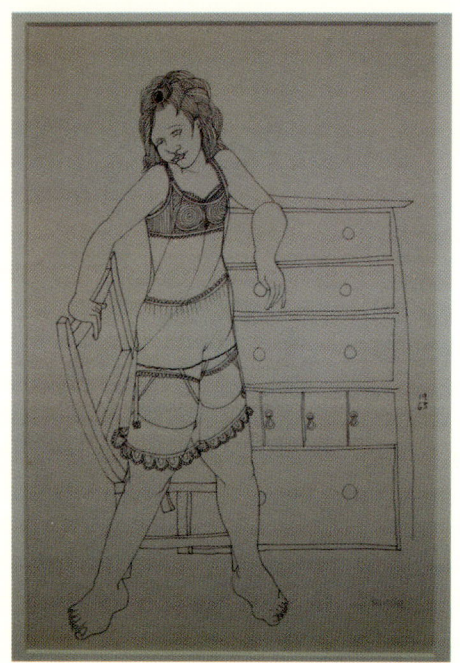

GIRL IN UNDERWEAR
1963 • ink • 18" x 12"
Travelling Collection

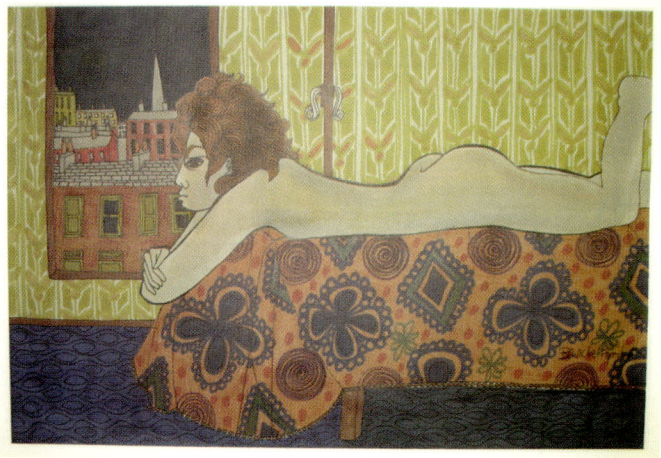

HER BEDSITTER
1963 • marker and ink • 12" x 18"
Waterford Collection

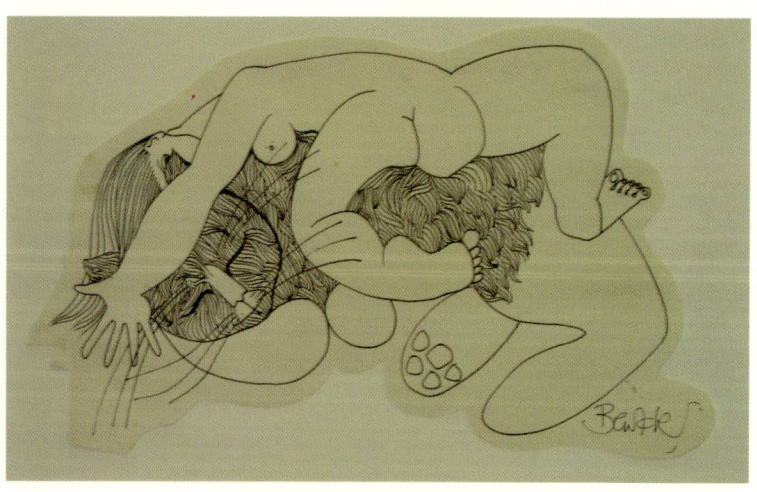

ON AN IMAGINARY ANIMAL
1963 • ink • 9" x 15"
Travelling Collection

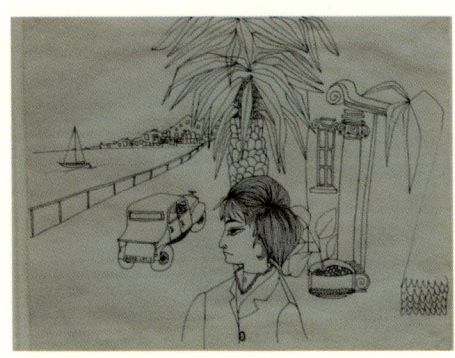

PROMENADE
1963 • ink • 13" x 16"
Travelling Collection

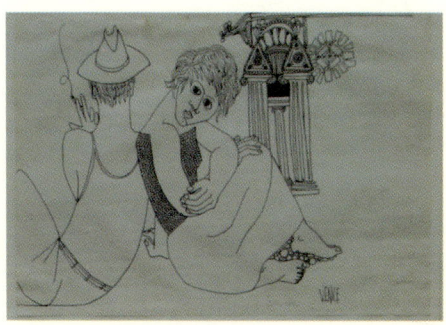

VENICE
1963 • ink • 13" x 16"
Travelling Collection

Pat and I got married. We honeymooned in the Alps, Nice, Paris and Italy.

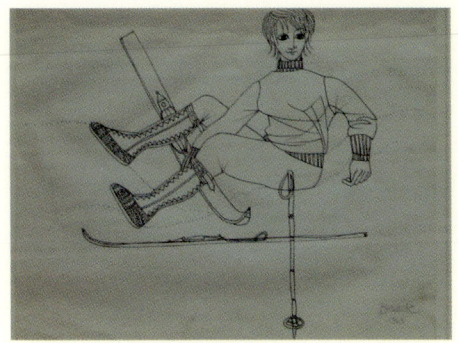

SKIING
1963 • ink • 13" x 16"
Travelling Collection

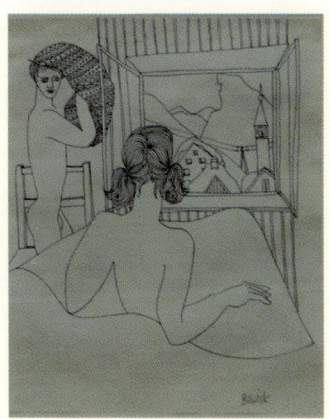

THE VIEW
1963 • ink • 13" x 13"
Travelling Collection

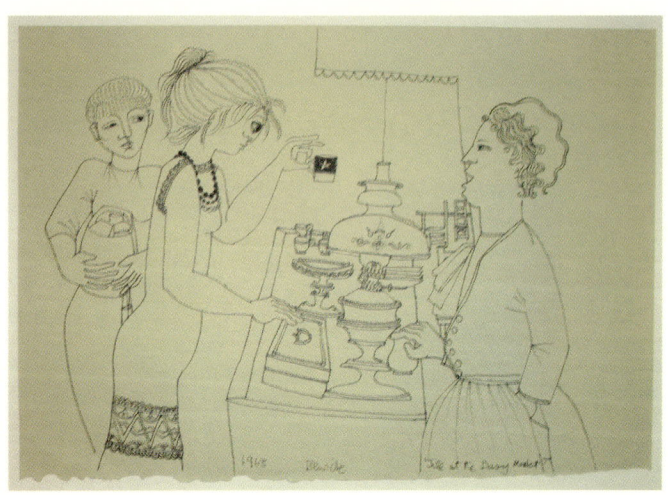

JILL AT THE DAISY MARKET
1963 • ink • 10" x 14"
Waterford Collection

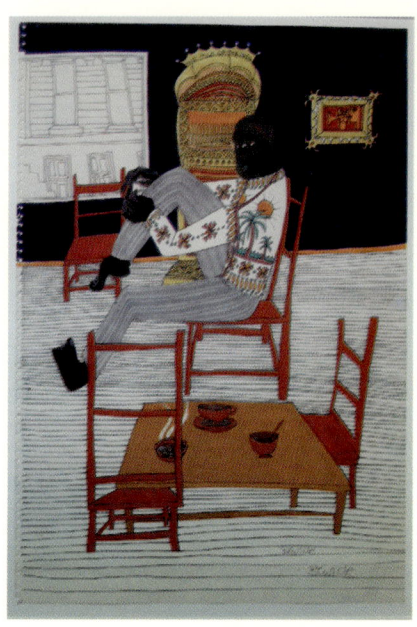

JUKEBOX
1963 • poster colour and marker • 21" x 14"
Waterford Collection

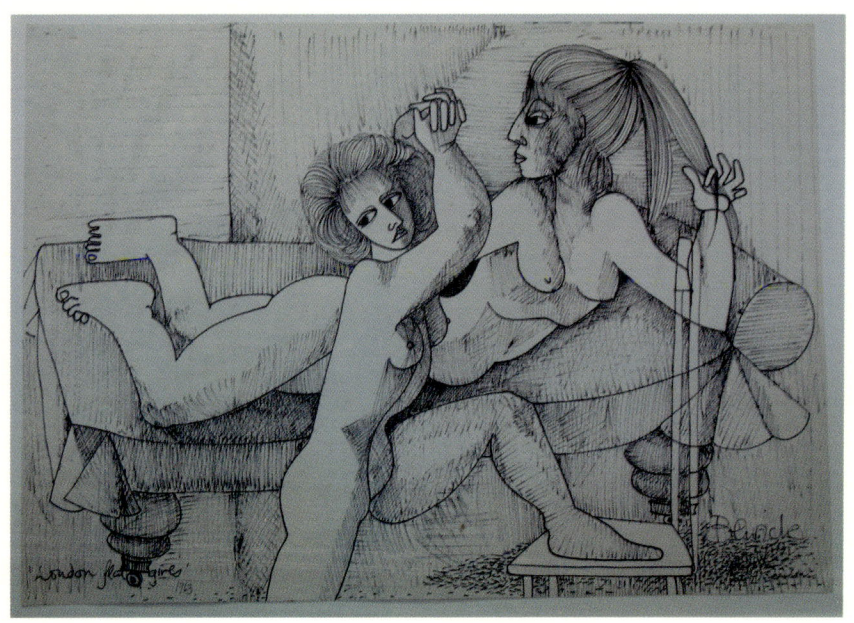

LONDON FLAT GIRLS
1963 • ink • 14" x 20"
Waterford Collection

Back to Beaufort Street.

Jill Neville, an author.

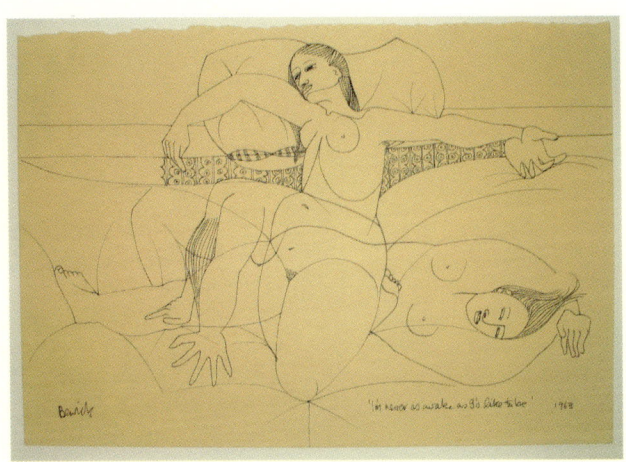

PIGGYBACK II
1963 • ink • 12" x 16"
Travelling Collection

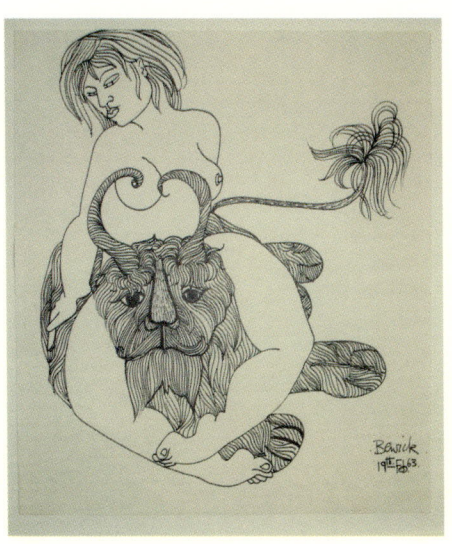

ON THE BACK OF AN IMAGINARY ANIMAL
1963 • ink • 12" x 11"
Waterford Collection

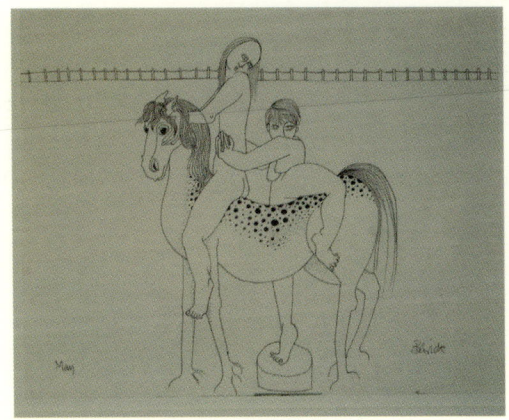

ON THE RACETRACK
1963 • ink • 14" x 18"
Waterford Collection

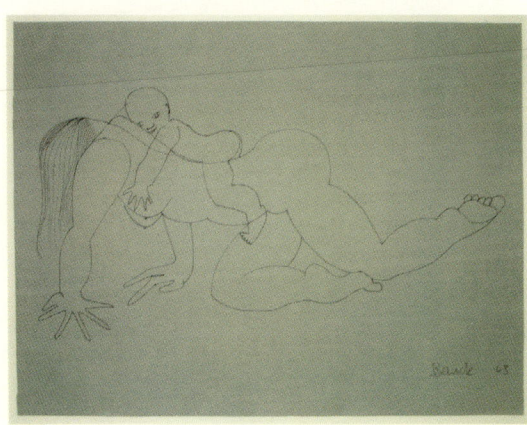

NEVER AWAKE AS I'D LIKE TO BE
1963 • ink • 10" x 14"
Travelling Collection

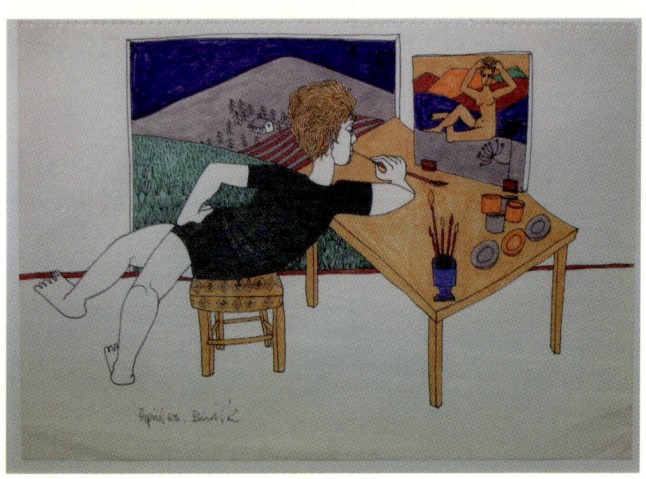

PAINTER
1963 • ink and marker • 14" x 21"
Waterford Collection

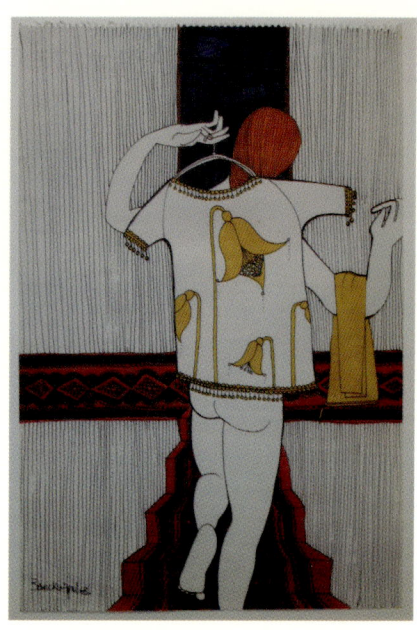

UP THE STAIRS
1963 • poster colour and marker • 18" x 12"
Travelling Collection

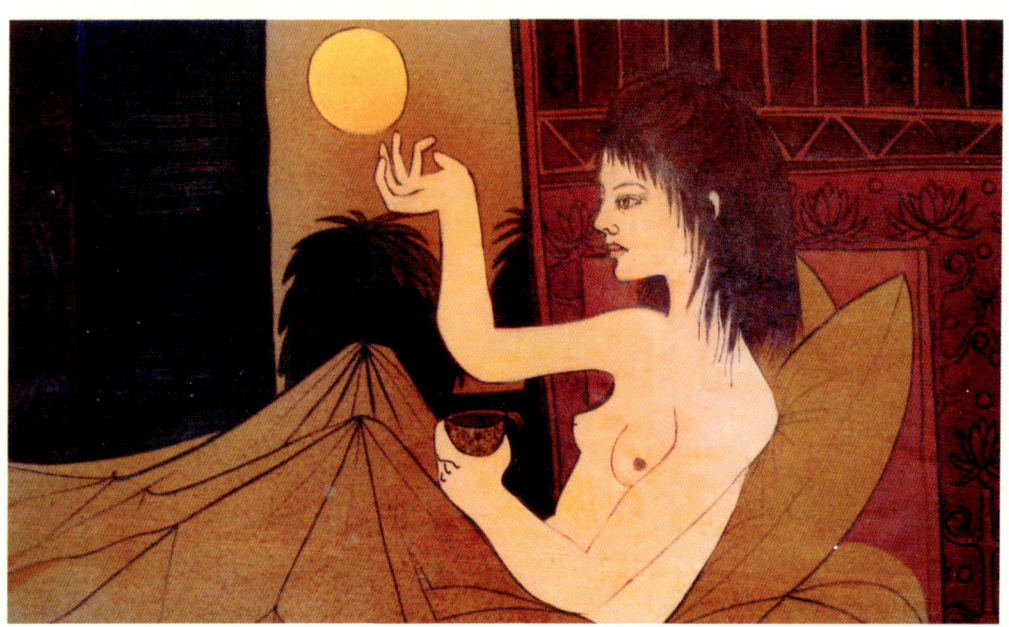

TROPICAL MOON
1963 • poster colour and ink • 12" x 19"
Kerry Collection

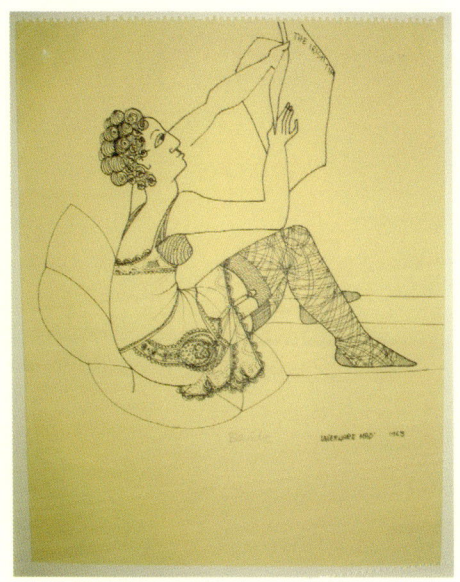

UNDERWEAR MAD
1963 • ink • 15" x 12"
Waterford Collection

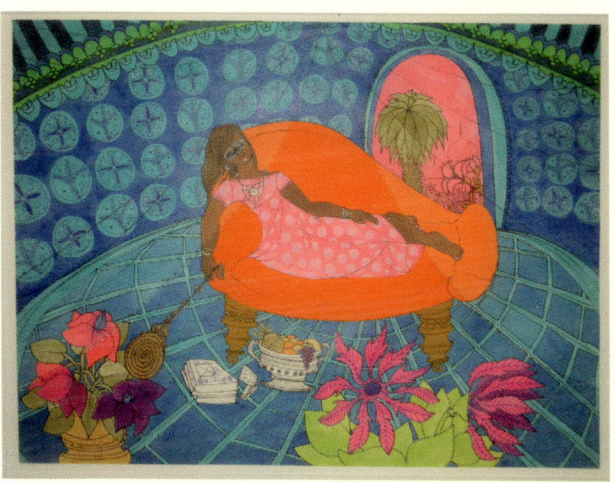

CHILITA IN DREAMLAND
1964 • poster colour and ink • 22" x 30"
Kerry Collection

In Dublin again, a poor monkey sat in a window day in day out.

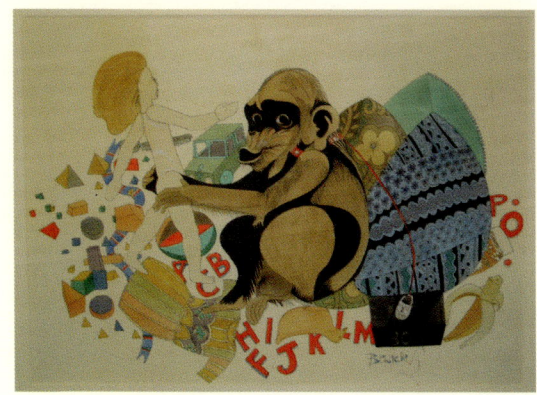

MONKEY IN DONNYBROOK
1964 • ink • 22" x 30"
Kerry Collection

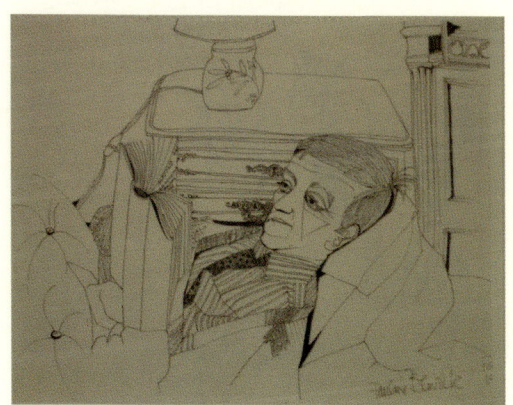

PAT READING
1964 • ink • 14" x 18"
Kerry Collection

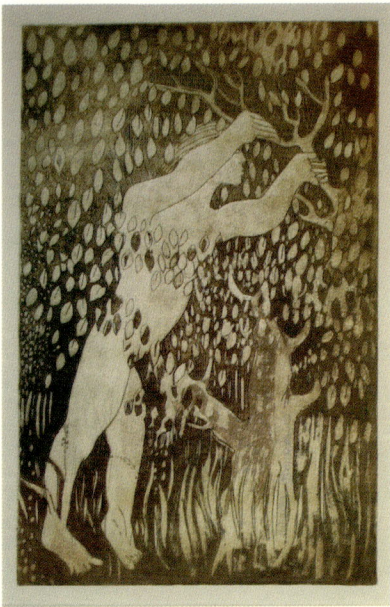

PULLING BRANCHES
1966 • etching • 12" x 9"
Waterford Collection

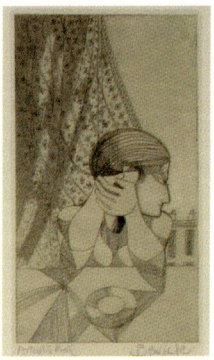

A CUP OF TEA
1965 • etching • 7" x 4"
Waterford Collection

Joined the Graphic Studios in Upper Mount Street to learn to etch.
Sugar tinting, the smell of printing ink, John Behan, Brian Bourke,
Patrick Hickey, Elizabeth Rivers, John Kelly, Charlie Cullen and many
more worked alongside each other.

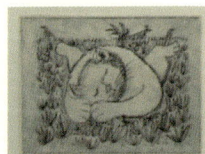

SLEEPING CAT, COCK AND HENS
1964 • etching • 3" x 4"
Waterford Collection

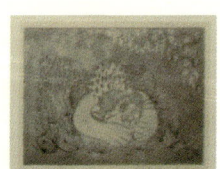

SLEEPING CAT
1964 • etching • 3" x 4"
Waterford Collection

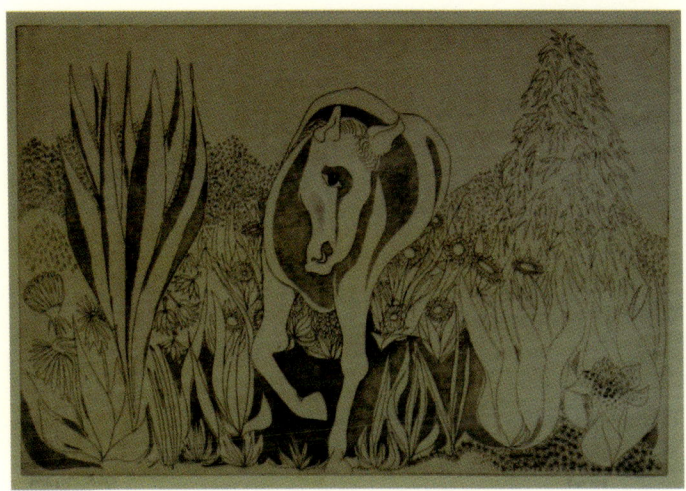

HORSE AND FLOWERS
1964 • etching • 13" x 18"
Kerry Collection

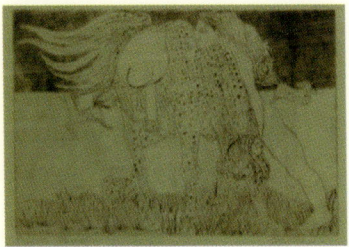

WOMAN AND HORSE
1964 • etching • 7" x 10"
Kerry Collection

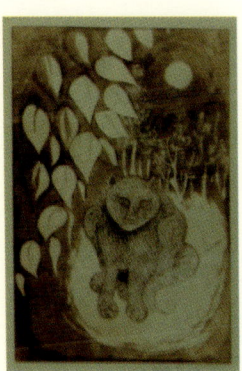

CAT IN A WOOD
1964 • etching • 10" x 7"
Kerry Collection

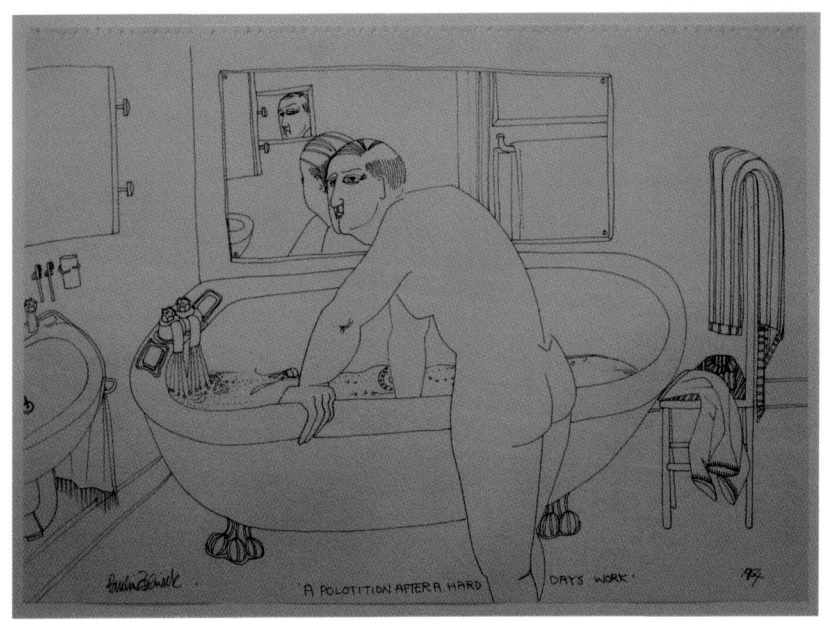

A POLITICIAN AFTER A HARD DAY'S WORK
1964 • ink • 14" x 21"
Waterford Collection

Still thinking about having babies.

Our artists' group held life classes in Leslie McWeeney's flat in Upper Mount Street.
Chilita, our Spanish dancer friend posed for us.

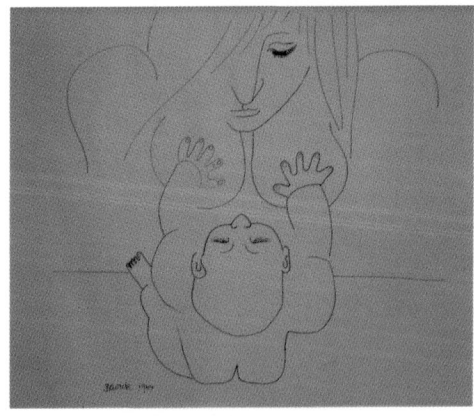

AT THE BREAST
1964 • ink • 20" x 25"
Travelling Collection

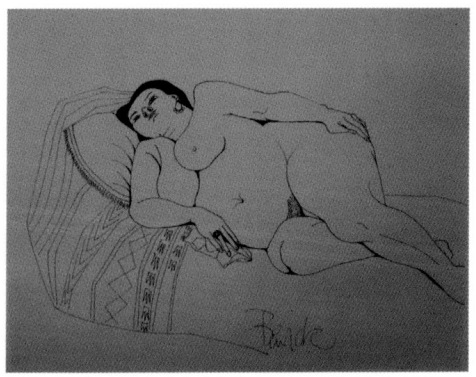

CHILITA IN LIFE CLASS
1964 • ink • 14" x 18"
Travelling Collection

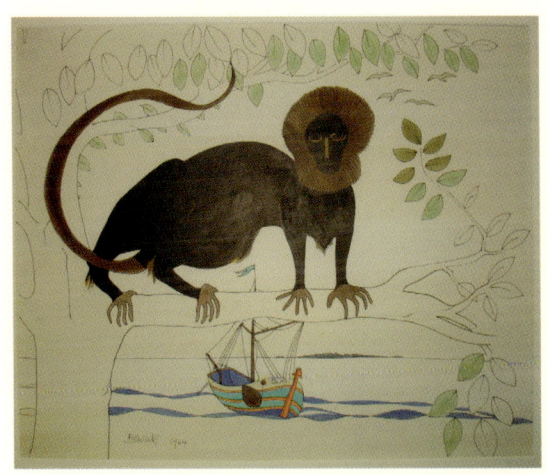

MONKEY ON A LIMB
1964 • poster colour and ink • 21" x 25"
Waterford Collection

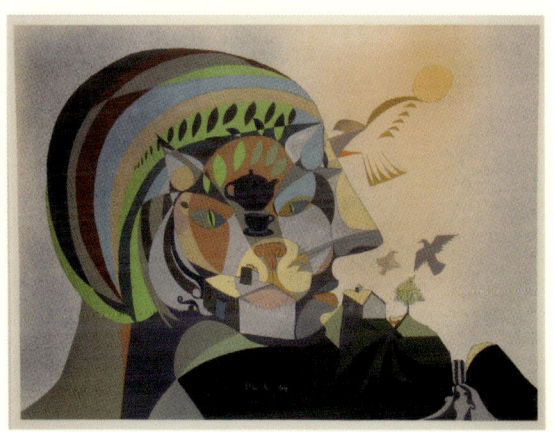

THINKING OF MARRIAGE
1964 • poster colour and ink • 22" x 30"
Waterford Collection

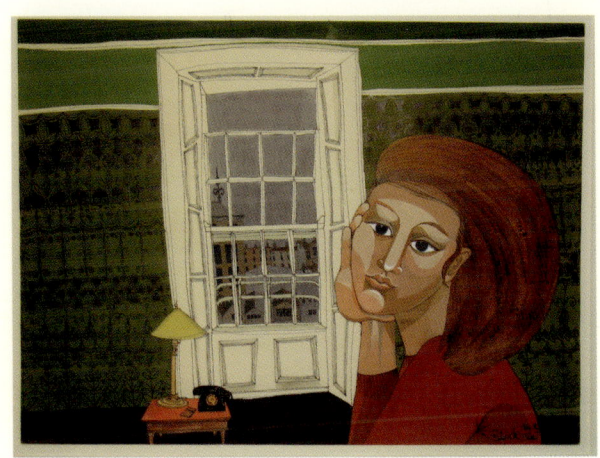

THINKING IN UPPER MOUNT STREET
1964 • watercolour and ink • 22" x 30"
Travelling Collection

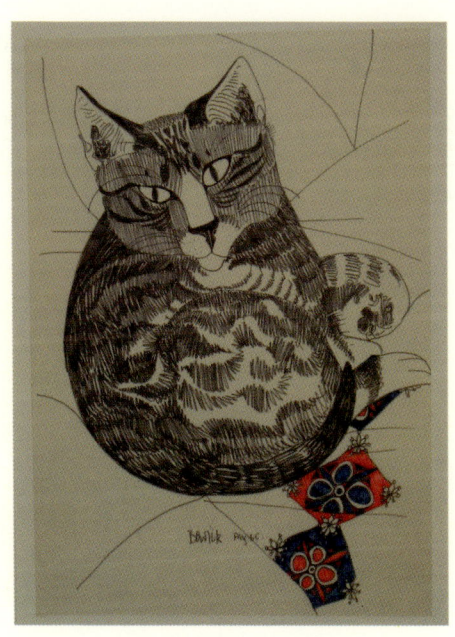

CAT
1965 • marker • 16" x 12"
Kerry Collection

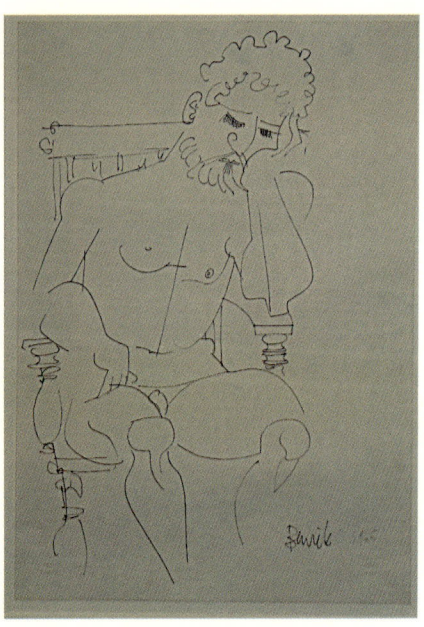

BRIAN BOURKE LIFECLASS I
1965 - ink • 20" x 14"
Kerry Collection

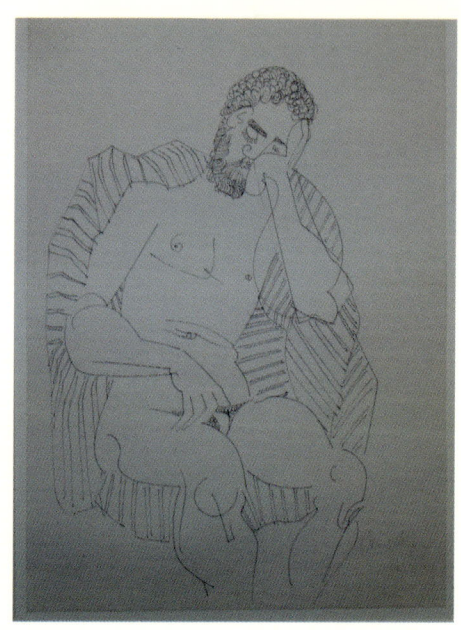

BRIAN BOURKE LIFECLASS II
1965 • ink • 20" x 14"
Waterford Collection

Four poses of Brian Bourke at our life class.

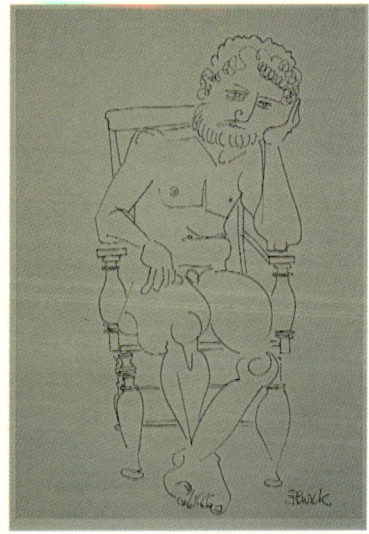

BRIAN BOURKE LIFECLASS III
1965 • ink • 20" x 14"
Travelling Collection

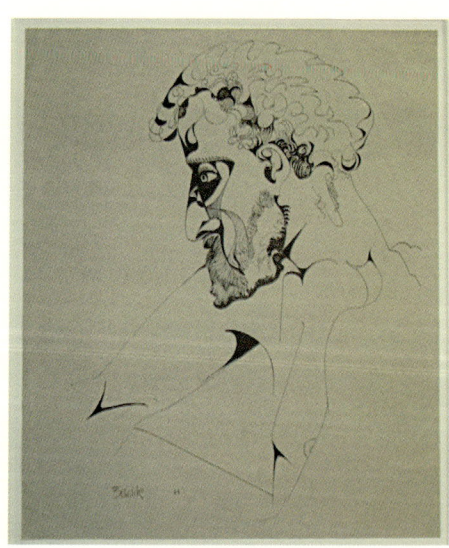

BRIAN BOURKE LIFECLASS IV
1965 - ink • 22" x 19"
Waterford Collection

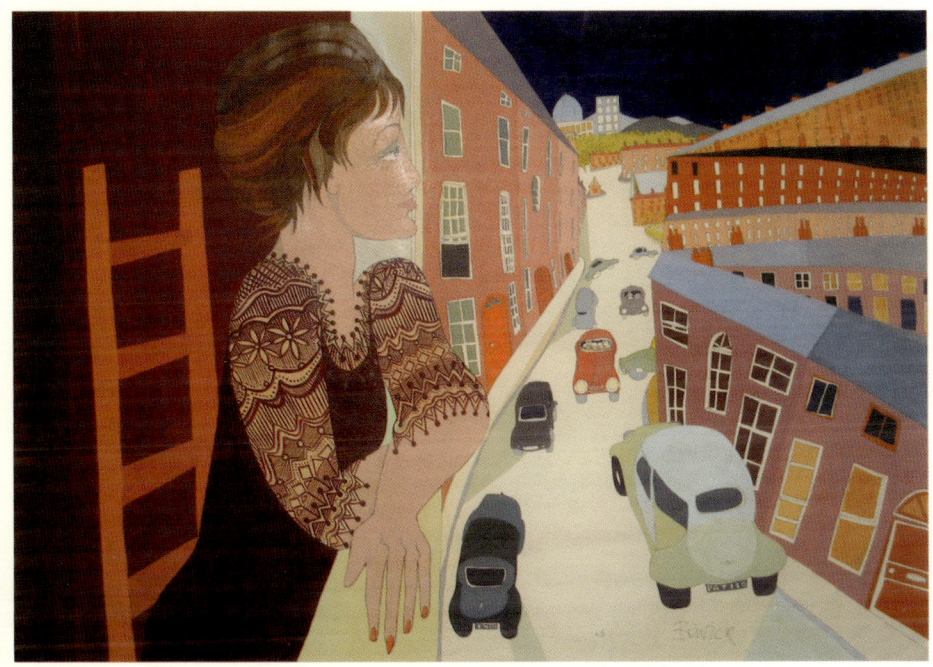

FITZWILLIAM SQUARE
1965 • ink • 27" x 39"
Kerry Collection

Shopping, nappies, prams seemed so boring
compared to the life I was having.

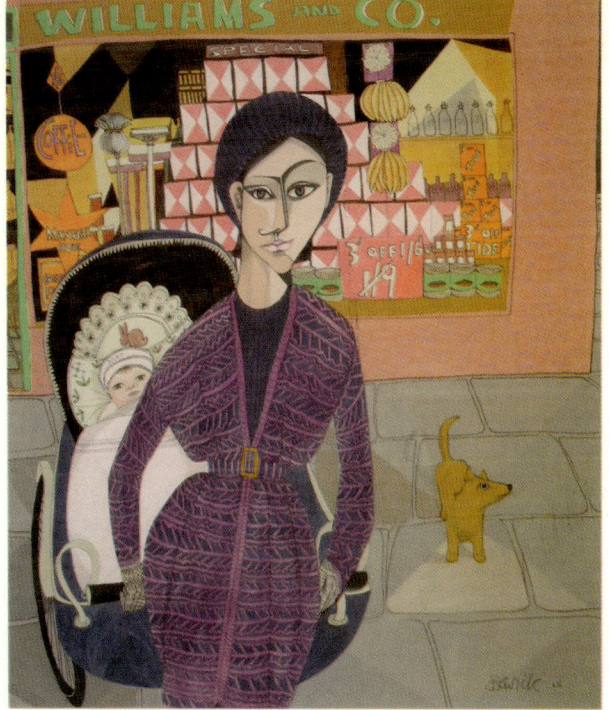

WOMAN AND BABY OUTSIDE WILLIAMS, BAGGOT STREET
1965 • poster colour and ink • 28" x 25"
Travelling Collection

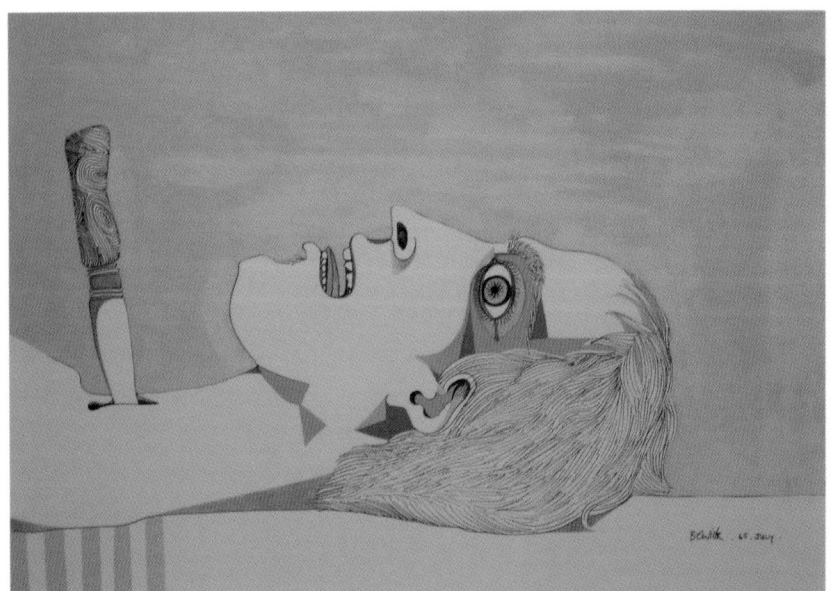

KNIFE
1965 • poster colour and ink • 15" x 22"
Travelling Collection

Barry and Philip bought a house in Villefranche.

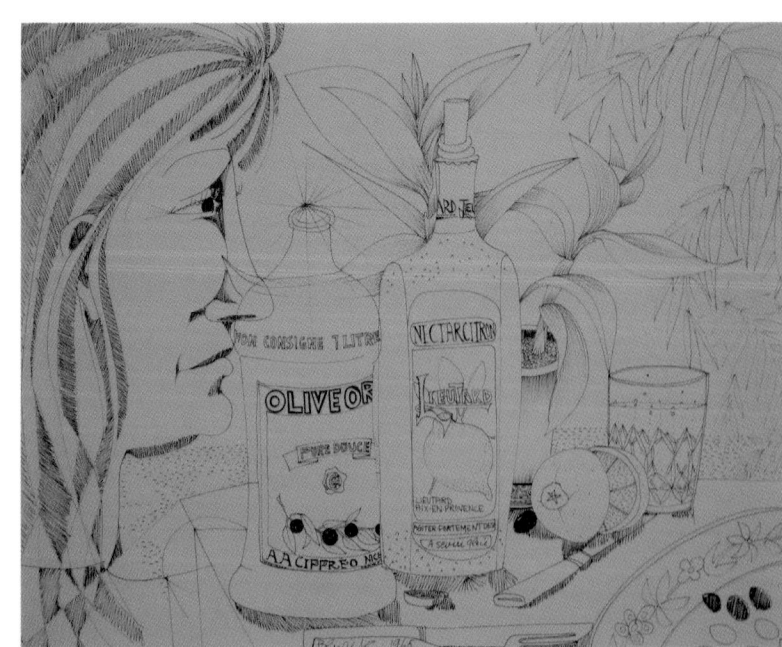

IN THE SOUTH OF FRANCE
1965 • ink • 19" x 24"
Waterford Collection

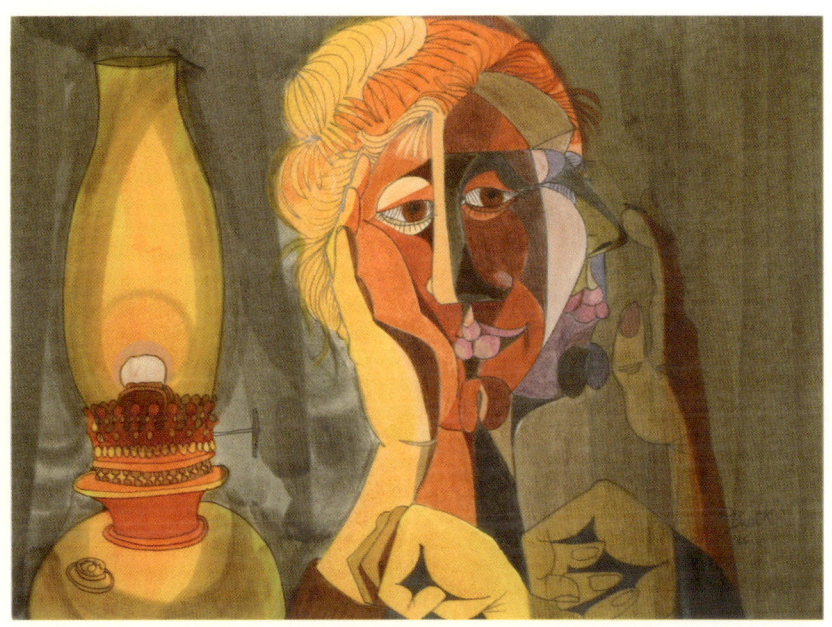

BY LAMPLIGHT
1966 • ink • 15" x 20"
Kerry Collection

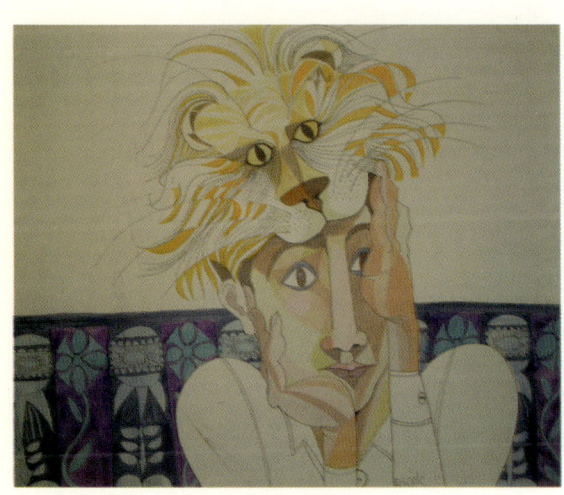

LION MASK
1966 • ink • 20" x 25"
Kerry Collection

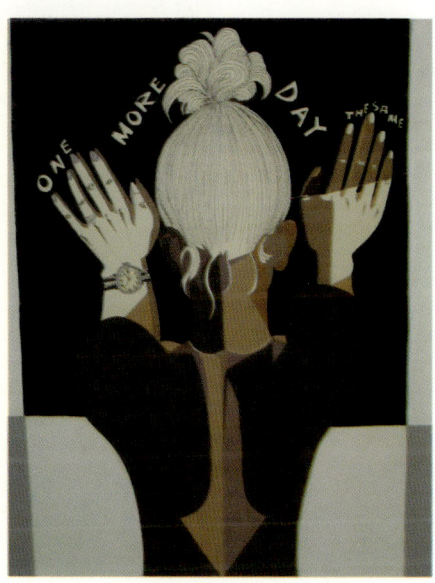

ONE MORE DAY THE SAME
1966 • poster colour and ink • 22" x 17"
Kerry Collection

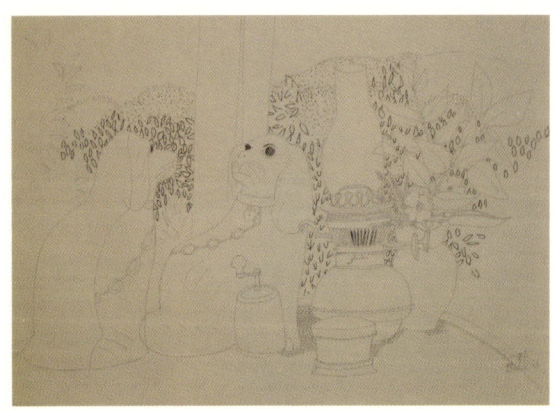

TWO STAFFORDSHIRE DOGS
1966 • ink • 15" x 21"
Kerry Collection

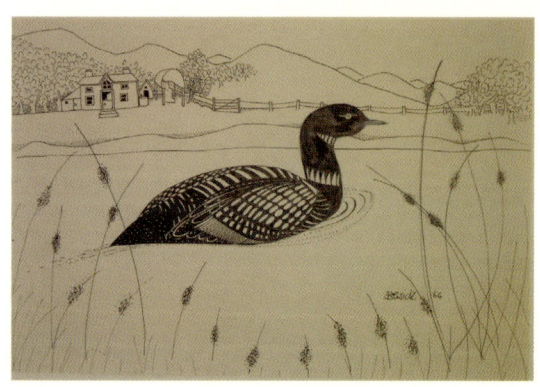

WATERBIRD
1966 • ink • 15" x 22"
Kerry Collection

When we visited Barry and Philip in Villefranche.

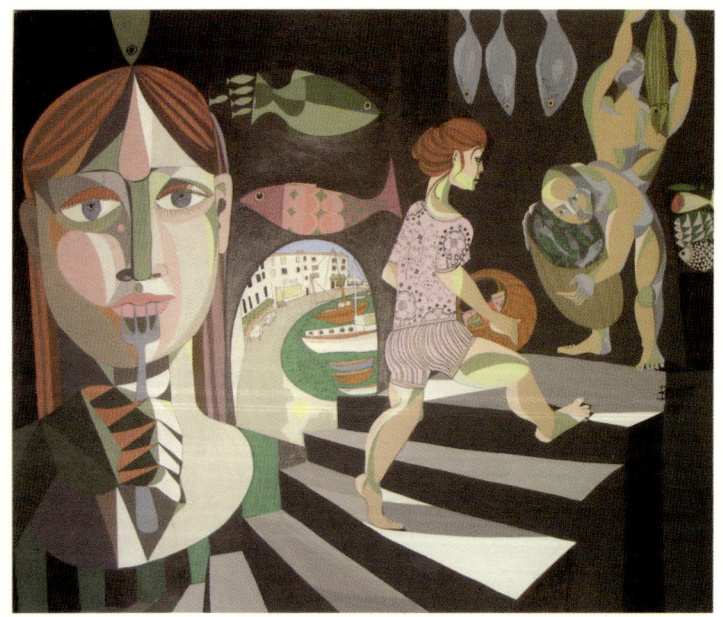

FISHING PORT
1966 • poster colour and ink • 21" x 25"
Waterford Collection

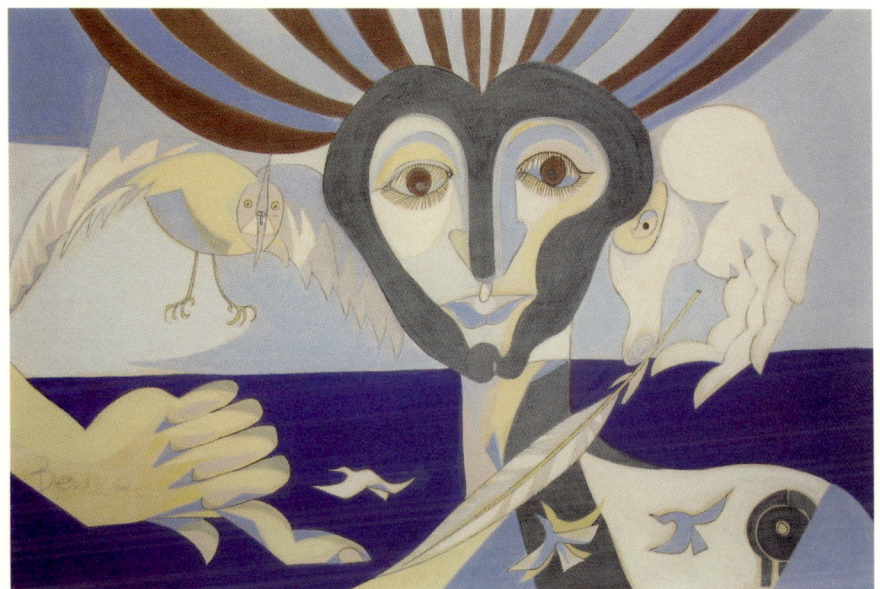

GOD
1966 • poster colour and ink • 14" x 21"
Waterford Collection

What I imagined God would look like, if he existed.

Poppy was our first born.

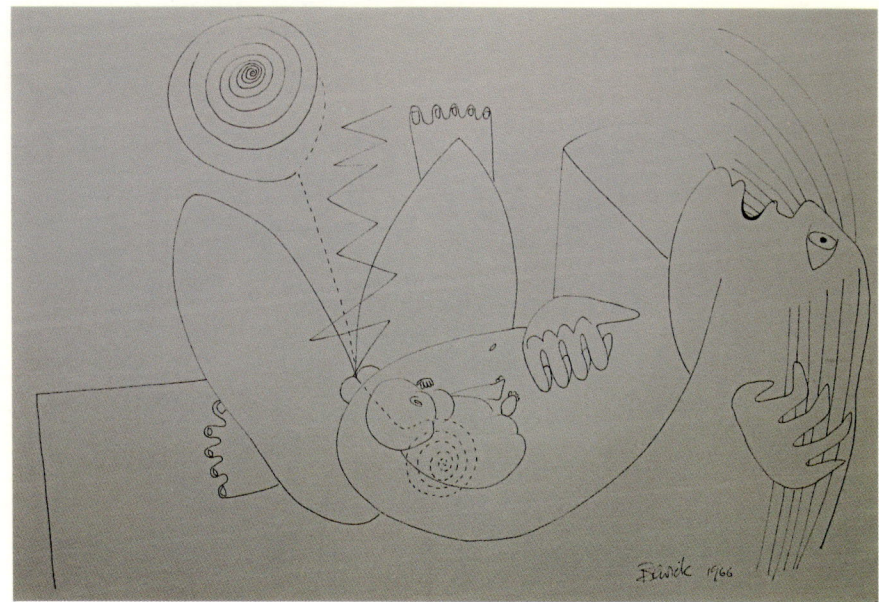

IN LABOUR
1966 • ink • 15" x 22"
Waterford Collection

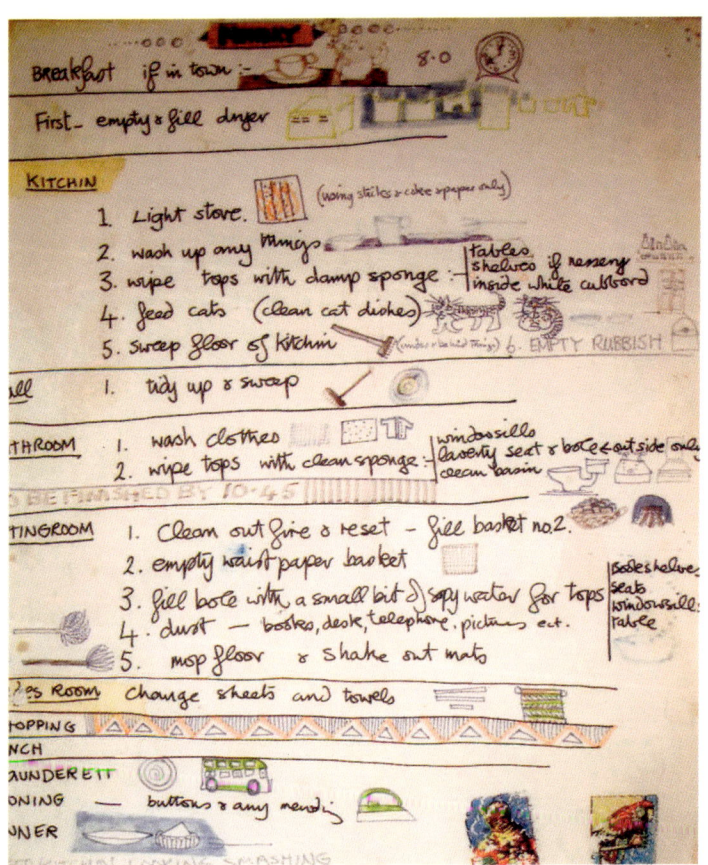

MADGE'S WEEK'S WORK I: MONDAY
1966 • ink • 12" x 10"
Travelling Collection

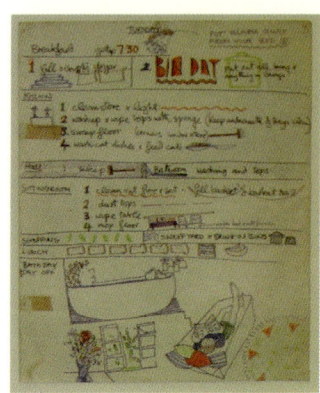

MADGE'S WEEK'S WORK II: TUESDAY
1966 • ink • 12" x 10"
Travelling Collection

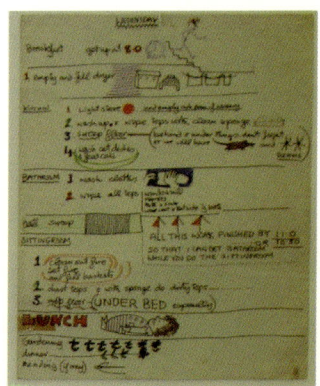

MADGE'S WEEK'S WORK III: WEDNESDAY
1966 • ink • 13" x 10"
Travelling Collection

We employed Madge from Laragh. She was only 16. She had a lovely relaxed nature to be around children.

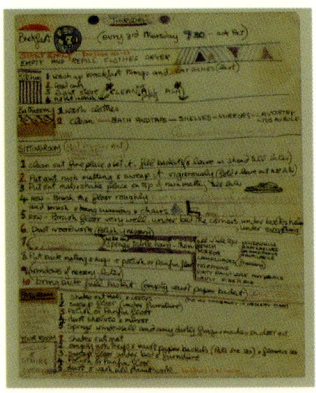

MADGE'S WEEK'S WORK IV: THURSDAY
1966 • ink • 13" x 10"
Travelling Collection

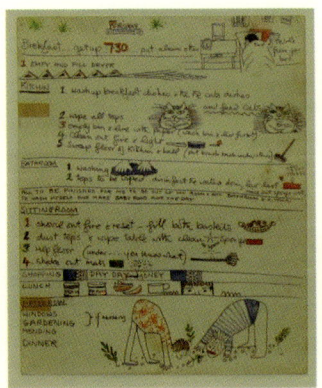

MADGE'S WEEK'S WORK V: FRIDAY
1966 • ink • 13" x 10"
Travelling Collection

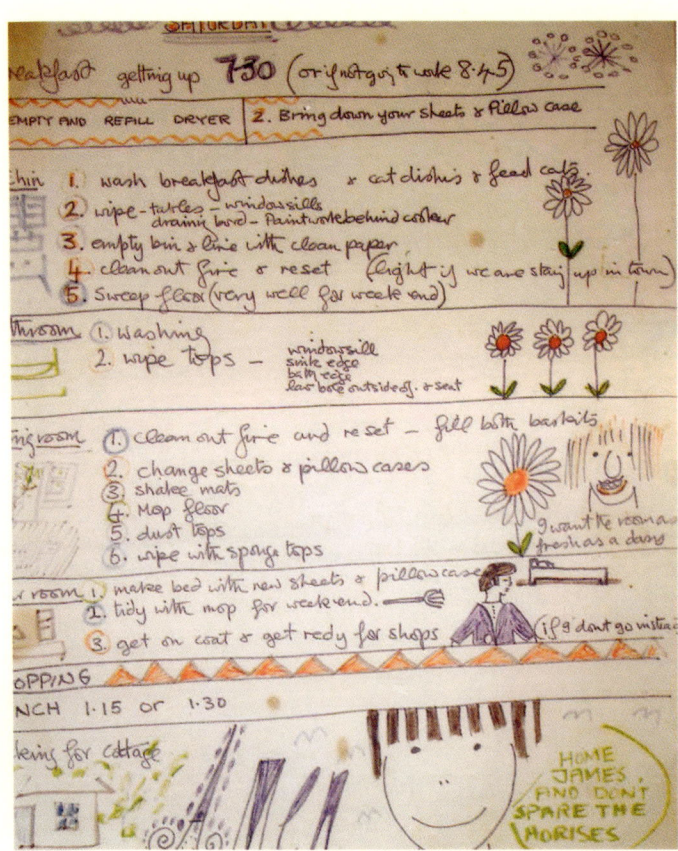

MADGE'S WEEK'S WORK VI: SATURDAY
1966 • ink • 12" x 10"
Travelling Collection

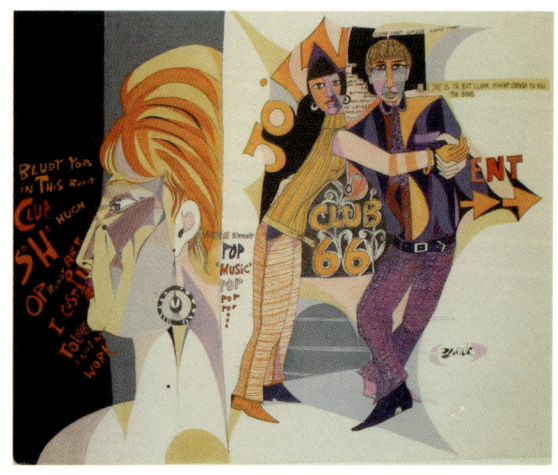

NIGHT CLUB
1966 • poster colour and ink • 19" x 24"
Travelling Collection

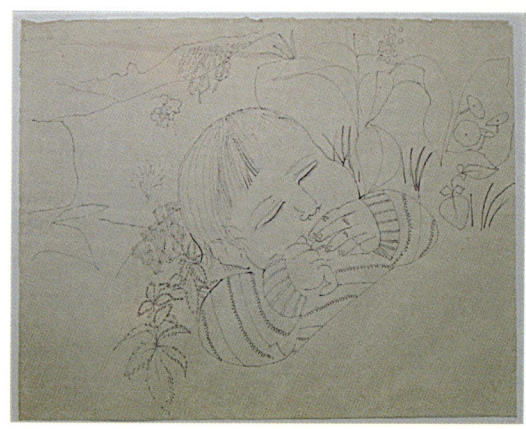

POPPY
1966 • ink • 14" x 18"
Travelling Collection

I loved Poppy. The small world of the baby and the family became my big world.
No longer concerned about atom bombs.
A sty in Poppy's eye became a problem vaster than any bomb.

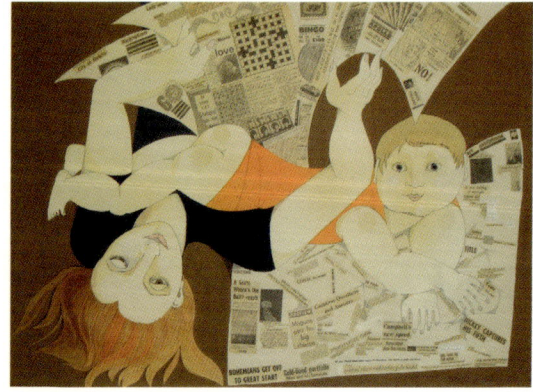

READING REVIEWS
1966 • poster colour and ink collage • 27" x 37"
Waterford Collection

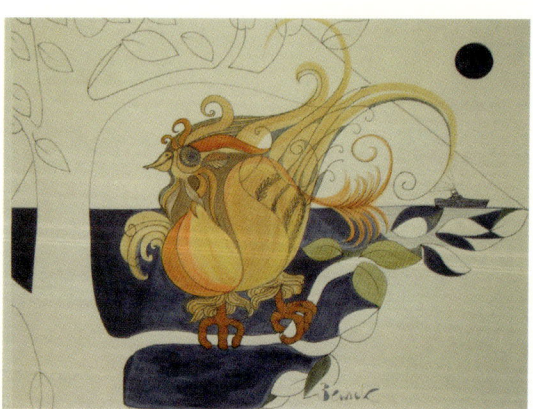

STRANGE BIRD
1966 • ink • 17" x 22"
Travelling Collection

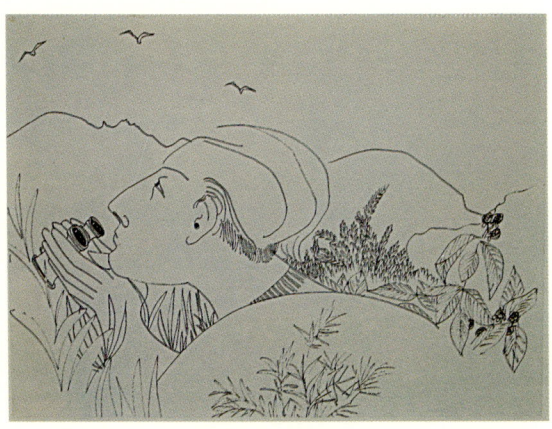

BIRD WATCHING
1967 • ink • 17" x 22"
Kerry Collection

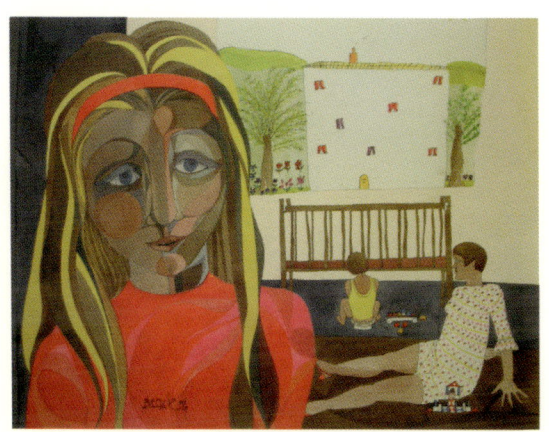

TRINIE WITH HER PICTURE
1967 • ink • 22" x 30"
Kerry Collection

Trinie was one of Chilita's daughters.

Pat ate sheep's balls in Paris.

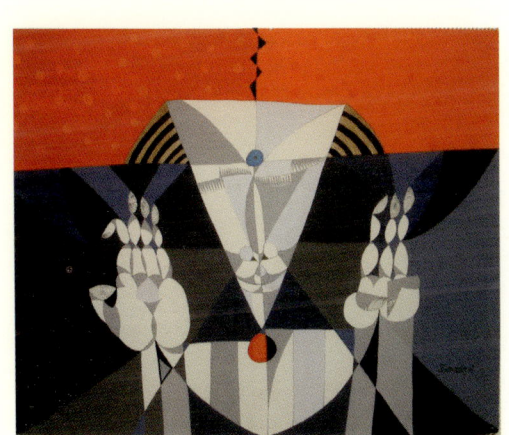

MIDDLE EYE
1967 • poster colour • 19" x 24"
Kerry Collection

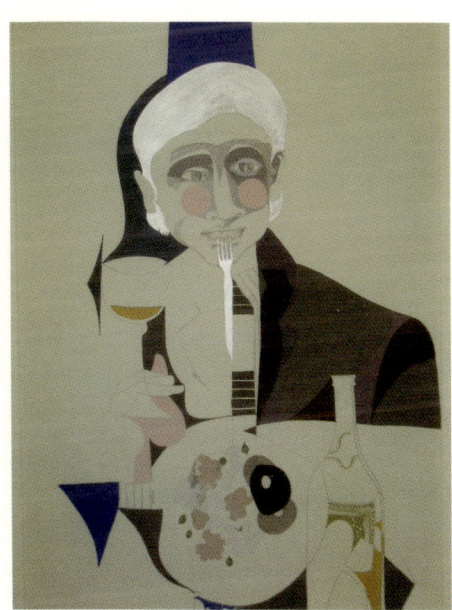

MAN EATING CEREVELLES
1967 • ink • 41" x 28"
Kerry Collection

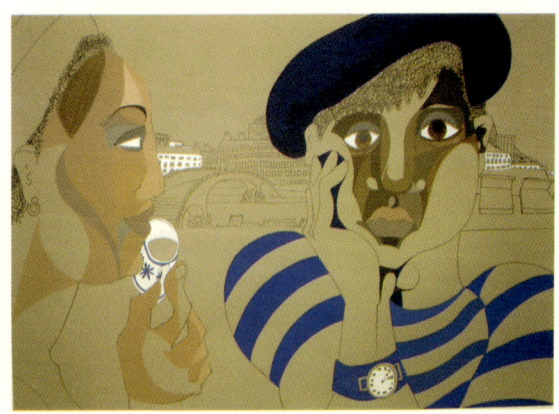

BLACK COUPLE IN PARIS
1967 • poster colour and ink • 17" x 23"
Waterford Collection

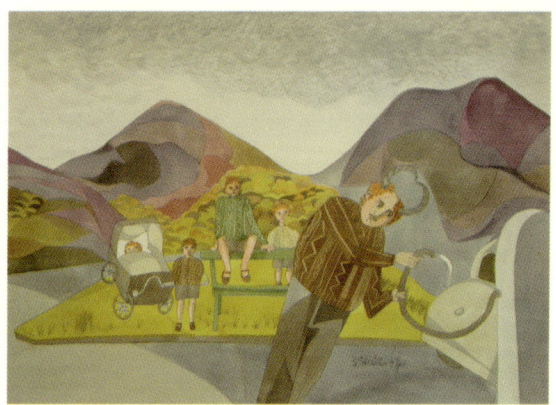

EUGENE AND FAMILY
1967 • ink • 27" x 38"
Travelling Collection

Eugene owned the petrol pumps and shop in Laragh near Harry's glasshouse.
She had endless hippy admirers call on her.

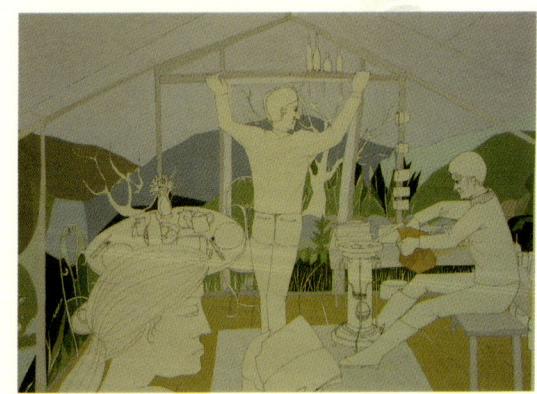

HARRY'S GLASSHOUSE
1967 • poster colour and ink • 22" x 30"
Waterford Collection

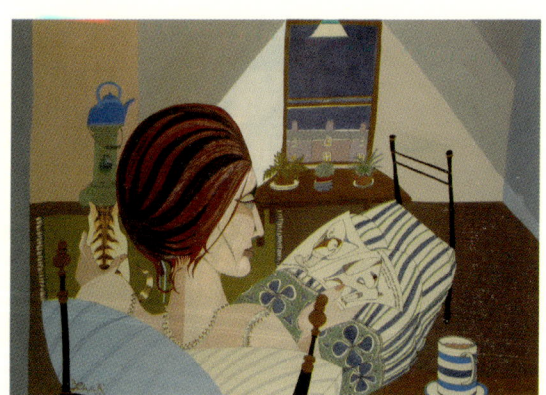

JENNY
1967 • poster colour • 32" x 44"
Waterford Collection

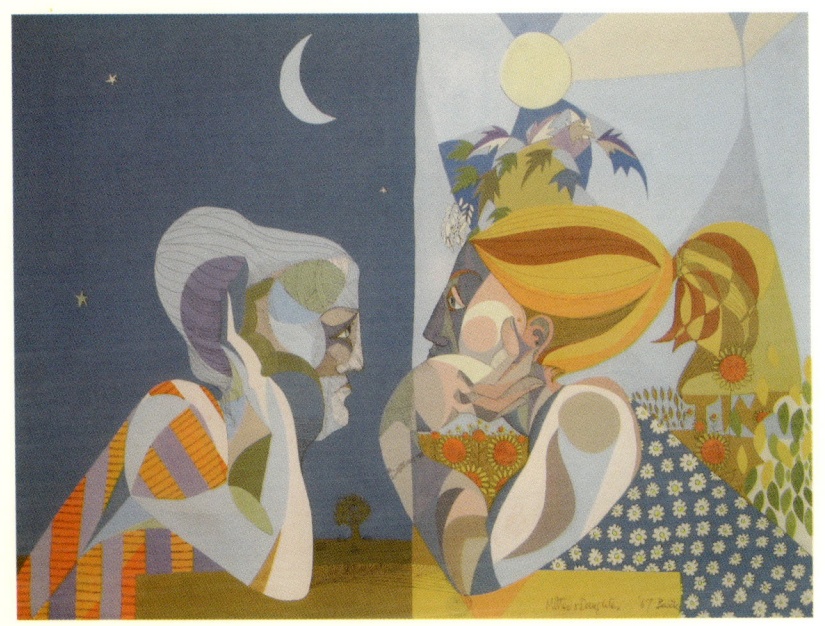

MOTHER AND DAUGHTER
1967 • poster colour • 22" x 30"
Travelling Collection

Harry and I disagreeing. Pat and I having babies
threw Harry into a strange mood. 'I'll take Pauline
[Poppy] and bring her up in Laragh where she'll get
good country air. You're only thinking of yourself
keeping her in Dublin'. I had become an adult, and
adults were her least favourite people.

Pat wouldn't read to me.

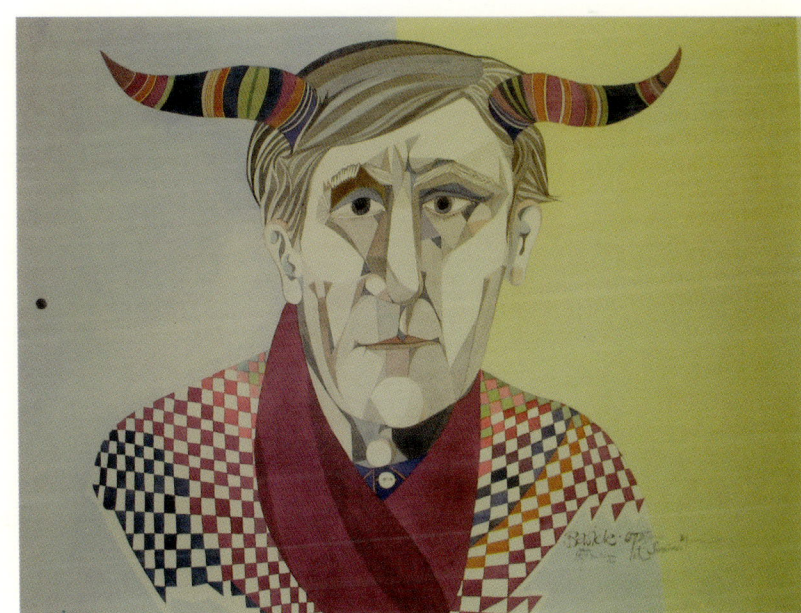

PAT WITH HORNS
1967 • ink • 22" x 30"
Travelling Collection

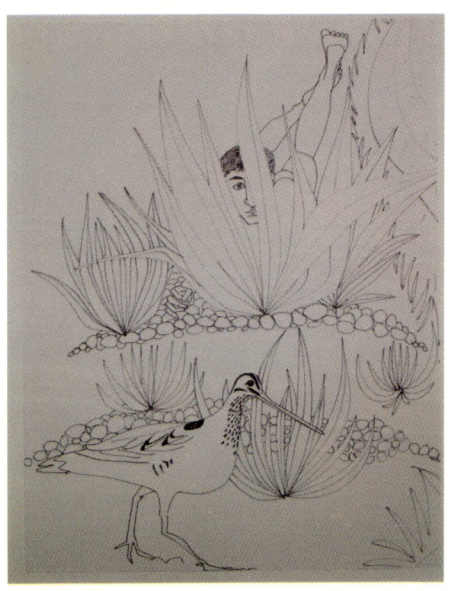

MAN SPOTTING SNIPE
1967 • ink • 18" x 14"
Waterford Collection

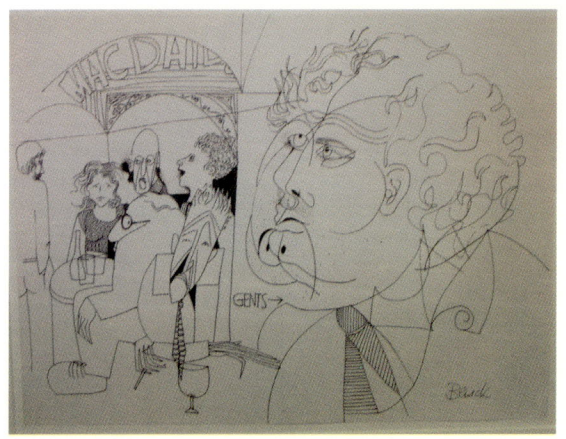

McDAID'S
1967 • ink • 17" x 23"
Travelling Collection

Patrick Kavanagh, Tony Cronin, Leland Bardwell and many other writers and artists
all met in McDaid's for uproarious conversations.

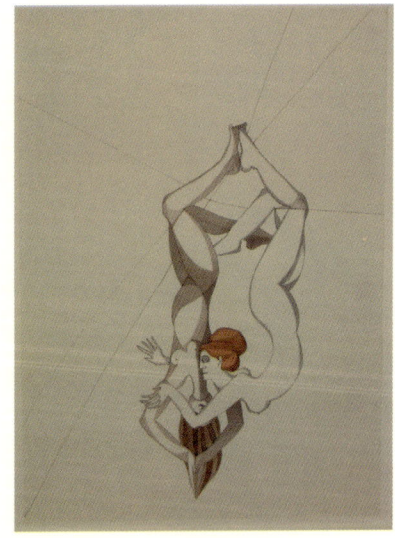

ACROBATS
1968 • ink • 22" x 16"
Kerry Collection

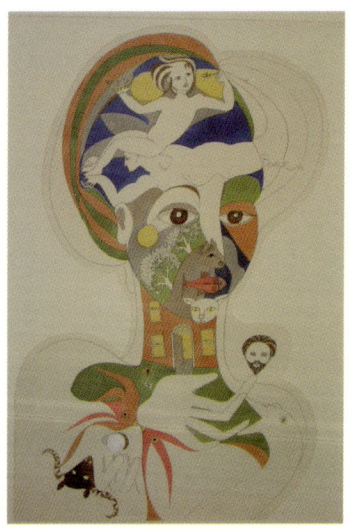

BITS OF LIFE
1968 • ink • 39" x 25"
Kerry Collection

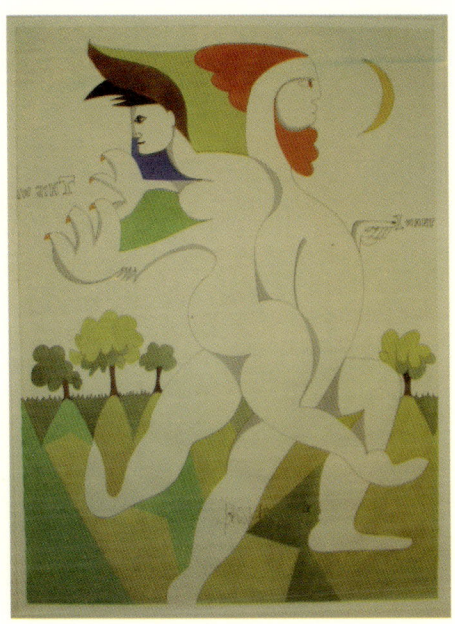

I WANT THIS
1968 • ink • 30" x 22"
Kerry Collection

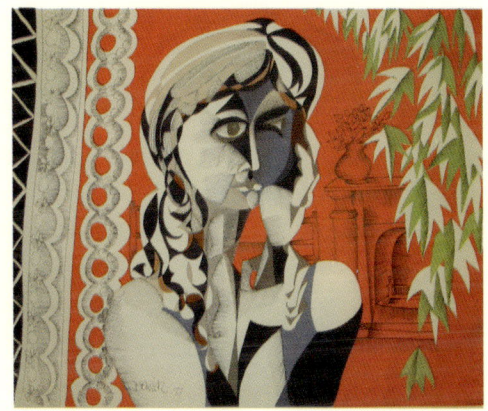

LOOKING OUT, THINKING IN
1967 • poster colour and ink • 19 " x 24"
Kerry Collection

Alex Zadkovski, a Russian artist lived in Zurich. He influenced the very heavy lead pencil drawings I did. He sent me a bundle of pencils from Zurich.

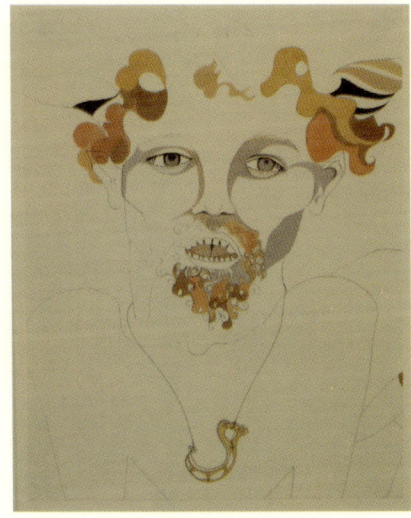

LUKE
1968 • ink • 18" x 14"
Kerry Collection

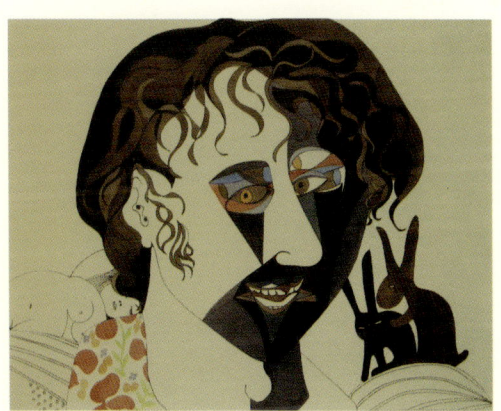

ALEX
1968 • ink • 14" x 18"
Waterford Collection

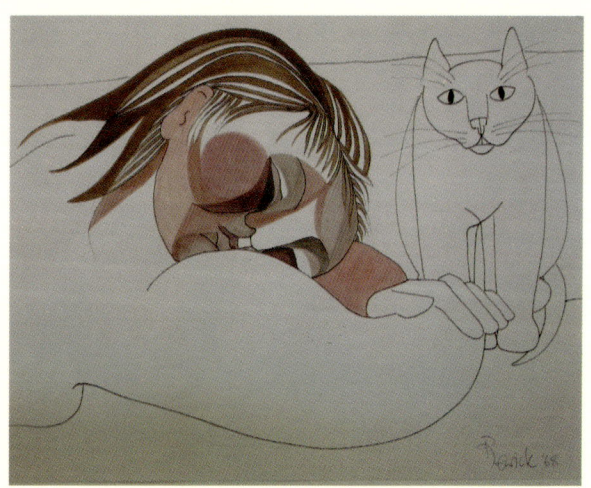

ASLEEP WITH THE CAT
1968 • ink • 14" x 18"
Travelling Collection

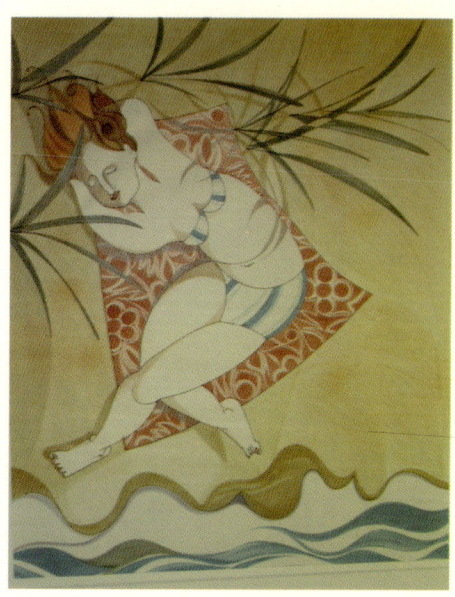

ASLEEP BY THE SEA
1968 • ink • 20" x 25"
Waterford Collection

Rainer singed Luke Kelly's hair. It was impossible to cut with scissors.

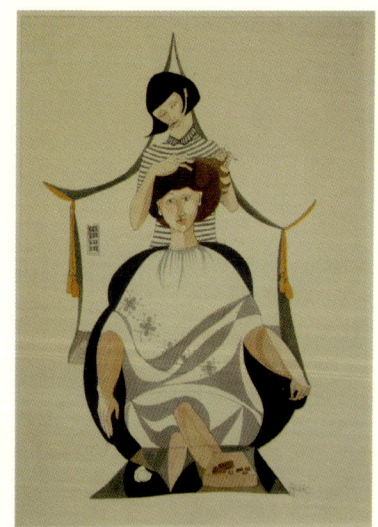

RAINER'S HAIRDRESSING SALON
1968 • ink • 39" x 28"
Waterford Collection

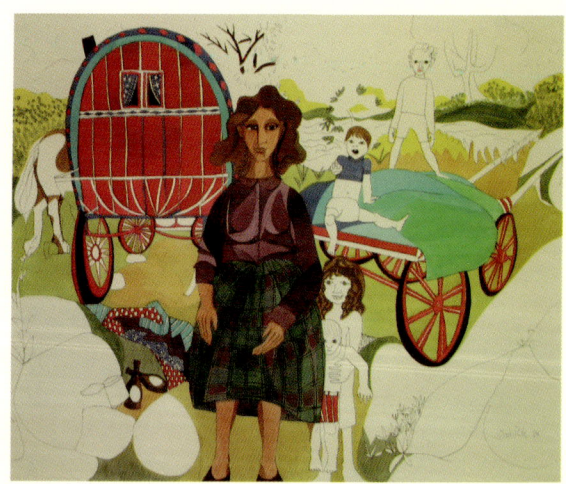

THE CARAVAN WE BOUGHT
1968 • ink • 20" x 25"
Waterford Collection

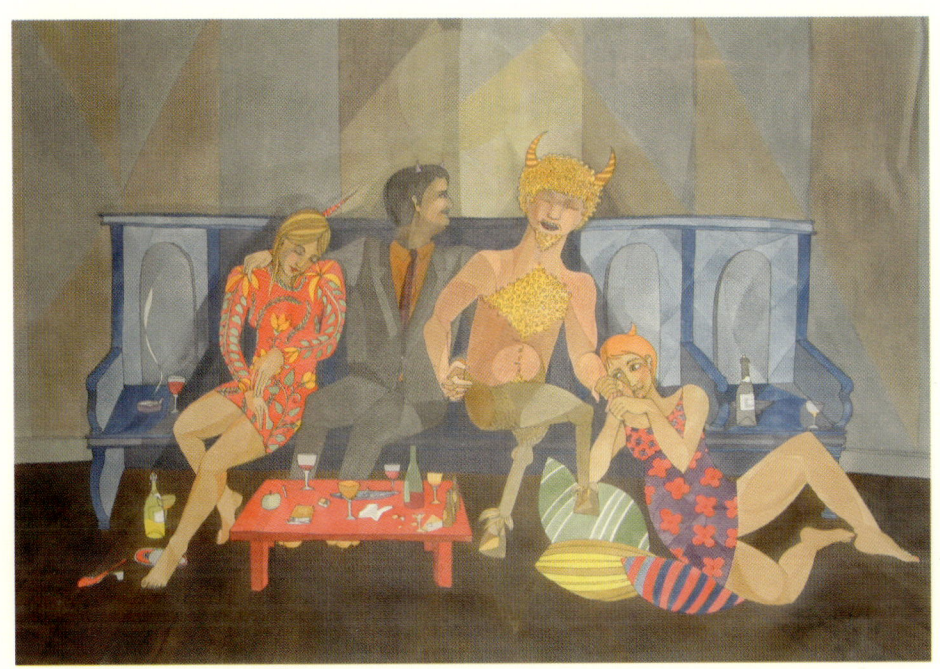

HEYTESBURY LANE PARTY
1968 • watercolour and ink • 28" x 42"
Travelling Collection

Sean Mac Reamoinn, Jenny and I
listening to Luke singing Raglan Road.

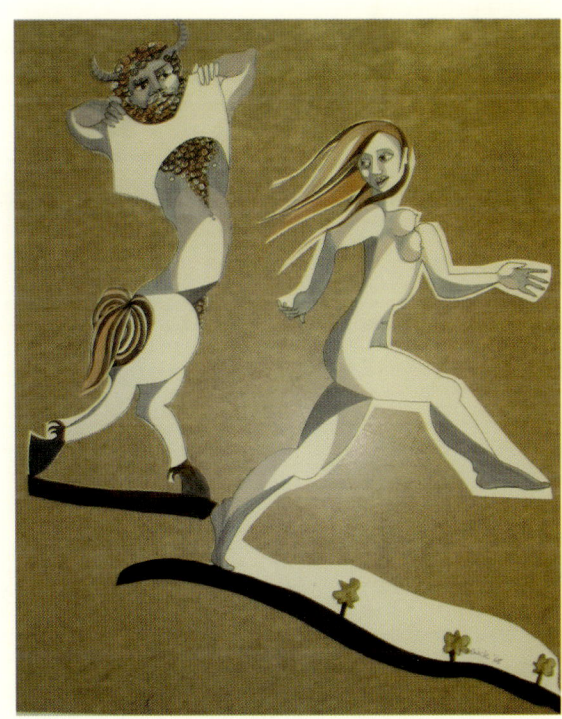

THE CHASE
1968 • ink • 25" x 20"
Travelling Collection

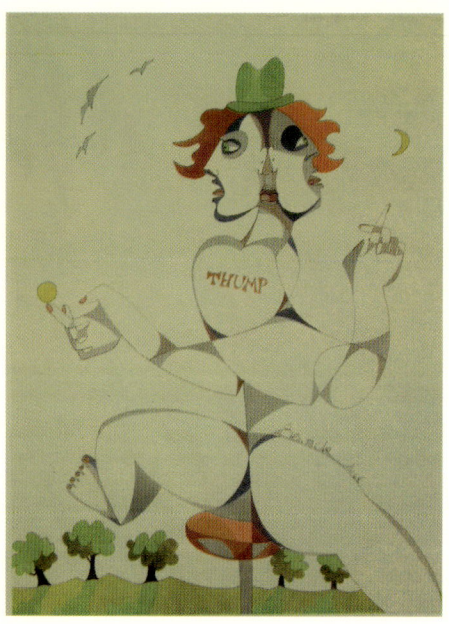

THUMP MAN
1968 • ink • 30" x 22"
Travelling Collection

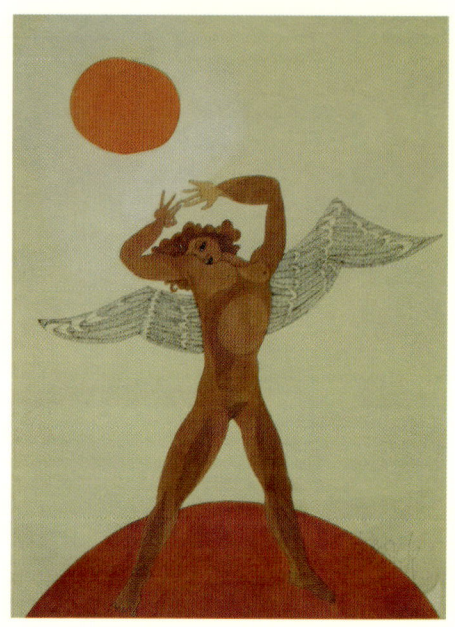

WOMAN ON THE WORLD
1968 • ink • 30" x 22"
Travelling Collection

The dilemma about which way to go …

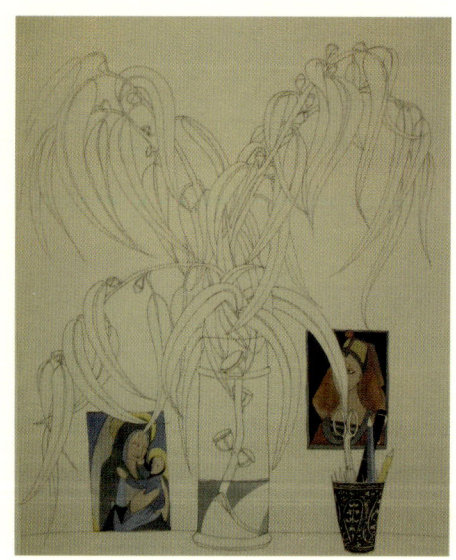

EUCALYPTUS LEAVES
1969 • ink • 25" x 20"
Kerry Collection

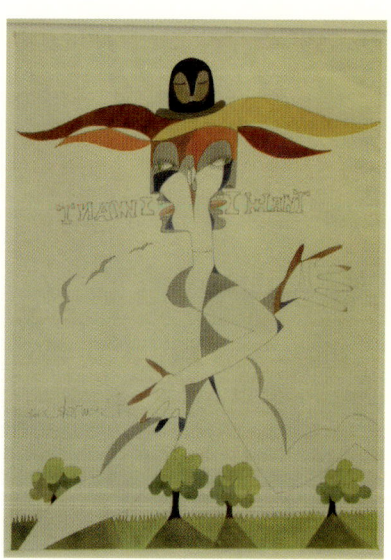

I WANT, I WANT
1968 • ink • 30" x 22"
Waterford Collection

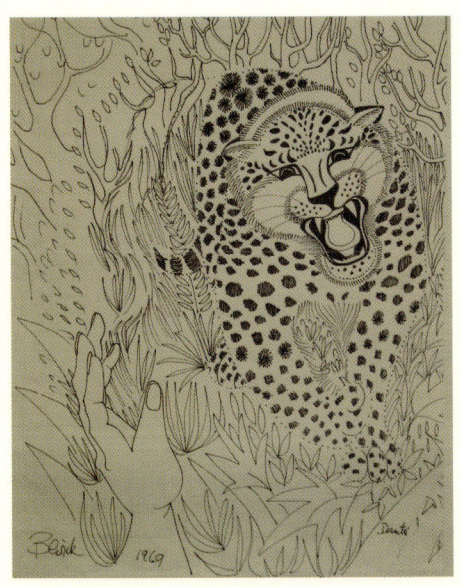

DANTE
1969 • ink • 18" x 14"
Kerry Collection

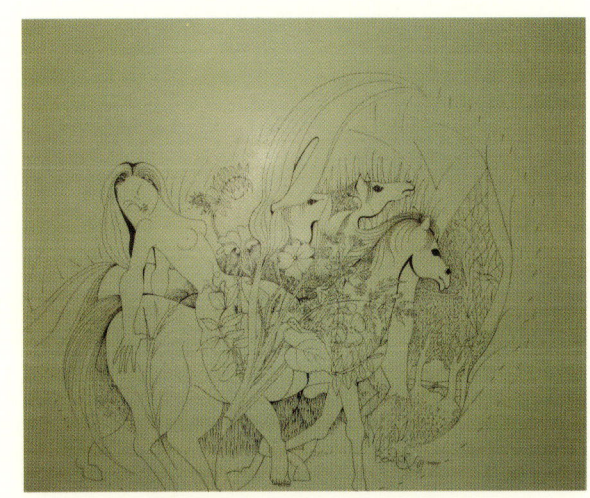

RIDING THROUGH WILD FLOWERS
1969 • ink • 20" x 25"
Kerry Collection

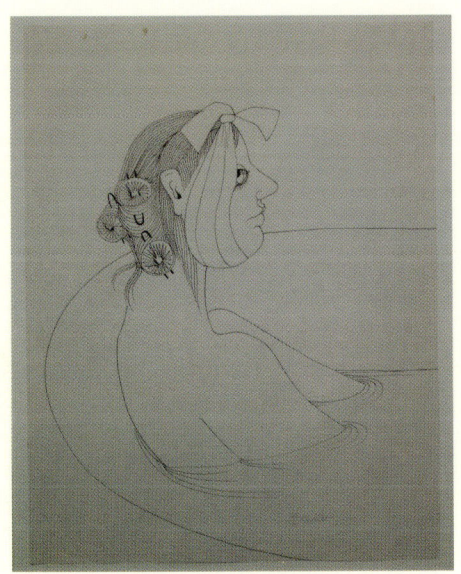

BEAUTY TREATMENT
1969 • ink • 18" x 14"
Travelling Collection

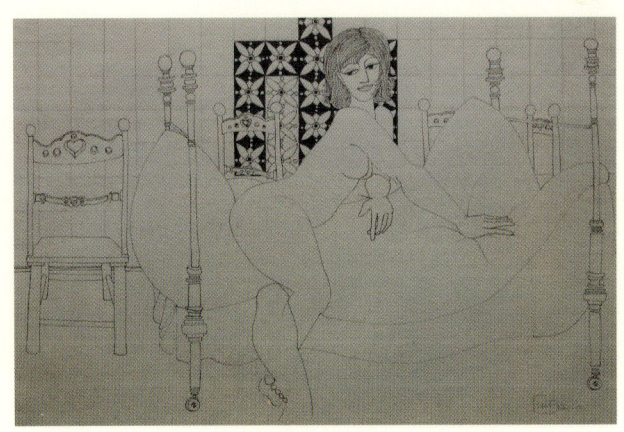

HAPPY GIRL
1969 • ink • 12" x 18"
Waterford Collection

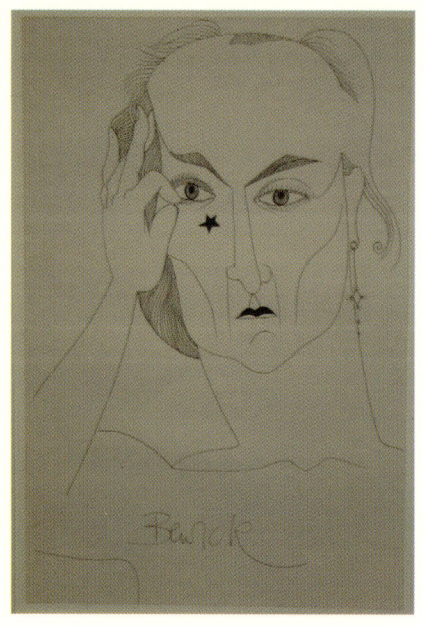

GAY BOY I
1969 • ink • 22" x 14"
Kerry Collection

Mr Pussy imitated Mae West, Elizabeth Taylor and other glamorous women. 'Is that a bottle in your pocket or are you glad to see me?'

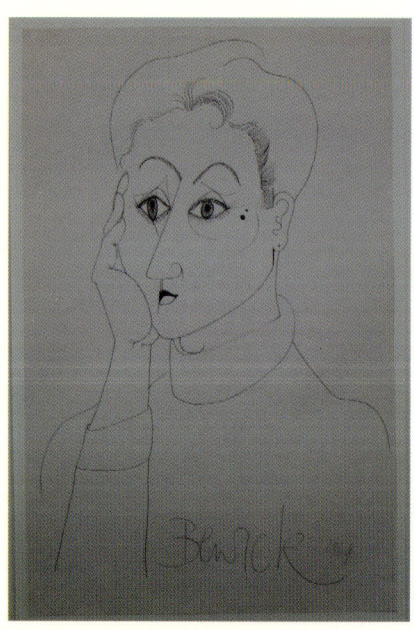

GAY BOY II
1969 • ink • 22" x 14"
Waterford Collection

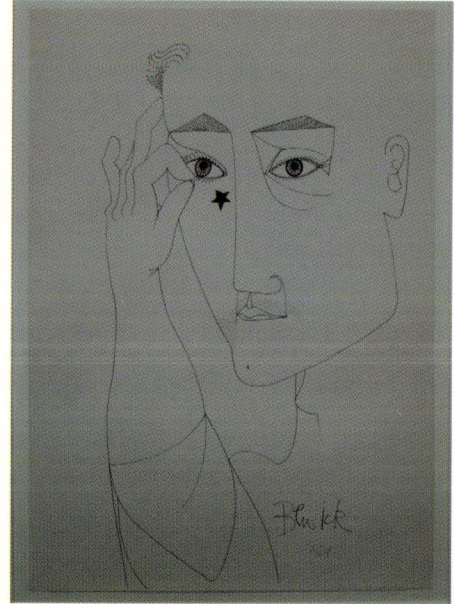

MAKEUP MAN
1969 • ink • 21" x 15"
Travelling Collection

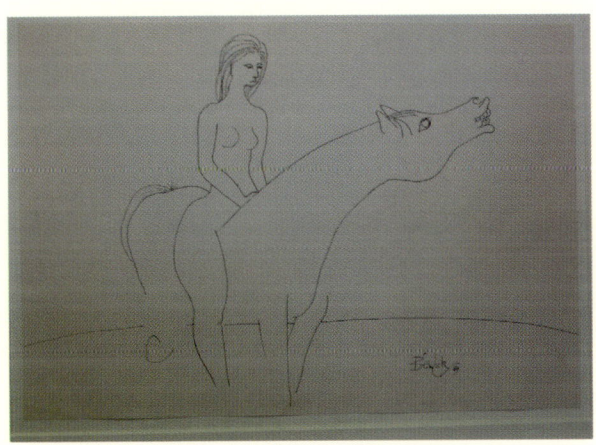

HORSE RIDER
1969 • ink • 15" x 22"
Travelling Collection

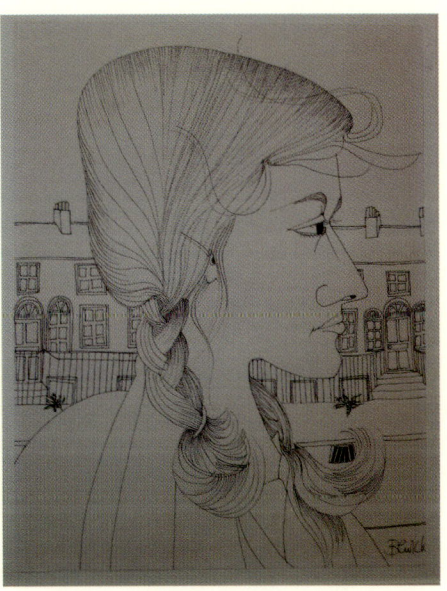

WILHEMENA
1969 • ink • 18" x 14"
Waterford Collection

A visiting Dutch tourist.

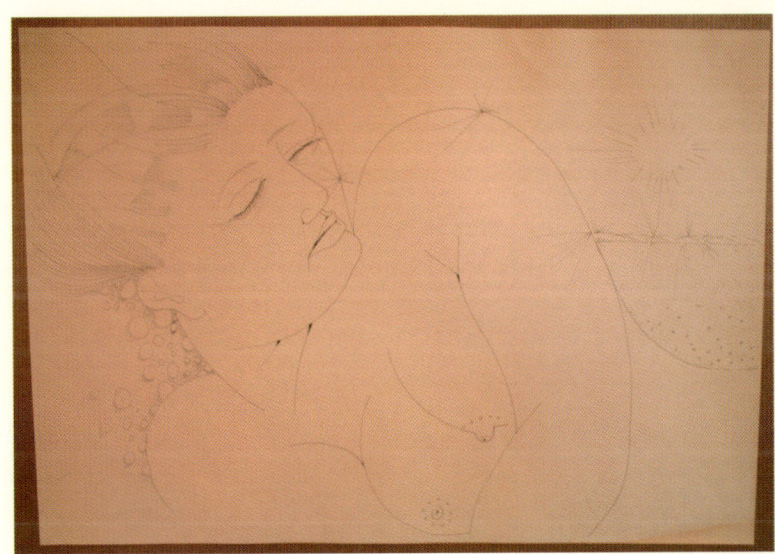

MORNING SUN
1970 • pencil • 15" x 22"
Kerry Collection

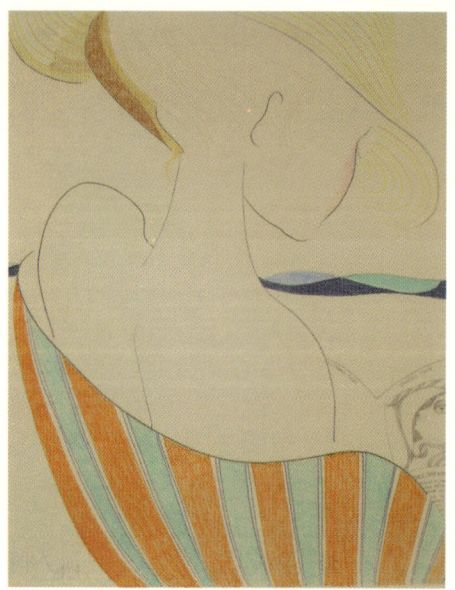

READING IN A HAT
1969 • pencil • 25" x 20"
Waterford Collection

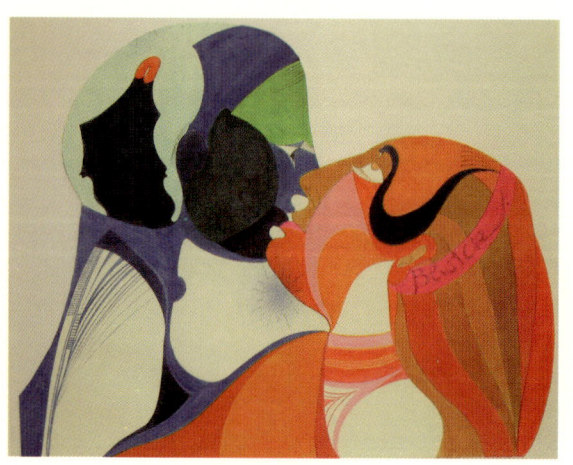

THE KISS
1969 • ink • 20" x 25"
Travelling Collection

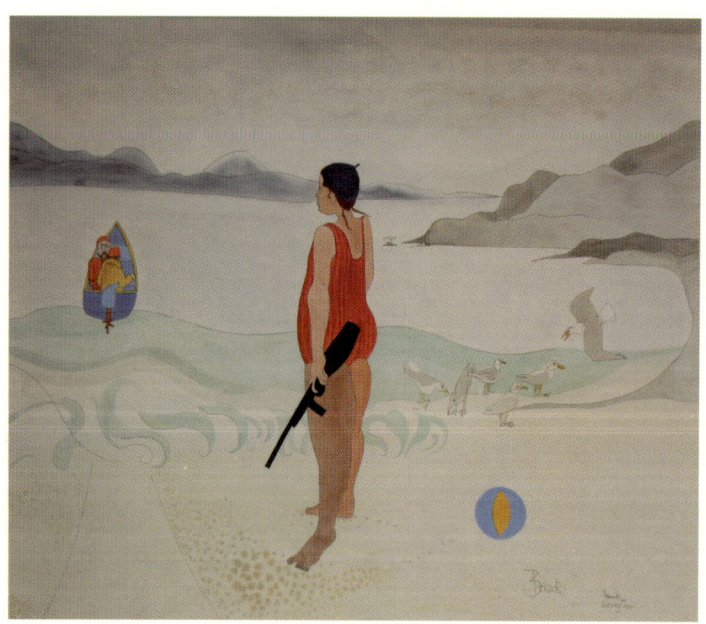

THREE TOURISTS IN KERRY
1970 • watercolour • 27" x 36"
Kerry Collection

Shocking to see in such a beautiful setting this girl playing gun games.

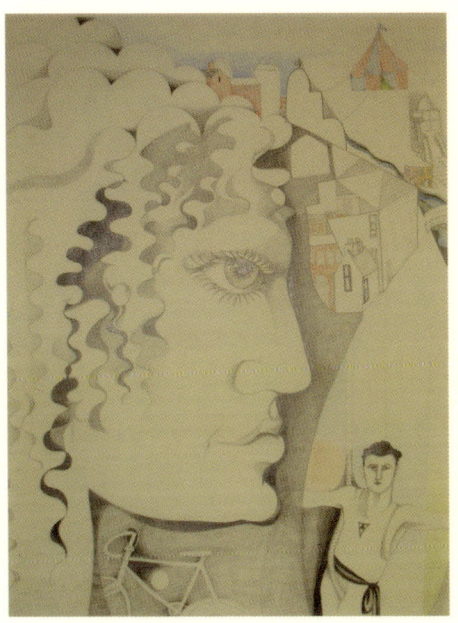

CIRCUS IN CORK
1970 • pencil • 35" x 26"
Travelling Collection

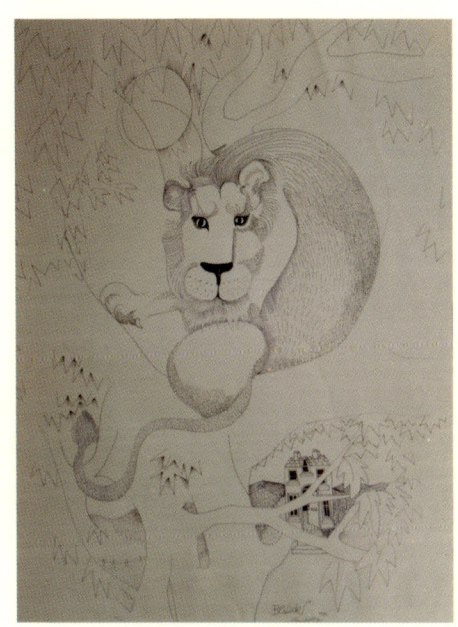

LION IN KERRY
1970 • ink • 30" x 22"
Kerry Collection

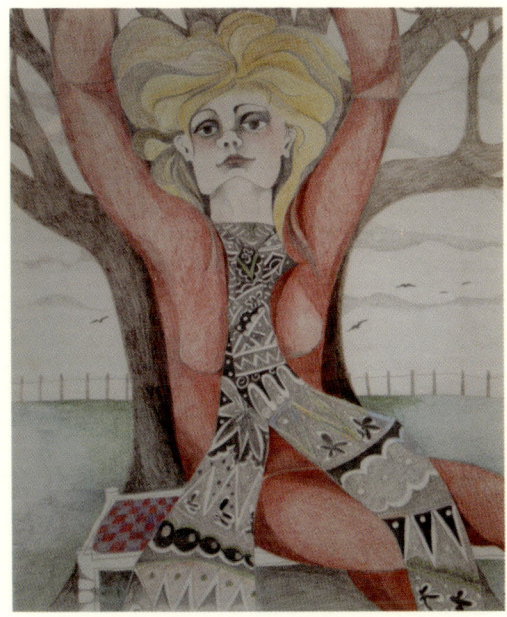

GIRL IN VELVET SUIT
1970 • coloured pencil • 25" x 20"
Kerry Collection

Leo Smyth said it was like being with a pink elephant. I wore this outfit when we visited Sybil Connolly, dress designer. He loved to pull one down.

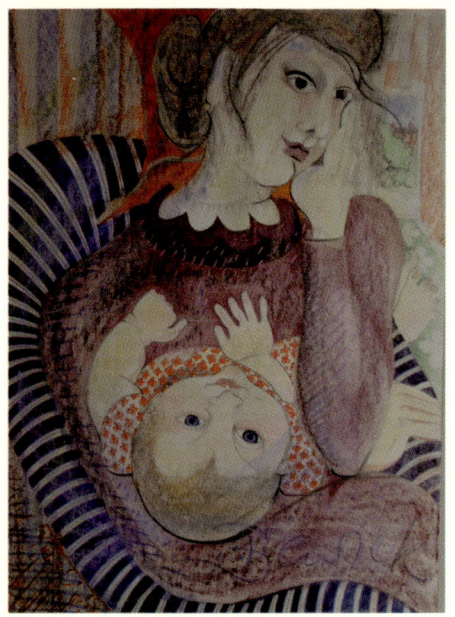

MOTHER AND CHILD
1971 • crayon • 30" x 22"
Kerry Collection

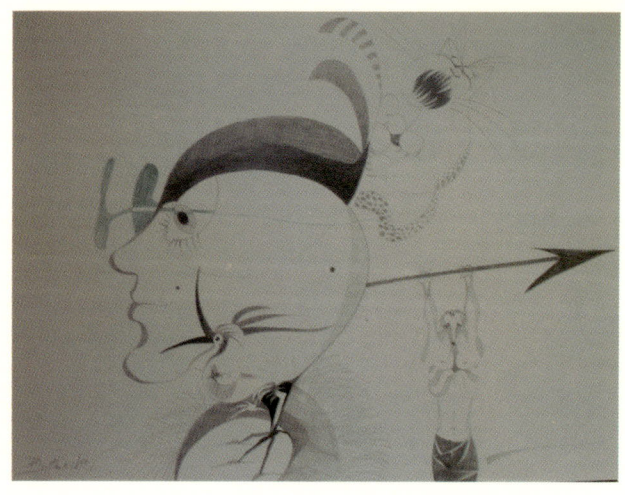

PORTRAIT OF HER THOUGHTS
1970 • pencil • 27" x 37"
Kerry Collection

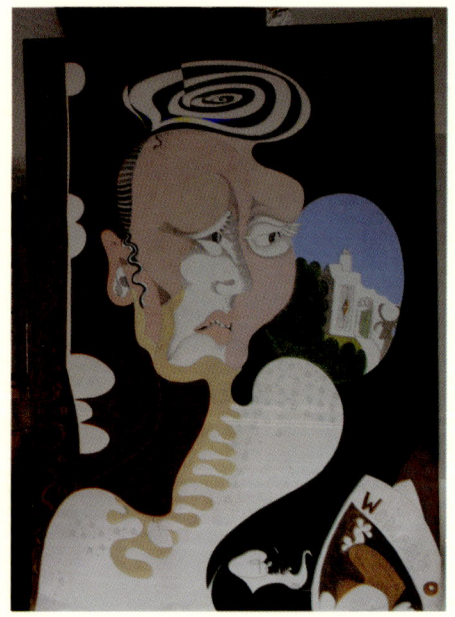

READING WOMAN'S OWN
1970 • acrylic and pencil • 44" x 32"
Kerry Collection

The thoughts of Leslie McWeeney.

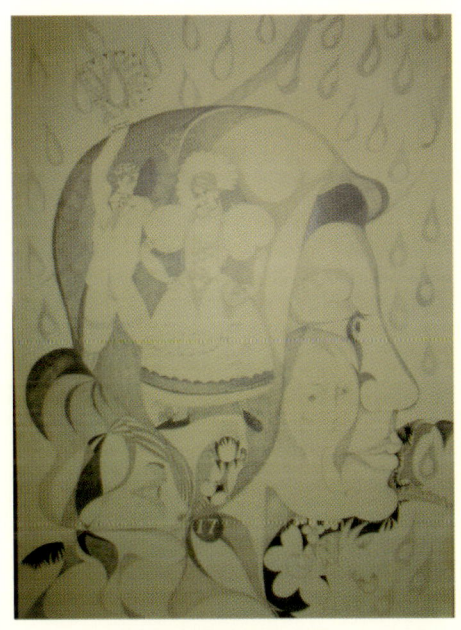

THE WEDDING
1970 • pencil • 44" x 32"
Waterford Collection

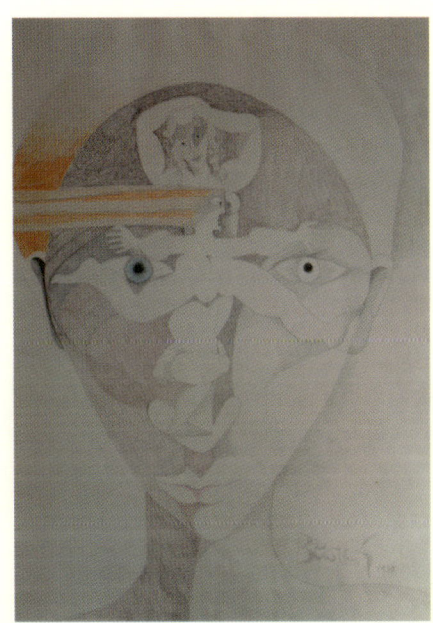

TO RUN AWAY?
1970 • pencil • 30" x 22"
Kerry Collection

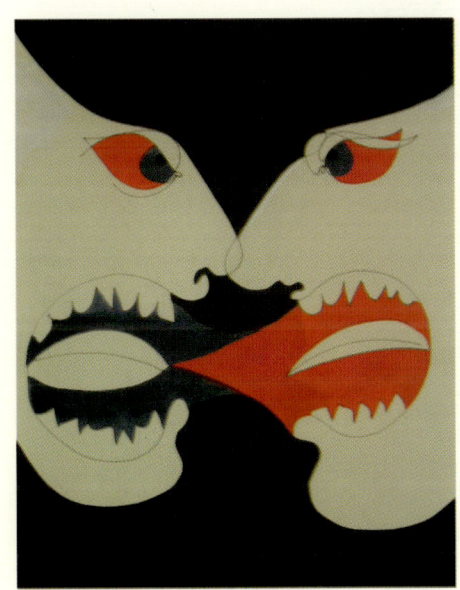

ARGUMENT
1970 • ink • 18" x 14"
Waterford Collection

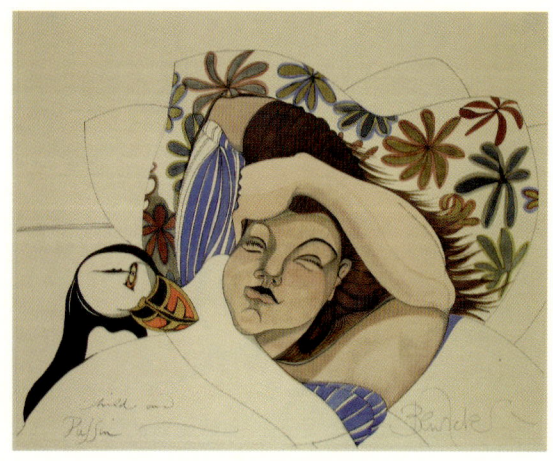

CHILD AND PUFFIN
1970 • watercolour • 21" x 25"
Travelling Collection

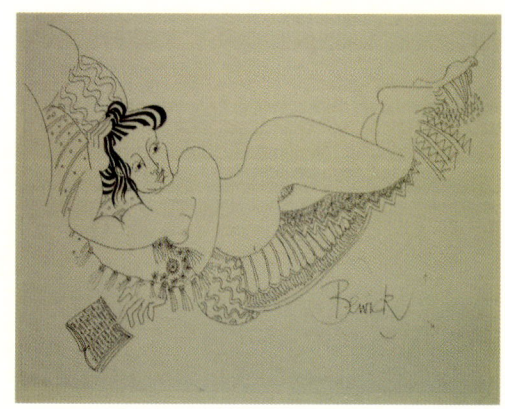

CONTENTED READER
1970 • pencils • 14" x 18"
Travelling Collection

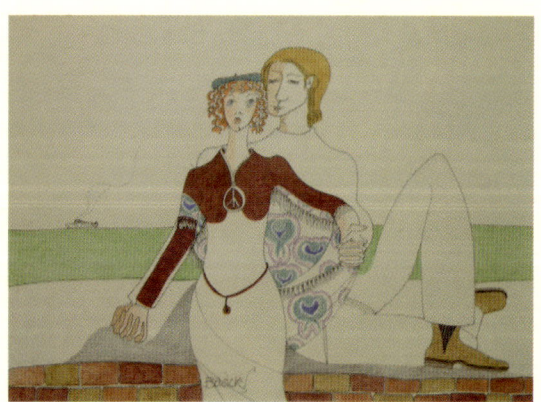

COUPLE BY THE SEA
1970 • pencils • 17" x 23"
Waterford Collection

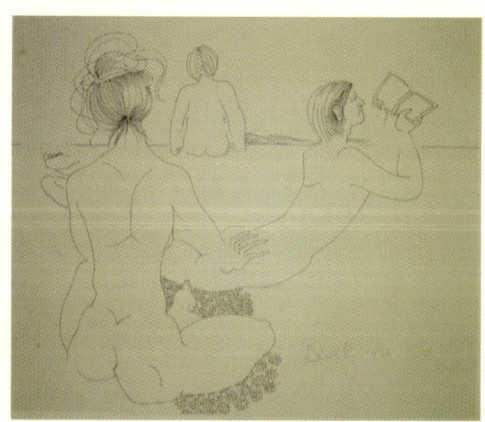

FAMILY BY THE SEA
1970 • ink • 21" x 25"
Waterford Collection

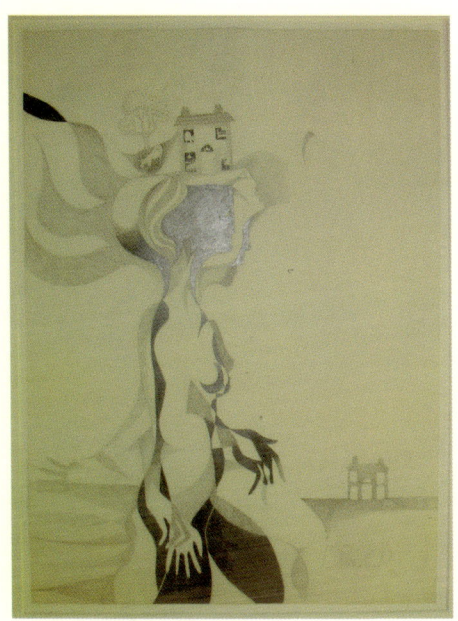

GOING HOME
1970 • pencil • 30" x 22"
Waterford Collection

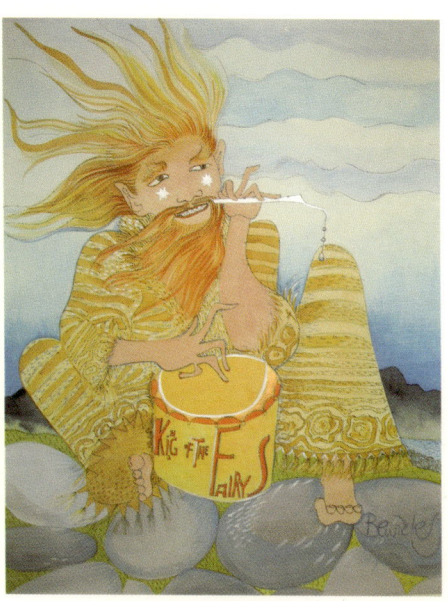

KING OF THE FAIRIES
1970 • watercolour • 25" x 20"
Travelling Collection

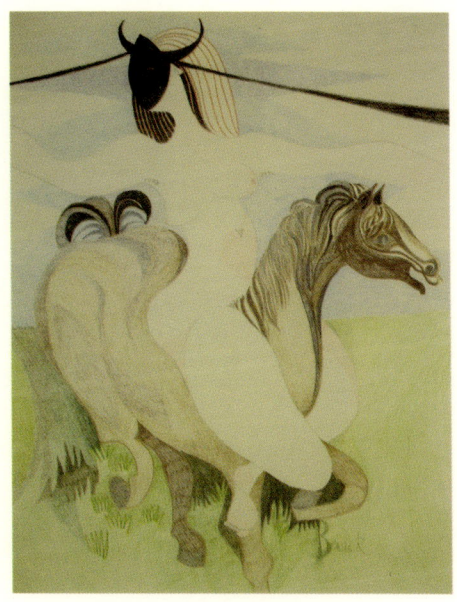

MASKED RIDER
1970 • crayon • 24" x 20"
Waterford Collection

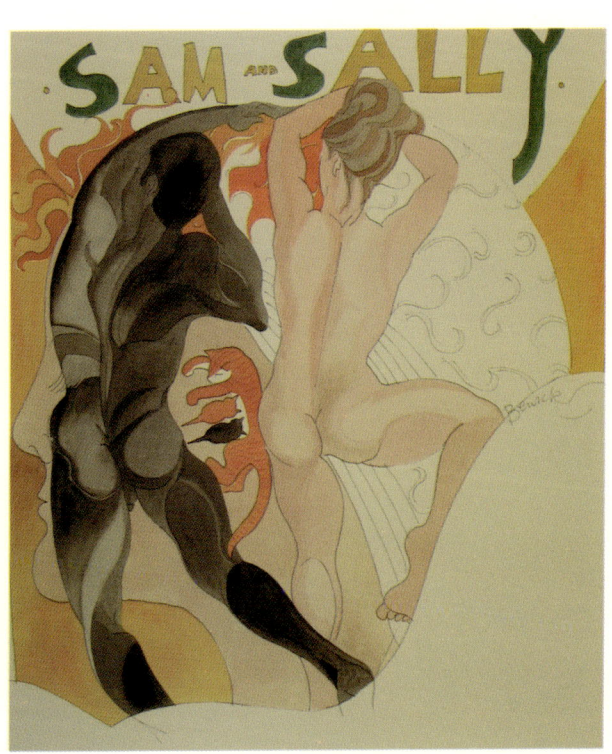

REMEMBERING SAM AND SALLY
1970 • ink • 22" x 19"
Travelling Collection

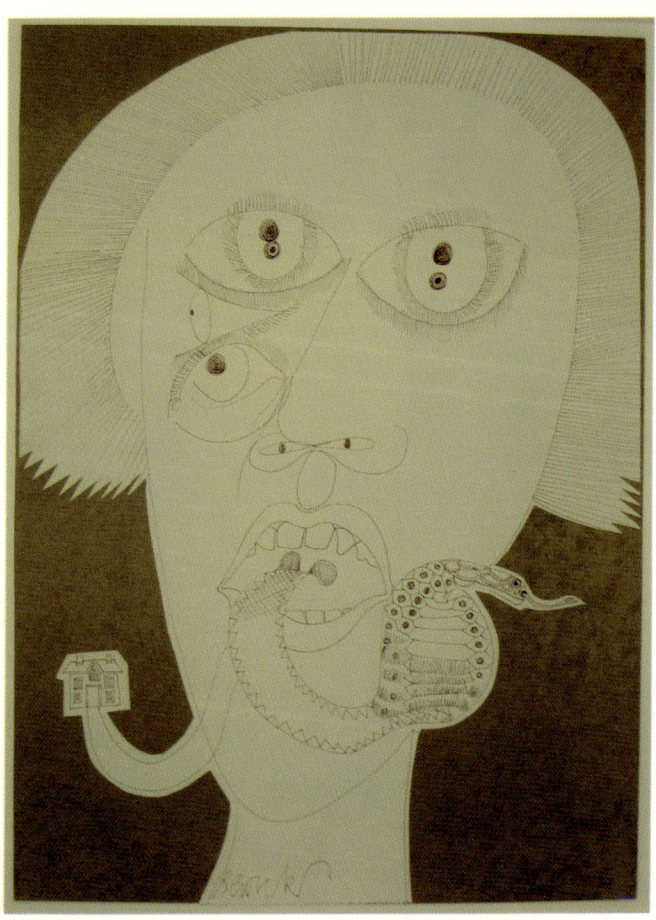

SPEAKING WITH FORKED TONGUE
1970 • ink • 30" x 22"
Travelling Collection

I shared a mews with Sally Travers, Michael Mac Liammoir's niece.
She loved coloured men.
MacLiammoir lay on her *chaise longue* and dramatically stated:
'Visiting here is like a game of chess, with the whites losing'.

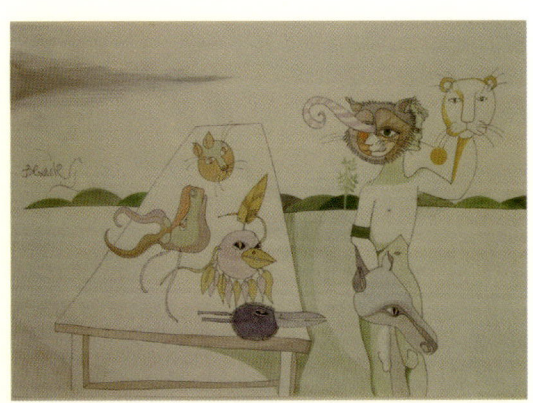

VARIOUS MASKS
1970 • watercolour • 16" x 23"
Travelling Collection

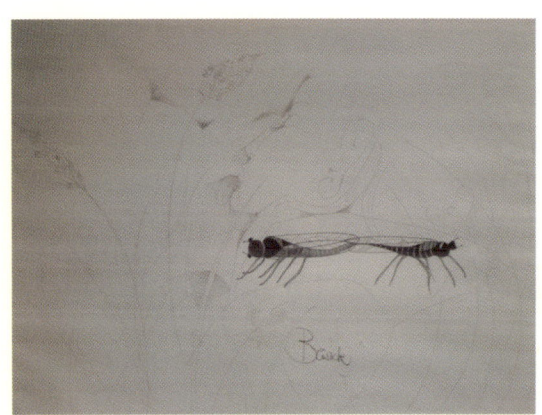

ASLEEP WITH INSECTS
1971 • pencil • 22" x 30"
Kerry Collection

Adorable, selfish suckling babies.

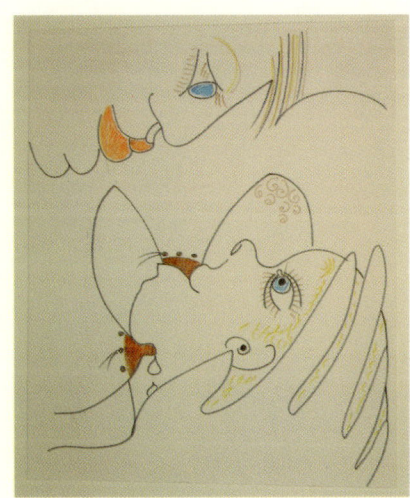

BABY SUCKLING
1971 • marker • 12" x 10"
Travelling Collection

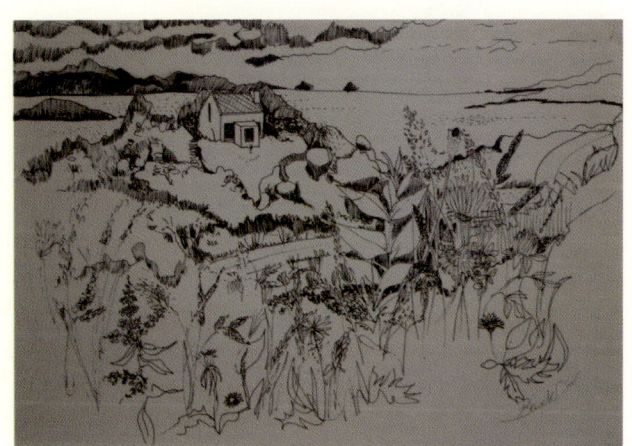

GLEESK, COUNTY KERRY
1971 • ink • 15" x 22"
Kerry Collection

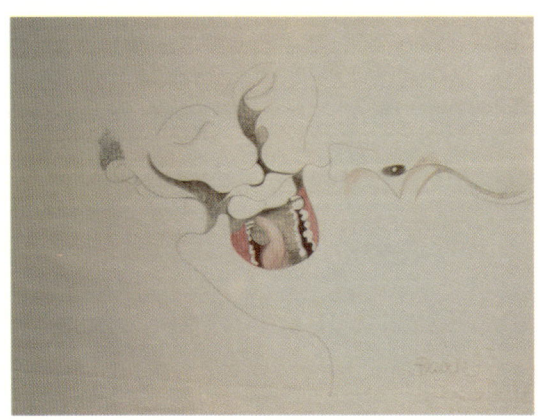

GREED
1971 • pencil • 22" x 30"
Kerry Collection

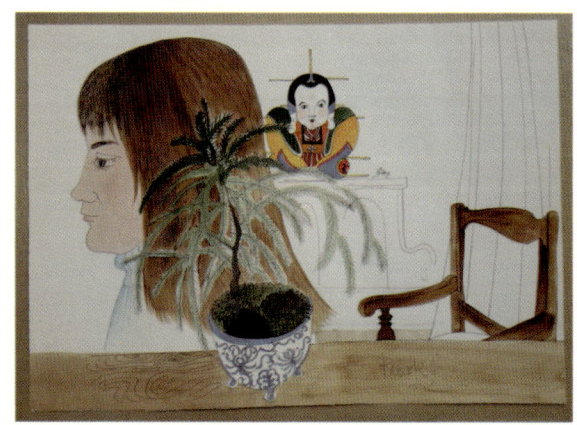

POPPY AND BONSAI
1971 • ink • 15" x 22"
Kerry Collection

Having children and the threat of atom bombs was a constant fear.

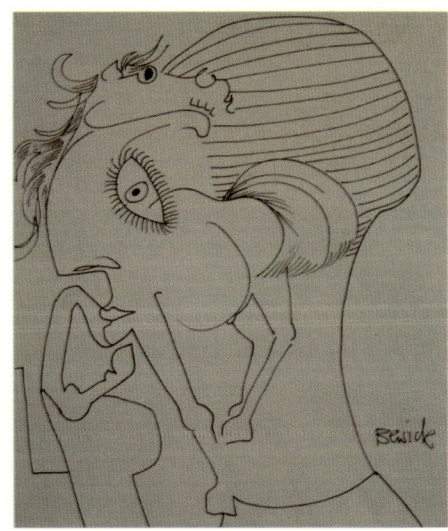

WOMAN AND HORSE
1971 • ink • 12" x 11"
Kerry Collection

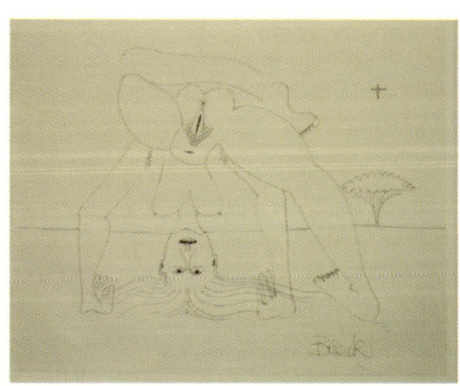

ATOM BOMB
1971 • ink • 15" x 20"
Waterford Collection

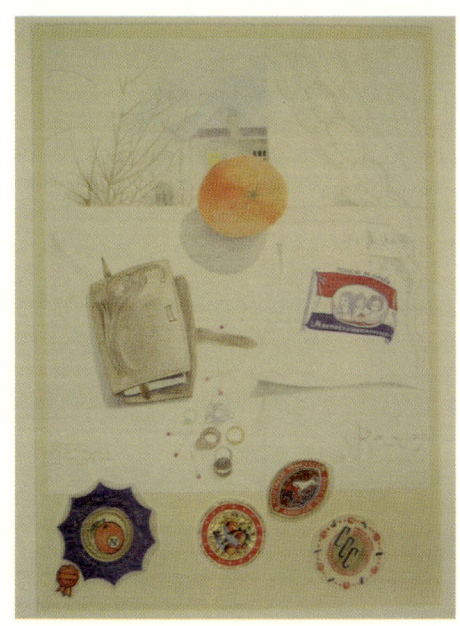

DIARY AND ORANGE
1971 • pencils • 27" x 19"
Waterford Collection

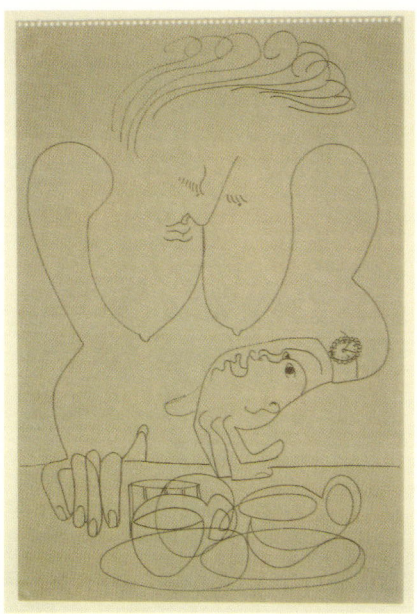

FEEDING TIME
1971 • ink • 18" x 12"
Travelling Collection

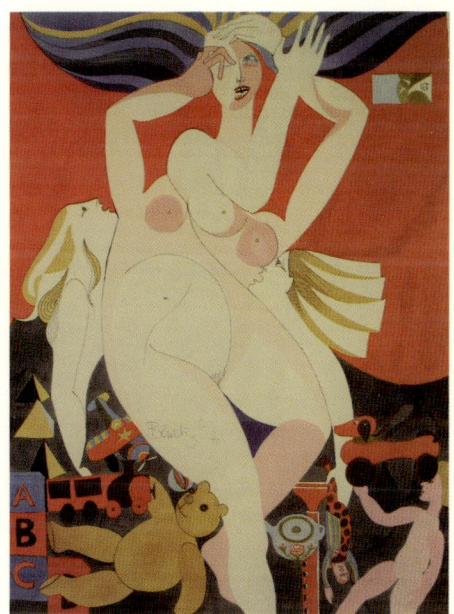

FRUSTRATED MOTHER
1971 • watercolour and ink • 31" x 23"-
Waterford Collection

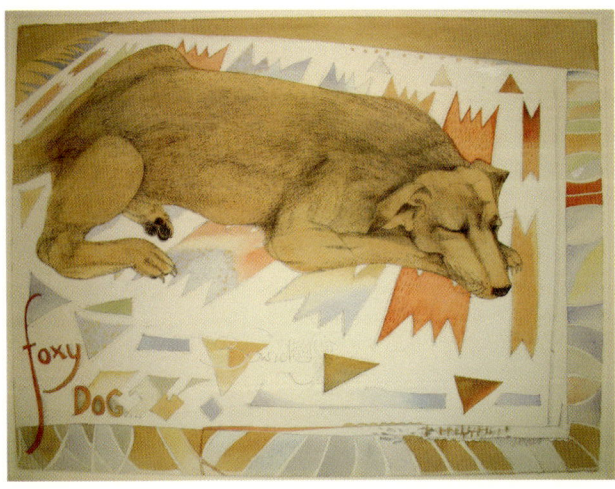

FOXY DOG
1971 • pencils • 23" x 31"
Travelling Collection

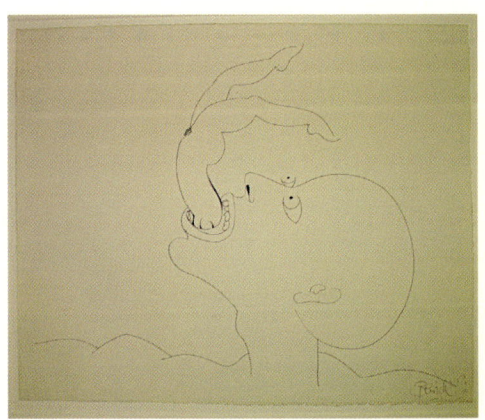

GREEDY FOR LOVE
1971 • ink • 20" x 25"
Travelling Collection

'In a nuclear war, put your head under the sand and mind your babies,
even though you may get my bum blown off!', said Sally.

Foxy joined me while painting in the Demesne, Killarney. He followed me home, so we kept him.

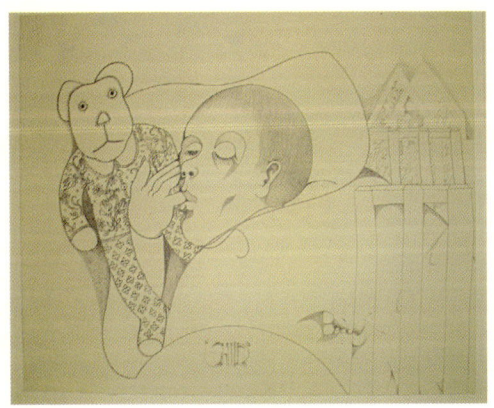

HOLLY AND TEDDY
1971 • pencil • 20" x 25"
Waterford Collection

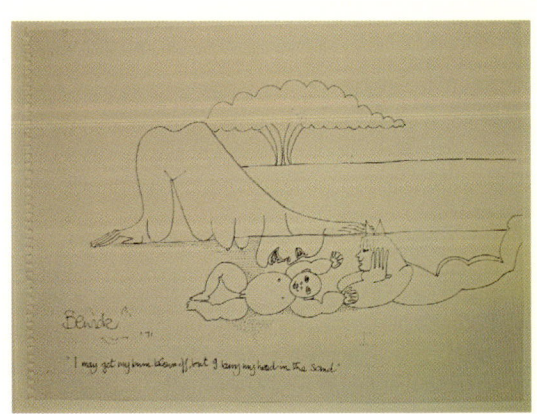

I MAY GET MY BUM BLOWN OFF
1971 • ink • 14" x 20"
Travelling Collection

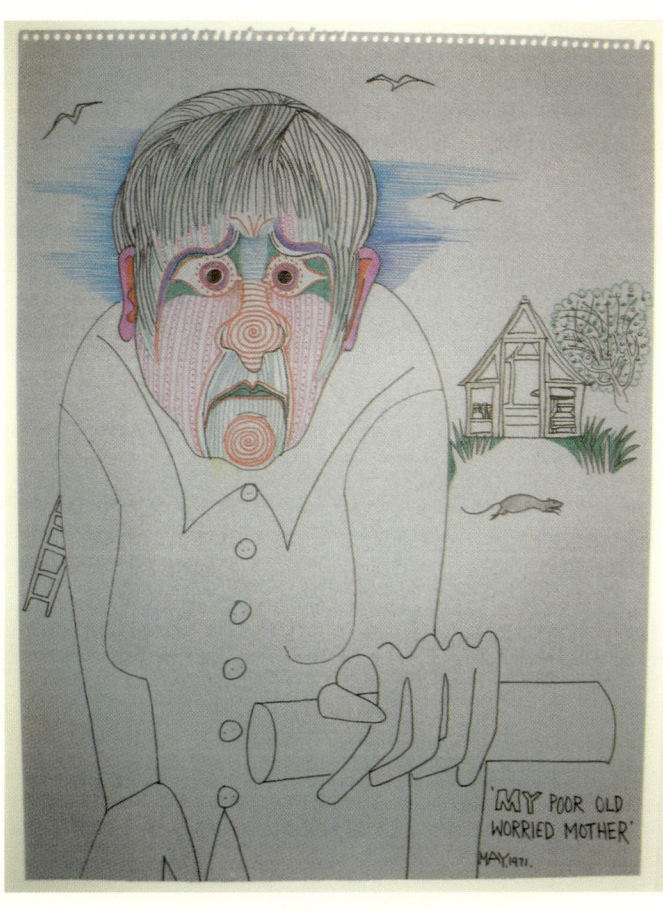

My Poor Old Worried Mother
1971 • marker • 15" x 12"
Travelling Collection

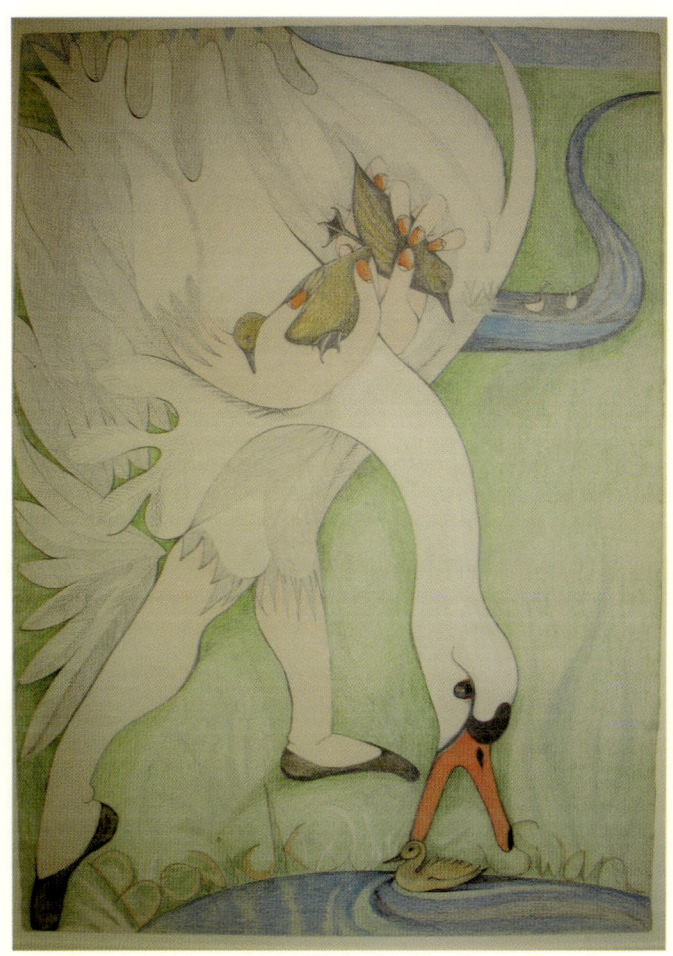

Swan Mother
1971 • pencils • 41" x 23"
Travelling Collection

Harry didn't like to hear us correcting the children.

Swan mother protecting, like all birds and beasts, our young.

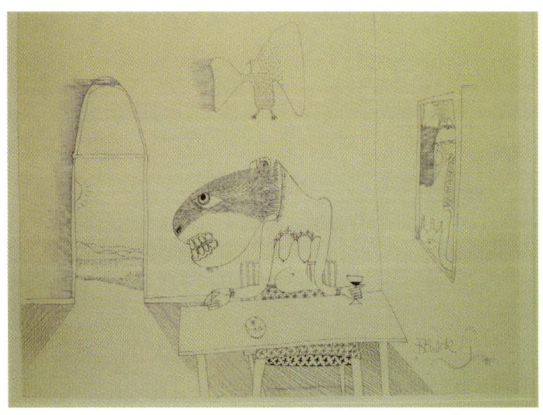

MADAME RAT
1972 • ink • 22" x 30"
Waterford Collection

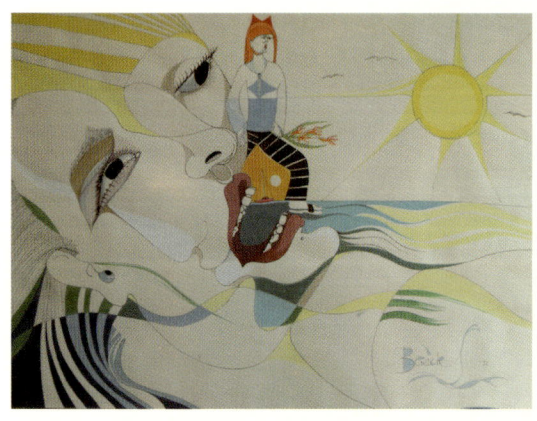

SHE LIVED AT GLEESK
1971 • watercolour • 22" x 30"
Kerry Collection

Holidaying at John Watling's house Gleesk, County Kerry, we watched a red-haired eccentric woman dancing to the sun each day.

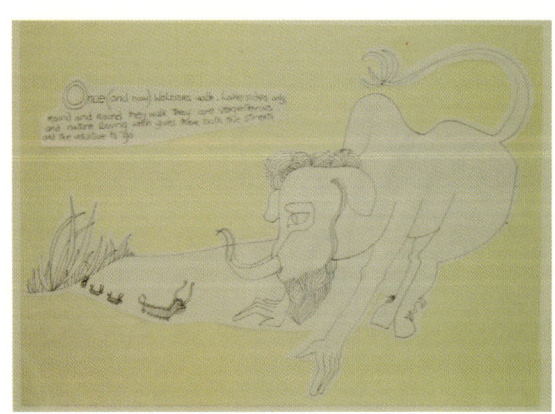

WALTER'S WALK
1971 • ink • 17" x 24"
Travelling Collection

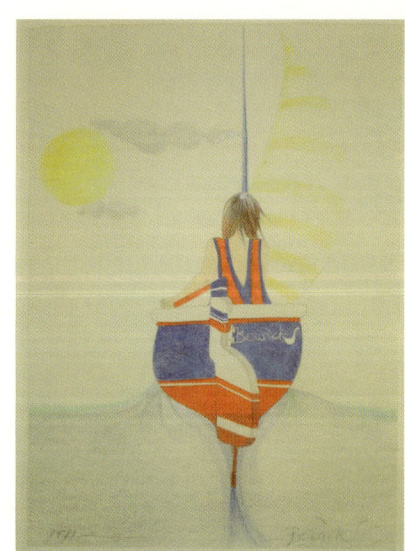

WOMAN AND BOAT
1971 • crayon • 21" x 15"
Waterford Collection

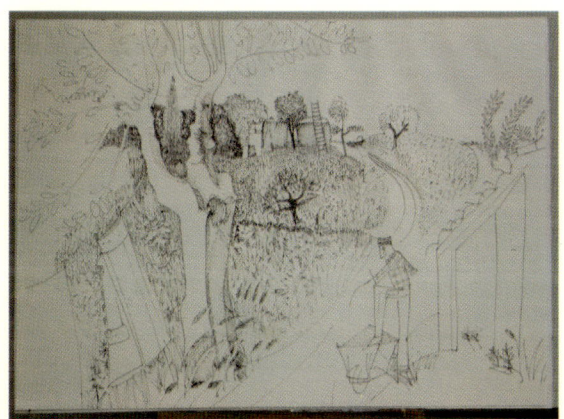

BRICCIANO, TUSCANY
1972 • pencil • 16" x 23"
Kerry Collection

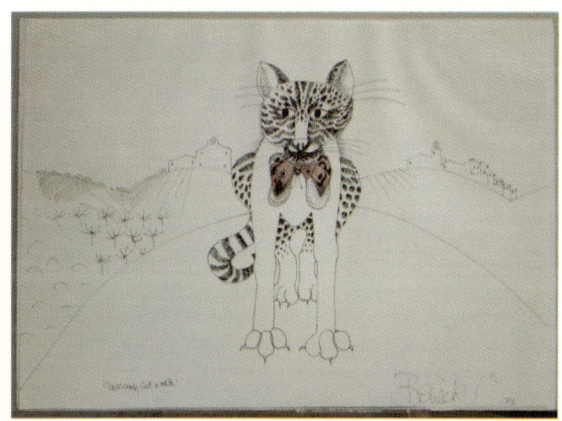

CAT AND MOTH, TUSCANY
1972 • ink and pencil • 16" x 23"
Kerry Collection

Our first trip to Italy. Barry had persuaded us at last to visit her place in Tuscany, opening a new world. Instead of visiting the museums in Siena and Florence the immediate area around Bricciano was far more interesting.

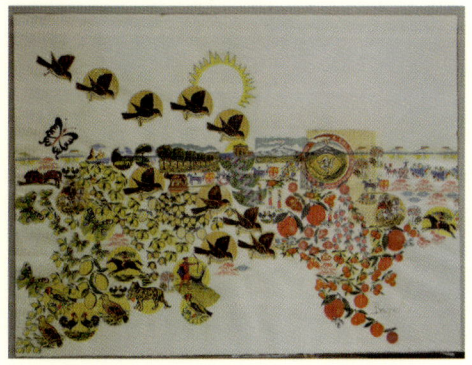

MOUNT ETNA IN ORANGE PAPERS
1972 • orange papers • 22" x 30"
Kerry Collection

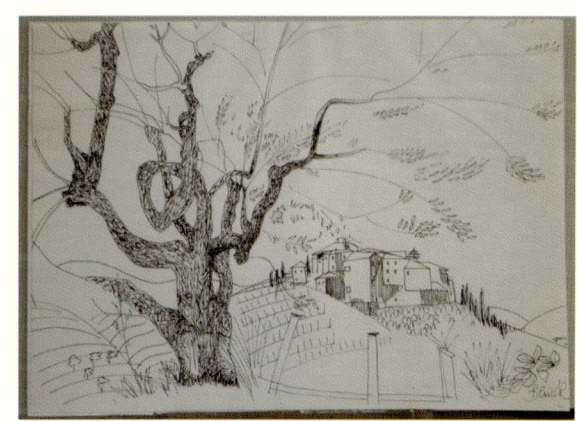

OLIVE TREE
1972 • pencils • 16" x 23"
Kerry Collection

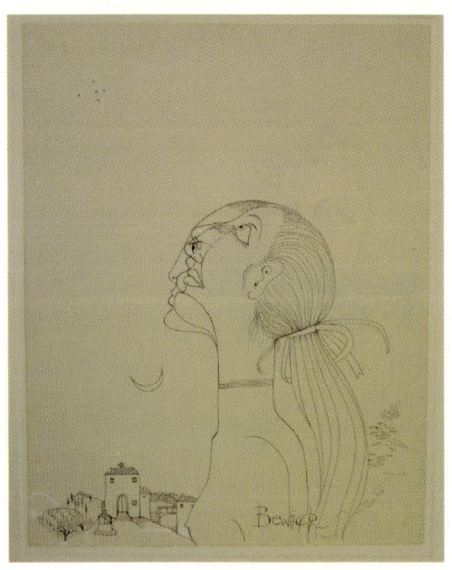

AEROPLANE LIGHTS
1972 • pencil • 25" x 20"
Travelling Collection

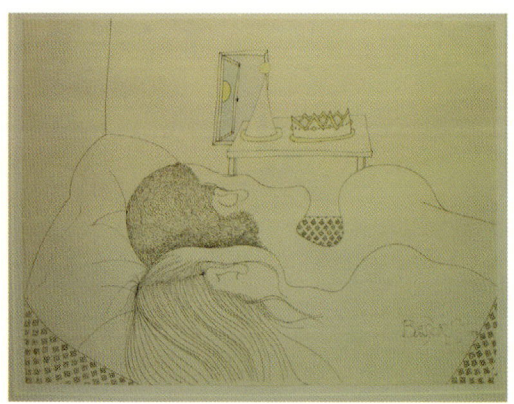

AFTER THE PARTY
1972 • ink • 22" x 30"
Travelling Collection

Our curtains were red, white and blue, I dyed them purple after the British Embassy was attacked.

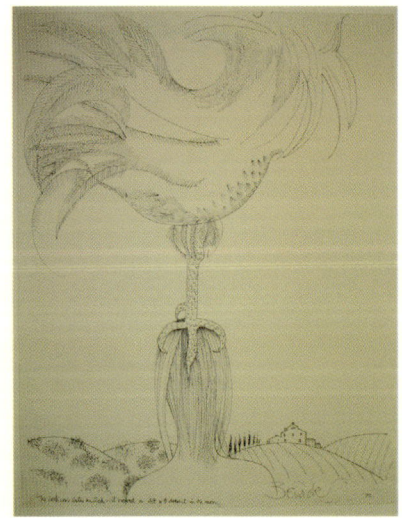

COCKEREL ON HER HEAD
1972 • ink • 25" x 20"
Waterford Collection

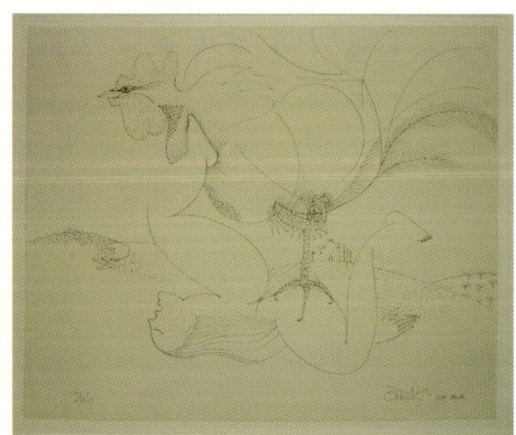

COCKEREL AND WOMAN
1972 • ink • 20" x 25"
Waterford Collection

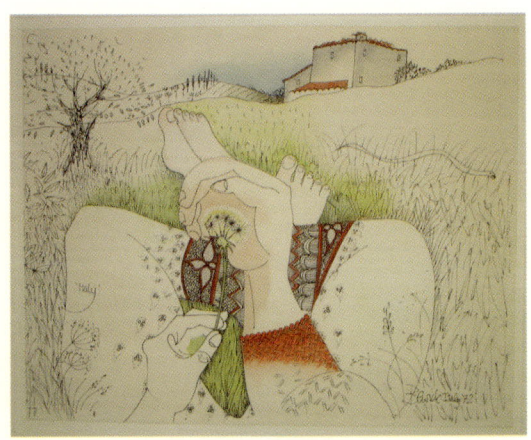

DANDELION CLOCK
1972 • pencils and ink • 19" x 24"
Waterford Collection

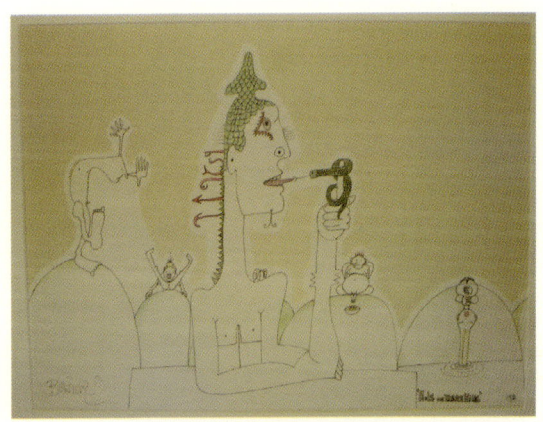

FOOLS ON THEIR HILLS
1972 • pencils • 21" x 30"
Travelling Collection

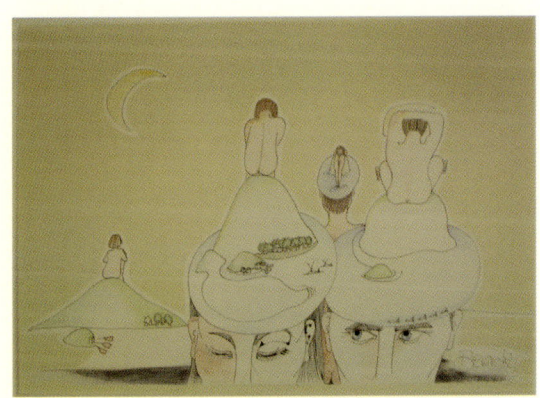

ISLAND OF HATS
1972 • pencils • 18" x 30"
Travelling Collection

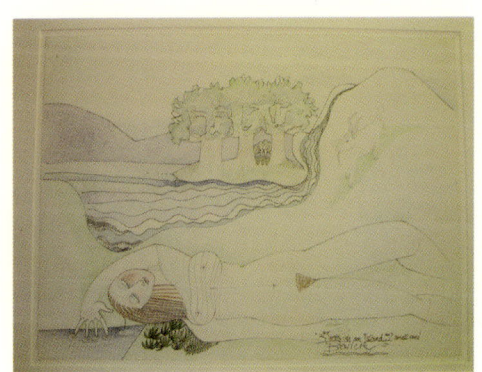

THREE BIG TRESS ON AN ISLAND
1972 • pencils • 23" x 31"
Waterford Collection

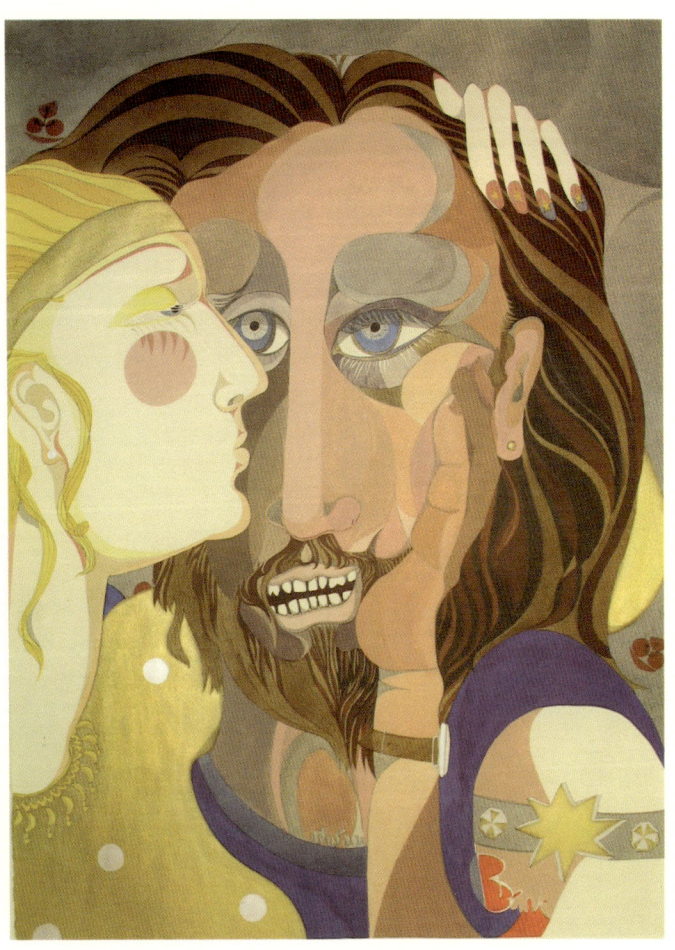

HIPPY COUPLE
1972 • ink and gouache • 30" x 22"
Waterford Collection

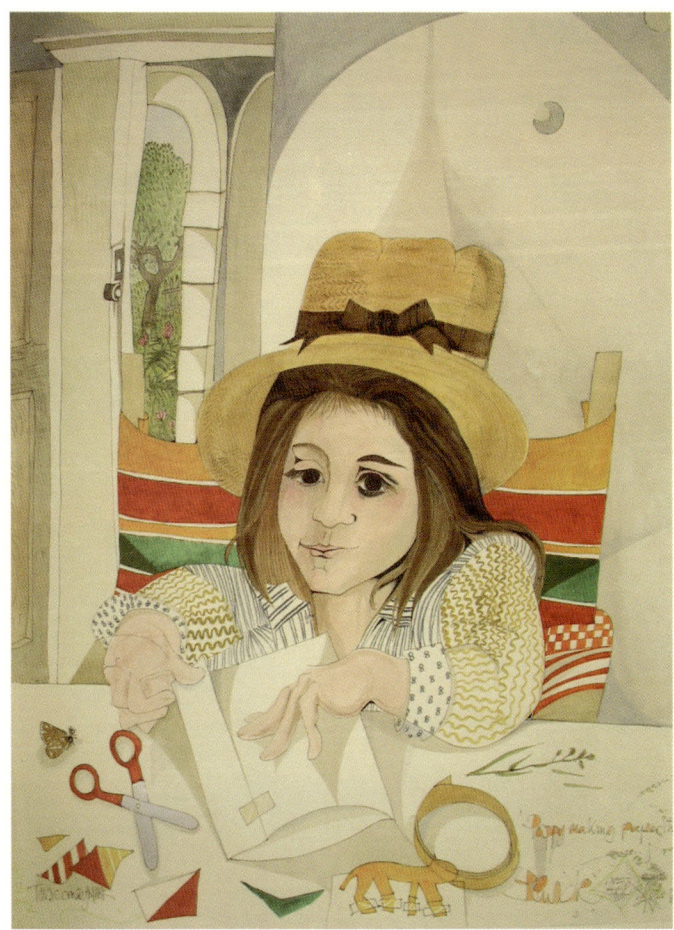

POPPY MAKING THINGS
1972 • watercolour • 31" x 33"
Travelling Collection

We stayed in Tuscany for three months helping the neighbours load hay and drive their white oxen.
Ribauld picnics in the chestnut woods, wild boar ran from us in fright.

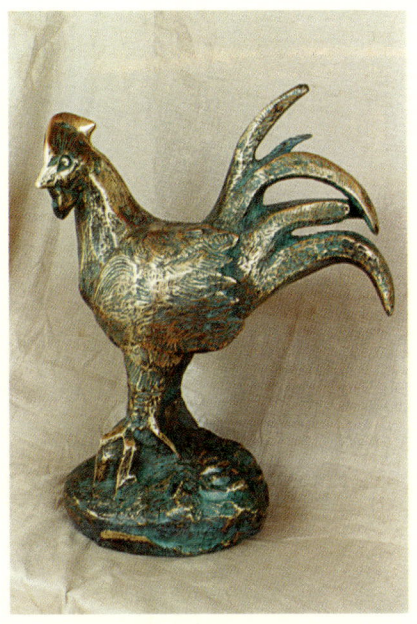

THE COCKEREL
1972 • bronze sculpture • 22" high
Waterford Collection

The cock strutted around Bricciano as if he owned it, the owls were in the roof with their young squaking each night.

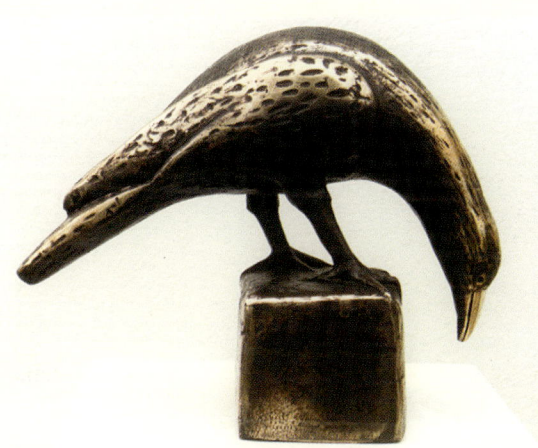

GREYBACK CROW
1974 • bronze sculpture • 10" high
Waterford Collection

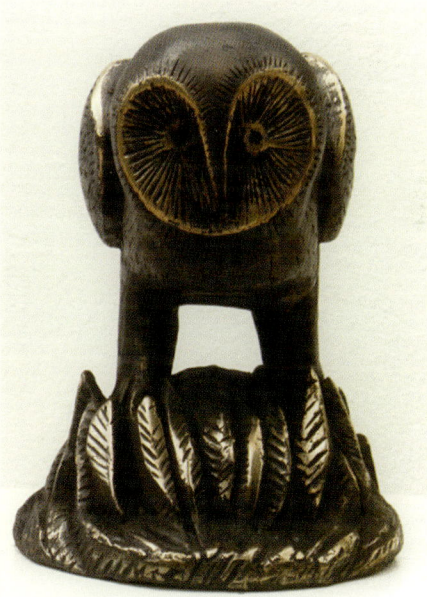

THE OWL
1972 • bronze sculpture • 12" high
Waterford Collection

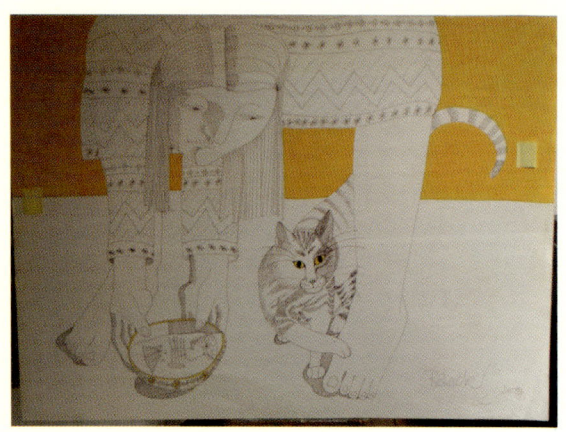

ANNE AND THE CAT
1973 • ink • 32" x 44"
Kerry Collection

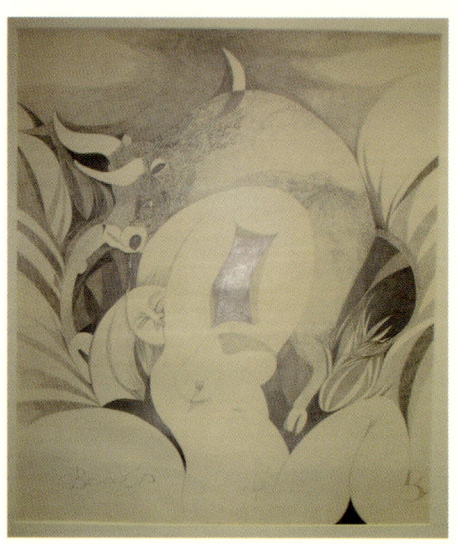

BULL AND WOMAN
1973 • pencil • 32" x 28"
Travelling Collection

Alex's pencils were used for these.

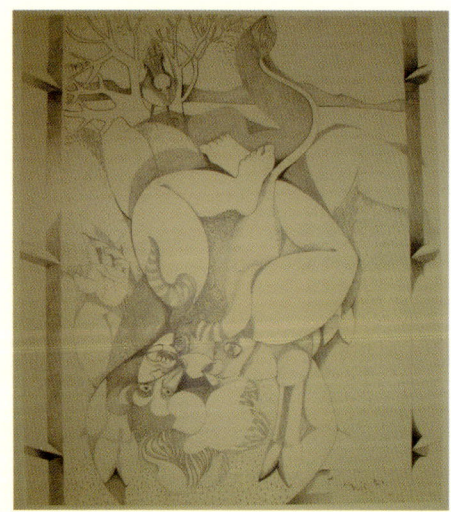

BULL
1973 • pencil
Waterford Collection

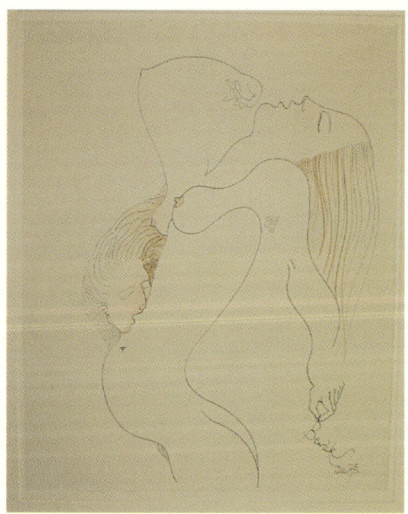

LOVERS
1973 • pencils and ink • 24" x 20"
Travelling Collection

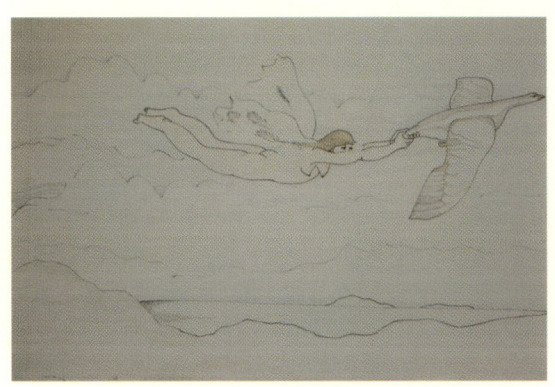

FLYING WITH A GOOSE TO KERRY
1973 • pencils and ink • 16" x 24"
Kerry Collection

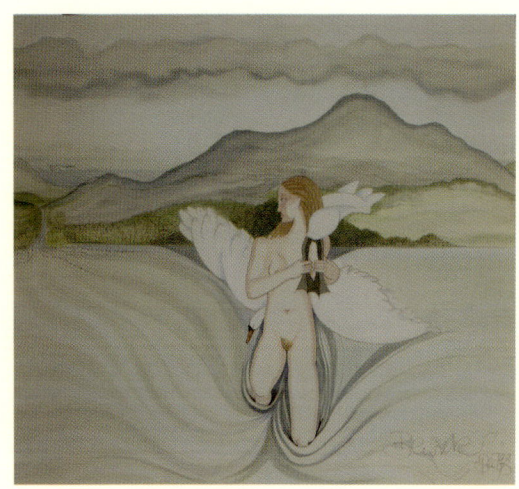

WOMAN AND SWAN
1973 • ink • 26" x 39"
Kerry Collection

The move to Killarney. Pat got a job in St Finian's and they gave us a house until we found our own.

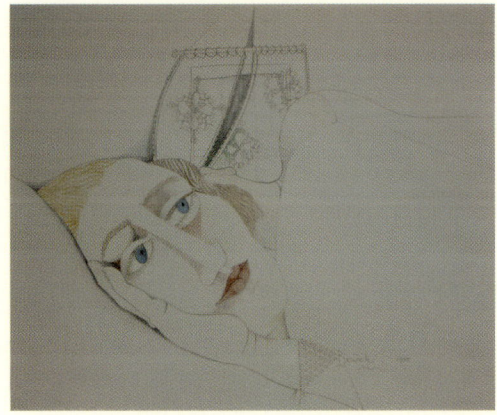

WIFE THINKING
1973 • pencils • 20" x 25"
Kerry Collection

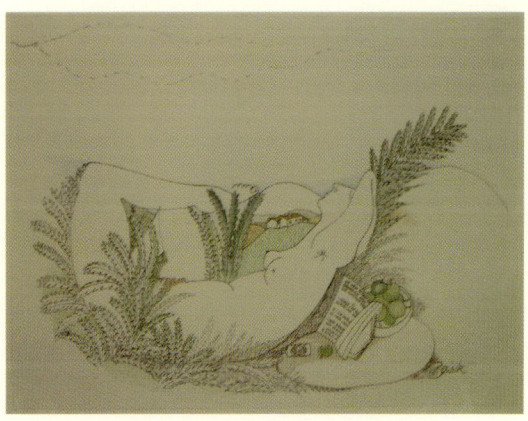

READING SEAMUS HEANEY
1973 • ink and pencil • 17" x 22"
Waterford Collection

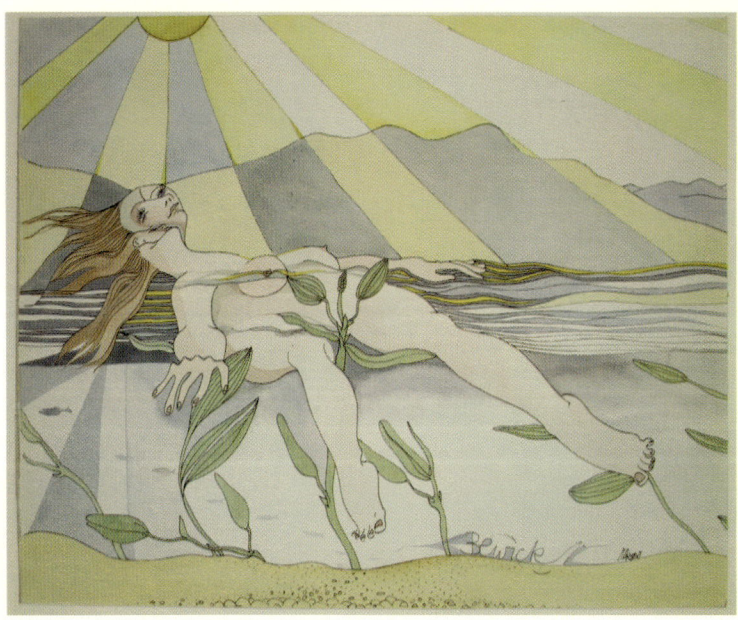

FLOATING IN LOUGH LEANE
1974 • watercolour • 19" x 24"
Travelling Collection

The Killarney lakes give a strange dreamlike quality.

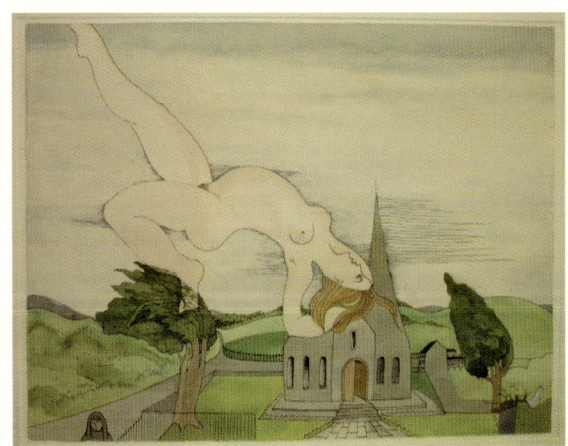

FLYING OVER THE CATHEDRAL
1973 • watercolour • 23" x 30"
Travelling Collection

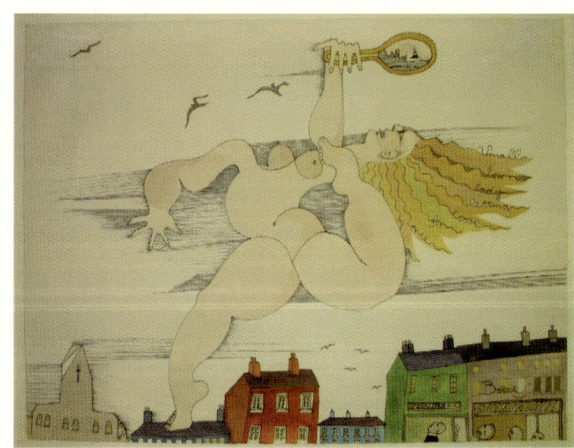

SMALL TOWN LADY LETTING LOOSE
1973 • watercolour • 23" x 31"
Waterford Collection

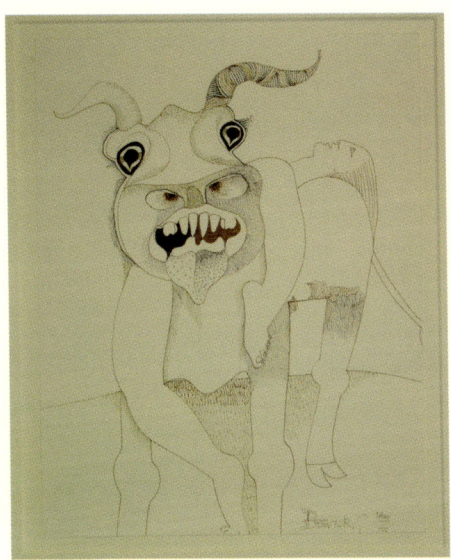

HER BEAST
1973 • ink • 18" x 14"
Travelling Collection

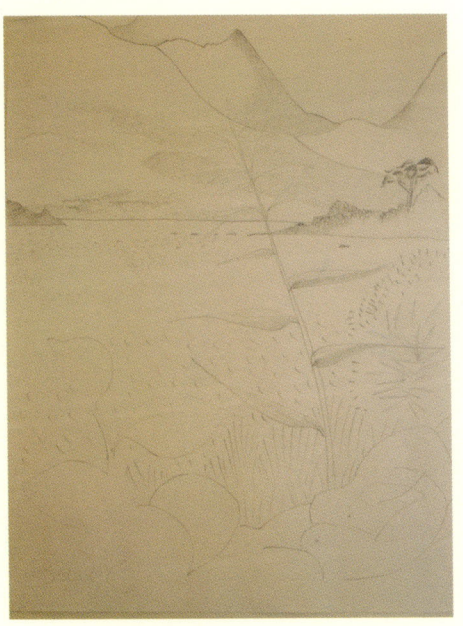

KILLARNEY LAKESIDE
1973 • pencil • 15" x 12"
Kerry Collection

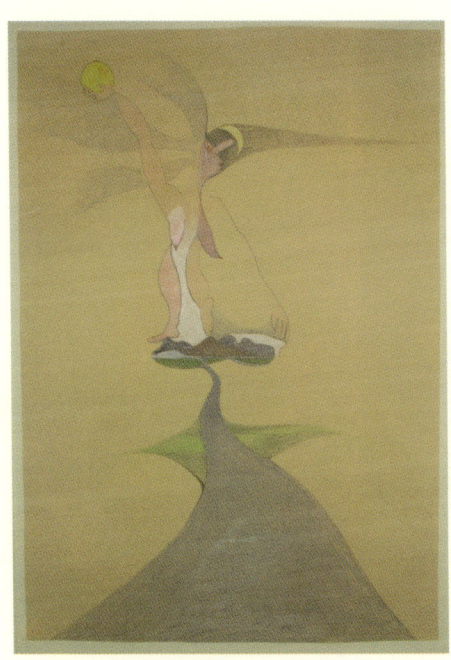

KILLARNEY DUBLIN ROAD
1973 • pencil • 24" x 17"
Waterford Collection

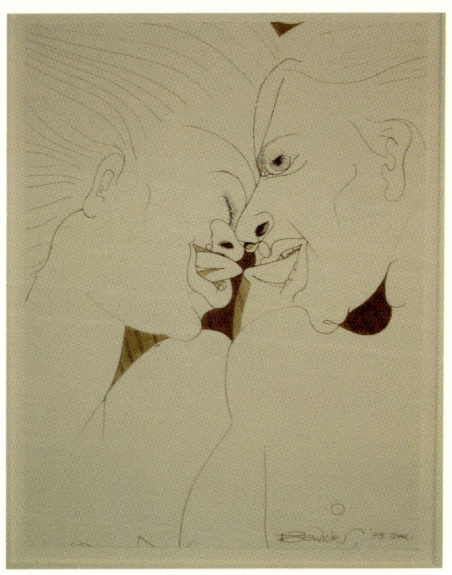

TIPPING TONGUES
1973 • sepia ink • 18" x 14"
Travelling Collection

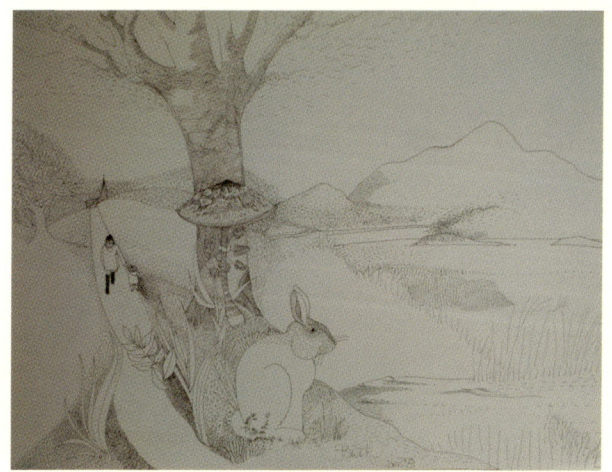

WALKING IN THE DEMESNE, KILLARNEY
1973 • ink • 32" x 44"
Kerry Collection

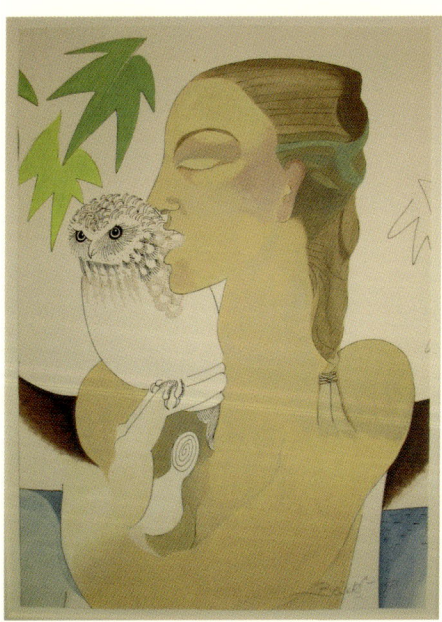

WOMAN AND OWL
1973 • acrylic • 22" x 16"
Waterford Collection

Picking edible mushrooms, painting and lying by the lake, and Pat working in St Finian's was our Killarney life.

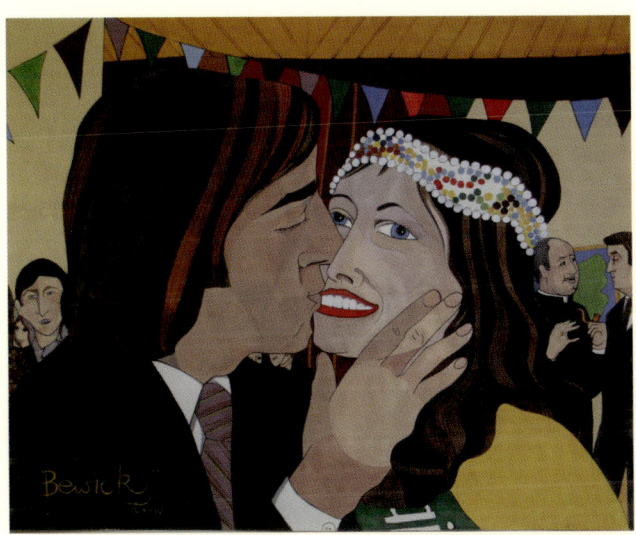

BENJY AND THE QUEEN OF THE MOUNTAIN
1974 • gouache • 20" x 25"
Kerry Collection

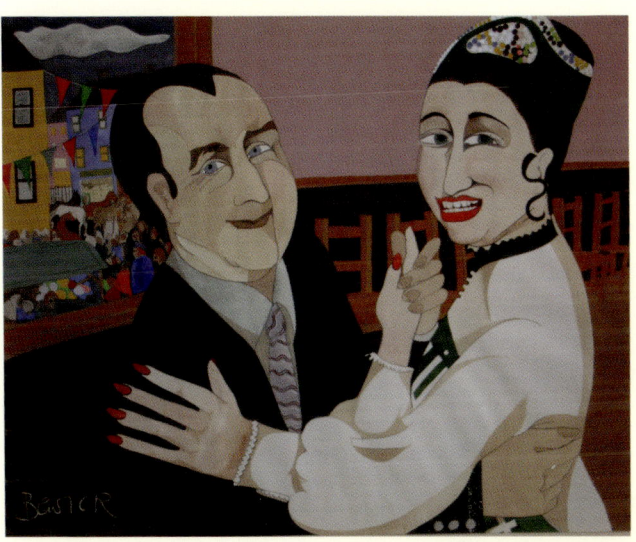

DANCING WITH THE QUEEN OF THE MOUNTAIN
1974 • gouache • 20" x 25"
Kerry Collection

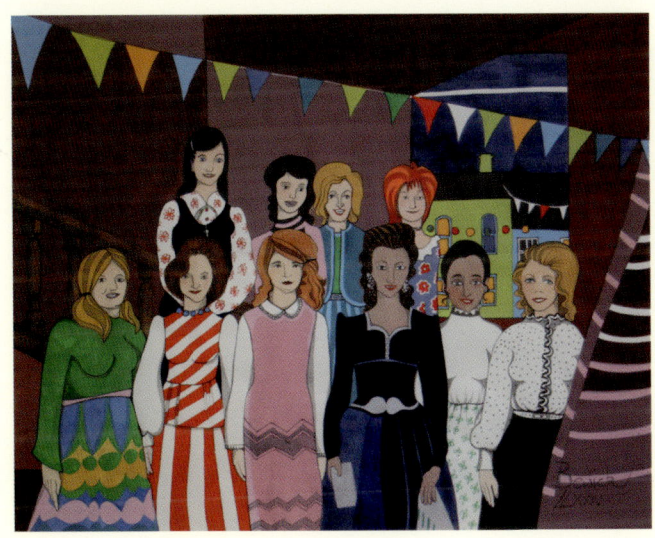

CONTESTANTS FOR THE QUEEN OF THE MOUNTAIN
1974 • gouache • 20" x 25"
Kerry Collection

Festivals such as Puck Fair, the Rose of Tralee and Queen of the Mountains abound in Kerry. Bengy of *The Riordans* was the judge.

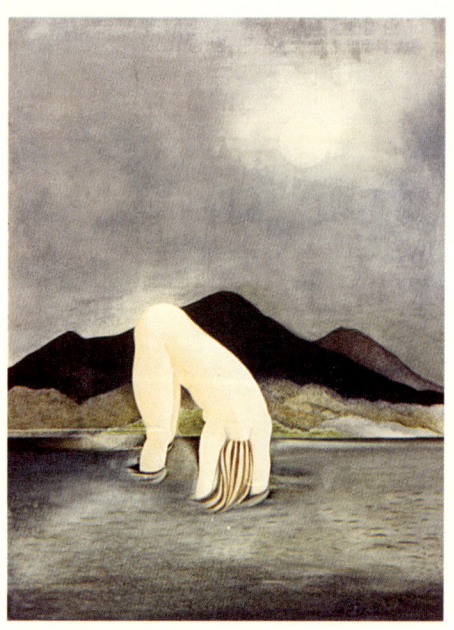

DIPPING HER HAIR
1974 • ink on board • 31" x 23"
Waterford Collection

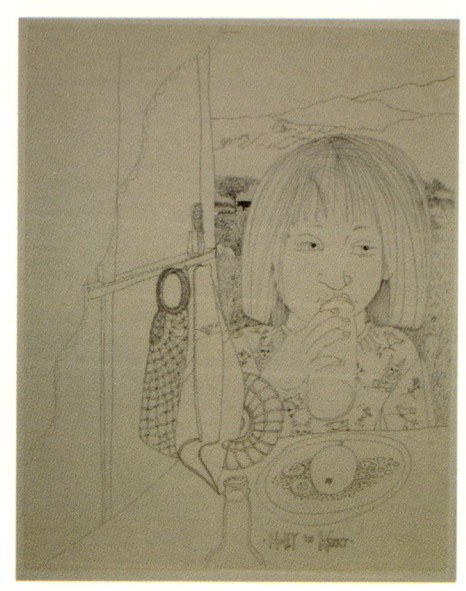

HOLLY IN KERRY
1974 • ink • 25" x 20"
Travelling Collection

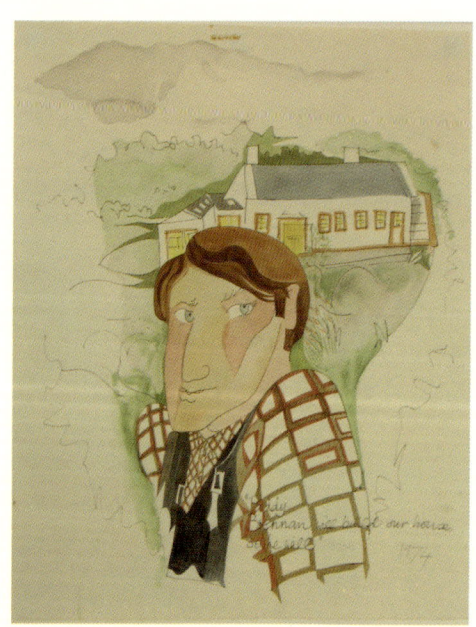

PADDY BRENNAN WILL BUILD OUR HOUSE,
SO HE WILL
1974 • watercolour • 25" x 20"
Travelling Collection

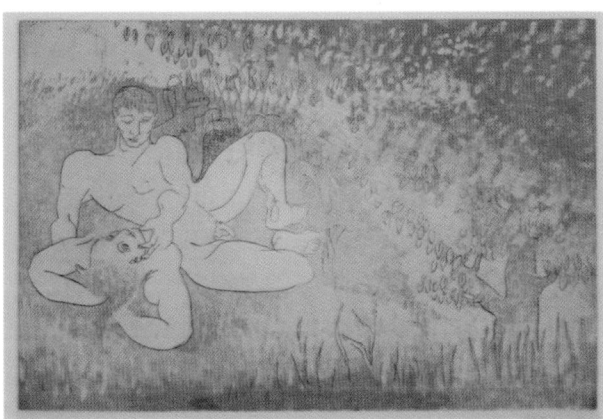

LOVERS (early design stage)
1974 etching
Travelling Collection

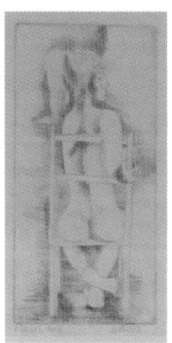

SEATED NUDE (early design stage)
1974 • etching
Travelling Collection

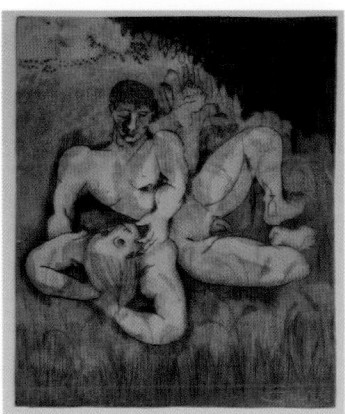

LOVERS
1974 etching
Travelling Collection

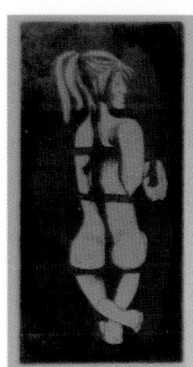

SEATED NUDE
1974 • etching
Travelling Collection

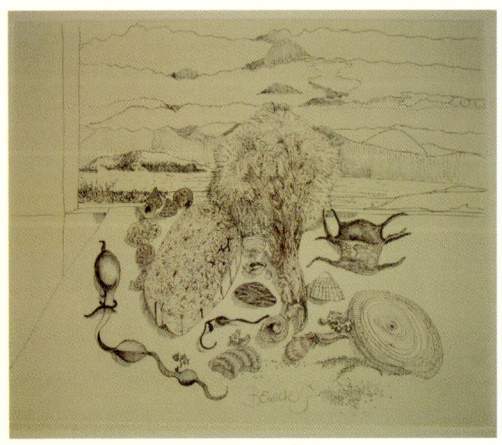

SEAWRACK
1974 • ink • 20" x 25"
Waterford Collection

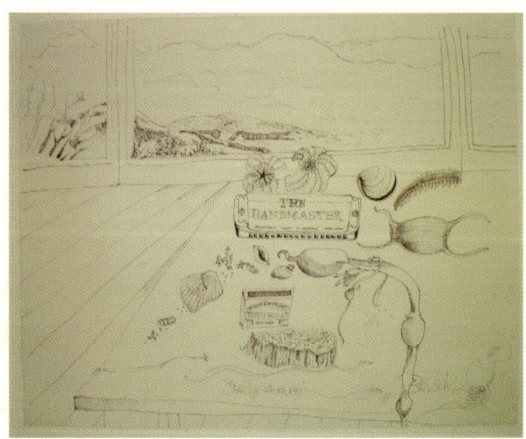

STILL LIFE WITH SEA AND SKY
1974 • ink • 20" x 25"
Waterford Collection

Ella Coffey, a traveller living in Tralee was often on the road.
She made many embroidered dresses for me and Maria Simonds-Gooding.

Alfonso worked with the stained glass artist Harry Clarke. Here in my studio sketching he kept saying:
'This is Heaven, Heaven'.

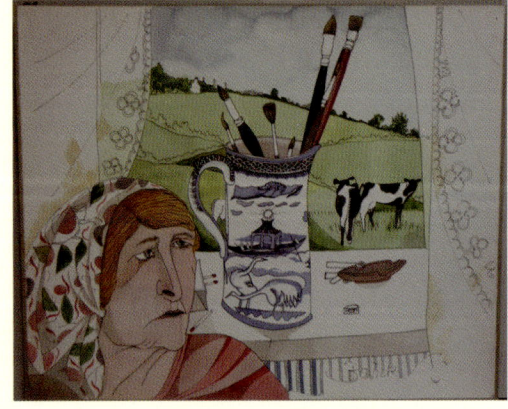

ELLA COFFEY
1975 • watercolour • 20" x 25"
Kerry Collection

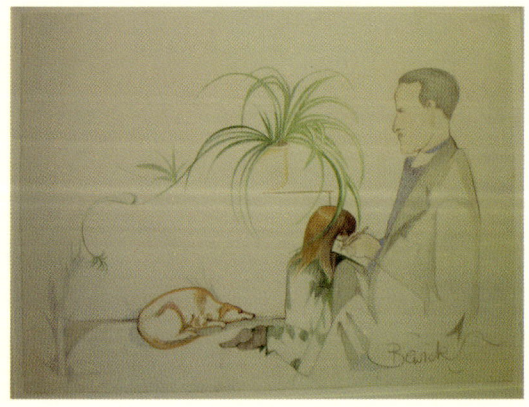

ALFONSO
1975 • pencils • 22" x 30"
Travelling Collection

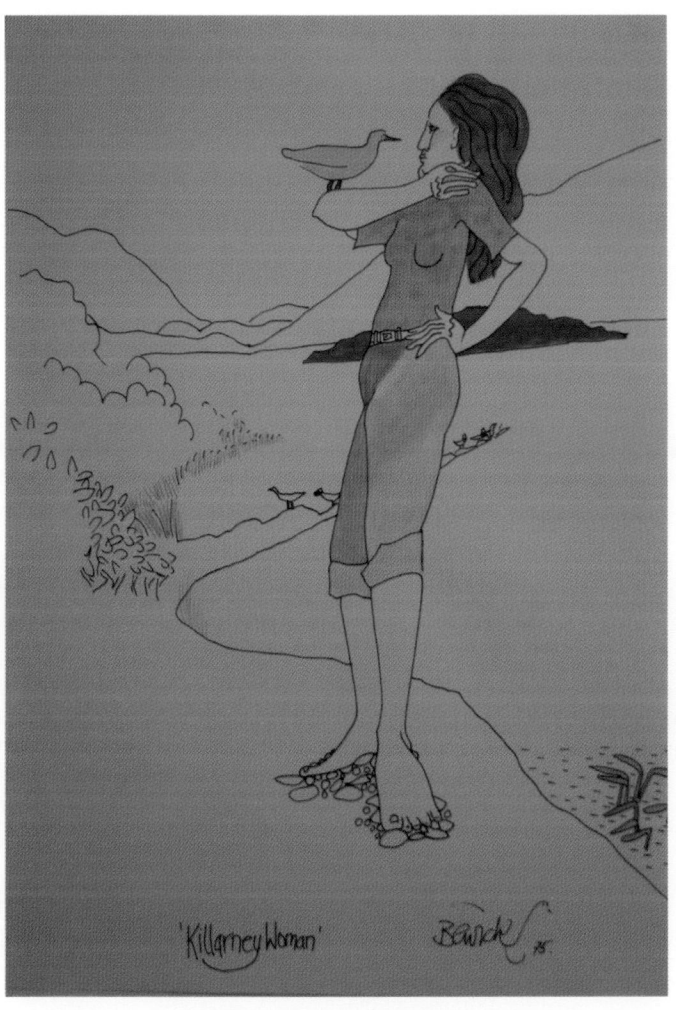

KILLARNEY WOMAN
1975 • watercolour • 24" x 17"
Kerry Collection

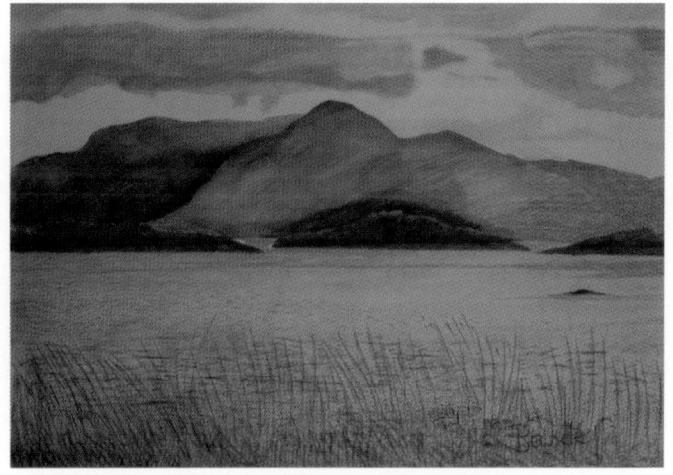

TWOMIES MOUNTAIN, KILLARNEY
1975 • ink • 16" x 23"
Kerry Collection

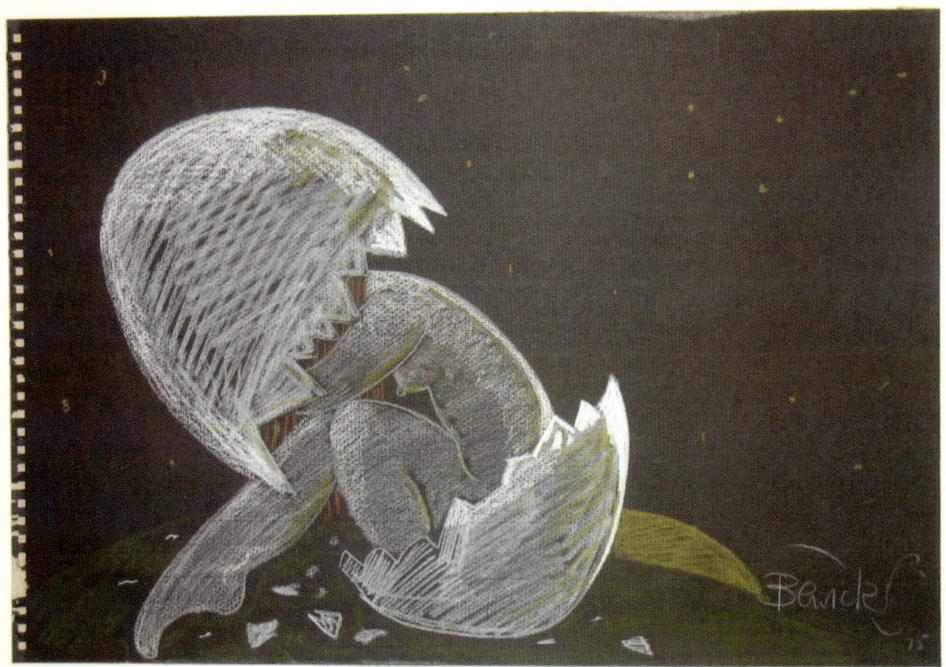

WAKING WOMAN
1975 • pastel • 12" x 18"
Waterford Collection

John Mulcahy, editor of *Hibernia*, commissioned a cover for International Women's Year, 1975.
I did two sketches, followed by a linocut which he used.

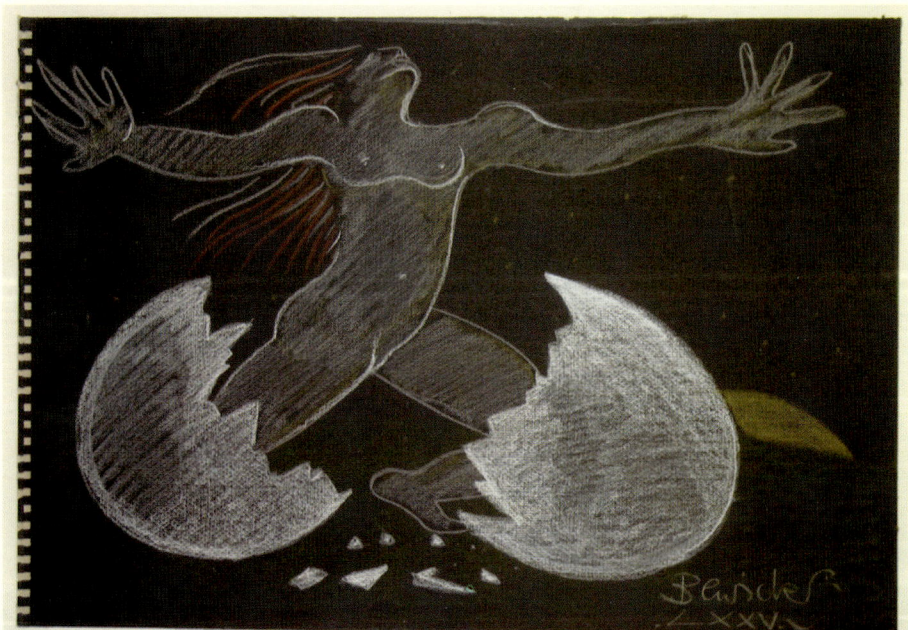

WOMAN AWAKE
1975 • pastel • 12" x 18"
Waterford Collection

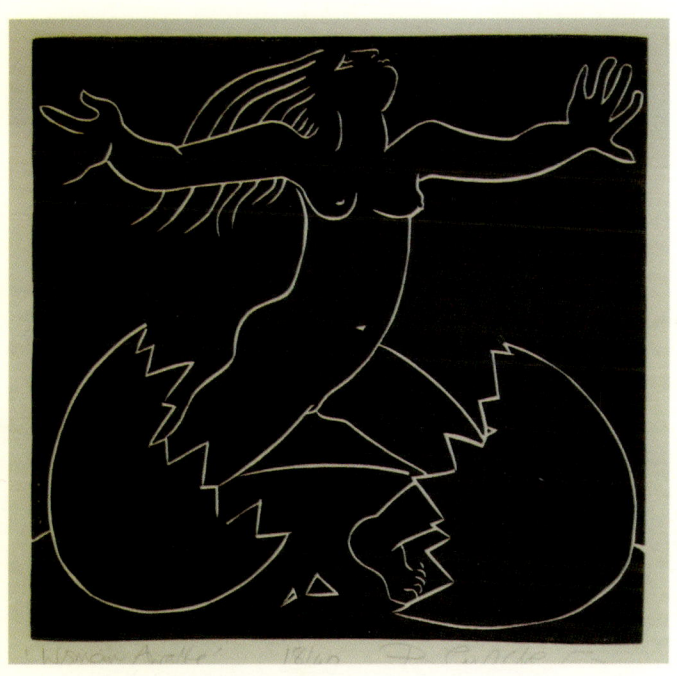

WOMAN AWAKE, BLACK (LTD. ED. OF 40)
1975 • lino cut • 21" x 16"
all Collections

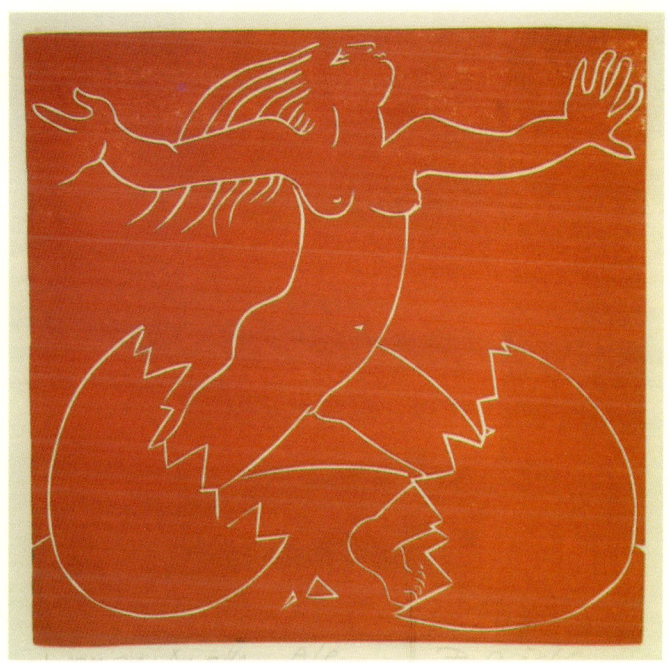

WOMAN AWAKE, RED (LTD. ED. OF 6)
1975 • lino cut • 21" x 16"
all Collections

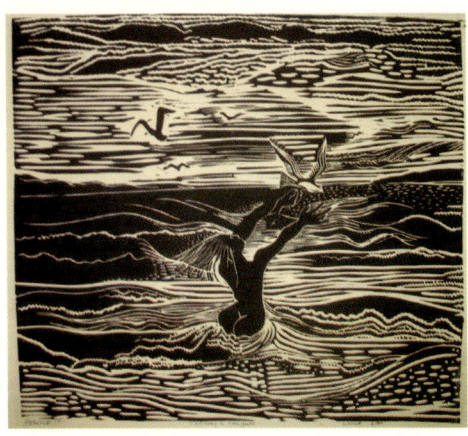

CATCHING A SEAGULL
1975 • lino cut • 23" x 27"
Kerry Collection

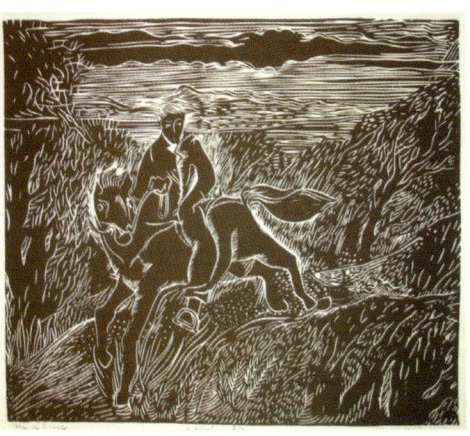

MAN ON HORSE
1975 • lino cut • 23" x 26"
Waterford Collection

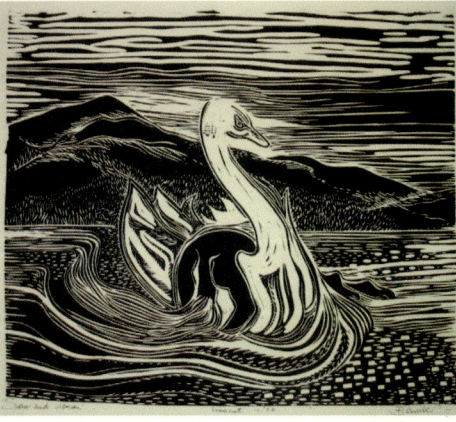

SWAN AND WOMAN
1975 • lino cut • 19" x 23"
Kerry and Travelling Collections

Life around Rossbeigh, Killarney and the Lakes was gouged out of scrap battleship lino bought in a coal-yard in Dublin. The high heel marks dictated where to cut.

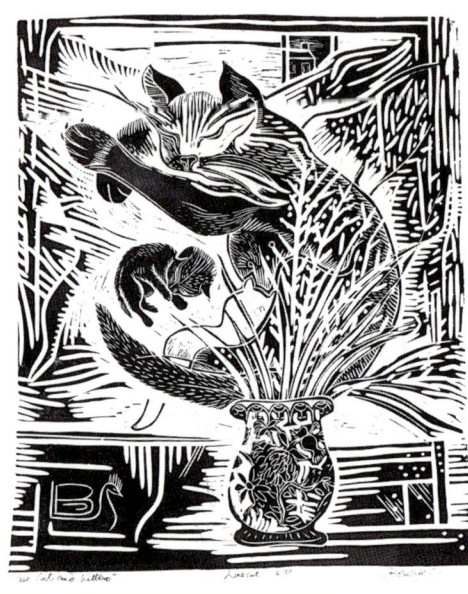

CAT AND VASE
1975 • lino cut • 28" x 23"
Waterford Collection

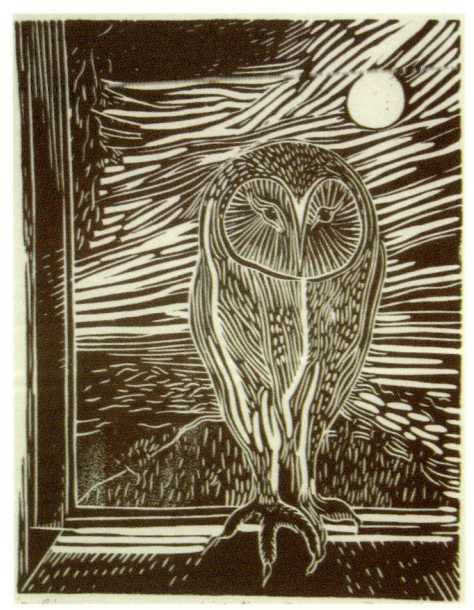

THE OWL
1975 • linocut • 18" x 14"
Travelling Collection

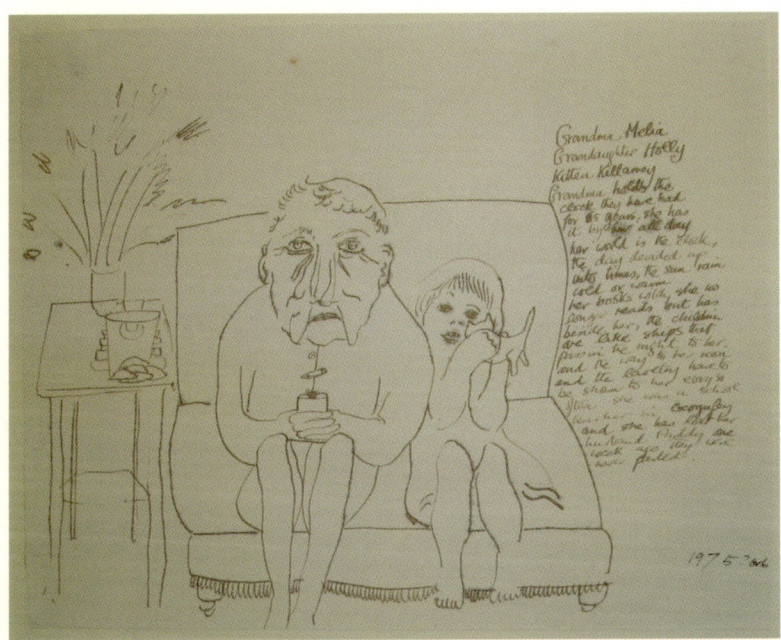

GRANDMA
1975 • ink • 14" x 18"
Travelling Collection

Pat's mother came to live with us. 'I *am* his wife, you know', she said to me.

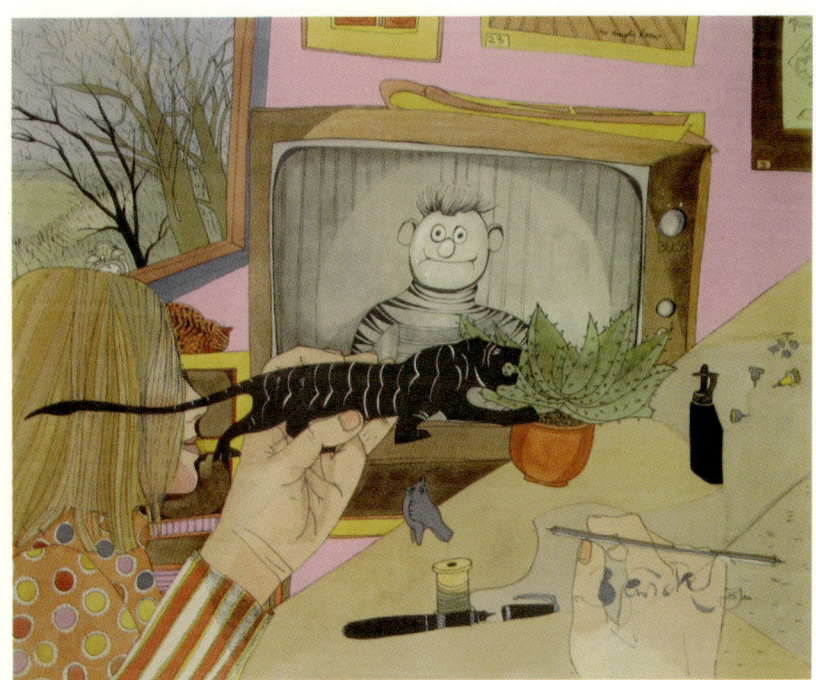

WATCHING SESAME STREET
1975 • watercolour • 20" x 25"
Travelling Collection

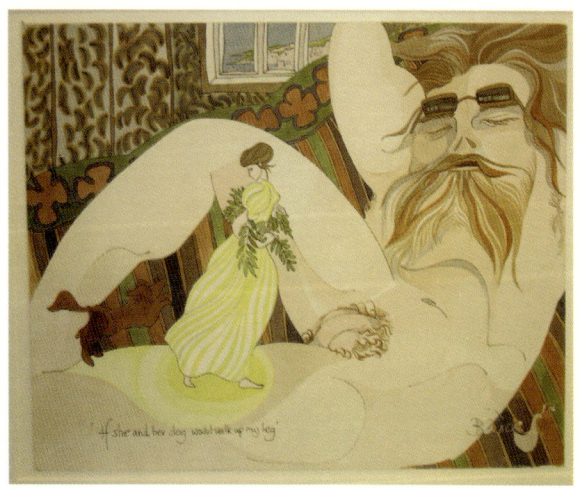

IRISH POET
1975 • watercolour • 19" x 24"
Waterford Collection

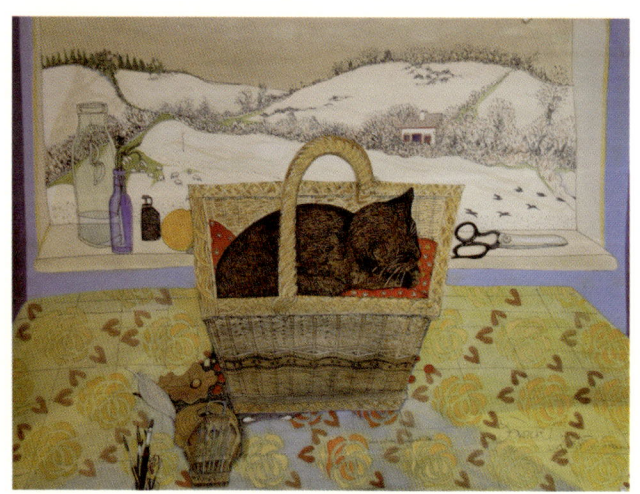

CAT IN A BASKET, AGHADOE
1976 • watercolour • 32" x 44"
Kerry Collection

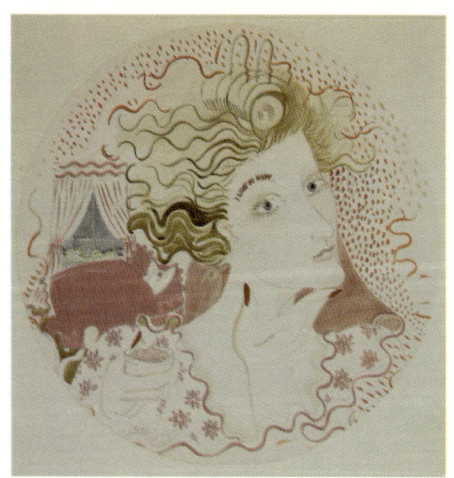

I LIVE IN HOPE
1976 • watercolour • 25" x 25"
Waterford Collection

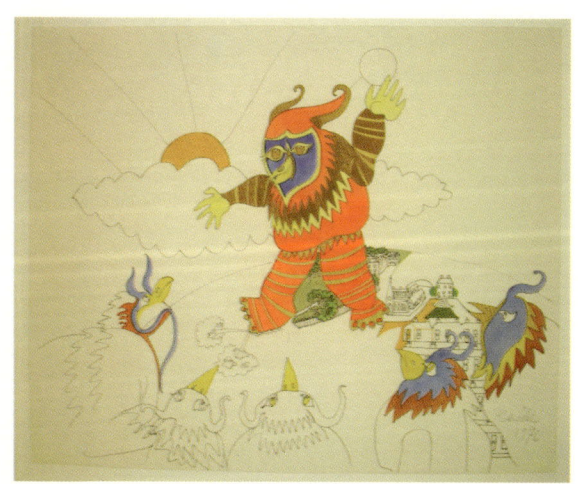

AMUSING THE CHILDREN AGAIN
1976 • watercolour • 20" x 25"
Waterford Collection

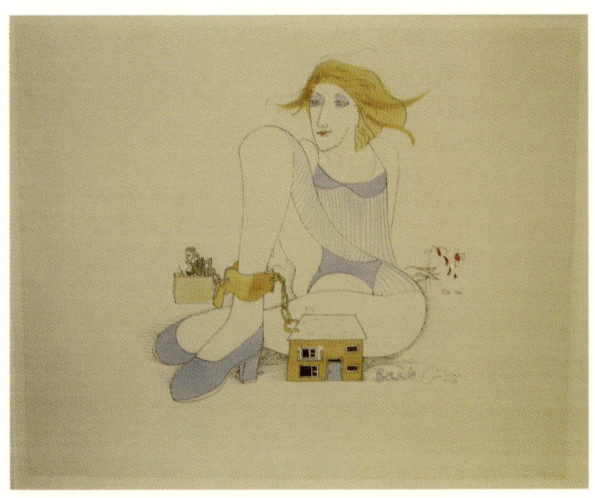

HOME AND OFFICE
1976 • watercolour • 20" x 25"
Travelling Collection

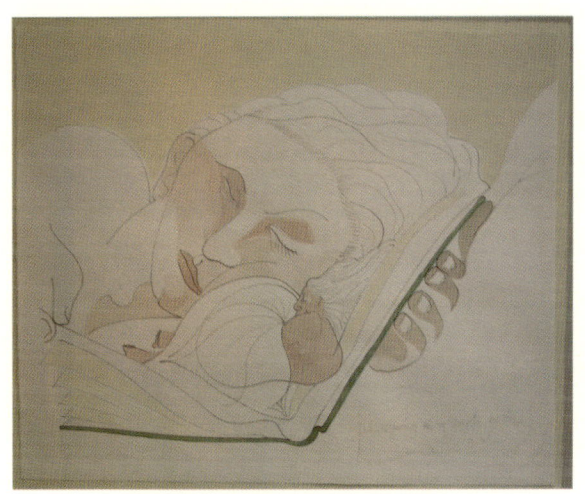

SLEEPING IN A POET'S BOOK
1976 • ink and watercolour • 19" x 24"
Kerry Collection

The neighbours came into manys the painting.

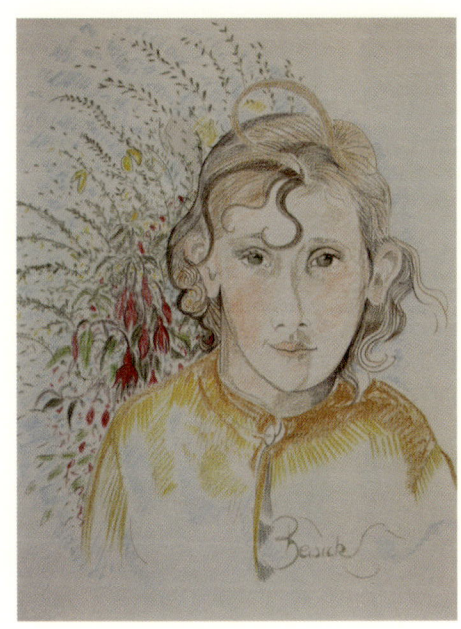

EILEEN
1977 • pastel • 22" x 18"
Kerry Collection

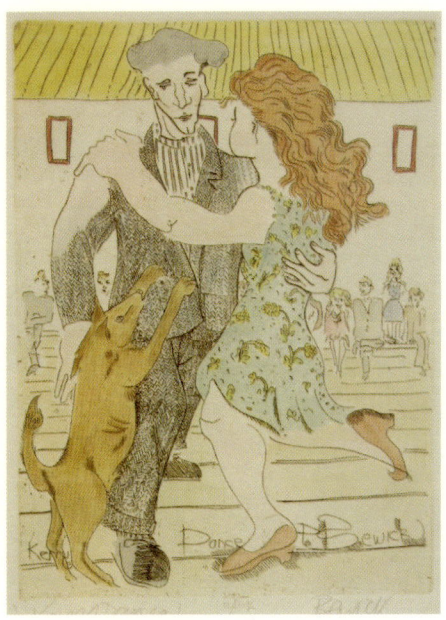

KERRY DANCE, Artist's Proof
1977 • hand coloured etching • 17" x 13"
Kerry Collection

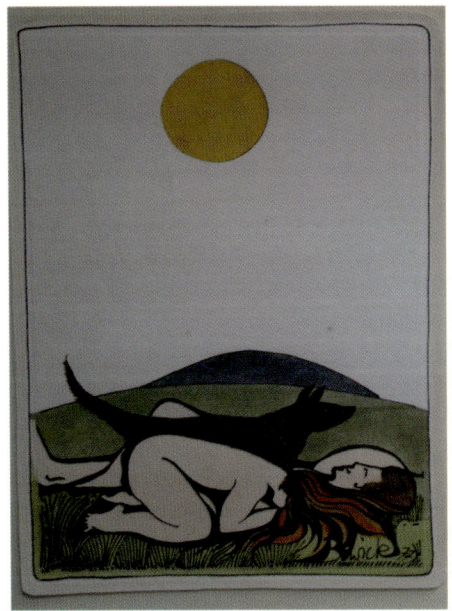

ON A HILL I
1977 • pastel • 11" x 8"
Kerry Collection

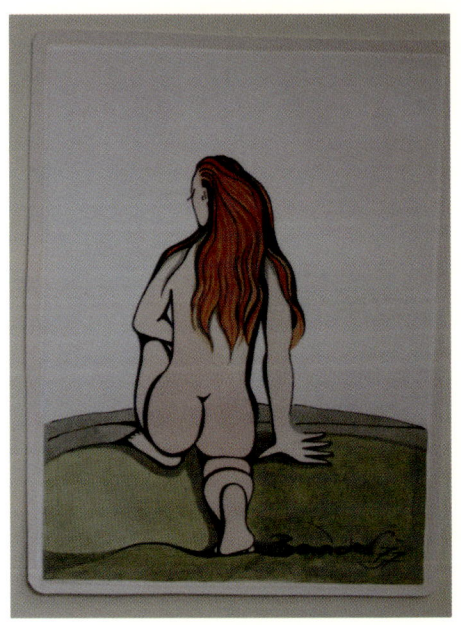

ON A HILL II
1977 • pastel • 11" x 8"
Kerry Collection

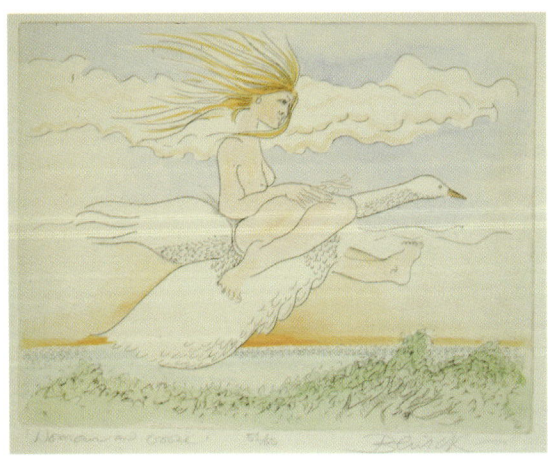

WOMAN AND GOOSE, Artist's Proof
1977 • hand coloured etching • 14" x 16"
Waterford Collection

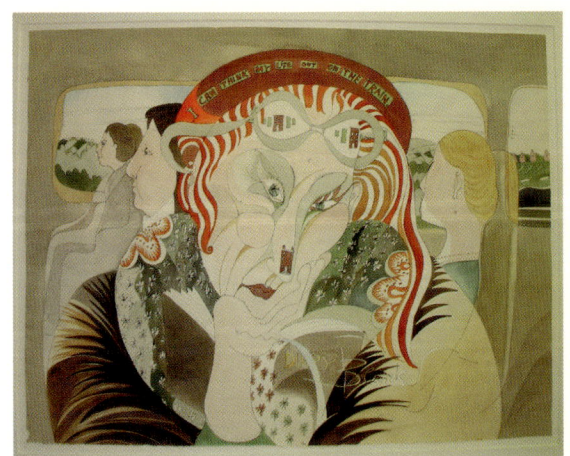

THINKING ON THE TRAIN
1977 • watercolour • 22" x 30"
Waterford Collection

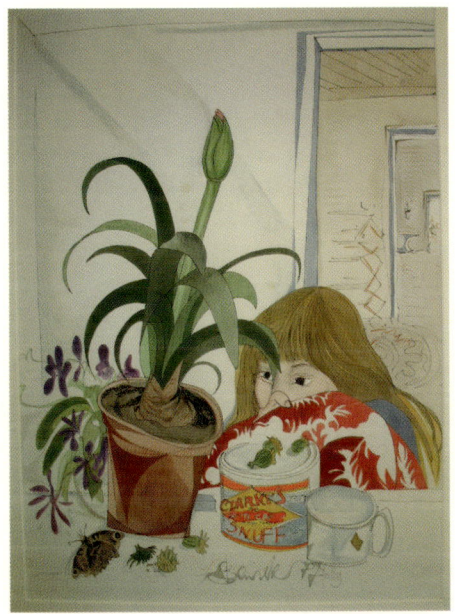

Two Buds, Holly and Amaryllis
1977 • watercolour • 30" x 22"
Travelling Collection

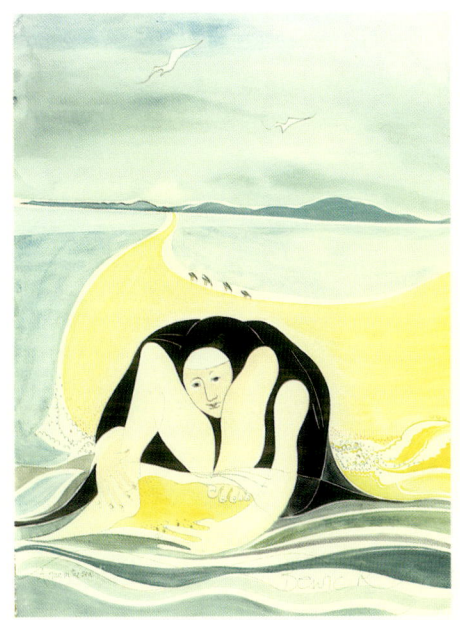

Nun at Rossbeigh
1978 • watercolour • 30" x 22"
Kerry Collection

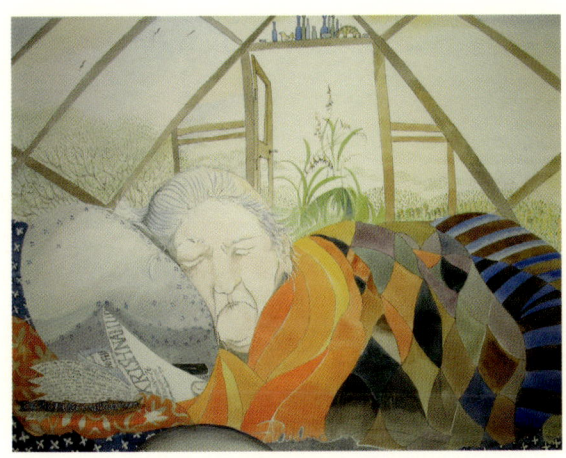

Harry and Krishnamurti
1978 • watercolour • 23" x 31"
Travelling Collection

Harry read all Krishnamurti's philosophies.
'What does he say?'
'Nothing, absolutely nothing. He's wonderful'.

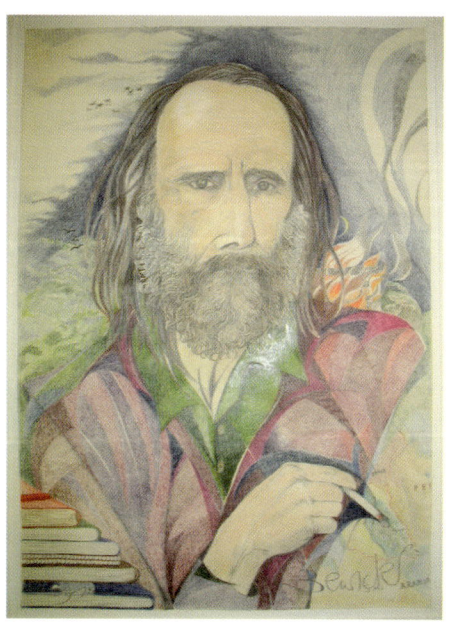

JOHN KILBRACKEN
1978 • pencils • 31" x 22"
Waterford Collection

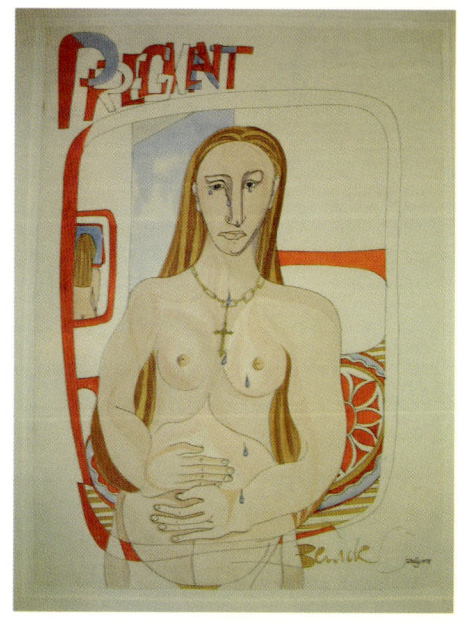

PREGNANT
1978 • watercolour • 30" x 22"
Travelling Collection

John Kilbracken visited us and slept with not a chink of light coming into his room.
He would get up for sittings of this portrait telling me the story of Kiligar being burnt to the ground.
I saw different scenes between the strands of his thin hair.

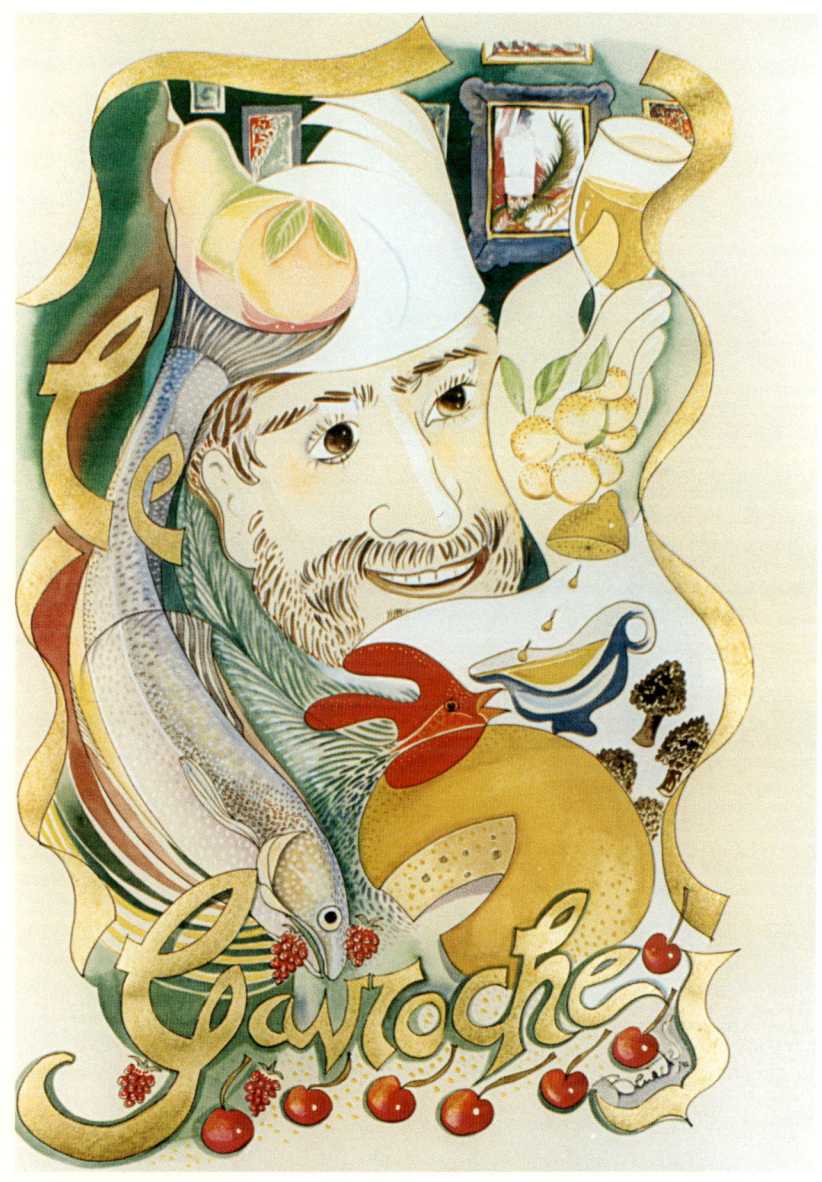

CHEF, LE GAVROCHE
1979 • watercolour, goldleaf and acrylic • 26" x 20"
Travelling Collection

The Roux Family of Le Gavroche, London use this image on their ceramics.

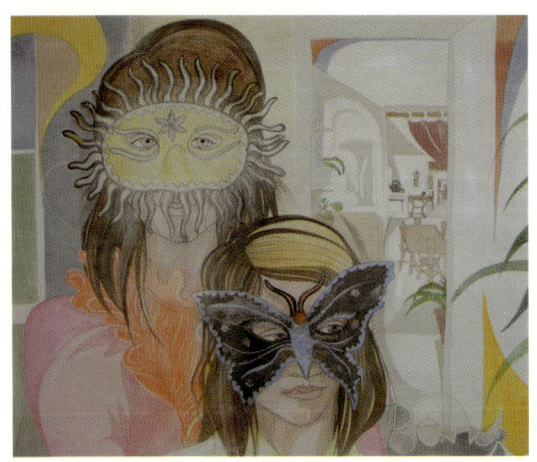

PANTOMIME MASKS
1979 • watercolour • 20" x 25"
Kerry Collection

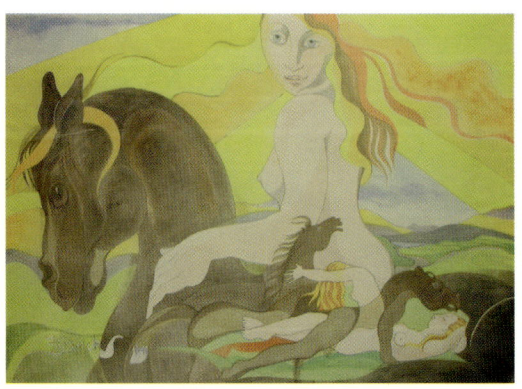

WOMAN AND HORSE
1979 • watercolour • 22" x 31"
Waterford Collection

Cinderella, directed by me, was acted out with Holly and Poppy's school friends. 'If the shoe fits, wear it', 'Where's my hairy molly, I'm off to the ball'.

A recurring dream a journalist told me about. The rabbis got nowhere, paddling against each other.

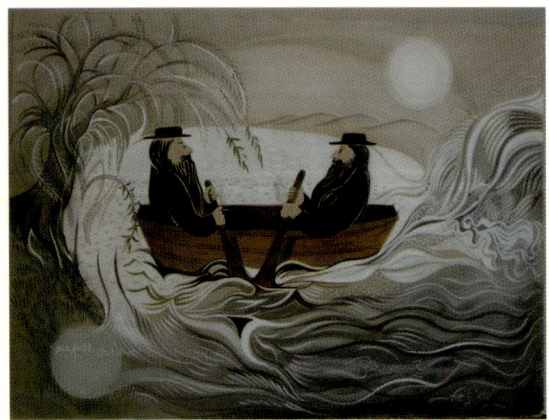

TWO RABBIS IN A BOAT
1982 • watercolour • 23" x 32"
Kerry Collection

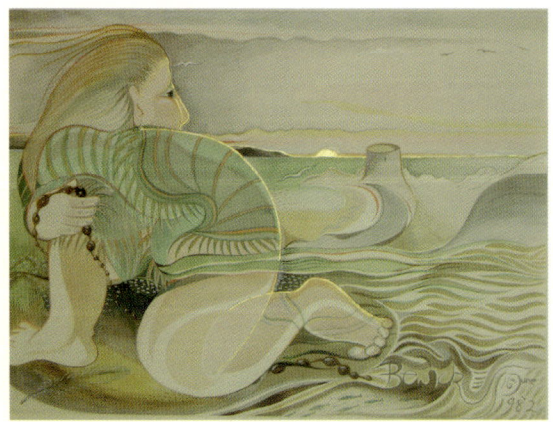

JOYCE'S TOWER
1982 • watercolour • 22" x 31"
Waterford Collection

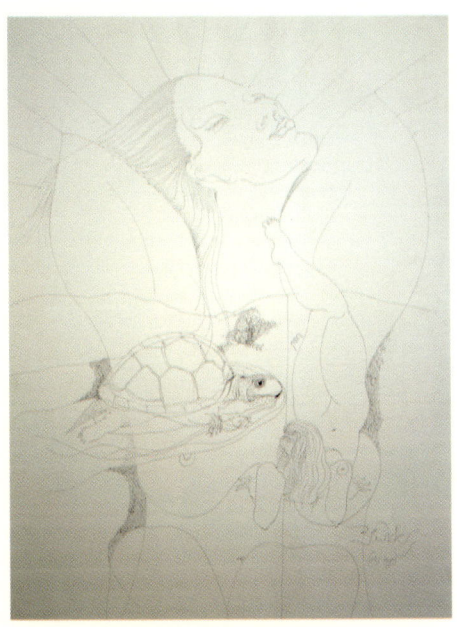

WOMAN AND TORTOISE
1980 • ink • 30" x 22"
Waterford Collection

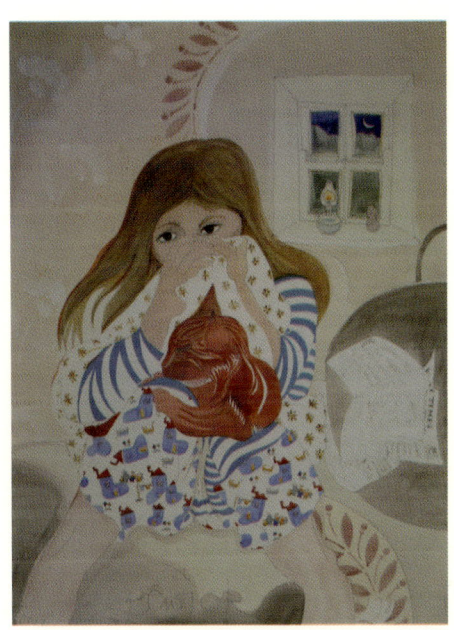

HOLLY AND CAT
1981 • watercolour • 32" x 23"
Kerry Collection

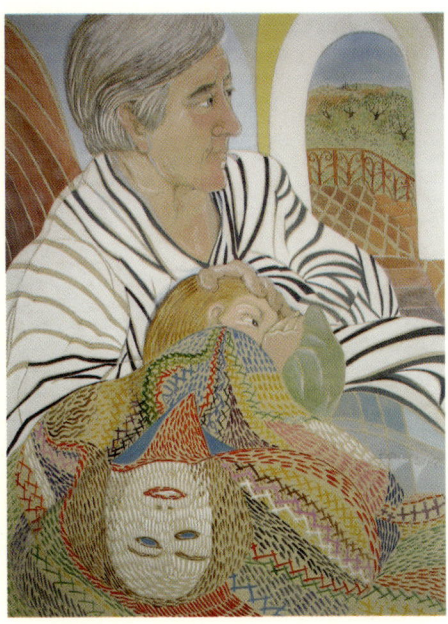

HOLLY AND PAT IN TUSCANY
1983 • watercolour • 30" x 22"
Travelling Collection

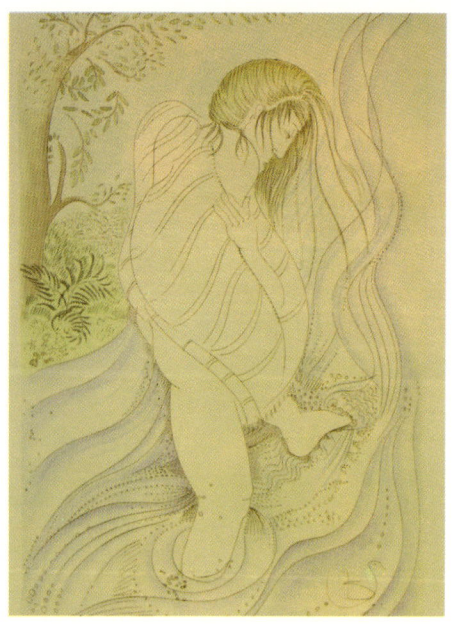

KICKING WATER, Artist's Proof
1983 • hand coloured etching • 30" x 22"
Waterford Collection

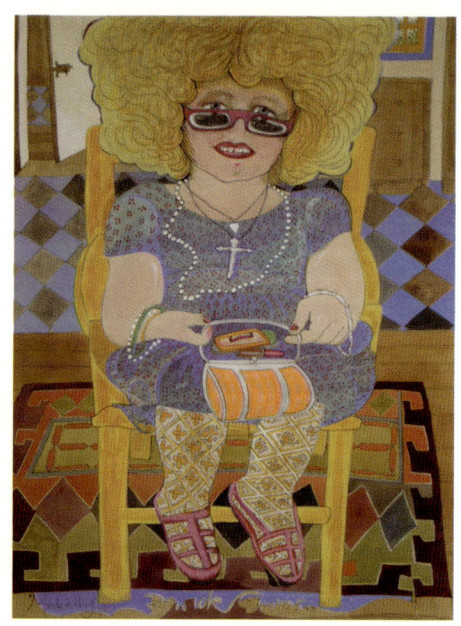

MANDY DRESSING UP
1985 • watercolour • 31" x 23"
Kerry Collection

Our neighbour Mandy routed in the dressing up box to look like this.

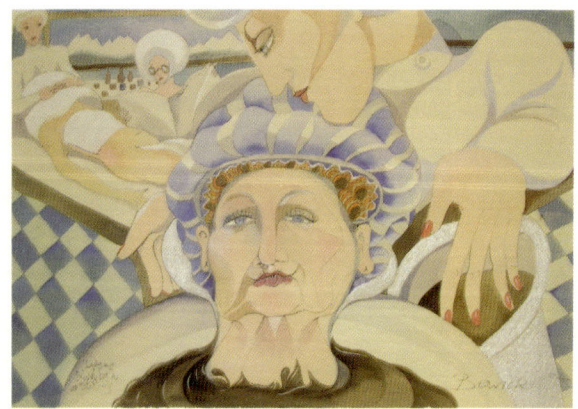

LADY IN MUD BATH, ST MORITZ
1986 • watercolour • 15" x 23"
Travelling Collection

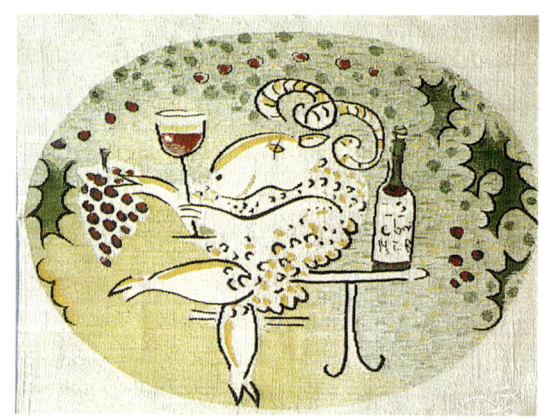

RAM AND WINE
1984 • silk tapestry • 26" x 37"
woven by Regine Bartsch
Travelling Collection

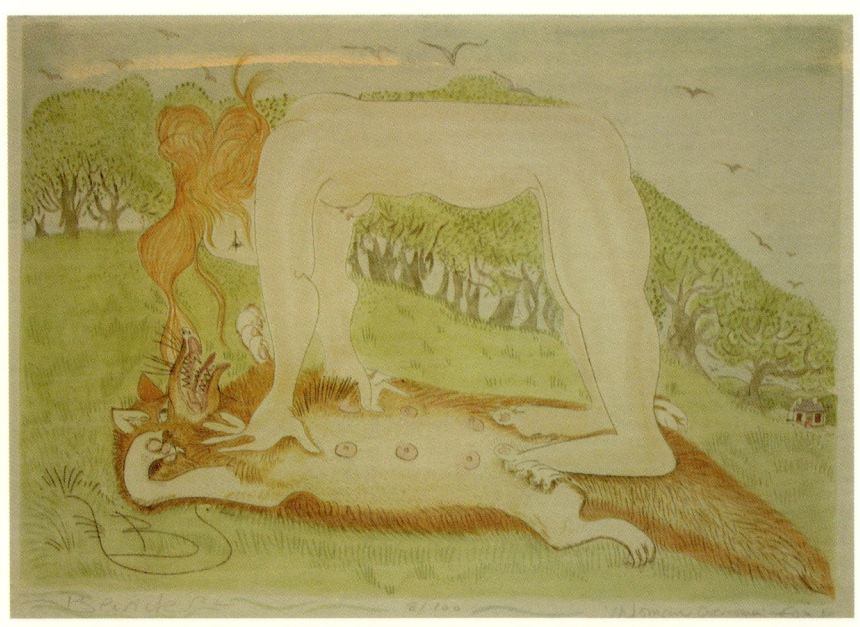

WOMAN OVERCOMING FOX, Artist's Proof
1987 • hand coloured etching • 20" x 27"
Travelling Collection

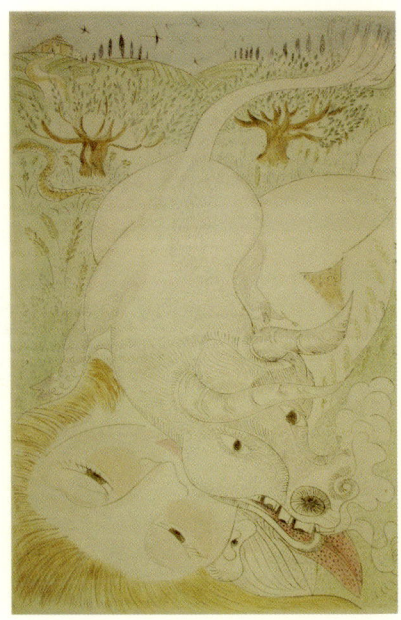

WOMAN AND BEAST, Artist's Proof
1987 • hand coloured etching • 27" x 20"
Travelling Collection

A fox came and took our cock in broad daylight. He dropped it when I made very loud banging noises, sauntering off leaving the cock gasping.

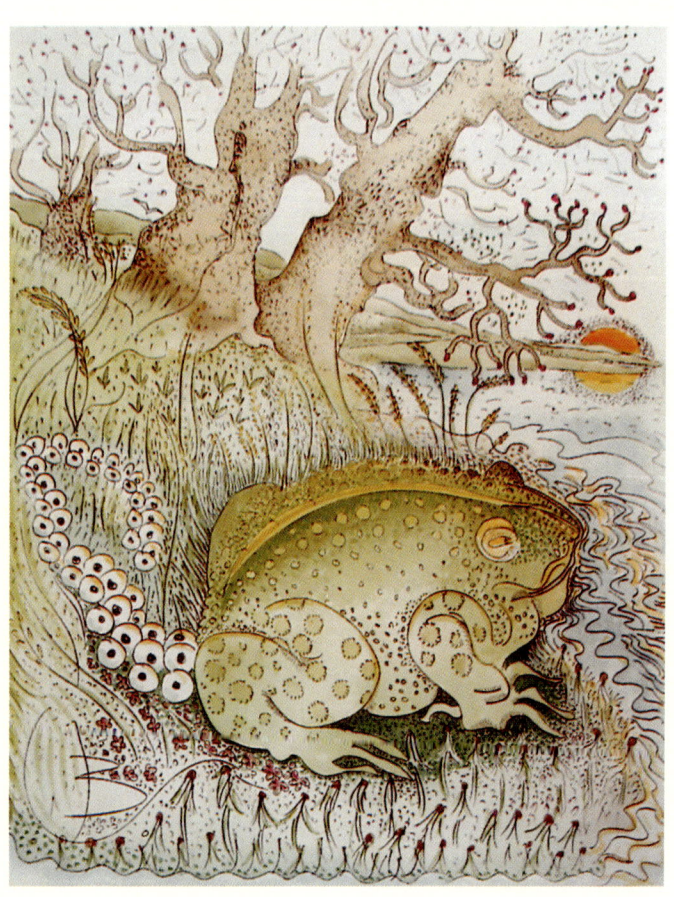

NATTERJACK TOAD, Artist's Proof
1987 • hand coloured etching • 26" x 20"
Kerry Collection

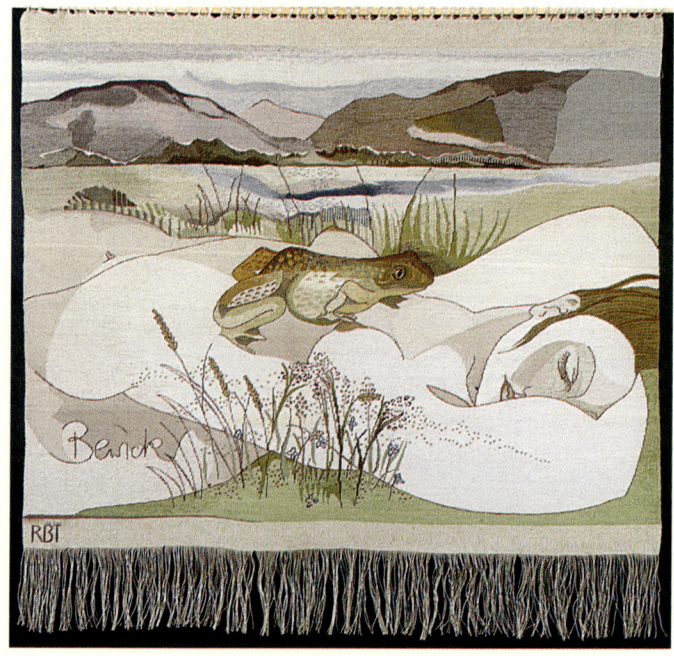

WOMAN AND FROG, CARAGH LAKE
1984 • wool tapestry limited edition of six • 38" x 48"
woven by Regine Bartsch
Travelling Collection

The Natterjack toad is peculiar to Dooks, Glenbeigh.

To be so at ease lying in nature is a dream.

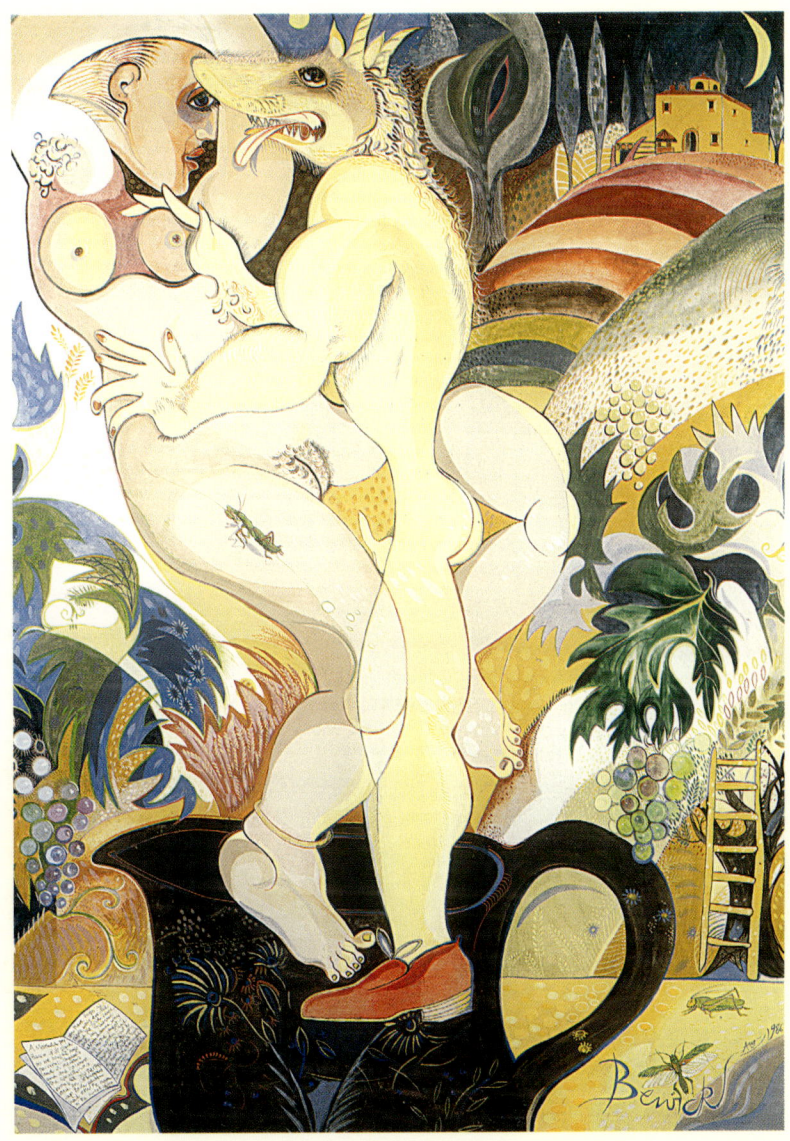

TUSCAN DREAM
1985 • pigment acrylic on canvas • 105" x 78"
pure Irish linen frame surround
Travelling Collection

Painted after a picnic in the woods with the local people of Tuscany.
I had a fear of wolves that had been released by the government into the countryside,
coupled with the flirtatious men.

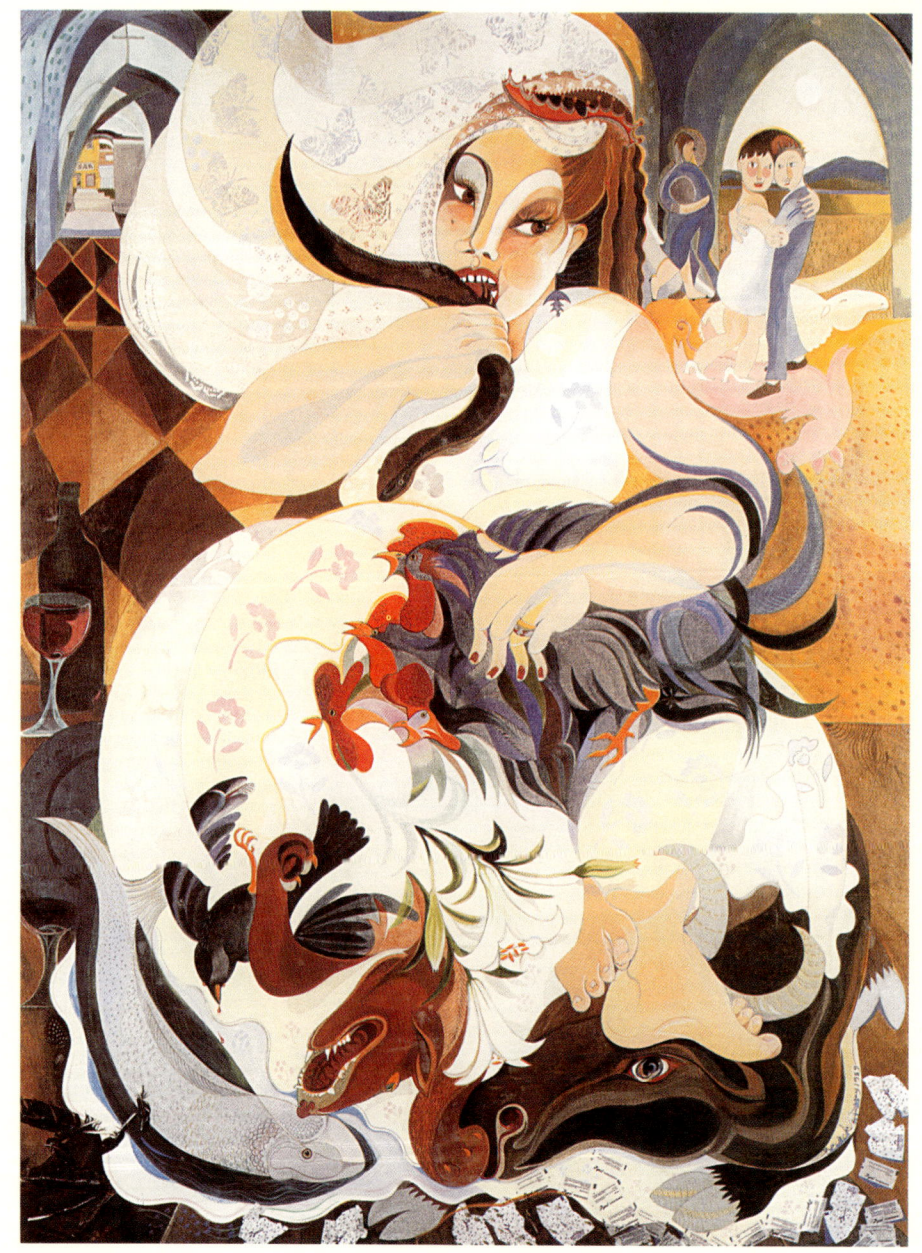

THE GREEDY BRIDE
1989 • acrylic • 90" x 66"
Kerry Collection

Thinking of a woman more interested in the material side of marriage.

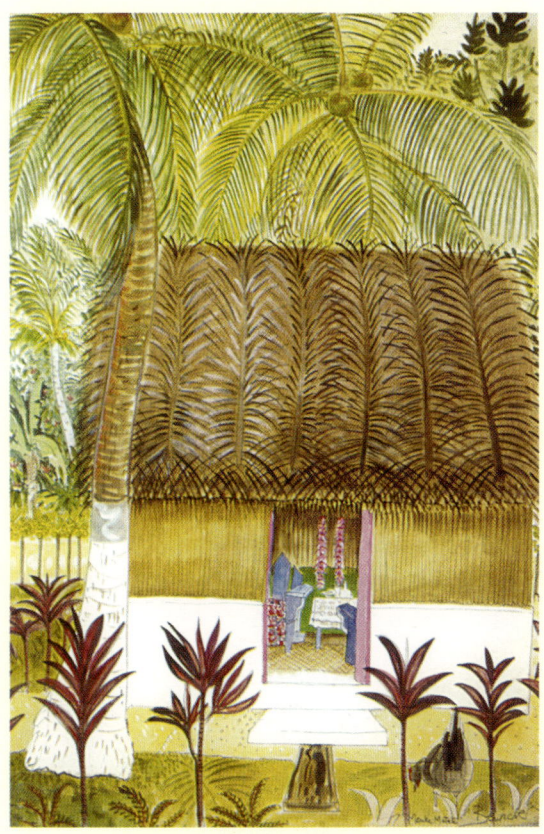

MOTEL MAUKE
1990 • watercolour • 30" x 20"
Kerry Collection

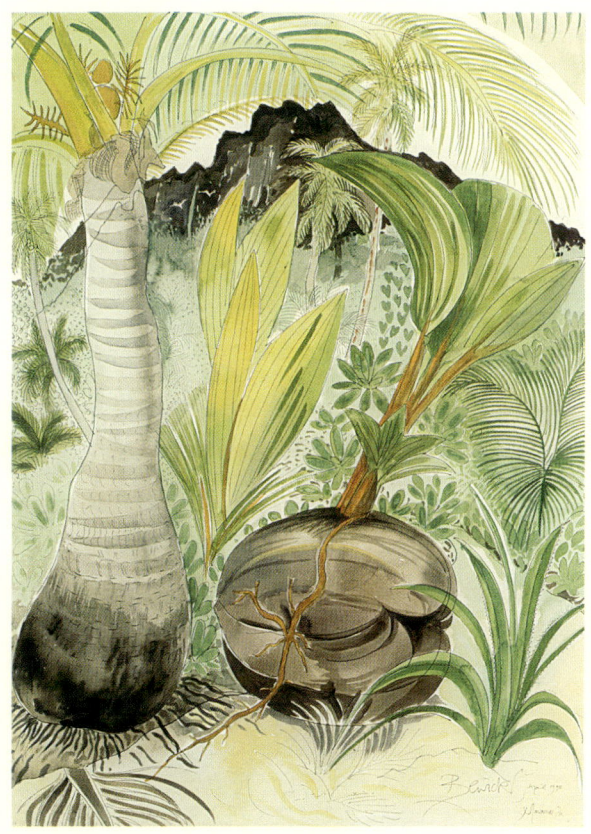

COCONUT AND TREE, MAINGAPU
1990 • watercolour • 31" x 23"
Waterford Collection

The one truck on the island brought us from the airport hut to this 'motel', necklaces of flowers awaited us.

The coconut bobs over the sea, is swept onto the sand, and grows into a tree. All the islanders feed from these trees.

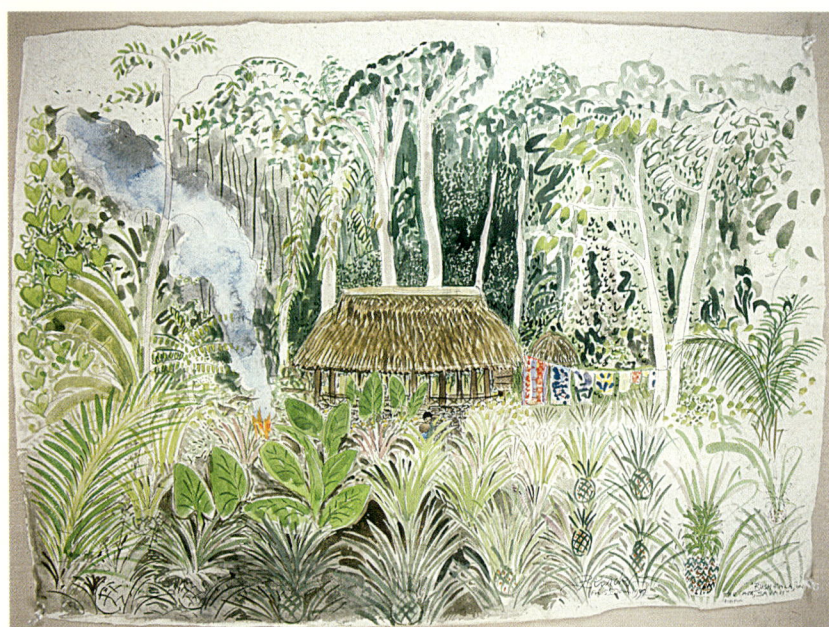

BUSH FALE WITH OUTDOOR FIRE
1990 • watercolour • 23" x 31"
Waterford Collection

Pineapples in rows growing on the black volcanic dust
Each house's roof was supported by poles.
No such thing as doors.

'Why did you paint her? She has no title',
Moelagi, the lady chief, said.

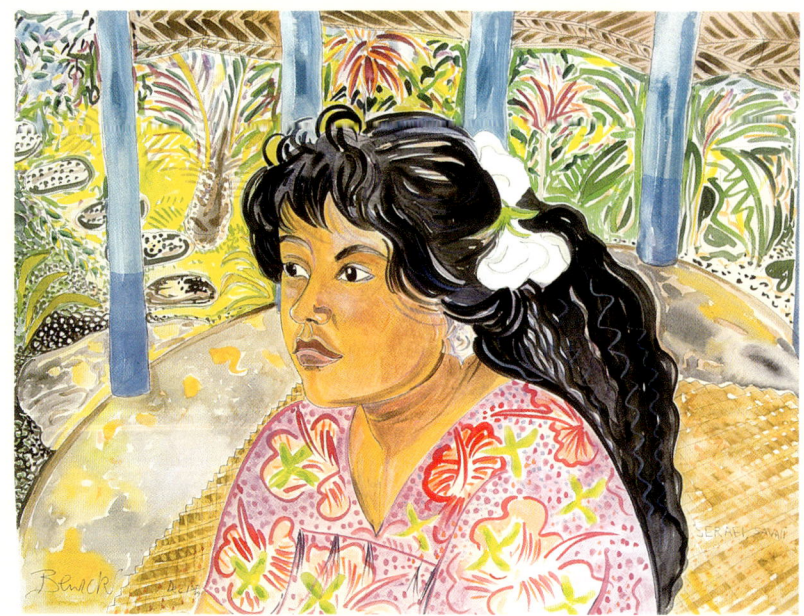

SARAFI IN HER FALE
1990 • watercolour • 22" x 30"
Travelling Collection

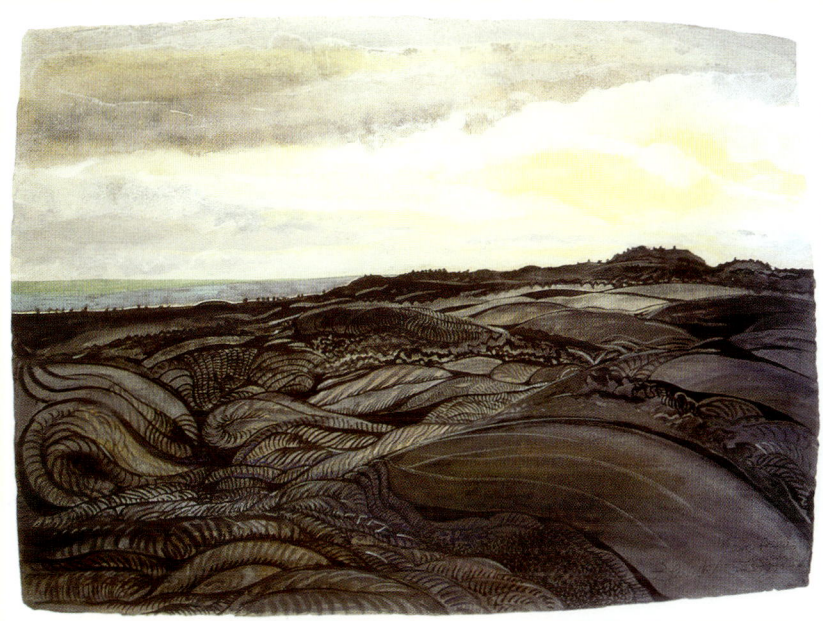

LAVA FIELDS
1990 • watercolour • 23" x 31"
Waterford Collection

Through shaded jungle out to a vast flat volcanic mass of black twisted lava bunched, lumped and coiled towards the sea. Precious green olivins shine on the black cinders. We greedily gather them to take home.

A group of young people hold babies and welcome us to their fale. Behind them an old woman sits cross-legged. 'She's blind. She's had her day'.

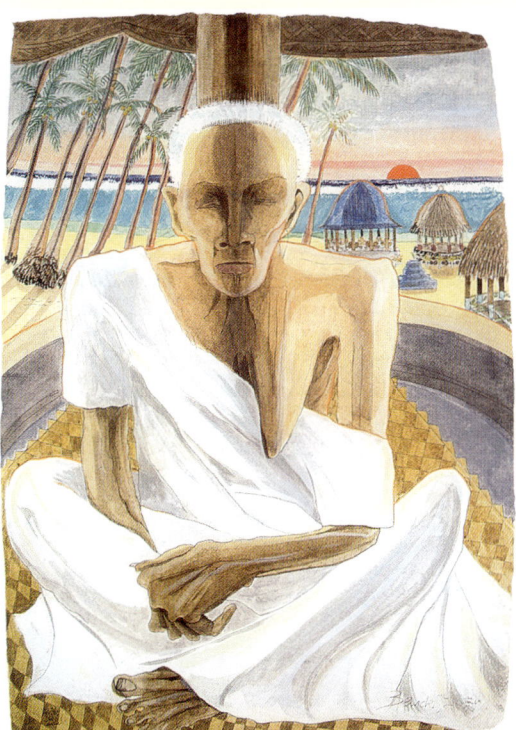

OLD WOMAN, SAVAI'I
1990 • watercolour • 30" x 22"
Waterford Collection

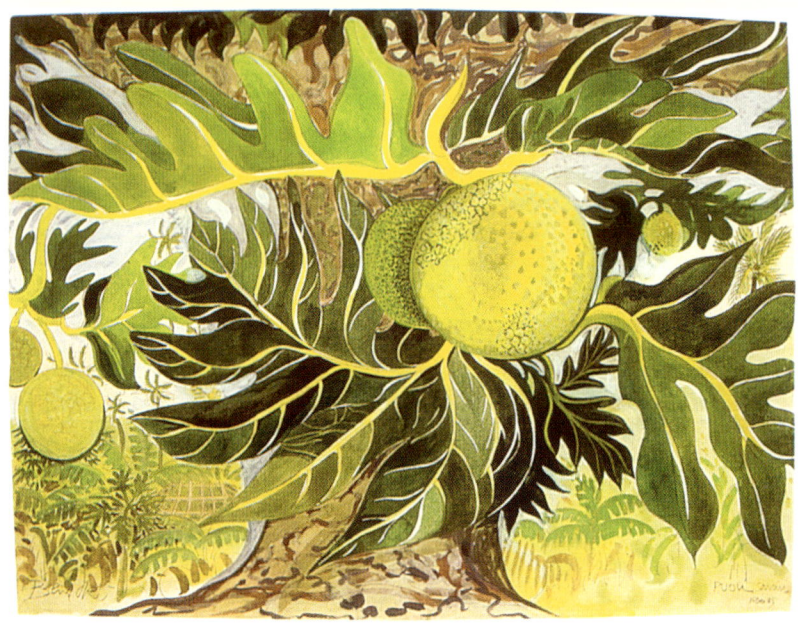

BREADFRUIT TREE
1990 • watercolour • 22" x 30"
Kerry Collection

I wanted to show the close-up details of the fruit, the tree shape recedes into the background.

Smoking fags and flowers seemed a funny mixture.

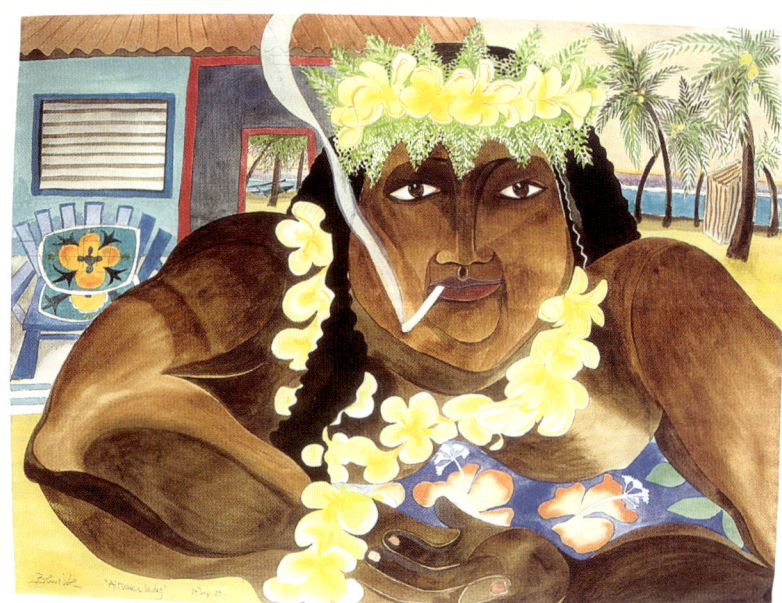

AITUTAKI WOMAN SMOKING
1990 • watercolour • 22" x 29"
Kerry Collection

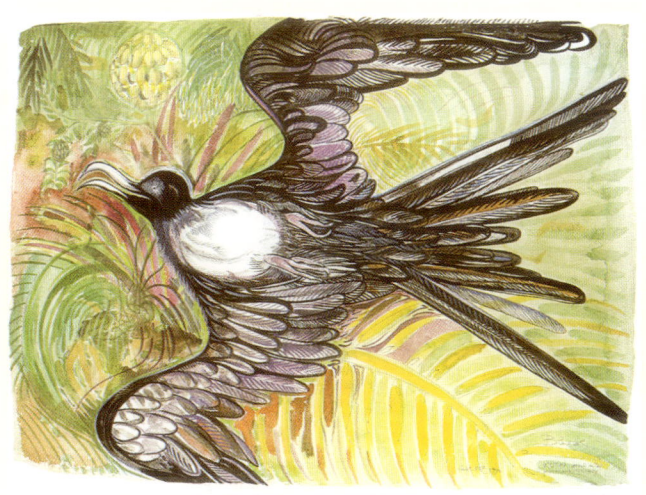

HURRICANE BIRD
1990 • watercolour • 23" x 31"
Travelling Collection

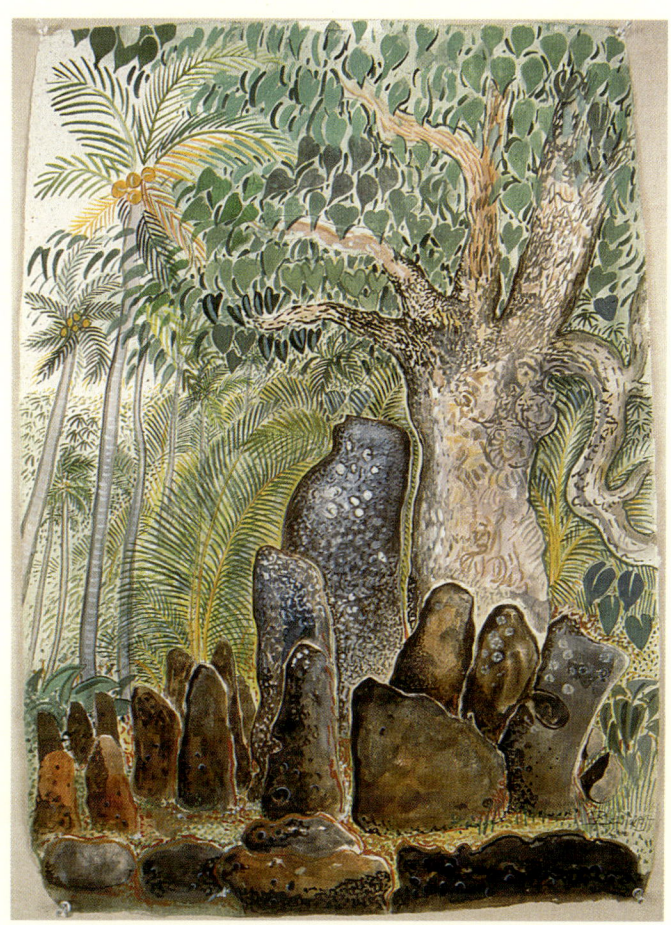

MARAE ON AITUTAKI
1990 • watercolour • 30" x 22"
Travelling Collection

A huge hurricane bird lay dead by a veranda. Its navy blue wings stretched four feet.

The chief stood behind the tallest stone to give his sermon.

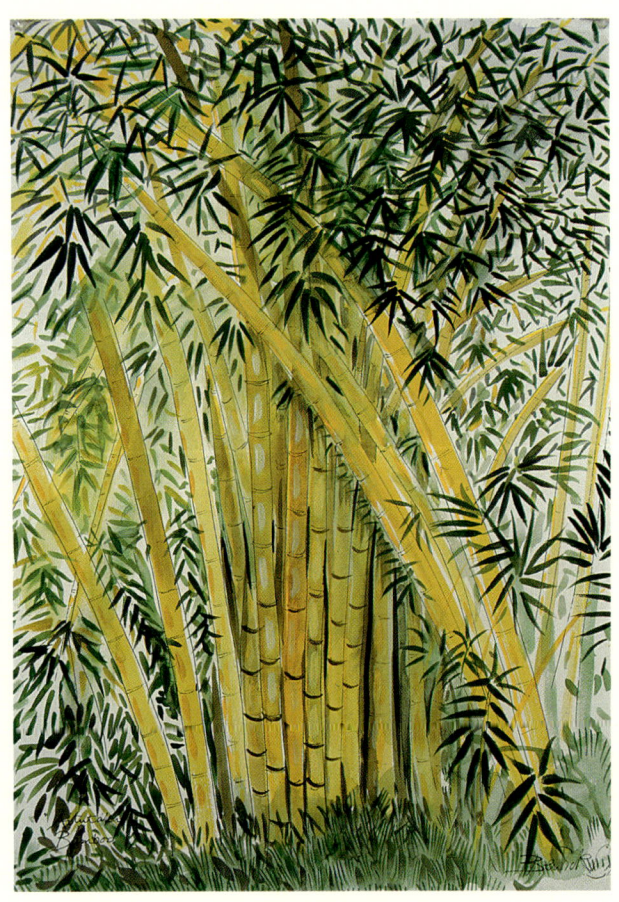

BAMBOO
1990 • watercolour • 31" x 23"
Kerry Collection

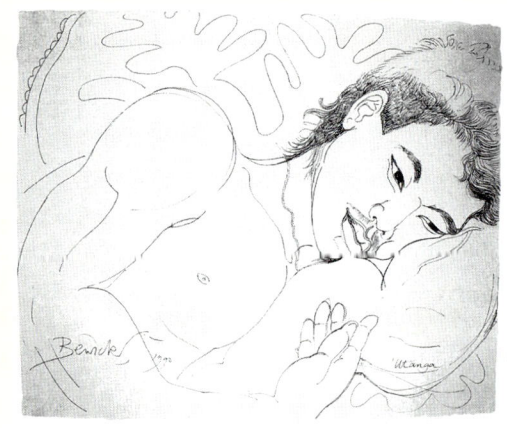

UTANGA ALMOST ASLEEP
1990 • ink • 21" x 26"
Travelling Collection

We all slept out under the stars. When the snoring got too loud, I escaped indoors.

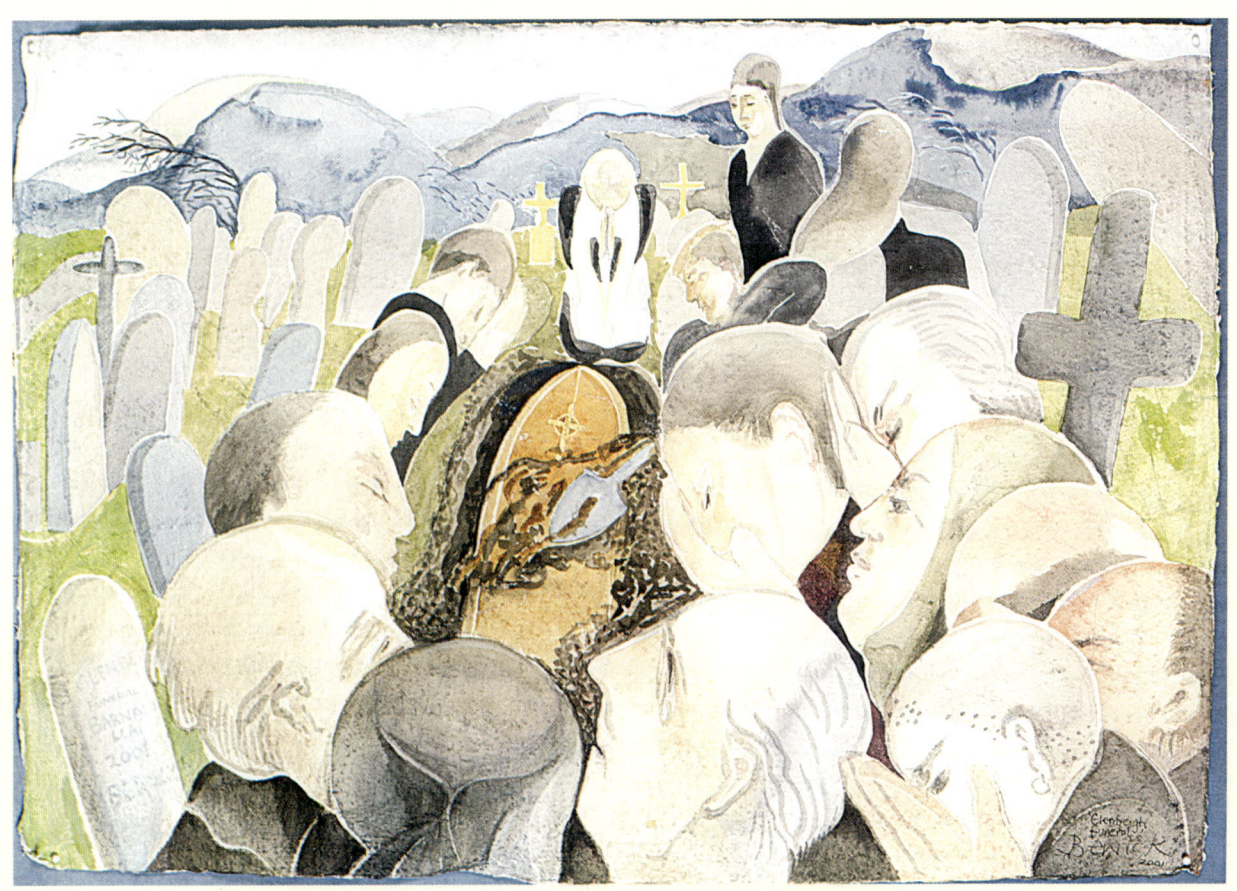

GLENBEIGH FUNERAL
1990 • watercolour and acrylic • 29" x 42"
Kerry Collection

The tree bent like the people's heads over the tragic death of a neighbour.

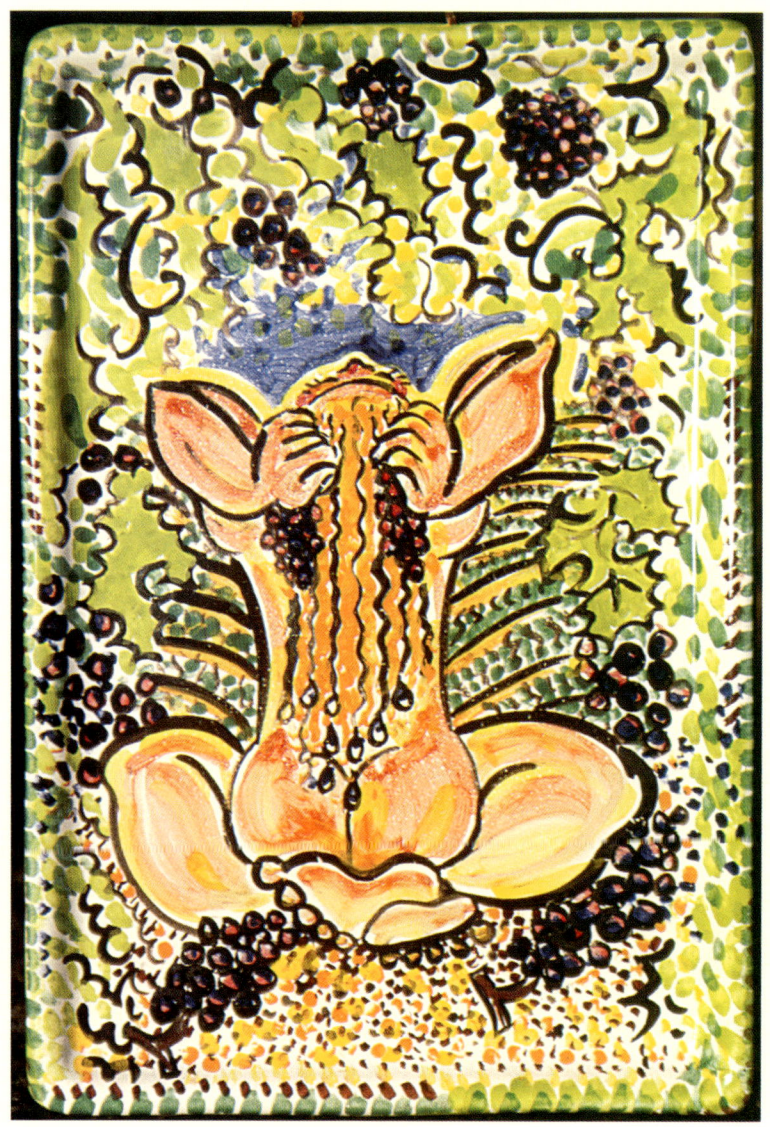

GRAPEJUICE DOWN HER BACK
1993 • majolica glazed tile • 6" x 4"
Travelling Collection

Painted in the Rampini Studios, Tuscany.

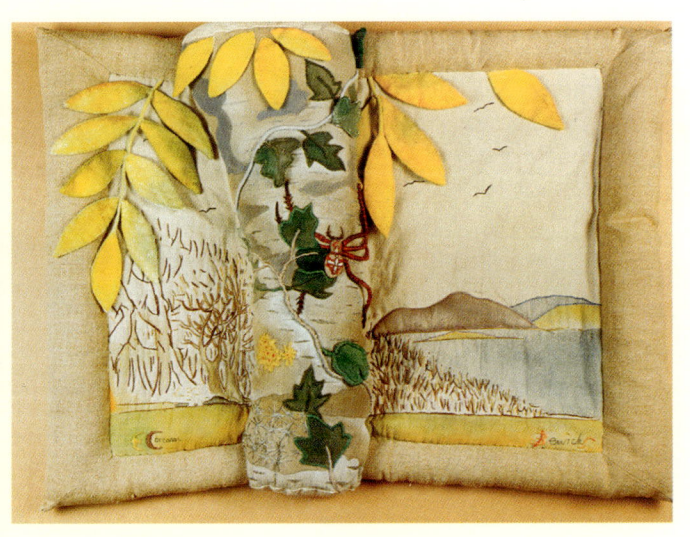

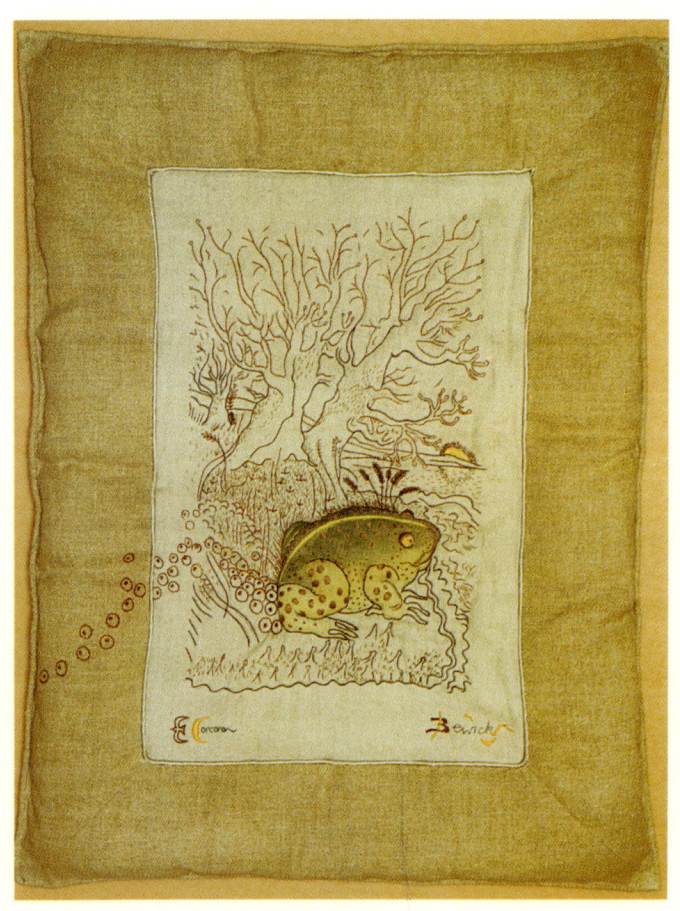

SPIDER
1994 • linen, silk, wool and acrylic wash • 28" x 31"
Travelling Collection

NATTERJACK TOAD
1994 • linen, silk and acrylic wash • 27" x 21"
Travelling Collection

Edwina Corcoran stitched all the padded wall hangings.

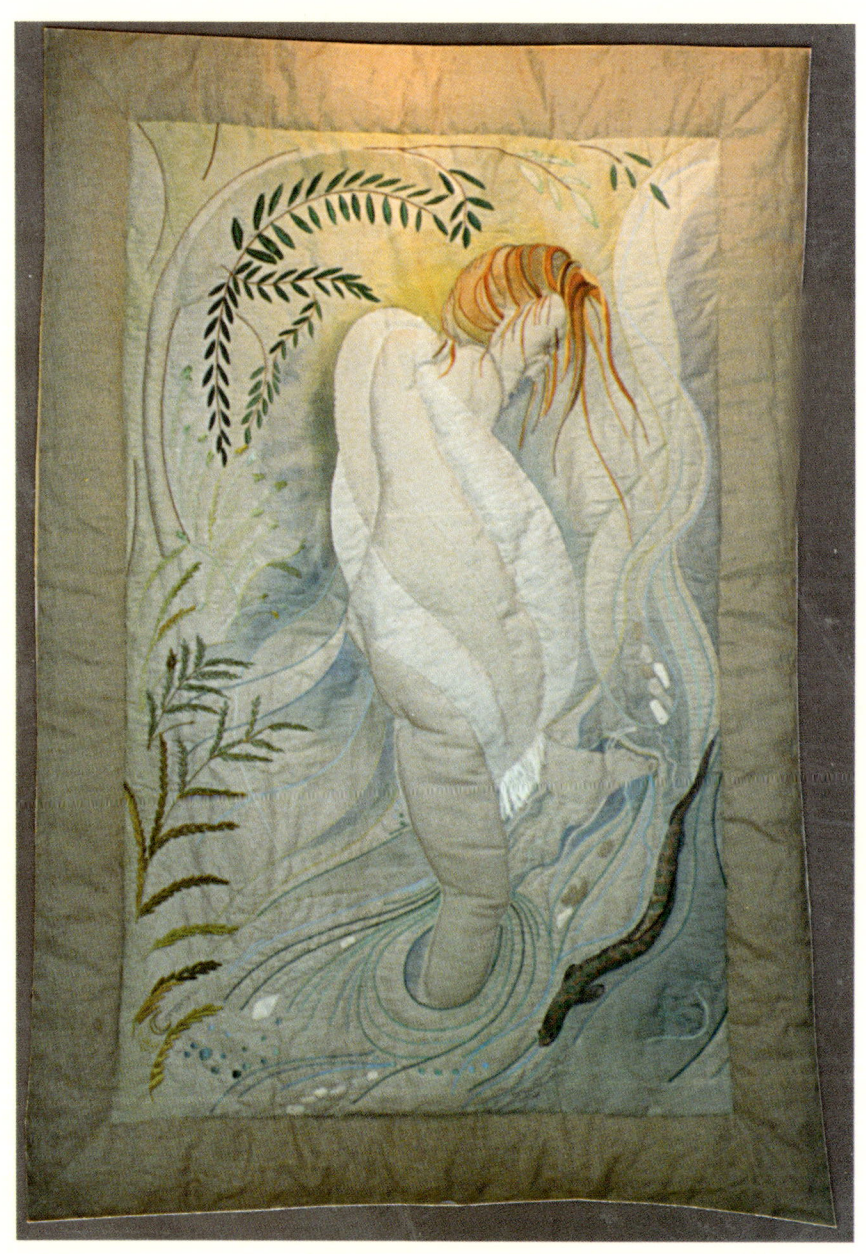

Woman and Eel
1995 • linen, silk, wool and acrylic wash • 77" x 50"
Kerry Collection

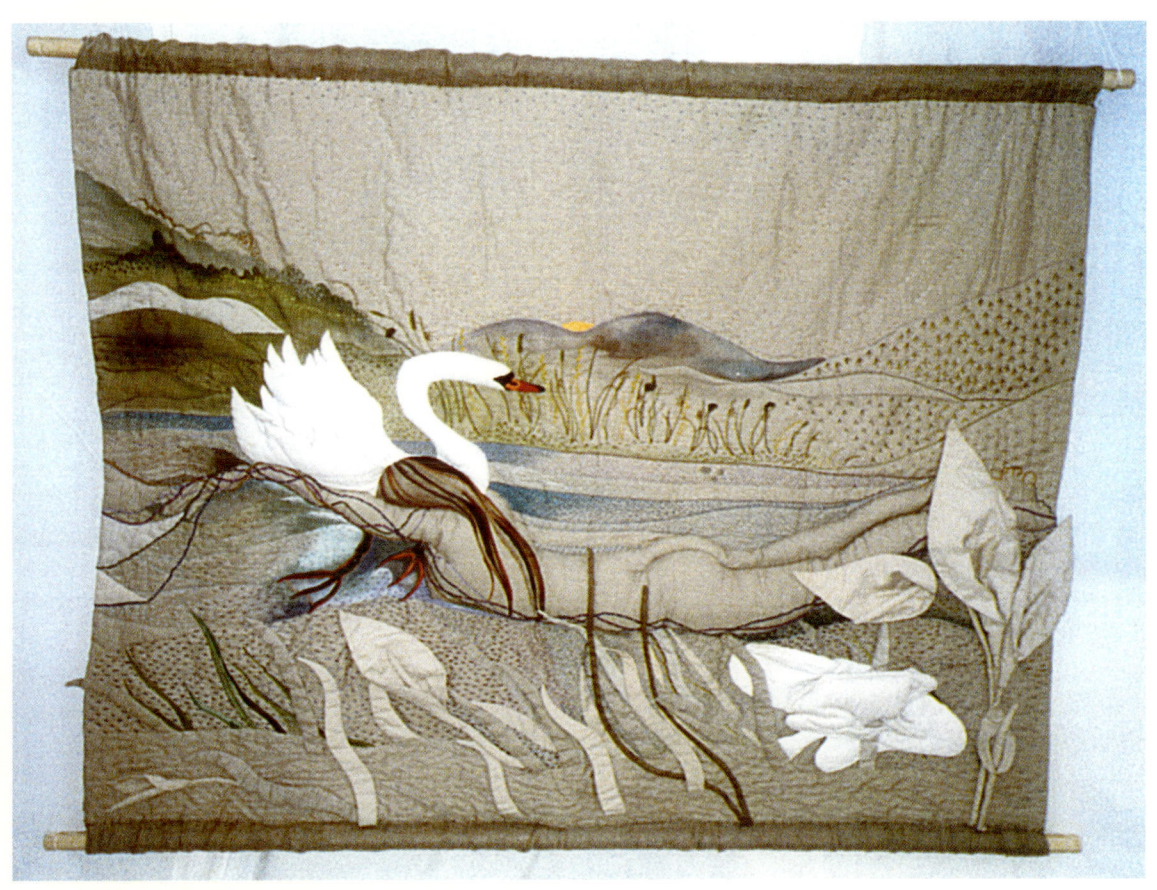

SWIMMING TO A SWAN
1995 • linen, silk, wool and acrylic wash • 78" x 60"
Waterford Collection

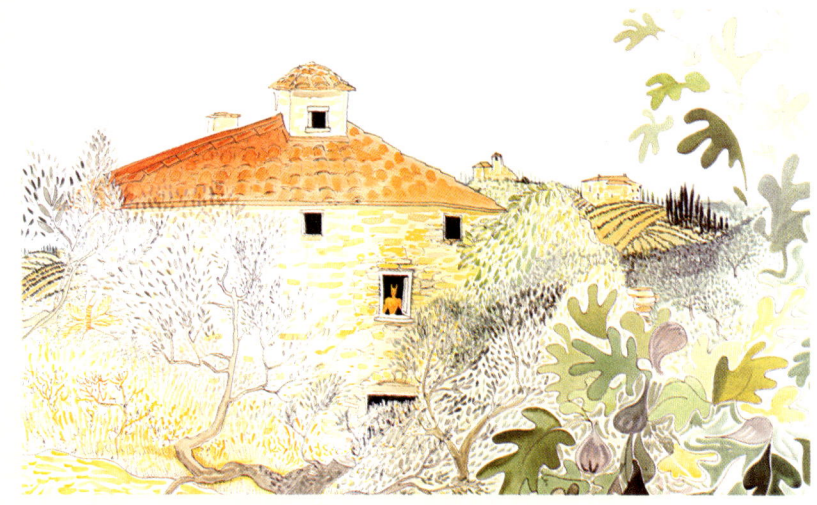

YELLOW MAN AT HIS WINDOW LOOKING OUT AT FIGS
watercolour • 23" x 31"
Travelling Collection

The Yellow Man lives alone in an old farmhouse in Tuscany.

After looking at the vineyards from his window, the Yellow Man goes outside.

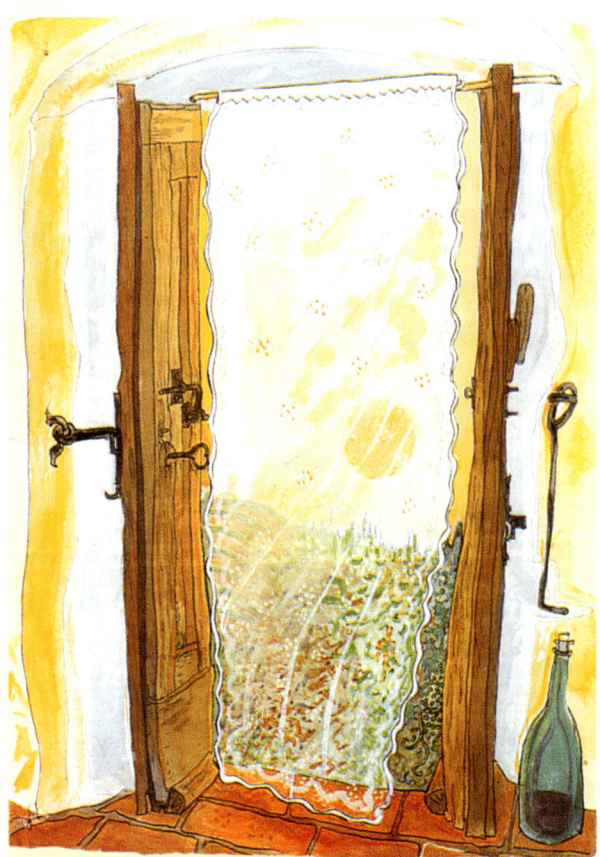

YELLOW MAN'S DOOR
watercolour • 16" x 13"
Kerry Collection

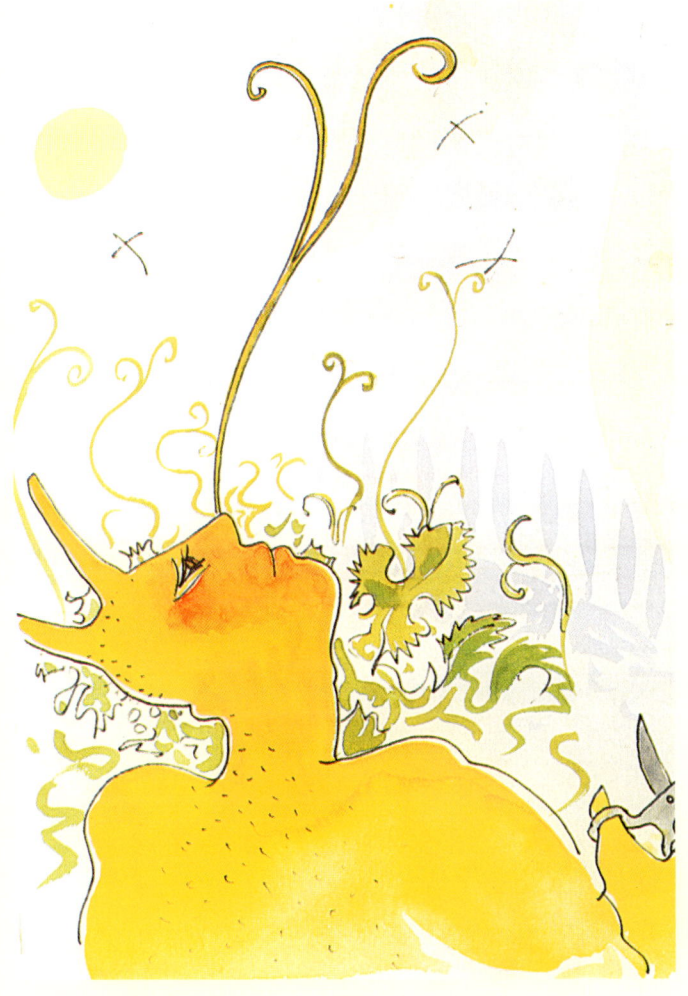

YELLOW MAN CUTTING CREEPERS
watercolour • 13" x 8"
Waterford Collection

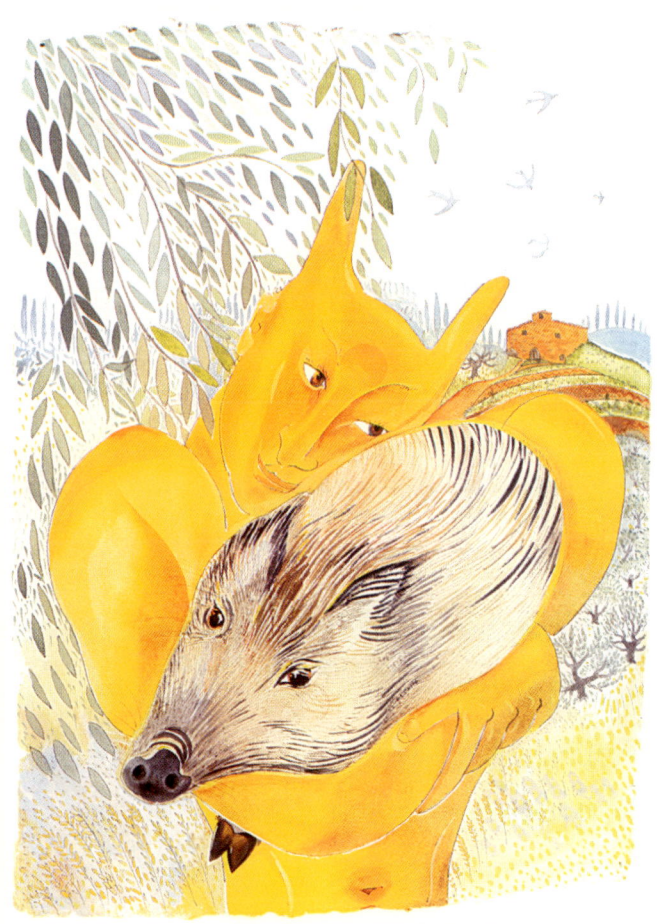

YELLOW MAN HUGGING A BOAR
watercolour • 31" x 23"
Waterford Collection

Today he clips the overcrowded shoots from the vines.

He loves the strong smell of wild boar.

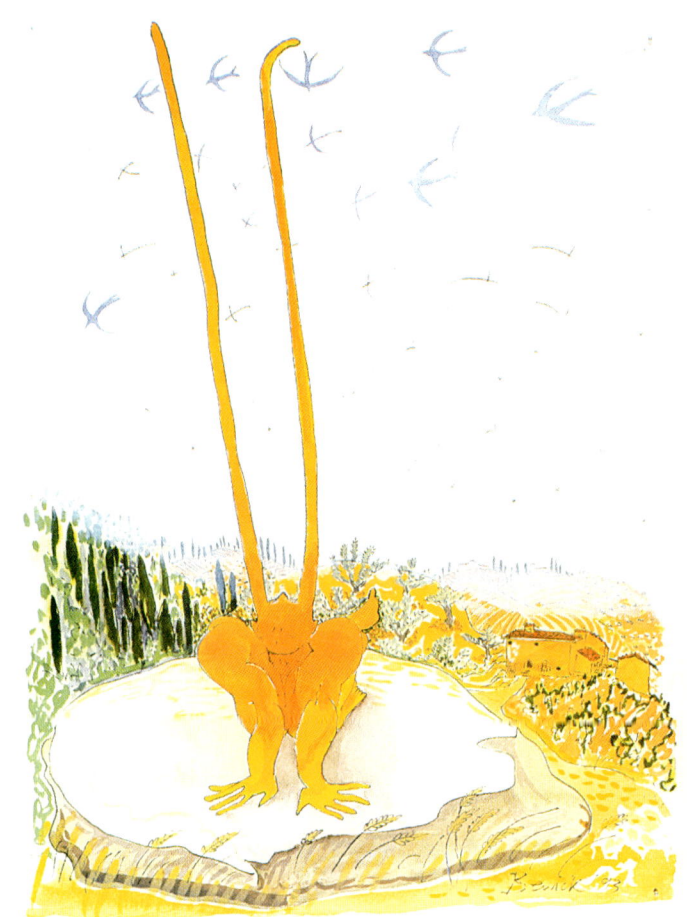

YELLOW MAN WITH SWIFTS
AND LONG ANTENNAE
watercolour • 16" x 13"
Waterford Collection

The sun shines and the swifts fly.
The Yellow Man's antennae extend to touch the swifts.

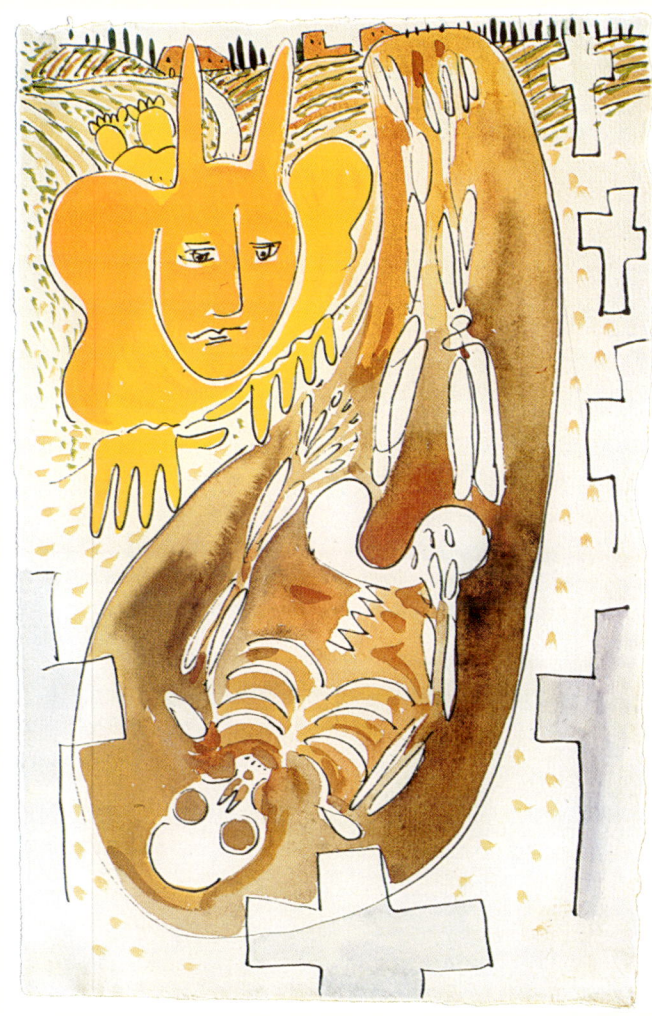

YELLOW MAN LOOKING AT A SKELETON
watercolour • 8" x 12"
Waterford Collection

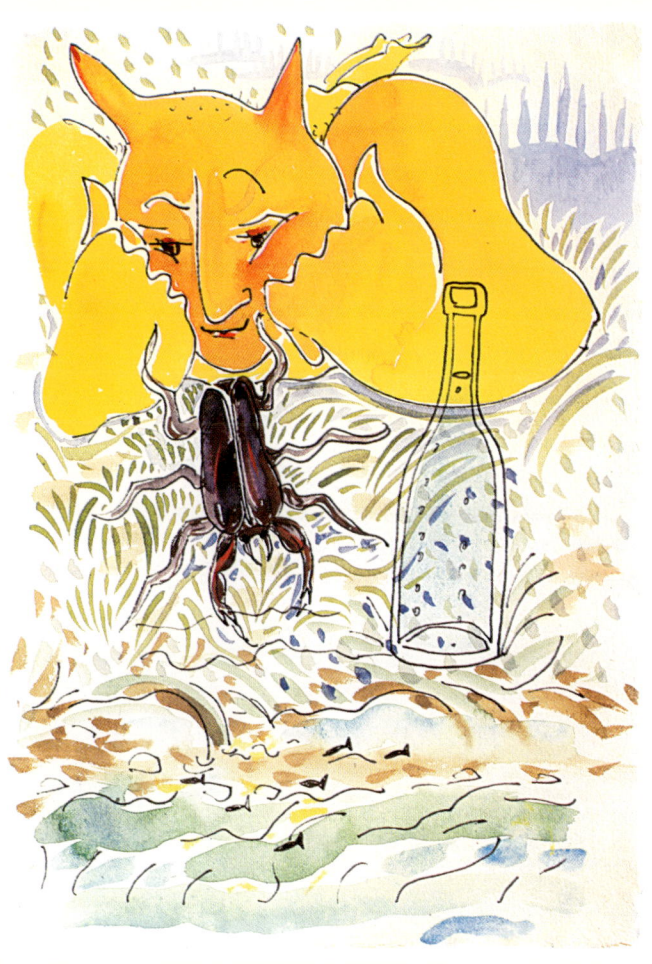

YELLOW MAN LOOKING AT A BEETLE
watercolour • 12" x 8"
Waterford Collection

The Yellow Man digs and loosens the soil to allow the seeds to spread their shoots. He digs up a human skeleton. Has this seed done with spreading its shoots?

A beetle's life walks on six legs. 'I bet it's going to eat some of the seeds I've set'.

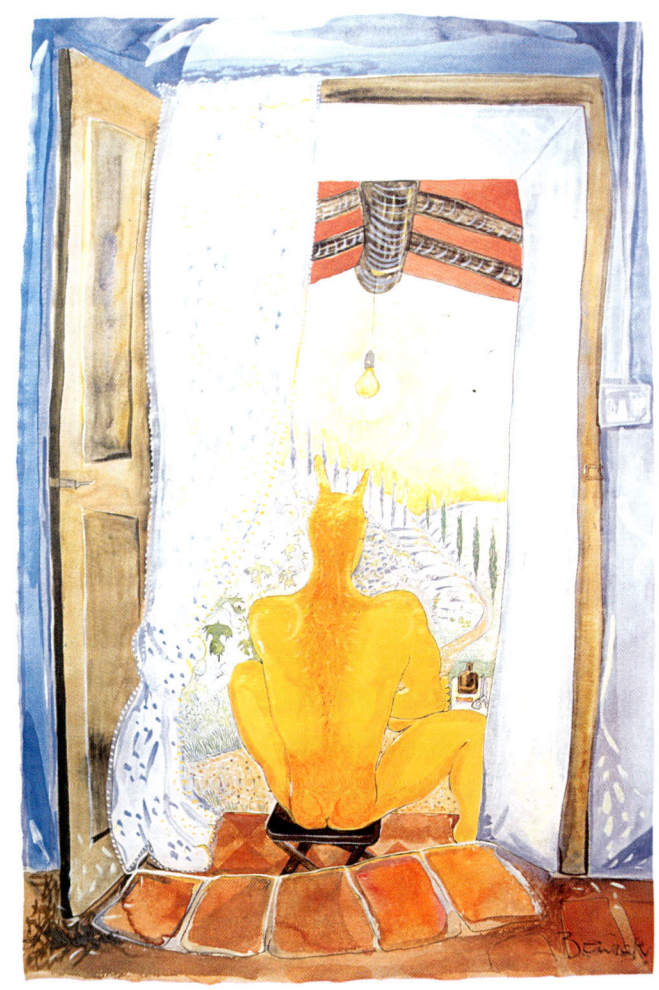

YELLOW MAN GETTING READY FOR A
TRIP TO SIENA
watercolour • 30" x 20"
Kerry Collection

The Yellow Man decides to visit Siena. He washes and cuts his nails.

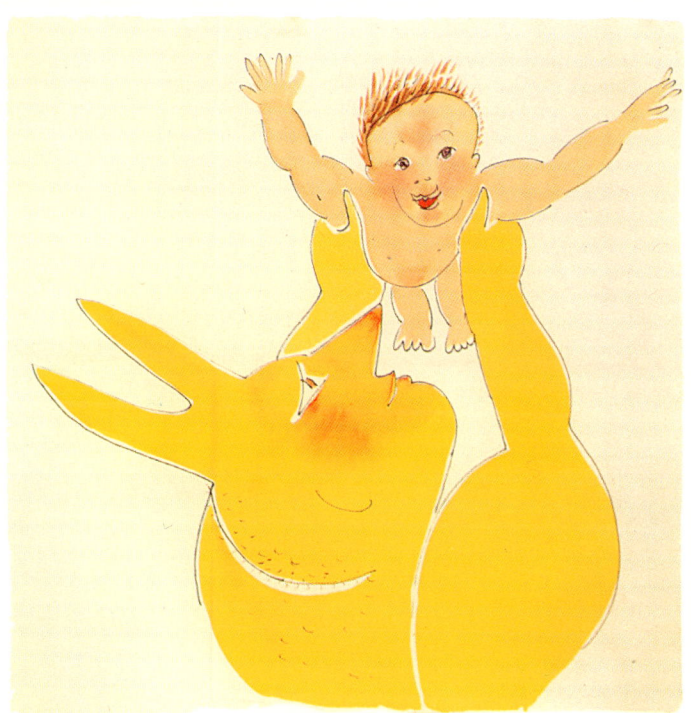

YELLOW MAN LIFTS UP BABY
watercolour • 13" x 16"
Travelling Collection

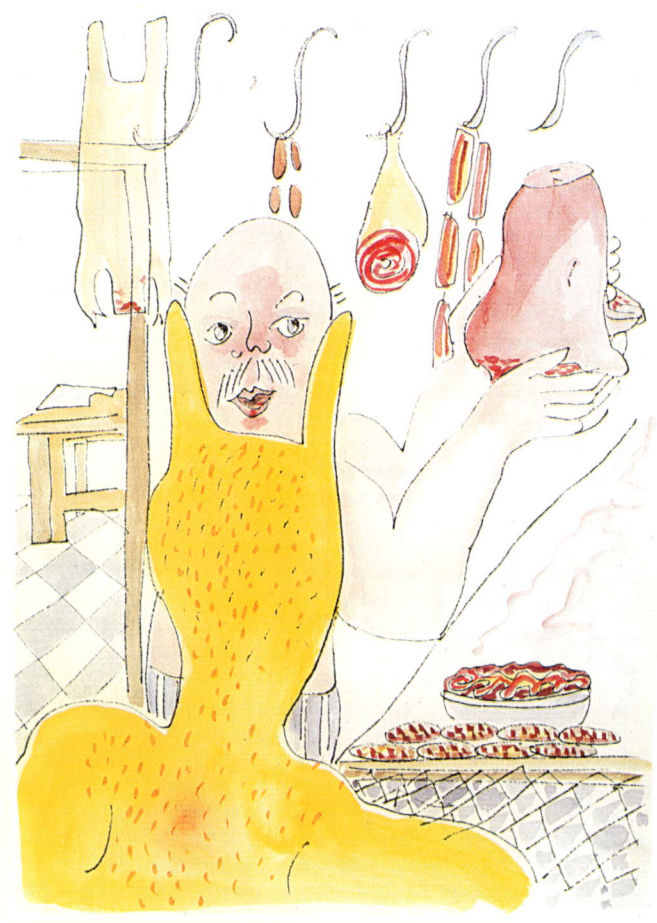

YELLOW MAN IN BUTCHER'S SHOP
watercolour • 11" x 8"
Kerry Collection

In the city park a mother and father share their baby with the Yellow Man.

The butcher holds up a pig's head. It puts the Yellow Man off meat today.

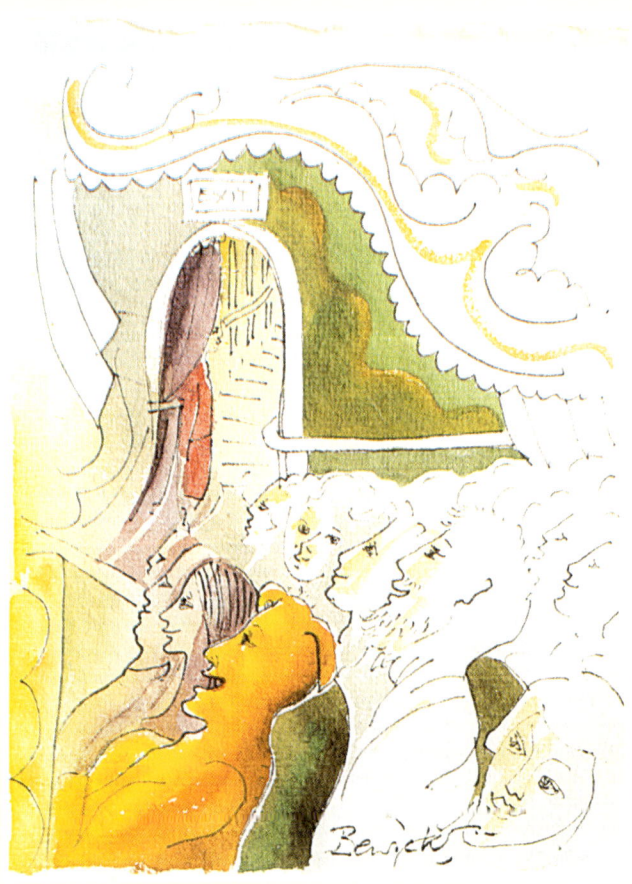

YELLOW MAN AT THE THEATRE
watercolour • 6" x 5"
Travelling Collection

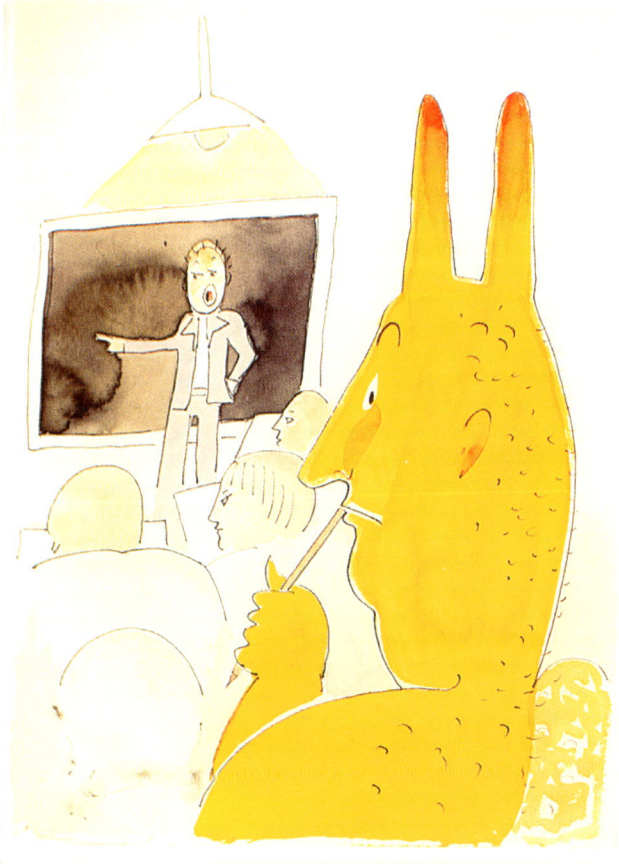

YELLOW MAN SCHOOL LESSON
watercolour • 13" x 8"
Waterford Collection

The Yellow Man goes to the theatre. He thinks the play is fascinating. It is about two tramps waiting for somebody who never turns up.

He visits a school. The lesson has no connection with the Yellow Man's life.
So he leaves …

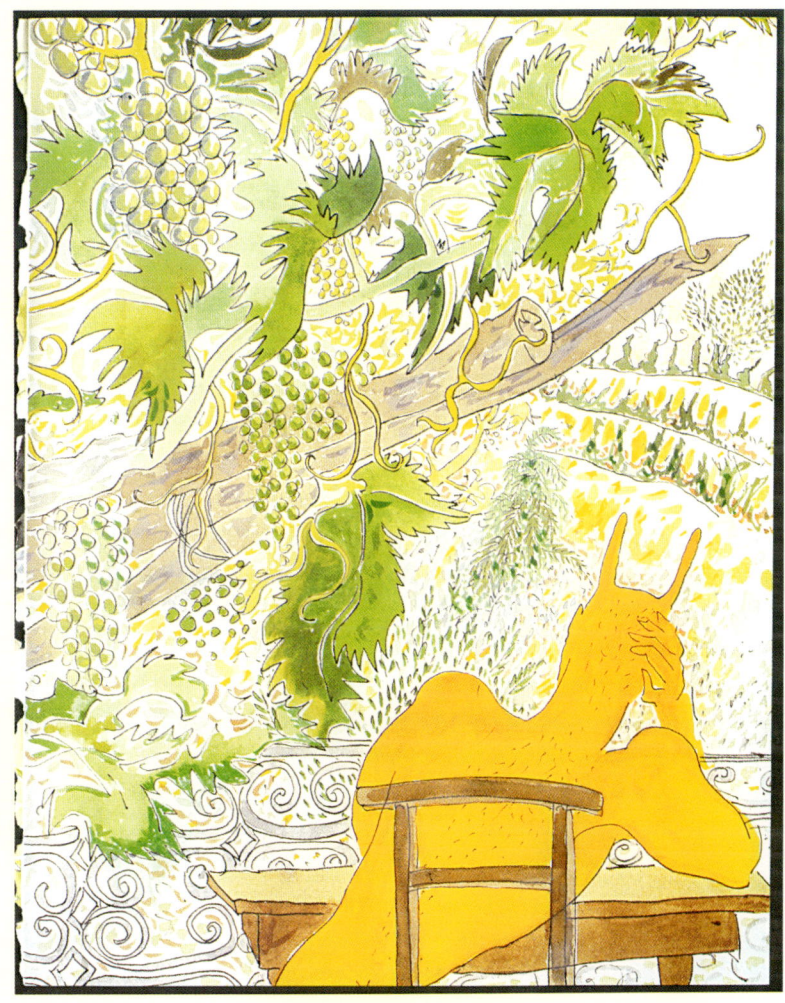

YELLOW MAN THINKING
UNDER A GRAPEVINE
watercolour • 16" x 13"
Kerry Collection

The Yellow Man often sits by his house in the shade of an aged, fertile vine, its clumps of young grapes dulled with bloom. The vine-leaves curl. Acid green shoots each skywards and onwards from its gnarled grey trunk. Crickets grate their monotonous call. Year in, year out, the Yellow Man lives alone. No-one comments on the colour of his skin, his nakedness or his antennae. Maybe it's because he doesn't make judgements, is not grasping. Like nature he is just there, simply there. He has no history. His vision is unattached to the past. He looks at an object without knowledge of it. His questions don't demand an answer. He is complete, yet open for more. His changing body doesn't surprise him. He's young, old, blushing, excited; his antennae flush, shrink and grow. He lives his silent life observing, alert, empty, without guilt, unconditioned – yet in tune, alone.

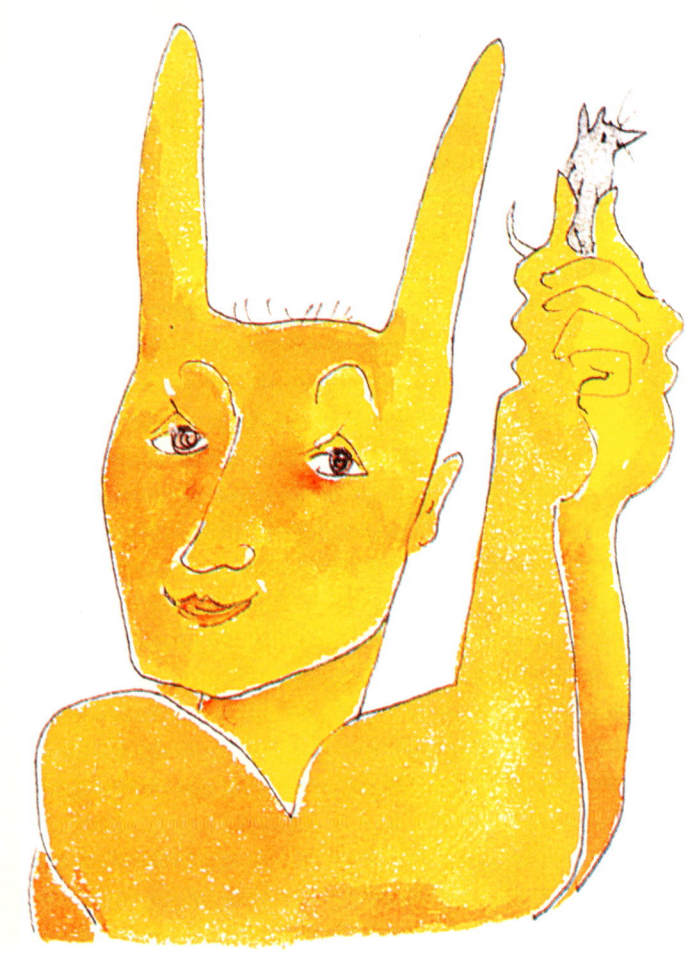

YELLOW MAN AND MOUSE
watercolour 6" x 5"
Travelling Collection

I am yellow, but a mouse sees me as grey.

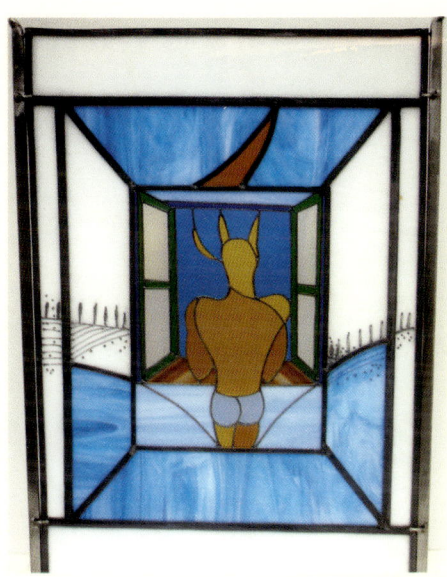

YELLOW MAN AT HIS WINDOW
stained glass • 27" x 18"
Kerry Collection

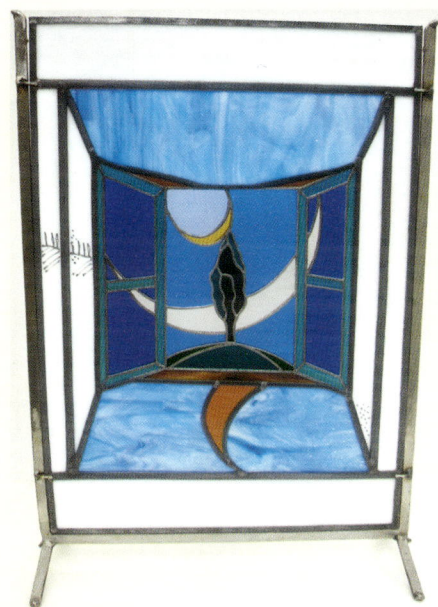

YELLOW MAN'S WINDOW
stained glass • 27" x 18"
Kerry Collection

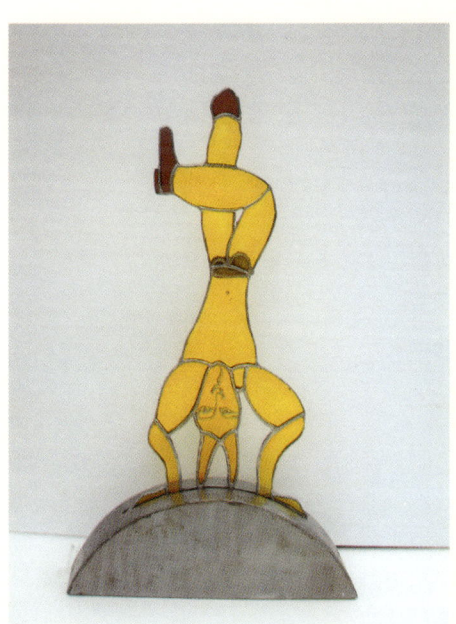

YELLOW MAN ON THE WORLD
stained glass • 20" x 12"
Kerry Collection

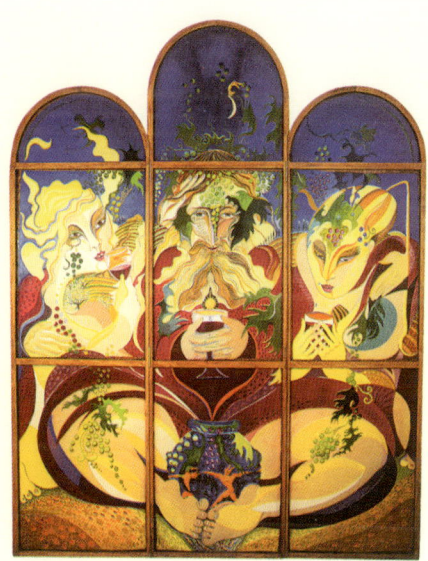

BACCHUS, WINE URN AND TWO WOMEN
acrylic on carved wood screen
Travelling Collection

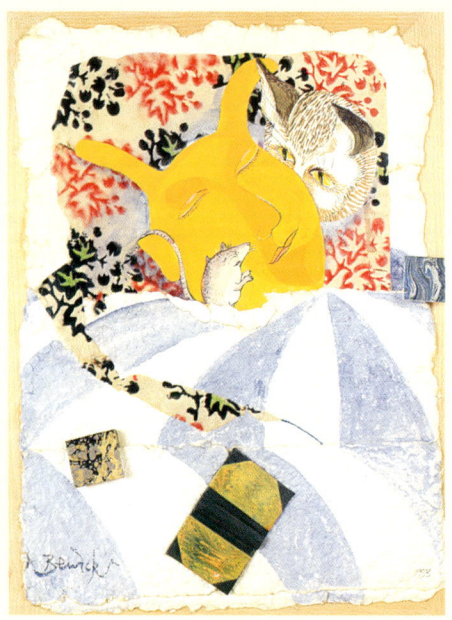

YELLOW MAN ASLEEP
WITH CAT AND MOUSE
acrylic and collage • 29" x 23"
Kerry Collection

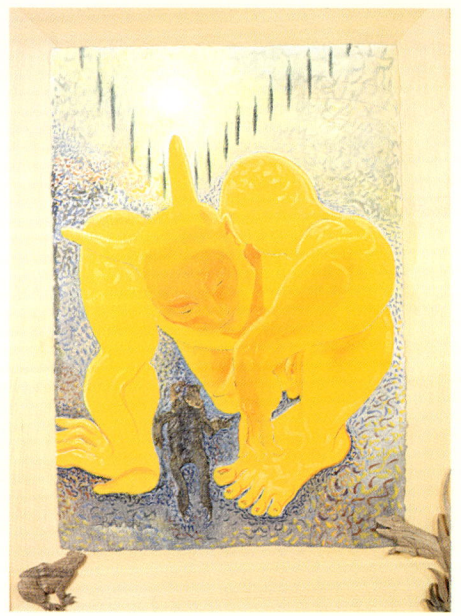

YELLOW MAN WITH A DEAD FROG
acrylic • 41" x 31"
Waterford Collection

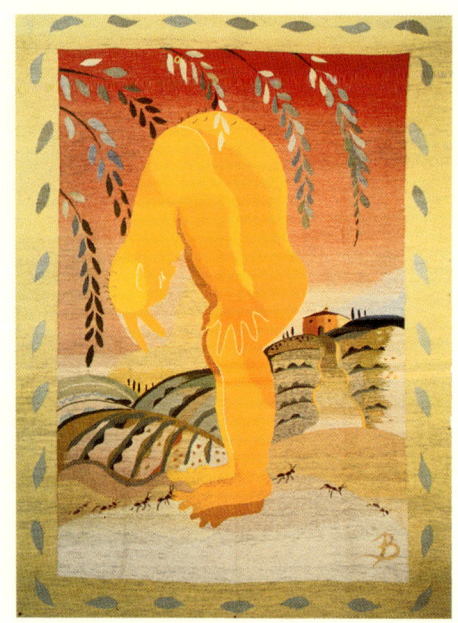

YELLOW MAN LOOKING AT ANTS
silk and linen tapestry • 92" x 72"
woven by Regine Bartsch
Travelling Collection

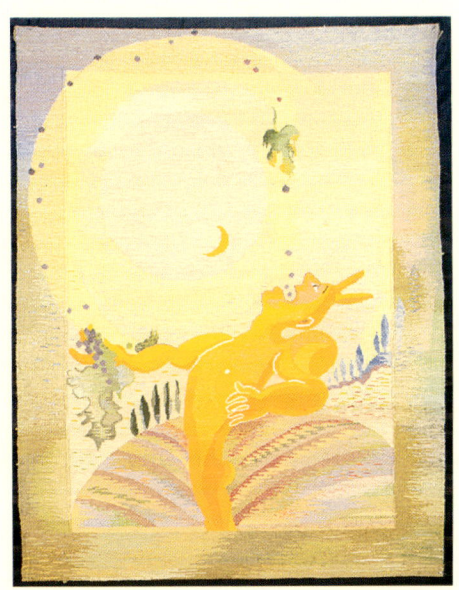

YELLOW MAN THROWING UP GRAPES
design for tapestry • 60" x 32"
Waterford Collection

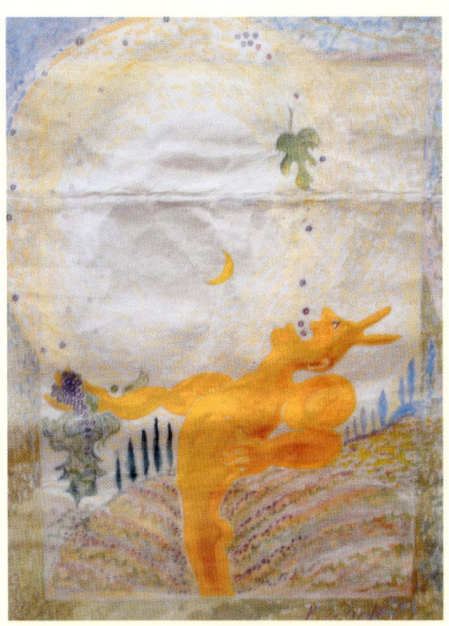

YELLOW MAN THROWING UP GRAPES
silk and linen tapestry • 48" x 36"
woven by Regine Bartsch
Waterford Collection

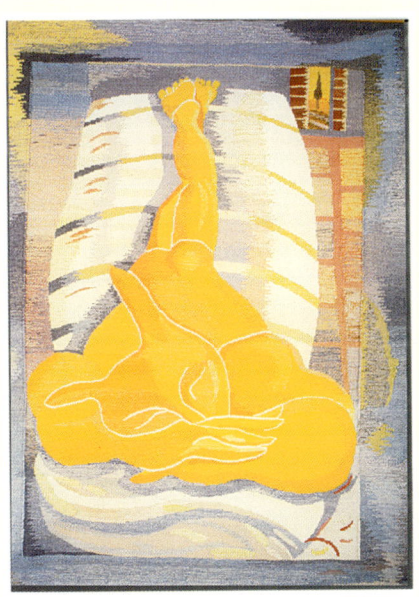

DESIGN FOR TAPESTRY OF
YELLOW MAN ASLEEP
watercolour in carved frame • 45" x 33"
Kerry Collection

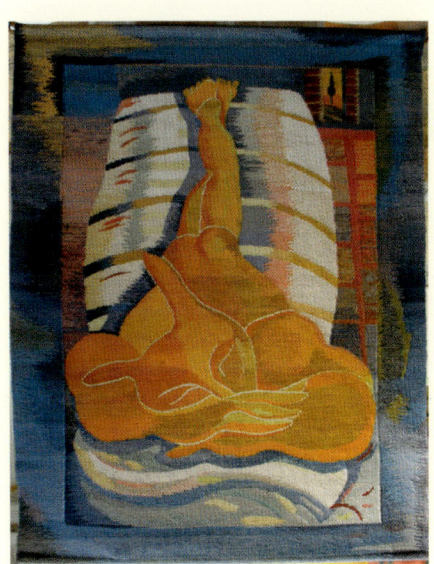

YELLOW MAN ASLEEP
silk and linen tapestry • 48" x 36"
woven by Regine Bartsch
Kerry Collection

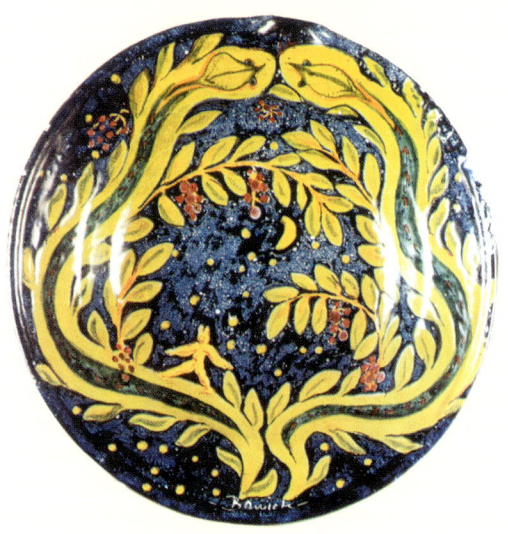

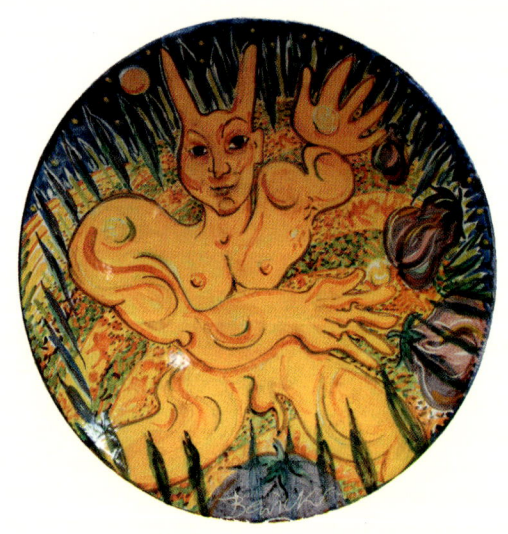

TWO SNAKES IN THE BLUE NIGHT
terracotta glazed pouring dish 4" high, 6" diameter
Waterford Collection

YELLOW MAN WITH AN AUBERGINE BY MOONLIGHT
terracotta glazed dish • 24" diameter, 6" deep
Kerry Collection

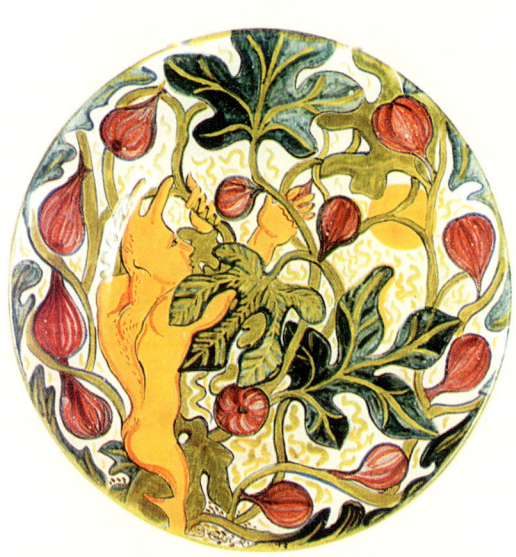

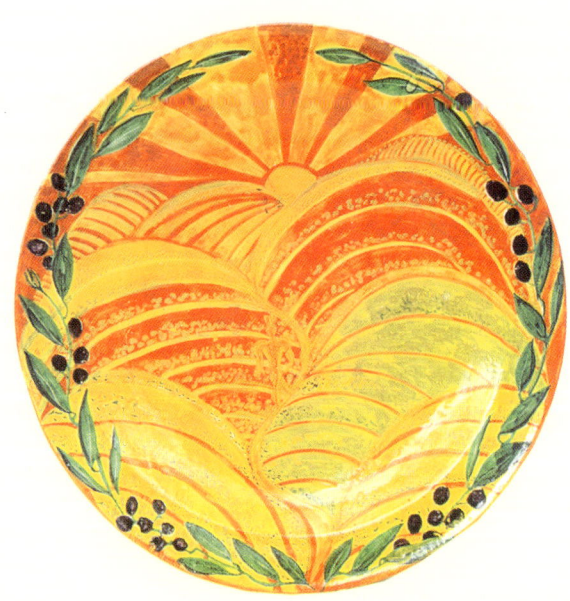

YELLOW MAN PICKING FIGS
terracotta glazed dish 3" high
Travelling Collection

YELLOW MAN AND SUNSET
terracotta glazed dish • 24" diameter, 3" high
Kerry Collection
cracked by the artist

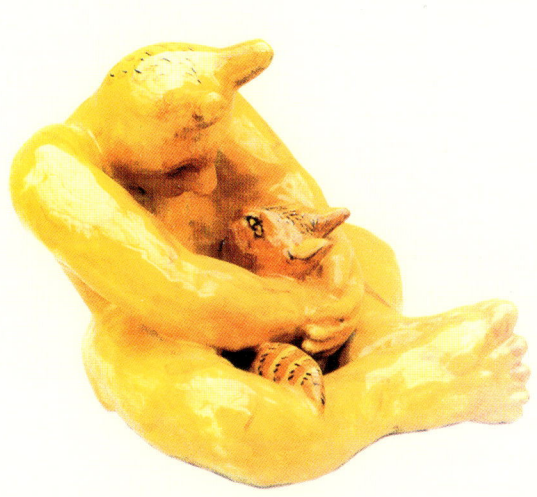

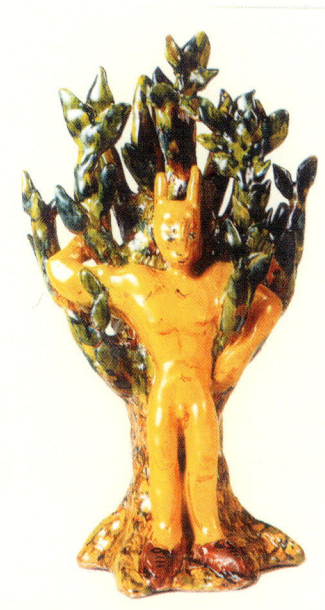

YELLOW MAN AND CAT
terracotta glazed figure • 6" x 8"
Kerry Collection

YELLOW MAN STANDING IN A TREE
terracotta glazed figure • 11" x 6"
Waterford Collection

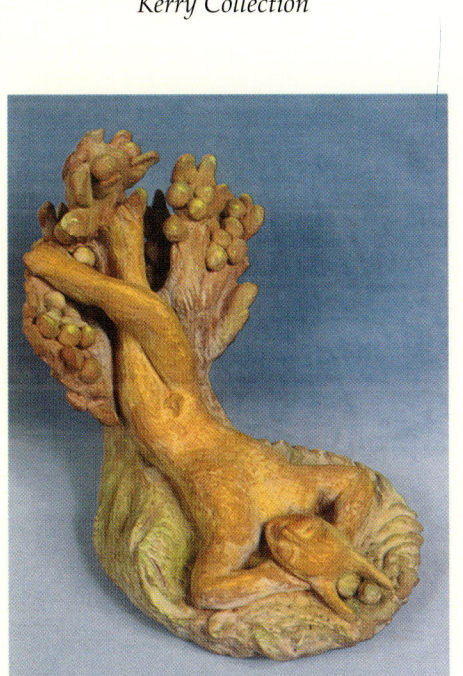

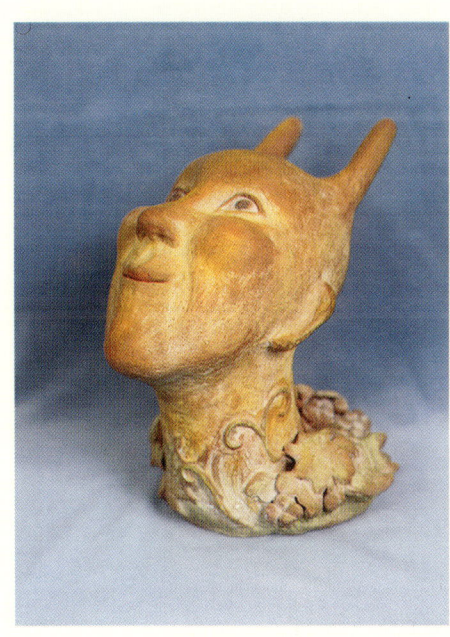

YM ASLEEP UNDER AN APPLE TREE
terracotta figure, powder pigment • 10" x 10"
Kerry Collection

YELLOW MAN LOOKING UP AT THE SKY
terracotta figure, powder pigment • 12" x 13"
Waterford Collection

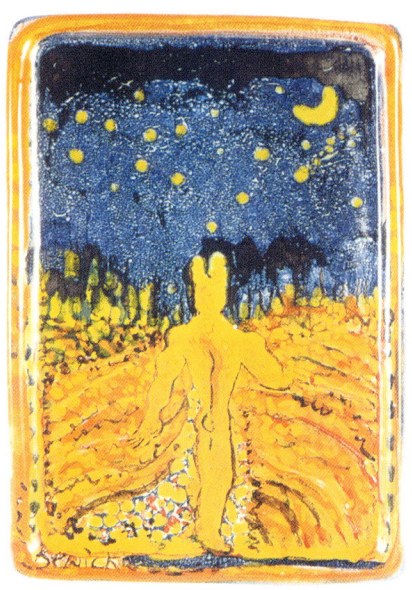

YELLOW MAN ON A NIGHT WALK
terracotta glazed wall plate • 10" x 7"
Travelling Colleciton

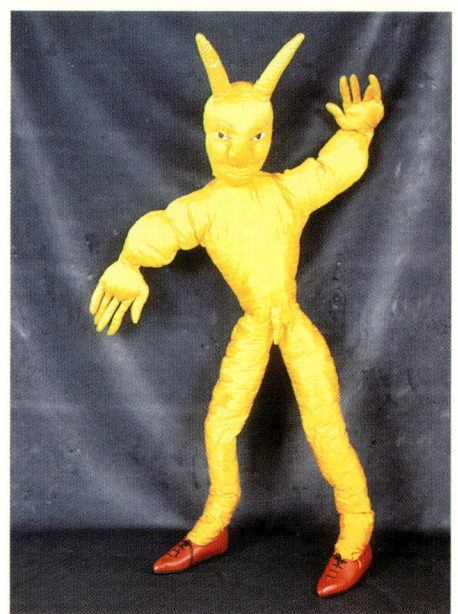

YELLOW MAN SILK DOLL, RED SHOES
Doll executed by Aisling Nelson,
shoes by Mr Tutti of Naas • 4"
Travelling Collection

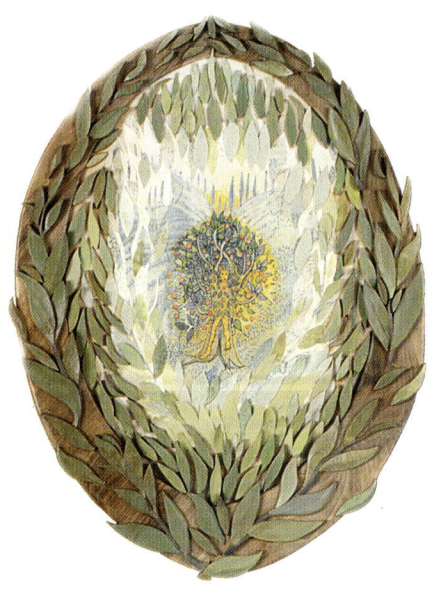

YELLOW MAN DREAMS
HE IS AN ORANGE TREE
acrylic in a carved frame • 27" x 21"
Travelling Collection

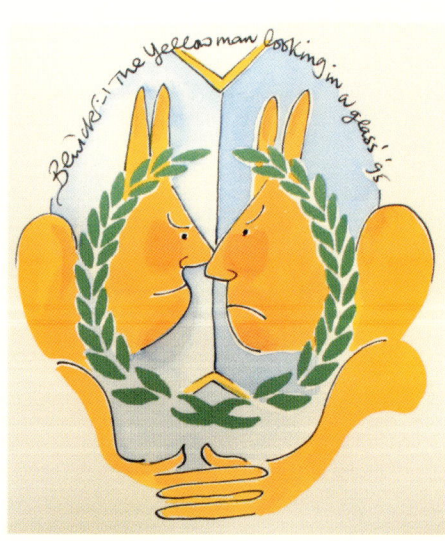

YELLOW MAN LOOKING IN A GLASS
watercolour in a limited edition book
Waterford Collection

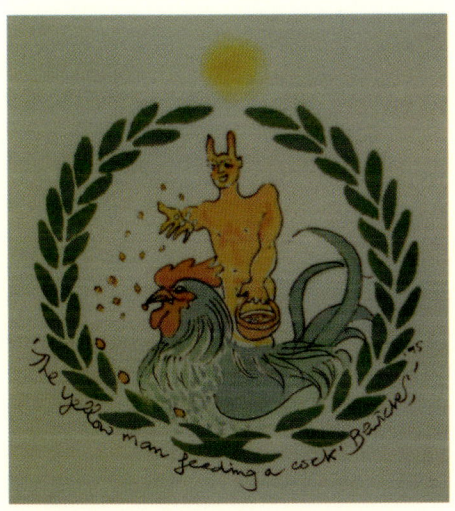

YELLOW MAN FEEDING A COCK
watercolour
Travelling Collection

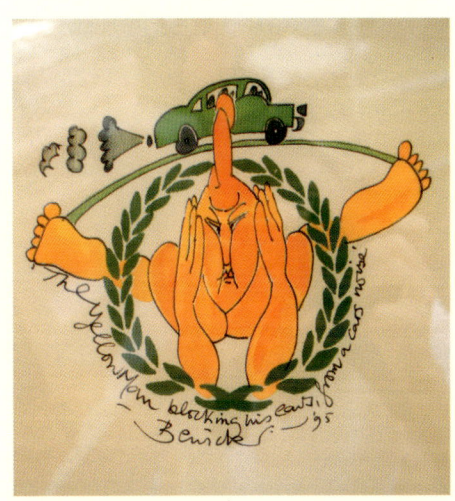

YELLOW MAN AND CAR
watercolour • 8" x 8"
Waterford Collection

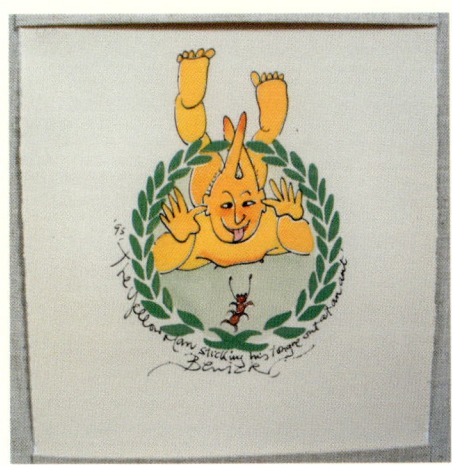

YELLOW MAN STICKING HIS TONGUE
OUT AT AN ANT
watercolourin a limited edition book
Kerry Collection

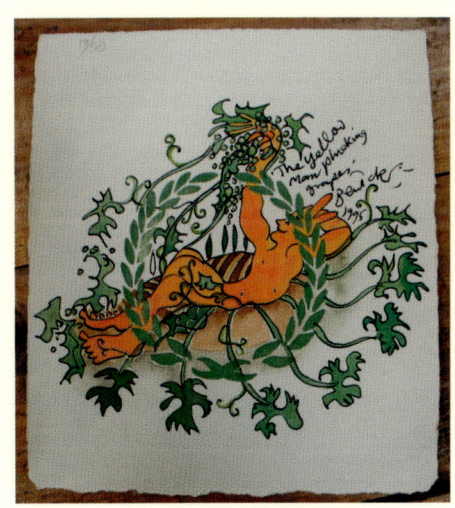

YELLOW MAN PICKING GRapes
watercolour in a limited edition book
Travelling Collection

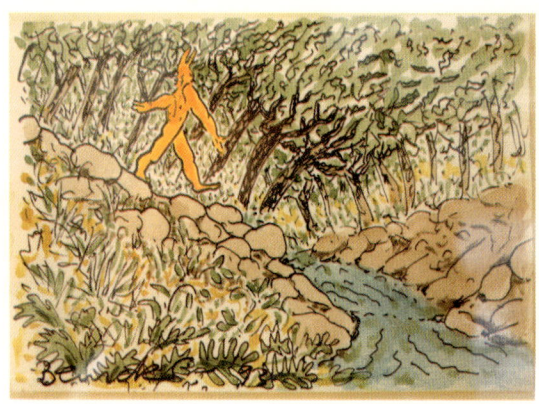

YELLOW MAN WALKING TO THE STREAM
watercolour
Kerry Collection

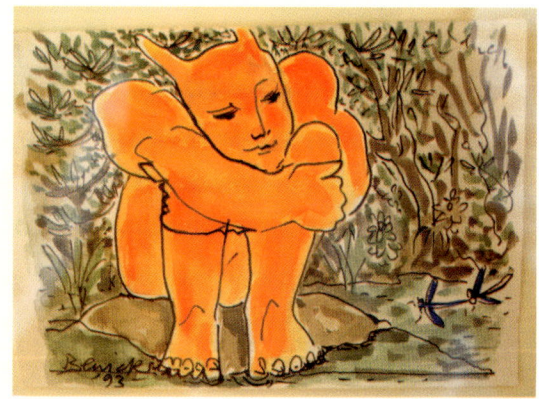

YELLOW MAN LOOKING AT A DRAGONFLY
watercolour
Kerry Collection

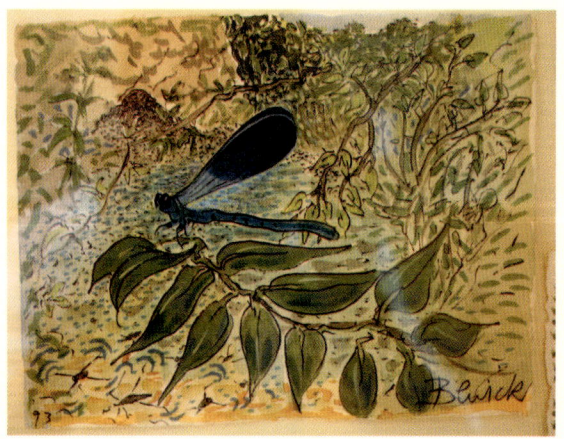

DRAGONFLY
watercolour
Kerry Collection

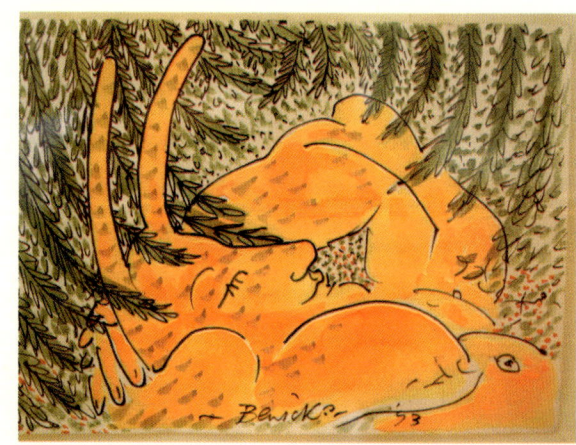

YELLOW MAN ASLEEP
watercolour
Kerry Collection

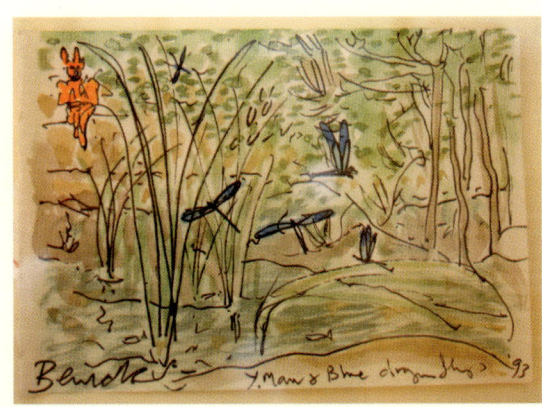

YELLOW MAN AND BLUE DRAGONFLIES
watercolour
Kerry Collection

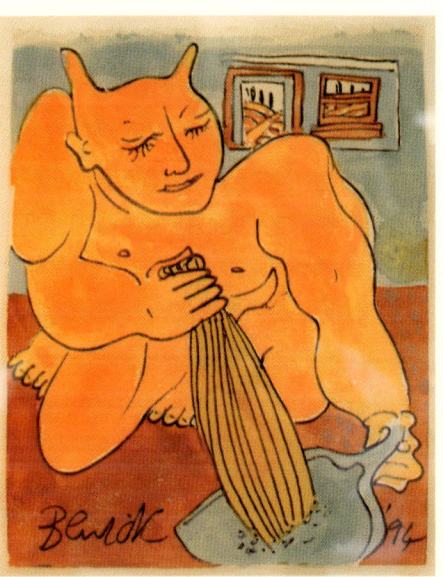

YELLOW MAN SWEEPING THE FLOOR
watercolour
Waterford Collection

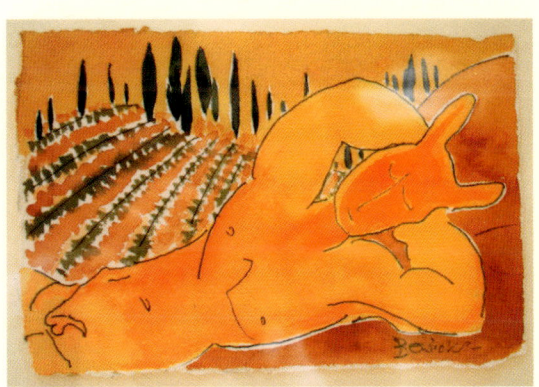

YELLOW MAN ASLEEP IN THE VINEYARD
watercolour
Waterford Collection

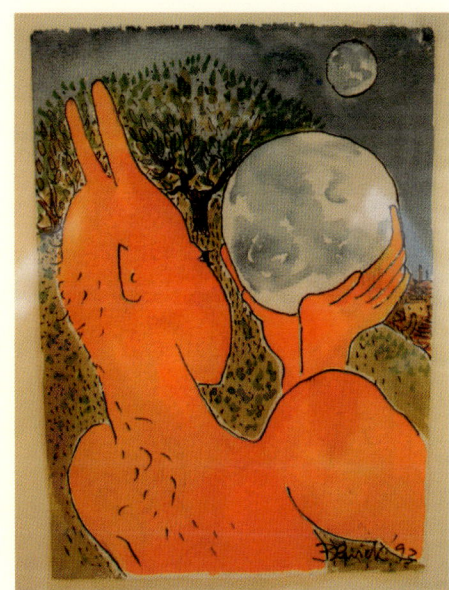

YELLOW MAN HOLDING THE MOON
watercolour
Waterford Collection

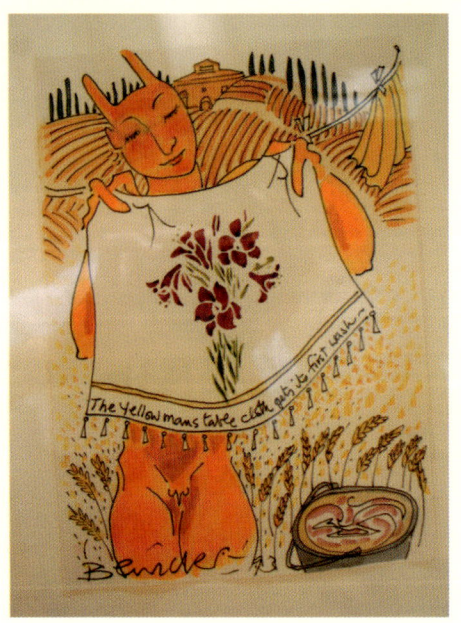

YELLOW MAN WITH A TABLECLOTH
watercolour
Waterford Collection

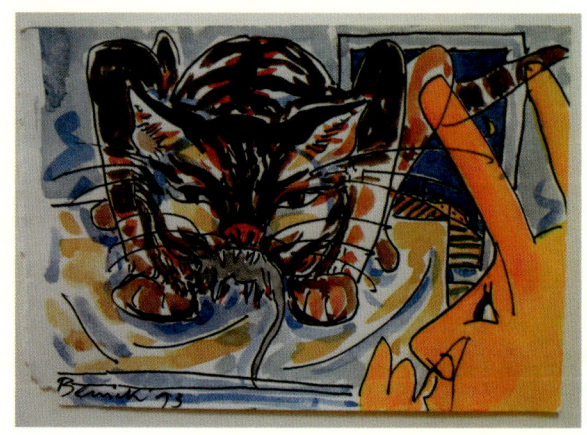

YELLOW MAN WITH CAT AND RAT
watercolour
Waterford Collection

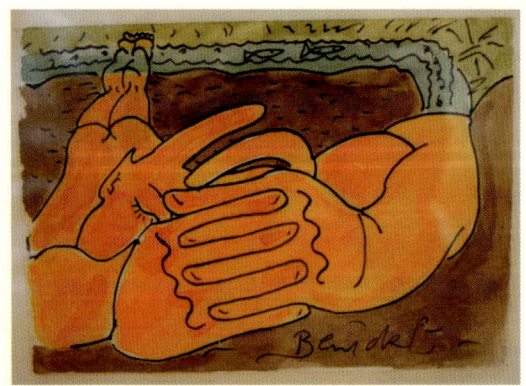

YELLOW MAN ASLEEP BY THE STREAM
watercolour
Waterford Collection

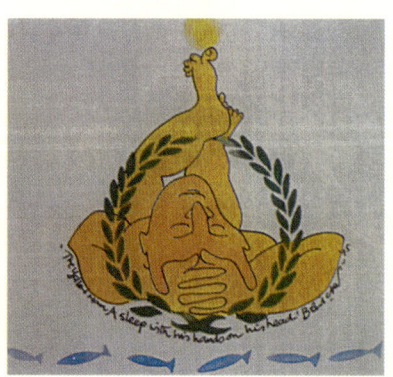

YELLOW MAN ASLEEP
WITH HIS HANDS ON HIS HEAD
watercolour • 8" x 8"
Kerry Collection

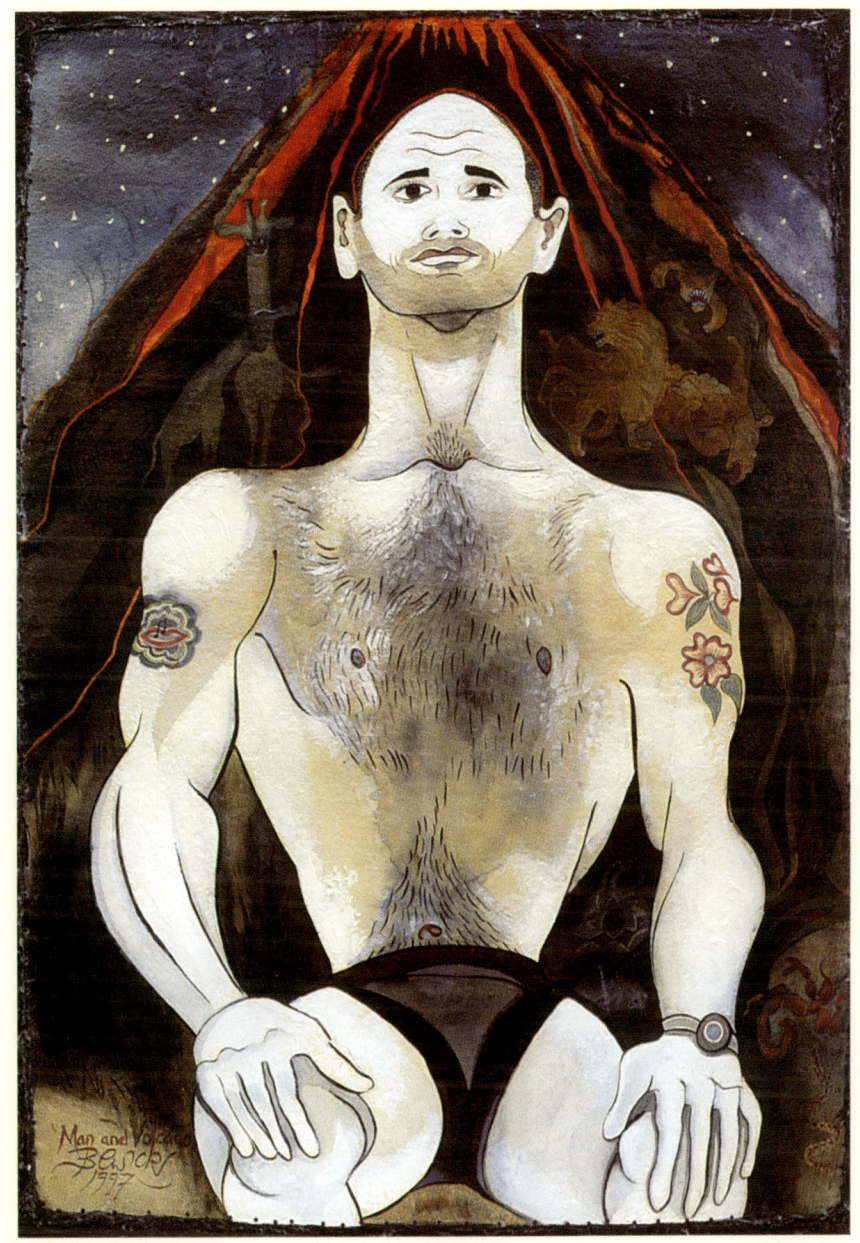

WHITE MAN AND VOLCANO
1997 • acrylic • 57" x 41"
Waterford Collection

Christian expressed all the fears of the world that came into my mind.

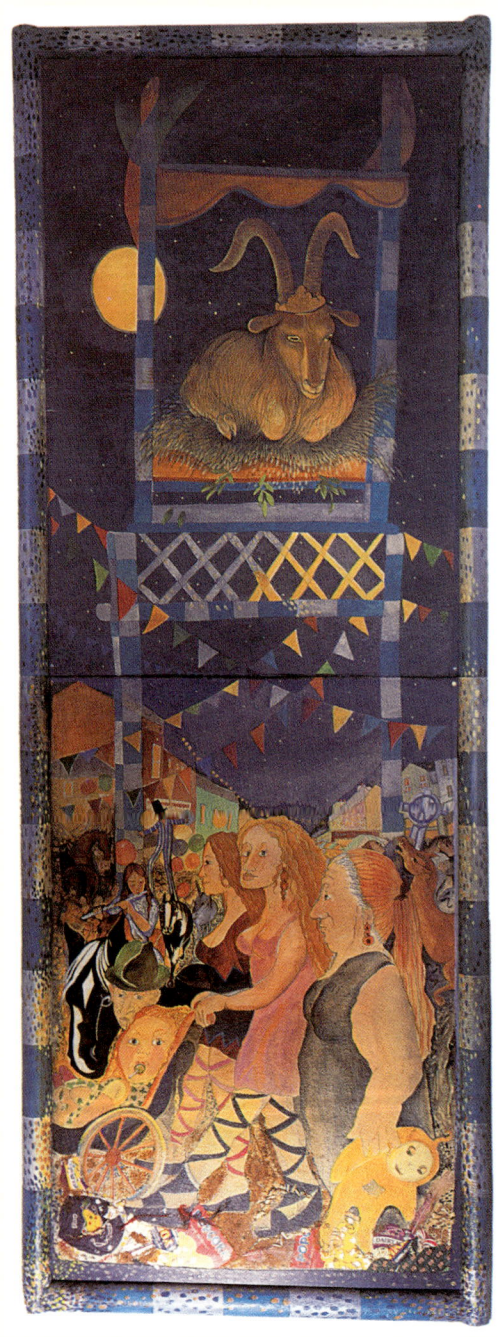

PUCK FAIR
2000 • mixed media acrylic and street rubbish varnished
120" x 48"
Kerry Collection

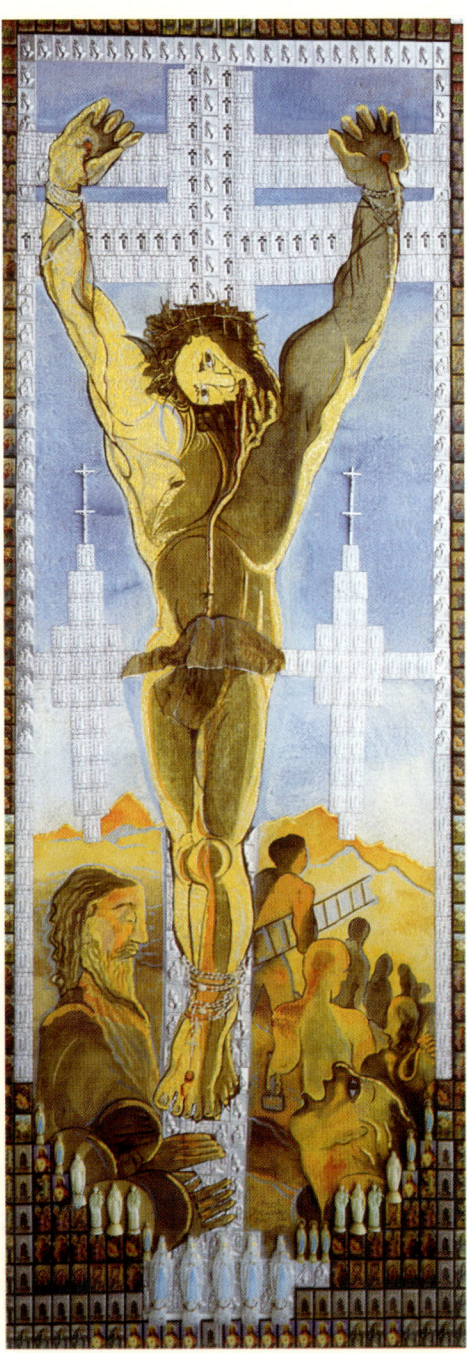

CRUCIFIXION
2001 • mixed media, artefacts, acrylic and goldleaf
111" x 42"
Waterford Collection

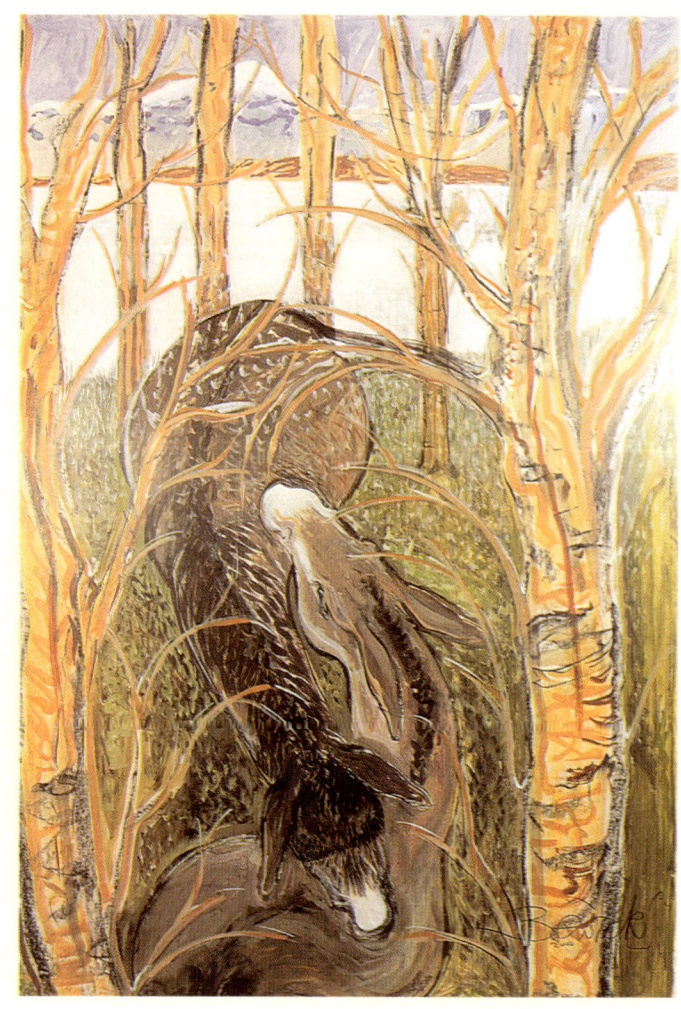

TWO DONKEYS
2000 • acrylic and charcoal • 72" x 53"
Kerry Collection

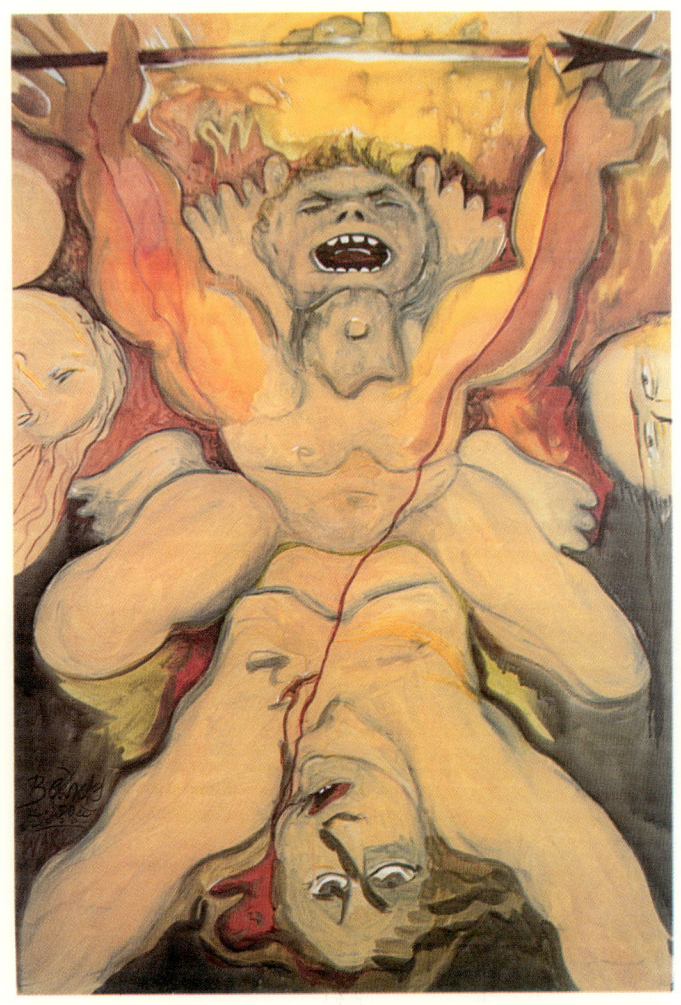

War
2000 • oil • 49" x 35"
Travelling Collection

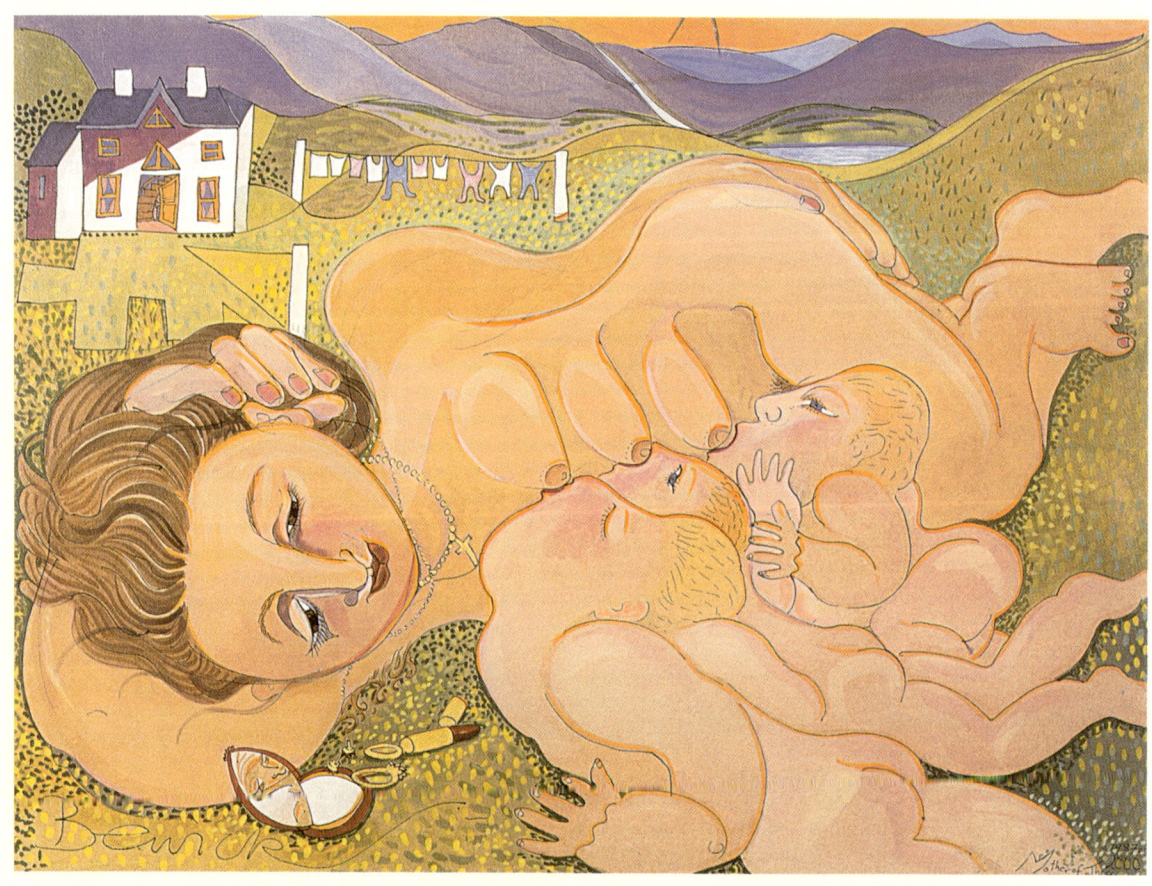

MOTHER OF THREE
1987/2000 • acrylic and grass seed • 24" x 32"
Travelling Collection

It's rare that a visitor finds me without an appointment. A couple walked up the drive carrying a newborn baby. 'Darling, his nappy needs changing'. 'Lay him there beside Pauline's picture'. After the smell had died down, 'Darling, I think he needs a feed'. She leant over him on the table, her breast dangling into his mouth, first one breast, then the other, milk dribbling down the side of his mouth. After they left, all thoughts of the previous painting were banished, and out came this.

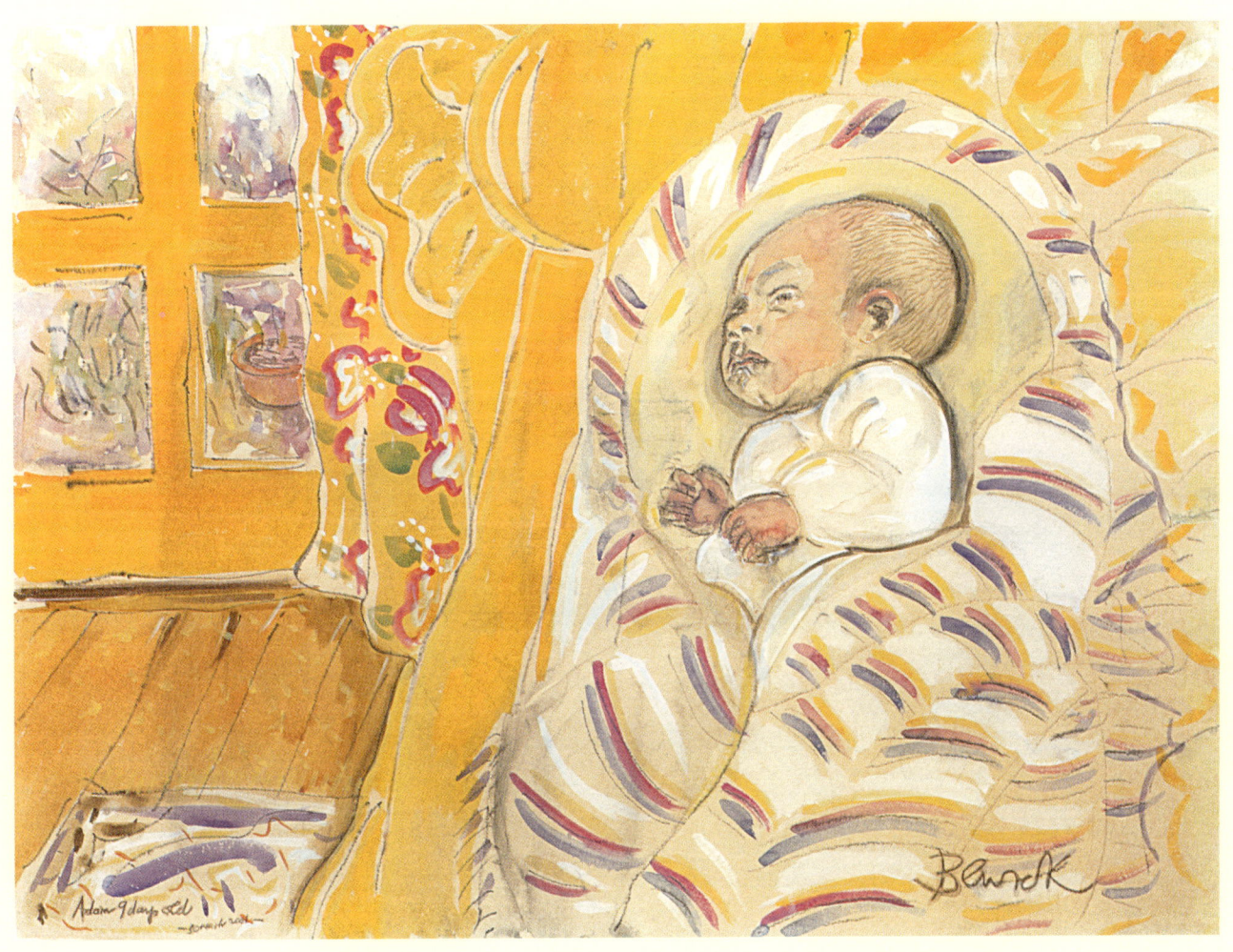

ADAM, NINE DAYS OLD
2001 • watercolour and acrylic • 24" x 32"
Travelling Collection

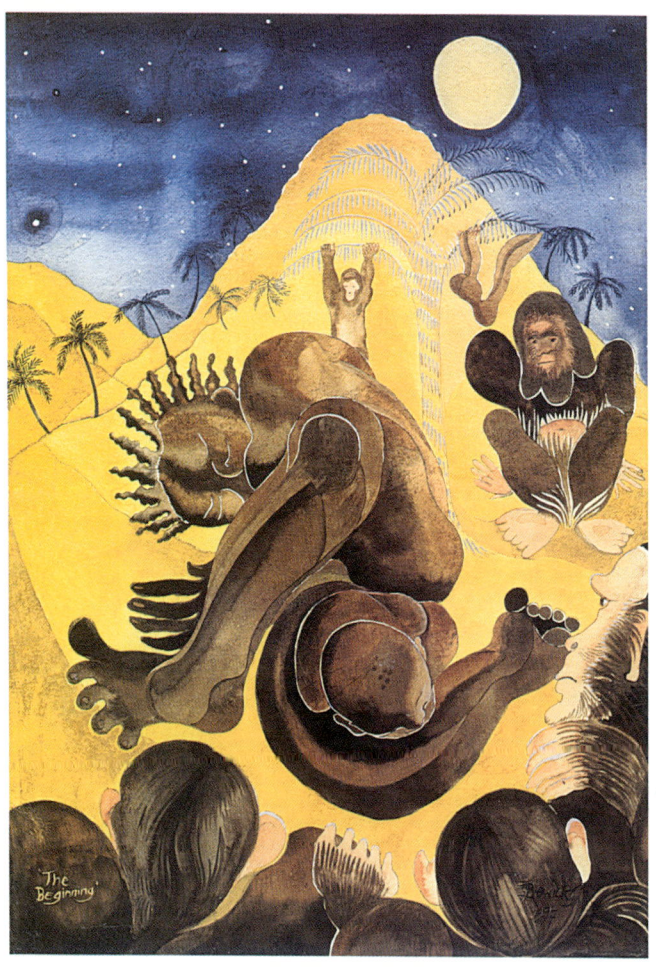

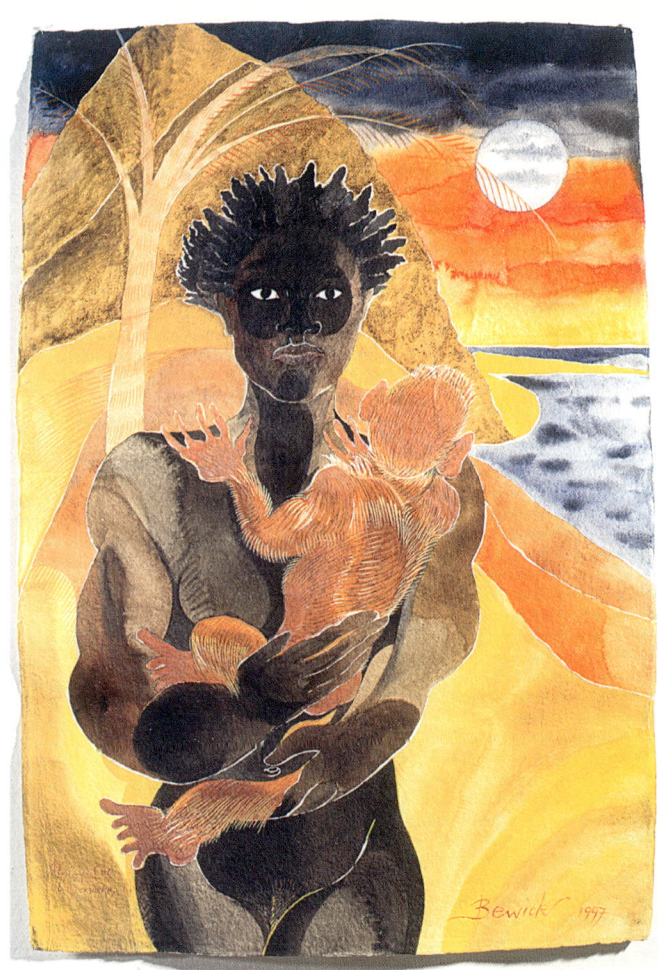

AFRICAN EVE: THE BEGINNING
2000 • acrylic • 60" x 45"
Waterford Collection

AFRICAN EVE AND MONKEY
2000 • acrylic • 63" x 48"
Kerry Collection

Richard Dawkin's writing on African Eve inspired these two paintings.

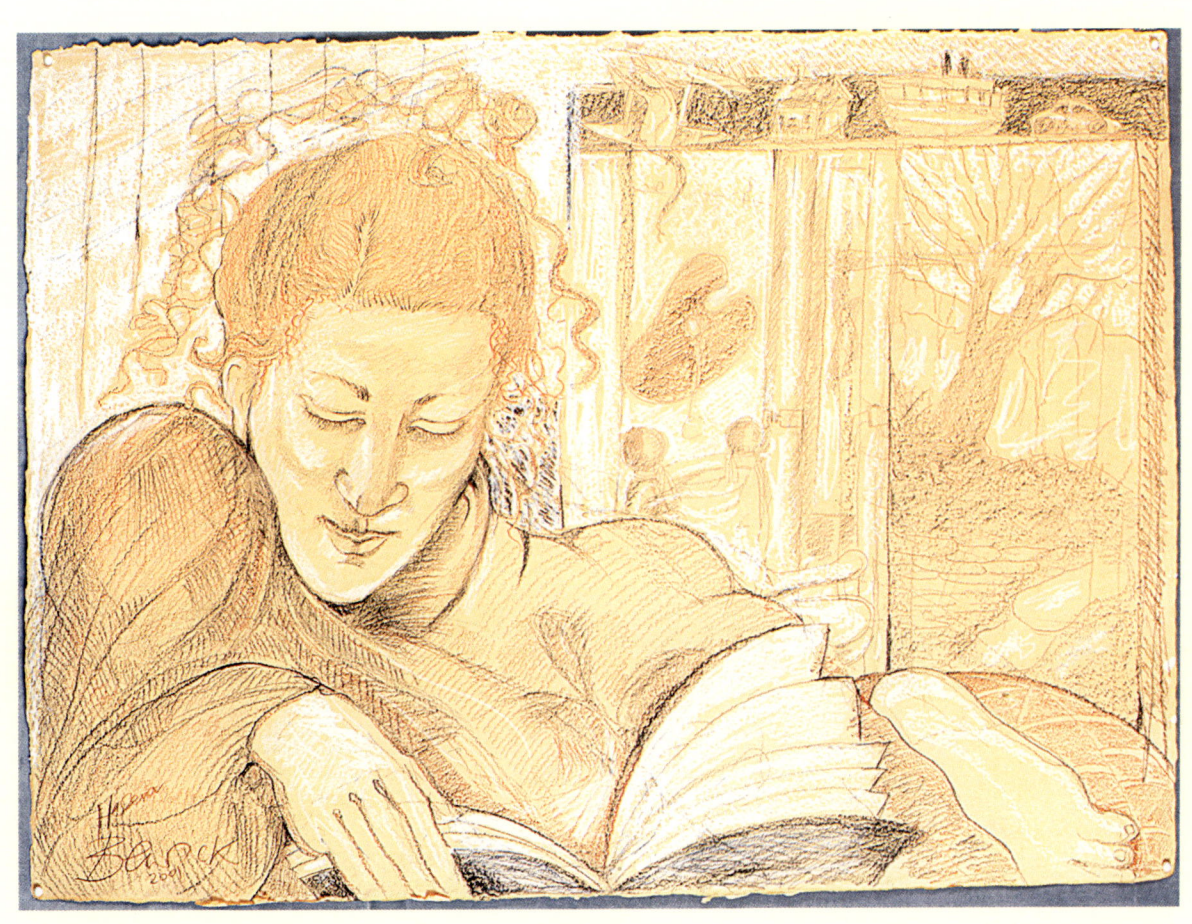

HELENA
2001 • conte • 24" x 32"
Kerry Collection

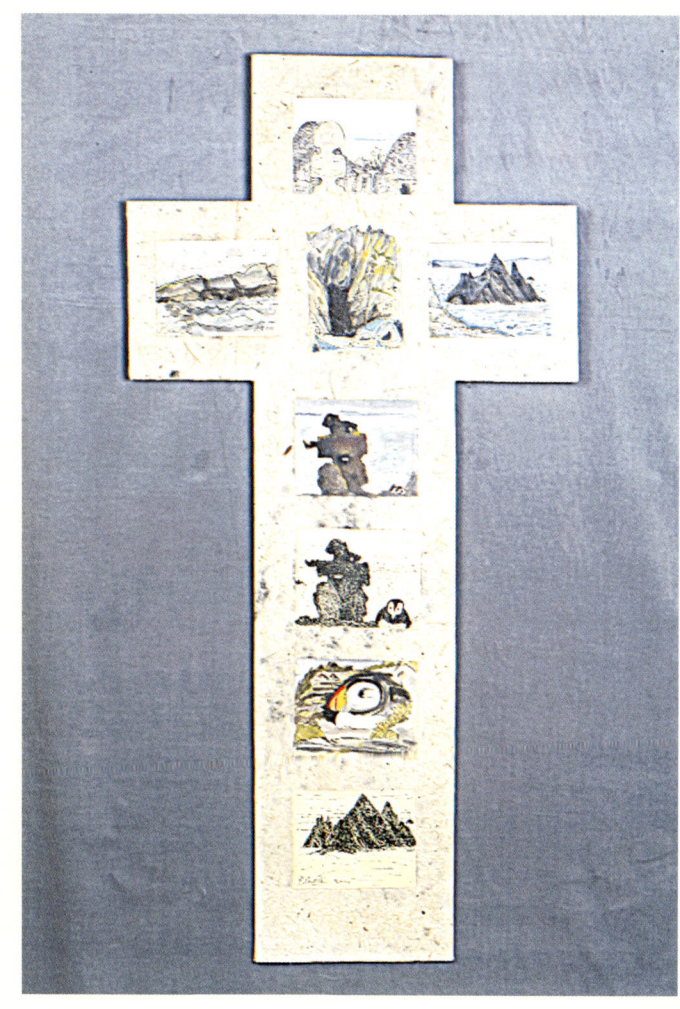

SKELLIG CROSS
2002 • watercolour, hand made paper on board varnished
50" x 24"
Kerry Collection

Kate Kennelly took a group of writers, sculptors and painters on an inspirational trip to the Skelligs.

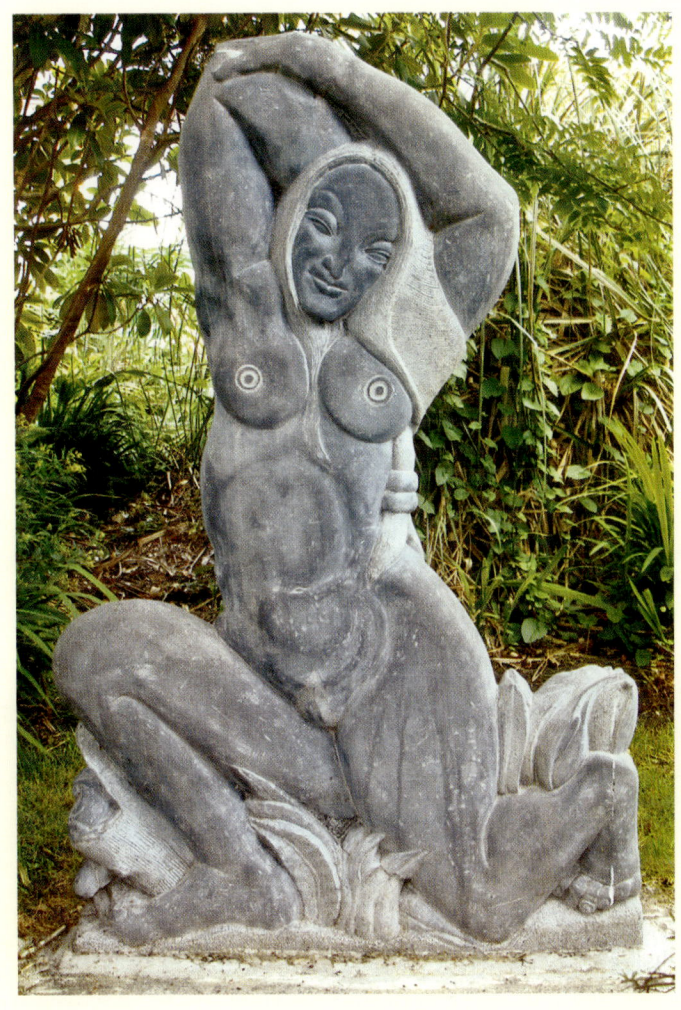

NIAMH
2002 • sculpture
Kerry Collection

Niamh is from Tir na nOg. Legend says the entrance lies between Inch and Rossbeigh.

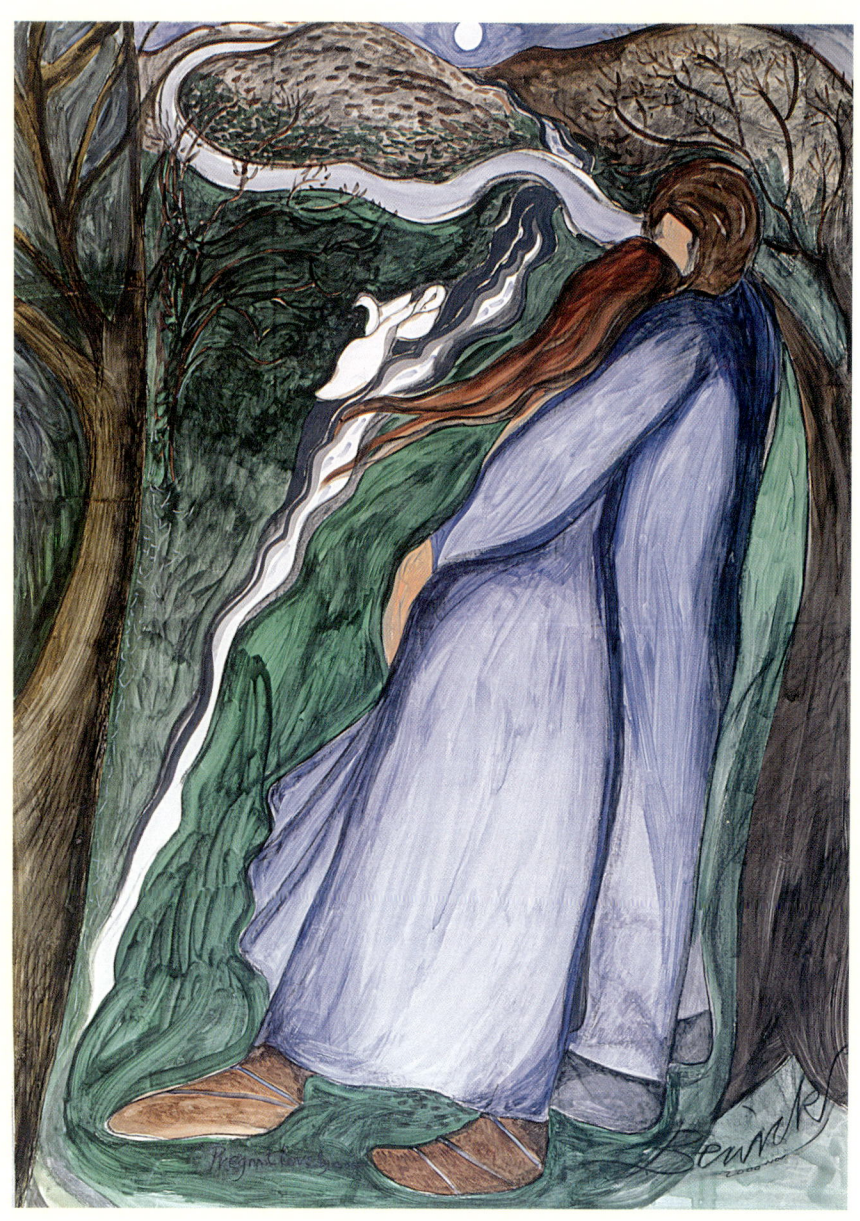

LOVERS BY A STREAM
2002 • acrylic • 73" x 54"
Waterford Collection

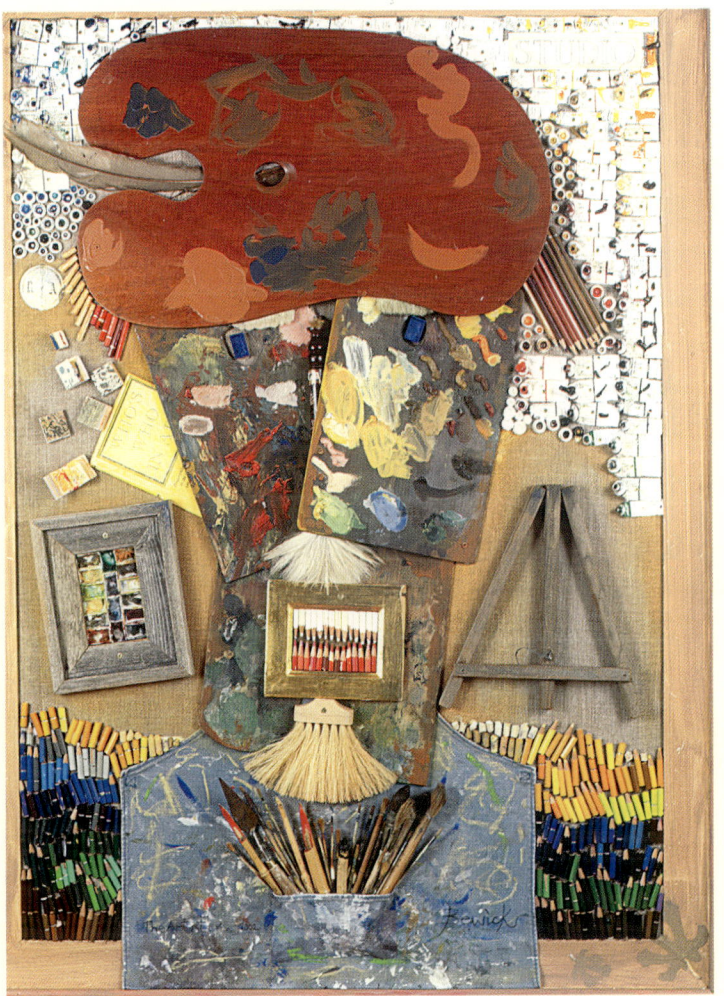

THE ARTIST
2002 • mixed media collage • 54" x 41"
Waterford Collection

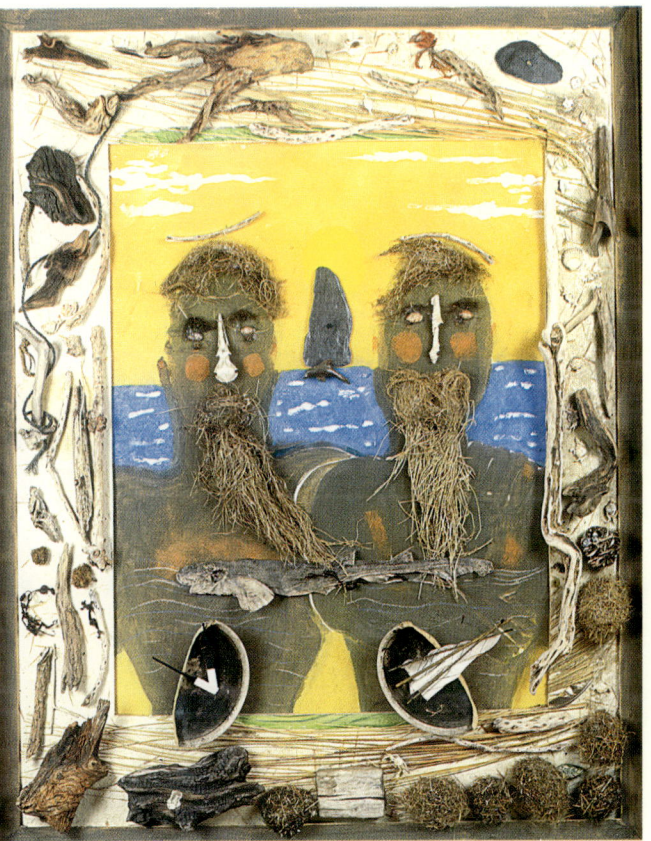

FLOTSAM AND JETSAM
2002 • mixed media collage • 56" x 46"
Kerry Collection

I used all the old artist material lying around.

Flotsam and jetsam found on beaches.

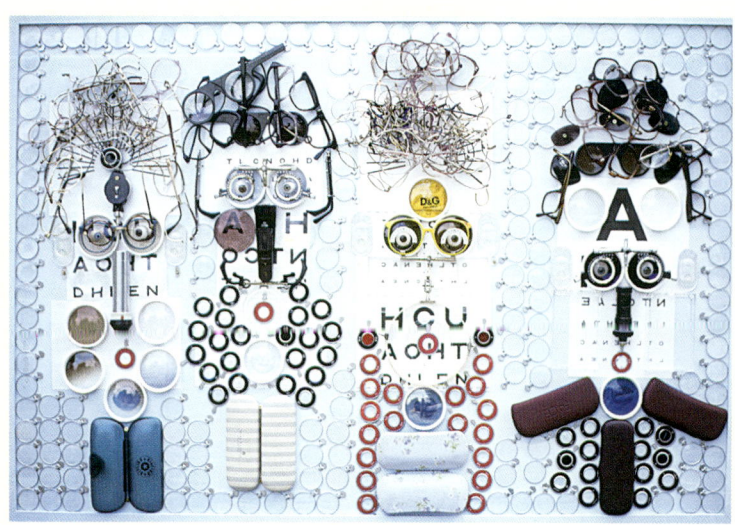

OPTICIAN'S CONFERENCE
2002 • mixed media collage • 34" x 50"
Waterford Collection

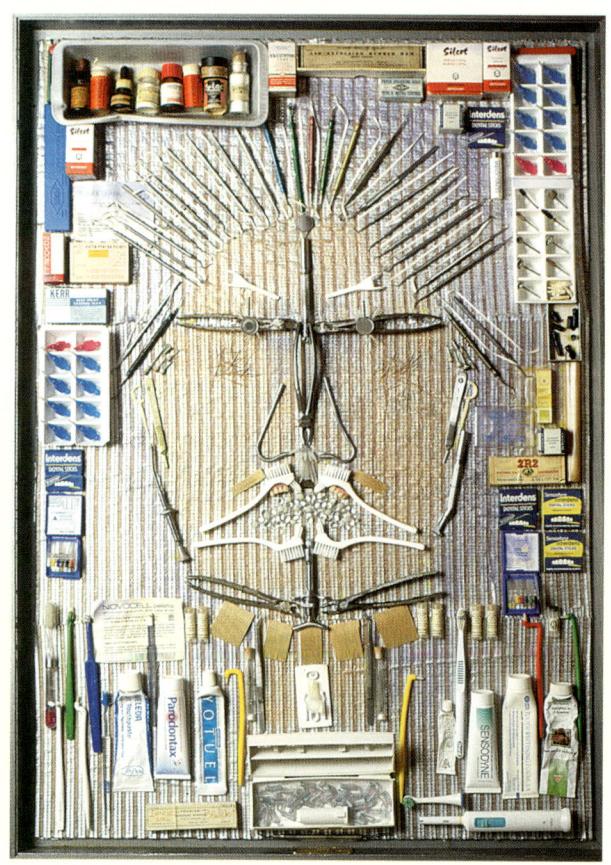

THE DENTIST
2002 • mixed media collage • 46" x 34"
Kerry Collection

I asked Patrick O'Donoghue our optician if he had any material, he gave me boxes and boxes.

Our dentist Brendan Coffey gave me all his dentist's tools from his student days. This is his portrait.

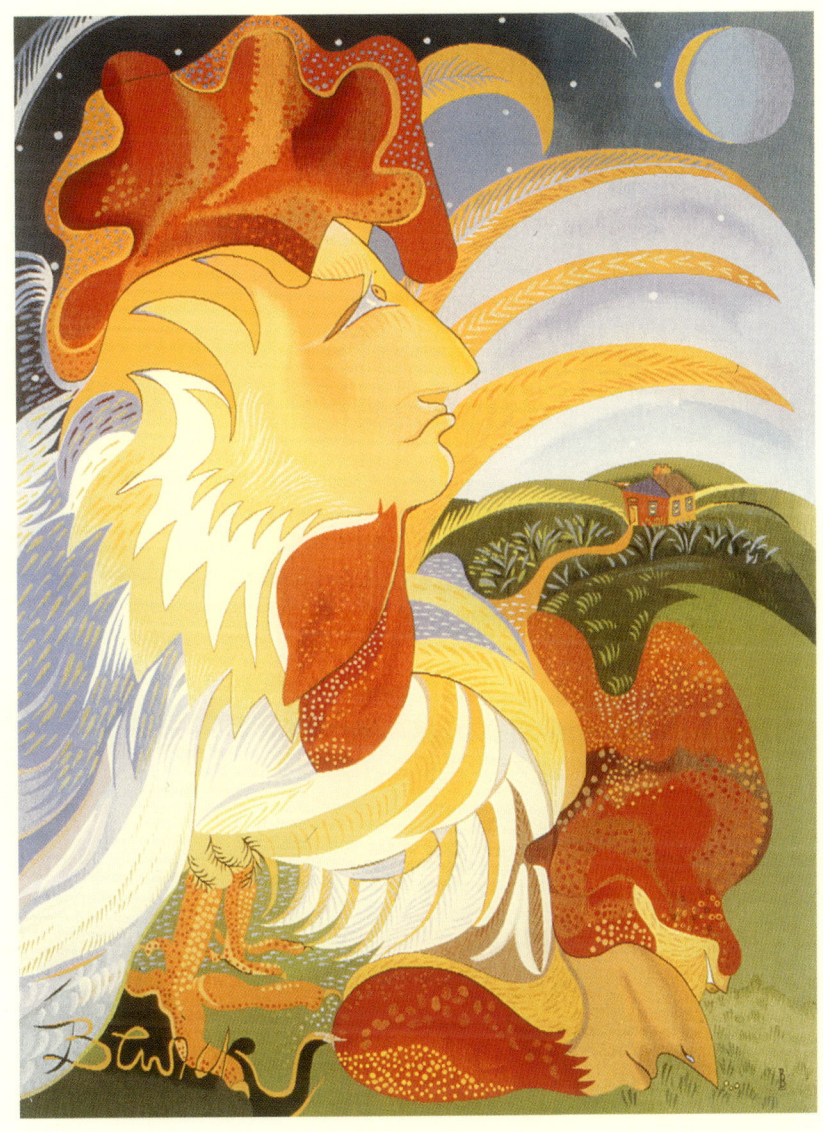

THE COCK, THE FOX AND THE MOON
2003 • Aubusson tapestry wool and linen • 90" x 67"
Kerry Collection

This expresses our lives: the fox our predator, the house our home, and we peck, peck, peck our food.

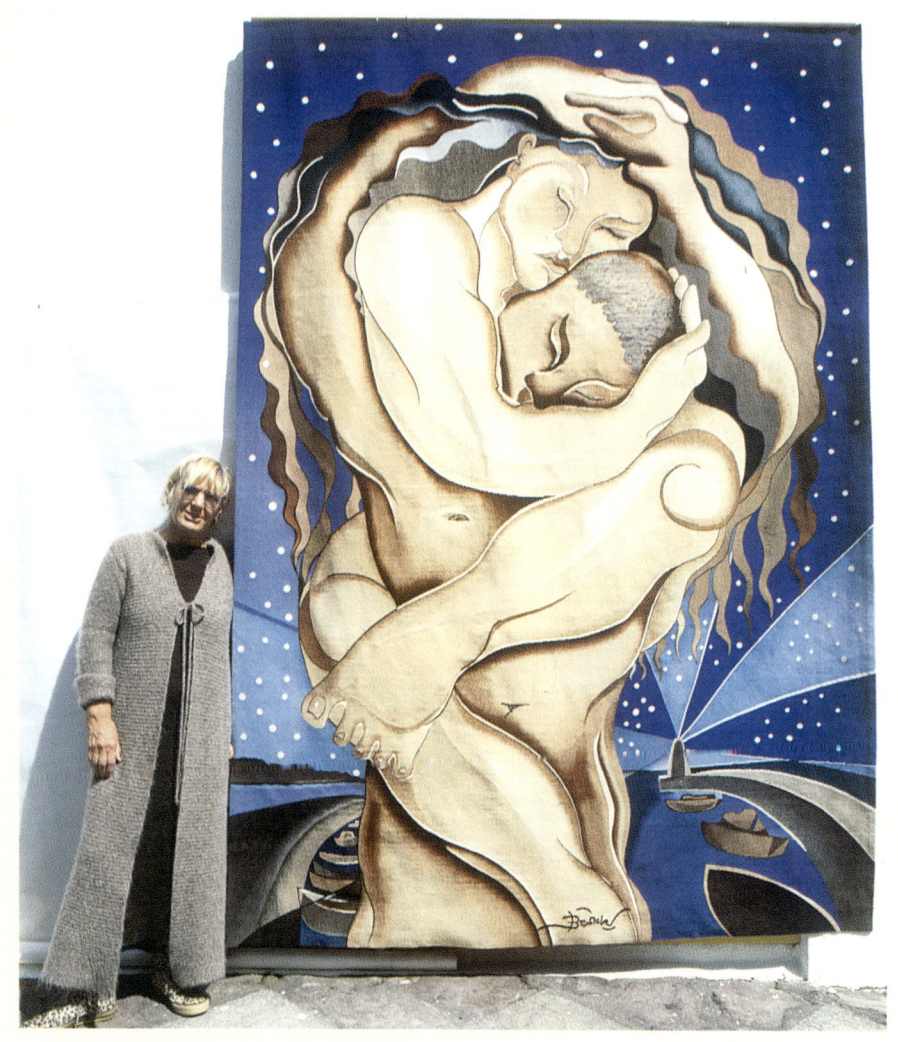

LOVERS AND STARS
2003 • Aubusson tapestry wool and linen • 118" x 85"
Waterford Collection

Universal love … the world goes round.

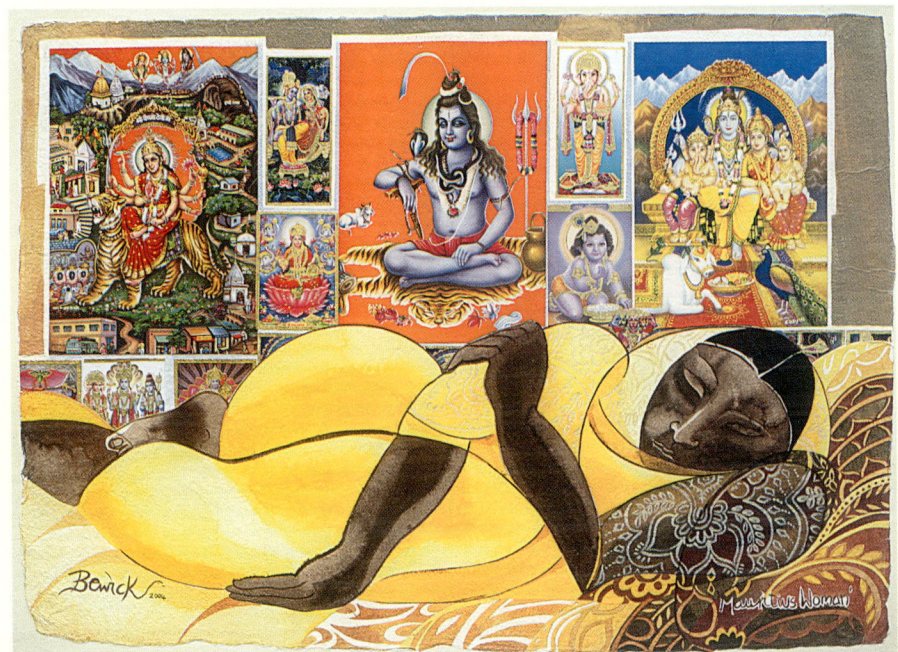

MAURITIUS WOMAN
2003 • acrylic and collage • 41" x 57"
Kerry Collection

Five religions co-exist peacefully on Mauritius.

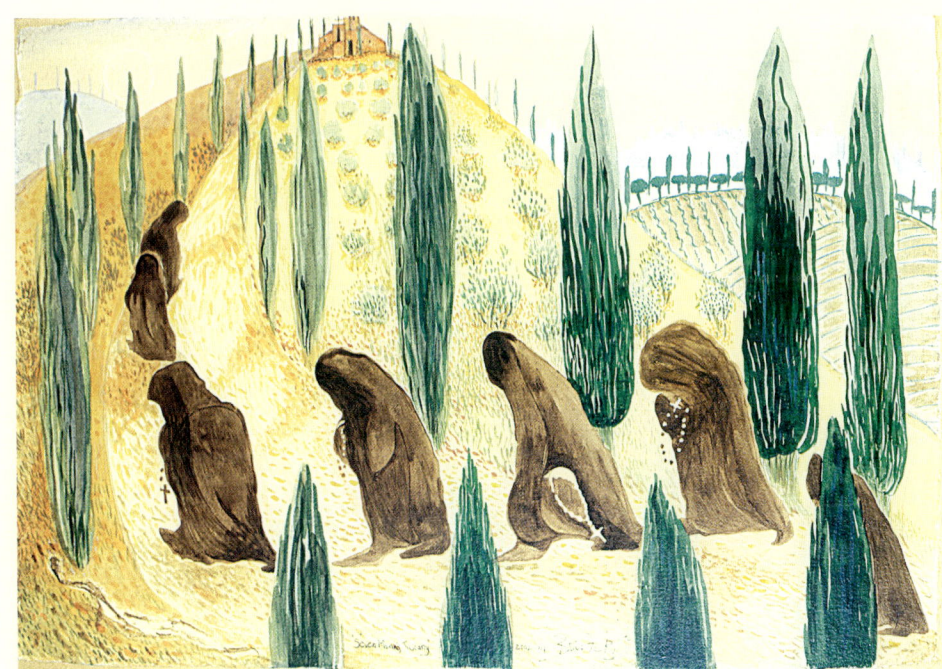

SEVEN MONKS, TUSCANY
2003 • acrylic • 35" x 49"
Waterford Collection

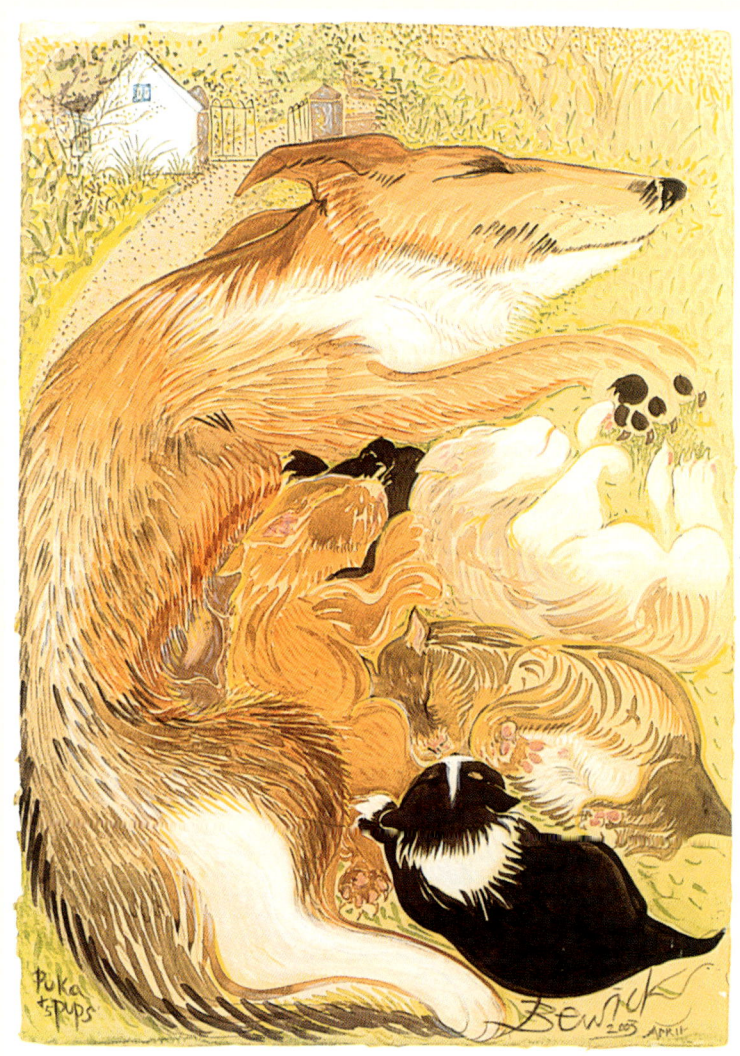

PUKA AND PUPS
2003 • watercolour • 32" x 23"
Waterford Collection

Puka could open and close the front door.

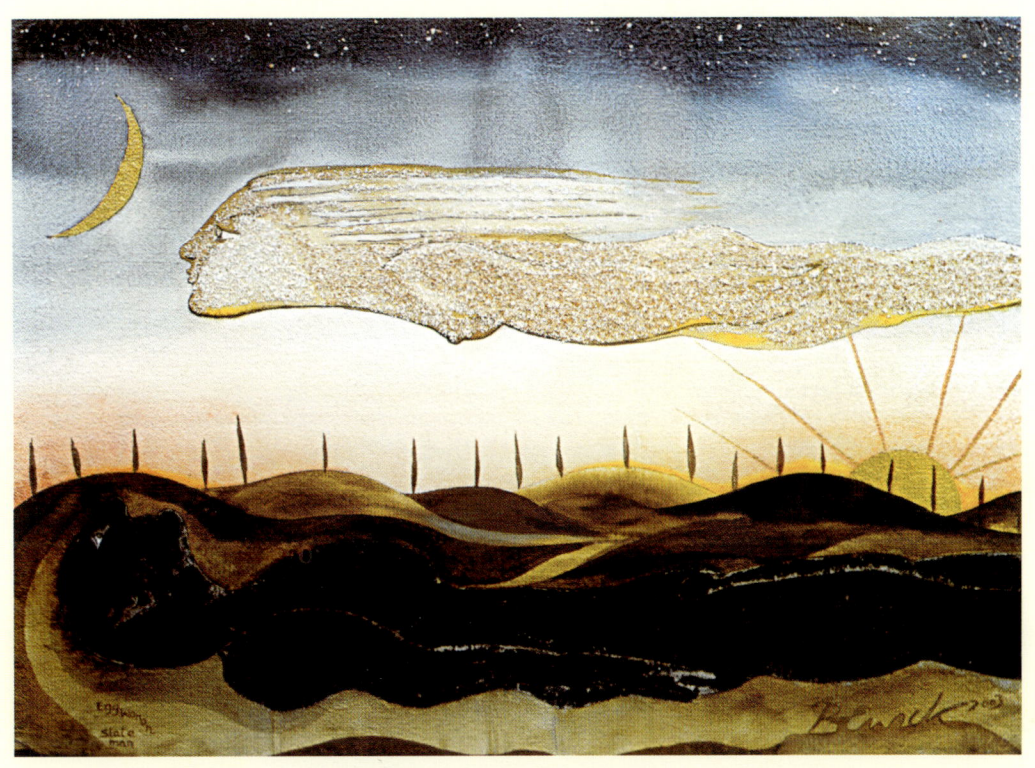

EGGSHELL WOMAN, SLATE MAN
2003 • Eggshell, Slate Dust, Acrylic and Goldleaf • 42" x 57"
Waterford Collection

All eggshells were collected, brown, white and duck-egg, I spread glue on the surface of the woman and covered her in broken shells. The man was covered in Valentia slate dust, the moon is 24 carot gold.

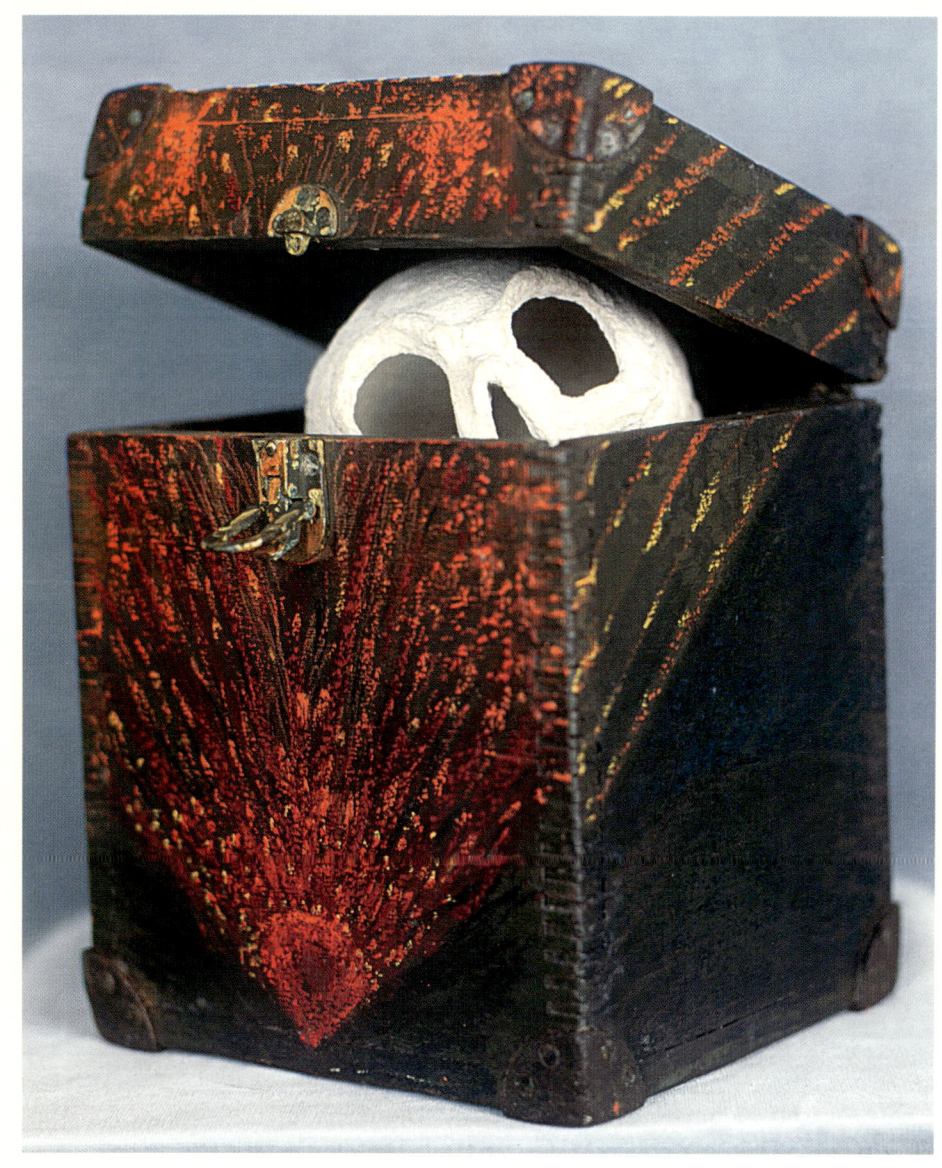

EXPLOSION BOX AND SKULL
2003 • box painted in crayon and acrylic,
papier mache skull inside • 8" x 8", 10" high
Travelling Collection

Having bought what I thought was a pretty box, it turned out that it had been used on the battlefield as a telephone box.

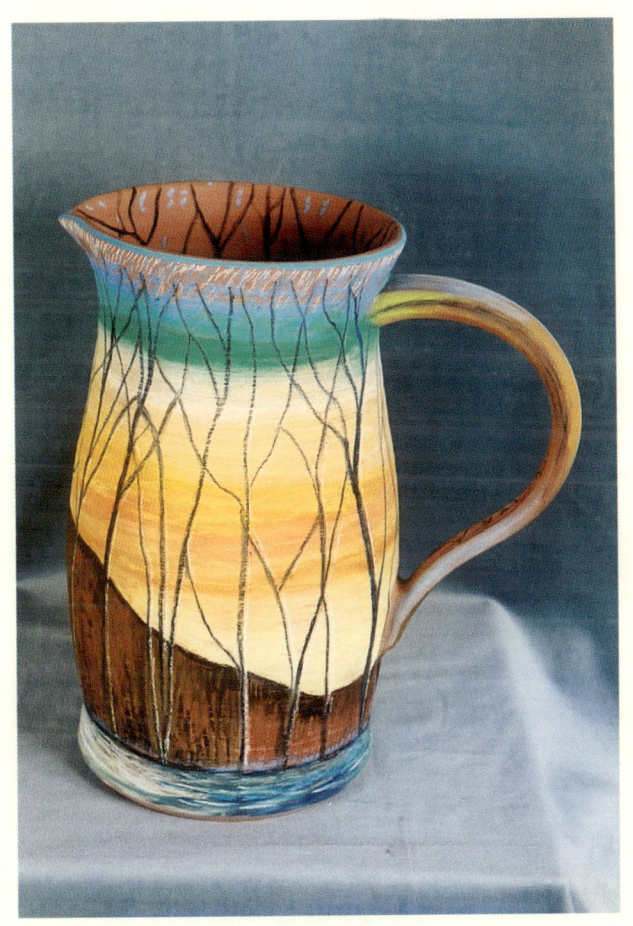

ON THE ROAD AT SUNSET
2003 • biscuitware jug, crayon
and acrylic varnished• 11" x 11"
Kerry Collection

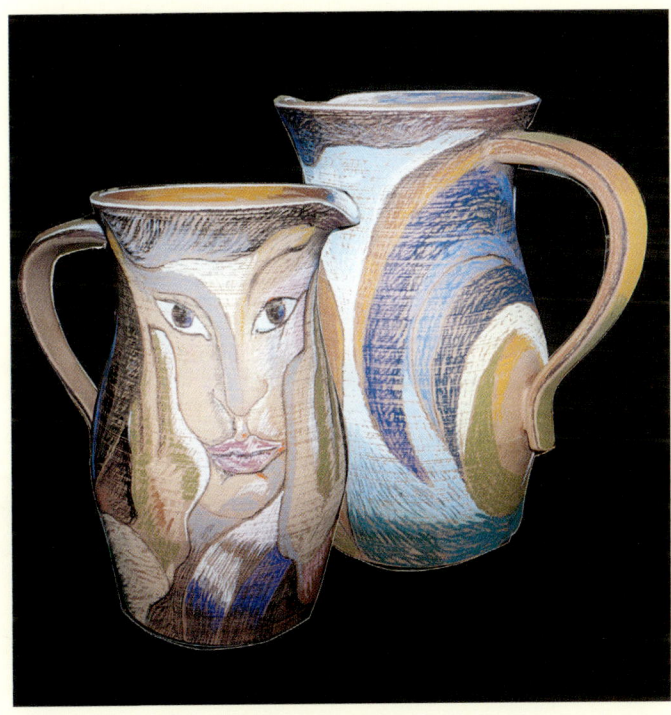

HANDS ON HER CHIN
2003 • crayon and acrylic varnished
on biscuitware • 13 " x 13"
Waterford Collection

These ceramic bases were made by Eddie Thadier of Glenbeigh.
I used white glaze on some, and varnished pastel on others.
The biscuitware sucked in the varnish holding the colour.

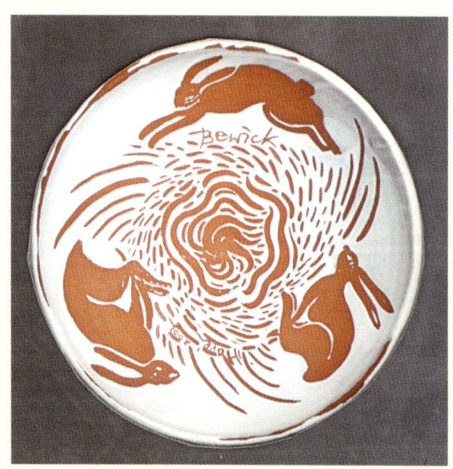

HARE PLATTER
2003 • biscuitware and white glaze
15" diameter
Waterford Collection

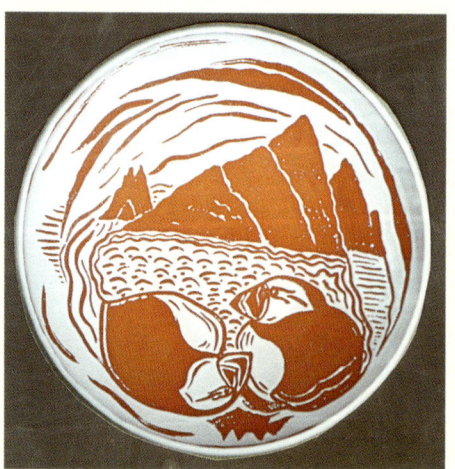

PUFFIN PLATTER
2003 • biscuitware and white glaze
15" diameter
Kerry Collection

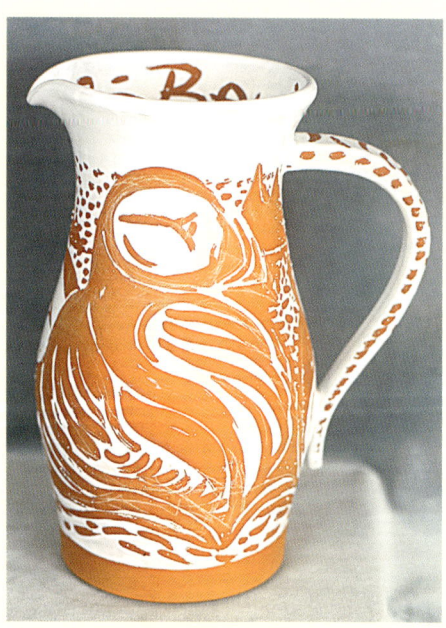

PUFFIN JUG
2003 • biscuitware and white glaze
13" x 11"
Kerry Collection

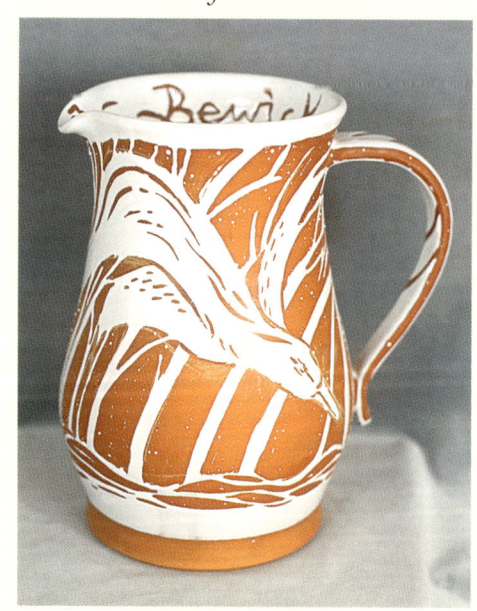

BIRDS AND TREES
2003 • biscuitware jug
Waterford Collection

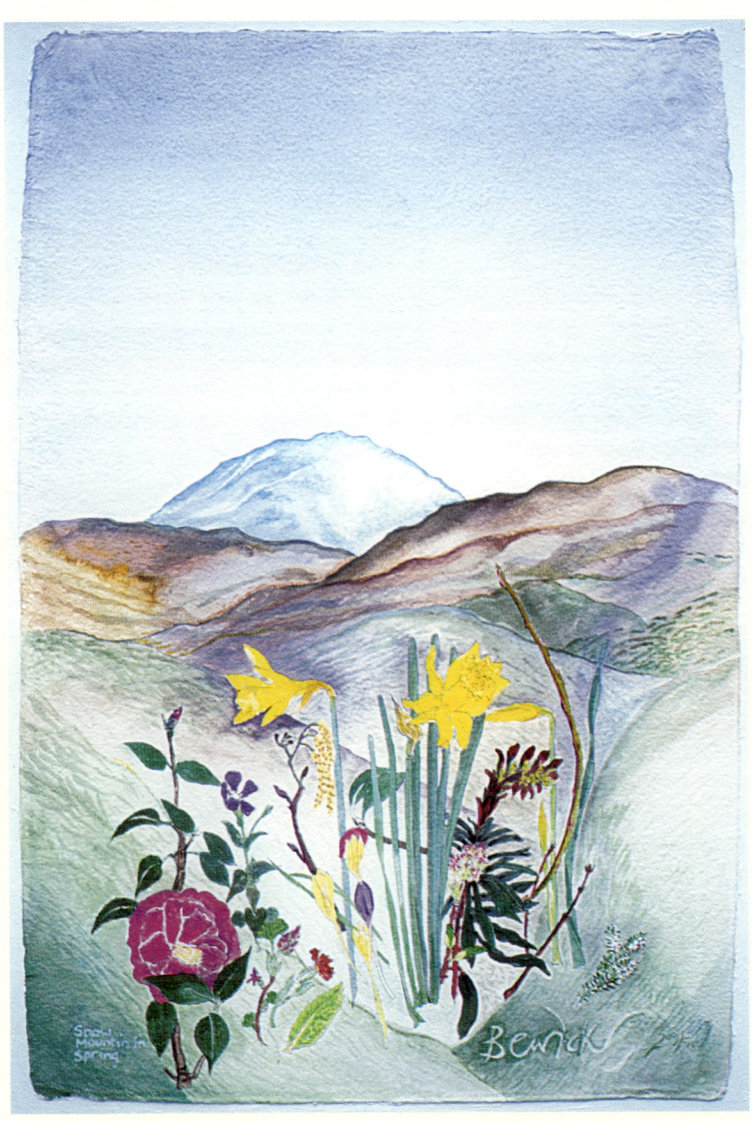

SNOW MOUNTAIN IN SPRING
2004 • watercolour • 40" x 28"
Waterford Collection

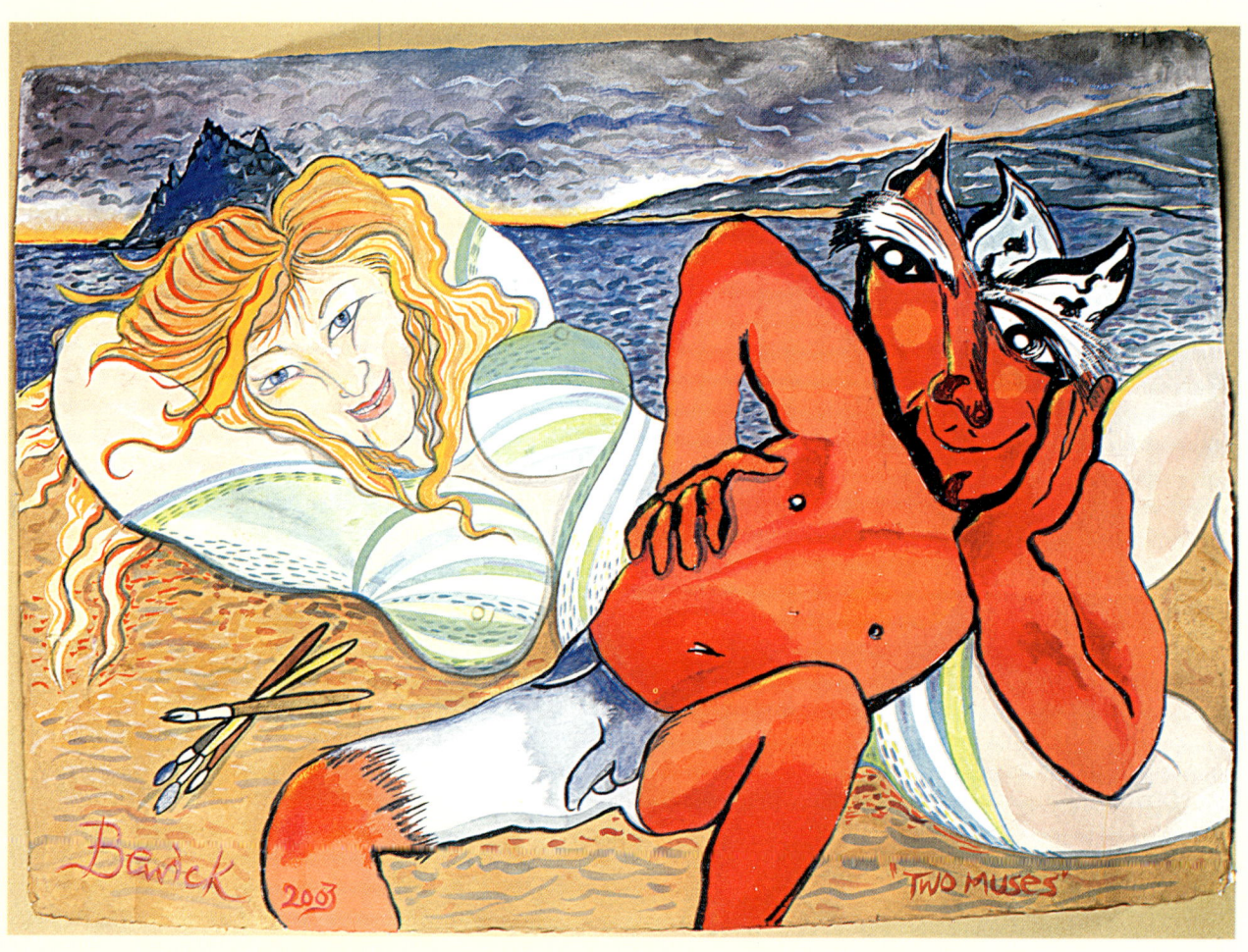

TWO MUSES BY THE SKELLIGS
2004 • acrylic • 41" x 57"
Waterford Collection

Once upon a time Lainey Keogh and Mick Mulcahy fell in love.
'You've made my dick too small', said Mick.

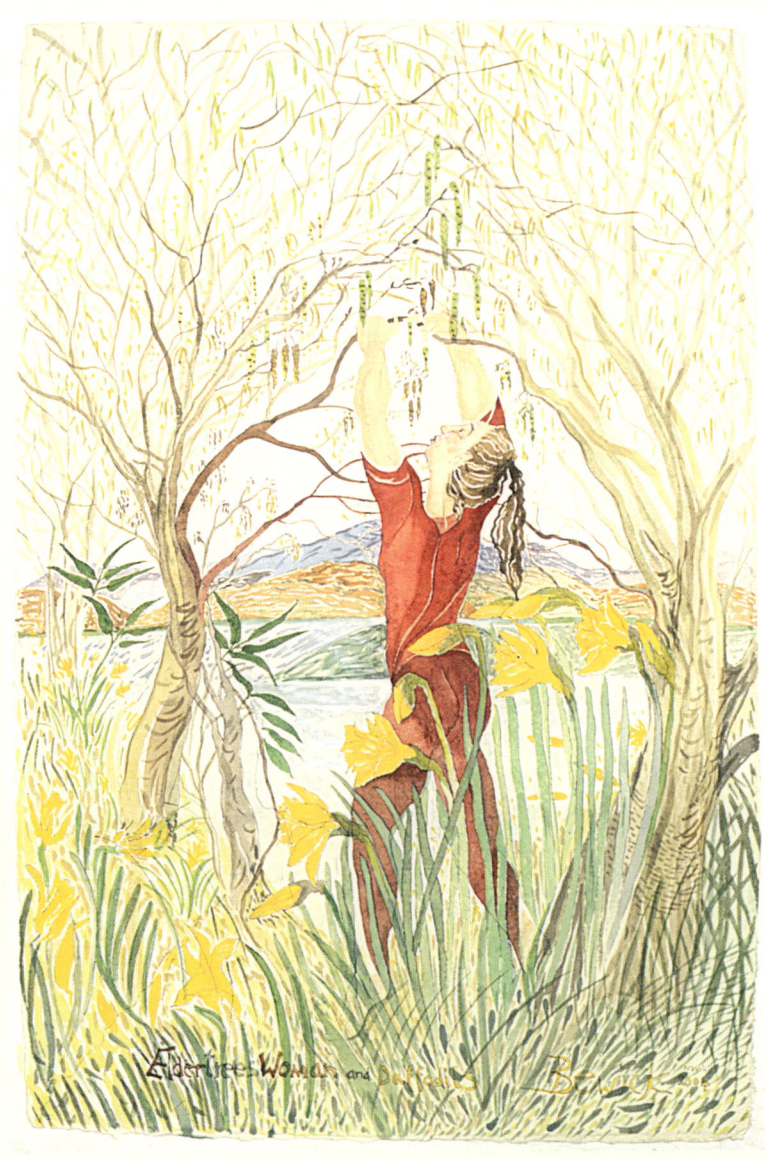

WOMAN, ALDER AND DAFFODILS
2004 • watercolour and acrylic finish • 40" x 28"
Travelling Collection

A week at Birr Castle, County Offaly. Regine and I painted from morning until night.

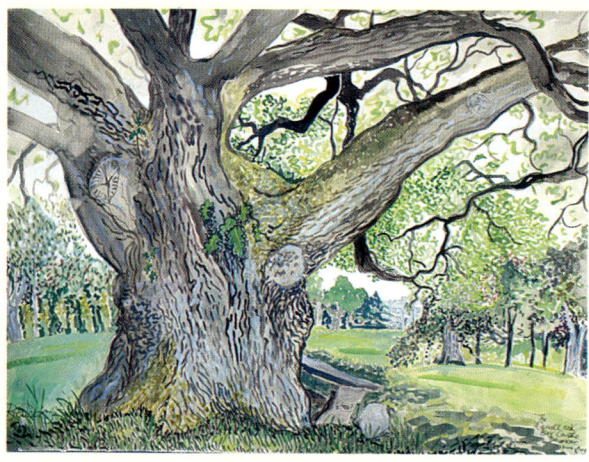

BIRR OAK TREE
2004 • watercolour • 23" x 32"
Kerry Collection

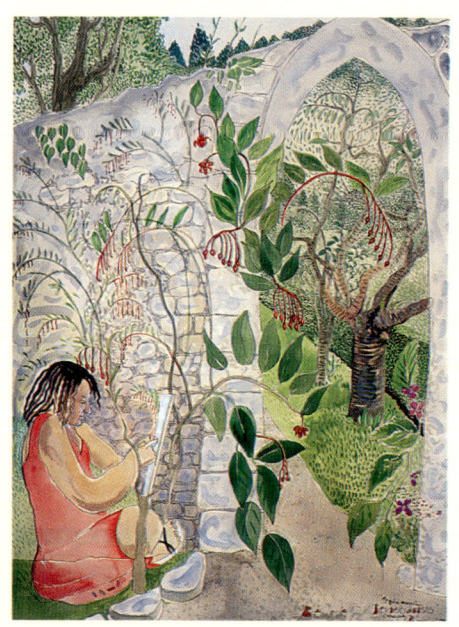

BIRR GARDENS AND REGINE
2004 • watercolour • 32" x 23"
Waterford Collection

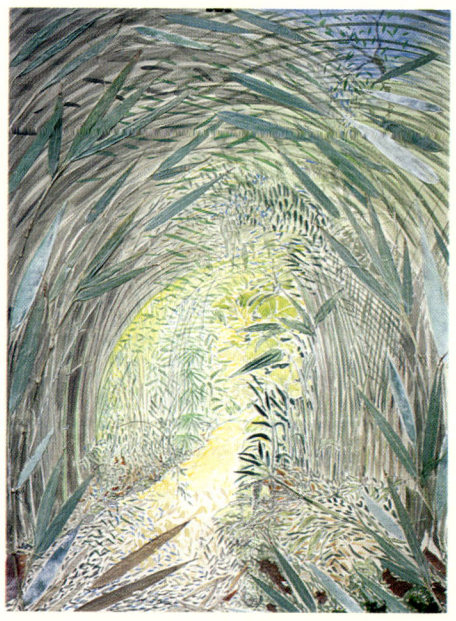

BIRR BAMBOO PASSAGE
2004 • watercolour • 23" x 32"
Travelling Collection

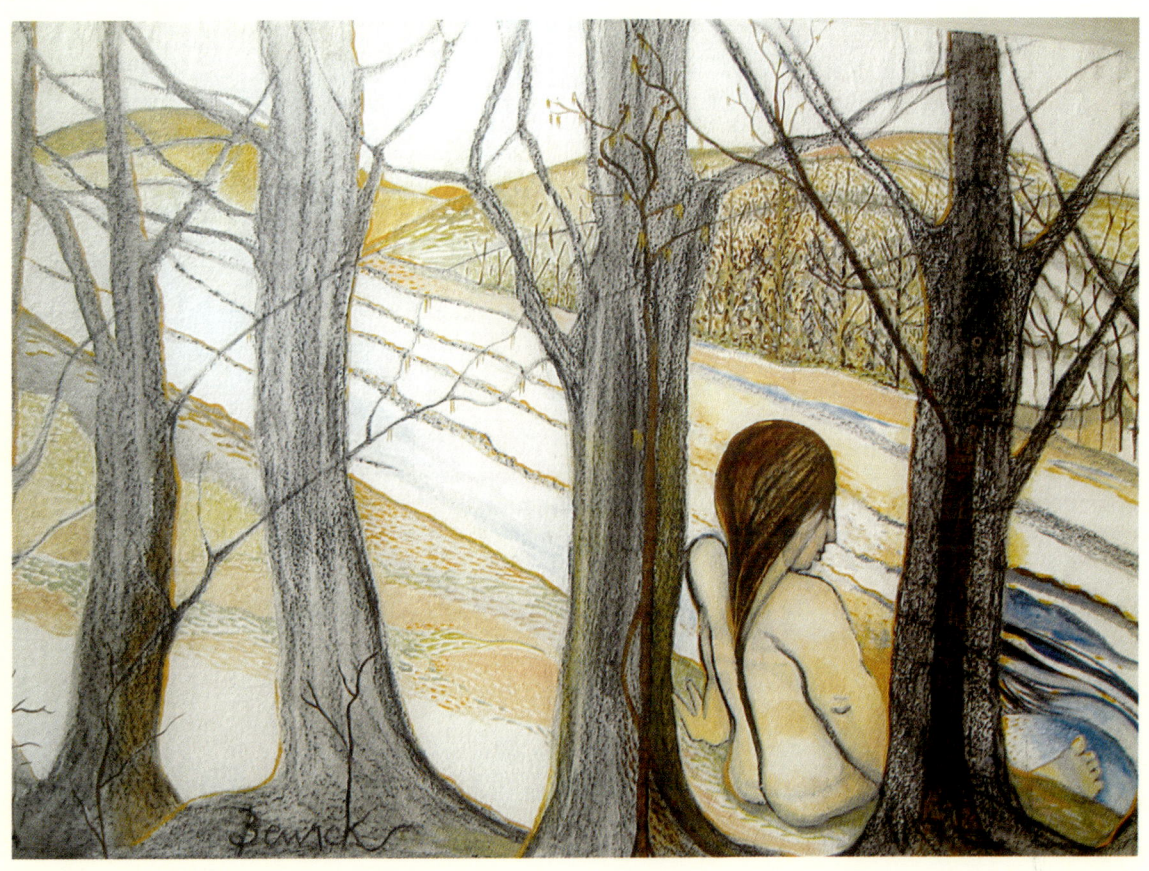

AFTER MIDDAY, FRANCE
2005 • oil and charcoal • 44" x 59"
Travelling Collection

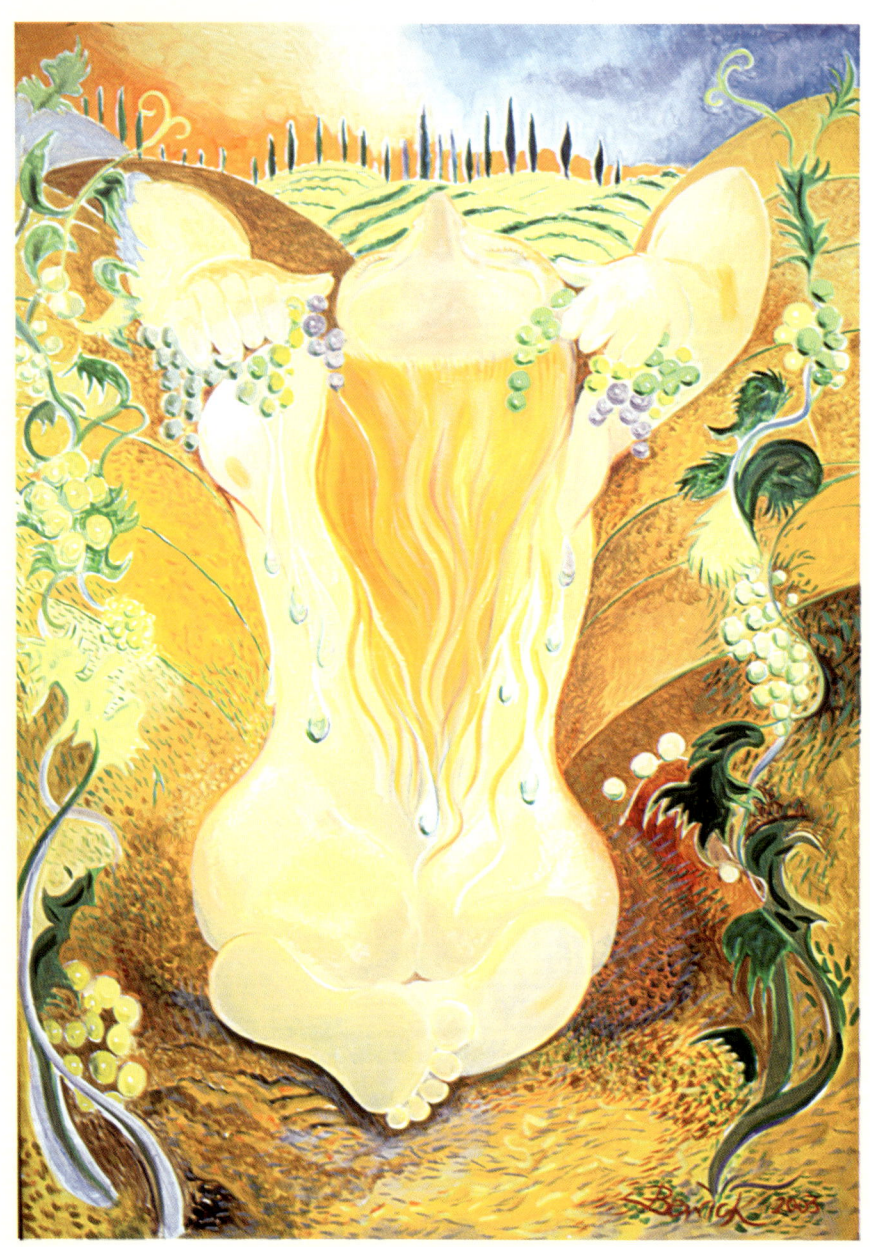

GRAPEJUICE DOWN HER BACK
2005 • oil • 48" x 34"
Kerry Collection

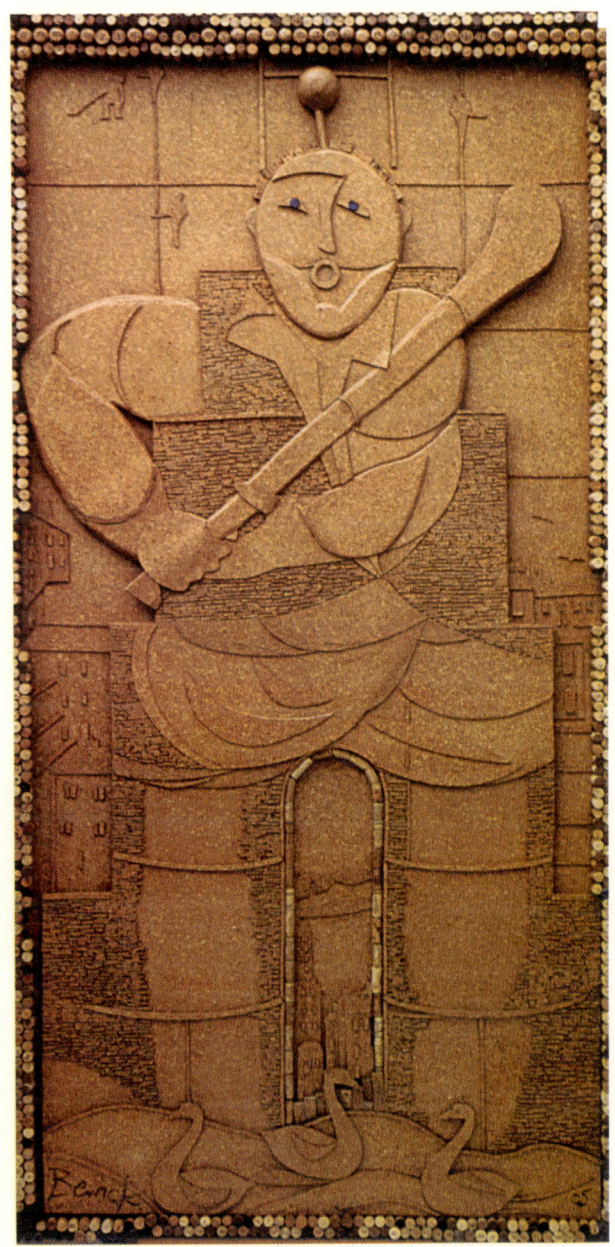

THE CORK HURLER
2005 • mixed media • 96" x 48"
Waterford Collection

'Christy Ring' assembled for the Cork Year of Culture 2005.

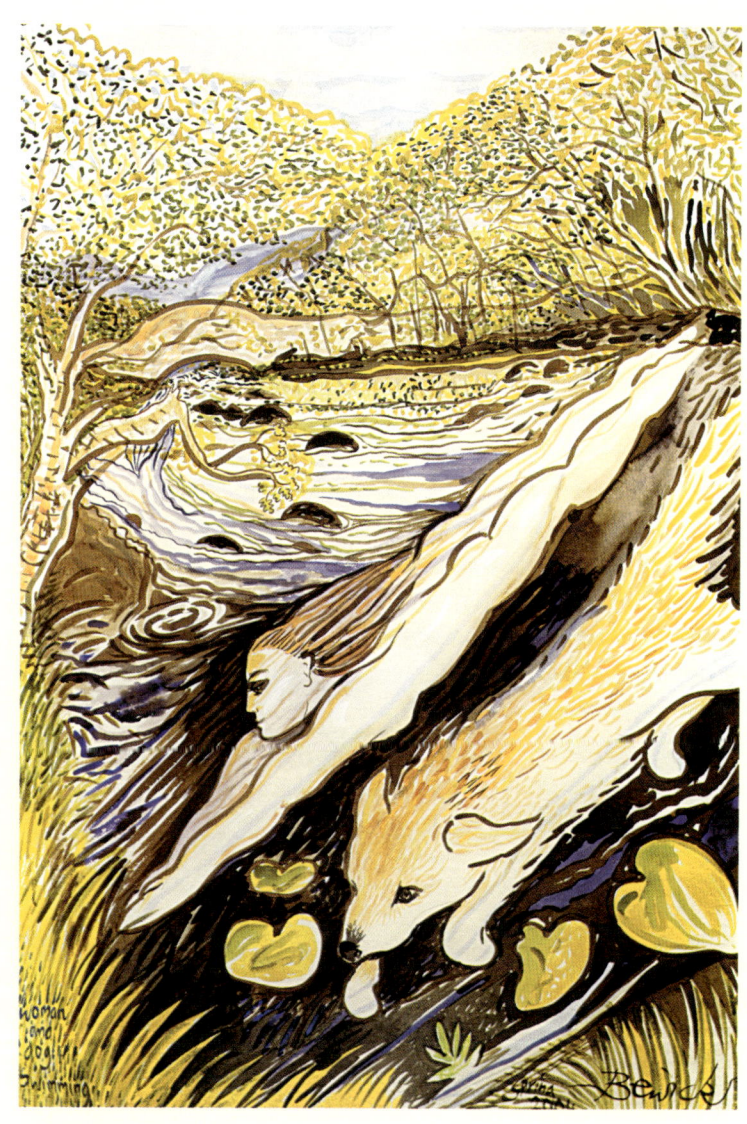

DIVING WITH MY DOG
2004/2005 • watercolour and acrylic • 53" x 39"
Kerry Collection

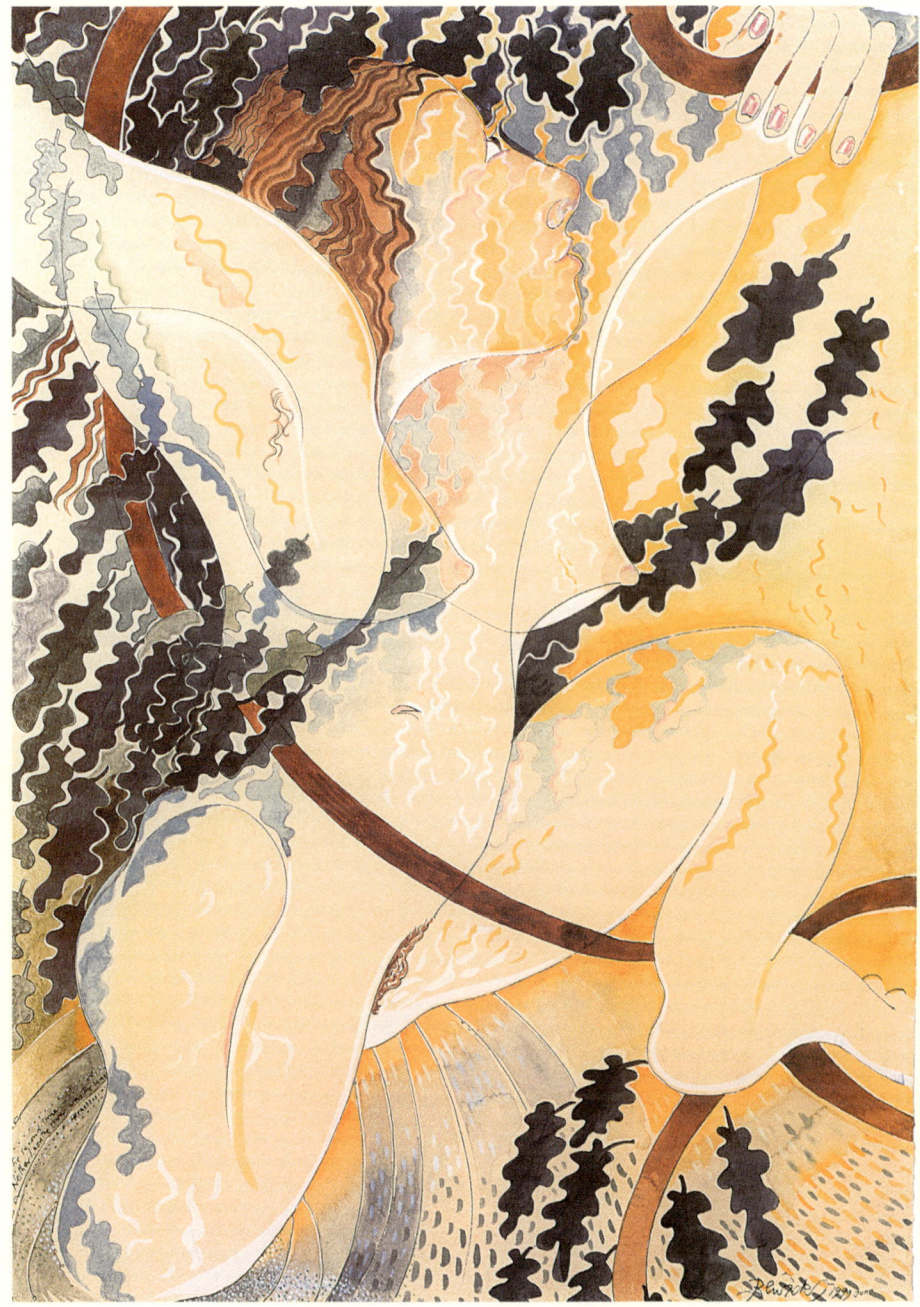

WOMAN, WATER AND OAK TREE
2006 • Aubusson tapestry, wool and linen • 90" x 67"
Travelling Collection

'The second time neither I nor the river was the same' - Heraclitas

A week spent in Cill Rialaig with Regine inspired these pastels.
The dramatic changes from the sky to the sea was rushed onto glass paper with unison pastels.

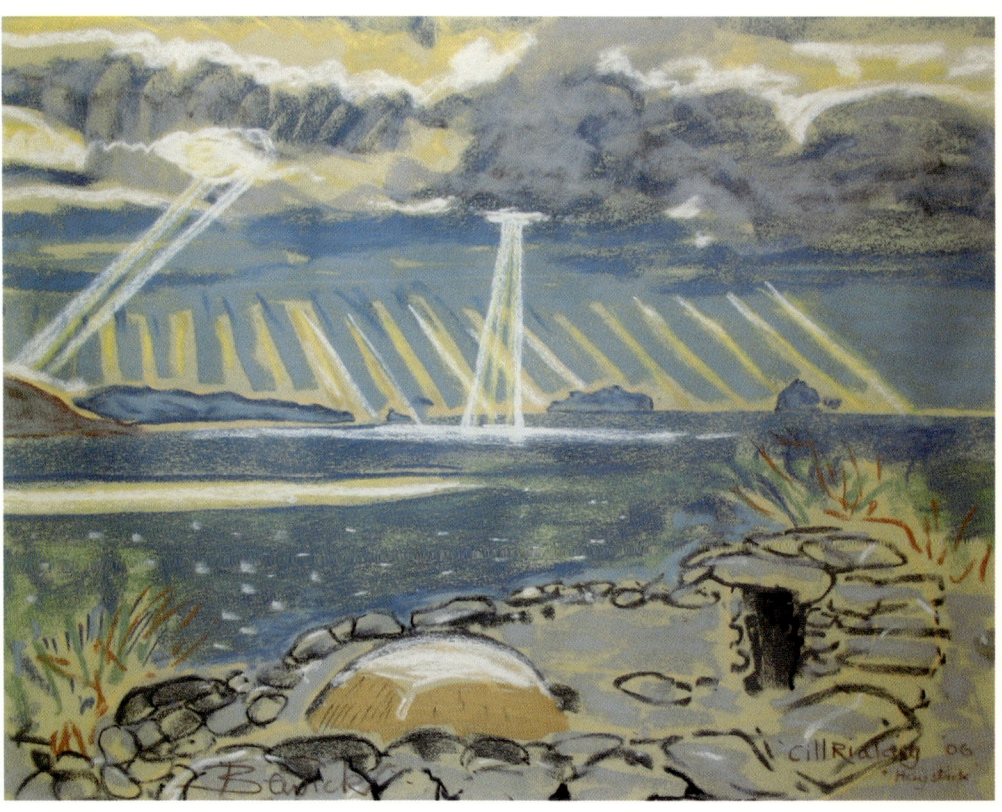

CIL RIALAIG AND HAYSTACK
2006 • pastel • 20" x 26"
Travelling Collection

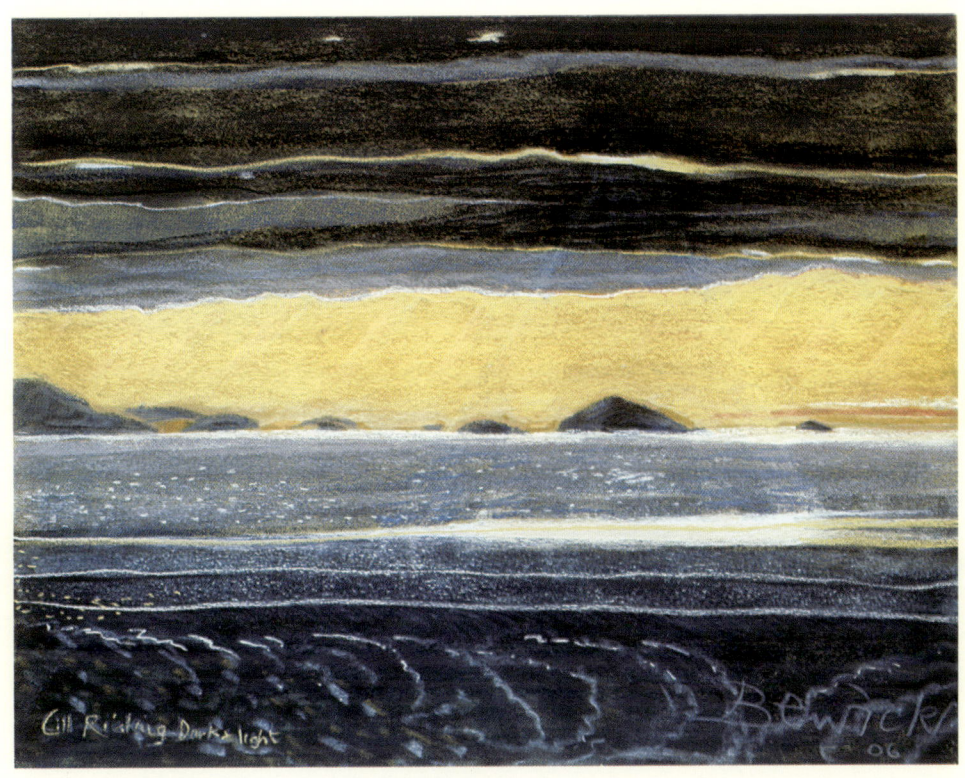

CILL RIALAIG DARK AND LIGHT
2006 • pastel • 20" x 26"
Kerry Collection

The sky expressed all emotions, ominous, light and dark.

A pink happy evening.

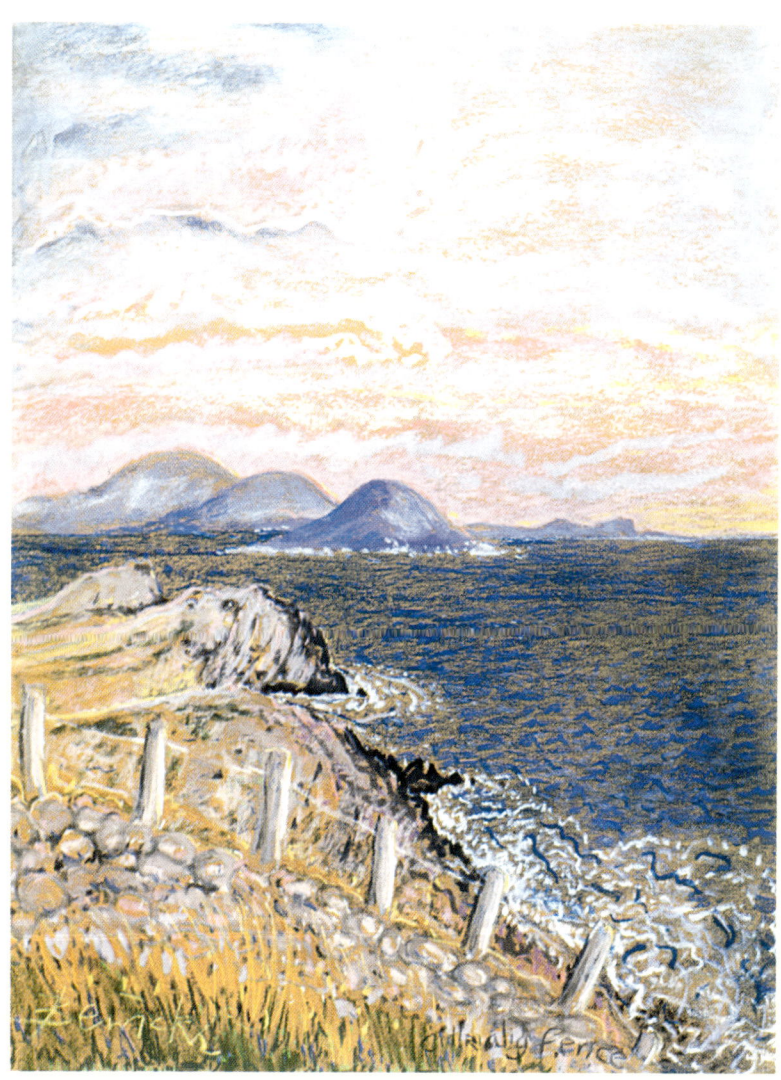

CILL RIALAIG AND FENCE
2006 • pastel • 26" x 20"
Waterford Collection

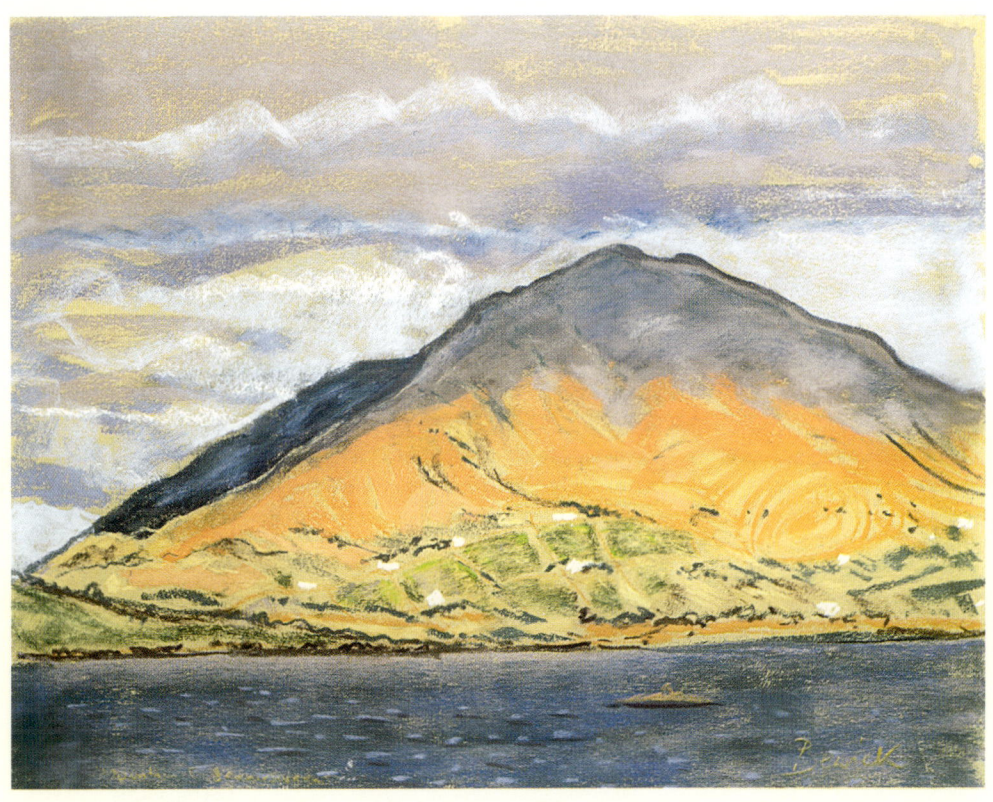

E. Mountain, Caherciveen
2006 • pastel • 20" x 26"
Kerry Collection

Stopping on the way home, I couldn't resist the light on the mountains outside Cahersiveen.

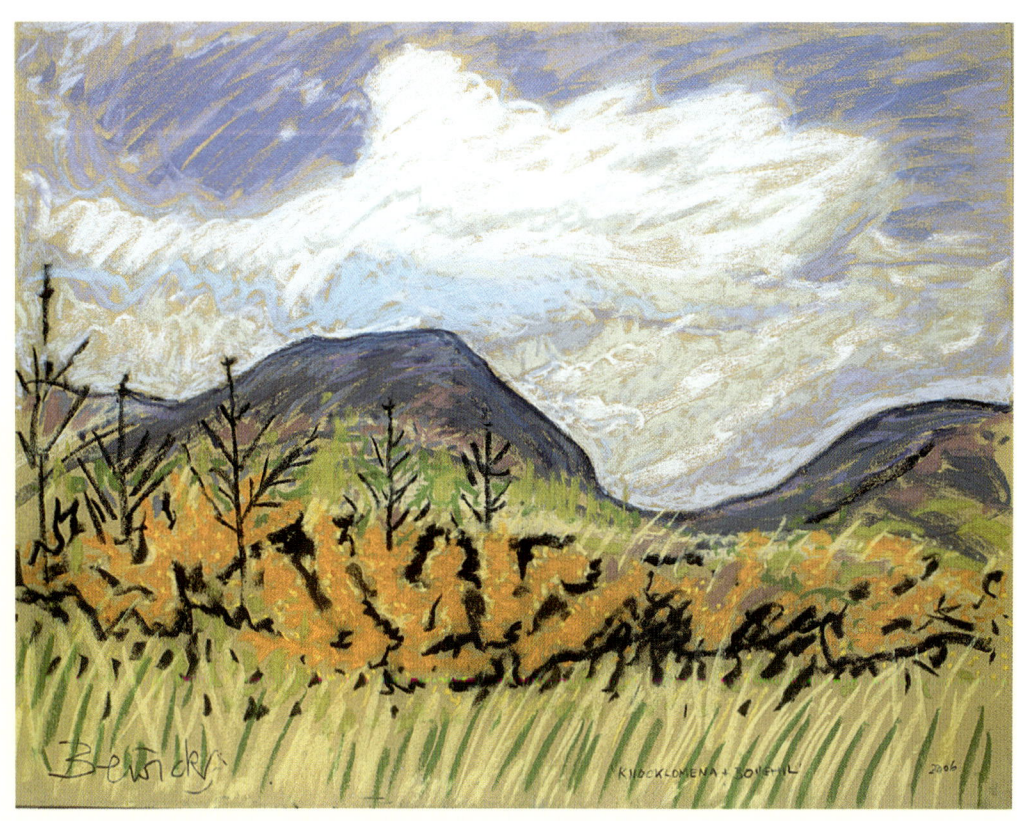

KNOCKLOMENA AND BOUGHIL
2006 • pastel • 20" x 26"
Kerry Collection

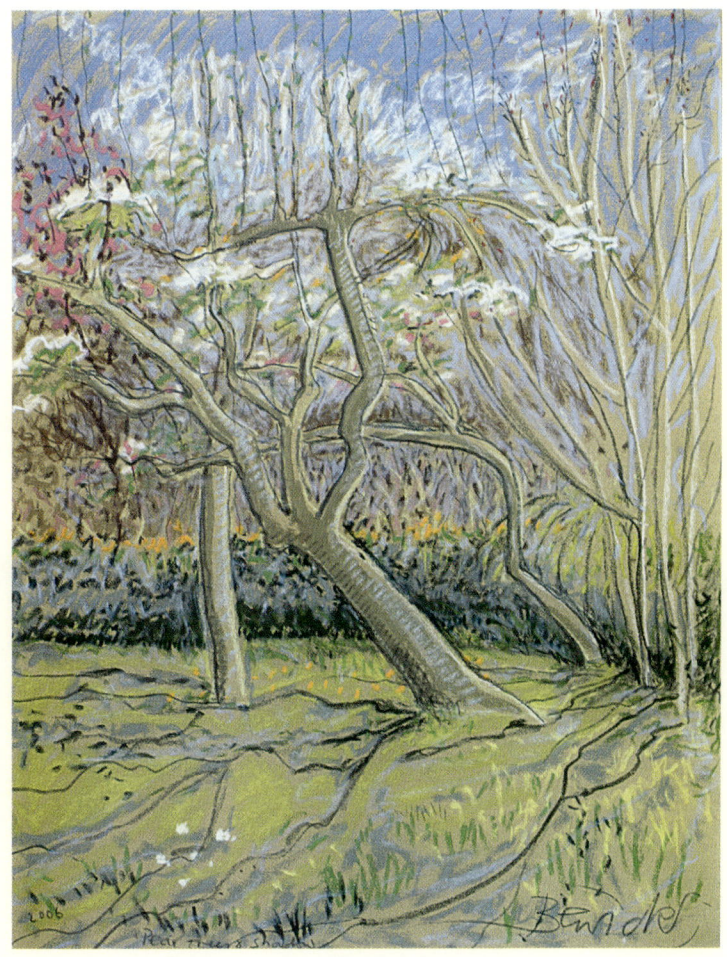

PEAR TREES AND SHADOWS
2006 • pastel • 26" x 20"
Waterford Collection

The west wind blows some trees to the east.

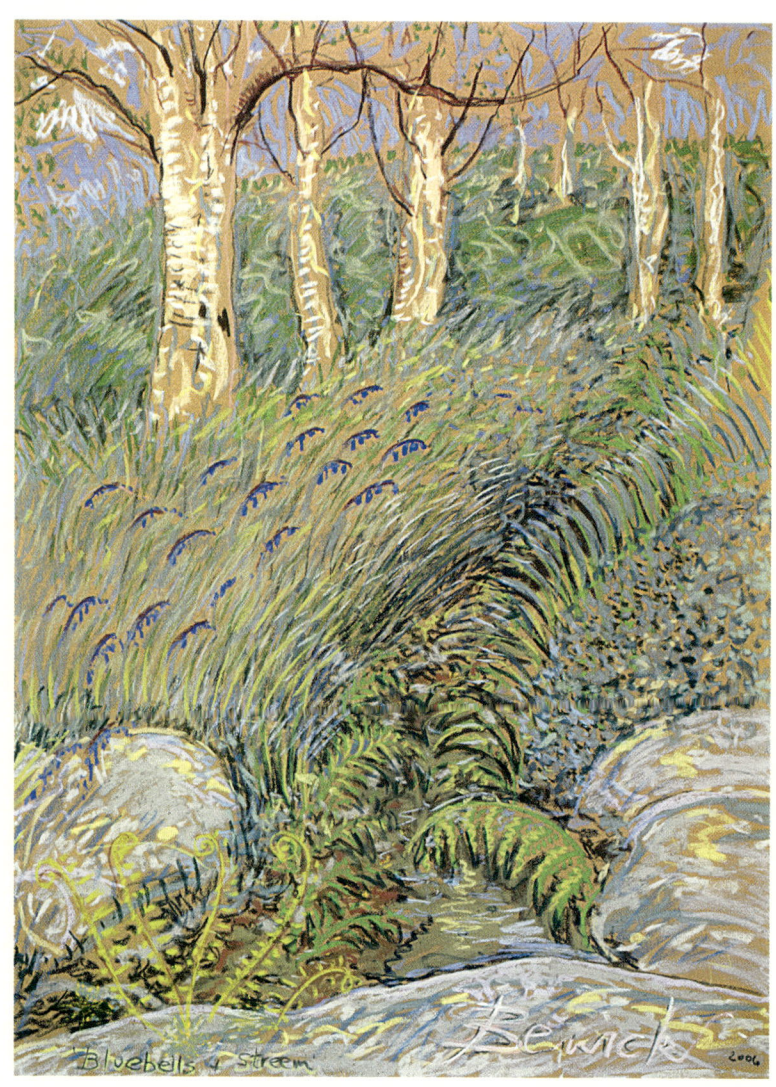

BLUEBELLS AND STREAM
2006 • pastel • 32" x 24"
Travelling Collection

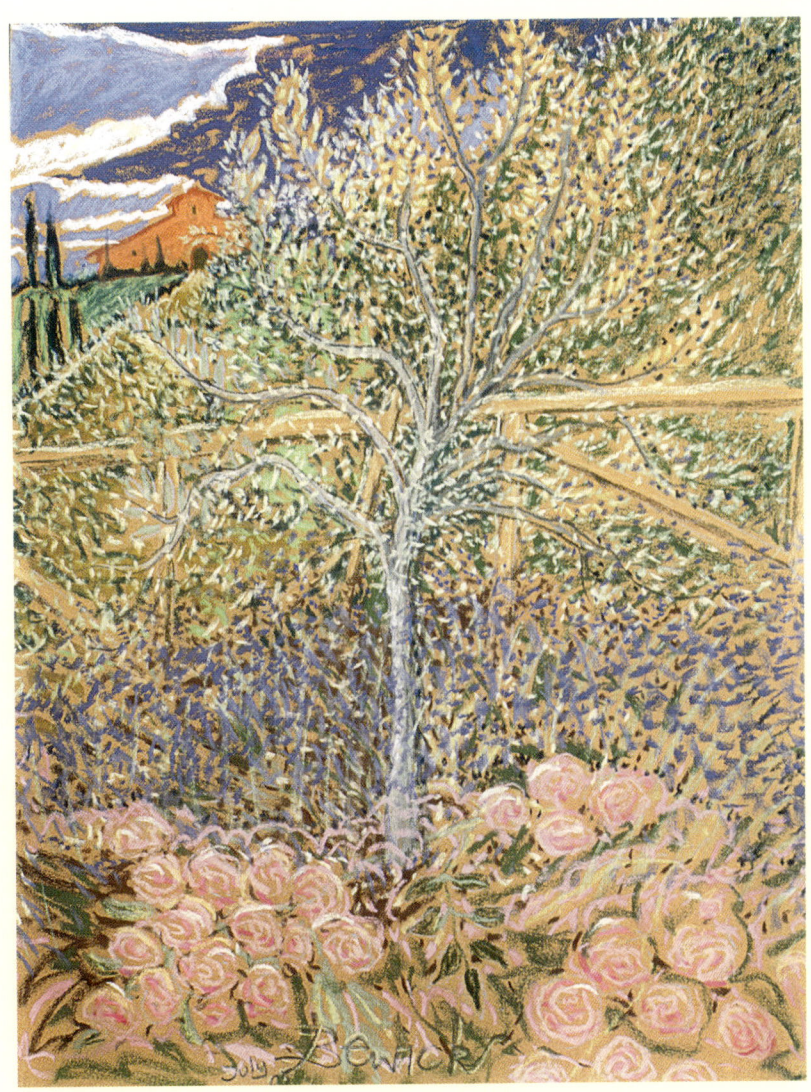

ROSES, LAVENDER AND OLIVE TREES
2006 • pastel • 26" x 20"
Waterford Collection

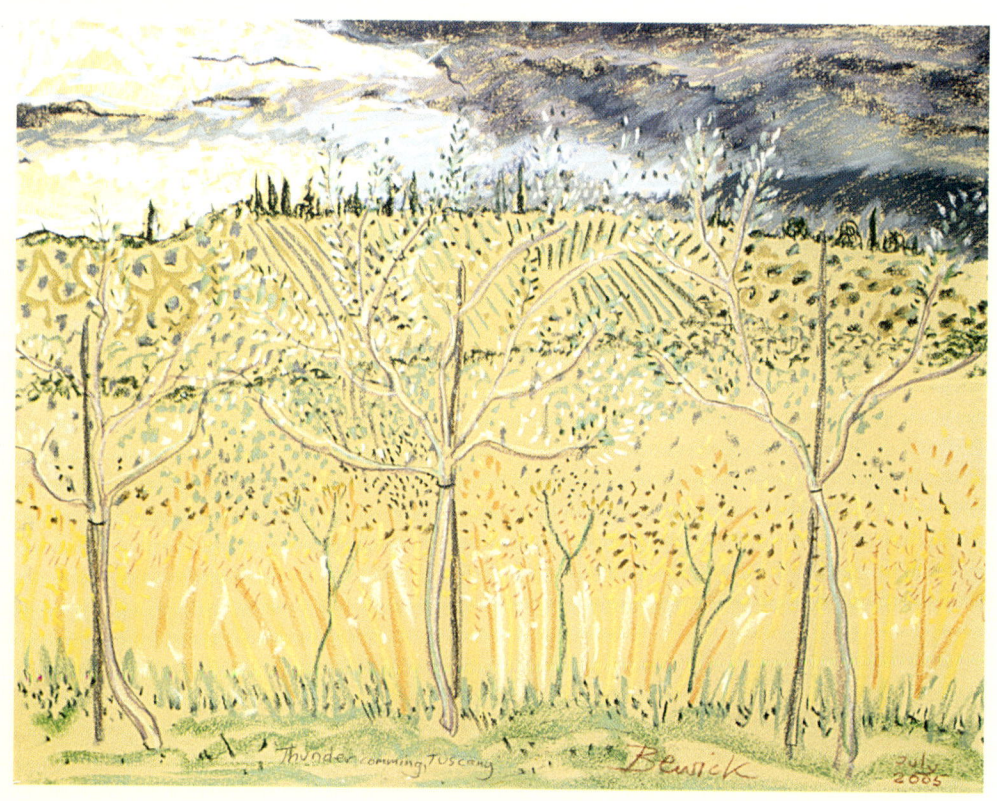

THUNDER COMING TUSCANY
2006 • pastel • 20" x 26"
Travelling Collection

A new way of looking at Tuscany with pastels.
Details in watercolours require excellent eyesight,
pastel gives an all-over impression of light and dark

Alan Hayes

Pauline Bewick: A Life in Painting

Pauline Bewick announced in autumn 2005 on Pat Kenny's *Late Late Show* that she was to donate a major collection of her paintings to the State. This book catalogues the donation. From her first sketch at the age of 2½ in 1938, Pauline's mother Harry encouraged her art and kept all her finished work in a battered suitcase, carried around on all their journeys. When Pauline grew up she also continued to keep her work, either in its master form or some record of it. She also kept all the correspondence of her career, letters, diaries and published work, which has now become quite a sizeable archive. However, it is clear when talking to the artist that she has very little interest in the past, or in her own history. She lives in the present and talks about the future. Pauline's history is fascinating to all of us who ask to hear it, but it doesn't seem to matter to her. It seems Harry was the same, she had no interest in the past, or what they did then, but only the now and what is to come.

Pauline Bewick's Seven Ages is arranged as a chronological journey from the age of two to seventy, ranging from the artist's first small sketches created on a farm in Kerry in the late 1930s to the huge pieces she currently paints in that same county. In between, in the many intervening years, we journey with the artist across Wales and England to progressive schools with her mother, their return to Ireland and life in Dublin, her teenage years and twenties working as an artist in Dublin and London, falling in love with Patrick Melia, starting a family and moving back to a permanent home in Kerry, while also encompassing international perspectives, in particular from journeys to the South Seas and Tuscany. Throughout all this time, Bewick has represented her life in sketchbooks, sculpture, on paper, canvas, etc, etc, pouring out her emotional and intellectual dreams, and building an empathy with those who have followed her journeys.

Pauline Bewick was born on 4 September 1935 in Northumbria, England into a family descended from the naturalist and wood engraver Thomas Bewick. However the formative influence in her life was not from her father John Corbett Bewick, but her mother, Harry, a creative, unconventional character. Her birth name was Alice, but she was told her real name was unlucky and that the name 'Harry' suited her better. So that was it, and for the rest of her life she was known as Harry Bewick. Having run away from her husband and the Bewick family, Harry chanced on meeting Pat Newling, a Kerry woman running a hotel in Letchworth, who told her of her orphaned niece and nephew living on a small farm in the wilds of Kerry. Harry offered there and then that she would move to Kerry and foster the two children, Lucy and Michael. So started the journey to Ireland which was to shape Pauline Bewick's life in such a distinctive way. "Harry believed in living in the present and throwing the past away, but she kept all my early paintings in a battered suitcase which she brought on all our journeys". These paintings were de-acidified and preserved by the National Gallery and are now part of this permanent Seven Ages collection.

It all started in Kenmare when Harry gave Pauline a little book with blue striped lines, and in that book in 1938, at the tender age of 2½, Pauline did her very first sketch, a dancing girl. She later recalled that she felt so happy there, and so was drawing her own feelings at the time. A memorable visit to the Lansdowne Arms Hotel in Kenmare for lunch, where as a vegetarian Harry asked the bemused staff for raw vegetables only, resulted in the sketch 'Waitress in Cafe'. "I remember seeing this wedding in Kenmare when I was four, and Harry gave me huge praise for being able to do a side-view of the bride". 'Pat Newling Smoking' represents a visit by Lucy and Michael's aunt home to Kerry (where incidentally she was very happy with the care given by Harry to the fostered children). At the age of six, and with a packet of Harry's old oil paints and some scrap wood, Pauline secretly painted 'Bogac - Our Bog' as a surprise for Harry's birthday. For most paintings Harry saw the work in progress, but the artist remembers she didn't interfere, except to write the Irish words. "Harry had fallen madly in love with Ireland, and she would write the title of each painting in Irish. I was too young to write. Everything my sister Hazel and I painted was 'totally brilliant' in her view. She was a huge support to us both". Pauline's artistic skills were developing and she was being exposed to interesting and engaging images, such as visiting travellers, friendships with Kerry characters, the Kenmare regatta and the classics presented by Anew McMaster's travelling repertory company. Her early days in Dourus school were memorable because of a sympathetic teacher, Miss Murphy, who recognised that Pauline had a learning disability and encouraged her artistic skills. In the last painting of these early Kerry years, 'Theatre at the Carnegie Library Kenmare' (1943, aged eight), a noted development is the more grown-up faces of the characters from the match-stick-men-like ones of earlier drawings. Hidden in Bewick's loft in Kerry there remain early photos of this Kenmare experience, including one of Hazel and Pauline with their horse Shamrock.

These happy times ended when Lucy suddenly died from galloping meningitis and it was decided to send Michael to Switzerland 'for the air' to prevent him developing TB. (Michael did live to a good age and he had loving memories of Harry and those happy years living together as a family). After Lucy's death and with Michael gone to Switzerland, Harry felt it was time to move on, and a nomadic existence commenced. Over the following years they lived in a houseboat, a caravan, a railway carriage, a gate lodge, a workman's hut and a suburban house. They lived in Belfast, Portrush and Derry for a brief period before deciding to return to Britain. Between 1944-1948 Pauline attended progressive schools and conventional schools in Wales and England - times which were both exciting and thought-provoking for the young artist. She went to progressive schools at Blackbrook, Monmouthshire and St Catherine's in Bristol. "At the second progressive school in Bristol, I remember dancing naked on the lawn to Tchaikovsky's Dance of the Sugar Plum Fairy, thinking how wonderful and graceful I was!" They met 'John Watling' there, Pauline's favourite teacher and a life-long friend - here he is represented solemnly

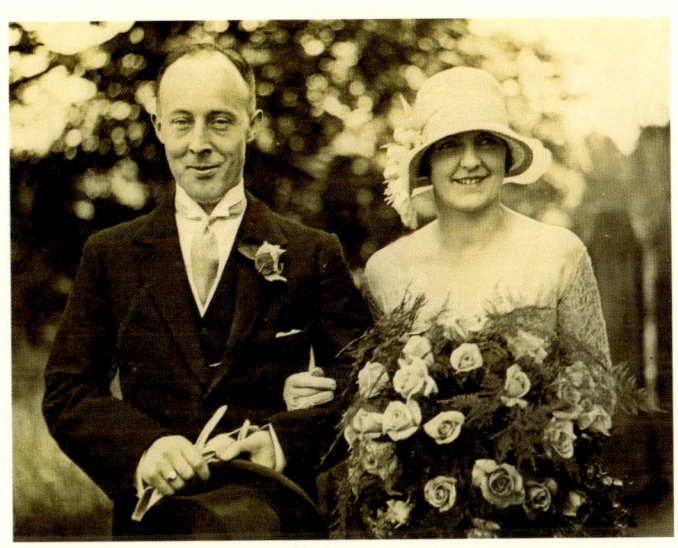

John Corbett Bewick and Alice Graham on their
wedding day, c. 1929

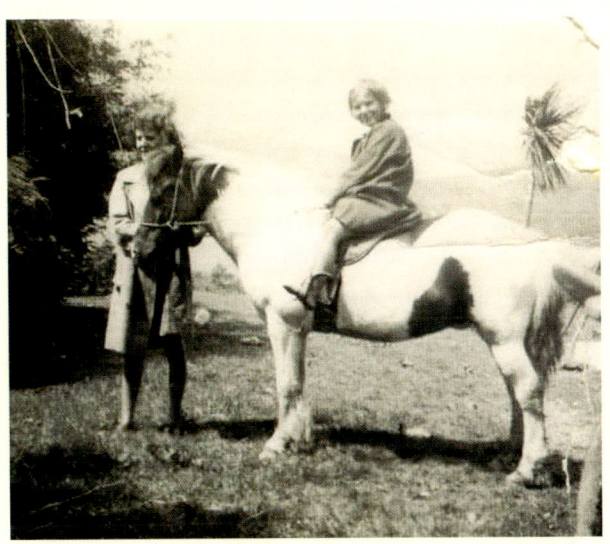

Hazel with Pauline on their horse Shamrock,
Kenmare, c 1942

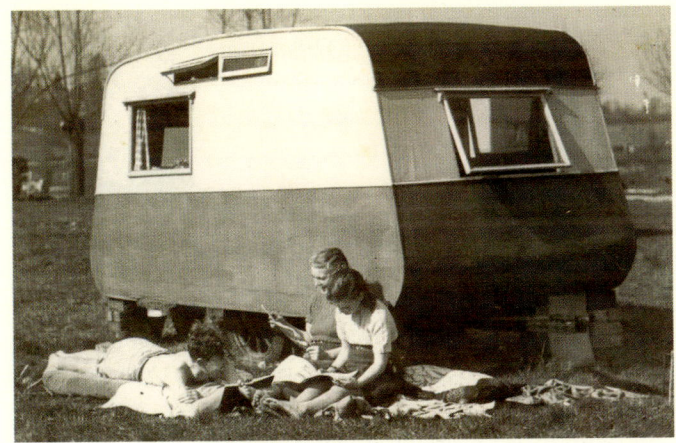

John Watling, Harry and Pauline at their caravan, c. 1946

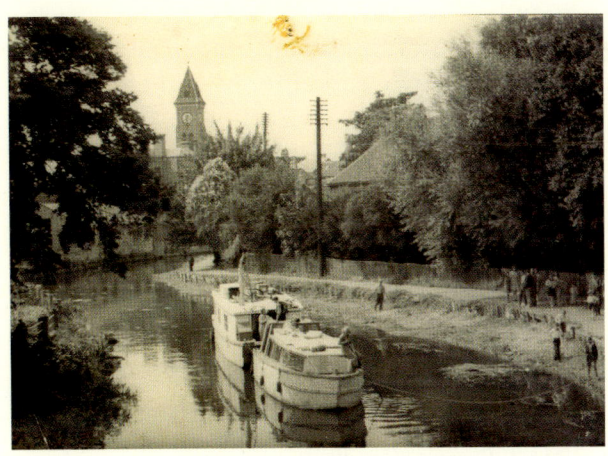

Harry and Pauline's riverboat on the Kennet and
Avon Canal, England c. 1947

in charcoal. "This image makes him look horrific which is sad, because he was one of the nicest people I ever met. There had been no male influences apart from Michael, who was a boy, so John was the earliest father figure in my life". Leaving the progressive school they lived in a caravan in Saltford before travelling the Kennet and Avon Canal in a houseboat called Janty and settling in Henley-on-Thames. Living on that houseboat Pauline painted many of the images and ideas she was exposed to, always encouraged and supported by her mother. Harry, however, did not want Pauline to sign her paintings 'Bewick', and encouraged her to use her middle name, and sign herself as 'Pauline Gale' or 'Pauline G'. The young artist only started using her proper name on her work after enrolling in the Dublin Art School in 1950. "I thought a lot about what went on around me and the unusual conversations Harry was having with progressive school teachers on subjects like conscientious objectors and abortion. Painting ideas was a way of sussing out things I couldn't understand".

She painted a two-faced woman after hearing a conversation about a hypocrite. She admired local Quaker women who shared each others' children, the 'Phoney Twins' were objects of hilarity, while progressive school teacher 'Mr Butterfield', who taught the largely irrelevant subject of ship-building and couldn't sew the holes in his socks properly, was a figure of fun. "Harry often talked about the South Seas and of Margaret Mead's studies of the people there, so I painted what I thought were South Seas people. Harry wore a lipstick called Tahiti Pink in those days". 'Abortion' was her representation of a concept she didn't understand.

John Watling fell in love with Nicandra McCarthy, Augustus John's model, who joined them on their journeys and was drawn with Harry and Pauline. Back in Ireland in 1949 they travelled around in a van, looking for somewhere to settle, singing songs like "Two tomcats by the fireside sat/said one tomcat to the other tomcat/Let's char/coal each others'/arsehole/char/coal/arse/hole/arse/hole/char/coal" and so on. After her unconventional schooling Harry decided to enroll Pauline in art school. A visit to the Cork Art School ended swiftly when Harry was told that life drawing wasn't allowed. "That is ridiculous", Harry informed them. The Dublin Art School accepted Pauline, and Harry bought a house in Frankfort Avenue with a loan from the Building Society where she rented rooms to students and opened a vegetarian restaurant in her kitchen (Sheila Fitzgerald was the only customer). Pauline painted the images of this period – life in art school and at home, making new friends, beginning to fall in love, "cuddling up, dancing, wearing big hoopy earrings and going to hops". Pat Cahill, one of Harry's tenants, would tell their fortunes. These years marked the ending of childhood and the beginnings of adulthood.

Leaving Art School Bewick began making connections in the creative world in Dublin. She worked as a singer in the Clover nightclub in O'Connell Street and met Carolyn Swift and Alan Simpson of the Pike Theatre. She started working in the theatre as a designer and actor. Working in stage set she painted the irises of artificial eyes and drew advertisements. She painted 'Hoddy', jazz critic of the *Irish Times* ("Although I never saw him in the bath!"), she did cover illustrations for *Icarus*, a Trinity College magazine, and soon was given a commission by the Dolmen Press to illustrate Thomas Kinsella's *Thirty Three Triads*. Her growing interest in the wider world is clear with work that encompasses themes of race, sexuality and gender during this period. A hectic cultural life

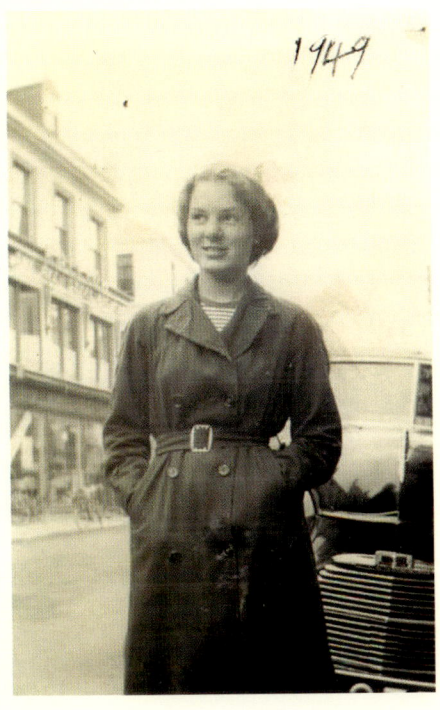

Pauline back in Killarney, 1949

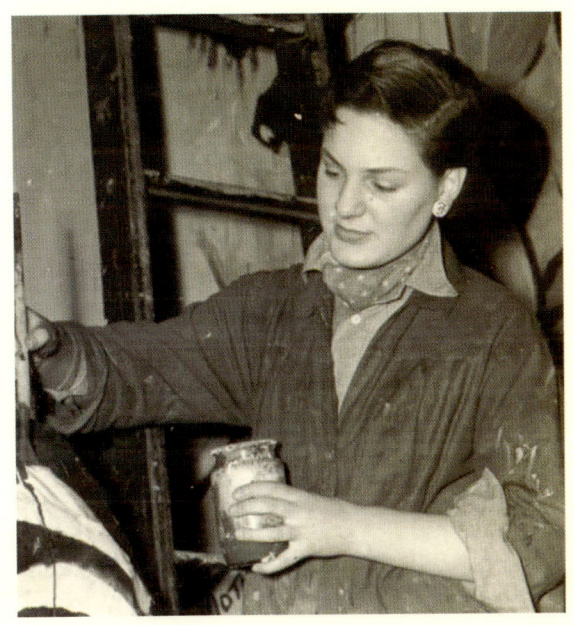

Student days in the Dublin Art School, 1950

Hazel, Harry and Pauline during a visit to England for Hazel's wedding, c. 1950s

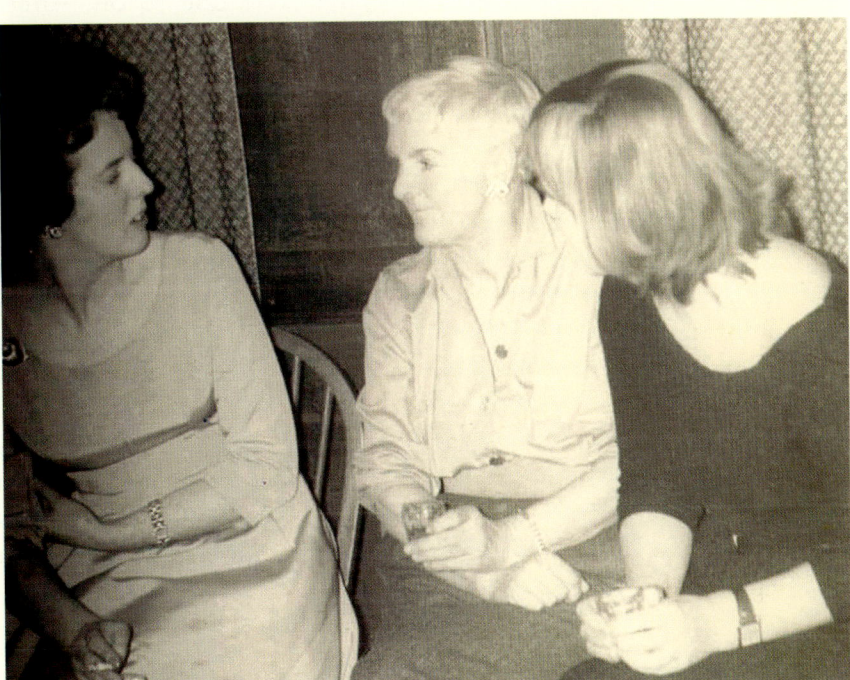

is represented by trips to the theatre and clubs seeing Marcel Marceau and the Kabuki dancers. During her first trip to Paris, she watched Sidney Bechet's mistress stir the bubbles out of his champagne.

Friendships developed with Dublin with characters like John Molloy, Desmond Barry, Sebastian Ryan and Jewish poet Leslie Daiken. A lifelong friendship began in art school with Barry Laverty, daughter of the writer Maura Laverty, and with Barry's future husband, the artist Philip Castle. The entry of Pat Melia, a young student at Trinity, into her life started a relationship which has lasted almost 55 years, with few hiccups, and is going stronger than ever. 'Marriage at Woodlands' painted in 1954 is a fictional representation of their marriage, which didn't actually take place until 1963.

By the late 1950s, Bewick accepted that she couldn't make a living as an artist in Dublin, and so moved to London. There she shared a house with Sally Travers who had an interesting social life centring around exotic men friends. When Travers' uncle Michael MacLiammoir visited he would entertain and perform for the two young women. The gay characters she sketched were representations of Mr Pussy. "I had a very good gay friend and we often went to gay clubs and West Indian clubs". In 1960 Bewick was commissioned by the BBC to sketch a new children's TV show, *Little Jimmy* which received great ratings and was a critical success. The money earned from the BBC paid for Bewick to go on a Mediterranean cruise with Barry Laverty and Philip Castle who had married. In Greece she met 'Costos' and fell in love with him. "I had a wild streak in me and fell for wild men". But Costos "was a bit too macho ... I couldn't live with a man who was dictatorial, and so I picked Pat". Her painting of 'Brow Beating' doesn't represent either Costos or Pat, but relationships in general.

On returning to Dublin, Pauline Bewick and Pat Melia lived in a flat in Upper Mount Street, before borrowing money and buying a house in Heytesbury Lane. Bewick then started mulling over whether or not to have babies. While she was concerned about over-population and the dangers of nuclear war, they decided to go ahead. Pregnancy and early motherhood were strange experiences for Bewick, "hormones made me feel quite strange and lonely ... I found bringing up little babies boring. It wasn't very stimulating! Didn't thrill the boots off me! I painted the conflict inside women", most significantly in 'Williams, Baggot Street' and 'Another Child'.

Their first daughter, Poppy, was born in 1966, and Holly in 1970. Both girls were painted regularly throughout their childhoods, as has Pat Melia been over the past fifty years. The painting of 'Pat with Horns' shows the artist's reliance on her husband to read to her because of her dyslexia. "He can be very self-willed and I can be quite bossy, and when he wouldn't read to me one night, I painted him with horns". Luke Kelly and Sean MacReamoinn were painted with hooves and horns in 'Heytesbury Lane Party' and the former solo in 'King of the Fairies'. "Luke Kelly was fascinating to me. He just represented Dublin to me. Once I met him on Stephen's Green and he had lost his two front teeth and I thought it was just like the old Georgian houses crumbling".

After decades of a semi-nomadic lifestyle, a permanent move came in 1973 when Pat Melia was offered a job in Killarney Psychiatric Hospital and the family moved to Kerry. It was thirty-five years from Bewick's first journey

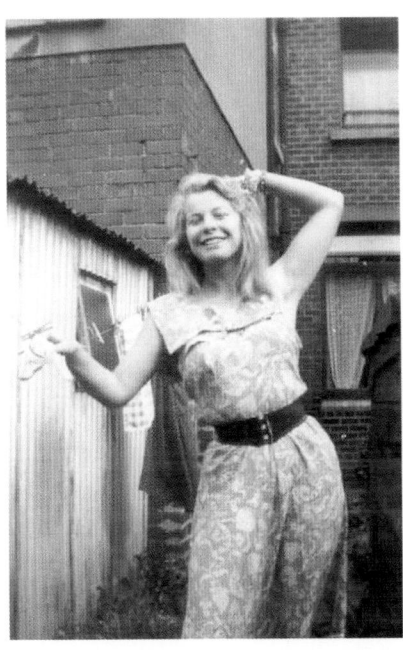

Pat Cahill, Harry's tenant, at 51
Frankfort Avenue, c. 1952

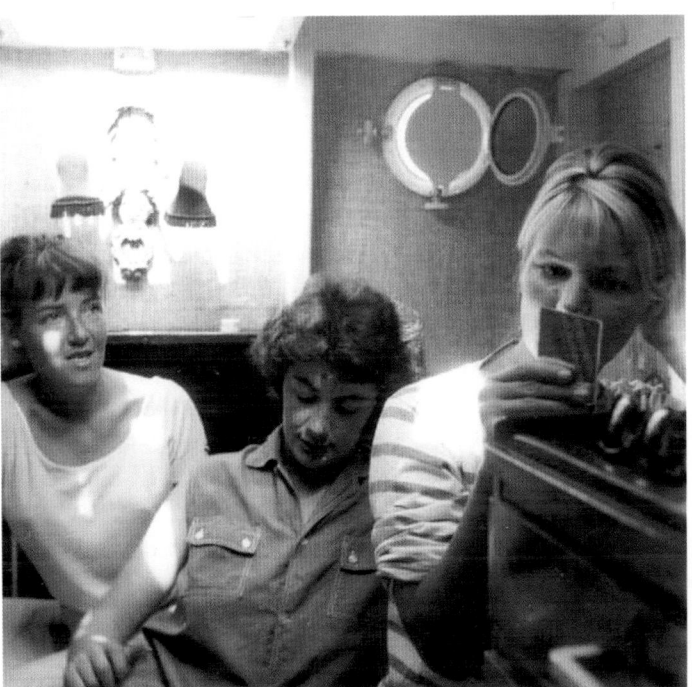

Barry Laverty, Nuala O Faolain and Pauline on their
Mediterranean cruise, c. 1962

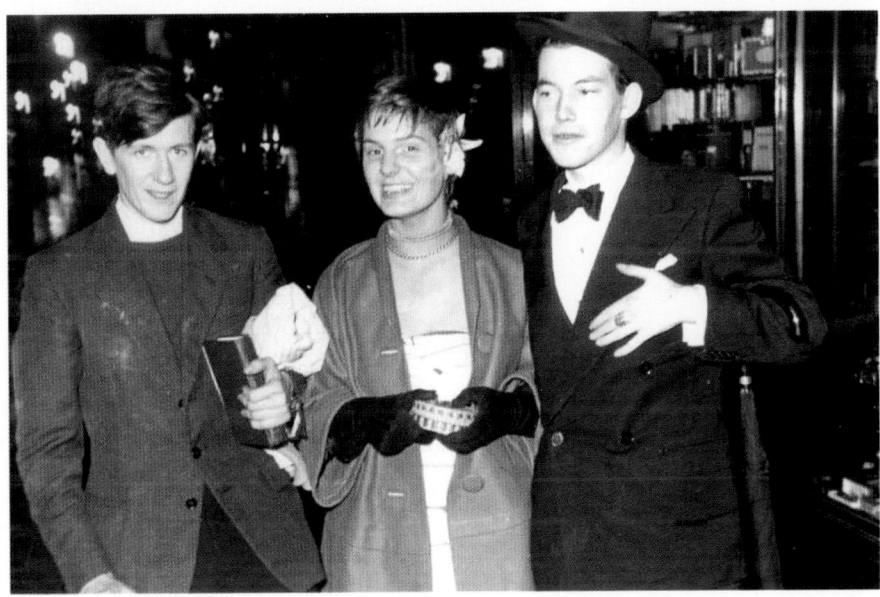

Pat Melia, Pauline and Sebastian Ryan, c 1952

to that county. The family lived firstly in Killarney town. Bewick felt self-conscious and shy there. In their front garden she crafted a sculpture of a pig much to some passerbys' dismay! Her three famous paintings 'Floating in Lough Leane', 'Small Town Lady Letting Loose' and 'Flying over the Cathedral' are great representations of women, who, feeling repressed, decide to set themselves free. Bewick got great pleasure when one of the earliest women to be ordained to the priesthood in England choose the latter painting as the cover of her ordination missal. And Bewick found it amusing when the English establishment got upset at the reproduction of the image of a naked nun flying over a cathedral at the distinguished (and already controversial) priestly ordination.

Leaving Killarney, the family moved to their idyllic home in Glenbeigh in 1976. There, over the last thirty years, Bewick has been inspired to paint the images which have made her an international name. These dream-like, hypnotic images of the beauty and cruelty of nature, female (and sometimes male) sexuality, fascination with cultures and religion, are images which will remain forever an integral part of the artistic canon which Ireland has given to the world. Many of these paintings are now part of Bewick's permanent donation to the State.

Over these years she has experimented with a number of different media, creating designs for wine labels, linocuts, bronzes, ceramics, collages, wall hangings, and, in particular, tapestries, some of which were woven in the 1980s by a local artist Regine Bartsch. In 2002 while driving through France, an unexpected opportunity arose to visit Aubusson, world-famous for tapestries. Since the 1950s Bewick had admired tapestries created in Aubusson and she used this opportunity to commission new ones from a master weaver, Bernard Battu, based on her 'Life of Cocks and Hens', 'Lovers and Stars' and 'Woman, Water and Oak Tree' paintings.

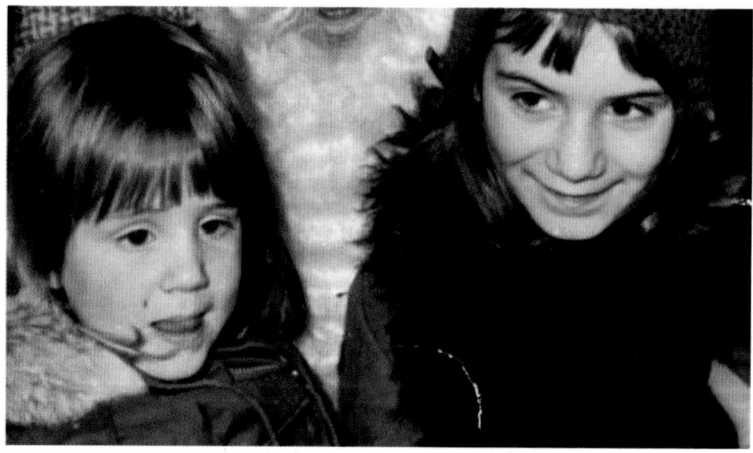

Daughters, Holly and Poppy, c 1973

310

In the early 1970s Pat Melia and Pauline Bewick visited their artist friends Barry Laverty and Philip Castle in Tuscany, fell in love with the area, and bought their own house there. They regularly visit Tuscany where daughter Holly now lives with Tuscan husband Luca and two children. The stunning Tuscan landscapes are a great contrast with the Kerry landscapes painted regularly over these decades. The artist believes "you have to go out and experience nature, rather than just paint it in your head". She also enjoys representing human lives in nature, turning humans into other animals.

Her fiftieth year, 1985, was a major creative year for Bewick, inspiring her to compile a huge retrospective exhibition of 1500 pieces, 'From Two to Fifty', shown in the Guinness Hop Stores, Dublin, the Crawford Municipal Gallery, Cork and the Ulster Museum, Belfast. David Shaw-Smith made a documentary on her work, shown internationally on television and in film festivals, and Dr James White published the first critical examination of the artist, *Pauline Bewick: Painting a Life*. In the late 1980s in Tuscany, Bewick created the initial sketches for her ideal character, the Yellow Man. At this stage of her life she was trying to find both her ideal human being, and the ideal society. Inspired by the many conversations Harry had had about the South Seas way back in the 1940s, Bewick decided to move there for one year, not as a tourist, but to live in community with the locals. She was embraced by the islanders and witnessed many of their customs and ways of life, again seeing at close hand the beauty and cruelty of humans and nature. Life was hard, sometimes they were hungry, and she discovered it was not an ideal society, but she was happy. Bewick made many friends and had a relationship with Utanga. After that first year, she made another return journey for a year to finish writing her book, *The South Seas and a Box of Paints*.

Since returning to Ireland, Pauline Bewick has found her greatest happiness and contentment with Pat Melia in Kerry. She continued to work on her Yellow Man concept, mounting a huge record-breaking exhibition in the RHA, Dublin and writing and illustrating a book, *The Yellow Man*. In that book, Bewick writes of the Yellow Man's life in starkly spiritual text which reveals her own philosophies of life. And as always the humour continues in her life and work. "I've painted a lot of scary big women. Where they came from, you would need an analyst!"

All the paintings in this book are now housed in the Waterford Institute of Technology and in the Killorglin Town Centre, with a third collection travelling the world. Bewick's offer of this master collection to the State was warmly accepted by John O'Donoghue TD, Minister for Arts, Sports and Tourism at the Abbey Theatre in November 2005. "For almost seventy years she has drawn much of her inspiration for her art from her Kerry surroundings and from Irish life and mythology. Pauline is an extremely talented and extraordinarily prolific painter. While we are gathered this evening to mark the occasion of this wonderful publication of Pauline's works, I must refer to her recent display of enormous generosity in donating the works from her master collection to the State. On behalf of the Irish people I would like to thank Pauline for this overwhelmingly generous gift". These paintings form a unique record of one woman's life to date and are an invaluable social record of twentieth-century Ireland. They are now available for the perpetual enjoyment of the Irish public and international audiences.

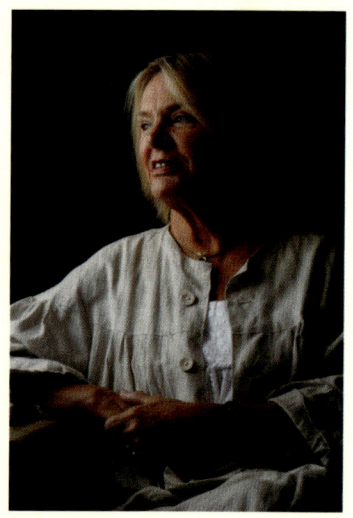

PAULINE BEWICK, 2006
courtesy of Nina Finn-Kelcey

ACKNOWLEDGEMENTS

Pat Melia for numerous help throughout, including the 'Seven Ages' title
Michael Diggin, John Trelaor, Nina Finn-Kelcey, Danny Fernandez – photography
John Trelaor – conservation framing
Martin Bell – exhibition design
Antoinette O'Shea – image archivist
Kate Landers – administration and preparation of collections for Pauline Bewick
Dr Abdul and Katharine Bulbulia
Francis and Catherine Fitzpatrick Hayes
Adrienne Foran, the staff at Betaprint and DP Imaging

The quotes appearing in this book are taken from interviews, lectures, broadcasts and previous publications over many years.

www.soloarte.ie are the exclusive agents for Pauline Bewick's Seven Ages travelling exhibition